Georgia
and the American Experience

Bonnie Bullard London

CLAIRMONT PRESS

Atlanta, Georgia

AUTHOR

BONNIE BULLARD LONDON grew up in historic Wilmington, North Carolina, where she first developed her love of history. She graduated from Sullins College and the University of Georgia. She received an M.Ed. from Georgia State University. Bonnie taught in the Atlanta Public Schools and Georgia history at Booker T. Washington High School. She has also been an instructor with the Governor's Honors Program. In addition, she served as an elementary principal in the Atlanta City Schools and Clarke County. As a consultant in curriculum, she served with the Northeast Georgia RESA and the Georgia State Department of Education. Presently, she is an education instructor with Coastal Georgia Community College and Armstrong Atlantic State University. She is also president of London Limited and conducts staff development throughout the state of Georgia. In addition to authoring a number of articles and student ancillary materials in the area of Georgia studies and language arts, this is her third Georgia Studies textbook.

CONSULTANT

GLEN BLANKENSHIP, Senior Development Consultant, is the Program Director at the Georgia Council on Economic Education in Atlanta, Georgia. He taught 8th grade Georgia Studies at Renfroe Middle School,

in Decatur, Georgia. Dr. Blankenship is a frequent presenter at state, regional, and national conferences and consults with school districts across the nation to develop curriculum and improve student learning. Dr. Blankenship earned his B.A. and M.Ed. in Political Science from Georgia State University, and a Ph.D. in Educational Leadership from Emory University.

CONTRIBUTORS

PATRICIA H. GUILLORY, Multicultural Author and Consultant, is currently Director of Social Studies for Fulton County Schools in Atlanta. She received a B.A. and M.Ed. from the State University of West Georgia. She received her Ph.D. from Georgia State University. She has spent the entire twenty-five years of her career in Fulton County, first as a classroom social studies teacher and department chair and the last ten years as Director of K-12 Social Studies Curriculum. In addition, Pat is a trainer for the Southern Center for International Studies and a trainer and district coordinator for the Center for Civic Education. She is past president of the Georgia Council for the Social Studies and president of the National Social Studies Supervisors Association.

BARBARA HADLEY MATHIS received a B.A. from the University of Georgia and an M.Ed. from Georgia State University. She taught in Grades 7-12 in Florida and in Harris, Troup, Cobb, and Camden counties, Georgia. She served as the State English Coordinator for the Georgia Department of Education and as an English Coordinator for the Governor's Honors Program. Mrs. Mathis worked with the development of Georgia's Criterion-Referenced Tests for pupils in Grades 5 and 8, the Regents' Writing Examination, and Georgia's Teacher Competency Testing Program for Certification. She has served on the adjunct faculties of Georgia Military College, Valdosta State University, and Coastal Georgia Community College, where she currently teaches English. She is a member of the National Council of Teachers of English Conference on College Composition.

ACKNOWLEDGMENTS

As with any textbook, *Georgia and the American Experience* is the result of the collaborative efforts of many individuals. I particularly owe a debt of gratitude to Barbara Mathis for her countless hours working on the manuscript, her English expertise, and assistance in collecting and generating materials. Special acknowledgments are given to Susan Akers, Glynn County Schools, and Myra Glisson, Charlton County Schools for their invaluable suggestions along with those eighth-grade teachers from Glynn, Bullock, and Murray counties who took time to share suggestions and comments. I also thank the Coastal Georgia Community College librarians for their help in literally "gathering" materials. I so appreciate the research assistance of Jennifer Hutchinson, Kim Gordon, Reverend Frank Logue, Linda Wilson, and my AASU students and Dr. Pat Parsons who were always on the lookout for interesting items and shared them generously. I also send special thanks to family and friends for their support and encouragement. But none of this could have been done without the constant assistance of Mark Mathis who, because of his expertise with computers and his love of, and interest in history, enabled this book to become a reality and made writing it so much easier and certainly more fun.

—*Bonnie Bullard London*

Clairmont Press is grateful to the following educators who reviewed the manuscript for this textbook. Much appreciation goes to each for their incisive comments and suggestions.

Dr. Eddie Bennett
Director of Social Studies, K-12,
Cobb County Schools

Ms. Sharon Coleman
Social Studies Consultant, Okefenokee RESA

Dr. Deborah E. Daniell
Instruction Coordinator for Social Studies, K-12,
Gwinnett County Schools

Ms. Lynn McCoy
Social Studies Consultant, Southwest RESA

Ms. Carmen Perkins
Teacher, Double Churches Middle School,
Muscogee County Schools

Mr. Scott Roberts
Teacher, Summerour Middle School,
Gwinnett County Schools

Mr. Larry Smith
Heritage Education Teacher,
Savannah-Chatham Schools

Executive Editor: Kathleen Conway

Design: Robin McDonald

Photo Research: Robin McDonald

Maps: Lee Windham

Cover photos: North Georgia mountains from Brasstown Bald (background); Georgia State Capitol (front cover inset); Georgia peach (front cover); the Old Pink House in Savannah (back cover inset, above); Chattahoochee river bridge, Columbus (back cover inset, below).

ISBN: 1-56733-100-9   Printed in the U.S.A.   Sixth Printing

Introduction

According to historian Kenneth Stampp, "With the historian, it is an article of faith that knowledge of the past is the key to understanding the present." Not only is understanding history, particularly the history of the state in which you live, important to having a well-rounded education, it can also become an open door to your future. Arnold Toynbee stated "History is a Greek word which means, literally, just 'investigation.'" And that is what I invite you to do. Investigate our state's past. Learn from our mistakes and accomplishments. Learn about the relationship of cause-and-effect both in terms of past events and your life today. Why? Fifteen years ago, in the first book in this series, *A History of Georgia*, I said to students, "You will be featured in the next adventure story." And so they are in this book. Then they were 12, today they are 27 and teaching school or making laws, serving the public as attorneys or transportation workers, raising families, continuing their studies, or just being good neighbors. They are making important decisions through voting, serving on committees, or sharing their opinions about ways to improve their community.

Now it is your turn. What will future history books say about you and your contributions? As you read through the text and complete the accompanying activities, keep asking yourself—in what ways can I become a proud part of this great state in which I live? It's up to you. Go for it!

Above: Needwood Baptist Church near Darien, organized in 1866 as Broadfield Baptist Church on the nearby Broadfield rice plantation. This building, dating from the mid-1870s, was moved from the plantation to this location in 1886. Example of early African American vernacular architecture. Page i: A quilting demonstration at Georgia Agrirama in Tifton. Pages ii-iii: North Georgia hills, Rabun County. Pages iv-v: Early Atlanta scene by Wilbur G. Kurz. Pages viii-ix An alley of live oaks leads to the old house at Hofwyl-Broadfield Plantation State Historic Site near Darien.

Contents

Maps

Figures (Charts, Tables, and Diagrams)

Special Features

Our Special State

Welcome to our Georgia! You may be a native Georgian. Or you may have arrived here from Mexico, Vietnam, India, Japan, Korea, or other nations and U.S. states. We are glad you are here and hope you enjoy learning more about your home.

In the two chapters of this unit, you will learn about our geographic regions, our climate, our waterways, and other natural resources of the state. You will also read about the many plants and animals you can see as you walk around your neighborhood, visit a public park, or travel on Georgia's back roads.

A special feature in this unit takes you on a visual trip to "Georgia's Wonders," seven unique places in our state that are the result of nature, time, and geography. But before we begin studying about the state we call home, let us look at what geography means.

Geography affects where people live and how they make a living. In the Blue Ridge region, most farms (left) are small. The geography of central and southern Georgia is good for growing peaches (above).

Where in the World is Georgia?

Chapter Preview

Georgia character word:
Responsibility

Geographic Terms: geography, relative location, absolute location, hemisphere, axis, equator, parallels, latitude, meridians, prime meridian, longitude, region, precipitation, wetland, barrier island, continental shelf, Fall Line, climate, weather, vertical climate, drought, wind current, trade winds, prevailing westerlies, ocean currents, hurricane, nor'easter, tornado, El Niño, La Niña, global warming

Places: Appalachian Plateau region, Ridge and Valley region, Blue Ridge region, Piedmont Plateau, Coastal Plain region, Okefenokee Swamp

Have you ever wondered why Georgia summers are so hot and sticky? Perhaps the local weather forecaster predicted snow, but you woke up to see nothing but a little frost on the ground. What would life be like if you lived on the beach or in the mountains? To answer these questions, we need to understand the six essential elements of geography and the role of geography in our lives.

Above: The Atlantic Ocean, seen here from Jekyll Island, brought European explorers and settlers to Georgia. **Left:** From a vantage point near Hiawassee, the Blue Ridge Mountains stretch off into the distance. The Blue Ridge are part of the Appalachian Mountains and run from northeastern Georgia up through Virginia.

Signs of the Times
Georgia Today

Vital Statistics:

Land area: 58,910 square miles
Inland water: 854 square miles
Number of bordering states: 5
Major bodies of water: 1
Number of islands: 18
Number of physiographic regions: 5
Number of counties: 159
Highest point: Brasstown Bald
Lowest point: Atlantic coastline

Location:

Latitude and longitude: 30°–35°N Latitude, 80°–85°W Longitude
Location within United States: South
Location within South: Southeast
East-West divider: Fall Line
Geographic center of state: Twiggs County
Driving time: 10 hours from northwest corner of state to southeast corner

Figure 1 Timeline: 1750–2000

1998 Severe flooding in southeastern part of state

1972 Cumberland Island established as national seashore

1952 Georgia record high of 112°F

1940 Georgia record low of −17°F

1893 Deadly hurricane hit Savannah

1850s Providence Canyon began forming due to erosion

1750	1800	1850	1900	1950	2000

1811 New Madrid, Missouri, earthquake

1764 Mason-Dixon Line established to separate North and South

1872 Acid rain first acknowledged

1896 "Greenhouse effect" first discovered

1816 Blizzards in northeastern U.S. in June and August

1980 Mt. St. Helens volcano erupted

1984 First hole in ozone layer discovered in Antarctica

1989 San Francisco earthquake

What is Geography?

The term *geography* comes from the Greek word *geographia* and means "Earth's description." Geography is the science of studying Earth as the home of humans. Geography helps us understand ourselves, the places where we live, our relationships with the natural environment, and our interdependence with other places and people in the United States and throughout the world. Studying Georgia's geography helps us answer such questions as why the Indians lived in certain areas of the state, why early settlers moved to particular areas, how the location of a town affects its economy, and even why department stores carry certain kinds of clothing.

Now that you can define the word *geography*, what do you need to know to become a "geographically informed" person?

Understand the world in spatial terms: Be able to use maps and other tools to acquire, process, and report information; use mental maps to organize information about people, places, and environments; analyze the spatial organization of people, places, and environments on Earth's surface;

Understand places and regions: Comprehend the physical and human characteristics of places; realize that people create regions to interpret Earth's complexity; know how culture and experience influence people's perceptions of places and regions;

Understand Earth's physical systems: Know the physical processes that shape the patterns of Earth's surface; understand the characteristics and spatial distribution of ecosystems on Earth's surface;

Understand the human systems of Earth: Know the characteristics, distribution, and migration of human populations on Earth; understand Earth's cultural mosaics, the concept of economic interdependence, the process, patterns, and functions of human settlement, and the influence of the forces of cooperation and conflict;

Understand environment and society: Comprehend how human actions modify the physical environment, how physical systems affect human systems, and the changes that occur in the meaning, use, distribution, and importance of resources; and, finally,

Understand the uses of geography: Realize how to apply geography to interpret the past, to understand the present, and to plan for the future.

Location, Location, Location

When we talk about studying geography, we are simply describing a particular part of Earth—Georgia. So, as geographers, where are we?

One basic geographic skill is the ability to describe where a place is located. Location is either relative or absolute. Relative location describes where a place

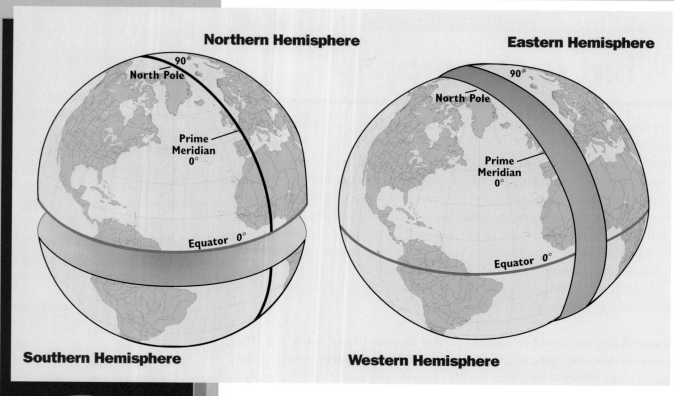

Northern Hemisphere

90°

North Pole

Prime
Meridian
0°

Equator 0°

Southern Hemisphere

Eastern Hemisphere

90°

North Pole

Prime
Meridian
0°

Equator 0°

Western Hemisphere

Map 1
The Hemispheres

Map Skill: What other countries in North America lie in the northern hemisphere?

is located compared with other places. For example, Darien is located near Brunswick; Dalton is located eighty-eight miles northwest of Atlanta; Fort Benning is southeast of Columbus. You might describe your school's location by saying that it is near a certain mall or a particular business. Now, you try it. What is the relative location of your house or apartment to your school?

Absolute location identifies a precise position on Earth's surface. In your hometown, your street address designates a *local location* and defines the absolute location of your home. To find the absolute location of states or countries, we use maps and globes and we need markers more precise than street addresses.

Globes are round in shape like a sphere and are scale models of Earth. Spheres can be divided into two halves called **hemispheres**. If you examine the globe in your classroom, you will see that the globe turns on an **axis**, an imaginary straight line around which an object rotates. The north end of the axis is called the North Pole. The south end of the axis is called the South Pole. The line that goes around the globe exactly halfway between the two poles is called the **equator**. It divides Earth into two hemispheres. Something that may surprise you is that right this minute you are actually moving about 1,000 miles per hour. That is because Earth, which is about 25,000 miles around at the equator, is moving on its axis every twenty-four hours. Now, that's something to think about!

The northern hemisphere extends from the equator to the North Pole, and the southern hemisphere extends from the equator to the South Pole. The United States is located in the northern hemisphere, but there is more to the absolute location of our state.

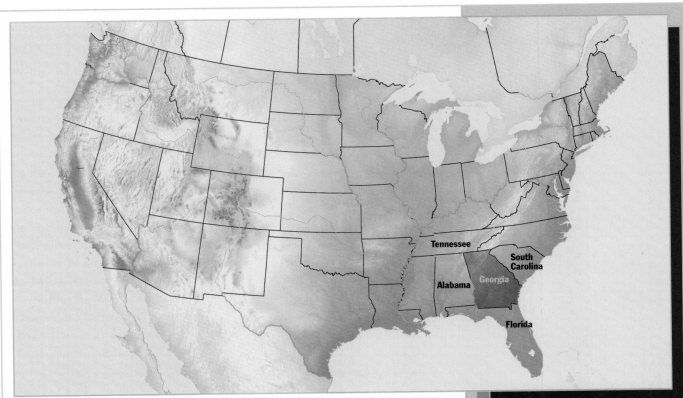

Latitude and Longitude

Examine the globe and you will find lines that run east and west side by side with the equator. These lines are called **parallels**. They are used to describe **latitude**, which is the distance north or south of the equator. Since there is only one equator, there is only one line on a globe which is 0° latitude. All of the other lines or parallels mark distances north (N) or south (S) of the equator.

These distances are measured in units called *degrees*. The North Pole is located at 90° N, and the South Pole is found at 90° S. Each degree can be divided into smaller measurements called *minutes* so that each degree contains 60 minutes. Each minute can be divided into even smaller measurements called *seconds*, so that each minute contains 60 seconds. Locations are usually written in just degree and minute designations. In expressing latitude, you must always add the letter *N* or *S* to the number of degrees. For example, the port of Savannah is located at latitude 32° 02' N. Georgia is located between 30° 21' and 35° N latitude. However, that is only one of the pieces of information needed for an absolute location.

Examine the globe again and you will find lines that run from one pole to the other. These lines running north and south are called

Did You Know?

The geographic center of North America is located in Rugby, North Dakota. Rugby is 1,500 miles from the Pacific Ocean, the Atlantic Ocean, the Arctic Ocean, and the Gulf of Mexico.

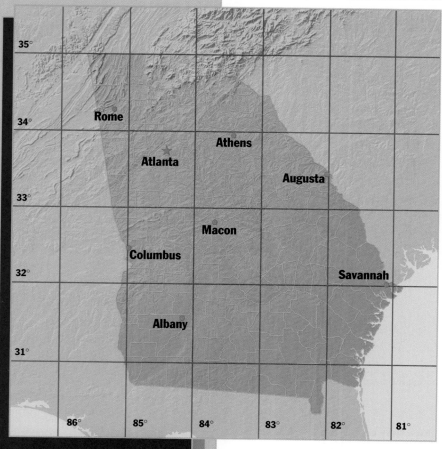

**Map 3
Latitude and
Longitude**

Map Skill: What Georgia
city is located at 33° 57' N
latitude and 84° 42' W
longitude?

meridians. The starting point for the meridians is the **prime meridian**, a line running from the North Pole through England and part of Africa to the South Pole. Meridians measure degrees of **longitude**, which tells how far east or west of the prime meridian a place is located. The prime meridian is located at 0° longitude. All locations west of the prime meridian are numbered and labeled with the letter *W*, and all locations east of the prime meridian are numbered and labeled with the letter *E*. Georgia is located between 80° 50' and 85° 36' W longitude.

If you wrote a pen pal in Australia and described where you lived, how would you describe Georgia's relative location? You might say that Georgia is located in the northern hemisphere, or in North America, or in the southeastern corner of the United States. You might add that five other states touch Georgia borders—Florida on the south, Alabama on the west, Tennessee and North Carolina on the north, and South Carolina along the Savannah River on the northeast. You can include that Georgia is also bordered by the Atlantic Ocean on the east.

However, if you wanted to share Georgia's absolute location with your pen pal, you would have to say that Georgia is located between 30° 21' and 35° N latitude and between 80° 50' and 85° 36' W longitude.

In terms of land area, Georgia is the largest state east of the Mississippi River. Its greatest length is 315 miles, and its greatest width is 250 miles. There are 58,910 square miles of land and 854 square miles of inland water in Georgia. The state has almost as much land as all of the New England states combined. The geographic center of the state is located at a point 18 miles southeast of Macon in Twiggs County.

It's Your Turn

1. What is your relative, absolute, and local location? Can you determine your absolute location from the map on this page?
2. Define latitude and longitude.
3. If you go to five different Internet sites, you will probably find five different figures for Georgia's land area. Why would that be the case? Check it out.

Section 2

Geographic Regions of Georgia

Section Preview

As you read, look for:
- the five regions of Georgia,
- the Fall Line, and
- vocabulary terms: **region, precipitation, wetland, barrier island, continental shelf,** and **Fall Line.**

A **region** is the basic unit of study in geography. It is an area on Earth's surface that is defined by certain unifying characteristics. These characteristics may be cultural, human, or physical. A region may be defined by a government (such as the United States), a common language, climate, situation, or even landforms or the physical topography. We live in several regions—in North America, in the United States, in the South, in the southeastern United States, in Georgia, and even in a particular region or section of the state.

The people who call Georgia home enjoy a wide range of geographic areas. There are twenty-four physiographic patterns (natural characteristics of Earth's surface) in Georgia. These natural divisions differ both in area and in their land base, which may be limestone, clay sediment, shale, or marsh. There are enough similarities among the twenty-four patterns, however, that they can be combined into five major physiographic regions: (1) the Appalachian Plateau region, (2) the Ridge and Valley region, (3) the Blue Ridge region, (4) the Piedmont Plateau, and (5) the Coastal Plain.

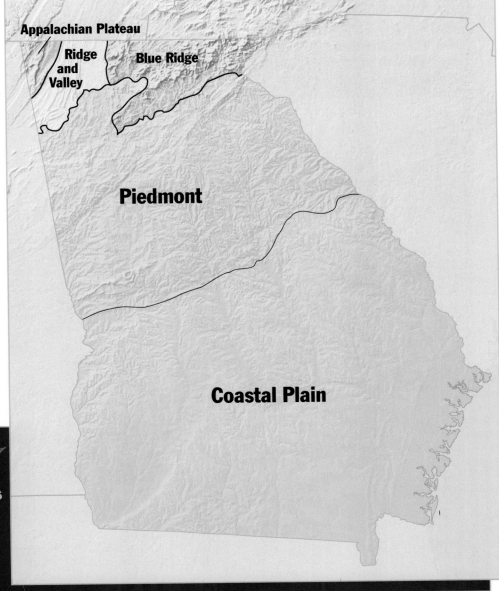

Appalachian Plateau

Ridge and Valley

Blue Ridge

Piedmont

Coastal Plain

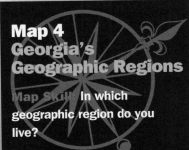

**Map 4
Georgia's
Geographic Regions**

Map Skill: In which geographic region do you live?

The Appalachian Plateau Region

The smallest of the physiographic areas, the Appalachian Plateau region is a maze of limestone caves, deep canyons, and interesting rock formations. Many people refer to this region in the far northwestern corner of the state as the "TAG Corner" because it is the point at which Tennessee, Alabama, and Georgia meet. Also sometimes called the Cumberland Plateau, the region has the broad, flat-topped, 100-mile-long Lookout Mountain on one side and Sand Mountain on the other, separated by ridges of limestone. In between these two mountains is a long, narrow valley. Soils in this region are a mixture of limestone, shale, and sandstone and are well suited for the region's hardwood forests and pastures.

With an elevation (the height above sea level) of up to 2,000 feet, this region is one of the most scenic but least traveled parts of the state. Civil War buffs frequent the Chickamauga and Chattanooga National Military Park, the site of historic Civil War battles. Cloudland Canyon, located between Trenton and Lafayette, has two beautiful waterfalls that cascade over layers of sandstone, dolomite, and shale millions of years old.

Cloudland Canyon (below) in Dade County is one of the Southeast's most beautiful natural sights. The steep, 1,980-foot canyon was cut by Sitton Gulch Creek (opposite page, below) over millions of years. Cloudland Canyon State Park is a favorite destination for hikers.

Visitors to the Chickamauga and Chattanooga National Military Park will see Civil War cannon (left) and monuments to the units that fought there (above).

The Ridge and Valley Region

Between the Blue Ridge Mountains and the Appalachian Plateau lies the Ridge and Valley region. This area of the state has low open valleys and narrow ridges that run parallel to the valleys. Elevation ranges from 700 to 1,600 feet above sea level. Most of the soil in the region is a mixture of shale and sandstone on the ridges and limestone and clay in the valleys. Forests and pastures dominate the region, but there are flat and fertile farmlands with fields of grain, pastures for cattle, and rows of apple orchards near Ellijay. The valleys are divided by steep and narrow ridges capped with limestone. The rocks that make up the ridges are very resistant to erosion. Ridges include Taylor Ridge and Pigeon Mountain.

The region runs from Polk and Bartow counties northward to Chattanooga, Tennessee. It is known for its industry, particularly textile and carpet manufacturing. Dalton, known as the "carpet capital of the world," leads the way.

A famous story told by the late Bernice McCullar in her *This Is Georgia* explained the northwest Georgia location of Plum Nelly reached over a winding two-lane road. People would refer to it as "plum outa Tennessee and nelly outa Georgia." Today Plum Nelly also the name of a well-known Appalachian folk art center.

Opposite page, above: Gilmer County in the Ridge and Valley Region is Georgia's "Apple Capital." Opposite page, below: Ten miles northeast of Dalton is Prater's Mill, built in 1855. Left: Shinbone Valley in Chattooga County is one of the many valleys in this region. Above: There are more than seventy carpet manufacturing plants in Dalton. Pictured is Shaw Industries.

PLUM NELLY

The Blue Ridge Region

The Blue Ridge region of Georgia is known for its rugged beauty. Located in the northeastern part of the state, it is part of the Appalachian Highlands that stretch from New York to Alabama. The Blue Ridge region is a hundred miles wide and has an area of about two thousand square miles. The highest and largest group of mountains in Georgia is in this region. These mountains are important to the rest of the state because they are the first barrier to warm, moist air rising from the Gulf of Mexico. When that air makes contact with the high mountains, it cools. The precipitation (rain, hail, sleet, or snow) that results provides water for the entire state. Here, precipitation can exceed 80 inches per year.

The region has a mixture of sandy loam (a blend of clay, sand, and organic matter) and clay. The shallow soil is easily eroded, and the steep slopes add to the erosion problems in the region. The area is well suited for hardwood forests, vegetable farming, and apples.

Brasstown Bald, the highest peak in the state, is located in this region. (In the South, high mountains that are treeless on top are often called "balds.") The peak is almost 5,000 feet high. If you climb to the top of the observation tower there, you can catch a glimpse of three surrounding states: North Carolina, South Carolina, and Tennessee.

The Ridge and Valley region marks the beginning of the Appalachian Trail at Springer Mountain, northeast of Dahlonega. Every year, outdoor adventurers begin the 2,144-mile hike, hoping to arrive at its end in Maine.

Above: Springer Mountain marks the southern end of the 2,015-mile Appalachian Trail. Above right: Markers like these guide hikers along the Trail. Right: Northeast Georgia's Blue Ridge Mountains draw visitors from all around the world. Opposite page, above: Helen's alpine village is a favorite tourist stop. Opposite page, below: The observation tower atop Brasstown Bald offers a 360-degree vista of North Georgia and neighboring states.

Travelers to this region can also visit other well-known Georgia landmarks including beautiful Amicalola Falls, which drops 729 feet; the 1,000-foot-deep Tallulah Gorge in Raburn County; and the alpine community of Helen in White County. In addition, this region is known for its many recreational opportunities.

Georgia's three northern regions are all part of the Appalachian Mountains. The story of the Appalachians began over 900 million years ago when the continents collided and created one giant continent. This collision also created the Appalachians. Over millions of years, the continents split apart and slowly moved away from each other. The first Appalachian Mountains eroded into what later became the Atlantic Ocean.

About 500 million years ago, the continents once again began to move back together. As the continents moved together, they pushed the sediment from the ocean floor back up and created the second Appalachian Mountains. Once again, the continents collided. The force of the collision caused Earth's crust to fold and more mountains to form. Each time the continents collided and formed more mountains, the existing mountains were pushed further west. That is why the Appalachians have several sets of parallel ridges.

About 200 million years ago, the continents began to drift apart again. Over the past 200 million years, the Appalachian Mountains have eroded from their original height. At times ice glaciers covered the mountain chain. The weight of the glaciers pushed down the mountains underneath. The ice carved valleys and pushed the eroded rock sediments as far south as the southeastern corner of the United States.

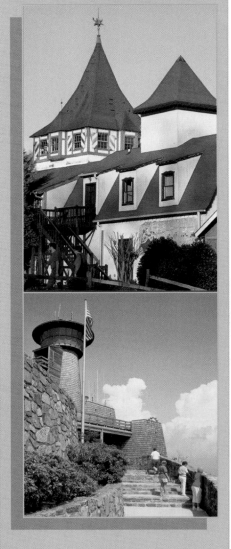

Did You Know?

Before one hundred million years of erosion wore away the Blue Ridge Mountains, they were 75 percent taller than they are today.

The Piedmont Plateau

The Piedmont Plateau begins in the mountain foot-hills of northern Georgia and goes to the central part of the state. It has gently sloping hills and valleys in the north and flatlands in the south. The region has well-drained soils, primarily sandy loam and clay, which are suitable for hardwood timber, pine, and agriculture.

Some Georgians refer to the gently rolling hills and southern flatlands as the "heartland" of the state. The term *Piedmont* means "foot of the mountain," but the plateau is so long that it actually runs from Alabama northward to Delaware. This granite-based landform makes up about one-third of the state's land area. In addition to the granite base, there is another familiar type of soil: clay. People new to the region often seem perplexed after a heavy rain and ask, "What is that red stuff?" Long-term residents usually simply smile and respond, "Well, that is our famous Georgia red clay."

About one-half of the state's population lives in the Piedmont region. It was the cotton belt during the period before the Civil War. Today, it is known for the production of wheat, soybeans, corn, poultry, and cattle. Business and industry also flourish throughout the area. The cities of Atlanta, Athens, Madison, and Milledgeville are among some of the densely populated areas criss-crossed by the Chattahoochee, Flint, Ocmulgee, and Oconee rivers.

Top: Stone Mountain is the world's largest mass of exposed granite, which underlies much of this region. **Above:** This gondola takes visitors to the top of Stone Mountain. **Right:** The region is characterized by gently rolling hills. **Opposite page, above:** Atlanta is the region's, and the state's, largest city. **Opposite page, below:** Erosion often exposes Georgia's famous red clay.

The Coastal Plain

The Coastal Plain, which occupies about three-fifths of the state, is the largest region. There are actually two parts of Georgia's Coastal Plain: the Inner Coastal Plain and the Outer Coastal Plain. The Inner Coastal Plain has a mild climate and a good supply of underground water. It is the major agricultural region of the state, with soil that varies from limestone to clay. The Vidalia Upland has become world famous for the unique sweet onions that grow there. The southwestern corner around Bainbridge and Albany is called the Dougherty Plain, in whose rich soil grow peanuts, corn, and pecan trees.

The Outer Coastal Plain does not have drained soil to provide fertile farmlands, but it is the center of naval stores and pulp production in the state. As you travel along the flat coastline area, which in some places

Above: This monument at the Early County Courthouse in Blakely honors the importance of the peanut to the area's economy. **Below:** Georgia poet Sidney Lanier was inspired to write "The Marshes of Glynn" after visiting the marshlands near Brunswick. **Opposite page, above:** The Inner Coastal Plain is the major agricultural region of the state.

Did You Know?

Living on the Outer Coastal Plain does have one unique disadvantage—sand gnats. When the elements are just right, these tiny nuisances love flying around your hair and face, and they can bite. But there is a cure— take a fresh clothes dryer sheet and rub it on your hair and face. It works to keep those pests away.

By the Side of the Road

SIDNEY LANIER
Georgia's Greatest Poet

← ✦ ✦

Was a guest in this home on many occasions in the 1870's. It was then the residence of his wife's brother, Henry C. Day. On these visits Lanier became acquainted with "THE MARSHES OF GLYNN" which he immortalized.

One of Georgia's most well-known and best-loved writers is poet Sidney Lanier. Born in Macon, Lanier often visited Brunswick and enjoyed the quiet beauty of the marshes that separated the Glynn County city from the barrier islands of Jekyll and St. Simons. To find out who he visited and how the marshes affected him, read the Historical Marker.

Want to see more? You can visit the Lanier Cottage in Macon where he was born. There you will see the desk where he worked, along with many personal items belonging to the poet. And, if you drive to Lakeland through Lanier County in southwest Georgia, you can learn even more about his life. Lanier will be discussed in greater detail later in your textbook. Watch for him!

Map 5
Georgia's Barrier Islands

Map Skill: How many barrier islands does Georgia have?

Right: Sapelo Island's coastal salt marshes are a nursery for fish and shellfish.

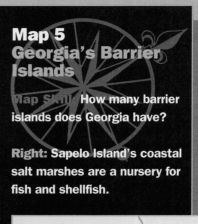

Ogeechee R.

Tybee Island
Little Tybee Island

Wassaw Island

Ossabaw Island

St. Catherines Island

Altamaha R.

Blackbeard Island

Sapelo Island

Wolf Island

Little St. Simons Island

Sea Island
St. Simons Island

Jekyll Island

Little Cumberland Island

Satilla R.

St. Marys R.

Cumberland Island

is fairly swampy and marshy, you are in the territory first visited by early explorers. One of the major features of the Outer Coastal Plain is the 681-square-mile Okefenokee Swamp located south of Waycross. The Okefenokee, the largest swamp in North America, is a freshwater wetland. A **wetland** is a low-lying land area where water lies close to the surface creating sloughs, swamps, bogs, ponds, and freshwater marshes. A wetland can also be a lowland that is influenced by tidal water flows to create salt marshes. Georgia ranks fourth in the nation in the number of acres of wetlands found in the state.

Along the coast, the deep harbors and barrier islands offer recreational facilities, seafood gathering and processing industries, and major shipyard ports. Here, for example, are cities such as Savannah, Darien, and Brunswick with their enduring, genteel beauty.

The coast is an interlocking chain of marshes, rivers, and tributaries that eventually flow into the Atlantic Ocean. The Spanish explorers called this subtropical region "Islands of Gold." Along the one-hundred mile shoreline is a group of **barrier islands**, so called because they protect the beaches by blocking much of the wind, sands, and water that could erode the mainland. Even today, this chain of islands offers much in terms of beauty, recreation, and tourism. Jekyll Island is primarily a state park, and Cumberland Island is a national seashore. Perhaps the greatest legacy of the barrier island group is that two-thirds of the land remains wilderness sanctuaries.

The **continental shelf** is the portion of the continent or the coastal plain that extends into the ocean. The continental shelf's outer edge, called the *continental slope,* drops away gradually. The continental slope is the actual edge of the continent. It falls into deep plateaus and eventually into the ocean depths two miles down.

Piedmont

Fall Line

Coastal Plain

Atlantic Ocean

The Fall Line

The Coastal Plain region is separated from the Piedmont Plateau by a natural boundary known as the Fall Line. The **Fall Line** is the point at which hilly or mountainous lands meet the coastal plain. This line runs from Columbus on the western side of the state, through Macon and into Augusta on the eastern side. Other cities located on the Fall Line are Milledgeville, Roberta, Thomson, and Warrenton. Rivers and creeks flowing from the rocky hill country cut deep channels in the softer soil of the plains. This drops the elevation and creates waterfalls. As early settlers began to leave the coastal regions and explore inland, many were forced to stop at the Fall Line because they could not travel over the steep and rushing falls. These early settlers, as well as Indians and traders, found the waterfalls an excellent power source and built settlements there.

Map 6
The Fall Line

Map Skill: Rivers above the fall line are fast moving, while rivers below the Fall Line are slower moving. Why do you think that is so?

Above: Fall Line waterfalls provide a source of power for businesses located along the Fall Line, including this textile mill in Columbus.

It's Your Turn

1. What are Georgia's five physiographic regions?
2. Which are Georgia's largest and smallest regions?
3. What is the difference between the Inner Coastal Plain and the Outer Coastal Plain?
4. What is the Fall Line and why is it important?
5. What are some of the cities located along the Fall Line?

Georgia's Climate

Section Preview

As you read, look for:
- the difference between weather and climate,
- the effect of weather conditions on the state,
- different types of weather phenomena, and
- vocabulary terms: climate, weather, vertical climate, drought, wind current, trade winds, prevailing westerlies, ocean currents, hurricane, nor'easter, tornado, El Niño, La Niña, and global warming.

One of the most distinguishing characteristics of Georgia's geographic regions is the climate of each area. But, what does that really mean? **Climate** refers to the type of weather a region experiences over a long period of time. **Weather** refers to the day-to-day conditions and changes in the atmosphere. While weather varies constantly, a region's climate remains stable. The climate of an region influences the types of homes built, the types of industries that develop, the clothing styles, and even what crops are grown. Weather extremes can produce devastating results—destruction of property and the environment, injuries, and deaths.

Look out of a window for a minute. What do you see? If the leaves are turning red, orange, and gold, it is probably fall regardless of which region you call home. However, the weather outside can differ tremendously based on where you are located. For example, in the north Georgia mountains, those beautiful autumn leaves indicate that snow is just around the corner. In south Georgia, however, fall leaves are an indicator to keep the umbrella handy as residents hope that hurricane season is finally ending and they can prepare for a dry month.

Below: Snowfall is rare in Atlanta. This photograph was taken at Piedmont Park.

Temperature

As a result of Georgia's latitude and longitude (and our nearness to the equator), the climate in our state overall is mild with a subtropical feel along the coast. We experience four distinct seasons: spring, summer, fall, and winter. In most places, summers are hot and humid while winters are mild. However, there is a narrow band across the north Georgia mountains that has warm summers and moderately cold winters because mountainous terrain also influences temperature. The higher the elevation, the colder the temperature. This phenomenon is sometimes referred to as **vertical climate**.

The highest temperatures in the state usually occur in July, and the coldest readings are normally in January. The average temperature for the year is 65°F (Fahrenheit). However, the mercury can fall below 0°F in the northern sections and rise above 100°F in the middle and southern regions of the state.

Several unlikely records have been set in the state. For example, on July 24, 1952, the town of Louisville had a temperature of 112°F. At the other end of the scale, Floyd County shivered on January 27, 1940, when the temperature plunged to -17°F.

Generally, though, temperatures are relatively comfortable through most of the year, which is one of the reasons why so many companies move into our state. Industries tend to favor mild climates because such weather equals lower costs for heating and air conditioning and fewer weather-related absences. Equally important, our mild climate generates longer growing seasons for a variety of crops. Even in today's modern Georgia, one in six Georgia jobs relates to agriculture or agri-business.

Precipitation

Precipitation is vital to Georgia's economy. Snow, which generally falls only in the mountain regions, melts and runs off into streams and lakes. Rainfall aids the growth of crops and forests. In a normal year, Georgia receives an average of 40 to 52 inches of rain in central and southern regions and 65 to 76 inches in the northern mountains, some of which is in the form of snow. July is the wettest month of the year, and October is the driest. Interestingly enough, all five areas of Georgia, including the Outer Coastal Plain, have experienced ice or snow, so a snow day from school really can happen even in Savannah, Brunswick, or the St. Marys area.

From 1998 through 2002, Georgia, like many other parts of the country, experienced a severe drought, with rainfall far below average. A **drought**

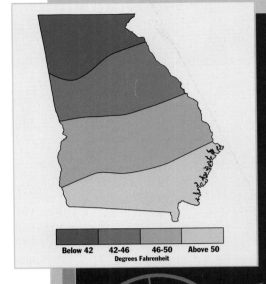

Map 7
Average January Temperatures

Map Skill What is the January temperature for where you live?

Below 42 | 42-46 | 46-50 | Above 50
Degrees Fahrenheit

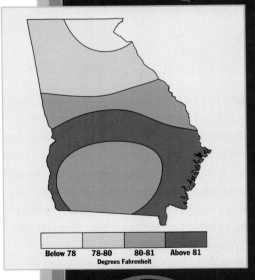

Map 8
Average July Temperatures

Map Skill What is the July temperature for the area where you live?

Below 78 | 78-80 | 80-81 | Above 81
Degrees Fahrenheit

Did You Know?

According to weather observers, if birds fly for cover when it starts raining, the rain will only last for a short time. But if they start flying around as usual in the rain, forget about the family picnic.

Spotlight on the Economy

Droughts

Above: Even irrigation equipment cannot help farmers' crops when a drought strikes.

Droughts impact us environmentally, socially, and economically. Businesses, industries, and home users are all affected by having less water. There is not as much water available to produce hydroelectric power. Forest fires become a constant threat, especially in heavily wooded areas of the state. Shortages of rainfall also mean fewer water-related recreational opportunities. Conservation becomes very important. But the most damaging impact of prolonged droughts is on agriculture.

Droughts limit agricultural production, so there is less harvest to sell to farmers' markets, food production companies, and grocery stores. Droughts also mean less grain for livestock. This affects beef, dairy, and poultry farms. Production goes down and prices go up. Everyone pays for the drought when they check out at their local supermarket.

To Georgia's economy, rain means more than carrying an umbrella. Snow means much more than a day out of school for students. Rain and snow mean economic survival. Sometimes, however, too much of a good thing can be trouble-some. In 1994, for example, all Georgia precipitation records were broken in most of the region from Bainbridge to Macon as over 23 inches of rain fell within a week's time. Thirty-two counties were declared disaster areas by the federal government. Officials in Albany, one of the hardest-hit areas, had to find shelter and food for 15,000 people. In Macon, 150,000 people were without water, while the town of Montezuma was virtually under water. Caring people along with various state and federal governmental agencies came to the aid of these Georgia citizens, many of whom lost everything they had worked so hard to attain.

Precipitation is also good or bad depending on the timing of the rains. The very rainfall that helped Georgia pull out of a five-year drought in 2003 also arrived a bit earlier than scheduled and damaged several major Georgia crops including watermelon production.

is a lack of precipitation over a period of time that results in water shortages. Lack of rainfall for even a short period of time can harm industries, farmers, and homeowners alike. A few weeks without rain and lawns begin to turn brown, plants and shrubs shrivel, fire warnings become common, and water conservation actions run full speed. The most famous drought in U.S. history may be the 1930s Dust Bowl when 50,000,000 acres of land became useless for farming and ranching. In the late 1980s, the country suffered the worst drought in 50 years, affecting at least 35 states. Crops and livestock died, some farm areas became deserts, and forest fires destroyed over 4,100,000 acres in 1988 alone. Half of Yellowstone National Park was charred.

Wind and Water Currents

When we think of Georgia and water, we certainly think of our coastline on the Atlantic Ocean. We know that the Atlantic has an influence on our state. But we often do not think about the influence the Gulf of Mexico has on Georgia since the Gulf is not directly on our border. Both have a strong influence on Georgia because of winds, wind currents, and ocean currents.

Winds

Winds influence the overall weather pattern of Georgia. Air masses that begin over the Gulf of Mexico and the Atlantic Ocean control summer's warm months. The winter months are controlled by air masses that start in the polar regions of Alaska and Canada. Wind patterns can bring moderate weather or intense storms in the forms of tornadoes and hurricanes.

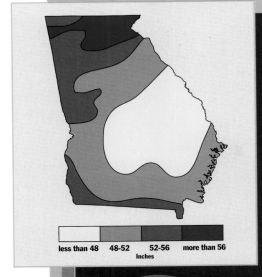

| less than 48 | 48-52 | 52-56 | more than 56 |

Inches

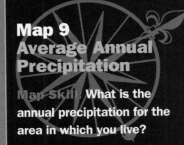

**Map 9
Average Annual
Precipitation**

Map Skill: What is the annual precipitation for the area in which you live?

Barrier islands, such as Cumberland Island shown here, are constantly changing due to the effects of wind and water currents.

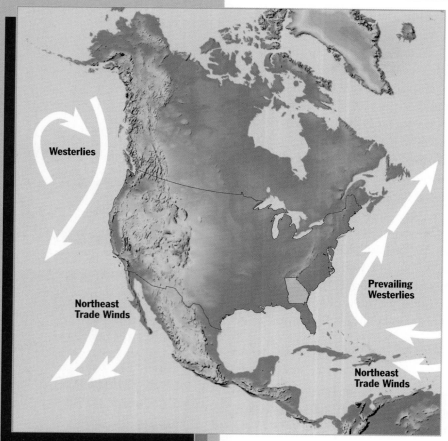

Westerlies

Northeast Trade Winds

Prevailing Westerlies

Northeast Trade Winds

Map 10 Wind Currents

Map Skills In which direction do the trade winds blow?

Wind Currents

The early explorers who traveled to Georgia and the rest of the southeastern area sought favorable wind currents to shorten their trip and to make for smoother sailing. A **wind current** is a continuous movement or flow of air. Surface winds from the equator to around 30° south latitude flow from the southeast. Winds from the equator to around 30° north latitude generally flow from the northeast. These winds are known as **trade winds**. The early navigators used the trade winds to sail westward to the New World.

Winds from around 30° to 60° latitude north and south of the equator generally blow from the west to the east. These winds, often called **prevailing westerlies**, were the winds used by explorers on their homebound trips, usually traveling a route slightly north of the trade winds. These areas are known as the *middle latitudes* and are prone to produce cyclones, which can bring winds from any direction as they pass. These westerly winds carry storms across the Atlantic, creating dangerous gales and heavy winds that are severe hazards to shipping.

The wind currents were important to early explorers visiting Georgia because they allowed ships to travel to the New World with settlers and with the supplies the colonists needed. They also allowed ships to travel from the New World back across the Atlantic carrying goods produced in the colonies.

Ocean Currents

About 71 percent of Earth is covered with water. Most of that water is in the oceans—the Atlantic, the Pacific, the Indian, the Arctic, and the Antarctic. The water in these oceans is constantly moving, and some of this movement forms rivers in the ocean. *Oceanographers* (scientists who study oceans) call these rivers of ocean water **ocean currents**. Strong ocean currents, especially the Canary Current and the Atlantic Equatorial Current, combined with the trade winds to push the explorers' ships south and west to the New World. On their homeward voyage, the ships were pushed to the east by the Gulf Stream.

Ocean currents are caused by the uneven heating of Earth's surface by the sun. Earth is hottest at the equator, where the sun shines most directly on Earth. Earth is coldest at the poles, where the sun shines less directly. Ocean currents contribute to the movement of heat from the equator to the poles, thus helping equalize Earth's surface temperatures. Ocean currents affect not only the routes chosen by ships carrying people and goods across the sea to the New World; they also influence climate and living conditions for the plants and animals on land.

Weather Phenomena

As you have already discovered, most of the time Georgia's climate is predictable—a few snow days from Atlanta and Athens northward in the winter, afternoon thunder showers and hot, hazy summer days in the coastal areas. However, there are also some unpredictable climate phenomena that occur with regularity in our state.

Hurricanes

Hurricanes are spawned when waters of 80°F or more transform the heat energy of tropical waters into strong winds and heavy waves. In our section of the world, the beginnings of these storms occur off the coast of Africa as depressions. It may take several weeks for a depression to turn into a tropical storm and eventually a hurricane.

The term *hurricane* comes from the Spanish word *huracan*, which means "big wind" and which was derived from the Indian word *huracan*, a reference to the evil spirit of storms. The season for these fierce storms is from the beginning of June to the end of November, and their devastation can be frightening. The devastation results from both wind and storm surge. The movement of water inland from coastlines, tidal rivers, and marsh areas can be as damaging as the fierce winds.

Georgia's most damaging hurricane-like storm in terms of loss of life came ashore in Savannah on August 27, 1893. Although the winds were not strong, 1,000 people died from flying debris and other storm-related causes. At that time, there were no reliable weather alerts for hurricanes, save word of mouth. Many people were simply unaware and

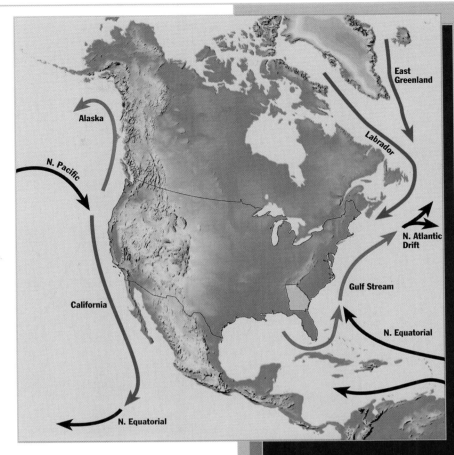

East Greenland

Alaska

Labrador

N. Pacific

N. Atlantic Drift

Gulf Stream

California

N. Equatorial

N. Equatorial

**Map 11
Ocean Currents**

Map Skill: What current runs along the east coast of North America?

Did You Know?

The costliest hurricane to hit the East Coast was Hurricane Andrew in 1992, which hit land in Dade County, Florida. Damages from this Category Four hurricane were over $25 billion.

unprepared for the 72-mile-per-hour storm.

Hurricane strength is registered on a score from one to five. A Category One hurricane has top winds of 74 to 95 miles an hour. A Category Five hurricane has winds of over 155 miles an hour and a water surge of more than 18 feet. Hurricanes are given names by the National Hurricane Center in Miami, Florida. The center usually chooses one name, either male or female from each letter of the alphabet, although occasionally a letter is skipped. Through years of experience, residents along the coast of the eastern United States have learned to pay close heed to tropical storm reports. The more you know about the various weather emergencies, the safer you and your family will be.

Nor'easters

A nor'easter ("northeaster") has the look of a hurricane. But it is really a gale wind that blows from the northern Atlantic and is often accompanied by large amounts of rainfall. Between October and April, areas of low pressure develop off the East Coast. The storm picks up warm air and moisture from the relatively warm Atlantic Ocean water. Strong northeast winds blow and pull the storm north along the Atlantic coast. At the same time, those northeast winds move cold air south. The combination of warm and cold air can produce a storm of snow, sleet, freezing rain, or heavy rains. When such storms move inland, they can produce rain or snow over coastal areas. The nor'easter is not, however, normally as strong or as devastating as a hurricane.

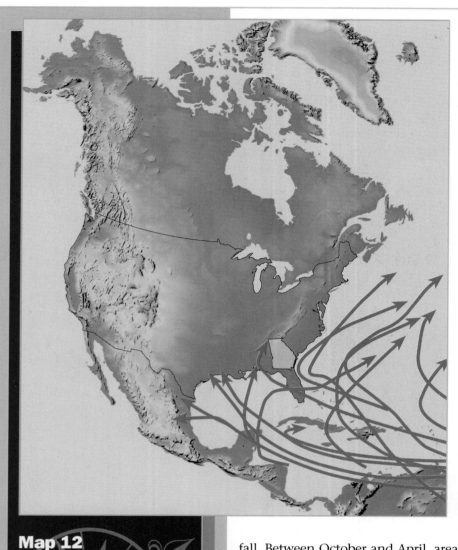

Map 12
Hurricane Paths

Map Skill: What area appears to be the most active for hurricanes?

Figure 2 Saffir-Simpson Hurricane Scale

Scale Number or Class	1	2	3	4	5
Wind Speeds (miles per hour)	74–95	96–110	111–130	131–155	Over 155
Storm Surge in Feet	4.0-4.9	5.0-7.9	8.0-11.9	12.0-18.0	Over 18.0
Expected Damage	Minimal	Moderate	Extensive	Extreme	Catastrophic

Tornadoes

Although Oklahoma has the most tornadoes in the United States, Georgia also has these funnel-shaped whirlwinds. When we see action movies or read about the excitement of storm chasers, we sometimes forget that these are dangerous, life-threatening cyclones. The word tornado comes from the Spanish word *tronada*, which means "thunderstorm." When warm, moist air mixes with a rapidly moving cold front, severe thunderstorms are possible. In the southeastern United States, these storms can produce tornadoes. Tornadoes are swirling cyclonic winds that, in our hemisphere, move in from southwest to northeast and spin in a counterclockwise motion. As the spinning increases, a column works itself down from the clouds. As it touches the ground, the tornado literally pulls debris up into the air.

Georgia has an average of twenty-one tornadoes a year, resulting in one to three deaths. Most tornadoes occur from March to May, but they can happen in any month. A tornado can last for a few minutes and travel as little as one-half mile with wind speeds up to 100 miles per hour. Larger tornadoes, called *maxis*, may travel over 200 miles during a three-hour period, with wind speeds of a shattering 250 miles per hour.

Tornadoes can cause extensive property damage, injuries, and loss of life. And they are unpredictable. Both large and small tornadoes seem to have minds of their own. They can move in a straight line, loop, hop over places, and even double-back on themselves. If you have seen pictures of damage after a tornado, you know that a line of houses can be totally crushed—with the single exception of one house in the middle of the storm path that

Above: When tornadoes touch down, the destruction can be horrific.

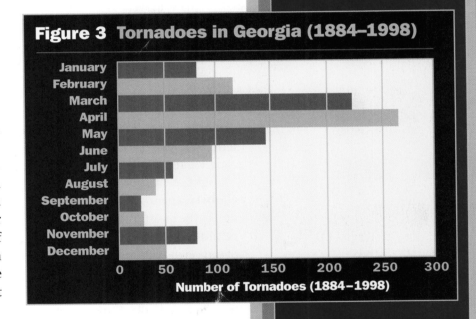

Figure 3 Tornadoes in Georgia (1884–1998)

Number of Tornadoes (1884–1998)

Rating	Wind Speeds (mph)	Expected Damage
Figure 4 Fujita Intensity Scale for Tornadoes		
F-0	40–72	Light: Loose Debris
F-1	73–112	Moderate: Broken Windows and Doors
F-2	113–157	Considerable: Trees Broken
F-3	158–206	Severe: Outer Walls Collapse
F-4	207–260	Devastating: Structural Damage
F-5	261–318	Incredible

Figure 5
What to Do During a Tornado

Because of the danger of tornadoes, it is important to know what to do if there is a tornado "warning." Schools practice tornado alerts each year, but what if you are home alone? Sometimes the sky will turn a dark green shade or large hail will begin to fall.

1. Stay away from windows.

2. Seek a safe shelter immediately. A basement is best or move to an interior room of your home. If necessary, wait out the storm in an interior bathroom (the plumbing helps strengthen walls).

3. If you hear a loud noise that sounds like a train, seek cover under a table, put a mattress over your head, or get inside the bathtub or shower and wait until the storm has passed and the sky brightens again.

stands without so much as a cracked window.

Georgia's most devastating tornado came on April 6, 1939. when a tornado touched down at 8:27 a.m. in Gainesville and Hall County. Over two hundred people were killed and over sixteen hundred were injured in that storm; much of downtown Gainesville was destroyed.

Changes in Weather Patterns

Much research is being conducted to determine how El Niño and La Niña affect Georgia's weather patterns. El Niño, which means "Little Boy," is warmer-than-normal Pacific Ocean surface temperatures. La Niña, which means "Little Girl," is colder-than-normal Pacific Ocean surface temperatures. El Niño seems to occur unusually strongly about once a decade, usually in December before Christmas. Both El Niño and La Niña bring climate havoc. For example, in the early 1980s, El Niño was 7°C (Celsius) warmer than normal and pumped heat energy into the atmosphere, altering weather patterns across three-fourths of the globe. There was flooding in North and South America and droughts in Africa, South Asia, and Australia.

Another phenomena influencing Georgia's climate is global warming. Global warming is the term that describes the raising of the average temperature on Earth due to an excess of carbon dioxide in the atmosphere. Researchers are finding rising temperatures and precipitation increases resulting from global warming.

A Final Note

Regardless of where you live in Georgia, people always talk about the weather. It is either too hot or too cold, too rainy or too dry. The next time you are tempted to complain, think about life in Antarctica. The coldest temperature is -126.0°F. An average summer day is 1°F. The average daily temperature of the six-month winter is -70°F. It's something to think about!

It's Your Turn

1. Why is Georgia's climate relatively mild?
2. Define the term *drought*.
3. Why is Georgia's limited annual snowfall so important?
4. How did wind and ocean currents influence the settlement of the New World?
5. Where do Atlantic coast hurricanes originate?
6. What is the difference between El Niño and La Niña?

Chapter Summary

- Geography helps us understand the world in spatial terms, places and regions, Earth's physical systems, the human systems of Earth, and environment and society.
- Latitude and longitude are used to locate a specific place on Earth. Georgia's absolute location on the globe is between 31°21' and 35° N latitude and between 80°50' and 80°36' W longitude.
- Georgia borders five other states—Florida, Alabama, Tennessee, South Carolina, and North Carolina—and it has 100 miles of coastline on the Atlantic Ocean.
- Georgia is the largest state east of the Mississippi River. It includes 58,910 square miles of land and 854 square miles of inland water.
- The geographic center of the state is located in rural Twiggs County, 18 miles southeast of Macon.
- Georgia's lowest point is sea level on the Atlantic coastline; the highest point is Brasstown Bald in Towns County with an elevation of 4,784 feet.
- Georgia contains five major physiographic regions: Appalachian Plateau region, Blue Ridge region, Ridge and Valley region, Piedmont Plateau, and Coastal Plain.
- A Fall Line crosses the state, separating the coastal plain from the hilly or mountainous areas.
- Georgia's average annual temperature is 65°F.
- Georgia's rainfall averages 40 to 52 inches in the central and southern parts of the state and 65 to 76 inches in the northern mountains.
- Wind currents, including trade winds and prevailing westerlies, provided power for early explorers to sail to the New World and return to homes across the Atlantic.
- Ocean currents also helped early explorers travel to the New World. In addition, they help stabilize Earth's temperature by moving heat from the equator to the North and South Poles.
- Georgia experiences such weather phenomena as hurricanes, nor'easters, and tornadoes.

Of Special Interest

The Official State Song of Georgia

Georgia, Georgia, the whole day through
Just an old sweet song keeps Georgia on my mind.
Georgia, Georgia, a song of you
Comes as sweet and clear as moonlight through the pines.
Other arms reach out to me
Other eyes smile tenderly
Still in peaceful dreams I see
The road leads back to you.
Georgia, Georgia, no peace I find
Just an old sweet song keeps Georgia on my mind.
Melodies bring memories
That linger in my heart
Make me think of Georgia
Why did we ever part?
Some sweet day when blossoms fall
And all the world's a song
I'll go back to Georgia
'Cause that's where I belong.

Source: "Georgia on My Mind" by Hoagy Carmichael and Stuart Gorrell Copyright © 1930 by Peermusic III, Lt. Copyright © Renewed. Used by Permission. All Rights Reserved.

*Chapter*Review

Reviewing People, Places, and Terms

Define, identify, or explain the importance of each of the following as it relates to this state we call home.

1. absolute location

2. hemisphere

3. longitude

4. bald

5. geography

6. responsibility

Developing Critical Thinking

1. Explain the different ways a prolonged drought can negatively impact the state's economy and its individual citizens.

2. In your opinion, which of the following Georgia regions is the most important to Georgia's agricultural economy—the Coastal Plain (Inner and Outer) or the Piedmont? Defend your choice.

3. Explain how wind and ocean currents influenced settlement in the New World.

Understanding the Facts

1. Which of Georgia's surrounding states touch only two other states?

2. Identify one way each of the state's five physiographic regions is unique.

3. What is the difference between the Inner Coastal Plain and the Outer Coastal Plain?

4. What are the barrier islands, and what purposes do they serve?

5. What do weather and climate have in common? In what ways are they different?

6. How do ocean currents help equalize Earth's temperature? Why is that necessary?

7. How many tornadoes does Georgia average a year?

8. Using a Venn diagram, compare and contrast El Niño and La Niña.

Checking It Out

1. Earthquakes in Georgia? Oh yes, and they occur more often than you know. Check out the when, where, and why using your research skills. While you are there, check out the 1811 New Madrid, Missouri, earthquake and see how it changed the Mississippi River.

2. Atlanta and Athens have also experienced some of a tornado's wrath. Use your research skills to find out more about these weather events. A clue to help you: the key phrase is "state of Georgia tornadoes." Also, check out what you need to do if you are in a car and see a tornado in the distance bearing down on you.

3. Research global warming and find one thing that you can do to help.

4. The United States has a "tornado alley." Identify the states in the alley and describe how your life might change if you lived there.

Writing Across the Curriculum

1. The date is December 15th, and you are a weather forecaster living in Athens. Everyone wants to know if there will be snow during winter break. Research the average monthly temperature and the average monthly precipitation for Athens. Based on what you have learned in your text and your research, write your weather forecast.

2. Develop a home safety booklet for your family to use during tornado season.

3. Your local Chamber of Commerce has asked you to write a brief ad proclaiming your geographic region the best place to live. Based on what you have read thus far, write that ad.

Exploring Technology

1. Using your favorite search engine on the Internet, look up the National Geography Standards. Decide which of the eighteen standards you think are the most important for young people to know. Explain your choices.

2. Check out the following statements to determine if they are true. Explain each.

    a. In 10 minutes, a hurricane can release more energy than all of the world's nuclear weapons combined.

    b. Lightning strikes about 6,000 times per minute on our planet.

3. There are all sorts of long-held folklore about the weather. Use the search words "weather folklore" to find three or four beliefs that you think are most interesting. Then determine through observations, interviews, or web searches if any of those beliefs are actually true.

Applying Your Skills

1. Research one of the historical sites found in the region in which you live. Interview local residents about their knowledge of the site. Use local library or media center resources to find out more about the site.

2. Research your area's weather patterns. Graph the weather of your hometown or community over the period of one year. (Note, this information is available from the University of Georgia.) What is the average temperature of your community? What are the coldest and hottest months? What are the wettest and driest months? What is the record precipitation for your community? Has your community experienced any weather problems in the past five years? What impact did these problems have on the people and the economy? Share your findings in a report to your classmates.

Just for Fun

You have heard the expression "It's raining cats and dogs." But did you know that it is possible? Research the expression to find out more.

Photo Question

In which one of Georgia's geographic regions are peanuts a major crop?

Georgia's Seven Wonders

Okefenokee Swamp (below) is the largest swamp in North America. Cypress trees (above) are known for their "knees," which help anchor them in unstable ground.

If you have taken a world history class, you may remember reading about the "Seven Wonders of the World," which included the Hanging Gardens of Babylon, the Great Pyramid, and the Colossus of Rhodes. But what you might not realize is that our state also has its own "seven natural wonders."

As you know, climate affects the natural features of a state over the centuries. Winds and water have eroded and shaped the state's topography (physical features such as mountains or plateaus). Among the many natural features of Georgia's topography, seven have been designated as natural wonders: the Okefenokee Swamp, Tallulah Gorge, Radium Springs, Warm Springs, Stone Mountain, Providence Canyon, and Amicalola Falls.

The Okefenokee Swamp, which was once part of the Atlantic Ocean floor, received its name from the Indian word *o-wa-qua-phenoga*, which means "land

of the trembling earth." The Okefenokee is filled with a shallow "black water" stained by the tannic acid of decaying vegetation. The swamp covers a half million acres (about seven hundred square miles) and is located in the Outer Coastal Plain near Waycross and Folkston. This primitive wetland is home to hundreds of species of plants, animals, and reptiles, many of whom are endangered. Throughout the area are about seventy "piney woods" islands, once home to Seminole Indians and settled by pioneer Georgians in the 1850s.

If you visit, you will enter a world of giant, 80-foot cypress trees draped with moss overhanging dark, murky waters filled with alligators, herons, egrets, and cranes. The swamp is also home to Georgia's native black bears—and the comic strip character "Pogo." So, if you like snakes, turtles, armadillos, otters, birds, deer, alligators, and frogs, take a guided trip on a tour boat and enjoy the sights and sounds. Oh, make sure you say hello to 15-foot, 900-pound "Oscar," the alligator.

Tallulah Gorge, located on U.S. 441, spans the border between Habersham and Rabun counties. One of the most spectacular gorges in the eastern United States, Tallulah Gorge is 3 miles long and nearly 1,200 feet deep. The hard granite walls form steep cliffs. The roar of the waters that cut the gorge could once be heard for miles and led to the nickname the "Niagara Falls of the South." Today the Tallulah River is silent because it was dammed to provide hydroelectric power for Atlanta's continuing growth. Because of the dam, you can now vacation on manmade Lake Rabun or Lake Burton.

Above: Spectacular vistas into Tallulah Gorge have drawn millions of visitors to this state park over the years.

Tallulah Gorge reached national prominence several times. In 1886, "Professor Leon" tightwalked across the gorge; 84 years later, Karl Wallenda repeated that walk. Wallenda stopped twice in crossing the falls to stand on his head.

Today, visitors are returning to the area to enjoy the many displays at the Jane Hurt Yarn Interpretive Center or to shop for handmade mountain handicrafts. Those who like hiking or mountain climbing can request special permission to practice those skills on the gorge.

Radium Springs, located near Albany in Lee County, is another of Georgia's wonders. First opened in 1927 as a resort casino, the springs feature sapphire-blue water flowing through a crystalline pool. Indians believed that this water had healing powers. Today, Radium Springs has largely dried

Top: Franklin D. Roosevelt built this six-room cottage in Warm Springs. It later came to be called the "Little White House." Above: FDR State Park in Warm Springs is one of the most beautiful of the state's parks.

up due to drought and algae. But there are fourteen other "blue holes" and caves hundreds of feet below Albany courtesy of the Flint River. They provide the city with clear, purified 68° water.

Radium Springs is no longer in operation although there is interest in converting it to a state park. And there has been some interest in restoring the former casino. What do you think?

Another site close to Radium Springs is an area of sand dunes. If you look closely, you may find sharks' teeth in the sand. Why? Many geologists believe that this area was the northern edge of the Gulf of Mexico millions of years ago. That is a wonder in itself.

In Meriwether County, near Pine Mountain, is one of Georgia's most famous natural wonders—**Warm Springs**. The warm mineral springs flow from the hillsides of Pine Mountain. The temperature of the pools of mineral springs average 88°, and the springs flow at a rate of 914 gallons a minute. The Creek and Iroquois Indians brought their sick and wounded to the springs to be "healed," much like those who visited Radium Springs.

Henry Clay and John C. Calhoun also visited the springs, but it was in 1924 that the area gained fame. Franklin Delano Roosevelt visited Warm Springs as treatment for his polio. The four-term president made so many trips to the

healing springs that he built a comfortable but small home there in 1932 . It eventually became known as the "Little White House." Today, the springs are part of a state rehabilitation center and are, along with nearby Callaway Gardens, a popular resort attraction.

Probably the best known of Georgia's seven wonders is **Stone Mountain** near Atlanta. This solid granite mountain rises 750 feet above the Georgia Piedmont and is 1,683 feet above sea level. It began to form over 300 million years ago when molten magma was pushed into existing rock about 10 miles below the surface. The surrounding rock layers eroded slowly, and the granite mass was uncovered about 15 million years ago. The 25-million-square-foot, 583-acre rock was a sacred place for the Creek Indians who settled the area.

Stone Mountain may be best known for its Confederate Memorial Carving, which is the largest raised sculpture in the world. The carving is more than 400 feet above the ground, measures 90 by 190 feet, and is recessed 42 feet into the mountain. The figures are as tall as a 90-foot building. The carving dates to 1912 when the United Daughters of the Confederacy acquired the north face of the mountain for a Civil War monument. The carving depicts Confederate President Jefferson Davis, General Robert E. Lee, and

Top: Stone Mountain was once described as "very high, shining when the sun set like a fire." Above: The Confederate Memorial Carving is larger than a football field.

Visitors to Providence Canyon (above and below) are amazed at the breathtaking colors exposed in the canyon walls.

Thomas J. "Stonewall" Jackson. It was begun by sculptor Gutzon Borgium (who went on to carve Mount Rushmore). Fifty-eight years and several other sculptors later the carving was completed.

Today, millions of visitors travel to the park each year to enjoy the lake, museums, and recreational facilities, to learn about unusual clams and fairy shrimp that lie in crater pools on the top of the mountain, or to see rare plants and flowers. During summer nights, the park comes alive with the magic of a laser light show unlike any in the world.

Providence Canyon near Lumpkin is Georgia's "Little Grand Canyon." This 1,108-acre state park contains sixteen canyons that have eroded 150 feet deep. The winding gullies display multicolored rock levels of tan, white, buff, pink, red, salmon, orange, and lavender hues (shades of color). The bottoms of the canyons are an ancient ocean floor where fossils exist. Some of the canyons are over a half-mile long and 300 feet across. The canyons were caused by the erosion that resulted when settlers cleared trees to farm the land in the mid-1800s. The farmers grew cotton in the same soil year after year without giving the soil time to rest and rejuvenate. Soon, the land was stripped of all vegetation. Then erosion—the enemy of all farmers—began to creep into a ditch that started out only about 5 feet deep. Eventually the canyons were created.

Today, trees and plants run throughout the state-operated park with seven miles of hiking trails. You can also wander through and explore the canyons.

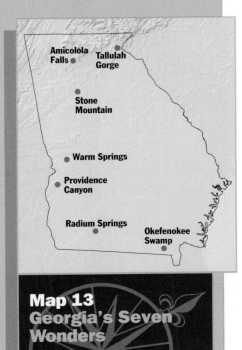

Map 13
Georgia's Seven Wonders

Map Skill: Which of Georgia's seven natural wonders is closest to where you live?

Left: Amicalola Falls is the highest waterfall east of the Mississippi.

The last of Georgia's seven natural wonders is **Amicalola Falls** near Dawsonville. It is located high in the watershed of a ridge known as Amicalola Mountain. In the Cherokee language, *Amicalola* means "tumbling water." A river runs along the western slope until it tumbles off. The falls provide an incredible 729-foot cascade of water, which drains into the Etowah River further south.

Amicalola is the southern end of the great Appalachian Mountain chain. The falls are just a few miles from the Southern Terminus Access Trail for the Appalachian Trail. Occasionally, you might see hikers leaving that point to begin their walk to Maine. Now, that's a hike! Can you guess the number of miles they must travel? Check it out.

This Place We Call Home

In Chapter One, you learned about our geographic regions and our state's climate. In this chapter, you will continue your geographic journey through Georgia by examining the plants and animals that live in our state, our mineral resources, and our waterways.

Top: Top: This baby alligator will grow into Georgia's largest reptile. **Above:** The dwarf crested iris is often found in Georgia's forests. **Left:** Lake Blackshear is an 8,000-acre reservoir in Georgia Veterans Memorial State Park. **Opposite page, above:** In March, you can often see peach trees in blossom. **Opposite page, below:** The Canada goose is quickly becoming a year-round resident.

Signs of the Times
Georgia Today

Georgia Resources:
Deep water ports: 2 (Savannah, Brunswick)
Inland barge terminal ports: 2 (Columbus, Bainbridge)
National forests: 2
   (Chattahoochee-Oconee National Forests)
Percentage of Georgia that is forested: Over 60 percent (Hardwoods, 53 percent, mostly maple, oak, sweetgum; Pine, 47 percent)
State parks: 39

Georgia Numbers:
Number of plant species in state: 3,000 +
Number of rare plant species: 105
Number of state symbols: 45
Number one pest plant: Kudzu
Number of acres entrusted to Nature Conservancy: 220,000

Figure 6 Timeline: 1800–2050

1936
Chattahoochee National Forest established

1930
Kudzu introduced into Georgia

1972
State Department of Natural Resources formed

1919
Marble from Tate Quarry used in Lincoln Monument in Washington, D.C.

1980
Severe energy crisis in Georgia and throughout nation

1830
Industry and air pollutants enter Georgia

1911
Forest Service bought 31,000 acres of Georgia land

2012
You will be in charge of solving environmental problems in Georgia

1800   **1850**   **1900**   **1950**   **2000**   **2050**

1845
Potato blight struck Ireland

1905
U.S. Forest Service created

1979
Three Mile Island accident

1872
Yellowstone Park, world's first national park, created

1972
DDT banned

1940
Bald Eagle Preservation Act passed

1970
Environmental Protection Agency formed

Section 1

Georgia's Flora and Fauna

Georgia's **flora** (its plants, flowers, and trees) and **fauna** (animals, reptiles, birds, and sea life) are among the most diverse in the United States.

Plant Life

Because of a 180-day growing period in the northern section of our state and a 270-day growing season along the coast, Georgia is home to hundreds of species of plants. They range from the hearty purple verbena found throughout the state to the rare and delicate trillium found only in the Tallulah Gorge. And few places can equal the beauty of Georgia's springtime at Callaway Gardens with azaleas, wild dogwood, iris, and daffodils. In the spring, Thomasville is ablaze with color from over five hundred species of roses.

Native plants in Georgia are not just for beauty. Some can be fun and useful. Most people have, at one time or another, picked a dandelion and blown the soft, feathery fuzz into the air. But did you know some families use the dandelion leaves for salad? Plants also serve medicinal purposes. Aloe plants, for example, are a mainstay in many kitchens as an immediate healing agent for burns.

Section Preview

As you read, look for:
• the variety of Georgia's plant and animal life, and
• vocabulary terms: flora and fauna.

Did You Know?

Thomasville is called the City of Roses, while Macon is called the City of Cherry Blossoms.

Wildflowers abound throughout the state. This photograph was taken on Sea Island.

Not all of our plants are popular. During the summer, you need not drive far to see a species of greenery that frustrates all farmers, gardeners, and Department of Transportation work crews. Kudzu has a long but less-than-distinguished career. In 1876, one hundred years after our nation's first birthday, Philadelphia hosted a Centennial Industrial Exposition. One hit of the fair was a bed of thick, green growth on display at the Japanese Exposition. The Japanese used the plant as both medicine and food flavoring. Because of its reputation as an agent in stopping soil erosion, kudzu plants were introduced into Georgia in 1930. Today, our state's neighbors to the north and south are finding out what Georgians quickly discovered. Not only does kudzu fail to stop soil erosion, the multileafed, cascading plant can grow up to one hundred feet during the summer months and is almost impossible to kill. But, the news is not all bad. Recently, scientists have found the leaves can be crushed into a powder and used as a cooking starch. It is also found in health foods and even made into kudzu candy.

Besides kudzu, there are other botanical invaders in our state. Botanists think that about 20 percent of plants found in the wild are foreign to Georgia soil, including privet, Japanese honeysuckle, chinaberry, and tallow trees.

Trees

Georgia has over 36 million acres of land. Over 23 million acres of that area is forested, which is twice the national average. To put it another way, over 60 percent of our state is forested. With over two hundred species of trees in Georgia and the southeastern United States, the variety seems endless. In the northern part of the state are hardwoods such as hickory, red spruce, white oak, beech, and maple. Loblolly, longleaf, slash, and other pines as well as the live oak are abundant in the Piedmont and parts of the Coastal Plain. Bald cypress and cedar cover large areas of the Okefenokee Swamp.

Some of our cities are known for their trees. Magnolias line many of the neighborhood streets in Augusta, while dogwoods abound in Atlanta. In the fall,

Top: The mountain laurel is one of Georgia's best loved native shrubs. **Center:** The fragile looking Indian pipe thrive in shady areas. **Above:** Kudzu has been nicknamed "the vine that ate the South!"

Did You Know?

Spanish moss is not really moss. It is an air plant related to the pineapple family. It lives on moisture in the air, has no roots, and can grow to be as long as twenty-five feet. Although beautiful to look at, do not touch this plant because most Spanish moss clumps are filled with chiggers.

A Mark on Georgia, the World, and Football

Charles Holmes Herty was born in Milledgeville in 1867. When Charles was only a few years younger than you are now (he was 11), he and his sister became orphans. They went to Athens to live with their aunt. Charles attended the University of Georgia and Johns Hopkins University. He returned to the University of Georgia in 1891 as a chemistry instructor. At the same time, he became the University's first football coach. In January 1892, Herty's young team played its first game against Mercer College, winning with a score of 52–0. A month later, the team traveled to Atlanta where they played a team from Auburn College. The team lost, but the game started the South's oldest football rivalry.

In 1899, Herty left the University to study in Europe. When he returned to the United States, he joined the U.S.

Above: Charles Holmes Herty's personal motto was "For Science and Country." The Georgia Section of the American Chemical Society honors him each year by awarding the prestigious Herty Medal to a chemist from the southeastern United States.

Forest Service to work on saving pine trees throughout the South. In 1929, Professor Herty designed a container for the naval stores industry that caused far less damage to the pine trees. By 1932, he had created a pulp and paper lab in Savannah that used pine trees to make newsprint. This led to many new jobs in the South.

Herty was the first president of the American Chemical Society and, with another scientist, helped establish an organization that led to the National Institutes of Health.

downtown Athens turns bright gold with the fan-shaped leaves of the gingko trees, and in the spring, thousands of visitors pour into Macon as the Yoshino cherry trees blossom. It is also difficult to imagine Savannah without thinking of its moss-laden, giant live oaks and palmetto. Then, of course, there are the two trees that are synonymous with Georgia: the peach tree and the pecan tree. Both contribute significantly to Georgia's economy. Interestingly, although Atlanta has fifty-five streets with the name of Peachtree, there are no peach groves within miles of the city.

The beautiful wooded areas of the state are a major advantage for Georgia's recreation and tourism industries. The Chattahoochee-Oconee National Forests are one of the protected forest areas of the state. But if you want to see something really unusual, drive to Rome. There you will find Marshall Forest, which is the only virgin forest within a city limits anywhere in the country. The 100-acre forest and surrounding acres are home to over 300 species of plants and were a gift to the Nature Conservancy. This generous gift is a National Natural Landmark, Georgia's first but hopefully not its last.

Wildlife

Georgia's fauna is as diverse as its flora. With enough land, varied physiographic features, and a moderate climate, Georgia is a natural home for wildlife. Among its fauna are mammals, birds, reptiles and amphibians, and fish.

Mammals

Over forty *species*, or kinds, of mammals are found in Georgia. One of them, prized by hunters and naturalists alike, is the whitetail deer. It was almost extinct by the early 1900s, but, thanks to careful management, whitetail deer can now be found in all 159 Georgia counties. But those soft-eyed, sweet looking creatures that remind us all of "Bambi" do not eat grazing food like hay. They seem to prefer the leaves and blooms of all woody plants and many of the blooms in our yards as well as fruits and nuts. However, the deer add a beauty and grace to our lives that we do not want to lose even if we lose a few plants along the way.

In addition to deer, squirrels, opossums, bats, rabbits, hares, raccoons, and foxes can be seen in most sections of the state. Bobcats are usually found in the forest mountain regions or in swamps. Wild hogs make their home in Coastal Plain river swamps, along with beavers, otters, armadillos, and minks. Wild horses still roam Cumberland Island.

Top: Whitetail deer feed on a wide variety of plants—including people's yard plantings and crops! Above: Foxes, like this gray fox, can be found throughout Georgia.

Georgia's state marine mammal is the right whale, considered to be one of the most endangered species in the world. Weighing up to seventy tons, the seventy-foot right whale is actually a baleen whale. It earned the name "right" during long-ago whaling days. Whalers claimed this species was "just right" in terms of weight, amount of oil for fuel and soap, and whalebone.

The pygmy sperm whale is the second most common whale off Georgia's coastal waters. Another common marine mammal is the bottle-nosed dolphin, which can be spotted along the ocean beaches and in tidal creeks and rivers. Lesser in number are the Atlantic spotted dolphins and the spinner dolphins, both of which are usually seen only several miles offshore.

One marine mammal facing grave danger of extinction in Georgia is the manatee. The West Indian manatee, commonly called a "sea cow," is a large seal-shaped creature with flippers as forelimbs and paddle-like, rounded tails. The manatee averages ten feet in length and adults weigh 1,000 to 2,500 pounds.

The manatee spend most of their time eating water plants, resting, or traveling in the rivers, estuaries, salt-water bays, creeks, and canals along Georgia's Atlantic coastline. Because they are so temperature sensitive, manatees congregate at warm water run-offs from plants along the coastline.

Marine conservationists estimate that fewer than 2,640 manatees are left in the United States. Like the right whale, the manatee suffers from boating collisions, the loss of a natural habitat, water pollution, and the ingestion of fish hooks and lines discarded in coastal waters. A rapidly growing segment of the population operate power boats and pleasure crafts in coastal waters, so the manatee must confront commercial and recreational boaters to survive.

Birds

Georgia is a year-round home for 170 species of birds, including robins, cardinals, blue jays, thrashers, and woodpeckers. Two hundred other species feed and nest in the state during spring and fall migrations. One of the most popular visitors is the ruby-throated hummingbird. Thousands of people place feeders of lightly sugared water in their yards each year hoping to attract the shy, tiny visitors as they migrate to South America.

There are also many game birds in Georgia. Quail, doves, ducks, and wild turkeys are the most popular with hunters. Georgia has joined at least forty-two other states in classifying the bald eagle as an endangered species. Hunting eagles is strictly forbidden by law. The state funds a program to feed the young eaglets until they are ready to live on their own. Extensive federal and state programs, along with caring private citizens, have resulted in a significant increase in the number of nesting bald eagles.

Reptiles and Amphibians

Forty species of snakes live in Georgia; all but six species are harmless. Poisonous snakes include the copperhead, cottonmouth (water moccasin), coral, and three types of rattlesnakes. It is important to remember that snakes do not automatically attack people; they strike to defend themselves. Since they can only strike a distance of about one-half of their body length, it is wise to remain at a safe distance of about 4 to 5 feet and be safe. Snakes are an important and valuable part of our environment since they keep down the population of rodents and insects that can make our lives miserable.

Did You Know?

Alligators **can run at a speed of 15 miles per hour, and** crocodiles **cannot stick out their tongues.**

The Coastal Plain region, particularly swampy areas such as Okefenokee, is home to the American alligator. Alligators grow to an adult length of six to twelve feet. Although they are protected by the federal government from unauthorized killing, they have become so numerous that Georgia now allows an alligator hunting season.

There are twenty-seven varieties of turtles in Georgia. The famous loggerhead sea turtles live on the barrier islands off Georgia's coast. From May through August, the loggerheads nest at night on the ocean and river beaches. The species is now endangered because recent developments on the coast have increased the artificial lighting and caused much damage to the nesting habitat. Visitors to a stream, marsh, or pond can easily find some of Georgia's other amphibians. The

Top: The bald eagle, our national symbol, usually nests near water. **Above** Visitors to the Lamar Q. Ball, Jr. Raptor Center in Statesboro can see raptors like this redtailed hawk "up close and personal."

By the Side of the Road

WORLD RECORD BASS

Approximately two miles from this spot, on June 2, 1932, George W. Perry, a 19-year old farm boy, caught what was to become America's most famous fish. The twenty-two pound four ounce largemouth bass (Micropterus salmoides) exceeded the existing record by more than two pounds and has retained the world record for more than fifty years. Perry and his friend, J. E. Page, were fishing in Montgomery Lake, a slough off the Ocmulgee River, not for trophies but to bring food to the table during those days of the great depression. The fish was caught on a Creek Chub Perch Scale Wigglefish, Perry's only lure, and was 32½ inches in length and 28½ inches in girth. The weight and measurements were taken, recorded and notarized in Helena, Georgia and Perry's only reward was seventy-five dollars in merchandise as first prize in Field and Stream Magazine's fishing contest. The longstanding record is one of the reasons that the largemouth bass was made Georgia's Official State Fish. Montgomery Lake is today part of the Department of Natural Resources' Horse Creek Wildlife Management Area.

124-4   GEORGIA HISTORIC MARKER   1984

On June 2, 1932, near Jacksonville, a nineteen-year-old farm boy named George W. Perry caught what was to become America's most famous fish. The twenty-two pound, four-ounce largemouth bass was the largest bass ever caught, heavier by more than two pounds. The record has stood for over fifty years.

Perry and a friend were fishing in Montgomery Lake, a slough off the Ocmulgee River, hoping to catch food for their tables during the Great Depression. Perry caught the record bass on a Creek Chub Perch Scale Wigglefish, his only lure. The bass was 32½ inches long and 28½ inches around. The size was notarized in Helena. His longstanding record is said to be one of the reasons the largemouth bass was made Georgia's official state fish.

The Spanish moss-draped oaks that surrounded Lake Montgomery when Perry caught his record fish are still there. But the water no longer winds in from the river, so the lake is much smaller and shallower. You can see a picture of Perry's lure on a giant sign that welcomes visitors to Jacksonville. According to local reports, Perry was a modest man and rarely bragged about his world record. Sadly, he died in an airplane crash in 1974.

Above: A hatchling loggerhead turtle makes its way toward the ocean in late summer.

state is a natural home for twenty-four types of frogs, four species of toads, and thirty-six kinds of salamanders.

Fish and Sea Life

If you ask Georgia fishers, "What do you like to catch?" you can almost guess the part of the state in which they fish by the answer they give. If they like trout, chances are they are from north Georgia. On April 1, they join scores of other people, equipped with handmade fishing flies or cans of corn, wading into the cold mountain streams. The state boasts four thousand miles of public and private trout streams. To Georgians in the middle and southern part of the state, nothing can match the fun of bringing in a largemouth bass from one of the thousands of ponds and lakes that dot the region. A number of state and national fish hatcheries ensure that our lakes and streams are always full of the hundreds of fish species available to sportspersons. Coastal fishers enjoy the challenge of bringing in red drum, spotted sea trout, sheepshead, and croaker. Locals along the Golden Isles frequently catch their dinner of blue crabs or pink shrimp. Offshore artificial reefs ensure that future generations enjoy an abundance of fish off the coastal shores. The Grays Reef National Marine Sanctuary, off Sapelo Island, is one of the largest bottom reefs in the southeastern United States. One of the most popular fish in the coastal area is catfish, which can be found in both freshwater and saltwater.

One other fish deserves recognition: shad. The Ogeechee River near Savannah is the home of this special delicacy. The season for shad runs from January 1 to March 31, and many fine restaurants in the coastal region feature this tasty, albeit expensive, delicacy. Shad roe, which is made up of millions of tiny eggs, is usually wrapped in bacon and baked as another unique coastal treat.

One of the most feared sea creatures off the Georgia coast is the shark. You have probably not confronted a shark in the water since they normally swim farther out from shore than beach-goers. But this fascinating fish is vitally important to our future. Scientists believe that sharks never get cancer, even though they live up to one hundred years and can survive for six weeks without eating. Scientists do not know if the absence of cancer is because the shark has no skeletal system (only cartilage) or if it has a natural immunity that can be used in research to find a cure for cancer.

Georgia's fishing industry, which produces about $45 million per year, is changing. As the shrimping industry slows due to decreasing numbers and size of shrimp and increased government regulations, Georgia's commercial fishers have turned to other fish markets. Asian markets rely on some foods not considered seafood staples in our country but considered to be delicacies in their culture. These new foods include welks and jellyfish. The latter is about 95 percent water, but the remaining part is made into "jelly balls." Fishermen are gathering these new sea foods for export overseas.

Top: This shrimper is sorting his catch. Georgia shrimp are considered by many to be the best in the world. Above: Jekyll Island is a favorite destination for surf fishing enthusiasts.

It's Your Turn

1. What percentage of Georgia's land is forested?
2. Find out which trees and plants dominate in your hometown. How does that differ from some other sections of the state? For example, salt marsh wiregrass does not grow in northern Georgia. It grows only in the long pine coastal areas of the state.
3. Which two endangered marine mammals make Georgia their home for a portion of the year?
4. What aspect of coastal area growth and development most hinders the endangered loggerhead sea turtles?
5. What potential does the shark hold for man's future?

Did You Know?

Georgia's fish serve many purposes. Most people do not realize that some lipsticks used the world over have fish scales in them.

Section Preview

As you read, look for:
- the state's mineral resources and
- uses for minerals mined in the state.

Georgia's Natural Resources

Because we have such a diverse state, we are fortunate in Georgia to have many natural resources. Our fauna and flora are a part of those resources, but we also have many rock and mineral resources.

Perhaps our best-known resource is marble, found primarily in Gilmer, Hall, and Pickens counties. In fact, Pickens County holds a Marble Festival each year where you can see a beautiful marble hotel and visit a school made out of marble. Both are located in Tate. Marble is used for buildings, monuments,

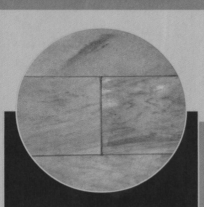

Right: The Tate House was built in 1925 by Colonel Sam Tate, the founder of the Georgia Marble Company. Georgia marble was used in the construction of the Lincoln Memorial. **Above:** The rare rose-colored marble used in the Tate House is responsible for its nickname of the "Pink Palace." **Below:** The Tate School, built of white marble, is the nation's only marble elementary school.

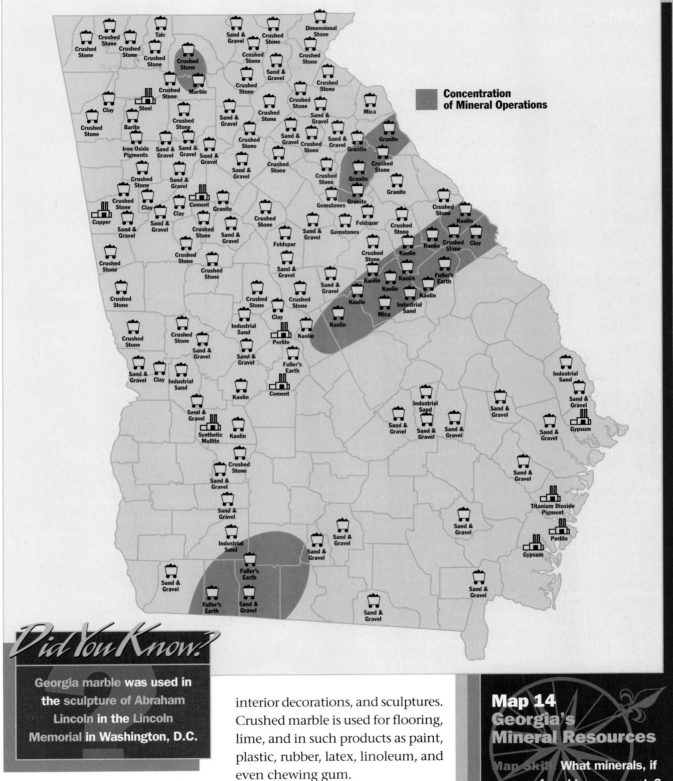

Concentration of Mineral Operations

interior decorations, and sculptures. Crushed marble is used for flooring, lime, and in such products as paint, plastic, rubber, latex, linoleum, and even chewing gum.

Another well-known stone product is granite, which is found mainly in Elbert and DeKalb counties. Granite is used for buildings, monuments, paving blocks, and curbs. Crushed it is used in concrete and concrete products

**Map 14
Georgia's
Mineral Resources**

Map Skill: What minerals, if any, are found in your county?

Figure 7　Other Mineral Resources of Georgia

Mineral	Uses	Primary Mining Area
Barite	Used in radiation shielding, as filler for brake shoes, in golf and bowling balls	Cartersville (Bartow County)
Feldspar	Used in ceramics, soaps, scouring powders, and electrical insulations	Jasper, Greene counties
Gold	Used in jewelry, electrical uses, covers dome of State Capitol	Dahlonega (Lumpkin County)
Limestone	Used in cement, highway material, agricultural lime	Much of northwest and Coastal Plain region
Muscovite mica	Used for roofing materials, joint cement, rubber, paint, well drilling compounds, and electrical insulations	Hartwell (Hart County), Washington, and Sandersville
Ocher	Coloring for bricks, mortar, cement, and linoleum	Cartersville (Bartow County)
Phosphate	Used in fertilizer, water softeners, baking powder, detergents, ceramics, and pharmaceuticals	Coastal Plain region
Quartzite	Used in landscaping, decorative stones, road material, industrial sand	Augusta (Richmond County)
Sandstone	Used for building stone, road material	Jasper, Pickens counties and Coastal Plain region
Shale	Cement, brick, tile, road materials, sewer pipe	Polk, Murray counties
Structural clays	Used in brick, tile, road materials, sewer pipe	Richmond, Bibb, Muscogee counties
Talc, soapstone	Used in roofing materials, cosmetics, steel pencils, paper, paint, rubber, insecticides	Murray County, much of north Georgia

including road paving materials. Limestone and slate are two additional stone products mined in Georgia.

It may come as a shock to many people, but the estimated value of nonfuel coal mined in Georgia is over $1.6 billion a year.

More profitable, however, are clay products called kaolin and fuller's earth. Fuller's earth is mined in Decatur, Grady, Jefferson, and Thomas counties. It

is used primarily for drilling muds, kitty litter, as an absorbent for oil or grease, and in soaps and medicines. The most valuable mineral in Georgia is kaolin, which is almost 54 percent of our nonfuel mineral production. Kaolin is mined in the Fall Line counties of the east-central Coastal Plain. It is used as a coating for paper, a filler for paint, plastics and rubber, as a base for porcelain products, in addition to other uses. Hard kaolin is also used for fire bricks, mortar, and cement.

There are many other minerals that are very important even though they may be mined in smaller quantities.

It's Your Turn

1. Name four minerals for which Georgia is nationally known.
2. You will read in upcoming chapters about Georgia's gold rush. Where is most of Georgia's gold found?
3. Go online with your favorite search engine and research Georgia's mineral resources. One good source is the U.S. Geological Survey. Identify the minerals associated with your own community. Which were mined in the past and which are still mined today?

Top: Kaolin mines are found along a 20-mile-wide, 60-mile-long strip running from Macon to Augusta. Above: Kaolin is often mixed with water and shipped in rail cars.

Georgia's Waterways

Below: The Atlantic Intracoastal Waterway is an important shipping lane for cargo ships.

Georgia's waterways provided transportation and food for early Indian tribes. When European settlers arrived, they set up trading posts and established temporary and permanent settlement sites on river *bluffs* (steep riverbanks). Today, the Atlantic Ocean and inland rivers, lakes, and streams are used for recreation, to make electricity, as inexpensive transportation resources for ships and barges, as ports for trade and commerce, as a food source (fishing), and, of course, as attractions for Georgia's tourism industry.

The Atlantic Ocean

Georgia has more than one hundred miles of coastline on the Atlantic Ocean, beginning at the Savannah River and going to the St. Marys River. Savannah and Brunswick are the state's two deepwater ports. Some parts of the coastline serve as wildlife refuges and others as commercial fishing and shrimping centers. There are harbors for the coming and going of luxury cruise ships and trading ships as well as miles of recreational beaches that draw tourists from far and near.

Georgia's barrier islands, are located several miles off the Atlantic coastline. These islands block ocean waves from directly hitting Georgia's mainland. Between the barrier islands and the mainland is the Atlantic Intracoastal

Waterway, a 1,000-mile inland waterway that runs from New York to Miami, Florida. The waterway gives commercial and recreational boating traffic safety from storms, strong currents, and waves of ocean routes.

Along the coastal area, Georgia has semidiurnal tides, or two high tides and two low tides each day. A tide is a rise or fall of the sea level caused by the gravitational pull of the sun and the moon. The coastline has six- to nine-foot tides, which are very unusual. As an example, Cape Hatteras, North Carolina, has two- to three-foot tides, and Miami, Florida, has one- to two-foot tides. The high tides and the gradual slope of the Coastal Plain allow tidal waters to flow far into the land, creating the most massive area of saltwater marshes on the entire Atlantic coastline. While Georgia's tides are considered high tides, they are not particularly strong or forceful, so they do not carry into shore the deeper, coarser grains of sand from the ocean. When ocean tides are at their highest, they are referred to as "spring tides" and when they are at their lowest, they are called "neap tides."

Coastal Waterways

Between the barrier islands and the mainland is a four- to six-mile band of saltwater marshes covering about a half-million acres. At least one-third of the salt marshes along the Atlantic coastline are in Georgia. The marshes, protected by the government, are home to many kinds of water life. Salt marshes extend well into Georgia's mainland by following the major rivers and occupying wetland areas. About 95 percent of the vegetation in the salt marshes is cordgrass, but there is also glasswort, saltwort, salt grass, and marsh lavender. Plant life is certainly not the only active life among the saltwater marshes. The rulers of the marshes are the sand fiddlers and mud fiddlers; they are joined by the snails and crabs that thrive in the harsh environment. The marshes are a food source for herons, egrets, ibis, sandpipers, and the endangered

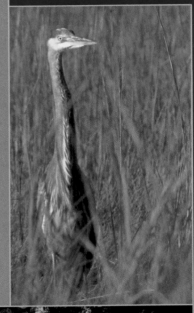

Below: The great blue heron can be seen throughout Georgia, except in the northeast. Bottom: Jekyll Island's saltwater marshes are home to many varieties of plants and fish.

Focus on the Environment

Endangered Marshes?

Are Georgia's 450,000 acres of saltwater marshes in trouble? In the spring of 2002, scientists along a six-county area of the coastal marshlands tried to find the reasons behind the sudden appearance of over five hundred acres of parched, browning and balding, dying marshes. At this point, there appear to be three possibilities for the frightening die-off in marsh areas: Georgia's severe droughts from the late 1990s and early 2000s, a new form of virus attacking the marshlands, or, pollution from manmade problems such as chemical spills.

During the same time period, the state's blue crab population was severely decreasing as were coastal shrimp resources. Are the three problems related? No one knows for sure, but if Georgia loses the salt marshes, it would have a horrendous impact on shellfish and other wildlife that depend on the marshlands for home, protection, and food. In addition, the loss of the recreational use of the marshlands would be devastating to local economies and tourism. This situation is an example of the " If ..., then ..." proposition. Why?

Use your research skills to follow-up on the causes and solutions for the marsh die-off. Are there things that you can do to harm or to protect one of Georgia's most beautiful resources?

wood storks so popular among coastal birdwatchers.

Freshwater sloughs (pronounced "slaws") are small ponds, freshwater marshes, and swamps. Sloughs also develop from marsh creeks that lose their tidal flow. Within the maritime forests, a number of freshwater sloughs serve as a source of fresh water for the wildlife of the forests.

Estuaries are bodies of water where freshwater rivers and salt water mix. Sounds, marsh creeks, and tidal rivers are examples of estuaries along Georgia's coastline. These estuaries are nurseries for crabs, shrimp, fish, and shellfish. When these animals are young, they are known as plankton, tiny microscopic organisms. They are among the few creatures that thrive in the harsh environment of the estuaries. The *salinity* (salt level) of the sea water decreases as it moves into the interior marshes, creeks, and rivers. The salinity also changes regularly because of the tides and rainfall. Changes in salinity are one factor in making the marshlands a difficult environment for plant and marine life.

The many different elements of the coastal area are interdependent. The sandy beaches and dunes protect the islands from erosion and flooding. The barrier islands protect the salt marshes from storms and ocean currents. The salt marshes are feeding grounds for aquatic life, which are, in turn, food for larger marine life. They provide nurseries and nesting sites for coastal birds. As tides flow in and out of the marshes twice daily, they remove marsh waste and circulate valuable nutrients and organisms.

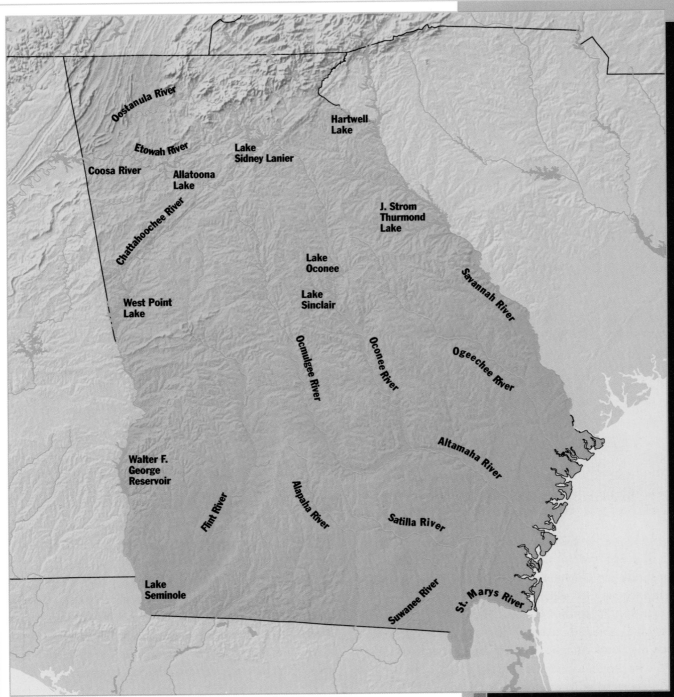

Oostanula River

Etowah River

Coosa River

Allatoona Lake

Chattahoochee River

Lake Sidney Lanier

Hartwell Lake

J. Strom Thurmond Lake

Lake Oconee

Lake Sinclair

West Point Lake

Savannah River

Ocmulgee River

Oconee River

Ogeechee River

Altamaha River

Walter F. George Reservoir

Flint River

Alapaha River

Satilla River

Lake Seminole

Suwanee River

St. Marys River

Rivers

Georgia has twelve principal river systems. The Savannah, Ogeechee, Altamaha (which combines the Oconee and Ocmulgee rivers), and Satilla rivers flow directly into the Atlantic Ocean. Western rivers, including the Chattahoochee and Flint, become part of the Gulf of Mexico. In the northern part of the state, the Etowah and Oostanula rivers form the Coosa River, which flows through Alabama into the Gulf. The Alapaha, the Suwannee, and the St. Marys, located in south Georgia, flow across the Georgia-Florida border.

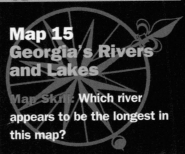

Map 15
Georgia's Rivers and Lakes

Map Skill: Which river appears to be the longest in this map?

Georgia's Ports

Georgia's has two major deepwater seaports, **Savannah** and **Brunswick**, and two inland barge terminals, **Bainbridge** and **Columbus**. The economic impact of these ports exceeds $1.8 billion in annual income. They account for over 81,000 jobs and pay over $585 million in state and local taxes. Over 90 steamship lines serve Georgia, which leads the South Atlantic region in foreign cargo handled.

The key to the economic success of Georgia's ports is the transportation infrastructure supporting those ports. The ports of Brunswick and Savannah are located close to two major interstate highways (I-95 and I-16) and to key railroad hubs. From Georgia, goods are two truckload days from 82 percent of the U.S. industrial marketplace and 79 percent of the nation's largest consumer markets. Over 100 motor freight carriers serve the metropolitan areas of Georgia. The state has 35 scheduled carriers, 2,200 intrastate haulers, and 25,000 interstate truckers serving the state. In addition, two major railroad lines operate in the state.

Above: Savannah is one of the most important containerized ports in the United States.

Savannah's seaport concentrates on containerized cargo and is the fifth largest container port in the nation. The Brunswick port concentrates on auto shipping, heavy equipment, farm machinery, and luxury tour buses. In addition, shipping of bulk agricultural products has increased.

A massive amount of imports (goods and supplies shipped into the state) and exports (goods and supplies shipped out of state) flow through Georgia's seaports and inland barge terminals. In fact, the ship on the reverse side of Georgia's state seal represents the state's exports. Georgia has a history of product exporting. In 1788, it was the first state to export cotton to Great Britain. The first cattle exported from America left from Savannah's port.

Georgia's marketplace really is the world, and the state's seaports make that marketplace a viable enterprise.

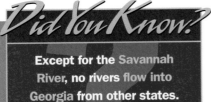
Georgia's major waterways have been important to the social, political, and economic growth of the state. In looking at a map of Georgia's river systems, it is notable that the names of more than half show an Indian influence. For example the Coosa River gets its name from the Choctaw. It means "kusha," or cane. The Choctaw used cane to make arrows, spears, and knives and as a container for fragile pieces of clothing. Altamaha is believed to mean "chief's lodge." Other smaller river systems have Indian names, including Apalachee, Towaliga, and Coosawatee. But the American influence can certainly be seen in river names like Rottenwood Creek, Settingdown, Potato Creek, and Mud Creek.

These rivers play important roles in recreation, in providing water sources for towns and cities, as sources for seafood, and as a boon to Georgia's economy through the economic benefits of inland barge terminals in Bainbridge and Columbus. The inland port terminals at Bainbridge and Columbus are located on the Apalachicola-Chattahoochee-Flint river system. They provide low-cost transportation services primarily for agricultural and industrial commodities to and from the Gulf of Mexico and major markets in the southeastern United States.

Above: Visitors to Etowah Mounds State Historic Site can see original Indian fish traps in the Etowah River.

The Savannah River

By the time Hernando de Soto reached the Savannah River in 1540, Indians had traveled the 314-mile-long waterway for many years. They called it the Isondega, meaning "blue water." Along the border of South Carolina, the river spreads into three lakes: J. Strom Thurmond Lake (formerly called Clark Hill Lake), Lake Russell, and Hartwell Lake. The Savannah is the only river that flows into Georgia from outside its borders. The headwaters of the Savannah River are in South Carolina.

Top: The Savannah River, seen here at Augusta, forms the border between Georgia and South Carolina. Above: The headwaters of the Chattahoochee River, seen here at Helen, are near Brasstown Bald

The Chattahoochee River

The name of the Chattahoochee comes from the Cherokee and means the "river of the painted rock." It was so named because of the colorful stones that lay across the riverbed. The river itself flows 436 miles from the mountains of North Georgia to the Gulf of Mexico. Part of the southern section forms the natural border between Georgia and Alabama. The chief cities along its banks include Gainesville, Atlanta, and Columbus. Major manmade lakes, including Lake Lanier, West Point Lake, and the Walter F. George Reservoir, are part of the Chattahoochee's winding path. In addition to supplying water

to Atlanta and Columbus, the river is a water source for Helen, Buford, LaGrange, and West Point.

The Flint River

The Flint River is one of Georgia's most picturesque and vital rivers. It runs parallel to the Chattahoochee from College Park, near Atlanta, until it empties into Lake Seminole at Bainbridge. Like all river basins, the Flint River basin is a **watershed**, an area that catches rain and snow, which then drains into marshes, streams, rivers, lakes, and groundwater. The Flint covers 8,460 square miles of Georgia's Piedmont and Coastal Plain regions. Interestingly enough, the river meanders (curves) so much that a boater can travel 350 miles although the river is actually only 212 miles long.

The Altamaha River

The Ocmulgee and Oconee rivers meet near Hazlehurst and Lumber City. They then flow into one of Georgia's most powerful rivers, the Altamaha. This muddy river is rich in fish and fertile swamps. It empties into the Atlantic Ocean near the coastal city of Darien.

Top: The mighty Altamaha River carries much silt downriver and, at Darien, has formed islands and a delta.
Above: The Flint River flows gently over boulders at Sprewell Bluff State Park.

Lake Chatuge was created in 1941 by the TVA.

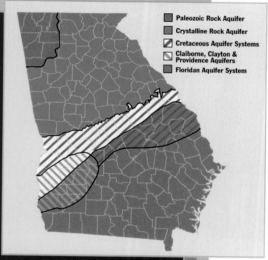

Paleozoic Rock Aquifer
Crystalline Rock Aquifer
Cretaceous Aquifer Systems
Claiborne, Clayton & Providence Aquifers
Floridan Aquifer System

Map 16
Georgia's Major Aquifers

Map Skill: What aquifer underlies most of the Coastal Plain?

Georgia's Major Lakes

Although Georgia does not have any large natural lakes, the state is fortunate to have excellent lakes created by the U.S. Corps of Engineers and the Georgia Power Company. There is also a network of lakes formed from Georgia's massive river systems. Whether manmade or natural, the state's lake system provides recreational areas, reservoirs, and hydroelectric power.

Allatoona, Carter Lake, Lake Lanier, Walter George, West Point, and Seminole all generate hydroelectric power, which provides us with the electricity we use in our homes. In later chapters, you will also read about the nuclear power plants that provide electricity for the state. In addition, J. Strom Thurmond Lake, Hartwell Lake, Oconee Lake, and others offer enjoyable fishing, camping, boating, and recreational shorelines.

Water — Not An Endless Resource

In the last chapter, you looked at the damaging effects a drought can have on our state. You also examined the importance of all forms of precipitation in providing water for our state. However, Georgia has water concerns even when there is no drought.

Much of the northern section of the state (the Appalachian Mountains regions of the Appalachian Plateau and the Ridge and Valley region, the Blue Ridge region, and the Piedmont Plateau) does not have groundwater because of the bedrock so close beneath the soil surface and because of the steep slopes of the mountainous areas. When this section receives precipitation, most of the water runs off and into the rivers of the area. Those rivers flow southward, carrying the water away from north Georgia and into the central and southern areas of the state and other states.

Since the northern half of our state relies on surface water to meet its water needs, a number of major **reservoirs**, or holding tanks, have been constructed in that section of Georgia. However, most of Georgia's population and much of the state's rapid growth have taken place in the metropolitan areas around Atlanta in the Piedmont Plateau. The area with the greatest water needs lies in the area with the least amount of water resources.

The southern half of our state, basically the Outer and Inner Coastal Plain areas, does have ground water. The major **aquifers** in our state serve as natural water storage tanks, but all four are located in the Coastal Plain. While they provide an abundant water supply for agriculture as well as southern residents and businesses, there are concerns about the aquifers as well. In the past one hundred years, increased usage of water has dropped the water level in these natural reservoirs. In some cases, the level has dropped enough that *brackish water* (a mixture of salt and fresh water) has flowed into the aquifers.

Water is not an endless resource. It is a resource that must be shared by all residents, businesses, and industries. In Georgia's case, that water must also be shared with Alabama, Florida, and South Carolina who are also served by some of the state's rivers and aquifers. Conservation of natural resources, including water, is the responsibility of every Georgian. What can you do to help preserve our water resources?

A Final Note

There is a one-of-a-kind water resource located in Augusta (Richmond County). It is a canal, a nine-mile transportation corridor that is the only canal of its kind in the southern United States. In the past, the Augusta Canal had different uses as you will learn in later chapters. Now it is a National Park Heritage Area. That canal changed the county and the state both before and after the Civil War. It is a source of pride for Augustonians.

It's Your Turn

1. What might happen if Georgia's barrier islands were all washed away?
2. What are estuaries? How do they protect Georgia's ecological balance?
3. How have Georgia's abundant water resources helped the state attract business and industry?
4. What are Georgia's natural water storage tanks and where are they located?

Chapter Summary

- Georgia has very diverse plant and animal life. Endangered species include the bald eagle, the right whale, and the manatee.
- Over 23 million acres of land in Georgia is forested, twice the national average.
- Georgia's natural resources include forests and minerals. Key minerals in Georgia are clays, kaolin, granite, and marble.
- A major waterway is the Atlantic Intracoastal Waterway, a 1,000-mile water highway running from New York to Florida.
- Georgia has semidiurnal tides (two high tides and two low tides daily).
- Major rivers include the Savannah, Ogeechee, Altamaha, and Satilla rivers, which flow directly into the Atlantic Ocean. The Chattahoochee and Flint rivers flow into the Gulf of Mexico. The Etowah and Oostanaula rivers form the Coosa river and flow through Alabama into the Gulf. The Alapaha, Suwannee, and St. Marys rivers flow across the Georgia-Florida border.
- Georgia's manmade lakes provide recreational facilities, water storage reservoirs, and hydroelectric power.
- The state's water resources were a major influence on settlement in the early days of Georgia's history and are a major influence attracting business and industry to the state today.
- Georgia has two deepwater seaports, Savannah and Brunswick, and two inland barge terminals, Bainbridge and Columbus.

ChapterReview

Reviewing People, Places, and Terms

Use each of the following terms in a sentence.

1. aquifer

2. Atlantic Intracoastal Waterway

3. estuaries

4. flora

5. fauna

6. inland barge terminal

7. reservoir

8. watershed

Understanding the Facts

1. What are some of the types of trees grown in the northern, coastal, and Okefenokee areas of the state?

2. Because of strong conservation efforts, what mammal is now found in all 159 of Georgia's counties?

3. Identify three of Georgia's endangered species.

4. What species of poisonous snakes are native to Georgia?

5. What are some of the most profitable mineral resources in Georgia's economy?

6. What are Georgia's inland port terminals and how do they strengthen the economy?

7. How many acres of saltwater marshland lie between Georgia's barrier islands and the state's mainland?

8. Which Georgia rivers flow into the Atlantic Ocean? Which Georgia rivers flow into the Gulf of Mexico?

9. What are the main benefits of Georgia's large lakes?

Developing Critical Thinking

1. How do Georgia's semidiurnal tides benefit coastal marine life?

2. Explain the differences between Georgia's manmade reservoirs and natural aquifers, and give examples of each.

3. Where are Georgia's seaports and how does the transportation infrastructure contribute to their success?

4. Based on what you have read in the chapter, discuss three ways you can become more "diligent" and three ways you can demonstrate "respect for the environment."

Checking It Out

1. History, including geography, always contains some mysteries. You have read about the bald eagles in our state and Georgia's efforts to preserve this endangered national symbol. The good news has one exception. During 2002, twenty-five eagles mysteriously died around Lake Thurmond. In addition, numbers of Canadian geese also died. Both fell victim to AVM (avian vacular myelinopathy), a fatal disease of unknown origin. Will this undo all of the efforts to save the bald eagle? Why are the

birds dying? The only clue experts had in 2002 was "the coots." Use the Internet and see if you can find out why the birds died and solve this mystery.

2. In addition to the Atlantic Ocean, which borders Georgia's east coast, what are the other oceans of the world? Find them on your maps or globe.

3. In addition to the minerals described in the chapter, Georgia has other minerals, some of which you can mine yourself. Which mineral deposits are located closest to your home? Which minerals are you likely to come across while "rock hunting"?

Writing Across the Curriculum

1. Write an 3-4 paragraph expository report for your class on ways of conserving water resources in Georgia. Your report's purpose is *to inform*. Organize the report with an introduction that states a specific point (called a *thesis sentence*). Then provide details (examples, evidence, authority information, facts, or statistics) to support your point (prove your thesis). End your report with a brief conclusion that restates or rephrases your thesis and summarizes the major supporting details presented. Of course, you will have to do a bit of research to gather information for your report. It should not be just personal opinions, but should be based on factual data.

Exploring Technology

1. Use your favorite search engine to find the names and locations of all of Georgia's state and national parks. Make an alphabetical chart of the cities and towns in which these parks are located. What types of activities are available in each park?

2. If you are interested in sea creatures that live deep in the ocean and are never seen, go to a website such as www.oceans.gov. Find three of the creatures that you think are the most interesting to share with your classmates. Also check out "aquatic nuisance species" to see what we need to do to manage these damaging entities.

Applying your Skills

1. Georgia has over 180 festivals each year celebrating local flora, fauna, and history. After researching Georgia festivals, record on a state map the festivals and dates of celebrations that will be taking place within about 65 miles of your home (that's about an hour's drive away).

2. National Arbor Day, a day set aside to encourage the planting of trees, is in April. Georgia's Arbor Day is in February. Find out what accounts for this difference.

3. Georgia's granite industry employs about 2,400 people for a payroll of just over $57 million. What would be the average salary if everyone was equally paid?

Photo Question

This lake was created when the Chattahoochee River was dammed. What is it?

Above: The blockhouse at Fort King George was recreated
in 1988. These cannon are on the second floor of the blockhouse.
Opposite page: This is the entrance to the ceremonial earthlodge at Ocmulgee National Monument.

From Exploration Through Independence

People have lived on the North American continent for the past 12,000 to 30,000 years. Anthropologists believe that these Native Americans arrived during the last great Ice Age, that period when much of Earth's water was frozen in glaciers. They probably came over land bridges that connected North America and Asia as they followed large herds of animals. These prehistoric peoples spread over the areas we now know as North, Central, and South America.

When the European explorers arrived in the New World, including the Spanish explorers at St. Augustine and the English explorers at Jamestown, they found many different tribes of Native Americans. They called them all "Indians."

Although several European nations had earlier explored and made attempts at starting colonies in what is today Georgia, the actual colonial period in the state lasted only fifty years. It began in 1733 when the first English colonists set foot on Georgia soil with James Oglethorpe. It lasted until 1783 when the Treaty of Paris was signed ending the American Revolution.

During this period, many different cultures came together, primarily the Native American cultures and those of the French, Spanish, and British explorers and settlers. These original Georgians found and built new homes in the wilderness, fought a war for their independence from Great Britain, and laid the foundation of a new nation—the United States of America.

The Land and Its Early People

Chapter Preview

Georgia character word:
Honesty

Terms: archaeologist, artifact, shale, anthropologist, culture, horticulture, tribe, antiquities, clan

People: Paleo Indians, Archaic Indians, Woodland Indians, Mississippian Indians, Creek, Cherokee

Places: Bering Strait, Etowah Indian Mounds, Kolomoki Indian Mounds

Section 1	How Did We Learn About the Earliest People?
Section 2	Indian Nations in Georgia

During the last Ice Age, the sea level was much lower than it is today. Scientists believe that a land bridge connected Asia and America across what is now the Bering Strait, the narrow body of water that separate Alaska and Russia. Bands of people crossed the land bridge in search of animals for food. We can only imagine their reaction when they traveled to the plains region (what is now the central United States). In this wilderness area, beavers were as large as today's bears, and some birds had wing spans of over 15 feet. Lions, camels, zebras, and saber-toothed tigers roamed alongside bison, deer, moose, and foxes. Animals that we once thought lived only in Africa and Asia once lived here in North America too.

Map 17
Bering Land Bridge

Map Skill: Why is the Bering Strait important in understanding how some of the earliest people came to America?

Asia

Bering Land Bridge

North Pole

Migration Routes

☐ Present Day Landmass
☐ Landmass existing 20,000 Years Ago

North America

Left: Cartersville's Etowah Indian Mounds Historic Site is one of the best examples of the Mississippian mound-builder culture in existence. The temple mound is on the right. Opposite page, above: This arrowhead is just one of the artifacts discovered at Etowah Mounds.

Signs of the Times
c. 10,000 B.C.–1732 A.D.

Population: 22,000 Cherokee in North Georgia and with an unknown number of Creek

Average Salary: None by our standards

Life Expectancy: Males, around 25 years; Females, somewhat older

Food Costs: Time needed to hunt, plant, and gather; visiting groups would barter for items wanted

Trade "Prices": Beaver furs, canoes, deer skins, corn kernels, arrowheads, beads and other items considered of value to the trader

Art/Architecture: Intricate ceremonial jewelry, statues particularly those of a spiritual nature

Literature: Songs and stories handed down from one generation to another

Music: Drums, chants, songs and dances

Fashion: Ranged from simple animal skin coverings to intricately beaded handsewn garments and headdresses made from softened animal skins

Fads: Rare. Indian cultures valued traditions passed down from earlier generations. Games and tournaments of skill were very popular.

People/Personalities: The tribe's peace chief and war chief; there were also "fanners," messengers, speakers, chief priest, and chief for sacrifices. One of the most important personalities was that of War Woman or Beloved Woman.

Education: Oral history from elders. By the time children were 12 or 13, their education was completed and they began life learning from experiences. For boys, "vision quests" were important.

Figure 8 Timeline: 10,000 B.C. – 1500 A.D.

800 A.D. – 1600 A.D.
Mississippian culture

10000 B.C. – 8000 B.C
Paleo culture

200 B.C. – 400 A.D.
Hopewell culture at its zenith

8000 B.C. – 1000 B.C.
Archaic culture

1000 B.C. – 1000 A.D.
Woodland culture

10,000 B.C. 8,000 B.C. 6,000 B.C. 4,000 B.C. 2,000 B.C. 0 2,000 A.D.

1500 B.C.
Metal work began in New World

1000 A.D.
Leif Ericson explored Vinland

30,000 B.C. – 10,000 B.C.
First people crossed land bridge into what is now North America

1492 A.D.
Columbus arrived in the Bahamas

How Did We Learn About the Earliest People?

Section Preview

As you read, look for:
• how archaeologists and anthropologists learn about ancient peoples,
• the four prehistoric Indian cultures,
• where Native American mounds and artifacts have been found in Georgia, and
• vocabulary terms: archaeologist, artifact, shale, anthropologist, culture, horticulture, tribe, and antiquities.

Systems of writing, which began in Africa, are only 6,000 years old. Before that time, early civilizations depended on *oral traditions*. The oral tradition was a system in which older persons in a family or other members of a group repeated narratives of events over and over until the younger generations learned them by heart. As succeeding generations grew up, they passed down the traditions, beliefs, and folklore. Later civilizations used cave walls, animal hides, or tree bark to record stories of past events, first in crude drawings, then pictographs, and then in symbols representing sounds. To understand the past, we need to call on experts in other fields in the social sciences.

Archaeologists dig into the earth to find artifacts that will tell us something about early inhabitants. **Artifacts** are pottery shards (pieces), weapons, tools, jewelry, or any items that were made by people. Artifacts can also include *fossils* (the traces or remains of once-living things). Fossils can tell us much about the lives of animals, birds, and even people. Some of the most successful archeological digs during the past ten years have been in shale. **Shale** is a type of rock that is formed in successive layers. Although thin and easy to break, two pieces of shale can encase the total body of a bird or a prehistoric animal.

Sometimes archaeologists can tell how old a prehistoric site is because they know when particular tools, weapons, or pottery found there were used. They may also choose to use the carbon 14 test to help date things they find. Radioactive carbon is in all living things. When an animal or plant dies, it begins to lose this carbon at a known rate. By learning how much carbon is left in the remains, scientists can tell, within about two hundred years, when it lived. The carbon 14 test can also be used to date artifacts such as clothing or written records.

Anthropologists use these artifacts along with cave drawings, well-traveled pathways, and oral history to study the culture of a group. **Culture** is a term that describes the beliefs, traditions, music, art, and social institutions of a group of people who share common experiences. Anthropologists may also study artifacts and fossils to find out how groups of people lived. There are, for example, many types of projectile points, or arrowheads. By studying a particular point, looking at its type, size, markings, and stone composition, an-

Above: We can learn a lot from the artifacts left behind by ancient peoples. This Woodland culture ceramic owl figurine was excavated at Kolomoki Mounds.

Did You Know?

B.C. stands for "before Christ" and means the number of years before the birth of Jesus Christ. *A.D.* means "Anno Domini," Latin for "in the year of our Lord."

thropologists can guess what size animals hunters killed with the point. Projectile points, remains of camp sites, and other evidence indicate that, when the food was gone in one area, the people moved to another.

What archaeologists have learned about prehistoric times is not identified by the names of the groups we know today, such as Cherokee or Creek. Instead, early people are identified by cultural periods. No two cultures were exactly alike, and changes took place slowly. People learned from those who lived before, discovered new things, and taught what they knew to their children. Although cultural periods in history overlap, archaeologists have grouped prehistoric people in the following cultures: Paleo, Archaic, Woodland, and Mississippian.

Paleo Indians

The earliest known culture is that of the Paleo Indians, whose culture lasted until about 10,000 years ago. The word *Paleo* comes from the Greek and means "very old" or "long ago." Early people sometimes can be identified by the material they used to make knives, scrapers, and points for spears. Because most tools and spear points used by the people of this culture were made of stone, this period is referred to as the *paleolithic* (old stone) age.

Above: These spear points were made during the Paleo culture. **Below:** Paleo people hunted large animals like the wooly mammoth.

The Atlatl

The atlatl allowed hunters to throw spears or darts a greater distance. The hunters no longer had to get so close to their prey.

Above: These spear points were made during the Archaic Indian period.

The Paleo culture also used an amazing invention called an *atlatl*. This smooth stone sling-like implement threw darts far more accurately than if they were thrown by hand. It was like a human missile launcher. It enabled the Paleo hunters to kill animals for food from far away rather than forcing them to get too close to their prey.

The Paleo people were nomadic (roaming) hunters who wandered from place to place following herds of large animals. Hunters used long wooden spears to kill large animals such as mammoths, bison, ground sloths, and mastodons, which they then used for food. Archaeologists have also found large numbers of animal bones at the bases of cliffs. This leads them to believe that, at times, the hunters chased the animals over the cliffs to kill them for food.

Remains of their dwelling places indicate that Paleo people lived in groups of 25 to 50 people. Because these people moved around, however, they did not leave many artifacts in any one place. Only a few Paleo sites have been found in Georgia. Archaeologists have uncovered artifacts from the Paleo period in the Savannah River area, in the Ocmulgee River area, and in the Flint River at Albany.

Archaic Indians

The Archaic period (from the word *archaic*, meaning "old") included three distinct time spans: early, middle, and late.

Early Archaic Period

During the early Archaic period, from about 8000 B.C. to about 5000 B.C., the people still hunted large game. These animals, however, slowly became extinct either because of climate changes or because too many of them were killed. Whatever the reason, Archaic Indians began hunting smaller game, such as deer, bear, turkey, and rabbit. Hunters made their spears and points smaller. The people also began to eat reptiles, game birds, and fish.

The early Archaic people invented useful items, such as choppers, drills, and chipping tools made from deer antlers. Some of the stone artifacts found in Georgia are made from rock not often found in this state but common in other parts of the country. This has led archaeologists to think there was some trading among different groups of Indians.

Archaeological evidence also indicates that the early Archaic people moved each season. During the fall, they lived where berries, nuts, and fruits were plentiful. In summer, they moved to good fishing locations. They also migrated during spring and winter. The moves, however, were always for the same reason: to find food for their people.

Middle Archaic Period

Geographers tell us that by 5000 B.C., when the middle Archaic period began, the area grew warm and dry. Water levels along rivers and the coastal

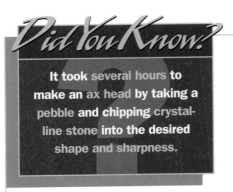
areas receded (moved back), and the people began to eat shellfish, such as mussels and clams. Scientists have found hooks made from animal bones that came from this period. These hooks were sometimes on the ends of long spears that were weighted in the middle with polished stones. Because hunters could throw the weighted spears long distances, food became easier to get. Finding more food meant the people did not need to move as often as they once had. Evidence also suggests that several small groups joined together to establish camps.

Late Archaic Period

A common artifact from the late Archaic period (4000 B.C. to 1000 B.C.) is the grooved axe. Indians made this tool by putting a stone axe head on a wooden handle. Excavations (archaeological diggings) of late Archaic settlements indicate that axes were used to clear trees and bushes around the camp.

The late Archaic people also saved seed to plant in the next growing season. It is thought that horticulture, the science of cultivating plants and trees, began in the late Archaic period.

Below: This campsite was typical of the Archaic people who relied on gathering natural food and hunting smaller animals after the large game had died out. They also began to plant some crops.

By 2500 B.C., the climate had become cooler and wetter, much like the climate of Georgia today. Water filled rivers, streams, and lakes, and the Archaic people of this period depended on shellfish for most of their food. On Stallings Island, a few miles north of Augusta on the Savannah River, archaeologists discovered a mound of mussel and clam shells. The mound was 512 feet long, 300 feet wide, and 23 feet higher than the depth of the river! Also at the Stallings site were remains of burial grounds, fire hearths, pipes, axes, shell beads, bone pins and needles, bone hooks, and many different spear points. Because of these discoveries, historians think late Archaic villages were more permanent than those of any group before them.

The way food was prepared also changed. Pottery shards dating from the Archaic period indicate that clay containers were used for storing, cooking, and serving food. Archaeologists think learning to make and use pottery may be one of the greatest contributions the Archaic people made to Native American culture.

Other archaeological finds help us understand the lives of Archaic people. They may have used a grinding stone found in Fayette County to crush nuts into a type of flour. Scientists believe that a nutting stone found in Coweta County was used by Indians to hammer nuts in order to get the meat and oil from them.

Woodland Indians

The Woodland culture developed about 1000 B.C. and lasted until about 1000 A.D. Evidence suggests that, during that period, several hundred families began banding together to form tribes. A **tribe** is a group of people who

Above: This Woodland period artifact is a ceramic duck figurine with cutouts. **Below:** This is the main temple mound at Kolomoki.

Top: The Woodland people lived in villages. Above: This is an example of a Woodland culture spear point.

share a common ancestry, name, and way of living. The tribes lived in villages and built huts as houses. The Woodland people used small trees and bark to build dome-shaped huts. They stuck the trees into the ground on one end, then bent them forward at the top and tied them together. They then wove sticks in and out between the trees to form walls. Sometimes they covered the sides of their huts with cane mats or tree bark. They made roofs of grass or pieces of bark and left a small opening in the top of the hut so smoke from cooking fires could get out. They also put fiber mats on the dirt floors for sleeping and sitting.

Hunting became easier for the Woodland culture, a period during which the bow and arrow came into use. Arrow points were made out of stone, shark teeth, or deer antlers. Fishing, hunting, and gathering nuts and berries remained important ways of getting food. The people also grew such things as squash, wild greens, and sunflowers.

The Woodland people learned to make pottery last longer. They found clay along river banks and mixed it with sand. They rolled the mixture into strips and coiled the strips on top of each other into the shape they wanted. They then made the clay smooth with a rock and water. They used wooden paddles to make designs on the pottery. After the clay containers dried in the sun, they were baked in a hot fire to make them hard enough to use for cooking.

Did You Know?

We southerners can thank the Woodland culture for giving us a special dish of beans, corn, and other vegetables. Its Algonquian name is *succotash*.

Elaborate religious ceremonies were introduced during the Woodland period. These ceremonies were spread through trade among different tribes. The Hopewell culture in Ohio, for example, had many of the same ceremonies used by the Woodland people in Georgia.

During this period, the Woodland people built cone-shaped burial mounds for the dead. They adorned bodies with necklaces, bracelets, rings, and copper or bone combs. When Woodland people were buried, their families and friends put special funeral pottery, tools, tobacco pipes, and weapons in the graves with them. These artifacts cause archaeologists and anthropologists to think this group of people believed in some type of life after death.

Mississippian Indians

The Mississippian culture is considered to be the highest prehistoric civilization in Georgia. The culture, which started about 700 A.D., is so called because the first things learned about it were from villages excavated along the Mississippi River. The Mississippian age, sometimes called the Temple Mound period, was a time when the people lived in villages, farmed, and were very religious.

From archaeological sites, we learn much about how the Mississippians lived. We know, for example, that the people grew most of their food. Maize (corn), beans, pumpkins, and squash were all planted together in hills. They grew tobacco to use in ceremonies. The Mississippians planted in different fields each year so the soil would stay fertile. They prepared the land with stone or bone hoes and digging sticks.

The Mississippians began to dress and fix their hair differently. Their clothes were less simple, and they wore beads and ear ornaments. Sometimes they

Below: These 4-foot high statues are from Etowah Mounds. **Bottom:** Artifacts at the Etowah museum include discs the Indians used to play a game called "chunky."

NACOOCHEE INDIAN MOUND

Nacoochee Indian Mound was the center of the ancient Cherokee town of Gauxule, visited by DeSoto in 1540 in his search for gold, according to legend. On this ceremonial mound, 190 feet long, 150 feet wide and 20 feet high, stood the Town House where a sacred fire burned unceasingly. Ceremonial dances were performed in and around the Town House. Residents of the town lived on the flat land surrounding the mound. The findings of Heye Foundation archaeologists who explored the mound in 1915 indicate the advanced cultural development of the builders.

To examine the lives of Georgia's earliest natives, we turn to two primary sources of information—archaeological evidence and oral traditions. One archaeological site is located in White County on Rte. 17 just east of Rte. 75 near Helen. The mound rises from the flat pastureland. Built by the Mississippian culture, the mound was partially excavated in 1915. A white latticework gazebo sits on top of it today.

painted or tattooed their bodies. They also began wearing feather headdresses.

Villages grew, and several thousand families might live in a single settlement. They built centers for religious ceremonies and as a home for the priest-chief, who was the head of the village. Moats and palisades (wooden fences) often protected the villages. In some Georgia villages, guard towers have been found 100 feet apart along the palisades, indicating that they needed to defend themselves against tribal enemies.

About 1600 A.D., something mysterious happened. The people left the villages, and there is nothing to tell us where they went. Did disease wipe out whole settlements? Did tribal enemies kill all the people in the villages? Did family units decide to migrate to other areas and become part of a new tribe? Because this was in the prehistoric period (before written history), we may never learn what happened to the Mississippians.

Above: The main temple mound at Etowah, called Mound A, is six stories above the countryside. Its flat top spans a half-acre.

Archaeological Finds

Much of what we know about the early Native Americans is based on the major Mississippian archaeological sites in our state. Figure 9 lists a few prehistoric and historic Indian sites in our state. Find the one closest to your home and continue reading to find out more about these incredible **antiquities** (ancient relics).

Top: The Rock Eagle effigy measures 102 feet from head to tail and 120 feet from wingtip to wingtip. Above: This 800-foot rock wall at Fort Mountain State Park may have been for ceremonial or defense purposes.

Middens are a treasure trove for archaeologists. Basically, a *midden* is a garbage pile. Just as our garbage can tell a lot about us—what we like to eat, messages or mail we read, whether or not we drink alcohol or grape punch—late Archaic shell middens tell us about those who came before us. The large shell midden on coastal Skidaway Island, near Savannah, lets us know whether early peoples ate mussels, clams, or oysters.

Middens dated to the Woodland and Mississippian periods reveal much about what the people ate, how they used fire, what they used for cooking vessels, and so on. You can still see these middens today along the barrier islands near Fort Pulaski and along several major rivers. We can only wonder what people 50,000 years from now will learn about us from our middens!

Excavations at Ocmulgee National Monument near Macon led to the discovery of a large ceremonial lodge built of red clay in the shape of a circle. It is about 45 feet across and has a 6-inch-high bench around the inner wall. Archaeologists believe the bench, which is divided into 47 sections, was for seating tribal nobles. There is a large eagle-shaped clay platform with seats for the priest-chief and two assistants. A fire pit is in the center of the floor. Archaeologists and anthropologists think the lodge was probably used for both religious and village ceremonies and for other meetings. In Early County (Blakely), one of the oldest counties in our state, is the Kolomoki site, which covers over 300 acres. Here, in the far southwest portion of our state, is a temple mound that is about 50 feet high, 320 feet long, and 200 feet wide.

In Bartow County at Cartersville, the 40-acre Etowah site has seven of these pyramid-shaped mounds. Located at the junction of the Etowah River and Pumpkinvine Creek are borrow pits (the holes left from the excava-

Figure 9 Georgia Archaeological Sites

County/City	Indian Site	What's There
Bartow/Cartersville	Etowah Mounds	Pyramid shaped burial mound, jewelry, headdresses, earthen ware
Early/Blakely	Kolomoki Mounds	300-acre burial mound area
Putnam/Eatonton	Rock Eagle	Huge eagle effigy made from rocks
Bibb/Macon	Ocmulgee Mounds	Ceremonial lodge
Richmond/Augusta	Stallings Island	Shell middens
Murray/Chatsworth	Fort Mountain	Rock wall

tion), a plaza, parts of the original village, and a museum. One of the mounds is 53 feet high and has steps leading to the top. Graves have been found along the base of a single mound, and bodies have been discovered in the tops of the mounds. The bodies were dressed in fine clothes, and beads and feather or copper headdresses had been placed on them. Some of the intricately designed copper head-dresses weighed almost 100 pounds. Carved marble statues also have been found at some of the burial sites. One of the best parts about the Bartow County site is that you can spend the night there; it is a state park.

Just a word of caution. Some of the archaeological sites in our state are endangered because of looting. Our character education term for this chapter, honesty, is vitally important in this situation. Anyone who walks through a historical site, sees something really neat, and decides to pick it up and pocket it is not being honest. That person is also ruining the chance for others to enjoy looking at the arrowhead, pottery piece, or jewelry.

**Map 18
Georgia Mound Sites**

Map Skill Are there any mound sites in your county?

It's Your Turn

1. Why is oral history important? Are there stories in your family that have been passed down from generation to generation? Ask a grandparent or great aunt or uncle.
2. What is the difference between artifacts and fossils?
3. Name at least one thing that separated the Archaic period from the Woodland period.
4. If you had to choose, which one of the four periods would you have wanted to live in and why?

Indian Nations in Georgia

After the Mississipians disappeared, we entered the "historic" period, so called because Europeans began to keep records of the Native Americans they met. There have been numerous tribal nations in Georgia. However, the two largest tribes in Georgia were the Creek and the Cherokee.

The Creek

Fourteen tribes with names such as Yamacraw, Yamasee, Ocmulgee, Oconee, Chiaha, and Apalachicola made up the Creek Confederacy, or nation. Even though the tribes had different names, their language and culture were much the same. According to Creek legends, the tribes had moved into the Southeast from what is now the southwestern United States. Small tribes banded together in the confederacy to protect themselves against larger tribes of the area.

The true name for the Creek was *Muscogee*, and they were known for being brave and for carrying on the ways of their fathers. During the early days of exploration, Europeans discovered a tribe living on the banks of the Ocheese Creek, which today is the Ocmulgee River. The explorers did not know the Indians' tribal name, so they called them Creek. As time passed, that term was applied to all of the tribes within the confederacy. Their language was Muskogean. They lived in permanent settlements or villages known as *italwa*. Those villages were surrounded by smaller villages known as *talofa*, an arrangement similar to our modern city surrounded by suburbs.

In the center of the village was a plaza area where religious ceremonies and games took place. A rotunda (a round building made of

As you read, look for:
• the two main Native American tribal nations living in Georgia,
• the Cherokee clan system,
• various parts of Cherokee culture, and
• vocabulary term: clan.

Did You Know?

It is estimated that in the 1400s, as many as 850,000 Native Americans lived in what is now the United States. Today, the Cherokee is the largest tribe and the Navajo second.

poles and mud) was located in the center of the plaza and used for council meetings. Individual family huts were built around the village plaza. Because the Creek had tools such as axes, their homes were either huts with wooden shingle or grass roofs or log cabins with chimneys.

When Creek villages reached a population of four hundred to six hundred people, the village split. Half of the people moved to a new site and settled a new village. While the new village developed its own plaza, held its own ceremonies, and had its own life, it retained a strong link to the "mother village" from which it had split. In this manner, the different villages of the Creek nation maintained strong ties and became a confederacy.

As the Creek began to grow more of their foods, farmlands surrounded villages and family homes were separated by a mile or more of crops. The Creek used the plow and ax and were successful farmers. They also raised livestock, which reduced the need for hunting.

Cherokee Tribal Clan Wheel

DEER WOLF WILD POTATO PAINT BLUE LONG HAIR BIRD

Above: This is the reconstruction of a Cherokee council house. Notice the benches along the walls.

The Cherokee

This proud tribe lived in the northwestern mountain region of the state. There were about 22,000 Cherokee in the southeastern United States during this time period. They called themselves *Awi-yum-wija*, which meant "real people" or "principal people." Since the Cherokee are most closely identified with Georgia, we will examine their culture in detail.

Tribal Clans

Within a tribe were **clans**, groups of people who believed themselves related by blood. There are seven Cherokee clans that continue today. Examine Figure 10 and decide to which tribe you would most like to belong.

Each clan had its own symbols and traditions, but jealousy was rare between clans. No one clan was considered "better" than another, and each clan was represented in the tribal council. During some meetings, the council members would wear different color feathers to represent their own clan. Council members who spoke up were representing the rest of the clan, so they spoke carefully.

Cherokee Government

Most tribes had two chiefs, one for making war and one for making decisions during peaceful times. Within the community was a council house built close to a stream. Council members could purify themselves in the water before, during, and after ceremonies. The council house was the largest building and could hold up to five hundred people. Although only council members could actually take part in the meetings, each clan was represented, and the ideas shared were many.

Clans governed on the local level. Each clan took care of its own affairs, deciding who could marry and who should be punished for wrongs.

A village was ruled by a headman. He was assisted by a righthand man, a messenger, and a chief of sacrifice in addition to other assistants. The village headman and other respected elders made up a council, which advised the tribal chief. The chief rarely made an important decision without talking to the village council. Decisions at council meetings were reached by agreement rather than by a majority vote. At some point in the discussions, the council simply agreed on the best thing to do.

Figure 10   Cherokee Clan Symbols

Clan	Color	Wood	Other names	Description
Blue clan (Ani Sahoni)	Blue	Ash	Panther, Wild Cat	Responsible for making a blue medicine from a special plant called blue holly that would keep the children well. Keepers of all children's medicines and the tribe's medicinal herb garden.
Long Hair clan (Ani Gilohi)	Yellow	Beech	Twister, Wind, Hair Hanging Down, Stranger	The teachers and keepers of tribal traditions. Also took in POWs, orphans, or those without a clan. Were said to have elaborate twisted hairdos. A peace clan, peace chiefs came from this group, and the chief often wore a white robe made up of bird feathers.
Bird clan (Ani Tsisqua)	Purple	Maple	None	Responsible for keeping birds and sacred feathers. Only clan that could kill or snare birds and gather eagle feathers to present to other clan members for some special feat or accomplishment.
Deer clan (Ani Kawi)	Brown	Oak	None	Keepers of the deer, deer hunters, tanners, and seamers. Also cared for all animals living on tribal grounds. Were often the faster runners of the tribes and would take messages from one tribe to another. This is a peace clan.
Wolf clan (Ani Wahhya)	Red	Hickory	None	Known for its chiefs and warriors. As the wolf is known as a protector, so is this clan considered protectors. Only clan that can track or kill a wolf.
Wild Potato clan (Ani Gatogewi)	Green	Birch	Bear, Raccoon, Blind Savannah	The farmers and gatherers of the wild potato plants from swamps and alongside streams. The potatoes were used to make flour for bread. They were considered to be the nurturers, keepers, and protectors of Earth. Are also the white peace clan.
Paint clan (Ani Wadi)	White	Locust	None	Responsible for making red paint used in ceremonies and as face and body decorations. They were also the medicine people and carriers of medicinal herbs and sacred objects when the tribe traveled to battle.

The Family

Central to the clan was the family. Cherokee society was considered to be *matrilineal*; that is, family lines were traced through the mother. A child was related by blood only to the mother, not to the father or the father's family as we have in much of our society today. A mother's extended family, including nieces and nephews, were the closest relatives of her children. Children could not marry anyone in that extended family. Nor could they marry close relatives in their natural father's clan. At any given time, there could be lots of relatives living within the same walls and helping each other.

The mother's brothers were responsible for raising her children. Usually, parents were loving and easygoing and disciplined their children very little, preferring that they develop an inner sense of what was right and wrong and take responsibility for the consequences of their actions.

In addition to preparing food, mothers also tended the garden, helped tan skins, and sewed outfits appropriate for the different seasons in north Georgia. Most importantly, they made baskets and pottery containers that were used in every facet of their lives. Fathers were frequently gone, either hunting for deer and moose or trading along the river.

Children played at games that helped them learn their adult roles. Boys learned to use the bow and arrow, and girls learned to cook and tend small children. Sometimes fun was just that—fun. For boys, there were fishing, bow and arrow target practice, tug of war, or foot races. Stick ball was very popular, as was marbles. For girls, there were tag, chasing rabbits, or picking

Top: A Cherokee woman prepares food in front of a traditional Cherokee house. Above: Cherokee boys learned to make arrow shafts and bows from hickory wood.

up shells from the river. Swimming and wading were favorites for both as was hide-and-seek.

Games that children played helped them grow up. Mud ball fights were common, and children were taught not to cry when hit. Hide-and-seek taught the skills of searching and evading. Wrestling was meant to build strength and quickness. These games and sports were common to all tribes, much as the Olympic sports are common to many nations.

Special ceremonies marked the time when girls became women and boys became men. Men and women married at different ages. Women just past the age of puberty were ready for marriage. Men were usually older, having had to prove themselves at hunting and war. A man and a woman who wanted to marry usually asked permission of the woman's family. After a small ceremony, the husband went to live with his wife's family and clan. In many situations, if the woman wanted a divorce, she simply put the husband's belongings outside the house to indicate an end to the partnership. But, more often than not, in the Cherokee culture, the two would agree to dissolve the union without hard feelings and the husband would return to his own mother's clan to live.

Homes

Most tribes built their villages on high banks or hills along rivers and streams. This position gave them rich soil, enough water, fish for food, and a good place from which to defend themselves.

Below: This Cherokee girl is demonstrating basket-making. **Bottom:** This lithograph of an early Cherokee village shows that they built their homes near rivers and streams.

Spotlight on the Economy

The Barter Economy

Early in America's history, money did not exist in the same form that it does today. Native Americans and even early colonists did not have currency or coins to exchange for products they wanted or needed. Instead, they used an economic system called a **barter economy**. The term *barter* simply means to trade or exchange goods or services without the use of money. Suppose you have a new CD that you cannot enjoy because your CD player is broken. Suppose too that your friend has a VHS tape that he cannot watch because his tape player is broken. If you and your friend agreed to exchange the CD and the VHS tape, you have used the barter system.

Bartering is a traditional form of economics. Actually, it is probably the oldest form of economics because people were exchanging goods and services without money for thousands of years before anyone thought to invent money. A **good** is any item that can be bought, sold, or traded. A **service** is any action that one does for another in exchange for some form of payment. (Payment does not have to be money; it can be another service or a product.)

Bartering worked well as the initial economic system in the New World. People traded goods that they had, such as tools or weapons or deerskins or shells, for other goods that they wanted or needed. Since both parties agreed to the exchange, it was usually an equitable (or fair) exchange. Any item could be a **medium of exchange** because someone would want or need it. The more people who wanted or needed the item, the higher its value. Good fishermen might have extra fish to exchange for seed or corn or vegetables grown by someone else who was a good farmer. Hunters or trappers might have bear skins, deer skins, or beaver pelts to exchange. A **resource** is anything used to produce a good or service. Resources that are plentiful or abundant are not as valuable as resources that are scarce (in limited supply).

Above: This Cherokee man is making a spear point, which would have been a good in a barter economy.

Economics is the study of how we made decisions to allocated limited resources (natural, human, capital) in order to meet our unlimited wants. As you read ahead in your history textbook, you will see how the United States moved away from the traditional barter economy into a market economy. But some things did not change. Scarce resources are still more valuable than plentiful resources. Goods and services are still the products that satisfy our wants. Watch for the changes in our economy as you move into the next chapters of Georgia's colonial days.

Their shelters were made from materials at hand. Some houses were round, others rectangular. Home construction began with a framework of tree poles, which they then covered with bark and woven vines or saplings. They plastered the outside with mud to keep the rain and cold out. Inside were benches for sleeping and sitting. Because fleas were numerous, they built the benches higher than a flea could jump. Other furnishings included woven mats, pottery, baskets, and wooden utensils. Fires were built in the middle of the dirt floors. During the summer, the sides were opened to let in cool air. During the winter, the sides were closed to hold in the heat.

The Cherokee built log houses for winter living. A small fire kept the house very warm but filled it with smoke. This warmth was useful when they wanted to make the body sweat out impurities. The Indians also built council houses for meetings. These council houses were larger versions of their dwellings.

Food

All of the Native Americans including the Cherokee fished and hunted animals to obtain meat. Deer was their main meat, but they also ate rabbit, squirrel, turkey, raccoon, and small birds. Meat was often cooked by roasting it over an open fire. This was the origin of barbecuing, a popular way of cooking meat although Spanish explorers introduced some different ways of roasting and actually gave us the word *barbeque*. Nothing was ever wasted from a kill. For example, fat from bear meat made a grease that was used for frying fish, waterproofing skin boots, or even as a tinder for fires. Bear skins were used as floor coverings, and claws were made into jewelry.

Fish were an important part of the Native Americans' diet. They used various methods to catch fish: hook and line, traps, spearing, and nets. On inland streams, they built V-shaped rock dams with traps at the pointed end of the V. You can still see the remains of some of those dams in mountain rivers. At night, they would build fires on piles of sand in their canoes. The firelight attracted fish like flounder and sea trout, which they then speared.

Of Special Interest

A Tale of Love

A legend is a story that can neither be proved or disproved but continues to be told through generations. Such is a legend of love that was denied. It is called The Legend of Sautee Nacoochee.

Many Native Americans inhabited a region along the Chattahoochee River in north Georgia in what is now the Nacoochee Valley. At some point in time, there was a young Choctaw brave called Sautee who fell deeply in love with a Cherokee princess called Nacoochee, or "Evening Star." The beautiful young girl was forbidden to marry Sautee because their tribes were enemies. Unable to stay apart, the two eloped one night. Quickly, the Cherokee chieftain sent many braves to pursue the two and bring his daughter home. After several days, they found the pair huddled on the slope of Mount Yonah, which was considered to be a sacred mountain with spiritual powers. The angry chief ordered that Sautee be thrown over a cliff to his death because of his disrespect for the chief's wishes. Before she could be stopped, Nacoochee likewise flung herself over the cliff to join her loyal brave.

All too late, the chief realized how much they truly loved each other. In his sorrow. he instructed that they be buried together along the Chattahoochee River. Two nearby valleys were named after them. Today, you can visit Habersham and White counties in the area of Sautee-Nacoochee where these moundbuilders once lived and loved. In the middle of a field is a white gazebo (a small roofed building used for rest and shade) commemorating the star-crossed couple.

Should legends be shared? Why or why not?

Photo: The Chattahoochee River between Sautee and Nacoochee.

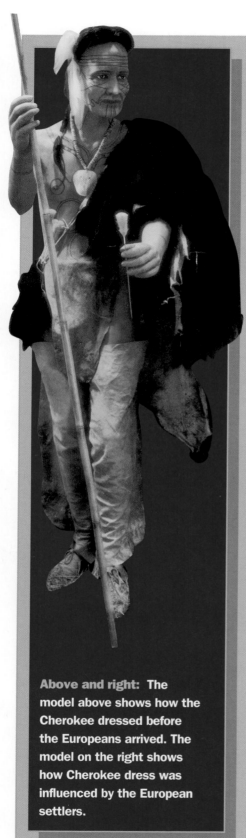

The tribes also grew a number of crops. Their chief crop was corn, which they called *maize*. Corn was prepared in many ways: ground into meal for bread, cooked in wood-ash water to make hominy, or roasted by the ear over a fire. During the winter, dried corn was stored in an airtight crib built high above the ground.

Other crops included squash, pumpkins, beans, and sunflowers. The main fruit tree they grew was the peach. Now you can really appreciate why Georgia is called the "Peach State." Honey and berries, fruits, and nuts gathered from the wild rounded out their diet. They made a delicious vegetable oil for cooking and seasoning by boiling crushed hickory nuts.

Clothing

The Native Americans wore little clothing during Georgia's warmer months. Tanned deerskins provided breechcloths for men and apron-skirts for women. Small children often wore no clothes. During warm weather, no one wore shoes. During cold weather, they wore moccasins, leggings made from soft deerskin, and match-coats for warmth. Match-coats were long, very warm capes made of furs or feathers. An early explorer who lived among the Cherokee for several years was amazed that they could sleep on the ground at night with no match-coat or other cover.

Spiritual Belief Systems

All Native Americans believed that many gods and spirits affected them whether in planting crops, hunting, fighting an enemy in battle, or just being. They believed that they must cleanse themselves inside and out to purify their spirits. Usually this was done with water or with smoke. The majority of tribes believed in an

Above and right: The model above shows how the Cherokee dressed before the Europeans arrived. The model on the right shows how Cherokee dress was influenced by the European settlers.

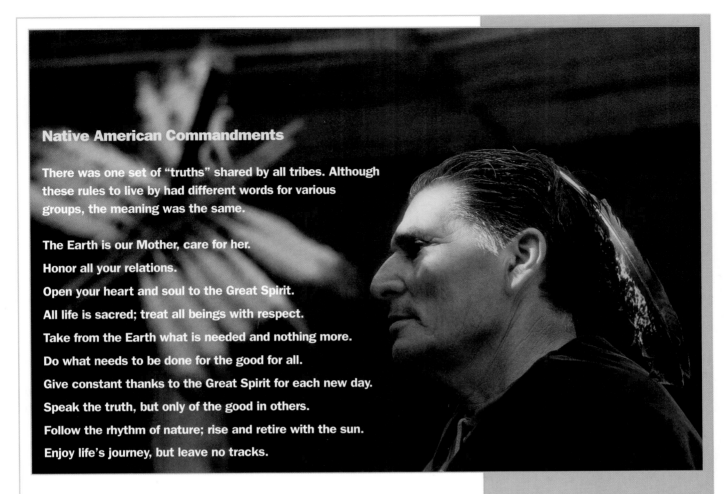

Native American Commandments

There was one set of "truths" shared by all tribes. Although these rules to live by had different words for various groups, the meaning was the same.

The Earth is our Mother, care for her.

Honor all your relations.

Open your heart and soul to the Great Spirit.

All life is sacred; treat all beings with respect.

Take from the Earth what is needed and nothing more.

Do what needs to be done for the good for all.

Give constant thanks to the Great Spirit for each new day.

Speak the truth, but only of the good in others.

Follow the rhythm of nature; rise and retire with the sun.

Enjoy life's journey, but leave no tracks.

afterlife where brave warriors and faithful women were rewarded and cowards and thieves were punished.

Three Worlds

The Cherokee believed that Earth was a large island resting on the waters. Each tribe thought that it was at the center of the Earth, which it called "This World." Above This World was the "Upper World," which was cleaner and purer than This World. The Upper World represented order and expectation. Below the waters on which the Earth rested was the "Under World," a place of disorder and change.

The Cherokee believed This World was usually orderly and predictable. As long as people stayed pure and behaved themselves and kept nature in balance, the spirits treated them justly. But illness and bad luck could come to people who misbehaved and polluted the world around them.

Gods

The chief gods, who were found in the Upper World, were the Sun and the Moon. The Sun was the main god, and she had the power of night and day, of life and breath. As a symbol of the Sun, the Cherokee kept a sacred fire burning. Keepers of the fire fed it some cornmeal or animal meat every day. The Cherokee believed that the Sun was kindhearted and watched over

This World. In darkness, however, she was not watching and bad things could happen. The Moon was also a god, the Sun's brother. He represented rain and fertility.

The Power of Beings

The Cherokee believed that just as certain humans had special powers so did some animals and plants. One of the most honored animals was the deer. When tracking the deer, hunters often donned a deer face and, before killing it, asked the deer's permission and forgiveness for taking its life. Failure to do this, they believed, resulted in painful joint conditions that kept the hunter from feeding his family. Only for hunger was the deer sacrificed.

Birds were also important animals because they came in contact with the Upper World. Their feathers were often used in ceremonies. The most important bird was the eagle, which stood for peace and order. Its tail feathers were highly prized, and it was an honor to wear them. Falcon feathers were used to improve eyesight. Turkey buzzard feathers helped healing. The Cherokee associated the turkey and the red-bellied woodpecker with war.

By the same token, there were things that needed to be avoided. Snakes were not killed because they

Top: For the Cherokee, the rattlesnake was special. They used its rattles in ceremonies. Top, right: The bear too was a special case. Above: This "buffalo man" mask was worn to depict the existence of evil spirits.

Did You Know?

The Cherokee believed that, when the moon darkened from an eclipse, a giant frog was trying to swallow the moon. They made noises to scare the frog into releasing the moon. It always worked.

might want revenge. The rattlesnake, however, was different. The Cherokee believed it was once a man sent to This World to save humans from disease caused by the Sun. Eating its meat would make one fierce. Its rattles were used to scare enemies, its oil was good for sore joints, its fangs were used to draw blood during healing, and its bones were made into necklaces.

The bear was also a special case, for it stood on two legs like a man. The Cherokee believed that bears were once men who failed to avenge wrongs done to their people. Because this was a great crime, the men were turned into bears. Before the Cherokee killed any animal, they asked the animal's spirit to forgive them. But not the bear. Bear-men who would not avenge wrongs did not deserve respect.

Honesty

In the belief system of almost all tribes, honesty was extremely important. From an early age, children were taught the dishonor resulting from stealing, cheating, or going back on your word. In fact, for adults, the punishment for stealing or cheating was often death.

Remembering that honesty is our character education term for this chapter, what does honesty mean to you? To the Cherokee, a person's word when he or she promised to do something meant nothing without honesty. It is certainly something to think about.

Plants

Considered friends of humans, plants were used for food and to fight disease and bring healing. Native Americans had over two hundred plants they used for medicine. Priests or medicine men often made a ceremony of giving out medicines. The root of bear grass was used against snakebite and rheumatism. To ease shortness of breath and to stop bleeding, the Cherokee drank a potion containing ginseng. Angelica root was good for back pain, while spicebush tea cleaned the blood. Horsemint tea brought on sweating and reduced swelling in the legs. The roots of the Venus's flytrap and the pitcher plant were thought to have unusual powers because the plants fed on dead insects.

Tobacco was a special plant. When smoked in a pipe, its pure, white smoke rose up to the Upper World. As a result, the Cherokee, and most other tribes, used tobacco on ceremonial occasions when asking for blessings from the gods.

The most important plant and main source of food was corn. To give thanks for the corn, the tribe celebrated with the Green Corn Ceremony. People in the tribe came from near and far to take part in the ceremony. It usually took place at the first full moon after the late corn ripened. The first day was spent feasting, cleaning all the buildings, and putting out all fires.

Above: As they developed agriculture, corn became the Cherokee's most important crop, a symbol of life. The Green Corn Ceremony was one of the most important of the year.

The second day was a day of fasting. The men drank tea to cleanse themselves. During the second day, the men forgave wrongs done to them. (Murder, however, was not forgiven.) On the morning of the third day, everyone feasted again. That afternoon, the priest lit a new fire and carried it to the ceremonial center. From that fire, the village fires were restarted. All wrongs were forgiven, and the priest urged the people to remain pure so they would have good luck. Then the women joined the men in dancing.

On the fourth day, they feasted, danced, painted themselves with white clay, and took a ceremonial bath in a stream. Some Native Americans still practice this ceremony.

Law of Retaliation

Native Americans had few laws. The most important was the law of retaliation. *Retaliation* means "the act of striking back or getting even." The law of retaliation was actually used to prevent feuds and preserve peace within the tribe. For example, if one person killed another, the spirit of that person would not rest until relatives avenged the death. The dead person's kin did this by killing the killer or a close relative. The matter was then considered settled.

When one tribe killed people from another tribe, war often resulted. The Cherokee looked upon war as a way to avenge deaths and terrorize the enemy. Native Americans did not often go to war to gain territory or property. Raiding the enemy was voluntary and a way to win honor. Warriors prepared for it by purifying themselves. Then, in small groups, they crept up on and attacked their enemies, taking trophies to show their people that the deaths were avenged.

When tribes wanted to make peace, they asked a neutral tribe to arrange peace talks.

Top: This Cherokee sweat lodge was used to cleanse the body, mind, and spirit. **Above:** The wind chimes outside a traditional Cherokee house warn of the entrance of evil spirits.

It's Your Turn

1. How was the Creek village organized?
2. Why were the clans so important in the Cherokee culture?
3. In what ways did the childhood games of Native Americans prepare them for adulthood?
4. Name three foods eaten by Native Americans that are still enjoyed by Georgians today.
5. What was the most important crop to the Cherokee?
6. What is your opinion of the Native American commandments?

A Final Note

Naturalist William Bartram traveled through north Georgia during the Revolutionary War and gave us a view of the life and culture of Native Americans. He wrote,

There were . . . many very magnificent monuments of the power and industry of the ancient inhabitants of these lands. . . . I observed a stupendous conical pyramid, or artificial mound of earth, vast tetragon terraces, and a large sunken area, of a cubic form, encompassed with banks of earth; and certain traces of a larger Indian town, the work of a powerful nation, whose period of grandeur perhaps long preceded the discovery of this continent.

The European explorers and settlers did not share that sentiment. It would be a mere 106 years before the Native American presence in Georgia was almost completely wiped out. During that time period, the Creek and Cherokee in our state, especially the Cherokee, built a continuously enriched culture, government, and language. But at the same time, they suffered numerous hardships, loss of land and homes, near starvation, imprisonment, and constant fear. Finally, most of the Native Americans were removed from Georgia.

Above: In the 1770s, William Bartram explored the southeastern United States, collecting seeds and specimens of the flora in the area. In 1791, he published a book on his travels. In 1803, he accompanied Lewis and Clark on their exploration of the Louisiana Territory.

Chapter Summary

- To learn about prehistoric people, we depend on the findings of archaeologists and anthropologists.

- The first settlers in our country are believed to be Asians who came to North America over a land bridge across what is now the Bering Strait.

- Scientists group prehistoric people into four cultures and time periods: Paleo, Archaic, Woodland, and Mississippian.

- The Mississippian was the most advanced of the four cultures.

- The two largest tribes in what is now Georgia were the Cherokee and the Creek.

- The Cherokee and the Creek had a rich culture with strong belief, family, and government systems.

- The Cherokee Nation was made up of seven clans.

ChapterReview

Reviewing People, Places, and Terms

Match each of the following words with the definitions that follow.

A. anthropologist

B. archaeologist

C. artifacts

D. clans

E. culture

F. tribe

1. A scientist who studies how human cultures began and developed

2. A group of people who share a common ancestry, name, and way of living

3. A scientist who studies the items left behind by ancient people to determine how they lived

4. A term that describes the beliefs, traditions, music, art, and social institutions of a group of people

5. Groups of people who believe themselves related by blood

6. Things, such as pottery, tools, or weapons, that were made by humans

Understanding the Facts

1. What is the carbon 14 test?

2. In what period do scientists believe horticulture began?

3. During which period did the bow and arrow come into use?

4. List the differences between each of the Archaic periods.

5. How many tribes made up the Creek Nation or Confederacy?

6. What is meant by a mother-centered family system?

7. In what ways did Cherokee homes differ from the homes of the Plains Indians, which are the ones usually shown in movies?

8. What were three uses of plants by Native Americans?

Developing Critical Thinking

1. How can archaeologists tell about early cultures? What items do they study to learn about the past?

2. What could have happened to cause some of the Mississippian tribes to disappear?

3. Compare and contrast the methods of obtaining food in each of the four prehistoric cultural groups.

4. In what ways do you think "civilized" society has demonstrated the Native Americans' law of retaliation?

5. How are the games played by today's boys and girls different from those played by the Cherokee children? How are they the same?

Checking It Out

1. Native Americans have left their mark on Georgia. The state is full of communities, rivers, and attractions that bear descriptive Indian names. For example, Dahlonega, in Lumpkin County, comes from the Cherokee *atela-dalaniger*, meaning "yellow money." The Chickamauga River, which flows through Catoosa, Walker, and Whitfield counties, comes from the Muskogean *Tchiskamaga*, which means "sluggish or dead water." In Towns County, the name of the Nantahala Mountains comes from the Cherokee *nan-tah-ee-yah-heh-lik*, or "sun in the middle noon.

   Use your local Chamber of Commerce, school media center, Internet sources, and local historical society to find out the Native American heritage of any names in your community or area. Make a listing for the class and include a description of each site.

2. How do you prepare to become an archaeologist or an anthropologist? What type of schooling and licensing or credentials are required? Use your school career counselor and career information center to research these two fields of study and the job markets for them. Would you be interested in either career?

Writing Across the Curriculum

1. After reading "A Tale of Love" or other Native American legend, write a legend about how a place in your county got its name.

Exploring Technology

1. Research the Hopewell culture on the Internet. Identify ways in which their culture was advanced.

2. Many tribes believed that the world was divided into three parts: This World, the Upper World, and the Lower World. Use your Internet search skills to find information about each of these areas and report your findings to your classmates.

Applying your Skills

1. Sign language was important to Native American culture and is still a method of communication between people who cannot hear or who do not speak the same language. Develop a short story to present to your class and create signs with your hands that will represent the major people, places, and things in your story.

2. What do you think archaeologists and anthropologists of future centuries will think about today's eighth graders and their schools? What artifacts do you think might be used as evidence to describe your social and tribal life?

3. Using William Bertram's description, draw or make what he saw. *Note:* You may need to look up some of the words before starting.

Photo Question

This Woodland period pot was excavated at a mound site in Early County. What is the name of the site?

Settlement of the Thirteenth Colony

Historical accounts tell us that, from the beginning of time, both man and animal have traveled from place to place. Sometimes the travel was a search for better or more food or a search for warmth during an ice age. In some cases, bigger or stronger predators or neighbors forced others to travel. Later, people traveled in search of something better—better spices, gold, riches, land, freedom from fear, or just because it was possible to do it. During the rest of the book, we will examine these urges to search for something, understanding that each and every search has a different reason and often a price far more than just money.

Below: James Edward Oglethorpe built Fort Frederica, whose wall you see here, in 1736 to defend the new colony of Georgia from the Spanish in Florida.

Signs of the Times
1733-1752

Population: From 114-120 people in 1733 to approximately 5,000 colonists in 1752

Children: Life was relatively difficult. Once children reached 6 or 7, they were expected to work either at home or in the fields. "Lolling around" was considered a sign of sin or weakness. They were expected to dress in the same fashion as their parents. During free times, they played "scotch hoppers" (hop-scotch), cat's cradle, or kite flying. Children not in the upper class played with cornhusk dolls or used corn cobs to build houses and forts.

Life Expectancy: Males, around 30-40; Females, much earlier

Food: Rice; waterfowl; meat from hunted deer, turkeys, and wild boars; fish and shrimp; corn; homegrown fruits and vegetables like sweet potatoes and beans; beef from South Carolina; grits

Annual Rent: About 20 shillings sterling for every hundred acres of land

Literature: Each colonist received a Bible and a prayer book after landing. Other popular authors included Samuel Pepys, New England writer Anne Bradstreet, Samuel Hardy, John Bunyan, Jonathan Edwards, Cotton Mather, and Benjamin Franklin.

Art/Architecture: Many homes on the "squares" were two-story brick homes with wrought iron grilling and porches on both floors. Brick roads led to the commercial center of town along the river. Art in the homes might be pastoral scenes or portraits of family members painted by traveling artists.

Music: "Forester's Reel," "Soldiers Joy," "Gaspe Reel," and similar dance tunes. Hymns were also popular including John Wesley's "Charleston Hymnal."

Fashion: There were work clothes and social clothes, the latter being of fine cloth. Women's dresses were long and made from good cloth or silks with hats or umbrellas to protect their skin from the bright Georgia sun. Clothes were dyed bright colors.

Education: Georgia had the first agricultural experimental education in the country. Three Italians came with the colonists to teach them how to grow silkworms; the colonists also experimented with grapes, oranges, and corn. For children, there was a schoolmaster or apprenticeships. Boys were trained in the classics (Latin and Greek) or French and liberal arts; girls learned homemaking skills, writing, and reading. Later, some boys of wealthy landowners were sent back to England to be educated.

Fads: Dancing, especially "reels" popular in the colonies and the minuet, a slow intricate dance from Europe.

Figure 11 Timeline: 1500 – 1750

1752
Trustees returned colony to King George II

1742
Battle of Bloody Marsh

1540
Spaniard Hernando de Soto began exploring Georgia

1566
Spanish mission of Santa Catalina founded on St. Catherines Island

1739
War of Jenkins's Ear

1733
Oglethorpe and colonists arrived in Georgia

1663
England claimed Georgia

1732
Georgia charter signed by King George II

1721
Fort King George built near Darien

1500	1550	1600	1650	1700	1750

1492
Columbus made first voyage to New World

1607
Jamestown established

1707
Great Britain formed

1538
"America" used for first time on map

1588
Spanish Armada defeated

1718
New Orleans founded

1565
Spain founded St. Augustine

1741
Alaska discovered

Section Preview

As you read, look for:
- **the reasons for the explorations of the 1400s and 1500s,**
- **the early Spanish settlements, and**
- **vocabulary term: middleman, monarch, and colony.**

An Age of Exploration

For centuries, Europeans had traded with Asia through such Mediterranean ports as Venice and Constantinople and along a land route known as the Silk Road. Many middlemen took part in the Far Eastern trade. A middleman is a trader who buys goods from producers and sells them to other traders and consumers. The middlemen drove up the prices of such luxury items as dyes, silk, perfumes, drugs, gold, jewels, and spices such as pepper, cinnamon, nutmeg, and cloves.

In 1477, the publication of Marco Polo's *Travels* led many Europeans to believe that China's fabulous riches could be reached by ship. The riches of the East Indies, Polo said, were "something wonderful, whether in gold or precious stones, or in all manner of spicery." First, however, Europeans had to find a shorter trade route to the Orient before they could make these items more available to the people.

The Search for New Trade Routes

Among those looking for a trade route to the Far East was Prince Henry the Navigator of Portugal. During the early to mid-1400s, Prince Henry sent ships along the southern coast of Africa in search of an eastern passage to the Indian Ocean. But it was not until 1488, long after Prince Henry's death, that Bartholomew Diaz rounded the southern tip of Africa at the Cape of Good Hope.

Another European sea captain, Christopher Columbus, believed that the route to the Far East lay to the west. Like other experienced navigators of his day, Columbus believed that Earth was round. Columbus thought that the distance from Portugal to Japan was less than 3,000 miles. (It was really 12,000 miles.) He also believed that no land mass barred his way to the Orient. For years, Columbus tried to get support for his plan from the monarchs (kings and queens) of France,

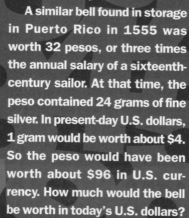

History by the Numbers

A Million Dollar Bell

In the summer of 1994, a diver found what is purported to be the bronze bell from Columbus's 1492 journey on the *Santa Maria*. The 31-pound, 10-inch tall, 10-inch diameter bell was found in 25 feet of water only 150 yards from the beach. It had spent 450 years under water.

The bronze bell was scheduled to be auctioned in Madrid, Spain, in 2003. Bids were to start at $1 million. However, Portuguese authorities stopped the auction to verify its authenticity.

A similar bell found in storage in Puerto Rico in 1555 was worth 32 pesos, or three times the annual salary of a sixteenth-century sailor. At that time, the peso contained 24 grams of fine silver. In present-day U.S. dollars, 1 gram would be worth about $4. So the peso would have been worth about $96 in U.S. currency. How much would the bell be worth in today's U.S. dollars?

Portugal, and England. Finally, Queen Isabella and King Ferdinand of Spain agreed to finance his voyage.

On August 3, 1492, Columbus, a 41-year-old Italian, set sail from Palos, Spain, hoping to reach China and the East Indies. His ships were named the *Pinta*, the *Niña*, and the *Santa Maria*. On one of the best-known dates in American history—October 12, 1492—Columbus landed on a Caribbean island he named San Salvador (now one of the Bahama Islands).

Columbus believed that the islands he had found lay off the coast of India. As you learned in a previous chapter, he even called the friendly and gentle natives he met "Indians." He believed that they could easily be converted to Christianity and hoped to make them faithful subjects of the Spanish monarchs.

In all, Columbus made four voyages to the western hemisphere (1492, 1493, 1498, and 1502). In his later voyages, he explored along the coasts of Central and South America and was the first European to visit Puerto Rico, Jamaica, and the Virgin Islands. In his reports, he described the extraordinary beauty of the "New World" he found. (Europe was the "Old World.") When he died in 1506, Columbus still believed that he had discovered a westward route to the Far East's riches. Vast stores of gold and spices, he insisted, lay close at hand.

John Cabot, who like Columbus was from Genoa, Italy, also sailed west. In 1497, sailing under an English flag, he discovered Newfoundland in

Top: This mural in the U.S. Capitol commemorates Christopher Columbus's first voyage to the New World. **Above:** America was named for the explorer Amerigo Vespucci.

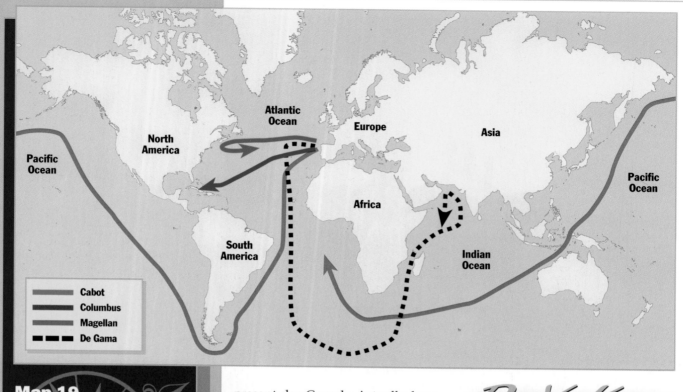

Map 19
Early Explorers and Their Routes

Map Skill: How many voyages are shown on this map?

Cabot
Columbus
Magellan
De Gama

Above: In 1498 Vasco da Gama reached India by sailing to the east, around Africa.

present-day Canada. Actually, however, he rediscovered it. Norsemen led by Leif Ericsson had landed in Labrador in the year 1001. They established a settlement in a region they called *Vinland*. After trying several times to colonize the area, the Norsemen fled back to Greenland. Unfriendly natives helped hasten their departure.

In 1498, Vasco da Gama sailed around Africa and reached India. An ocean trade route to the Orient had finally been found.

Did You Know?

Spanish explorer Christopher Columbus kept two sets of logbooks on his voyage to the New World. One logbook was public, the other was private. Columbus believed that the crew would panic if they knew how far they were actually sailing.

Amerigo Vespucci, an Italian navigator, had the honor of giving his name to the New World. In 1499, Vespucci sailed along the coast of South America. His writings caught the attention of a mapmaker who, in 1507, named the new land *America*.

In 1522, Ferdinand Magellan succeeded in reaching Asia by sailing west. However, his route around the southern tip of South America was long and hard. Europeans wanted an easier route to China and India. They were looking for the so-called *Northwest Passage*, an all-water route to Asia through the North American continent.

In the fifty years after Columbus's first voyage, European explorers continued to search for a shorter and easier route to the East Indies. King Francis I of France backed Giovanni Verrazano, who sighted land in March 1524 near

what is now Cape Fear, North Carolina. He followed the coastline south for about 150 miles before turning to the north again. Verrazano did not continue farther south because he was afraid he would run into the Spanish.

Spanish Exploration of the New World

Spanish explorers searched the Caribbean for wealth. In 1513, Juan Ponce de León discovered Florida, and Vasco Nuñez de Balboa crossed the Isthmus of Panama to reach the Pacific Ocean. (An *isthmus* is a narrow strip of land, with water on both sides, that connects two larger pieces of land.)

Another Spanish explorer, Hernando Cortés, was the first to live up to Spanish dreams of tremendous wealth. In 1519, he landed in what is now Mexico. Within two years, Cortés had conquered the native Aztec Indians, killed their ruler Montezuma, and won a treasure in gold and silver. Hearing of the wealth of the Incas in Peru, Francisco Pizarro set out for the western coast of South America. In 1535, in the Andes, Pizarro defeated the Incas. In doing so, he captured the richest silver mines in the world.

Spanish Exploration of Georgia

In 1539, the Spanish explorer Hernando de Soto left Havana, Cuba, with a huge group: over six hundred men, two hundred horses, and other animals such as mules and dogs. They landed in Florida and marched north. In 1540, they entered the southwestern part of Georgia, close to present-day Albany.

De Soto and his army wanted one thing as they moved across the state: to find gold. When de Soto arrived in Georgia, the native tribes saw white men and horses for the first time. De Soto had only a small number of men to face thousands of American Indians, but his weapons were better. His army

Top: Before the coming of the Spanish conquistadores, the Aztec capital of Tenochtitlan was a thriving city of 100,000 people. Smallpox so weakened the inhabitants that they surrendered the city to Cortez. **Above:** In 1513 Vasco Nunez de Balboa crossed the Isthmus of Panama and discovered the Pacific Ocean.

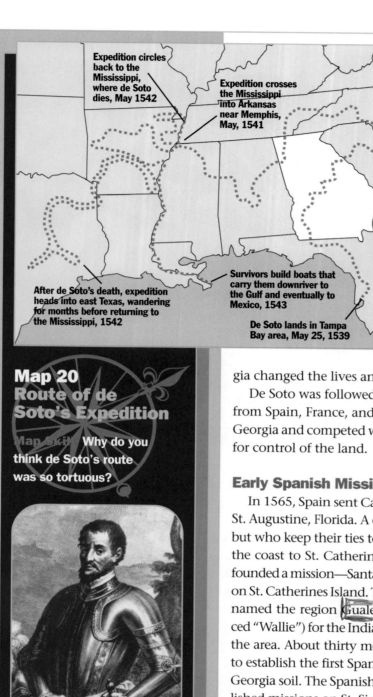

Expedition circles back to the Mississippi, where de Soto dies, May 1542

Expedition crosses the Mississippi into Arkansas near Memphis, May, 1541

After de Soto's death, expedition heads into east Texas, wandering for months before returning to the Mississippi, 1542

Survivors build boats that carry them downriver to the Gulf and eventually to Mexico, 1543

De Soto lands in Tampa Bay area, May 25, 1539

Map 20 Route of de Soto's Expedition

Map Skill: Why do you think de Soto's route was so tortuous?

Above: A skilled swordsman, horseman, and explorer, Hernando de Soto had little trouble enlisting young Spaniards to travel with him to Florida in search of gold.

had guns and crossbows, and his soldiers rode horses. The Spanish also wore plated armor, which arrows could not pierce.

During de Soto's search for gold in Georgia, his soldiers killed thousands of American Indians. Many more Indians died from diseases brought to the New World by the Spanish and other explorers. Some historians believe almost half the Native American population died from measles, smallpox, influenza, and whooping cough.

De Soto's expedition into North America was a failure. He found no gold or treasure. Most of his army was lost to starvation and disease. De Soto himself died somewhere along the Mississippi River. However, his march through Georgia changed the lives and culture of the American Indians forever.

De Soto was followed by many other European explorers, most of them from Spain, France, and England. These nations established settlements in Georgia and competed with each other and with the Native American tribes for control of the land.

Early Spanish Missions

In 1565, Spain sent Captain General Pedro Menéndez to begin a colony in St. Augustine, Florida. A **colony** is a group of people who settle in a new land but who keep their ties to their homeland. In 1566, the Spaniards moved up the coast to St. Catherines and Cumberland islands. That year the Spanish founded a mission—Santa Catalina—on St. Catherines Island. The Spanish named the region Guale (pronounced "Wallie") for the Indians living in the area. About thirty men were left to establish the first Spanish post on Georgia soil. The Spanish later established missions on St. Simons Island and at Sapelo at the mouth of the Altamaha River.

For most of the 1500s, Spain's hold over the missions and colonies it established made it an important player in the race for control of the New World. As a result of the gold it took from the New World, Spain became rich and powerful. But this wealth also brought with it the re-

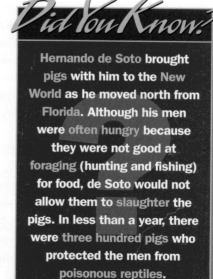

Did You Know?

Hernando de Soto **brought** pigs with him to the New World as he moved north from Florida. Although his men were often hungry because they were not good at foraging (hunting and fishing) for food, de Soto would not allow them to slaughter the pigs. In less than a year, there were three hundred pigs who protected the men from poisonous reptiles.

sentiment of other European nations. During the coming years, as Spain fought to hold onto its gains, the English and the French fought to gain a share of the treasures.

At sea, the conflict between Spain and England had already turned into an undeclared war by the end of the 1500s. English sea captains, men such as John Hawkins, Francis Drake, and Richard Greenville, captured Spanish treasure ships filled with gold, silver, and other valuable goods. They also attacked and burned Spanish settlements in the New World.

To counter these attacks, Spanish King Phillip II plotted to invade England, using a huge fleet of ships that the Spanish called the "Invincible Armada." The plot failed as the English, who had superior seamen and faster ships, destroyed or ran off much of the Armada. The Armada was damaged further by fierce storms.

It's Your Turn

1. On what date did Columbus land at San Salvador?
2. What explorer tried to establish a settlement in Labrador in 1001?
3. For whom was the New World named?
4. What was de Soto searching for in Georgia?
5. Where was the region called Guale located?

English Settlement of the New World

Section Preview

As you read, look for:
- the reasons why Great Britain established colonies in the New World,
- the first British garrison in what would become Georgia,
- the beneficial exchanges between Old and New World, and
- vocabulary terms: mercantilism, indentured servant, slave, and garrison.

After England defeated the Spanish Armada in 1588, it gained undisputed control of the seas and was ready to pursue its interest in the New World. Like most Europeans, the English believed there were large amounts of gold, silver, and exotic foods in the New World. They thought the country that claimed this new land would become even more powerful.

In the 1600s, the English began permanent settlements along the coast of the New World. They founded a colony first in Virginia, then Massachusetts. By the close of the 1600s, England had established twelve colonies along the Atlantic coastline.

Some of the colonies were begun by refugees from religious persecution; others were primarily settled for economic gain. Among the colonists, the

Spotlight on the Economy

Mercantilism

Great Britain began establishing colonies in America during a period of world history known for exploration and colonization. All of the European countries wanted colonies so they could be more powerful.

During the 1500s to 1700s, Great Britain—and the other nations of Europe—followed policies that came to be known as *mercantilism*. An important goal was to make Great Britain largely self-sufficient. To do that, the monarchy needed to create a "favorable balance of trade" by exporting more goods than it imported. A favorable balance of trade would bring gold and silver into Great Britain and make it militarily and economically strong. Laws were enacted to regulate trade. They made it difficult for foreign merchants to import goods into Great Britain. British merchants were told to export goods only in British ships.

Colonies were to help Great Britain gain that favorable balance of trade. They were sources of such raw materials and foods as sugar, timber, rice, tobacco, and cotton, thus ending any need to import these goods from other countries. Colonies were also markets for goods manufactured in Great Britain.

Captain John Smith, a founder of the Virginia colony, clearly understood the purpose of mercantilism. He viewed the colony as "a nurse for soldiers, a practice for mariners, [and] a trade for merchants."

Above: Cultivation of tobacco was very important to the success of Great Britain's southern colonies.

reasons for moving to the New World were as different as the people. Some came so they could have religious freedom. A few felt a spiritual "calling" to bring Christianity to the Native Americans. Others wanted adventure and the chance to make a new start. Almost everyone thought that, with hard work, they could have a better life. Most of the settlers did, indeed, face a variety of hardships before they succeeded.

For its part, England hoped to establish a system of **mercantilism**, a part of which was a trade policy that England should export more than it imported. Among the things it had to buy from other countries were cotton, forest products, tobacco, and some foods. Under a system of mercantilism, its colonies would produce raw materials and ship them to England. There, English citizens could use the raw materials to make finished goods, such as furniture, clothing, tools, and sugar. England could then sell those items to other nations and strengthen its own economy.

Top and above: James Fort is a recreation of the original Jamestown settlement. Costumed interpreters like these demonstrate to visitors what life in the fort was like.

Permanent Settlements

Permanent colonization of the New World began in 1607 with the English settlement of Jamestown, in what we now call Virginia. From the beginning, Jamestown, which was named after King James I, had its troubles. The 104 settlers who survived the transatlantic crossing arrived too late to plant crops. Because Jamestown was located beside a swamp, malaria swept through the village during the colonists' first year. By the end of that

Matoaka

Every now and then historical events are told and re-told in such a way that the facts become convoluted or tangled. Thus is the case of one Matoaka, who was the daughter of the Powhatan chief of the powerful Algonquian tribe. You probably know her better as Pocahontas, which was a nickname meaning "the naughty one" or "spoiled child." According to most historians and the Powhatan nation, the story of the 12-year-old throwing herself over the body of British explorer John Smith to save him from certain execution is untrue. We do know that the two met and initially were friends.

So, what was the true story? Accounts differ about the relationship of the Powhatan tribe and Jamestown settlers from 1607 to 1613 and about the life of Matoaka. In 1612, the bright and friendly 17-year-old young woman was captured by the Jamestown settlers. She was held captive for a year after the friendly relations between the tribe and settlers soured. During that time, 28-year-old John Rolfe, a tobacco planter, became enamored of the attractive prisoner and asked her to marry him. She agreed, was released from prison, and assumed the name of Rebecca Rolfe after being baptized in the Christian faith. Two years later, she traveled to Great Britain with her husband and her son Thomas. There she was wined and dined and put on display to support the Virginia colony. Her brightness and beauty captured the hearts of the English. On two occasions she met John Smith but refused to speak to him in the first incident and called him a liar in the second. In March 1617, the family was returning to their home in Jamestown when Pocahontas was taken ill and put ashore in Gravesend, England, where she died at age 21.

Above: This is the only known portrait of Matoaka (Pocahontas). It was painted in England in 1616.

year, only 38 settlers remained alive. The colony survived, however, and flourished, especially after the settlers discovered that tobacco grew well in the land. Soon other settlers were attracted to Jamestown.

The cultivation of tobacco created a need for labor, a need that was met by Dutch traders. In 1619, these traders introduced Africans into Virginia, most of whom were indentured servants. **Indentured servants** agreed to work for someone for a set period of time (usually 4 to 7 years) in return for passage to the New World. At the end of that time, indentured servants were free to do anything they wished. As the seventeenth century wore on, however, Africans more and more were treated as slaves. **Slaves** had few rights and spent their entire lives in service to others.

English explorers also established settlements in New England and the Carolinas. Since the Spanish were already in Guale, conflicts arose between the English and Spanish settlers. But by 1686, the Spanish had retreated south to St. Augustine. England realized that it needed a "buffer" between its colonies and the Spanish settlements in Florida. Georgia was to become that buffer.

Fort King George

Although Spain had moved out of Guale, more than one country claimed the land. France was establishing colonies along the Gulf Coast and in northern Alabama. Both the French and the Spanish posed a threat to the British colonies.

Colonel John "Tuscarora Jack" Barnwell, a wealthy South Carolina planter, traveled to London to ask that a fort be built at the mouth of the Altamaha River. The Crown approved the construction of the fort. In 1721, the **garrison** (a fort where troops are housed) was finished. Fort King George became the British "warning point" for invaders. Although abandoned in 1727 due to Indian raids, swampy conditions, and sickness, Fort King George established the English presence in Georgia. Today, you can see what the fort was like by visiting Darien.

New World-Old World Exchanges

Both the New World and the Old World benefitted from the exploration of the New World. Besides the riches they gained, the European nations were able to spread their Christian beliefs to the new continent. Foods, plants, and animals were exchanged between the Old and the New Worlds. Corn, the white potato (misknown as the Irish potato), sweet potatoes or yams, peanuts, turkeys, and pumpkins were some of the foods transported from the New World to Europe. Rye, radishes, beets, sugar cane, rice, peaches, and wheat were among the plants that came from Europe to the New World. The Europeans also brought horses, chickens, pigs, oxen, sheep, goats, and cattle to the New World. Many of these animals destroyed the native ground cover and led to the extinction of some native animals. However, the animals thrived here.

Top and above:
Fort King George was reconstructed and is now a state historic site.

Did You Know?

Many of the soldiers at Fort King George suffered from trench mouth, a painful condition. It was caused by the soldiers eating out of a "trencher," a piece of wood with the middle scooped out as a bowl. Because the bowls were rarely washed, the men got ulcers on the mouth and tongue.

It's Your Turn

1. Why did England want to establish colonies in North America?
2. What crop led to the use of indentured servants and slaves in the New World?

Section 3

The Colonization of Georgia

As you read, look for:
- reasons for establishing a colony in Georgia,
- James Edward Oglethorpe and his plans,
- the Georgia charter,
- the arrival of the *Ann* in Georgia, and
- vocabulary terms: trustee, charter, and regulations.

Section Preview

Great Britain first claimed Georgia in 1663, but it was not until 1717 that the British made plans to settle there. Sir Robert Montgomery, a nobleman from Skelmony, Scotland, and two partners, poet Aaron Hill and merchant Amos Kettleby, wanted to create the "Margravate of Azilia," a new colony. Montgomery's dream was to have "the most delightful country of the universe [where] coffee, tea, figs, currants, olives, rice, almonds and silk" would be produced for British markets. Montgomery proposed to settle an area that lay west of the Savannah River and ran to the Altamaha River. He promised to give land, gold, silver, and precious stones to those who would move to this "paradise."

Montgomery's plan seemed good, but he did not have enough financial backing to carry it out. After a few years, Montgomery's dream of a "future Eden" died.

In the years that followed, there were several other proposals to settle the area for Great Britain. None was successful until the late 1720s, when James Edward Oglethorpe began to talk of a colony for the "working poor."

James Edward Oglethorpe

James Edward Oglethorpe, born in London in 1696, was a member of an influential family. He was well educated and wealthy. He cared greatly about people in trouble and tried to find ways to help them. In 1722, he became a member of Parliament's House of Commons.

During that time, Great Britain was faced with many problems. There were more people than there were jobs. Many citizens, including some well-known ones, could not pay their debts. Laws concerning debtors were strict and harsh, and those who could not pay went to jail. Among those jailed was Oglethorpe's friend, architect Robert Castell.

Oglethorpe was on a committee studying prison reform when he learned that Castell had died of smallpox. Oglethorpe was angry because he believed debtors should not have to go to jail. He believed that his friend had died needlessly in a dirty prison. Stirred to action, Oglethorpe worked

> *A Plan representing the Form of Setting, the Districts, or County Divisions in the Margravate of Azilia.*

Above: Sir Robert Montgomery proposed a Georgia settlement called Margravate of Azilia, envisioning a heavily fortified settlement with intricate homesteads and pasture land.

to get laws passed that both improved prison conditions and let thousands of prisoners go free.

Unfortunately, just letting people out of prison did not help them. There were no jobs for them, and, without work, they still could not pay their debts. Dr. Thomas Bray, a clergyman and active humanitarian, proposed that a colony be founded to help these people.

Bray died before his proposal was acted on. However, James Oglethorpe, Lord John Percival, and nineteen other men outlined a plan that promised a fresh start in the New World to "unfortunate but worthy individuals."

A Dream Becomes a Reality

In the summer of 1730, Oglethorpe's group of twenty-one men asked King George II for a tract of land "southwest of Carolina for settling poor persons of London." The group knew Great Britain's two main reasons for beginning new colonies were (1) a balanced trading policy to make Great Britain self-sufficient and (2) defensive buffers to protect British colonies from the French, Spanish, and Native Americans. They proposed ways for their new colony to carry out those goals.

The new settlement could defend the southern Carolinas from Spanish Florida. It could also provide protection from the French, who were pushing east from the Mississippi River valley. Oglethorpe's group also listed economic reasons for the proposed settlement. France and Spain made money trading with the Native Americans who lived between the Atlantic Ocean and the Mississippi River. Great Britain could share in this. Oglethorpe and his supporters also said the new colony could produce silk, cotton dyes, and wine —three items Great Britain was importing from France, Russia, and Spain. They promised to send spices and semitropical fruit to Great Britain. British merchants were pleased with the idea of getting a good supply of raw materials while having a new market for their manufactured goods. Georgia, like other American colonies, would offer religious freedom to Protestants who were being mistreated by the Catholic Church in Europe. The king also liked the idea of more land and greater power for Great Britain.

On June 7, 1732, King George II granted a charter making Oglethorpe's group of twenty-one trustees responsible for establishing the

Above: Oglethorpe was shocked at the inhumane treatment of debtors he visited in prison and wanted to pass laws to help them. Not only were thousands arrested each year for not paying their debts, but many were charged a fee for being in jail. The death of his friend, Robert Castell, while in debtor's prison led Oglethorpe to demand reforms.

Did You Know?

In 1707, Great Britain was formed. It included England, Scotland, and Wales.

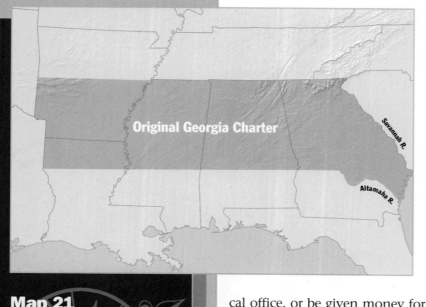

Original Georgia Charter

Savannah R.

Altamaha R.

Map 21
The Original Georgia Charter

Map Skills: What other current states did Georgia's charter include?

COLONIA GEORGIA AUG.

Above: The seal of the Trustees of Georgia. The cornucopia stands for "plenty" and was used to indicate that money would be made from the settlement of Georgia. The figures with water jars represent the Savannah and Altamaha rivers.

colony of Georgia and for managing it for twenty-one years. Trustees are people who hold responsibility on behalf of others. The charter, which is a legal document that grants special rights and privileges, noted that the grant covered an area of "all those lands, Countries, and Territories" between the Savannah and the Altamaha rivers extending westward "to the South Seas" (the Pacific Ocean).

Georgia's Charter

The charter had six thousand words and many limits. The king stated that the trustees could not own land, hold political office, or be given money for their work. "Papists" (Catholics), blacks, liquor dealers, and lawyers could not become colonists. Catholics were excluded because of a longstanding division between the Catholic Church and the Church of England. Blacks were not admitted so as not to introduce slavery to the colony. The trustees feared settlers would not work if liquor was permitted. They wanted colonists to settle their differences out of court and did not think lawyers would allow them to do this.

The colony belonged to the Crown, so the trustees were to get instructions from King George II. They could pass no laws unless the king agreed. The trustees worked around some of the rules by not having a governor and by using regulations, or government orders, instead of laws.

In allowing settlement of the colony, King George limited the trustees' authority, made them managers for a definite period of time, and said they could make no profit. In spite of the limits, excitement grew as the trustees developed the "Georgia Plan for Colonization."

Preparation for the Voyage

A search began to find settlers for the newest colony. Newspapers told of a land with mild temperatures and rich soil and the promise of a new start in life. Sir Robert Montgomery's description of it as the "most delightful Country of the Universe" was widely accepted as fact. Clergymen preached sermons, wrote religious books, and raised a great deal of money by talking about the goodness of the proposed colony.

The trustees talked with applicants and planned for the voyage and settlement. Unfortunately, debtors and former prisoners did not get to go. This meant the humanitarian reasons for the proposal were all but forgotten. Only a few of those chosen had ever been in debtors' prison, and no one got out of jail to make the trip. All who applied were carefully investigated. Those chosen were promised fifty acres of land, tools, and enough food for one year. Potential colonists who could pay their own way received five hundred acres of land and permission to take ten indentured servants.

In exchange, colonists had to agree to the following: (1) Each man was to defend the new colony against all enemies. (2) Land given to colonists could not be sold, and no money could be borrowed on it. It could, however, be passed on to a male heir. (3) Each colonist was to receive seeds and agricultural tools and was to use them in cultivating the lands of the new settlement. (4) Colonists were to use a portion of their land to grow mulberry trees so that silkworms would eat the leaves and make cocoons for the production of silk. (5) Each colonist was to obey all regulations established by the trustees.

Even though the agreement was strict, the fever of settling in the new colony grew. On October 24, 1732, the chosen settlers met to receive instructions for their voyage to Georgia.

The Voyage on the Ship *Ann*

When the settlers gathered on the London docks, they were both excited and a little afraid of the adventure ahead. Historians do not agree on the exact number of men, women, and children who traveled from Gravesend, England, to Georgia. But between 114 and 125 people left London on November 17, 1732. Their voyage to the New World took eighty-eight days.

Besides its passengers and crew, the *Ann* carried sheep, hogs, ducks, geese, and several dogs. There is no record of the ship being uncomfortable, but it was probably crowded with all the people and their belongings. The ship stopped in Madeira to take on five barrels of wine to go along with the ten barrels of Alderman Parson's best beer already on board. Food was simple, mostly salted pork and peas or dried beef and sweet pudding. Bread and hard cider were served with meals. There were few fresh vegetables other than carrots and onions. Fish were caught and cooked whenever possible.

Only two deaths were reported among the colonists on the trip, both of them infants. The passengers spent their days playing games, talking together, and planning what they would do when the voyage was over. Finally, land was sighted, and the *Ann* docked at Charleston, South Carolina. The ship stayed in Charleston one day, then put in at Port Royal (Beaufort), South Carolina, on January 14, 1733.

Above: As a man who possessed the virtues of kindness, compassion, and leadership, James Oglethorpe was a commendable choice to lead the settlers to their new home.

Did You Know?

In some books, you will find writers call the ship Oglethorpe traveled on as the *Anne* rather than the correct spelling *Ann*. One explanation for this error could be that the queen who ruled Great Britain from 1702 to 1714 was named Anne. Later writers just assumed the ship was named after the queen.

Right: When Tomochichi, chief of the Yamacraws, met James Oglethorpe, leader of the settlement, little did they know they were to become lifelong friends. **Above:** Chief Tomochichi with his nephew, who was probably the chief's sister's son. Notice the intricate designs on the chest of the chief.

Before the *Ann* could set anchor, Oglethorpe had to make friends with the Yamacraw Indians through their chief, Tomochichi. Oglethorpe went to the trading post in the Yamacraw village to find an interpreter. The trading post was operated by John Musgrove and his wife Mary, who was part Native American and part British. Oglethorpe offered John Musgrove about 100 British pounds a year to interpret for the Yamacraw and settlers. John agreed to act as interpreter, but Mary soon took over for him. With Mary's help, Oglethorpe and Chief Tomochichi established a close friendship that lasted until the chief's death in 1739. The South Carolina colonists, delighted to have new neighbors, loaded the ship with barrels of rice, a hundred cows, thirty hogs, sheep, and oxen and 2,000 British pounds. One South Carolinian, Mr. Hume, even sent along a silver baby spoon to honor the first child born in the new colony.

By the Side of the Road

Savannah Waterfront

The colony of Georgia began on Savannah's waterfront in 1733. The riverfront has always played an important role in Georgia, whether as colonial port, exporter of cotton, or tourist destination. The first commercial house below the bluff opened in 1744. Cotton dominated Savannah's exports throughout the nineteenth century. Construction began in the early 1800s for the multi-storied warehouses and "Factor's Walk," named for the cotton brokers whose offices were in the upper floors. River Street was created in 1834 and cobbled with ballast stones. The last cotton office on the waterfront closed in 1956. River Street's revitalization began in 1977.

Erected by The Georgia Historical Society and the Savannah Waterfront Association

2001.3   25-7

James Oglethorpe and his first group of settlers left the *Ann* on the Savannah River at a spot that is now the Savannah Visitor's Center behind City Hall. Even then, Oglethorpe knew the importance of placing the colony's first town on the river's edge to allow shipping to and from Great Britain. When you visit Savannah, read the historical marker now in place where Oglethorpe first landed to begin our state.

Today, Savannah's waterfront attracts tourists from all over the world.

The passengers waited on board while Oglethorpe and his staff searched for a permanent settlement site. The place decided on was about eighteen miles from the mouth of the Savannah River.

On February 12, 1733, Chief Tomochichi allowed the *Ann*'s passengers to land on sandy Yamacraw Bluff overlooking the Savannah River. According to the report sent to the trustees, Oglethorpe said:

I chose this Situation for the Town upon an high Ground, forty feet perpendicular above High Water Mark; The Soil dry and Sandy, the Water of the River Fresh, Springs coming out from the Sides of the Hills. I pitched upon this Place not only from the Pleasantness of the Situation, but because from the above mentioned and other Signs, I thought it healthy; For it is sheltered from the Western and southern Winds (the worst in this Country) by vast Woods of Pine Trees, many of which are an hundred, and few under seventy feet high. The last and fullest consideration of the Healthfulness of the place was that an Indian nation, who knew the Nature of this Country, chose it for their Habitation.

The settlement they established was the thirteenth English colony in the New World. Georgia's citizens were added to over 650,000 other colonists spread from Massachusetts through the Carolinas.

It's Your Turn

1. What was the "Margravate of Azilia"?
2. Who first proposed a colony for debtors?
3. What problems in England led Oglethorpe to plan for the new colony?
4. What were some reasons Great Britain wanted to settle Georgia?
5. What were some of the rules to which the first colonists had to agree?
6. What Indian chief was a friend to the Georgia settlers?

Section Preview

As you read, look for:
• the struggles of the settlers to build the new colony,
• the first settlements in Georgia,
• conflict with the Spanish,
• why the trustees returned the colony to the king, and
• vocabulary terms: artisan and militia.

Building a New Home

The colonists put up four large tents for shelter. Then they began getting the land ready for planting and preparing timber to build permanent homes. Most of the settlers had lived in the city and were **artisans** (craftsmen). They were not used to hard physical labor. Within two weeks, however, they began building the first permanent homes.

Oglethorpe had no title and only limited power, but he was accepted as the leader of the colony. During the early months, he got grants of land and made treaties with the Native Americans. He had a small fort built on the bank of the river and trained a **militia**, or citizen army, to defend the settlement. Oglethorpe gave advice to local leaders and encouraged the new colonists. He also worked with Colonel William Bull and surveyor Noble Jones to design the future city of Savannah. The basic pattern of this first planned city in the colonies was after a design by Robert Castell, Oglethorpe's friend who had died in a British debtors' prison.

The plan was for Savannah to have four squares. On the north and south sides of each square were twenty lots sixty by ninety feet. On the east and west sides, four larger lots were set aside for such buildings as churches or stores. The center of each square was for social, political, and religious gatherings. The squares were divided into blocks, which were called *tythings*, and wards. There were ten houses in each block and four blocks in each ward.

An examination of a present-day map of Savannah shows the influence of Jones, Bull, Castell, and Oglethorpe. Modern Savannah, with a population of over 146,000, is built much the same as the city that was planned over 255 years ago. Today, twenty-one of Oglethorpe's original twenty-four squares remain. What a monument to his planning!

Each settler was expected to care for his house in Savannah, his five-acre garden plot on the edge of town, and his forty-five farm acres in the country. During the first months, the colonists cultivated mulberry trees to

Above: At Fort King George State Historic Site, visitors can see this re-creation of an early settler's camp.

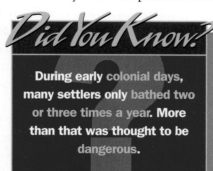

Did You Know?

During early colonial days, many settlers only bathed two or three times a year. More than that was thought to be dangerous.

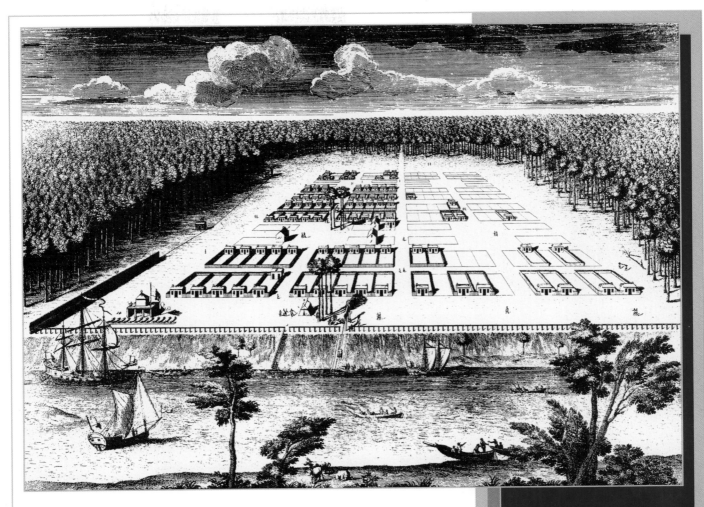

Above: Peter Gordon, an upholsterer by trade, kept a journal describing the crossing of the Atlantic on the *Ann* and providing us with the earliest view of the layout of Savannah.

feed silkworms. They also built a sundial for telling time, a gristmill for grinding corn into meal, a courthouse, a water well, and a bakery.

Work was done in spite of growing medical problems. Oglethorpe thought the use of rum caused the people to be sick. However, the scurvy, dysentery, and fever were more likely caused by a lack of fresh vegetables, changes in the climate, poor sanitation, and hard physical labor. Forty settlers died in the first year. That number might have been greater if new colonists had not arrived.

The Arrival of New Colonists

In July 1733, when the sickness was worst, a ship carrying forty-two Jews landed in Savannah's harbor. The passengers asked to join the settlement. Because Catholics were the only religious group not allowed by the charter, Oglethorpe agreed. He needed to replace the colony's only doctor, who had died earlier. He also needed more able-bodied men in the militia. Because of the services of Dr. Samuel Nunis, the newly arrived doctor, Georgia's first medical crisis passed.

In March 1734, Oglethorpe was planning to leave for Great Britain to report to the colony's trustees when more new settlers arrived. A group of German Protestants had been forced to leave Salzburg, which was then controlled by Catholics. They were led by John Martin Bolzius, and they asked to

Above: On June 28, 1734, Oglethorpe and his party of nine Indian guests, including Chief Tomochichi, reached London. They were entertained with many parties and dinners during their stay. The meeting of the Indians and the Trustees of Georgia was painted by Willem Verelst.

live in Georgia. Oglethorpe carried the Salzburgers to a place twenty-five miles from Savannah. There they began a town called Ebenezer, which means "the Rock of Help." They spoke a different language from the other settlers, so they stayed mostly to themselves. However, they worked hard and were busy colonists. Because the land was marshy with poor soil for crops, the Salzburgers asked Oglethorpe for a better site. In 1736, they moved to Red Bluff on the Savannah River. There they built another town, which they called New Ebenezer.

When the Salzburgers were settled, Oglethorpe left for Great Britain. He took with him Chief Tomochichi, the chief's wife, his grandnephew, and five other members of the tribe. The British liked the Yamacraw and held parties

and receptions in their honor. The Indians were presented to King George II and the Archbishop of Canterbury. His countrymen thought Oglethorpe was a hero, and excitement about the newest British colony grew. The visit strengthened Indian-British relationships, and Oglethorpe went back to Georgia with the full support of the trustees.

Oglethorpe reached Savannah in early February 1736, and he brought three hundred new colonists with him. Included were another group of Salzburgers, some Moravians (Protestants who banded together in Saxony, Germany, in 1722), and two religious leaders, John and Charles Wesley.

During his visit to Great Britain, the trustees gave Oglethorpe a large amount of money to make the frontier borders stronger. They also agreed

Fort Federica: Today the Fort Frederica National Monument on St. Simons Island is an archaeological site. Visitors can see artifacts such as this wine bottle (top, left), the remains of the fort's barracks (top, right), and the foundations of one of the houses (above).

with three new regulations Oglethorpe wanted to introduce. Upon his return, Oglethorpe first helped the Salzburgers move to Frederica on St. Simons Island. Then he began to present the three new regulations to Georgia's settlers: Buying rum was to be against the law, and alcohol could not be used in trading with the Native Americans. Slavery was not allowed because Oglethorpe thought it caused landowners to be idle while, at the same time, made them want more land. Trade with the Native Americans was to be watched carefully.

Discontentment among the Settlers

Oglethorpe's new regulations were not popular. The regulations, plus the earlier one about passing on land only to male heirs, began to divide the colonists. They were already facing economic hardships. Their mulberry trees were the wrong kind for producing large amounts of silk. The colonists were not able to grow hemp, flax, indigo (a plant used to make blue dyes), or grapes for wine. To make the discontent worse, their South Carolina neighbors, who had large amounts of land, slaves, and rum, were doing well. They were growing rice, cotton, and tobacco, and their success was due, in part, to the use of slave labor.

The Salzburgers and the Highland Scots, who had settled in Darien in 1735, opposed slavery. However, growing numbers of British settlers wanted slaves. There was less and less support for the trustees' regulations. Many Georgia settlers moved to places where they could live more nearly as they wished. When Oglethorpe returned to Georgia after one of his trips to Great Britain, he found upset people all over the colony.

Oglethorpe, however, had little time to listen to the colonists. In the fall of 1739, a war broke out between Great Britain and Spain. Great Britain controlled Georgia's borders, and Spain controlled Florida's. There seemed to be no way to keep the two groups from fighting.

The Spanish Invasion

The war was called the "War of Jenkins's Ear." Several years earlier, Spanish sailors were said to have cut off the ear of Robert Jenkins, an British seaman, to serve as a warning to British ship captains smuggling goods off the Florida coast. Oglethorpe welcomed the war. It gave him a good reason to invade neighboring Florida. A force of about two thousand men, mostly Native Americans and settlers from Georgia and South Carolina, was quickly organized. They tried to take major Spanish forts in Florida, particularly St. Augustine. However, a well-organized Spanish militia met Oglethorpe and his soldiers with a surprise attack on June 15, 1740. The Spanish won, and

Above: This map, drawn in about 1735, shows the young colony of Georgia. Notice the roads and settlements that had grown outside the planned community of Savannah.

Left: The English victory in the Battle of Bloody Marsh on July 7, 1742, helped secure the frontier boundaries against future Spanish invasions. The battle was fought between the St. Simons lighthouse and Fort Frederica. Below: This monument on St. Simons Island marks the site where Oglethorpe's forces surprised the Spanish troops during the Battle of Bloody Marsh.

Oglethorpe's forces had to retreat to St. Simons Island.

During the next two years, there were numerous attacks and counterattacks between the Spanish and British settlers, with neither side gaining much ground. In July 1742, Oglethorpe got the opportunity he needed. His forces, assisted by the Highland Scots, waited in the dense woods along the marshes on St. Simons Island. Spanish troops who came that way were caught completely by surprise and forced back across the Florida border. Even though the action was known as the Battle of Bloody Marsh, it was neither big nor very bloody. It did, however, mark the beginning of a safe southern frontier for the British.

After that battle, Oglethorpe had another plan. One of his soldiers had deserted and gone to the Spanish. Oglethorpe had a released Spanish prisoner carry a note to the deserter. The note, which was taken away from the prisoner by Spanish troops, said that British warships were on their way to begin a great battle against the Spanish settlers. The "warships" were really trading vessels, which quickly moved to safe waters the first time they met the Spanish Navy. The Spanish troops,

A Past and a Mission

We Georgians owe a great deal to James Oglethorpe. He had the interest and compassion to help people and the ability to work untiringly to fulfill a dream. Before he knew he would be reimbursed, Oglethorpe spent well over 100,000 pounds of his own money (which today would be $165,000 in American money) to make his dream come true and protect his charges. In 1910, a statue of James Oglethorpe was unveiled in Savannah's Chippewa Square. David Bottoms, Georgia's poet laureate wrote a poem about Oglethorpe that was printed in the book *Oglethorpe's Dream*. The following excerpts are from the section of the poem entitled "A Past and a Mission."

Do you revere the dead?
Do you revere the ways the dead have revered you?

A man stood on the bluff of a river
and imagined a city.

The river here forms a Half-moon,
around the southside of which the banks are about forty feet high,
and on the top a flat, which they call a bluff . . . .
Seven weeks and not a calm crossing. Two infants lost to sickness,
though otherwise no calamity.

but not a calm crossing.
Seven weeks of winter on the frigate *Ann,*
and a hundred or so colonists with their thick Protestant Bibles,
their axes, muskets, plows,
10 tons of Alderman Parson's best beer . . .

The Savannah River formed a half-moon,
the banks were high.

Upon the riverside in the center of the plain,
I have laid out the town, opposite
to which is an island of very rich pasturage.
. . .

A dream owned him.
It was a new idea, fragile, perhaps old-fashioned. He thought it good.
His dream was rich soil and sunlight. Rain and hard labor,
the free farmer on his own land.
His dream was opportunity.
He lived it by his labor. Hard work,
the free man and the free woman
working their own farmland.
Slavery, he wrote, is against the Gospel,
as well as the fundamental law of England. We refused as trustees
to make a law permitting such a horrid crime.

He made enemies.

Did You Know?

Although silk production was limited in the colony, some of the first spun silk was sent to the Queen of England for a royal dress.

however, did not know this. Because they thought they were outnumbered, the Spanish chose to leave the area for good.

The End of the Dream

In 1743, Oglethorpe was called to Great Britain to answer charges that he had not acted correctly when he failed to capture Spanish-held St. Augustine. Oglethorpe was cleared of the charges, but he did not return to Georgia. Instead, he remained in Great Britain, married a young heiress, and settled down to life as a patron of the arts.

William Stephens, the trustees' secretary, was named president of a colony filled with disagreement. Efforts to keep rum from being sold had been stopped in 1742. The people still wanted to own more land and to have slaves. By 1750, this was allowed. The regulation against slavery was repealed, along with the one that allowed a colonist to own only five hundred acres of land. When President Stephens retired in 1751, he was replaced by his assistant, Henry Parker. President Parker died a year later. Over the next three years (1752-1754), Georgia was led by President Patrick Graham. During his tenure, many settlers who had left under the rule of the trustees returned to the colony. At about this same time, the British Parliament decided not to set aside enough money to take care of the colony's needs. In 1752, one year

Top: The ruins of Horton House on Jekyll Island, built by Major William Horton in 1740. It is one of only two pre-Revolutionary tabby structures still standing in Georgia. **Above:** This is a close-up of tabby, a mixture of shells, lime, sand, and water. Tabby was a popular building material along the Georgia and Florida coasts.

before the charter's end, the trustees returned Georgia to the authority of King George II. A new era was about to begin.

A Last Look at the Charter Colony

The idealistic vision of society that had been shared by the trustees of the colony was never fulfilled. Few debtors reached Georgia's shores, and the colony was an economic failure. Many unhappy settlers moved elsewhere, and the dissension in the colony continued. Rum was freely imported, and slavery was introduced. By the time the Georgia charter ended, nearly one-third of the population of three thousand were slaves. Finally, the colony suffered from a lack of continuity in leadership. But with all its failures, the colony had made progress.

During the twenty years of the original charter, 5,500 people had settled in Georgia. They had built new homes and started new lives. Although some left the colony to go elsewhere, they still made an imprint on the society and culture.

A large number of settlers were European Protestants who came to the colony to escape religious persecution. In Georgia, they were able to practice their beliefs without fear of punishment.

Treaties with the American Indians and the elimination of the threat of Spanish invasion ended the need for British military protection. Georgia was a safe haven on the southern frontier.

There were also noteworthy religious, social, and political accomplishments in the colony's short history. Evangelist George Whitfield established the Bethesda Orphans Home in Ebenezer. The home served as a refuge for children without parents. Later, the home was expanded into a school and renamed Bethesda House. The school provided a basic education for many of Georgia's future leaders. In Savannah, John and Charles Wesley established the first Sunday school in America. They also founded the Methodist Church.

The court system, established during the early days of the settlement, was still functioning. By 1750, when the colonists gained outright ownership of the land, women were able to inherit property.

Perhaps the trustees' greatest accomplishment was their ability to enable the Georgia colony to survive the many hardships encountered during the first twenty years. The survival set the stage for Georgia to become a successful and profitable royal colony.

Above: Chief Tomochichi asked Oglethorpe to bring a minister to the colonies to serve his tribe. John Wesley, a young Church of England minister, volunteered. During his brief one-year stay, Wesley preached to the Indians and colonists. He conducted Bible study classes for the children every Sunday. Those classes are believed to be the first "Sunday School" held in the colonies.

It's Your Turn

1. How was Robert Castell important to the settlement of Savannah?
2. Why was Dr. Samuel Nunis important to Georgia's history?
3. What were the three regulations Oglethorpe introduced after his first trip to England?
4. Where was the Battle of Bloody Marsh fought?
5. When did the trustees return Georgia to King George II?

A Final Note

As we look back on the Georgia colony, it is important to remember the state motto, *Non Sibi Sed Allis*, which is Latin for "Not for themselves but for others." From that standpoint, we have only to look around us and know they were very successful.

Chapter Summary

- European explorers searched for all-water routes to reach the riches of the East Indies and expand trade.

- Many countries explored the New World including Spain, France, and England.

- In 1540, Hernando de Soto, a Spanish explorer, traveled through present-day Georgia searching for gold.

- Europeans brought to the New World a variety of new plants, animals, foods, and diseases. In return, they carried new plants, foods, and animals from the New World back to the Old World (Europe).

- In 1732, King George II granted twenty-one trustees, including James Oglethorpe, the right to settle a colony in what is now Georgia.

- Great Britain hoped that the new colony would defend its other colonies from the attacks of the French, Spanish, and Native Americans. Great Britain also planned for the colony to produce and ship raw materials it would otherwise have to buy from other countries.

- Led by James Oglethorpe, a group of settlers landed on a site near the mouth of the Savannah River. Some of the settlers were looking for religious freedom, while others wanted adventure and the opportunity to make a fresh start in life.

- The charter contained many limits on the freedom of the colonists, who were expected to defend the new colony and obey all regulations.

- Land was given to the colonists. However, they could not sell it, borrow money on it, or pass it on to anyone other than a male heir.

- Later regulations, including a ban on slavery, caused discontentment among the settlers, who needed additional help to work their properties.

- Although the original ideals for the colony were never fulfilled, the colony made progress and survived.

Above: After serving Georgia for ten years, Oglethorpe left in 1743 to return to England. Until his death in 1785, at the age of 88, Oglethorpe continued to work in many charities while living the life of a country gentleman.

Chapter Review

Reviewing People, Places, and Terms

On a separate sheet of paper, write the words that best complete each of the following sentences.

1. An artisan is (a) a recording star, (b) a craftsperson, (c) a small farmer.

2. Georgia's charter (a) was granted in 1732, (b) was issued by Prince Phillip, (c) established the Margravate of Azilia.

3. An indentured servant (a) was responsible for tending the mulberry trees, (b) offered to work for someone in exchange for passage to America, (c) is someone who handles the affairs of a group.

4. Mercantilism (a) involves establishing rules or laws, (b) grants certain rights to those who want to establish a colony, (c) is an economic and trade policy.

5. A monarch is (a) one who sponsors an expedition, (b) a type of ship, (c) a king or queen.

6. James Edward Oglethorpe (a) favored the use of slaves in the new colony, (b) wanted to help debtors, (c) was the captain of the *Ann*.

7. Slaves (a) were initially forbidden in Georgia, (b) were paid for their services, (c) both A and B.

8. Tomochichi (a) was the father of Matoaka, (b) was the chief of the Cherokee, (c) made a trip to Great Britain with Oglethorpe.

Understanding the Facts

1. Why did England expand the colonies it established in the New World?

2. Which foods and animals were exchanged between the New World and the Old World?

3. When did England first claim Georgia?

4. Why did King George II want to establish the thirteenth colony?

5. How many trustees were responsible for establishing and managing the colony of Georgia? For how many years were the trustees supposed to manage the colony?

6. What was the purpose for planting mulberry trees?

7. Why did many Georgia settlers want to introduce slavery into the colony?

8. In what year were the people in the colony allowed to own more land and have slaves?

Developing Critical Thinking

1. If you had been a citizen of London when Oglethorpe was looking for colonists for Georgia, would you have been willing to travel to a new land? Why or why not? What parts of the trip would have been the most exciting for you? What parts of the settlement process would have been the most frightening for you?

2. Suppose the initial regulations governing the colony had been upheld. Would life in the colony have been different? Explain.

Checking It Out

1. Use your research skills to find out more about the voyage of the *Ann* to the new colony. Who were the passengers on the *Ann*? What types of skills did they have? What could they contribute to the success of a new colony?

2. Use your research skills to find out more about the diseases that Europeans introduced into the New World and for which the Native Americans had no immunity. Which diseases were the most deadly and why? How long was it before these key diseases were controlled in the New World?

Writing Across the Curriculum

1. Imagine that you are a 14-year-old who made the voyage across the Atlantic on the *Ann*. Write a letter to a friend back in Great Britain describing life on board the ship and the excitement of landing in the new colony. Write a second letter, one year later, describing the pleasures and difficulties of living in the new colony.

Exploring Technology

1. The European nations that controlled settlements in the New World were all male-dominated societies. However, in the Native American and African societies, women played much more important roles. Use your favorite search engine to find out about the role of women in these three cultures. How did the activities and roles of colonial women differ from the activities and roles of Native American women in their matrilineal society, which you studied in the last chapter?

2. Use your favorite search engine to examine the exchange of plants and animals between Europe and the New World. (Use the key words "Columbian Exchange.") Did you know, for example, that the so-called Irish potato came from the New World? Did you know that the famed bluegrass of Kentucky came from Europe? Learn which of our common plants were native to the New World and which came from Europe.

Applying Your Skills

1. Using a United States map, outline the original land area granted to Oglethorpe and the other trustees.

2. Using a current map of Savannah, examine the layout of the early colony and compare it to modern Savannah. How are the maps similar and different? How do current street names indicate a sense of the history of the early settlement?

3. On a blank Georgia county map, locate Savannah, Ebenezer, Darien, and St. Simons Island.

4. Draw what you think would be a good layout for Savannah. How does your design differ from that used by Oglethorpe?

Just for Fun

Riddles were very popular during the colonial period. Try your hand at a few. You will need to keep a colonial "frame of mind."

1. What flies up but is always down?

2. When is a boy most like a bear?

3. What has a tongue but cannot talk?

From Royalty to Independence

The period after Georgia returned its charter and became a British royal colony until the end of the American Revolution was a time of unrest and turmoil in Georgia and in the other colonies. As you read more, it is important to remember that in 1763, when the trouble really started, Georgia was only 30 years old. Virginia and Massachusetts and other colonies had been colonies for 100 to 150 years. That is quite a difference in both experience and outlook.

Below: This painting by John Trumball is of the signing of the Declaration of Independence in what is now Independence Hall in Philadelphia. The painting includes portraits of 42 of the 56 signers and 5 other patriots. It can be seen in the rotunda of the U.S. Capitol Building.

Signs of the Times
1752-1783

Population: About 10,000 by 1759 in Georgia, including approximately 3,600 slaves

Life Expectancy: 37, if a child lived past 5

Wages: Plantation owners could make over 1,000 pounds a year. A skilled craftsman might earn about 85 pounds a year. The average laborer made 30 pounds; a journeyman (a skilled artisan who worked in various shops) made 40 to 45 pounds. The annual pay for a ship's boy was 2 pounds, 10 shillings. In the South, workers might be paid in farm goods, particularly tobacco.

Cost of Living: A supper of bread, cheese, and beer cost around 3 pence (pennies). If meat was added, it was just under a shilling (12 pennies). A day's worth of coal cost 1 pence. A yard of good cloth cost about 12 shillings. Knit stockings were 2 shillings. In the South, a good flintlock musket cost less than 1 pound. For 16 shillings, one could buy a new saddle, a dictionary, a table or a chair, or a nice winter coat. For 200 pounds, one could purchase or build a nice home.

Art/Architecture: Important American painters of the period were Benjamin West, John Singleton Copley, and Charles Wilson Peale. Homes became more ornate. The kitchen was often in a separate building, as was the "necessary house." Farmhouses had 3-4 small bedrooms downstairs, a combined family room-kitchen, and two small bedrooms upstairs or up the ladder to a loft area.

Literature: Books that were popular for adults to read to their children included *Robinson Crusoe*, *Gulliver's Travels*, and *Aesop's Fables*. Phillis Wheatley, a gifted black poet from Boston, had a book of her poems published in 1773.

Music: Revolutionary War favorites included "Johnny Had Gone for a Soldier," "The Foggy, Foggy Dew," "All the Pretty Little Horses," "The Rebels," and "God Save the King." British soldiers sang "The Yankeys Return from Camp" to make fun of the colonists. Today it is known as "Yankee Doodle."

Leisure Time: Horse racing was popular throughout the colonies. Popular games in cities included tennis, badminton, whist (a card game), cricket, and backgammon, checks (checkers), dominoes, jacks, marbles, spinning tops. Young people enjoyed fishing, kite flying, hopscotch, berry picking, tag, and blind man's bluff.

Fashion: Wealthy colonial women adopted the fashion of the "Tower." Hair was piled over crinoline pads until there were lots of curls. It was greased, powdered white, and decked with jewels, ribbons, vegetables, fruits, flowers, or lace. It literally took hours to complete the hair style, but it might last for 3 weeks.

Education: King's College (Columbia University) was founded in New York City in 1754. Harvard Medical School opened in 1782.

Science/Inventions: Benjamin Franklin performed his now-famous kite experiment in 1752. Franklin also designed Philadelphia's first street lights and invented bifocal glasses. In 1753, black inventor Benjamin Banneker built a wooden clock that kept time for fifty years. John Hobday invented a threshing machine in 1772 and was awarded a gold medal by the "Virginia Society for the Promotion of Usefull Knowledge."

Fads: "Bosom bottles" were worn for the first time in 1765. These small ribbon-decorated glasses became the first live "corsages."

Figure 12 Timeline: 1750 – 1800

1752 Georgia became a royal colony

1754 Reynolds became first royal governor

1757 Ellis named governor

1760 Wright appointed governor

1763 The Georgia Gazette was the first newspaper in the state

1765 Liberty Boys held first meeting in Savannah

1775 Georgia's Provincial Congress met

1777 First Georgia state constitution adopted

John Treutlen became governor

1778 British captured Savannah

1779 Battle of Kettle Creek, siege of Savannah

1750   1760   1770   1780   1790   1800

1754 French and Indian War began

1757 First street lights appeared in Philadelphia

1763 French and Indian War ended

1767 Mason-Dixon line established

1770 Boston Massacre

1773 Boston Tea Party

1774 First Continental Congress

1775 Revolutionary War began

1776 Declaration of Independence

1783 Treaty of Paris ended Revolutionary War

The Colonial Period

Much of the period from the mid-1700s until the outbreak of the Revolutionary War was overshadowed by the political events that led to the break between Great Britain and its colonies. But the concerns of most of the people in the thirteen colonies centered on the problems of everyday living.

The Colonial Economy

Great Britain's thirteen colonies could be divided into three groups. Although those within each group worked together, there was little cooperation and few similarities between the three sections even in terms of their economies. The New England Colonies were located in cold, rugged terrain with rocky soil. The people there made their living building ships, fishing, and whaling. They also engaged in buying, selling, and shipping goods, particularly fine, handcrafted furniture, to Great Britain and the other colonies.

The Middle Colonies had a milder climate and a rich soil for farming fruits and vegetables even though the farms were relatively small. Wheat was especially important in Pennsylvania and New York, leading to their nickname of the "breadbasket colonies." The Middle Colonies also prided themselves on the number of their industry including manufacturing, mining, textiles, and shipbuilding.

The third group of colonies—the Southern Colonies—includes the area where you live today. Here the climate was even milder, and the soil was rich. There were many large plantations. Farmers grew tobacco, indigo, silk, and rice. Forest products were a large part of the southern economy. Casks and barrels for shipping goods and naval stores were produced from the vast longleaf pine forests.

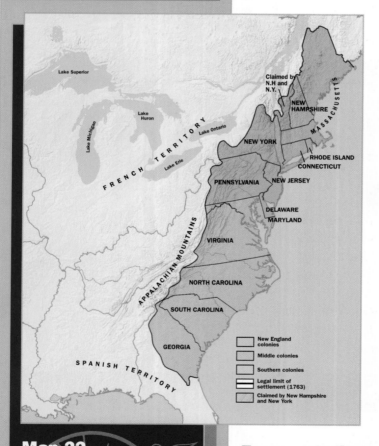

Map 22
The British Colonies in America

Map Skills Name the New England Colonies, the Middle Colonies, and the Southern Colonies.

Transportation and Communication

Transportation continued to be a problem. Colonists on foot or horseback still followed Indian paths, while boats delivered passengers and trade goods from port to port. Stagecoaches offered quick transportation among the colonies. That is, if you call the week it took to travel the ninety miles between New York and Philadelphia quick.

By the mid-1700s, most cities had cobblestone streets. Citizens, however, walked at their peril because some streets were used as garbage dumps. While

Did You Know?

Naval stores—tar, pitch,
rosin, and turpentine—were
used to preserve the wood
and ropes on ships.

watching where they stepped, the city dwellers also had to stay out of the way of wandering hogs and the occasional chicken.

Written communication was equally limited right before the Revolutionary War. People in the cities relied on newspapers for information. Those in rural areas had to wait for their newspapers, often as long as several weeks or months. Trading posts were sources of information, and bulletins and announcements were placed at the posts and in whatever local shops there were. In Savannah, the riverfront was also a source of information as ships came into port from Great Britain or from other colonies and shared the latest news. It was still news to the Southern Colonies even though much of the information was weeks old when it finally arrived at the Savannah port.

Education

For most children, schooling was something that occurred between daily chores. Seasonal agricultural needs took precedence. In the early days, most schooling took place either in the home or in the church. Boys were taught practical skills, such as farming or horseshoeing. If they lived in or near

Top: "Old field schools" were built in an old worn-out field that was good for nothing else. The one-room buildings were poorly heated and let in little light. Above: Punishment in colonial schools could be very harsh. Students could be caned for not knowing their lessons.

cities, they might be sent away to **apprentice** in a trade; that is, to learn a particular skill from a master craftsman. Girls learned homemaking skills, either to use in their own homes or working for others as "hired" hands.

When public schools first began in the New England Colonies, only boys attended. They studied the "3 Rs": reading, 'writing, and 'rithmetic. The alphabet included many religious and secular jingles to teach reading, religion, and community values. For example:

"A — Adam — In Adam's Fall, We sinned all."
"B — Bible — Thy Life to Mend, This Book Attend."

In some towns, both boys and girls could attend a "dame school," where a woman who was knowledgeable in the "3 Rs" opened her home as a school. Students carved their writing pens from goose quills and used ink made from boiled bark. Many boys continued on to Latin grammar schools to prepare for college. Colleges such as Yale, Harvard, Brown, Dartmouth, Princeton, and William and Mary opened in the colonies.

In the Middle Colonies, education was intended to prepare boys for a trade or skill. Most schools were run by different religious denominations. For those who could not afford to put their children in private schools, elementary school was considered adequate. There was very limited secondary level schooling.

Discipline in these early schools was very rigid. In many of the colonies, students were caned (whipped with a thick rod) if they could not show that they knew their lessons. Like many other things in their lives, going to school was not something to be treated lightly.

In the South, boys from wealthy families either had a *tutor* (a private teacher) or were sent overseas to be educated in Great Britain or France. "Old field schools" also became

Did You Know?

Education for wealthy young southern men included Latin, Greek, Hebrew, reading, writing, arithmetic, plane geometry, Italian bookkeeping, and navigation.

more common as small planters and farmers put up a one-room building in an abandoned tobacco shed. The schools charged a small fee, and students attended when they were not needed on the farms. Only the most basic education was provided. In some communities, parents banded together to pay someone, almost always a man, to teach the basics to their children.

Religion

Depending on the colony, church was generally both a place of worship and the center of community activity. In the stricter New England Colonies, church services often lasted three hours in the morning and three hours in the afternoon. The Puritans were especially demanding of their followers. **Puritans** were a group of people who had broken away from the Church of England because of religious differences. Those who did not observe the Puritan beliefs to the letter often received punishment ranging from caning to banishment from the area. For the Puritans, learning to read was extremely important in order to read the Scriptures. Although Puritanism eventually died out, many of the basic Puritan values, such as their work ethic and their strong determination in the face of challenges and adversity, became a part of early American culture.

In the Southern Colonies, although church attendance was expected, services tended to have more singing and shorter sermons. After-church socials were times for women to visit and chat while girls played hopscotch and boys played hoop ring or flew kites.

Georgia was a haven for such varied religious groups as the Moravians and the Jews. But the Anglican Church, or Church of England, was the major denomination. In fact, in 1758, it was made the official church of the colony of Georgia.

During the late colonial period, religion remained an important part of colonists' lives. New denominations appeared, and people slowly became more tolerant of the beliefs of others. To ensure there were enough ministers to serve the needs of the colonists, churches started colleges. The Baptists founded Brown University; the Presbyterians founded Princeton; the Congregationalists began Dartmouth; the Anglicans founded Columbia. Another consequence of the changes in religion during this period was that the colonists learned that they had more in common with each other than they had thought. Those commonalities would be important when it came time for action later.

Above: Midway Church was built by the Puritans who settled in the Midway area in the 1750s. This building was completed in 1792.

Leisure Time

Even recreation differed among the three regions. In the New England and the Middle colonies, most of the recreation centered around work and included such activities as barn raisings, quilting bees, and corn huskings. As they were in other aspects of their lives, the Puritans remained quite strict. People in their colonies were not allowed to gamble, dance, play cards, or wear frilly clothes. In the early colonial period, punishment for engaging in such activities had included public whippings, having one's legs locked in stocks, and being dunked into a pond or river while sitting in what was called the dunking chair. Later, strictness lessened considerably. One of the most popular leisure-time activities became horse racing. Balls and dinner parties were also popular activities.

In the Southern Colonies, fox hunting, horse races, and week-long parties with friends and relatives were a welcome change from the drudgery and isolation of farming or running a plantation. Food was always central to any large social gathering. Tables were laden with roasted pigs, pheasant, chicken, venison, wild turkeys, oysters, and fish. Vegetables included steamed pumpkin pudding, squash, corn, and succotash. Desserts included such treats as shoofly pie (a spice pie with molasses), slump (a fruit cobbler), and sweetmeats (candied nuts, fruits, or flowers).

For young people, games included jump rope, hoops, tennis, London bridge, hopscotch, leap frog, and other outdoor activities. Card games, if parents approved, were popular, as were yo-yo's and puzzles. Story telling was a great pastime.

Romance and Marriage

Romance during the late colonial period had a very different meaning than romance today. Girls could be "promised" in marriage as early as their birth, and they could be married by 14 or 15. A young man had to get permission from the father to call on a young woman. Courtships, such as they were, took place at dances, church, or carefully supervised home visits. Weddings were a time for great joy and celebration. Most ceremonies took place at 11:00 a.m. to allow a full day afterward for toasting, feasting, and entertainment.

For the wealthy families, marriage was primarily a business arrangement. For example, a father with a shipping company might marry his daughter to the son of another shipper. The two fathers could then merge their companies to form a larger business. Two plantations might be joined when the owners' children married. If the marriage resulted in a love relationship, so much the better. But love was not considered essential.

For less well-to-do families, marriage plans were much easier, and love often played a vital role in choosing a spouse. A social-class marriage was considered to be a lasting partnership. Divorce was a shocking rarity.

In these relationships, each spouse had a clearly defined role. Since women could not own property, their role was to provide a smoothly run home and well-behaved children. Many wives kept the family books, planned social gatherings, oversaw household servants, and taught their daughters the skills and arts needed for their future homemaking roles. Husbands were expected to be the providers and to be gallant and polite.

If her husband died, the surviving wife was expected to remarry after an appropriate mourning period of one or two months. Since half of all wives died in childbirth, men often had four or five wives.

Did You Know?

Since wedding guests often came from far away, wedding activities could last for weeks.

Below: Weddings were major events in the Southern Colonies. Dancing was an important part of the festivities, which often lasted until the early hours of the morning.

It's Your Turn

1. In what way were the economies of the colonies alike during this period?
2. In what ways did the Southern Colonies differ economically from the New England and Middle colonies?
3. What role did religion play in education during the colonial period?
4. What was the biggest difference in the leisure-time activities of young people in the colonial period and today?

Georgia Becomes a Royal Colony

In 1752, Georgia ceased to be a proprietary colony and became a royal colony. A proprietary colony was one that was governed by a board of trustees. A royal colony was one directly governed by the king.

During the two years before the first royal governor was appointed, some of the people who had left Georgia while it was a proprietary colony began to return. In 1752, Puritans from South Carolina bought 32,000 acres of land at Midway in present-day Liberty County. They moved there, bringing their slaves with them. Soon they began growing rice and indigo. A port was built nearby at Sunbury so the planters could ship their crops.

Did You Know?

By 1750, there were less than 80,000 Europeans in the entire land area of Canada, compared with 1.5 million settlers in the thirteen British colonies.

Georgia's First Royal Governor and First Government

On October 1, 1754, Georgians cheered when John Reynolds, their first royal governor, arrived. Because the trustees had believed that the first Georgia settlers were not able to govern themselves, they had not given them the right to vote, hold elections, or collect taxes. Reynolds, a navy captain, introduced the idea of self-government. Unlike the trustees, Governor Reynolds wanted the colonists to help run the government.

A *bicameral*, or two-chamber, legislature was set up to represent the eight parishes of the colony. A parish was both a church and a British government district. The lower house of the legislature was called the Commons House of Assembly; the upper house was called the Governor's Council. In order to vote, a settler had to own at least 50 acres of land. Those wishing to become a member of the Assembly, however, had to own at least 500 acres of land. Members of the Assembly could write and vote on bills before they became laws. The king of England appointed the members of the Governor's Council. The men selected were wealthy, influential landowners. They were to advise the governor, approve land grants, make laws, and, sometimes, act as judges in legal cases.

Governor Reynolds also set up a court system. When the colonists had differences with each other, they went before the Court of Conscience, over which presided a local justice of the peace. Cases that could not be settled in the Court of Conscience could be carried to the Governor's Council.

It was during this period that the French and Indian War began in a dispute over land in North America.

Top: The front of Georgia's colonial seal showed the colony giving the king silk spun in the colony. **Above:** The back had the coat of arms of the king.

The First Real World War

In 1754, three countries had settlements in North America. The Spanish had settlements in Florida and Mexico. The French controlled a vast area from Louisiana north to the Great Lakes, plus part of Canada. To protect their interests, the French had built forts, settlements, trading posts, and missions throughout the area, anchored by the cities of New Orleans and Detroit. The British had thirteen colonies along the Atlantic coast.

The **French and Indian War** was the result of disputes between France and Great Britain that had been going on for almost sixty-five years. The causes of the nine-year war that began in 1754 were greed and fear. The greed was a hope to capture the most land in the New World and control the treasures of the territory. The fear was that one country would gain more power than the other. With the exception of population differences in America, France and Great Britain were well matched. The British navy was the most powerful in the world, but France had the stronger army. Great Britain had a strong alliance with the six tribes of the Iroquois Confederacy, but the French were trading partners with many of the western tribes. The French had more experienced military leadership and, unlike the British colonists, the French settlers did not argue among themselves.

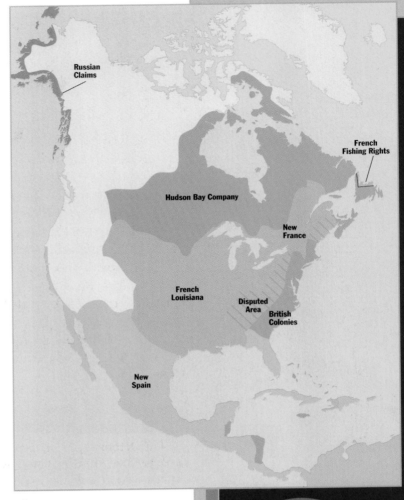

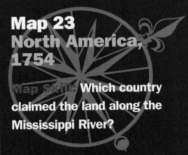

**Map 23
North America, 1754**

Map Skill: Which country claimed the land along the Mississippi River?

The Rivalry Intensifies

The tension between the two countries increased because both claimed the area of the Ohio River Valley. This frontier region was a huge area of about 200,000 square miles, which was about the size of France. British traders had formed profitable agreements with many tribes that had formerly traded only with the French.

At the same time, Virginia colonists were ready to move beyond the Allegheny Mountains into the Ohio River Valley. A group of businessmen had received a land grant of 500,000 acres in 1749, but the French continued to build forts throughout the area. This angered the Virginians.

In 1753, Virginia's governor sent a young George Washington to warn the French that the Ohio River Valley did not belong to them and to stop building forts there. Those demands were ignored, and Governor Dinwiddie warned his colony's government that the "Welfare of all the Colonies on the Continent were in grave danger from the French and Indian alliances."

Above: In 1754, a young George Washington was sent to tell the French to stay out of the Ohio River Valley.
Opposite page: British General Braddock was killed during a battle near Fort Duquesne in 1755.

Dinwiddie got the support he wanted. The following year, he again sent Washington to the French with a message. This time, however, Washington did not go alone.

War Erupts

Washington, a 22-year-old land surveyor and captain, led 150 Virginia militia troops to Fort Duquesne near the modern city of Pittsburgh. Washington's men set up a crude, round stockade of wooden stakes, which they named Fort Necessity. After a scout reported about 30 French soldiers in a nearby camp, Washington's men attacked, killing 10 and forcing the rest to surrender. As expected, the French attacked Fort Necessity a short time later. On July 3, 1754, severely outnumbered and having lost about one-third of his troops, Washington had no choice but to surrender to the French. The war had begun. It soon spread to Europe.

The first few years of the war in America consisted of a series of disappointing losses for the British and their colonies under the leadership of Major General Edward Braddock. The 60-year-old Braddock was a well-respected soldier, but he knew nothing about fighting the Indians. When he arrived, he decided to go to Fort Duquesne first in an attempt to defeat the French quickly. George Washington went with him as an aide. The colorful red uniforms of the British and the smart blue coats of the Virginia militia made good targets as the soldiers marched in long, straight lines through the forest. The French and the Indians hid among the trees. When the Indians screamed out their war cries, Washington wrote that the British lines broke and soldiers "ran as sheep pursued by dogs."

When the battle ended, General Braddock was dead and about two-thirds of his men were either killed or wounded. Although they were soundly defeated, Washington showed himself to be a brave military leader who had learned from Braddock's mistakes. He was made commander of a small Virginia force that now had to protect the colony along a 300-mile front.

As the war progressed, Great Britain continued to suffer losses both in the colonies and on the continent of Europe. In 1757, William Pitt was put in charge of the war effort. He used the strength of the British navy and was able to capture the key French Canadian cities of Quebec and Montreal. A year later, Washington again led troops to Fort Duquesne;

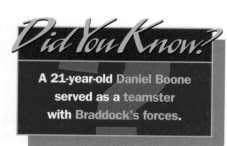

Did You Know?

A 21-year-old Daniel Boone served as a teamster with Braddock's forces.

this time he was victorious. The frontier was made safe and came under British control.

Georgia's Role in the War

Georgia did not take part in the war, but it was helped by the war. The Treaty of Paris of 1763, which formally ended the war, set Georgia's western boundary at the Mississippi River. A few months later, King George III issued the Proclamation of 1763. This proclamation moved the state's southern boundary to the St. Marys River. The Proclamation also forbade the colonists to settle west of the Appalachian Mountains. At the same time, the Cherokee and the Creek gave up all lands between the Ogeechee and Savannah rivers north to Augusta, which was Georgia's second oldest city. They also gave up the coastal land south of the Altamaha River.

Figure 13
Results of the French and Indian War

- The British gained control of Canada, which today continues to be a friend and trading partner of the United States.

- The western frontier—the Ohio River Valley and all lands east of the Mississippi River—was opened to Virginia and the other colonies.

- Great Britain obtained Florida from Spain, which had been an ally of the French during the war.

- For its help, France gave the Louisiana Territory to Spain.

- After 150 years of colonization, France lost all of its land in the area.

- Perhaps most importantly, the French and Indian War led to the American Revolution as Great Britain found itself left with a huge war debt.

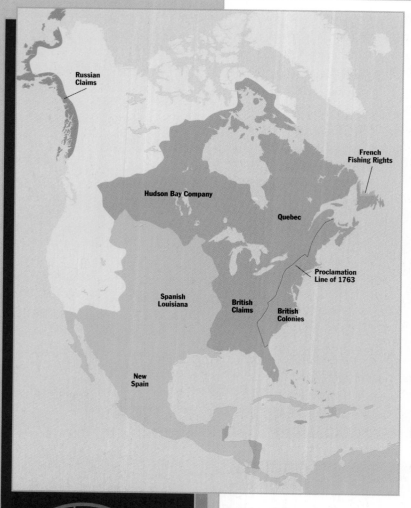

Russian Claims

French Fishing Rights

Hudson Bay Company

Quebec

Proclamation Line of 1763

Spanish Louisiana

British Claims

British Colonies

New Spain

Map 24 North America, 1763

Map Skill: What happened to France's territory in North America as a result of the war?

When the land came under Georgia's control, settlers began to migrate to the colony. The new boundaries were important to Georgia's growth. Not only did they provide water access for future shipping, but they also provided good farmland and dense forests with timber and naval stores resources.

Georgia's First Assembly

Georgia's new government met for the first time in 1755 in Savannah, the colony's capital and largest city. The delegates reorganized the state militia and passed bills so roads could be built and repaired. The colonial assembly also drew up codes that restricted the rights of slaves.

For a while, Governor Reynolds and the colonial assembly worked well together. However, during one legislative session, members of the Governor's Council could not agree on how much was needed to improve the military defenses of the colony. Governor Reynolds became so angry at their failure to agree that he stopped the meeting and sent the legislators home.

During the months that followed, Reynolds tried to govern Georgia by himself, leaving the colonists angry. There were arguments between those who thought he should leave and those who wanted him to remain. Many Georgians did not like having their right to self-government taken away and wrote to King George to complain. However, when Reynolds recommended moving Savannah to the Ogeechee River (close to today's Richmond Hill in Bryan County), we can guess that most of his limited support evaporated. Finally, after two years, the group who wanted self-government won. Georgia's first royal governor was replaced.

Governor Henry Ellis

In February 1757, the king chose Captain Henry Ellis as the next royal governor. Governor Ellis was a naturalist and a scientist who had led voyages to many different parts of the world. According to reports, he walked the streets of Savannah checking a thermometer that hung around his neck and making notes of its readings. Ellis believed that Savannah was one of the hottest places in the world, and he often carried an umbrella to protect himself from the sun.

Ellis learned quickly from Reynolds's mistakes. During his three years as governor, Ellis brought together people of many different political groups.

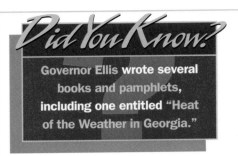
He sought the advice of the governor of the neighboring colony of South Carolina. He also depended on well-known and wealthy citizens to lead the colony.

While Ellis was governor, new colonists came to Georgia from South Carolina and the West Indies. Many of these new settlers brought slaves with them, and the governor granted the newcomers large amounts of land. By 1759, the population of the colony had grown to about 10,000, including 3,600 slaves.

Not all Georgians wanted slaves in the colony. The Highland Scots at Darien and the Salzburgers at New Ebenezer believed that hard work by the white settlers would result in the same economic growth as a system of slave labor.

Ellis was a popular governor, under whose direction the colony made economic gains. There were more and profitable farms. There were more merchants with a greater variety of items to sell. As a result, the colonists could buy the things they could not grow or manufacture, such as cloth, sugar, farming tools, and seeds for planting.

In 1759, Governor Ellis became ill, perhaps from heat-related problems, and asked to return to Great Britain. However, he was re-assigned to Nova Scotia as its royal governor in 1761.

A Savannah square was named for this "active, sensible, and honest man." Today there is discussion of whether to restore the square to its original appearance or to build a replica of the City Market, which once stood there.

Governor James Wright

After Henry Ellis left, the Honorable James Wright became governor. Wright was born in Charleston but educated in Great Britain. He had arrived in Georgia on October 11, 1760, to serve as lieutenant governor. Before coming to Georgia, he had been attorney general of South Carolina for twenty-one years. He was loyal to the king, but he also wanted the colonies to do well. He believed that Georgia would continue to grow if large farms were even bigger, if trading expanded, and if the western lands of the colony were opened to settlers. Wright agreed with the self-government program Governor Reynolds had started, and the colonists were pleased with him at first.

During his early years as governor, Wright completed the defenses around Savannah. Savannah was surrounded with **palisades**

Below: James Wright followed Henry Ellis as royal governor of Georgia. He served in that position until 1776.

Above: Indigo was one of Georgia's main crops before the American Revolution. The plant was used to create a blue dye.

(fences made of sharpened stakes), and the area forts were made stronger. The town of Sunbury grew and became the colony's official port of entry for ships arriving from other countries and colonies. Both houses of the colonial assembly worked together to promote Georgia's economic growth. Farmers were allowed to borrow more money, so they bought more land. The amount of owned land grew from 1 million acres to 7 million acres.

Rice and indigo became profitable crops. Enough silk was being produced so that, by 1767, almost a ton of it was exported to Great Britain each year. There were more schools, and more and more people were reading. Many books were sold, and, in 1763, the colony's first newspaper, *The Georgia Gazette*, was started. Many of the small frame houses were taken down. In their place, two-story houses were built of wood or tabby (a mixture of lime, crushed shells, sand, and water).

There was, however, another side to Georgia during these early years. Many mothers died in childbirth. School was mostly for children in the upper economic class. Also a group of what plantation owners called "undesirable people" moved from Virginia and the Carolinas to settle in the middle and western parts of the colony. These people became known as **crackers**. The term may have come from the cracking sounds of whips used on oxen or horses as these new settlers went to market to sell their goods. It may have come from the cracking of corn as they prepared corn meal. Some say the term came from a Scottish word that mean "boasters." No matter how it started, the term was meant as an insult for the lower classes. The crackers were thought of as people who did not obey the law and were not welcome in the colony.

During this time, other issues also grabbed Governor Wright's attention. There was no plan for defending the colony even after the forts had been strengthened. Also, a growing number of Georgians who were not wealthy began to ask for a greater voice in government. They were not alone. Shortly, their voices joined with others as the colonies began trying to gain **independence** (political or economic freedom) from Great Britain.

It's Your Turn

1. What were the results of the French and Indian War?
2. How did Georgia gain as a result of the French and Indian War?
3. When did Georgia's first legislature meet?
4. Who was Georgia's second governor? In your opinion, did he like his job? Defend your response.
5. What did Governor Wright succeed in doing that Governors Ellis and Reynolds had failed to accomplish?

The Call for Independence

Section Preview

As you read, look for:
- the reasons why the colonists became unhappy with Great Britain,
- how Georgians felt about the British taxes,
- the first Provincial Congress,
- vocabulary terms: Tories, Patriots, boycott, Proclamation of 1763, Sugar Act, Stamp Act, Liberty Boys, Townshend Acts, and Quartering Act.

Discontent in the Colonies

During the fifteen years before the American Revolution, many colonists began to tire of British rule and resent its policies. Although Great Britain had been victorious in the French and Indian War, the war had cost a great deal of money. Great Britain also had to pay soldiers to protect the colonies from any other aggressors. To the British, it seemed only logical to levy (impose) additional taxes on the colonies to cover these expenses.

When the American colonists complained about the unfairness of the new taxes, Great Britain passed some strict laws and started enforcing some old laws. The Navigation Acts, passed in the 1660s, said the colonies could only ship their goods on British vessels. This was not a problem for Georgia. Most of its trade was still with Great Britain, and British ships often sailed to and from Georgia. But those colonies that traded with several countries were no longer allowed to do so.

In 1764, Great Britain's increased tax on wine and imported goods received very little opposition in Georgia. Most of the money Georgia needed for its government was provided by Parliament, so the colony paid little tax to Great Britain. This was not true in the older colonies, and those colonies became very angry about the new tax. However, Georgia became more concerned when the Sugar Act was passed placing a tax on sugar and molasses imported from the West Indies. Georgia did a great deal of trading with sugar-producing countries such as Jamaica and Barbados.

In 1765, Parliament passed the Stamp Act in an attempt to raise money to pay for the French and Indian War. This act placed a tax on newspapers, legal documents, and licenses.

Figure 14 The Cast of Characters

As Georgia grew in population, the other colonies were growing in frustration. As you begin reading about the Revolutionary period, keep in mind the cast of characters. The 1.6 million people who lived in the colonies in the 1760s could be divided into many distinctive groups.

- The Tories (also called Loyalists, British Royalists, or "King's friends") were those who were loyal to the king of England, George III.

- The Patriots (also referred to as Whigs, Liberty Boys, Colonials, Sons and Daughters of Liberty) were those citizens ready to cut ties with Great Britain.

- Quakers, Mennonites, and Moravians (who left Georgia) were pacifists who did not believe in fighting and had religious objections to war.

- Redcoats and Lobsterbacks (so called because of their red uniforms) were British soldiers, some of whom were forced to fight against the Patriot colonists.

- The Council of Safety was set up by the Patriots in Georgia in 1775 when the Provincial Congress voted to join the other colonies in a boycott of trade with Great Britain. (A boycott is a protest in which people refuse to buy certain items until specific conditions are met.) The Council was to enforce the trade boycott. All of the colonies had similar groups.

- Finally, there were the fence sitters who, out of fear of choosing the losing side, would not commit to being Tory or Patriot or pacifist.

The Art of Politics

JOIN, or DIE.

This cartoon, created by Benjamin Franklin, is widely considered to be the first American political cartoon. It was published in Franklin's *Pennsylvania Gazette*.

Above: Noble Wimberly Jones was a member of the colonial assembly. In 1768 and 1769, he was elected as its speaker.

Throughout the colonies, the reaction to the Stamp Act was swift and sometimes violent.

A Stamp Act Congress met in Boston, Massachusetts, to speak against British taxes. The Georgia colonial assembly was not in session at the time, so it did not send a representative to the Stamp Act Congress. Nevertheless, on the day before it went into effect, a few Georgia citizens showed their dislike of the Stamp Act by burning an *effigy* (a likeness) of the stamp master in the streets of Savannah.

On November 6, a group of Georgians came together to oppose the Stamp Act. They called themselves the Liberty Boys. Older Georgians called them the "Liberty Brawlers" because they met in local taverns. Tondee's Tavern in Savannah was a favorite meeting spot. The Liberty Boys were part of a larger group, the Sons of Liberty, whose daring acts came to represent the spirit of the Revolution.

Although the taxes did not bother the average Georgian very much, the colony felt their effect. Georgia was the only colony that ever sold the stamps. Only a few were sold, but Georgia's neighbors in South Carolina, who were more directly affected, spoke out with anger against it. Also, Georgia's only newspaper, *The Georgia Gazette*, had to stop printing until the Stamp Act was repealed a year later.

Georgians Begin to React

During the next four years, many Georgians talked openly about their dislike of the strict new British laws. Between 1768 and 1772, members of the Georgia colonial assembly spoke against the Townshend Acts of 1767, which placed import taxes on tea, paper, glass, and coloring for paints. Later, without the approval of the governor, the assembly elected Noble Wimberly Jones as its speaker. Jones, a Patriot, was a second-generation colonist from Savannah. Unlike his father who was a Tory (as were many first-generation colonists), Jones was an outspoken leader of the discontented Georgians.

Governor Wright became upset with the growing discontent and particularly with the idea of having

Did You Know?

In some Savannah hotels, guests walked from their rooms through the windows and out onto the verandah. Since doors in hotels were taxed, hotels built more windows than doors and allowed guests to use the windows as passageways.

as the speaker of the assembly someone whose ideas were not the same as those of the king. Wright tried to end the protests by doing away with the assembly. However, the people were not so easily silenced.

Protests Increase

Protests against British taxes soon were more open in the other twelve colonies. The slogan "No taxation without representation" became a pre-Revolution war cry. Because the Townshend Acts had placed a tax on coloring for paints, the people stopped painting their homes. Because of the tax on tea, they quit drinking tea and turned to coffee. By 1770, the British Parliament had repealed the Townshend Acts, except for the tax on tea.

On a cold day in March 1770, some people in Boston threw snowballs at British soldiers and called them names. The soldiers fired into the crowd, killing five civilians, including a freed slave named Crispus Attucks. Unfortunately for the British, engraver Paul Revere made a copper etching of the event, which was reproduced again and again. As you can see, it shows a very different picture than what actually happened. But it was this view of a line of British soldiers calmly firing into the midst of innocent Boston citizens that helped ignite the cry for war.

In 1773, the East India Company had large amounts of tea it could not sell and was on the verge of bankruptcy. Parliament passed the Tea Act of 1773, which allowed the company to ship tea directly to the colonies. It could then sell the tea for less than colonial merchants could. The colonists looked on the law as a trick to get them to buy the tea and pay a lower tax. In December of that year, to protest the law, a group of Patriots (including Samuel Adams and Paul Revere) dressed as Mohawk Indians, boarded three British ships anchored in Boston harbor, and dumped 342 chests of tea into Boston bay. This action is remembered as "the Boston Tea Party."

The Intolerable Acts

To punish the colonists of Massachusetts for the actions of the Patriots, Parliament enacted four laws, which because of their harshness became known as the *Intolerable Acts*. Under one of the laws, the British closed the port of Boston until the citizens of Massachusetts paid for the tea. Under

Top: This is the etching of the Boston Massacre created by Paul Revere. Prints of the etching were distributed all over Boston. **Above:** Patriots at the Boston Tea Party took matters into their own hands when protesting the Tea Act.

another, Massachusetts colonists could not have a town meeting without the agreement of their governor, who was also the commander of the British troops. The operation of the court system was changed so that any British officials who committed capital crimes would be tried in Great Britain rather than by a colonial court. As a final punishment, Parliament passed the **Quartering Act**. Under this act, the citizens of all colonies had to house and feed British soldiers at their own expense.

Although the laws were aimed at Massachusetts, representatives of all the colonies except Georgia gathered in Philadelphia to protest them. On September 5, 1774, the delegates organized a *Continental Congress*. At this Congress, there were two major groups. One group wanted to pull away from Great Britain and seek independence. The other wanted to make changes but still remain under British rule. The colonists may not have been sure which group was right, but they agreed on one thing. Something had to be done, and it had to be done soon!

The Continental Congress agreed to stop all trade with Great Britain and urged each colony to set up *committees of safety*. These committees would enforce the boycott. Because its actions would have been called treason by the Crown, the Congress carried on its work in secret.

A Colony Divided

Anti-British sentiment was growing in Georgia, but the people still seemed to care more about which parish would have the most power in the Georgia assembly. Because the colony still depended on Great Britain, the assembly chose not to send a delegate to the Continental Congress. However, in August 1774, a group of Georgians met to discuss their reaction to the Intolerable Acts. After talking for a long time, they decided to send a resolution to Parliament demanding that citizens of the thirteen colonies have the same rights as British citizens living in Great Britain. They insisted that the Intolerable Acts did not agree with the "Rights and Privileges of an Englishman."

The assembly also decided to have a meeting in Georgia to talk about the growing unhappiness over their ties with Great Britain. This meeting, called the *Provincial Congress*, was held in Savannah in January 1775. Less than one-half of Georgia's parishes were represented, and the meeting ended without much being done.

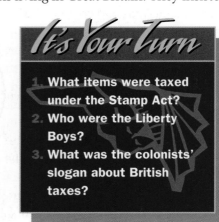

It's Your Turn

1. What items were taxed under the Stamp Act?
2. Who were the Liberty Boys?
3. What was the colonists' slogan about British taxes?

The Revolutionary War Period

Section Preview

As you read, look for:
• the steps taken by Georgia and Georgians before the American Revolution,
• the Declaration of Independence,
• the new government established by Georgia,
• Georgia's role in the American Revolution, and
• **vocabulary terms:** Second Continental Congress, Declaration of Independence, ratify, Articles of Confederation, siege, and Treaty of Paris (1783).

It took a long time for news to get around the colonies, so it was May before word reached Georgia of the battles of Lexington and Concord in Massachusetts on April 19, 1775. Poet Ralph Waldo Emerson described those battles as "Here once the embattled farmers stood/And fired the shot heard round the world." The battles marked the beginning of the Revolutionary War and forced Georgians to take a stand. In just a few days, a group of radicals broke into the royal arms storehouse in Savannah and stole 600 pounds of gunpowder.

Other protests followed quickly. Gunpowder used to fire cannon salutes on the king's birthday was tampered with and would not explode. A liberty pole was put up outside Tondee's Tavern. Tories were openly harassed. Guns were stolen from public warehouses, and no one paid any attention to what the governor said.

In September 1775, Georgia's Joseph Habersham and Captain Oliver Bowen captured a British schooner carrying gunpowder. Georgia kept 9,000 pounds and sent 5,000 pounds to the newly formed Continental Army.

Preparing for War

Three weeks after the battles at Lexington and Concord, the Second Continental Congress opened in Philadelphia. One of the early decisions made by the Congress was to send a petition to King George III, asking him to not take further unfriendly steps against the colonies. The king refused the petition. At the same time, the Congress also called for the creation of a Continental Army, which was to be led by George Washington of Virginia.

Georgia was absent for the first few days, but on May 13, 1775, Lyman Hall of Midway arrived in an unofficial capacity. The other colonies were furious with Georgia because it did not seem very supportive. Some members of the Congress even called for punishing the youngest colony.

Very shortly, however, Georgia was ready to act. In July 1775, a second Provincial Congress was held at Tondee's Tavern in Savannah. Unlike the

Figure 15 The Tories

About one-third of the colonists remained loyal to Great Britain, and many of those lived in Georgia. Their reasons for staying loyal to Great Britain were as varied as the people themselves.

● Some believed that since the British king was still paying money to support the colonies, he had the right to rule them.

● Some believed that the British had founded the colonies and had the right to govern them.

● Many colonists still had family or relatives in Great Britain, and they did not want to put them in danger or to cause them to lose the "perks" of royal approval. Some colonists even split their families by sending some members of the family back to Great Britain.

● Some colonists feared that life under the control of rich Patriots would be even harder than life under the control of the British.

● Finally, some colonists were simply afraid of the well-organized, well-equipped British soldiers.

Top: One of the first battles of the Revolutionary War was fought at Concord, Massachusetts in April 1775. Above: Lyman Hall was declared an "enemy of the crown" after signing the Declaration of Independence.

First Provincial Congress, this group was prepared to take positive steps. In addition to Lyman Hall, four others, all from Savannah, were chosen to go Philadelphia. In the group were Archibald Bulloch, John Houstoun, Noble Wimberly Jones, and Reverend John Zubly. The delegates were given no specific instructions to relay to the Continental Congress. Instead, they were asked to vote as they thought best for the common good of all Georgians. Finally, Georgia was ready to join ranks with the other colonies.

Earlier, shortly after the first shots had been fired at the battles of Lexington and Concord, a Council of Safety had met and prepared to form a new government. To show they meant what they said, the group officially withdrew from Great Britain. In so doing, the Patriots left Governor Wright without power. Wright was arrested in mid-January of 1776 by the Liberty Boys when he asked the Council of Safety to allow British vessels to purchase supplies from the colony. A month later, Wright escaped and fled to a waiting British warship, leaving the Council of Safety to govern the colony. In the following April, the Georgia Provincial Congress issued a series of guidelines, called "Rules and Regulations," which were to be used in governing Georgia until a more permanent document could be drawn up.

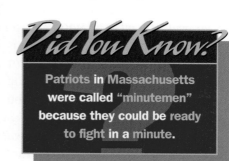

Did You Know?

Patriots in Massachusetts were called "minutemen" because they could be ready to fight in a minute.

The Declaration of Independence

In January 1776, Thomas Paine's pamphlet *Common Sense* appeared. In it, Paine urged the colonists to separate from Great Britain in language all people could understand. The pamphlet was a sensation and sold 120,000 copies in less than three months. By the end of the year, it had sold 500,000 copies. Paine quickly followed *Common Sense* with a series of pamphlets. In *The Crisis*, Paine wrote, "These are the times that try men's souls. The summer soldier and the sunshine patriot will, in this crisis, shrink from the service of their country; but he that stands it now, deserves the love and thanks of man and woman." Paine had a great deal of influence on the actions of the Second Continental Congress. John Adams said, "Without the pen of Paine, the sword of Washington would have been wielded in vain."

On July 4, 1776, over a year after the battles of Lexington and Concord, the Second Continental Congress approved the Declaration of Independence. When it was officially signed on August 2, 1776, the names of three Georgians—Lyman Hall, George Walton, and Button Gwinnett—appeared on the left side of the document, right below the signature of John Hancock. But it was over a month before Georgians found out how their representatives had voted or even what the Declaration said.

The 1,458-word document, written primarily by Thomas Jefferson, can be divided into three parts. The *Preamble*, or introduction, stated how the colonists felt about democracy. The second part, or body, listed twenty-seven grievances (complaints) against King George III and his government that led the colonists to seek independence from Great Britain. The third part, the conclusion, declared the colonies to be an independent nation for all future times.

The Declaration meant that the colonies we were one nation, still not in total agreement, but one nation nevertheless. When the Declaration of Independence was read in Georgia, it produced great excitement, although some colonists decided to return to Great Britain. Finally, Georgians began to prepare for war. They sent food and ammunition to the Continental Army and began to strengthen the home militia.

Political Changes in Georgia

Georgia joined the other colonies in celebrating the decision to become independent of Great Britain. The former colonies were tired of being governed and living under laws made by Great Britain, which they believed was both out of touch and too far away to understand their needs. The new goal

Top: George Walton, signer of the Declaration of Independence. Above: John Treutlen, Georgia's first governor.

History by the Numbers

The Dunlap Broadside

On the night of July 4, 1776, John Dunlap printed an unknown number of copies of the Declaration of Independence. Each document, called a *broadside*, was about 14 inches by 18 inches. Only 25 of those copies are known to exist.

On July 19, 1776, the Continental Congress ordered another printer, Timothy Matlack, to *engross* (print in final, legal form) the Declaration of Independence. Members of Congress who were present in Philadelphia signed the engrossed copy on August 2, 1776. Other members of Congress signed later. The signed, engrossed copy of the Declaration of Independence, which is 24½ inches by 29½ inches, is on permanent exhibit at the National Archives in Washington, D.C.

In 1989, a man bought a painting at a flea market for $4. Hidden in the painting's frame was an original Dunlap broadside of the Declaration of Independence. It was the 25th known copy of the document. It recently sold for $8.14 million, the highest price ever paid for an object sold at an Internet auction.

for each colony was statehood. Each new state was to develop its own method of governance and pass laws that met its needs.

Work was begun on a state constitution to replace the earlier "Rules and Regulations." Writing the new constitution was not easy. Some citizens wanted a government like the one already in place, with most of the power in the hands of a few wealthy landowners and merchants. The Whigs, a more extreme group, wanted to give all the people of Georgia a chance to govern themselves. The Whigs won, and Georgia decided on a government that would be based on the separation of powers and the rights of citizens to agree with how they were governed.

By May 1777, Georgia adopted its first state constitution at a constitutional convention held in Savannah. The parish system was done away with, and eight counties were formed. Burke, Camden, Chatham, Effingham, Glynn, Richmond, and Wilkes were named for British subjects who had been in favor of the Revolution; Liberty County was named in honor of American independence. **Liberty** is the character word for this chapter. What were the liberties that the young colonies wanted to secure for themselves?

However well meaning the lawmakers were in developing the 1777 constitution, there were problems. Rather than a bicameral legislature, the constitution of 1777 provided for a *unicameral*, or one-house, legislature. This single legislative body had very broad powers, including the ability to make appointments for the judicial branch (the courts) and the executive branch (the governor).

Stung by the loyalty of former governors to the king, the members of the constitutional convention wanted to limit severely the influence and power of the governor. They proposed a one-year term for the governor. The governor was to be selected by the legislature rather than voted on by the people. The actual power, therefore, was in the hands of twelve lawmakers from the legislature who served as an executive council. The executive council could accept or reject any proposals initiated by the governor. The constitutional convention selected John Treutlen, a Salzburger, as the first state governor over Button Gwinnett. It also adopted a new state seal.

Although the constitution of 1777 was changed in 1789, this first endeavor in providing for state's rights was an important step in Georgia's development.

On July 4, 1778, Georgians ratified (approved) the Articles of Confederation, which was the first constitution of the United States of America. The Articles did not go into effect until January 1781, when Virginia and Maryland ratified it.

The Revolutionary War in Georgia

During 1777 and 1778, Georgian members of the Continental Army made several unsuccessful attempts to capture British-held St. Augustine and parts of east Florida. Little other fighting took place in Georgia. In December 1778, however, British troops attacked and took control of Savannah. Soon there were reports of looting, burnings, and even murders at the hands of British troops as they tried to force Tories to put down their arms or flee the area. A month later, the British took the port of Sunbury. Before long, Augusta was under fire from British guns.

In all three cases, the poorly armed and understaffed Georgia militia could do little to stop the British. Georgia was once again under British military rule, and Governor Wright returned to Georgia to take charge of the government.

The Battle of Kettle Creek

Morale throughout the colonies was at an all-time low. Finally, in February 1779, Georgia had a victory. A rebel militia group led by Colonel Elijah Clarke (after whom Clarke County is named) defeated a force of more than 800 British troops at the Battle of Kettle Creek, about eight miles from Washington, Georgia.

The Battle of Kettle Creek was minor when compared to those fought in other parts of the country. It was, however, important to Georgia. The militia was able to take badly needed

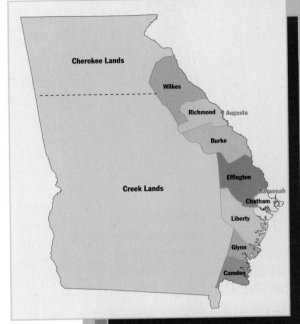

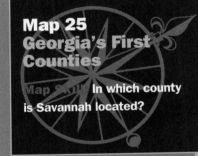

**Map 25
Georgia's First Counties**

Map Skill: In which county is Savannah located?

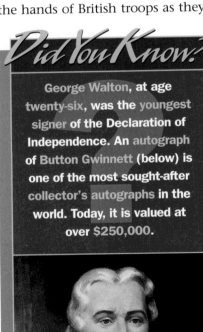

Did You Know?

George Walton, at age twenty-six, was the youngest signer of the Declaration of Independence. An autograph of Button Gwinnett (below) is one of the most sought-after collector's autographs in the world. Today, it is valued at over $250,000.

weapons and horses from the British soldiers, and the spirits of the Georgia militia were lifted by their victory.

The Siege of Savannah

In early September 1779, twenty-two French ships and 4,000 soldiers under the command of Charles Henri Comte d'Estaing arrived off Tybee Island. Those troops joined about 15,000 Americans under the command of General Benjamin Lincoln. The combined armies laid siege to Savannah. A **siege** occurs when forces try to capture a fortified fort or town by surrounding it and preventing any supplies from reaching it.

Finally, at daybreak on October 9, the American and French troops attacked British positions. The attack, which lasted only 45 minutes, failed. By the time it was over, more than 1,000 men with the American forces (821 of whom were French) and 40 British lay dead. Over 600 men were wounded. One of America's best foreign patriots, Polish Count Casimir Pulaski, had given his life for a country not his own. And, Savannah was set to remain in British hands for the next 3½ years.

Below: This French map, drawn in 1779, illustrates the French plans for the siege of Savannah. This battle marked the first time that American and French troops fought together. One of the heroes of the siege was Sergeant William Jasper.

PLAN DU SIEGE DE SAVANNAH
fait par les Troupes du Roy aux Ordres de Mr. le Cte. D'Estaing vice-Amiral de France en 7bre et 8bre 1779.

Nancy Hart

The Revolutionary War produced a number of heroes and heroines. One of those was a woman who was Georgia's most famous war heroine.

Around 1771, Benjamin and Nancy Hart and their eight children settled twelve miles outside of what we now call Elberton. Several legends surround Nancy Hart. Probably the most repeated one concerns Colonel John Dooley, a neighbor of the Harts who was killed by Tories. A few days after Dooley's murder, five of those Tories stopped by Nancy's home and demanded that she cook dinner for them. As the men talked, Nancy overheard them bragging about the murder.

Thinking quickly, Nancy brought out a jug of whiskey and offered it to the men. As they drank, they did not notice Nancy motioning to her daughters to go to the woods and sound the alarm for help. Enjoying their drink and food, they also did not realize that Nancy was quietly taking their rifles as she served them.

When Nancy pulled the third rifle away, one of the men finally noticed. As the men rushed her, Nancy calmly pulled the trigger and killed one of them. She grabbed a second rifle and held the other soldiers at gunpoint until help arrived. Some reports say she may have killed two of the soldiers; in any event, the rest were soon put on trial and hanged.

We may never know if the stories of Nancy Hart's courage are true. However, the legend of Nancy Hart remains as an example of the revolutionary spirit of Georgia. Hart County and its county seat, Hartwell, located in northeast Georgia, are named for her. Hart is the only county in Georgia named for a woman.

Financing the American Revolution

How did the newly formed United States of America manage to find the funds to pay for its war against Great Britain?

In 1775, as the Continental Congress began making plans for war, it decided to print and issue paper money called "Continentals" to pay for war materials, supplies, and soldiers' salaries. But by 1778, the nation faced serious economic problems. The Continentals were worthless because there was nothing (gold or silver) to back them up. To complicate the economic situation, each state began to print its own paper money. By 1780, the new nation had printed over $241 million Continentals, and the individual states had issued almost $210 million of their own paper notes. Congress realized that the Continentals were of little value and tried to take them out of circulation. It also began to collect taxes to help pay off some of its loans.

Loans and gifts from foreign countries helped the United States obtain the weapons, ammunition, and supplies it needed. Most of the loans were arranged by Robert Morris, a delegate to the Continental Congress who became special commissioner of finance in 1776. In 1781, Morris developed a plan for a national bank, the Bank of North America, to stabilize the economy and establish the credit of the new nation with the nations of Europe.

But Robert Morris was not alone in finding funds for the new nation. He was greatly helped by Haym Salomon. Salomon was a wealthy, successful businessman described as a "Broker to the Office of Finance," which meant that

Above: Pennsylvanian Robert Morris

he helped the new government obtain loans from European nations, banks, and merchants. Because he was a trusted businessman, European bankers would loan money to Salomon when they had refused to loan it to Congress. Both Morris and Salomon gave their own personal fortunes to support the Revolution.

Under the new Bank of North America, there was some relationship between the country's supply of gold and silver and its paper notes. As head of the Bank of North America, Morris issued treasury notes, called "Morris notes," that could be redeemed for hard currency. Congress also began to issue a new type of paper note that paid interest and that could be turned in for hard currency after a five-year period. The new government used the paper notes, the interest notes, and the treasury notes to pay for its revolution.

After the war, Alexander Hamilton became the financial planner for the new government. The new nation had accumulated almost $78 million in debts from the war, and it needed about $4 million to operate its new government. However, the country's income was very limited. The United States earned about $4.4 million in tariffs (taxes) on goods and about $19,000 from other sources for a total federal income of $4,418,000. The young nation began its life under a system of deficit spending, owing and spending more than was available. It is a system we understand well today. In 2001, for example, the federal government cost $1.8 trillion to operate.

Georgia was left in the hands of two governments, one royal and one rebel. Each government tried to take charge of the state, but neither was very effective. Some Georgians openly supported the king, while others just as openly supported the cause of independence. The major battles of the war were over, but guerrilla warfare—both political and military—continued in the backcountry of Georgia.

The Battle of Yorktown

In June 1781, Georgia's militia was again under the command of Colonel Clarke. With the help of Continental troops, Clarke took Augusta from the British. General George Washington, the commander of the Continental Army, was helped by French forces when he faced British General Lord Cornwallis in October 1781, at the Battle of Yorktown, Virginia. The American forces won that battle, forcing Cornwallis to surrender.

Cornwallis did not know that British ships carrying 6,000 men were on their way to help him. They arrived just six days after his surrender. Had the French not delayed the landing of the British ships, the results of the American Revolution might have been very different. By the spring of 1782, British forces in Georgia believed they could not defeat the Americans. They left Savannah, ending 3½ years of occupation.

The Treaty of Paris was signed by Great Britain, France, and the United States in September 1783. Independence was finally a reality. There were only eleven battles and skirmishes on Georgia's soil. However, Georgians could

Below: In October 1781, combined American and French forces trapped the British army at Yorktown, Virginia. British General Cornwallis surrendered on October 18, 1781.

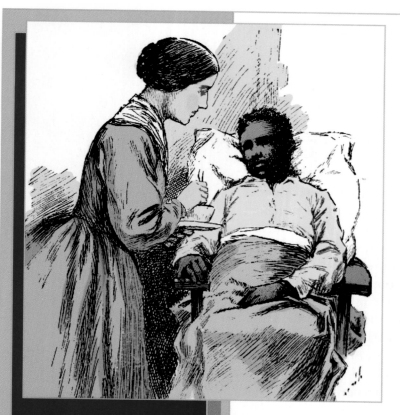

Above: During the heroic fighting at the Battle of Kettle Creek, Austin Dabney was hit by a rifle ball that passed through his thigh. Dabney is credited with saving the life of Elijah Clarke by giving the colonel a horse after his had been shot out from under him.

be proud of their part in the Revolutionary War as the work of building a new country began.

Blacks in the American Revolution

One of the men who followed Colonel Clarke at Kettle Creek was a Revolutionary War hero named Austin Dabney. Dabney was a freeborn *mulatto*, a child of mixed parentage. He arrived in Georgia just before the war with a man named Richard Aycock. Aycock, a white North Carolinian, was not known for his bravery. Instead of joining the Georgia militia himself, Aycock proposed that Austin Dabney take his place. After much discussion, some of which centered on whether he was freeborn or a slave, Dabney was accepted. He proved to be a good soldier at Kettle Creek and was wounded in action. A family named Harris cared for him while his wounds healed.

After the Revolutionary War, veterans were given plots of land as part payment for their military service. Many did not want Dabney to get his veteran's share of land. However, Governor George Gilmer and some members of the Georgia legislature praised Dabney as a patriot. After months of debate, Dabney received a valuable piece of land in Madison County. When he moved to his new home, he took the Harris family with him. Together, they made the property profitable. Austin Dabney died in 1834, fifty-five years after the Battle of Kettle Creek.

Dabney was just one of the many people of color who fought in the Revolutionary War. As early as the battles of Lexington and Concord, blacks took up arms against Great Britain in search of freedom. Thousands of slaves crossed over to British lines working as soldiers, boat pilots, cooks, musicians, and in many other jobs. The British both actively recruited blacks to serve as soldiers and captured slaves for use by the British Army. In November 1775, the British governor of Virginia offered freedom to all slaves willing to bear arms against the rebelling colonists. His proclamation led American leaders to accept blacks into the Continental Army, promising that they would receive freedom at the end of their enlistment. The government also made provisions to pay slave owners for all slaves freed in such a way. While there are

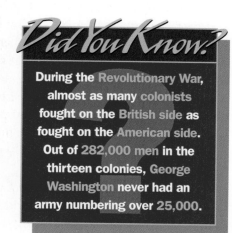

Did You Know?

During the Revolutionary War, almost as many colonists fought on the British side as fought on the American side. Out of 282,000 men in the thirteen colonies, George Washington never had an army numbering over 25,000.

no exact figures on the participation of blacks in the Continental Army, it has been estimated that about 5,000 served.

Although many blacks distinguished themselves in the Revolutionary War, support for their enlistment in the army varied. Southern states did not want to use slaves or freedmen as soldiers because the idea of recruiting and arming slaves raised fears of slave revolts.

General George Washington, himself a fourth-generation slave owner, questioned the wisdom of using black troops, but most of the former colonies began to enlist both slaves and free blacks in the armies. Georgia and South Carolina were the only two states to refuse to legalize slave enlistments in their militias.

Antislavery sentiment mounted after the war; in most states, public opinion turned strongly against slavery. In many states, blacks were given both their freedom and land at the end of the war. In the South, however, the decline of such staple crops as tobacco, indigo, and rice made the farmers reluctant to free their black slaves.

Looking Back at the Revolutionary War

When fighting broke out at Lexington and Concord, the British had a number of advantages in the coming military conflict. They had a strong central government, while the thirteen colonies were separate governments with no real central power. The British had a well-equipped, professional army; the colonies had eager citizen-volunteers with little training, discipline, and equipment and with limited experience. Fortunately, many experienced European soldiers seeking adventure came to join America's cause. The British had the world's most powerful navy; the colonies had only merchant ships. The Americans did commission four battle ships in 1775 and authorized private ships to attack the British Navy and keep any profits they made. The British were well financed by their government; the colonies had no major sources of revenue for their new government. Perhaps the most important British advantage was the divided loyalties of the colonists. Almost one-third of the colonists were neutral, and a large number, almost 20 percent of the population, remained loyal to Great Britain.

Despite the British military might, the colonists had four advantages that could not be overcome. First, they were fighting on their

Below: In 1775, General George Washington, leader of the Continental Army, recommended that blacks not be permitted to serve in the Continental Army.

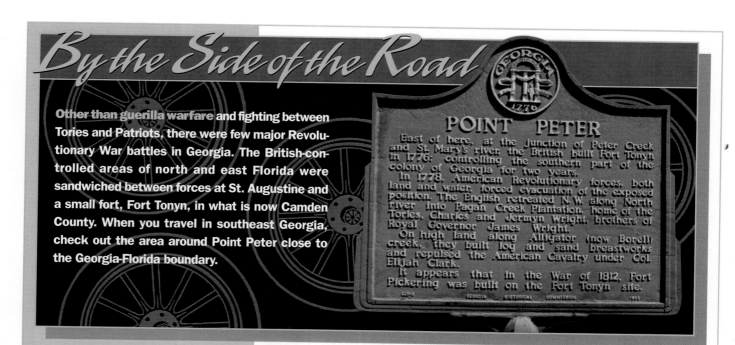

Other than guerilla warfare and fighting between Tories and Patriots, there were few major Revolutionary War battles in Georgia. The British-controlled areas of north and east Florida were sandwiched between forces at St. Augustine and a small fort, Fort Tonyn, in what is now Camden County. When you travel in southeast Georgia, check out the area around Point Peter close to the Georgia-Florida boundary.

POINT PETER

East of here, at the junction of Peter Creek and St. Mary's river, the British built Fort Tonyn in 1776; controlling the southern part of the colony of Georgia for two years.

In 1778, American Revolutionary forces, both land and water, forced evacuation of the exposed position. The English retreated N.W. along North river into Pagan Creek Plantation, home of the Tories, Charles and Jermyn Wright, brothers of Royal Governor James Wright.

On high land along Alligator (now Borell) creek, they built log and sand breastworks and repulsed the American Cavalry under Col. Elijah Clark.

It appears that in the War of 1812, Fort Pickering was built on the Fort Tonyn site.

Above: King Carlos III of Spain supported the colonies in their war for independence. He secretly shipped arms, munitions, cattle, uniforms, medicine, blankets, and money to the American colonies.

home soil. They were fighting not only for their belief in freedom but also for their own homes and farms and villages. Second, the British were fighting very far from home and had to deal with long and dangerous supply lines. Third, the colonies had no central area that could be captured to declare victory. Fighting was spread out among all thirteen colonies, along the Gulf of Mexico, the western frontier, and even north of the Great Lakes in Canada. Fourth, the battles were fought over the rugged terrain of forests and swamps familiar to the colonists and not the open, flat battlefields that the British were accustomed to using.

While everything seemed to favor the British over the colonists, the Americans won their Revolutionary War to become a new and independent nation.

With Thanks to Spain

Spain is an often forgotten ally in the American Revolution. Spain and France had been at war with Great Britain for almost one hundred years before the American Revolution. Spain was angry and embarrassed when it lost Florida and other territories at the end of the French and Indian War. It wanted revenge. Also, King Carlos III of Spain had become impressed with the colonials. Although he did not totally approve of the "idea of colonials seeking independence" since he himself had a number of colonies, he did want to help.

For over five years, Spain sent a great deal of money and supplies to support the colonists. The funds came from people living in what is now Texas, New Mexico, California, and Mexico. Men from Spanish possessions in the region fought with the colonists. Spain also provided invaluable information from a very effective spy network. Although Spain was not in a position to open defy Great Britain, it did a great deal behind the scenes.

Pedro Pablo of Bolea was the Spanish ambassador in France and met with Benjamin Franklin and others traveling to Europe to help break the British naval blockade. Bernardo de Galvez, the Spanish governor of Louisiana, provided military assistance against Great Britain in Florida, Louisiana, along the Gulf of Mexico, and in the Mississippi River Valley. He also helped the colonists move men, arms, and supplies through the Gulf of Mexico and on the Mississippi River while resisting British attempts to blockade the river.

A Final Note

The men who signed the Declaration of Independence showed extreme courage and took great risks. Had the colonists lost the war, each man who signed the document could have been shot for treason. Would you have been willing to risk your life and all that you owned for your belief in freedom?

Chapter Summary

- In the years before the Revolutionary War, everyday life in the thirteen colonies remained difficult.
- Georgia became a royal colony in 1752 and as such was governed directly by the British king.
- Georgia continued to prosper, and many people who had left the colony when it was under the rule of the trustees returned to the royal colony.
- A new group of settlers from South Carolina and the West Indies bought land and moved to Midway, bringing slaves with them.
- Governor John Reynolds was the first royal governor. He was followed as governor by Henry Ellis and James Wright.
- Georgia gained land at the end of the French and Indian War. Its southern boundary was set at the St. Marys River, and the Indians gave up lands north and east of the Ogeechee and Savannah rivers northward to Augusta and south of the Altamaha River.
- A series of laws imposed by the British on the colonies increased resentment against British rule.
- In 1775, the first shots of the Revolutionary War were fired during the Battles of Lexington and Concord.
- In July 1776, Georgia joined the other twelve colonies in declaring independence from Great Britain.
- Georgia was occupied by British forces for most of the war.
- Several battles were fought on Georgia soil, including the Battle of Kettle Creek.
- The final battle of the Revolutionary War took place at Yorktown, Virginia.
- The official end of the war came with the signing of the Treaty of Paris of 1783.
- People of color, including Austin Dabney, fought in the Continental Army.

It's Your Turn

1. Name the Georgia signers of the Declaration of Independence.
2. What was the purpose of the second part of the Declaration of Independence?
3. For whom were the original parishes of Georgia renamed as counties?
4. What was our country's first constitution called?

Above: Bernardo de Galvez, the Spanish governor of Louisiana, helped the American cause through diplomatic, financial and military exploits against Great Britain in the Mississippi River Valley, the Gulf Coast, Louisiana, and in the Gulf of Mexico.

ChapterReview

Reviewing People, Places, and Terms

Explain why each of the following people appears in a chapter on the Revolutionary War.

1. Elijah Clarke

2. Henry Ellis

3. Button Gwinnett

4. James Wright

5. Lyman Hall

6. John Treutlen

Understanding the Facts

1. Why did the South, unlike the other regions, have so many large plantations?

2. What was the difference between a royal colony and a proprietary colony?

3. What were the two chambers of Georgia's first legislature?

4. What areas of North America did Great Britain gain as a result of the French and Indian War?

5. In what city did Georgia's first legislature meet?

6. What was Georgia's first newspaper?

7. Name the six groups that existed in the colonies in the pre-Revolutionary War period.

8. What two things did the First Continental Congress agree to do?

9. What were the "Rules and Regulations" set forth by the Georgia Provincial Congress?

10. What advantages did the British have in the Revolutionary War and what advantages did the colonists enjoy?

Developing Critical Thinking

1. If you had lived in Georgia in 1772, would you have been a Patriot or a Tory? Why?

2. What does the slogan "No taxation without representation" mean? Can you think of some instances in the 1900s where this may have also been used?

3. Why do you think so few battles were fought on Georgia soil?

4. Suppose the British ships had broken through the French lines before Cornwallis surrendered at Yorktown. What might have happened and how would it have affected you today?

Checking It Out

1. Use your research skills to find out the role played by the French in America's war for independence. While gathering information, examine the role played by George Washington's good friend, the Marquis de Lafayette.

2. Use your research ability and find out why Georgia granted several hundred acres of land to Mordecai Sheftall for his sacrifices on behalf of independence. Sheftall, whose father was one of the original settlers of the Georgia colony, was a leader of Georgia's Jewish community.

Writing Across the Curriculum

1. Persuasive writing is meant to convince readers to think or act in a certain way. Try your hand at persuasive writing. Write a pamphlet for your community calling for support of any school program or activity that you think should be expanded or for any new program that should be developed.

2. Imagine that you are a newspaper writer in colonial and Revolutionary times. Write two newspaper articles. Write one for a colonial audience in Georgia describing the signing of the Declaration of Independence; write the other for a London newspaper describing the same event from a different perspective.

3. A *precis* is a concise summary of essential points. Read the Declaration of Independence and write a precis of the document using language more understandable to today's teenagers. Use standard English and punctuation and avoid slang.

Exploring Technology

1. All of the young nation's soldiers were not men, and a list of Revolutionary heroines does not stop at Nancy Hart. Use your favorite search engine to find out about Deborah Sampson, the woman who disguised herself as a man and served under General Washington for three years. Share your findings with your classmates.

2. Many of the heroes of America's revolution were about your age. One young man of 14 joined the privateer *Royal Louis* to fight the British. Use your favorite search engine to find out about the successes and bravery of this young lad, James Forten, a free black who became one of Philadelphia's most successful and influential citizens after the war.

3. Use your favorite search engine to solve this "history mystery." Who actually designed the American flag that is so associated with the name Betsy Ross? Share your findings with your classmates.

4. Research the Mennonites and Quakers. See if you can determine why they refused to fight. Do you agree or disagree with their beliefs? Explain.

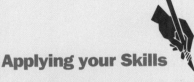

Applying your Skills

1. Which members of Georgia's delegation to the Second Continental Congress have counties named after them? Using a blank map on which the counties of Georgia are outlined, shade each of these counties. Then label the county seats. Which Georgia counties are named after Georgia's early governors? Label them on your map.

2. All five of Georgia's delegates to the Second Continental Congress either lived or worked in Savannah. On a modern-day map of the eastern United States, trace a land route from Savannah to Philadelphia and determine the number of miles. Also research the land routes that were available to the delegates at the time the Congress met.

Photo Question

Name this river which became the southern border of Georgia after the French and Indian War.

Testing a Nation

The fighting was over, and the United States was a free country. However, the new constitution—the Articles of Confederation—was not strong enough to hold the new states together. A new document and a greater commitment were needed for the new nation to survive. The path to the U.S. Constitution was not easy, but it resulted in a document that has served us well for over two hundred years.

While the United States was one nation, society, politics, economics, and culture were different in each major section of the country. The differences, perhaps, were sharpest between the northern and the southern states. From the early 1800s until the middle 1800s, people talked about these differences at socials and church meetings. Newspaper men wrote about them, and politicians made them the subject of speeches. The differences eventually led to conflict. That conflict led to secession, war, and Reconstruction, and marks one of the most difficult periods in Georgia's history.

Left: The home of secessionist and Confederate Secretary of State Robert Toombs in Washington, Ga. **Above:** Re-enactors of Battle of Chickamauga.

An Age of Expansion

Below: In 1825, the Cherokee Nation chose New Echota, near present-day Calhoun, to be its permanent capital. In 1830, the town had fifty residents, a main street sixty feet wide, and a two-acre town square. Prominent buildings included the Supreme Courthouse (right) and the office of the *Cherokee Phoenix* (below).

The Treaty of Paris of 1783 brought an end to the young nation's struggle for independence from Great Britain. In later years, the country adopted a new constitution, established the process for amending that constitution, and laid the foundation for a workable government. Georgia too rewrote its constitution.

The state worked to recover from the chaos of the war. Developments in farming and transportation improved the state's economy.

Georgia and the nation pushed their boundaries further west. In their desire for more land, the settlers pushed the Native Americans off their land and led eventually to the Trail of Tears.

Signs of the Times 1783-1838

Population: 516,823 in 1830, which was 4 percent of the U.S. population

Life Expectancy: 36 to 39 years

Wages: A young factory worker made about $3.50 a week. A child working in the New England textile mills made $.07 per day. An able seaman earned $12 a month.

Costs of Living: A loaf of bread cost $.03, a dozen eggs cost $.12, a pound of butter cost $.14, and a whole chicken cost $.15. People receiving mail paid postage of $.06 for up to 30 miles and $.25 for over 400 miles. An education at Harvard ran about $300 a year.

Art/Architecture: Successful artists of the day included Charles Peale and Ralph Earl. Federal style homes were popular. The English Gothic style was often used for churches, office buildings, and government buildings. Builders began adding landscaping to houses.

Literature: William Hill Brown published *The Power of Sympathy*, America's first novel. Washington Irving published *A History of New York* in 1809. Nathaniel Hawthorne published *Twice Told Tales*. Edgar Allan Poe published his first collections of poetry in 1827. The first "Mother Goose" stories were published in America.

Music: Band music was very popular as were the songs "Bound for the Promised Land," "Turkey in the Straw," "Oh Shenandoah," "Drink to Me Only With Thine Eyes," "Rock of Ages," and after the War of 1812, "The Star-Spangled Banner."

Fads: Political buttons first appeared. The game of craps, from a French game called "hazards," became a fad in New Orleans. Trotting contests in Boston became popular, and the winner was the horse who could run a mile in under three minutes. The first winner was a horse named Boston Blue.

Fashions: Moustaches became fashionable for men. The first shoes for right and left feet were introduced. After the invention of the cotton gin, cotton clothing became more popular. In towns and cities, men dressed in knee-high britches, white stockings, long tail coats, vests, and shirts. Women wore long gowns with three-quarter sleeves and low-cut bodices. Working women wore long skirts, petticoats, and jackets.

Science: Benjamin Franklin invented bifocals. Samuel Colt designed a pistol with a revolving cartridge. John Deere invented a steel plow. The Morse code was invented as F.B. Morse patented the electromagnetic telegraph.

Education: The first women's college opened in New York in 1821. The first public high school was established in Boston in 1821. In 1836, the first McGuffey reader was introduced as an elementary reading book. Massachusetts required children to attend school at least three months a year until age 15.

Transportation: Regular stagecoach routes linked New York City, Boston, and Philadelphia by 1785. The *Tom Thumb*, America's first steam-driven locomotive, began service on the Baltimore and Ohio Railroad. In 1832, the Erie Canal was completed. Robert Fulton's steamboat made its first trip from New York City to Albany.

Leisure Time: Golf was introduced in Georgia and South Carolina. Hunting and billiards were especially popular in the South, while cricket and competitive boat racing became popular in the North. Archery was introduced in America.

Figure 16 Timeline: 1780 – 1840

1788 Georgia ratified U.S. Constitution

1789 Georgia revised state constitution

1825 New Echota became Cherokee capital

1785 Capital moved to Augusta; University of Georgia chartered

1793 Eli Whitney invented cotton gin

1803 Georgia began land lottery

1828 *Cherokee Phoenix* first published

1795 Yazoo land fraud

1809 Sequoyah began syllabary

1829 Dahlonega gold rush

1838 Trail of Tears

1780   1790   1800   1810   1820   1830   1840

1787 Constitutional Convention met in Philadelphia

1791 U.S. Bill of Rights ratified

1830 Indian Removal Act passed

1823 Monroe Doctrine enacted

1789 French Revolution began; Washington elected president

1803 Louisiana Purchase

1815 Napoleon defeated at Battle of Waterloo

1812 War of 1812 began

1814 Francis Scott Key wrote *The Star-Spangled Banner*

Creating a New Government

Section Preview

As you read, look for:
* the new constitutions for the nation and state, and
* vocabulary terms: U.S. Constitution, Bill of Rights, and General Assembly.

The national government established by the Articles of Confederation had little power, which is what its authors wanted. Because of its weaknesses, the Confederation government could not make the thirteen separate states into one nation. In the summer of 1787, fifty-five delegates, representing every state except Rhode Island, met at Independence Hall in Philadelphia to revise the Articles of Confederation. William Few and Abraham Baldwin were Georgia's representatives to the Constitutional Convention. This closed-door meeting actually resulted not in the revision of the Articles but in the creation of an entirely new government.

The details of these efforts are described in Chapter 14, but the government set in motion in 1787 is the same one we have in our nation today.

The U.S. Constitution

The government that those fifty-five delegates created had three branches: executive, legislative, and judicial. The executive branch included a president, a vice president, and executive departments. The judicial branch provided for a system of courts to protect the rights of citizens. But it was the legislative branch that caused the most upheaval at the convention.

After months of arguing, the delegates determined that the legislative branch would have two houses: a Senate, with two delegates from each state, and a House of Representatives, with membership based on each state's population. With all of the slaves, the South had a larger population and would therefore have more representatives in the House. Delegates from the northern states did not want to count the slave population at all. Finally, the delegates compromised and decided that only three-fifths of the slave population would count toward representation.

Above: At the Constitutional Convention, Abraham Baldwin helped resolve the large state-small state representation crisis.

Did You Know?

Because he suffered from rheumatism and because he thought he needed to stay home to manage his plantation, George Washington almost refused to attend the Constitutional Convention. But he did go, and he served as its chairman.

Did You Know?

The **Constitutional Convention in Philadelphia was so secret that a full account of what went on there was not made public until almost sixty years later.**

The delegates also provided for a method of amending, or making changes or additions to, the **U.S. Constitution** as times and circumstances dictated. The first ten amendments to the Constitution were added only a few years after the document was written. They are known as the **Bill of Rights**.

The new constitution was ratified by 1788; Georgia was the fourth state to ratify it. The new government was in place the following year, and George Washington became the nation's first president. For that reason, he is called the "father of his country." Washington was not a particularly gifted public speaker or a farsighted innovator. In fact, John Adams called him "Old Muttonhead" behind his back. But Washington was beloved by his people and served as commander-in-chief for two terms. Washington never really wanted to be president. But he loved his new country, and he served as he was needed.

A New Start for Georgia Too

In Georgia, years of hardship and change followed the Revolutionary War. The war showed that the state government was poorly equipped to deal with many of its problems. The war ruined the state's economy and divided its people. Many of Georgia's men had left their farms to fight; because of this, food was limited. The new state government had to ensure that families in need received such basic items as flour and corn meal until they could plant and harvest their own crops. The state also had to honor its commitments to those who had served in the war by making good on its promise to provide them with land.

In 1785, the capital of Georgia moved from Savannah to Augusta. During 1788 and 1789, delegates met there to make changes in the state constitution. After those changes were made, the Georgia constitution was very much like the national one. To ensure the separation of powers, the state established three branches of government: legislative, executive, and judicial. But power, although separated, was not equally balanced.

The legislature, now called the **General Assembly**, was bicameral and included a senate and a house of representatives. Members were to be elected by popular vote. Legislators in the General Assembly selected the governor and other state officials, including the judges. More importantly, the legislators determined both how money was to be raised and how it was to be spent.

Above: William Few served in the Provincial Congress, the Georgia Assembly, and the Continental Congress before being named as a representative to the Constitutional Convention.

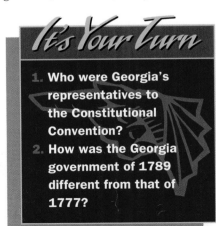

It's Your Turn

1. Who were Georgia's representatives to the Constitutional Convention?
2. How was the Georgia government of 1789 different from that of 1777?

American Spotlight

A Man Ahead of His Time

Benjamin Franklin was a writer, printer, inventor, scientist, historian, statesman, and diplomat. Born in Boston the fifteenth of seventeen children, Franklin was a self-educated man. At age 12, Franklin was indentured as an apprentice at his brother's newspapers. While the two brothers did not get along, the job provided young Franklin with two things. He loved reading, and he learned the in's and out's of the printing business.

Benjamin's brother would not let him write for his publication, *The New England Courant*. So Franklin began to write a series of letters to the paper using the pen name "Silence Dogood." The witty letters were quite popular and usually dealt with political issues and her "natural jealously for the rights and liberties of my country." Unfortunately, his brother discovered the trickery and silenced the young "Miss Dogood." But Ben had learned that he wanted to be a writer.

Franklin moved to Philadelphia, where he published his own newspaper, *The Pennsylvania Gazette.* His most remarkable publication was *Poor Richard's Almanack*, which was a collection of practical information and advice about the weather, planting, and the calendar as well as a collection of short, concise sayings expressing general wisdom. It was these sayings, called *aphorisms*, that made his almanac such a success. Many of his clever sayings are still used today: "A fool and his money are soon parted." "Early to bed, early to rise, makes a man healthy, wealthy, and wise." "No gains without pains."

After he sold his almanac, Franklin turned to science and the service of his county. His inventions improved people's lives and included the Franklin stove, a lightning rod, bifocal glasses, and a modern printing press. Franklin was also responsible for such innovations as Daylight Savings Time and the first free public library. He established the first public hospital in Philadelphia and founded the University of Pennsylvania. His leadership in his city led to the first paving and lighting of city streets and the first fire station. His

Above: Ben Franklin was one of the "founding fathers."

saying, "An ounce of prevention is worth a pound of cure" was related to fire safety, and he even established an insurance company to insure against home fire loss. That company is still in operation today.

Franklin worked hard for independence and was a representative to the Second Continental Congress. He edited the Declaration of Independence and was an ambassador to France, where he helped gain French support for the Revolutionary War.

Even in his late 70s, Franklin continued to try to help his country as a delegate to the Constitutional Convention. His last contribution was an antislavery paper written in 1789. When he died the following year, over 20,000 people came to pay tribute to this incredibly gifted man.

Land Fever in Georgia

Section Preview

As you read, look for:
• the ways settlers could get land in Georgia,
• the problems caused by the Yazoo land fraud, and
• vocabulary terms: headright system, Yazoo land fraud, and Louisiana Purchase.

Along with their hunger for independence from Great Britain, many Georgians of the late 1700s and early 1800s developed a huge appetite for land. During the settlement of the colony, much of the land east of the Oconee River belonging to the Indians was given to settlers by means of the **headright system**. Under this system, each white male counted as a "head" of a family and had the "right" to receive up to 1,000 acres. Although parts of this system lasted until the early twentieth century, it was largely replaced by a land lottery in 1803.

When *public domain* lands (lands owned by the state or federal government) were opened for settlement, Georgia surveyed land lots of different sizes. This so-called lottery land was located west of the Oconee River. For a small fee, any white male twenty-one years of age or older could buy a chance and, on the spin of a wheel, win land. Heads of households with children, war veterans, and widows were given extra chances in the land lotteries. Other states also had lotteries, and about 30 million acres of land were given away through them.

The Yazoo Land Fraud

Georgians' growing hunger for land reached a peak in 1795. At that time, Georgia's western borders were the Mississippi River and one of its *tributaries* (branches), the Yazoo River. Included in this territory were the present states of Mississippi and Alabama. Both South Carolina and Spain also claimed some of the same land, and the matter went to court for settlement.

Before any settlement was made, however, four land companies approached Governor George Mathews and members of the General Assembly and bribed them to pass a bill allowing the land companies to buy the western lands. When the Assembly enacted the bill, the land companies bought between 35 and 50 million acres of land for $500,000—about 1½ cents an acre.

The public quickly learned of this bargain basement sale, and there were protests all over the state. Newspapers printed articles telling what the legislators had done. Grand juries met to

Below: On February 21, 1796, all the records of the Yazoo land sales were collected and burned in front of the State Capitol building (then in Louisville). The "Holy Fire from Heaven" was started with the aid of a magnifying glass.

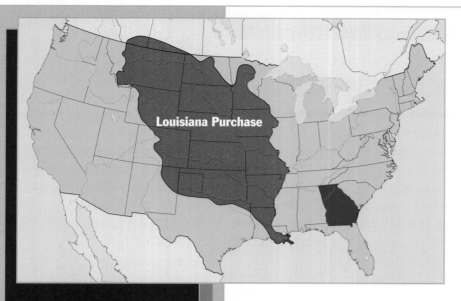

Louisiana Purchase

Map 26
The Louisiana Purchase

Map Skill What natural feature formed the eastern boundary of the Louisiana Purchase?

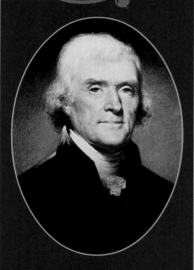

Above: In 1803, President Thomas Jefferson's desire to control the port of New Orleans led to the Louisiana Purchase.

look into both the law and the land sales. Many citizens called for the resignations of the legislators involved in what became known as the Yazoo land fraud.

As a result of public anger and pressure, the legislators involved were voted out of office. The new legislature repealed the law that had allowed the land to be sold. All records of these land sales were burned in public at Louisville, which had become the state capital of Georgia in 1796.

The state offered to refund the money from the land sales. However, there were many people who had bought land from the land companies and wanted to keep it. These people went to court. Finally, the federal government resolved the matter by paying over $4 million to settle the Yazoo land claims.

Georgia Cedes Western Land

Contrary to its initial hopes, Georgia lost rather than gained from the Yazoo land scheme. The state lost a large part of its land and a lot of money because of the failed plan. Also, after Spain renounced its claims to the area, the federal government contested Georgia's right to it. The long aftermath of the Yazoo affair created bad feelings among many of the state's citizens, and they appealed to the legislature to give in to the federal government. Therefore, in 1802, Georgia *ceded* (gave up) its land west of the Chattahoochee River to the federal government for $1.25 million, making the river Georgia's western boundary.

The new nation was acquiring land in other ways. Thomas Jefferson became the country's third president in 1800, succeeding John Adams. In 1803, President Jefferson bought the Louisiana Territory from France for $15 million. This transaction, which was known as the Louisiana Purchase, doubled the size of the country. The United States now extended west to the Rocky Mountains.

It's Your Turn

1. What two methods were used in Georgia to distribute land in the late 1700s and early 1800s?
2. What happened to the members of the Georgia legislature involved in the Yazoo land fraud?
3. What 1803 transaction between France and the United States doubled the land area of our country?

Section 3

Economic Growth in Georgia

Section Preview

As you read, look for:
• the impact of the cotton gin and mechanical reaper on agriculture,
• improvements in transportation, and
• vocabulary terms: depression and turnpike.

Above: In 1819, the *Savannah* was the first steamship to cross the Atlantic Ocean, sailing from Savannah, Georgia, to Liverpool, England.

As it had elsewhere in the new nation, the Revolutionary War brought financial chaos to Georgia. The state had no money to pay its huge war debts, and few citizens had money to pay taxes. When the British left Savannah toward the end of the war, one thousand Tories went with them. They took with them the equivalent of thousands of dollars, plus four to six thousand slaves and indentured servants.

But the period following the war also brought developments that made the future a little brighter for both Georgia and the rest of the nation. The development of mechanized farming tools, steamboats, and railroad engines and the many advances in industry, business, and commerce were all part of the Industrial Revolution in America.

Farming

Many of Georgia's rice and indigo plantations were in ruins after the war. There were also questions about who owned land. Tories, who had remained loyal to Great Britain, had their lands taken during the pre-Revolutionary

period. When the British were in charge of the state during the war, they returned the land to the Tories. After the war, lands were again taken from the Tories and given to former soldiers. In some cases, two or three families claimed the same piece of land. It took time to decide which family would keep the land.

Georgia at least had land and enough people to work it. It also had two agricultural crops that were soon in great demand: cotton and tobacco. Over the next thirty years, cotton became "king" in the South. This development greatly changed the lives of all Georgians, white and black.

A Man Named Eli

In 1793, Eli Whitney visited the home of Mrs. Catherine Greene Miller at Mulberry Grove Plantation near Savannah. Whitney, a friend of the family, was a schoolteacher and an inventor from Westborough, Massachusetts.

As the story goes, Mrs. Miller asked Whitney to repair a broken watch, which he agreed to do. Not long afterward, a visitor to the Miller home wished aloud for a machine to separate cotton fiber from its seed. Mrs. Miller, remembering the watch repair, asked Whitney if he could make a machine that would speed up the work done so slowly by hand.

After working several weeks, Whitney had developed a model for a cotton machine. He made the machine with wire teeth on a turning cylinder. It did separate the cotton from the seeds, but the lint got caught in the wire teeth and stopped up the machine. Several legends say that Mrs. Miller saw the machine's problem, took a clothes brush, and brushed the lint off the teeth. No one knows how much help Mrs. Miller really gave Whitney. In any event, before long, he built a factory near Augusta and had a working cotton engine, later shortened to just "gin."

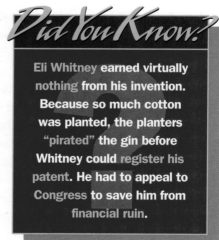

Top: Eli Whitney established the factory that was the first known example of mass production in America. Above: The cotton gin was cheap and easy to make and revolutionized the farming of cotton.

Did You Know?

Eli Whitney **earned virtually nothing from his invention. Because so much cotton was planted, the planters "pirated" the gin before Whitney could register his patent. He had to appeal to Congress to save him from financial ruin.**

Cotton growers welcomed Whitney's gin. Before its invention, a worker might have been able to separate six or seven pounds of cotton seed a day by hand. After the cotton gin's introduction, workers were able to separate about fifty pounds a day.

The Mechanical Reaper

Another agricultural invention, the mechanical reaper, further revolutionized the way work was done on a farm. The reaper, invented by Cyrus McCormick, had wooden paddles fastened to the harness of a horse. As a farmer guided the horse through his fields, the paddles turned and cut the grain. Using it, a farmer could cut six times more grain in a day than he could with a hand-held scythe.

Time- and labor-saving devices such as the cotton gin and grain reaper enabled Georgians to work larger and more profitable farms.

The Panic of 1837

Improved ways of farming helped Georgia's economy become strong after the Revolution. However, the boom period suddenly ended, causing the Panic of 1837. This was followed by a **depression** (a sharp economic downturn) that lasted into the early 1840s. During the depression years, many businesses failed, and many farmers and planters lost their land. Most banks did not have enough cash to pay out money that had been deposited with them. These banks failed, some closing for good. At the height of the depression, only eleven banks were open in Georgia.

Top: Cyrus McCormick was only 22 when he invented the mechanical reaper. **Above:** In 1851, McCormick's reaper won the highest award of the day, the Gold Medal, at London's Crystal Palace Exhibition.

Transportation

A major economic development during the early 1800s was the building of railroads. Before the railroads were built, people traveled on horses, boats, or stagecoaches. Freight was sent to market by riverboats, ferries, or wagon trains.

Many of Georgia's roads were stagecoach trails cut where Indian footpaths had been. Most of the roads ran from east to west. Stagecoaches ran regularly from Savannah to Athens in the north and Brunswick in the south. Augusta was the main east-west gateway into the state. A main stagecoach line connected Augusta and Columbus by way of Macon, but the stagecoaches could only cover thirty to forty miles a day.

Roads in wet, swampy places had logs across them and were known as *plank roads*. The federal government built some major highways in the early 1800s. These roads were called **turnpikes** because they had "pikes" or gates.

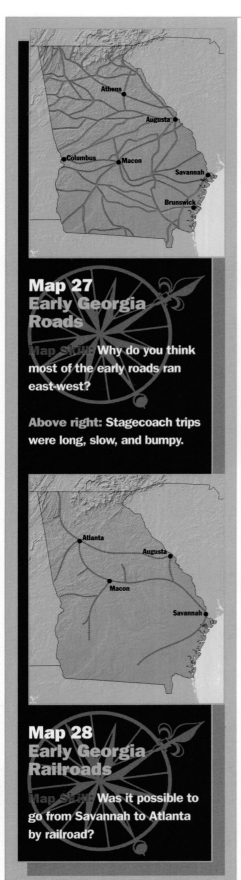

Map 27
Early Georgia Roads

Map Skill: Why do you think most of the early roads ran east-west?

Above right: Stagecoach trips were long, slow, and bumpy.

Map 28
Early Georgia Railroads

Map Skill: Was it possible to go from Savannah to Atlanta by railroad?

Did You Know?
In 1842, Terminus was renamed Marthasville, in honor of the daughter of former governor Wilson Lumpkin.

Travelers had to pay a fee at each pike to remain on the road, much like present-day toll roads. Among these turnpikes was the Old Federal Road, built in 1815 to run from Athens north through Cherokee territory into Tennessee. However, even the "good" roads were poor until the late 1800s.

Ferries were an important mode of transportation. These unique horse-drawn log rafts carried travelers across the rivers at their shallowest points, especially along the Flint River. In deeper river waters, the ferries used a pulley and cable system. That required a strong back and arm as the ferry operator pulled the raft across the river.

At first, rail travel was, perhaps, the least favored means of transportation. In 1830, there were only 13 miles of laid track in the United States, and those belonged to the Baltimore & Ohio Railroad. But just ten years later, there were 3,300 miles of track. Most of the track in Georgia belonged to the Western and Atlantic Railroad, which was chartered in 1836. The Western and Atlantic ran from a point near present-day Chattanooga, Tennessee, to a point on the southeastern bank of the Chattahoochee River. That point was called Terminus, which literally means the end of a railroad line. Today it is known as Atlanta. The railroads dramatically shortened travel time for both passengers and freight, reducing to hours trips that had previously taken days.

It's Your Turn

1. What two crops produced in Georgia were in great demand?
2. What was Eli Whitney's invention? How did it affect the growing of cotton?
3. Who demonstrated the first mechanical grain reaper?

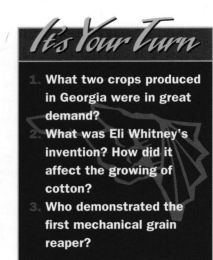

A Changing Economy

Two major changes took place in America's economy during this period—a change to commercial farming and the growth of factories. Both had a long-reaching impact on America's economy.

Farmers in America's early days grew just enough crops to feed their families. This practice was called *subsistence agriculture*. Later, farmers began to grow crops like wheat or cotton to sell at marketplaces. These crops were called cash crops and represented a different type of agriculture, *commercial agriculture*. Beginning in the early 1800s, farmers began to devote more of their time and land to commercial agriculture. Their cash crops were sold in local or distant markets. This change led to a market economy in the United States.

But there were great perils for farmers in a market economy. The movement into a market economy led farmers into debt and changed the agricultural practices of the young nation. Farmers often had to borrow money to survive and to resupply the farms until their crops were sold. Because crop prices rise and fall during the season, farmers had to hope that prices were high when it was time to take the crops to market. Farmers also bought more land to produce more crops for the marketplace, usually borrowing the money.

Also during the late 1700s and early 1800s, transportation improved with the use of canals, railroads, steamboats, and federal roads. As transportation became more available, trade among the states also increased.

New inventions, such as Whitney's cotton gin, McCormick's reaper, and water-powered cotton spinning machines, led to changes in manufacturing. During America's colonial period, most products were made by skilled artisans in homes or small shops. After 1800, modern manufacturing arrived.

In 1790, Samuel Slater, an English textile manufacturer, came to the United States and opened a mill to spin cotton into yarn. He contracted the weaving to women who worked in their homes to prepare clothing. More mills were built in New England, and young women were hired to work in these textile mills. As the machinery became more advanced, water was used to operate the spinning machines. Factories grew up around the water sources, and cities grew up around the factories.

The Industrial Revolution and the new market economy led to the use of many unskilled or semiskilled workers. As factories grew and equipment improved, there was an emphasis on making products quicker and cheaper to take advantage of prices at the marketplace and provide higher profits to investors and owners. The workers—women and children—did not fare as well.

These cheap workers often worked 12 to 15 hours a day, six days a week. Early efforts to organize workers met with little success because the factory owners had a large labor supply and could simply fire those who protested working conditions or wages.

America moved into the Industrial Age riding on the backs of innovators who developed new farming and manufacturing equipment, investors who expanded factories and production processes, and abundant power and labor supplies. However, the plight of workers and small farmers would lead to economic upheavals in America's future.

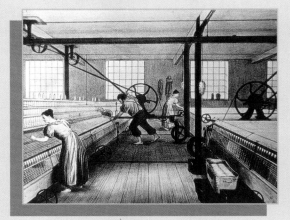

Above: Many young women found work in the textile mills.

Section 4

Georgia at the Dawn of a New Century

During this period, how people lived in Georgia depended on where they lived. There were two different Georgias in the late 1700s and early 1800s: the adventurous life of the frontier and the settled life of the growing towns.

It was a period of social growth. Membership in organized religions increased, and churches and synagogues played major roles in communities. There was more opportunity for formal education for more people.

Life on the Georgia Frontier

Frontier Georgia—the central and western parts of the state—was undeveloped land. Most of this land had been given away through the lottery, but there were few settlers. Some people attracted to the frontier were adventurers from settled towns such as Savannah and Augusta who wanted the excitement of frontier life. Some settlers migrated to the Georgia frontier from other states. They came over rough ground on roads that were little more than trails cut through thick brush and forests. During the early days on the frontier, far-flung trading posts were the only stores. Homesteads were often under the threat of attack from Native Americans, discontented Tories, or British soldiers.

As pioneers moved west in the early 1800s and left their towns behind, their kitchens were usually two iron pots and a memory of recipe rhymes learned during childhood. Clearing land, building cabins, tilling soil, putting up barns, digging wells, and all of the other chores of pioneer life were backbreaking labor leading to the old saying, "Them that works hard, eats hardy." Breakfast and the midday meal were the largest meals of the day.

Work also led to the major pioneer social activities. "Bean stringin's and corn shuckin's" were summer social occasions, while "apple parin's, cider

Above: Clearing land for a farm was hard, back-breaking work. Removing one tree stump could take as long as a month with the tools available.

makin's, and hog slaughterin's" were fall activities. The country store was central to frontier communities, but it carried only essential items such as coffee beans, salt, and flour. Luxury items were for special occasions and might have included cheese, peppermint balls, rice, and eggs for those families without laying hens. And, of course, the general store carried farm implements, seed, cloth, thread, and guns and ammunition.

Thirty years later, the frontier was dotted with farms, trading posts, taverns, and sometimes one-room schools. While everyday life continued to be rather difficult, improvements in agriculture and other aspects of life eased things considerably. Then, too, with the removal of British forces and the Tories, threats to the settlements decreased.

Life in Georgia's Towns

Life in Georgia's towns was quite different from life on the frontier. Cultural refinements were everywhere. The *Augusta Herald* and Savannah's *Gazette of the State of Georgia* were the two leading newspapers in the state. Newspapers were also published in Athens, Louisville, Milledgeville, and Sparta. Savannah had a theater where citizens could see plays by Shakespeare and more contemporary writers. People joined debating societies, went to concerts, or became members of a library society. They attended fancy dress balls and more informal gatherings such as barbecues and camp meetings. Horse racing drew large crowds in Augusta.

Food was cooked over an open hearth, and lucky families had an oven built into the chimney for cooking breads. The simpler meals consisted of stews, soups, sausages, roasted game, corn, dried vegetables, and cornbread or spoon bread. Foods served to guests were also simple. Beef, pork, and wild game were popular, and seafood, including shrimp, oysters, and fish, was a

Top: A 1785 cabin at Callaway Plantation. Above: The 1820 Davenport House in Savannah was designed and built by architect Isaiah Davenport.

favorite. Garden vegetables and sweet potatoes were served as side dishes. Many of the recipes used in southern homes today are the same as those enjoyed during the early 1800s.

In Georgia's small towns, communities provided for citizens with special needs. Orphanages cared for children without parents. A hospital for the mentally ill was opened in Milledgeville. A school for the deaf was started at Cave Springs. The Georgia Academy for the Blind was founded in Macon.

Religion

After the Revolutionary War, many ministers left America for Great Britain. Still, churches in Georgia grew, both in size and in importance to their communities. In addition to the Anglicans, Quakers, and Baptists, Methodist *circuit riders* (ministers who went from district to district) founded churches in the frontier region. Sometimes these ministers could have only one service a month for each church. However, they stayed in touch with the members and visited them as often as possible.

In 1787, free blacks founded the Springfield Baptist Church in Augusta. It is still located on the original site. The First African Baptist Church in Savannah was founded in 1788 under the leadership of Andrew Bryan. In Savannah, a Jewish synagogue had a small but committed membership. In 1796, Georgia's first Roman Catholic Church was established in Wilkes County. In 1801, a second parish was formed in Savannah.

Above: Rainy weather had little effect on Methodist preachers who traveled a circuit which could easily cover 500 miles.

During the first decade of the 1800s, towns such as Athens, Jefferson, Madison, Milledgeville, Monroe, and Monticello were established. As in Savannah and Augusta, churches in these new communities were an essential part of town life. There were Sunday and weekday worship services, and church buildings were often used for town meetings and social events.

In 1830, a religious group was formed that would have a major impact on America, and eventually the world. The founder of the Church was a young man named Joseph Smith. Born in Vermont into a large, religious family, Smith was only 14 when he received a vision of a new religion. By age 17,

Smith had had a second vision describing the beliefs of a new church. Smith started his new church, the Church of Jesus Christ of Latter Day Saints (or Mormons) with only six members, but the faith quickly grew. The Mormons, however, were persecuted and forced to relocate. They began settling in Utah in 1847.

Another important religious figure of the period was Richard Allen. Richard and his family were slaves and belonged to the chief justice of Pennsylvania, Benjamin Chew. Later they were sold to a Mr. Sturgis, who lived near Dover, Delaware. The family was allowed to attend the services of the Methodist Society. In 1777, at age 17, Richard Allen converted and became a member of the Society.

After purchasing his freedom, Richard became a preacher and traveled the Methodist circuit. Later he joined the congregation of St. George's Methodist Episcopal Church in Philadelphia. In 1784, the church licensed him to preach, but he had to hold his services at 5 a.m. Even that early hour did not deter the "colored people" who began to attend not only Allen's early services but the Sunday services as well. As membership grew, so did the uneasiness of the white congregation. Allen soon saw the need for a separate church for the "Africans," as they were called in the church.

In 1787, Richard Allen and two other members of the church, Absalom Jones and William White, led their followers out of the church. They immediately formed the Free African Society, a group dedicated to self-help and self-dependence for Africans. They also set about forming their own church.

Allen located a lot and the group found an old blacksmith building, which they hauled to the new site. In July 1794, the Bethel African Church opened for worship. By 1816, Allen had founded five other churches who wanted to join "Mother Bethel," as it was called, to form a new denomination. Its name was the African Methodist Episcopal (A.M.E.) Church. Richard Allen was consecrated as its first bishop. The church, then as well as today, adopted the teachings of John Wesley. Although four different buildings have served as the church, the lot that Allen purchased is the oldest piece of real estate owned continuously by African Americans in the United States. From this small group of believers came a worldwide church with over 1.2 million members. The first A.M.E. Church in Georgia was established in Savannah in 1865.

Education

Educational growth was slow during the post-Revolutionary War period. Some people received only a few years of elementary education. Often even the best farmers knew little, if anything, about reading or mathematics. Most of Georgia's citizens had not been to school at all. Governor Lyman Hall recommended that the state set aside land for schools, but few were built.

Even though the building of schools was slow, people believed in the value of education. In 1784, the government set aside twenty thousand acres of land for a state college. In 1785, the University of Georgia was chartered as a *land grant university* (a school for which the federal government donated the land). It is the oldest school of its kind in the nation. The university, which

Top: In 1830, Joseph Smith organized The Church of Jesus Christ of Latter-day Saints (Mormons) and became its first president. He was killed in 1844. Above: Richard Allen founded the African Methodist Episcopal Church and was its first bishop.

Above: The Academy of Richmond County, chartered in 1783, is the oldest educational institution in Georgia and one of the oldest in the nation. This building is listed on the National Register of Historic Places.

It's Your Turn

1. In what parts of Georgia was the frontier located?
2. What were the two leading newspapers in Georgia at the turn of the eighteenth century?
3. When was the Springfield Baptist Church founded?
4. What was the University of Georgia frequently called in its early days?

was to oversee all public schools in the state, opened for classes in 1801. The first building for the all-male, all-white student body was Franklin College, and for many years, the University of Georgia was frequently called Franklin College.

Did You Know?

Women were not admitted to the University of Georgia until 1918, 117 years after the college was opened to men.

In 1786, the Georgia legislature passed a law requiring each county to open *academies* (schools). But the lawmakers did not set aside money to build them. In 1820, there were only forty academies in the state. In 1822, some members of the legislature tried unsuccessfully to get money for public schools. However, money was placed in a special "state fund" to pay for the education of poor children.

In the early schools, such as the Academy of Richmond County founded in 1783, male students studied Greek, Latin, grammar, and mathematics. Females learned the arts and music. The Georgia Female College, later known as Wesleyan College, opened in Macon in 1836. There the girls had classes in French, literature, and science education. Tuition was $50 a year, and lessons in piano, art, or foreign languages were extra. Room and board was $15 a quarter, and there were extra charges for laundry and candles.

The cost does not seem great by today's standards, but only wealthier merchants and large landowners had enough money to send their daughters to Wesleyan. Many Georgia citizens saw no value in teaching females academic subjects, no matter what it cost. Instead, many young girls were taught sewing, cooking, child care, and music.

Section 5

The War of 1812

Section Preview

As you read, look for:
- reasons for the war of 1812,
- the effects of the war of 1812, and
- vocabulary term: embargo.

In his first inaugural speech, Thomas Jefferson declared: "Peace, commerce, and honest friendship with all nations, entangling alliances with none." Unfortunately, the United States found it very difficult to remain neutral while much of the world around it was at war.

An undeclared naval war with France that had broken out in 1798 was one of the problems that tested the young nation's ability to survive. Between 1793 and 1815, France and Great Britain were almost always at war. American merchants were caught in the middle as both countries tried to block the United States from trading with the other. Great Britain, which had the world's largest navy and controlled the Atlantic Ocean, even "impressed" American sailors. That is, British captains took sailors off American ships and made them serve in the British navy. Finally, in 1807, President Jefferson began an unsuccessful embargo to stop trade with foreign countries. Jefferson hoped the embargo would force Great Britain and France to change their policies. It did not. Instead, it had a disastrous effect on American shipping.

Americans also believed that Great Britain was stirring up the Indians in the western states and territories. In Congress, a group of land-hungry southerners and westerners known as the *War Hawks* wanted the United

Below: This painting shows the U.S.S. *Constitution* —"Old Ironsides"—defeating the H.M.S. *Guerriere* in the first decisive naval battle of the War of 1812.

In this 1811 political cartoon, the "Ograbme" (*embargo* spelled backwards) is trying to stop a man who is attempting to smuggle tobacco onto a British ship. Jefferson's embargo created an economic hardship for the country. The Ograbme was also called the "snapping turtle" or "terrapin," which is the reason for the image of the turtle in the cartoon.

States to declare war on Great Britain. They hoped to capture Canada and eliminate the British and Indian menace in the West. In June 1812, President James Madison asked Congress to declare war on Great Britain. By a narrow vote, Congress agreed.

Most citizens of the United States were not sure that Madison's decision was a good one. They thought the country was not prepared to fight against a major power such as Great Britain. The war lasted about two years, with neither side making any headway. In 1814, however, British forces invaded the Chesapeake Bay and made their way to Washington, which had become the young nation's capital. They burned much of the city, including the Capitol and the president's residence. Later the British were turned back as they tried to take control of Baltimore harbor. Although most people do not remember the battle at Fort McHenry, they do remember "The Star-Spangled Banner," which was composed at that battle.

One of the most memorable battles of the War of 1812 actually took place on January 8, 1815. This was several weeks *after* the Treaty of Ghent (in Belgium) was signed in 1814, ending the war. The soldiers at the Battle of New Orleans did not know that the war was over. The Americans, led by General Andrew Jackson, lost 13 men, while over 2,000 British soldiers were killed or wounded. The battle was recorded as a major American victory and has been remembered in songs. The battle also made Andrew Jackson a national hero.

The treaty that ended the war restored everything to what it had been before the war. The United States got no new land, but it gained in other ways. The war showed that the United States was willing to fight for its continued independence. Older nations started to pay attention to the young country. At the same time, the experience convinced the United States to stay away from European politics.

The war had other effects. The separate states truly began to feel united in one nation. The economy of the country started to change. When Americans could not get goods from abroad during the war,

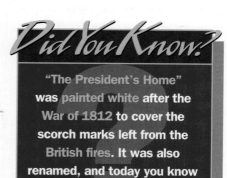

Did You Know?

"The President's Home" was painted white after the War of 1812 to cover the scorch marks left from the British fires. It was also renamed, and today you know it as the "White House."

they were forced to make them. Industry grew and, by 1815, the United States could supply many of its own needs, including such things as iron, textiles, wood, glassware, leather, and pottery. The War of 1812 was the last time American and British forces fought on opposite sides of a conflict. It also ended American hopes of gaining Canada as a part of our nation.

Shortly after the war ended, in 1817, President James Monroe asked Andrew Jackson to look into the problems that Georgians were having with the Seminole Indians. Instead of just investigating, Jackson invaded Florida and overthrew the Spanish governor. Spain agreed to sell Florida to the United States rather than fight. In 1819, the U.S. bought Florida for $5 million. Jackson was made governor of the newly acquired Florida Territory.

Above: The Battle of New Orleans was a stunning victory for the United States. Unknown to the two armies, the treaty to end the war had been signed in Paris two weeks earlier. In this depiction, General Andrew Jackson commands American troops from his white charger.

It's Your Turn

1. Why were Americans angry with the British at the beginning of the War of 1812?
2. How long did the War of 1812 last?
3. How did the War of 1812 help American industry?

Native Americans in Georgia

Native Americans had hunted in Georgia's forests and fished its streams and rivers for ten thousand years. The fifty-five years from 1783 to 1838 were one of the darkest periods in the history of these Native Americans. During this period, they were forced out of their traditional lands and moved to unknown territories.

The Cherokee

In 1800, most Native Americans in Georgia still made their living in the traditional ways—by hunting or farming. Some, however, were quick to learn from white settlers. The Cherokee, in particular, were considered to be the most advanced of the tribes. A few Cherokee, like Chief James Vann, lived in large houses. Located on the outskirts of Chatsworth, Vann's classic two-story brick mansion has been called the "Showcase of the Cherokee Nation." In addition to the main house, the homestead contained forty-two cabins, six barns, five smokehouses, a gristmill, a blacksmith, a foundry, a trading post, and a still. Vann believed that Christianity meant progress for the

Below and opposite page above: The Chief Vann House, exterior and interior, with a typical 18th century Cherokee log house on left.

Cherokee, and he brought in Moravian missionaries to teach his children and his people.

Sequoyah's Syllabary

One of the most important contributions to the advancement of Cherokee culture was made by George Gist, who was born around 1760. Gist's father was a Virginia scout and soldier, and his mother was a Cherokee princess. Gist's Indian name was Sequoyah, which meant "lonely lame one." Sequoyah was crippled, from either a childhood illness or a hunting accident, so he could no longer hunt or farm. Instead, he learned to work with silver. He also became a blacksmith.

Sequoyah was very interested in the white man's "talking leaves," pieces of paper with marks on them. He noticed that the papers could be carried many miles, and the people who used them could understand the meaning of the various marks. In 1809, Sequoyah began to make a syllabary. Unlike an alphabet of letters, a **syllabary** is a group of symbols that stand for whole syllables.

It took twelve years for Sequoyah to decide on the eighty-five symbols. According to legend, Sequoyah's wife, fearing that the white government would not like what he was doing, once burned all his work. Sequoyah spent more than a year reconstructing the syllabary, so dedicated was he to the task.

When he completed it, members of the tribal council at first made fun of the syllabary. However, after Sequoyah was able to teach his daughter and some young chiefs to write and understand the symbols within a few days, the council members changed their minds. They sent Sequoyah all over the territory to teach his method to other Cherokee. In about six months, most of the tribes could write and read the new symbols. As a result, the Cherokee were the first Indians to have their language in written form. Equally important, it demonstrated that Indians could communicate with each other without using the language of the white settlers.

People in the United States and Europe praised Sequoyah for his work. The Cherokee gave him a medal that he wore as long as he lived. The Cherokee Nation also rewarded him with a gift of about $500 a year for life. This gift, by the way, is the first record of a literary prize in America.

The *Cherokee Phoenix*

By 1828, Elias Boudinot, another Indian leader, became the editor of the first Indian newspaper. The paper, the *Cherokee Phoenix*, took its name from a legendary bird that burned itself and then rose from the ashes of the fire. The newspaper was printed in Cherokee and English. Perhaps its greatest

Sequoyah developed symbols to represent the 80 sounds of the tribe's language.

Top and above: This building is a reconstruction of the Cherokee Supreme Courthouse built in New Echota in 1829. The Cherokee Supreme Court heard 246 cases from 1823 to 1835.

achievement was that it was able to draw together the various tribes of the Cherokee Nation. The tribes were scattered in such far-flung places as Virginia, North Carolina, northeast Alabama, and Georgia. The newspaper made it possible to spread news among all of them.

Cherokee Capital Moves to New Echota

At one time, the capital of the Cherokee Nation was wherever the principal chief lived. In 1715, for example, it was in Stephens County, Georgia. At other times, the capital was in Tennessee or South Carolina. However, by 1825, the Cherokee had established a permanent capital at New Echota, near the present-day city of Calhoun.

New Echota was a thriving, bustling community. One of the twenty Cherokee government buildings in it was a print shop where the *Cherokee Phoenix* and textbooks for Indian schools were published and distributed. Other buildings included a Cherokee national library and a courthouse.

The Cherokee adopted a constitution similar to that of the United States. Their government also was organized along the lines of that of the United States and consisted of three branches: executive, legislative, and judicial. The principal chief and second chief were elected to their offices. Each October, Cherokee leaders, including those in the bicameral legislature and the superior court, met in New Echota to deal with tribal matters.

Did You Know?

By 1830, over 90 percent of the Cherokee could read and write.

The Creek

Tensions between the Creek and the settlers had grown during the late 1700s as pioneers kept pushing into Creek lands along the Oconee River. Tribes led by Chief Alexander McGillivray sent warriors against some of the pioneer settlements. The Indians burned houses, stole horses and cattle, and killed or captured over two hundred settlers. Georgia settlers got some men together and told them to kill on sight any Creek who were not members of friendly tribes. Although it was not quite a full-scale conflict, these skirmishes and attacks became known as the Oconee War.

Fighting between the settlers and the Creek went on for several years. In 1790, President Washington called Chief McGillivray to New York. The chief went, accompanied by twenty-three men of his tribe. President Washington and the chief talked and exchanged presents. McGillivray then signed the Treaty of New York, by which the Creek gave up all their land east of the Oconee River. They also promised to honor an earlier treaty in which they gave up lands through the Currahee Mountains to Tugaloo. In return, the United States government promised that no whites would go into land west of the boundary. The government also agreed to help the Creek start farms by giving them tools and farm animals.

When word of the treaty reached Georgians, they were very angry because it appeared to them that the federal government had taken the side of the Creek. Over the next few years, neither the Creek nor the Georgians paid any attention to the treaty. At one point, Governor Edward Telfair was ready to raise an army of 5,000 men to make war against the Creek, but President Washington talked him out of it. However, there were bad feelings between the tribes and the whites until both groups accepted other treaties. This "peace" lasted from 1797 until 1812.

It was during this time that the Yazoo land fraud took place. When the federal government stepped in and had Georgia give up all land west of the Chattahoochee River, it also promised to move the Native Americans out of the state. The federal government did little to carry out this promise. Then, in 1812, the United States was again at war.

The Creek War

Tecumseh, a Shawnee leader, tried to unite all Native Americans to fight for their land. The tribes in the Southeast split over this issue. Those who wanted war were called Red Sticks, and those who wanted peace were known as White Sticks.

During the War of 1812, many of the Red Stick Creek fought alongside the British. As you read earlier, the war ended with no real winner. However, something happened in 1813 that changed the future of the Creek Nation. On August 30, one thousand Red Sticks attacked Fort Mims in present-day

Top: In 1811, Tecumseh, a Shawnee, visited the Creek to recruit warriors and gain support for his plan. **Above:** Menawa was a leader of the Red Stick Creek. He led the party that killed Chief William McIntosh.

Alabama. About four hundred people, including women and children, died at the hands of the Red Sticks. Cries of "Remember Fort Mims" were heard all over the country.

Troops from Georgia, Tennessee, and the new Mississippi Territory began attacks in Creek territory. Many battles were fought during the next year, but the Creek were no match for the United States Army. The last battle of the Creek War began on March 27, 1814, at Horseshoe Bend, along the Tallapoosa River in Alabama. Over one thousand Red Sticks met two thousand troops led by General Andrew Jackson. With the help of White Stick Creek and Cherokee, Jackson defeated the Red Stick Creek.

In the following months, the Creek surrendered to Jackson and gave most of their lands to the United States government. Georgians were pleased with this outcome because it meant that the Creek owned no more land in southern Georgia.

Murder of Chief William McIntosh

As more and more of their land was ceded to the government, Creek tribes became separated from each other. There was little chance for them to talk together or to trade with each other. The strong Creek confederacy, which had united the tribes before the arrival of the settlers, was no more. Groups of Creek sometimes signed treaties without asking the tribes to agree. This practice led to the death of one well-known Creek leader.

By February 12, 1825, Creek Chief William McIntosh and his first cousin, Georgia Governor George Troup, had worked out the terms of the Treaty of Indian Springs in Butts County, Georgia. The United States paid McIntosh and a large group of Lower Creek chiefs $200,000 to cede (give up) the last Creek lands in Georgia to the federal government. The government, in turn, gave the use of that land to Georgia.

Groups of Creek who disagreed with the treaty met secretly to decide how to punish McIntosh. They agreed that, in accordance with Creek law, he should die. They sent a rival chief, Menawa, to execute him. According to reports, somewhere between 170 and 400 Creek marched single file to McIntosh's home in Butts County. After two days, they were a mile from McIntosh's house. Many reports say the Creek got close enough to hear

Above: Chief William McIntosh strongly believed that the Creek should sell their land to the government and take the money and land promised in the West. For that reason, he signed the Treaty of Indian Springs.

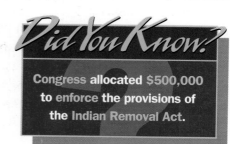

Did You Know?

Congress allocated $500,000 to enforce the provisions of the Indian Removal Act.

McIntosh and his son-in-law, Samuel Hawkins, talking. McIntosh did not know they were there.

At daybreak, the Creek set fire to the McIntosh home. They allowed the women and children to leave before they exchanged gunfire with the chief they had come to kill. Smoke and his wounds stopped McIntosh from fighting. The Creek dragged him from the house and stabbed him in the chest. McIntosh's scalp was taken as a warning to others who might want to give Creek land to white men.

The Indian Removal

In 1828, Andrew Jackson was elected president of the United States. Jackson had been friendly to the Native Americans, especially the Cherokee, when he needed their help to fight the Red Sticks. However, he was wise enough politically to know that white voters wanted the Native Americans removed from the southern states.

In 1830, Congress passed a bill, the Indian Removal Act, that called for all Native Americans to be moved to the western territories. There were strong feelings on both sides, and the bill passed by only fourteen votes. After Jackson signed the bill into law, however, there was no question about what would happen to the Southeast tribes.

Above: The Indian Removal Act was passed during the presidency of Andrew Jackson. Jackson believed that the Native Americans were children in need of guidance. He believed their removal would be beneficial.

Removal of the Creek

The Choctaw, who lived in the newly created states of Alabama and Mississippi, were the first of the tribes to be moved. Hearing that hundreds of Choctaw died during the march to the west, the Creek refused to leave the lands of their fathers. When they did this, Alabama took away all their legal rights. The Creek could not defend themselves against whites who moved in and took their lands.

The Creek in Georgia, who no longer had hunting lands, were hungry. Some reports say they stood in the streets of Columbus and begged for food. To add to their hardships, smallpox broke out among the tribes in 1831, and many died. In 1832, the Creek signed the Treaty of Washington, by which they ceded to the federal government the 5 million acres of land they still owned. In return, the government agreed to set aside 2 million acres on which the Creek would live and farm. The government would protect Creek life and property from whites. Creek could own land, but only after living on it for five years. Then they could choose to sell the land and move west. The decision to stay on reserved land or to move to the western territory was up to each individual.

Once signed, the treaty was broken almost at once. Creek homes were burned, items were stolen from their farms, and Indians were killed. By 1835, some Creek gave up and began the trip west. However, in 1836, bands of Lower Creek attacked whites between Tuskegee, Alabama, and Columbus, Georgia. Afraid of another Indian war, the U.S. Army captured over one thousand Creek and took them to the Indian Territory (present-day Oklahoma). During the next two years, a few Creek escaped and a few were made slaves, but the federal government forced thousands of them to move west.

Toward the end of the Creek removal in Georgia and Alabama, the United States became involved in another Indian war in Florida. They asked seven hundred Creek to help them fight the Seminole. After winning the war, the Creek returned to their families, who had been gathered in camps. Then the whole group, including those who had just fought with the army, was moved to the west.

Removal of the Cherokee

At the same time that the Creek were being moved, Georgia was also making plans to get rid of the Cherokee. Georgians wanted to homestead Cherokee land and also to mine the gold that had been found on Cherokee land.

Gold in Dahlonega

Gold was discovered in Dahlonega in the summer of 1829. In a matter of months, gold fever swept through the North Georgia mountain region. Although the Cherokee knew there was gold in the hills, the person given credit for the discovery was a farmer named Benjamin Parks. Parks found the valuable yellow metal while deer hunting in what was then Habersham (now White) County. Auraria, in nearby Lumpkin County, became the first gold mining center in the United States. Over ten thousand miners with gold pans, picks, and shovels moved onto Cherokee land.

The Georgia legislature passed a law that placed part of the Cherokee land under state control. It declared Cherokee laws null and void and would not let the Cherokee speak against white men in a court of law. This meant any white person could hurt or even kill a Cherokee without much fear of punishment. A second law, passed on December 19, 1829, refused the Cherokee any right to

Below: The discovery of gold in Dahlonega ended any hope of the Cherokee keeping their lands. Once the news spread, thousands swarmed onto Cherokee lands to make their fortune.

By the Side of the Road

The discovery of gold in northern Georgia in what was then Cherokee territory led to the eventual exodus of the Cherokee and the settlement of the area by white settlers. Most of the original gold mines have long since disappeared, but the most famous mine was the Calhoun mine. You can visit the site of the Calhoun Gold Mine today on U.S. Route 19 and GA 60 just outside Dahlonega.

CALHOUN GOLD MINE
← 1 Mi.

Famous Calhoun gold mine where it is said vein gold was first discovered in Georgia by white men.

In 1828 while deer hunting Benjamin Parks, of Dahlonega, accidentally found quartz gold in pockets or lodes. His find was so rich in gold that it was yellow like yolk of eggs.

Shortly after discovery this mine was sold to U. S. Senator John C. Calhoun, of South Carolina. It was operated by Thomas G. Clemson, son-in-law of Calhoun, and some of the gold was used to found Clemson College, S. C. Specimens from this mine are exhibited at the State Capitol in Atlanta.

Left: The old courthouse in Dahlonega, built in 1836, today serves as the Dahlonega Gold Museum.

gold mined in the Dahlonega area. While the miners searched the mountains and streams for "a spot that showed good color," the Cherokee were losing their homes, lands, and legal rights.

The Indians' Last Hope

Most Georgians did not care what happened to the Indians, but a group of white missionaries living in Cherokee territory did. To remove the missionaries, the Georgia legislature passed a law on December 22, 1830, which said a white person could not live on Cherokee land without taking an oath of allegiance to the governor. Eleven people, including the Reverend Samuel Worchester, postmaster at New Echota, refused to sign the oath and were jailed in March 1831. They were set free but arrested again in July. This time they were chained and made to walk from the North Georgia mountains to Lawrenceville. At their trial in September, the jury took only fifteen minutes to return a verdict of guilty. Gwinnett County Judge Augustin Clayton sentenced the group to four years at the state penitentiary in Milledgeville. Governor George Gilmer agreed to pardon anyone who would take an oath of loyalty to the state, and all but two agreed. Missionaries Worchester and Elizur Butler took their cases to the U.S. Supreme Court. Chief Justice John Marshall ruled that the decision of the Lawrenceville court could not stand because Cherokee territory was not subject to state law.

The Cherokee thought the ruling meant they could keep their land and government. Chief Justice Marshall ordered Butler and Worchester set free, but Judge Clayton refused. Georgia's newly elected governor, Wilson Lumpkin, would not take a stand against the judge. Even President Andrew Jackson refused to honor the Supreme Court order. Jackson thought that state governments should be in charge of Indian territories. He reportedly said, "John Marshall has rendered his 'decision'; now let him enforce it."

Cherokee lands were divided into lots of 40 and 160 acres. In 1832, the government held a state lottery to give the Cherokee lands to white men. Even then, the Cherokee refused to leave their home.

On January 9, 1833, Worchester and Butler gave up and told Governor Lumpkin that they would "abandon litigation." (**Litigation** is a legal court action.) The governor pardoned them and then said the two missionaries must leave the state and never return.

More and more, the Cherokee were run off their lands, whipped, and even killed. Chief John Ross made several trips to Washington to ask Congress for help. He wanted the Cherokee protected and the terms of past treaties honored. No help was given. Time was running out for the Cherokee Nation.

In December 1835, the Cherokee were told to come to their capital, New Echota. There they were to sign a treaty giving up all Cherokee land that remained in the Southeast. Any member of the tribe who did not come was considered to have agreed with the treaty. Three to five hundred Cherokee out of about seventeen thousand were at the meeting.

Top: Cherokee Chief John Ross took a petition to Congress with 15,000 signatures, 90 percent of all Cherokee, to protest the Indian removal. Above: Davy Crockett lost his seat in Congress for opposing Jackson's views on the Indian removal.

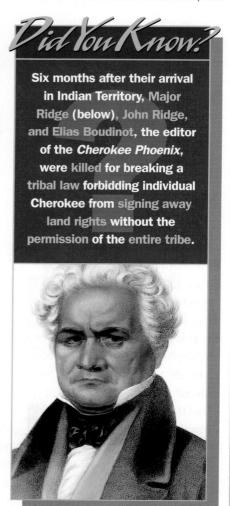

Did You Know?

Six months after their arrival in Indian Territory, Major Ridge (below), John Ridge, and Elias Boudinot, the editor of the *Cherokee Phoenix*, were killed for breaking a tribal law forbidding individual Cherokee from signing away land rights without the permission of the entire tribe.

Cherokee trader Major Ridge, his son John, and a small number of others agreed to sign the government's treaty. The treaty said the Cherokee would move west, and Georgia would give them a little money and food for the trip.

The Trail of Tears

After the treaty was signed, some national leaders like Henry Clay, Daniel Webster, and Davy Crockett tried to get the United States government to give the Cherokee the rights due them. No one listened. By May 1838, about two thousand Cherokee had gone. General Winfield Scott was ordered to remove the fifteen thousand or more Cherokee who refused to leave their home.

In May 1838, Scott and nearly seven thousand troops arrived in New Echota. The troops first built stockades to house the Cherokee. Then they went into homes and community buildings and forcibly moved the Cherokee to the stockades. Hundreds of men, women, and children died of cholera, dysentery, and fever while in the stockades. During the summer of 1838,

Map 29
The Trail of Tears

Map Skill: Through which states did the Cherokee have to travel to reach their new home?

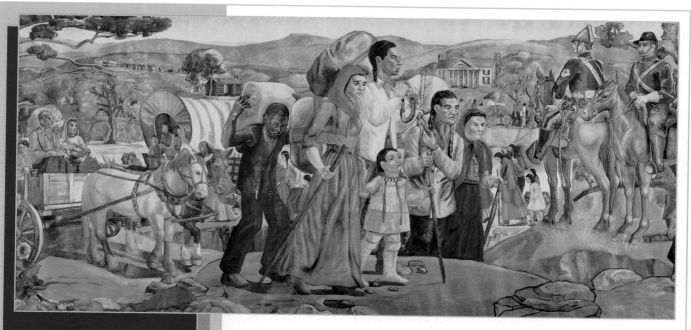

Above: This mural in the Oklahoma State Museum of History shows the family and servants of Chief John Ross leaving on the Trail of Tears.

the army loaded several thousand Cherokee onto crowded boats and sent them on the Tennessee, Mississippi, and Arkansas rivers to their new homes. The boats were dirty, and the food the government gave them was often not fit to eat. By the time these Indians arrived in Indian Territory, nearly one-third of the group had died.

A few Cherokee escaped and hid in the North Carolina mountains. The rest began a 700-800 mile walk to Indian Territory. It took some people six months to make the trip. Others were there in less time. However, winter winds, snow, and too little food led to the deaths of thousands of Cherokee. The exact number of how many were moved is not known, but about four thousand of this group died while they were in prison before they left or during the march west.

President Martin Van Buren, in his December 1838 address to Congress, said, "the measures of the Removal have had the happiest effect . . . the Cherokees have emigrated (moved out) without apparent reluctance." Today, we can only imagine the fear, despair, and hurt felt by those who had to leave the land of the "principal people." The Cherokee called the move to Indian Territory "ANuna-da-ut- sun'y," which means "the trail where they cried." To this day, the move is sadly remembered as the Trail of Tears.

It's Your Turn

1. What was Sequoyah's great contribution to the Cherokee?
2. Where was the Cherokee capital located in 1825?
3. Who were the Red Sticks?
4. What happened in Dahlonega in 1829?
5. Who was Samuel Worchester?

Between the Indian Removal Act of 1830 and the Trail of Tears, more than 100,000 Native Americans were displaced from 200 million acres of land that had been theirs for hundreds of years.

A Final Note

Before President John Adams fell asleep on his second night in the White House, he entered his thoughts into a journal. The November 2, 1800, entry reads, "I pray to Heaven to bestow the best Blessings on this House and all that shall hereafter inhabit it. May none but honest and wise men ever rule beneath this roof." In your opinion, has Adams's hope been realized?

Above: The outdoor drama "Unto These Hills" tells the story of the estimated 1,100 Cherokee who managed to escape into the mountains of western North Carolina. The escapees and others known as the Qualla Indians formed the Eastern Band of Cherokee, which exists to this day.

Chapter Summary

- In the period after the Revolutionary War, the U.S. Constitution was written, a new government established, and a Bill of Rights adopted. Georgia revised its state constitution.

- A fever for land gripped the people of Georgia and other parts of the country. Georgia ceded its western land to the federal government.

- The Louisiana Purchase doubled the land area of the new nation. Inventions such as the cotton gin and the mechanical reaper changed farming.

- At the end of the 1700s, life in Georgia was sharply different depending on whether one lived in the cities and towns or on the frontier.

- The United States fought Great Britain in the War of 1812.

- Although most Indians still followed traditional ways, some had made great advances. The Cherokee were especially quick to adopt the ways of the whites.

- Sequoyah invented a syllabary that enabled the Cherokee to communicate in writing.

- The Cherokee established a permanent capital at New Echota.

- The Treaty of New York ended the Oconee War and divided the Creek Nation.

- Greed for land and gold fever led to the Indian removal.

- U.S. treaties with the Indians were broken almost as soon as they were made.

- The Creek were forced west, and the Cherokee were gathered together and sent on their Trail of Tears to Indian Territory (present-day Oklahoma).

ChapterReview

Reviewing People, Places, and Terms

Use each of the following terms in a sentence.

1. embargo

2. headright system

3. syllabary

4. tariff

5. Yazoo land fraud

Understanding the Facts

1. What was the capital of Georgia in 1789?

2. What river became Georgia's western boundary after the settlement of the Yazoo land fraud?

3. What was the original name of the city of Atlanta?

4. Under what name is the Georgia Female College known today?

5. What was gained from the War of 1812?

6. How is a syllabary different from an alphabet?

7. In what month did Cherokee leaders meet at New Echota to deal with tribal matters?

8. What Indian chief signed the Treaty of New York?

9. How was the Creek chief who signed the Treaty of Indian Springs punished?

10. Who was president when the Indian Removal Act was passed?

11. Which tribes were the first to be removed?

Developing Critical Thinking

1. Why do you think the economy of Georgia was in ruins after the Revolutionary War?

2. Could something like the Yazoo land fraud happen today? Why or why not?

3. Sometimes we may think someone is not being fair, when in fact, we may just be looking at the situation from our own eyes rather than at the "big picture." Could that have been part of the situation with the removal of Georgia's Creek and Cherokee tribes—that no one stopped to look at the big picture? Using the character term *fairness*, jot down each instance when our state or nation was "unfair" to the Native Americans. Then decide what would have been fair? In your opinion, was the Indian removal right or wrong? Explain your answer.

4. Had you been a Cherokee living in Georgia during this time, would you have hidden in the mountains or traveled to Indian Territory? Suppose you were married and had a spouse and three children depending on you. Would that have changed your answer? Explain.

Checking It Out

1. Only history, and students of history such as yourself, can decide whether or not Andrew Jackson was a great military leader or a good president. But you will be hard-pressed to find a more intense, scandalous, or political love story among the inhabitants of America's White House. Use your research skills to find out about the love story between Andrew Jackson and

Rachael Donelson. Discover why their love story was such a political intrigue and share the information with your classmates.

2. Use your research skills to find out what happened to the Creek and the Cherokee who were forced to leave Georgia. Did all of them wind up in Indian Territory?

Writing Across the Curriculum

1. Benjamin Franklin was well known for his aphorisms. You may be familiar with many of his sayings. Try your hand at interpreting the following aphorisms: (a) Haste makes waste, (b) Love your neighbor, yet don't pull down your hedge, (c) A small leak will sink a great ship, (d) Well done is better than well said, (e) A good example is the best sermon, and, (f) Three may keep a secret if two of them are dead.

2. Try your hand at writing aphorisms. Imagine that you are preparing a series of inspirational posters for school. Phrase your advice in short, clever aphorisms.

Exploring Technology

1. Thomas Jefferson's epitaph omitted the fact that he had been president. Use your favorite search engine to check out Jefferson's epitaph. What did he write?

2. The War of 1812 has been commemorated by several songs including the popular "The Ballad of New Orleans." Use your favorite search engine to find the lyrics to the song and share with your classmates.

3. When Blackbeard the pirate was caught, 12-year-old Benjamin Franklin wrote a ballad about the infamous pirate. Use your favorite search engine to find the lyrics to that ballad and share it with your classmates.

Applying Your Skills

1. At various times, the capital of Georgia has moved from Savannah to Augusta, to Louisville, to Milledgeville, and, finally, to Atlanta. If distance from most parts of the state were the most important reason in choosing the site of a capital, in which of these locations should the capital be located? Why do you think it is not?

2. Using a U.S. map, what present-day states were acquired by the United States as a part of the Louisiana Purchase?

Photo Question

This is the living room of the "Showcase of the Cherokee Nation." Whose house was it?

Chapter 7

1838–1860

The Antebellum Era

Chapter Preview

Georgia character word:
Loyalty

Terms: antebellum, manifest destiny, annex, skirmish, states' rights, yeoman farmer, overseer, abolition, free state, slave state, Missouri Compromise, sectionalism, Compromise of 1850, Kansas-Nebraska Act, popular sovereignty, free soiler, driver, slave code, arsenal, underground railroad, Know Nothing party, Republican party, platform, secession, ordinance, Confederate States of America

People: William Lloyd Garrison, Harriet Beecher Stowe, Frederick Douglass, Dred Scott, John Brown, Harriet Tubman, Howell Cobb, Joseph E. Brown, Robert Toombs, John C. Fremont, Abraham Lincoln, Alexander H. Stephens

Places: Texas, Harpers Ferry, Marietta, Crawfordville

Historians differ as to the dates that make up the antebellum period (the period before the Civil War). For some, it was 1784 to 1860—the years after the American Revolution. Others set the period as 1823 to 1859. For the purpose of this textbook, we will use the period from 1838 to 1860. It was a time filled with turmoil, disagreement, and rapid change.

Below: Callaway Plantation House. Callaway got the last shipment of cotton off to England before the Civil War. His English broker sold the cotton and banked the money. Callaway used the money to finish the house in 1869.

Signs of the Times 1838-1860

Population: In 1840, Georgia's population was 691,392. In 1850, it stood at 906,185.

Life Expectancy: In 1850, it was 40 years for whites and 36 years for slaves.

Wages/Salary: A farmhand in the North earned $13 a month, a southern farmhand $9, a shoemaker $22, a male textile operator $26, an able seaman $18, and an ordinary seaman $14.

Costs of Living: A night's stay at a tavern cost 50 cents; food cost about 25 cents per person per meal. A woolen blanket cost $2.50. Flour cost $0.02 a pound, sugar $0.04 a pound, and salt $0.06 a pound.

Art/Architecture: Architecture changed drastically in 1848 when a builder constructed a five-story building using cast iron girders. The Hudson River School style of painting became popular.

Literature: Books of this period included James Fenimore Cooper's *The Pathfinder* and *The Deerslayer*, Henry David Thoreau's *Walden*, Herman Melville's *Moby Dick*, and Nathaniel Hawthorne's *The Scarlet Letter*. Improvements in printing presses made magazines and newspapers more popular. The number of magazines jumped from just over 100 in 1800 to over 3,700 by 1860.

Music: The New York Philharmonic Orchestra, the nation's oldest symphony orchestra, was founded in 1842. Popular songs included "Amazing Grace," "Michael Row the Boat Ashore," "Follow the Drinking Gourd," "Yellow Rose of Texas," "I've Been Working on the Railroad," and "Home on the Range."

Leisure Time: In 1839, Abner Doubleday laid out the first baseball diamond in Cooperstown, New York. The first baseball game was held in 1846 in Hoboken, New Jersey. In 1851, the schooner-yacht *America* won a 60-mile race against fourteen British yachts. The trophy became known as the America's Cup. Ted Turner won the America's Cup in 1977.

Fads/Fashions: Fashion arrived in baseball when the New York Knickerbockers began dressing in uniforms in 1851. Matrimonial agencies began to match eligible young women with "deserving" men. P. T. Barnum, known as the Greatest Showman on Earth, opened an exhibit in New York City. Audubon encouraged the fad of birdwatching when he published *Birds of North America*.

Science: Inventions of the period included soap powder, the safety pin, the washing machine, a pencil with an eraser on the end, and postage stamps with adhesive on the back. In 1856, Texan Gail Borden received a patent for condensing milk. Oil was used commercially for the first time—as medicine. The introduction of eyeglasses led some to think they would cure the blind.

Transportation: Charles Goodyear produced vulcanized rubber in 1839. The Baltimore & Ohio Railroad linked Chicago to the East. Stagecoach service and mail delivery connected St. Louis and San Francisco, a distance of 2,812 miles. In 1860, the Pony Express began service from St. Joseph, Missouri, to Sacramento, California.

Education: The U.S. Naval Academy opened at Annapolis in 1845. The City of Boston began giving written examinations for elementary children. In 1852, Massachusetts passed the first school attendance law requiring children ages 8-14 to attend school at least 12 weeks a year.

Religion: St. Patrick's Cathedral of New York was designed by James Renwick; today it remains one of the most famous churches in the nation. Beginning in 1858, religious revivals swept across the nation with daily prayer meetings in all major cities.

Figure 17 Timeline: 1840–1860

1842 Dr. Crawford W. Long of Jefferson first used ether as anesthetic

1846 Georgia sent over 2,000 men to fight in Mexican-American War

1849 Howell Cobb selected speaker of the U.S. House of Representatives.

1856 Savannah-born John Charles Fremont was unsuccessful Republican candidate for president

1858 Georgia's legislature allocated money to fund free elementary schools

1861 Georgia seceded from Union

1840 **1845** **1850** **1855** **1860**

1848 Gold discovered in California

1850 Compromise of 1850

1853 Gadsden Purchase

1854 Kansas-Nebraska Act passed; Republican party founded

1857 *Dred Scott* decision

1860 Abraham Lincoln elected president; South Carolina seceded from the Union

Manifest Destiny

In 1845, John O'Sullivan, a New York journalist, wrote that it was the **manifest destiny** of our country "to overspread the continent allotted by Providence for the free descendants of our yearly multiplying millions." Within months, what may have seemed to be greed for more land became instead a doctrine backed by religious zeal. In the words of President Polk, who had been elected in part because of his campaign promises to expand U.S. territory, "the world beholds the peaceful triumphs of . . . our emigrants. To us belongs the duty of protecting them . . . whenever they may be upon our soil." And, the hope was that the soil Polk referred to would be Texas, the Oregon territory, and California.

Texas

Mexico won its independence from Spain in 1821. Mexican territory included a huge tract of land that started where the Louisiana Purchase ended. The land was called "Texia" by the 30,000 plus Native Americans who lived there and "Tejax" by the few thousand Mexican Spanish inhabitants. Led by Stephen Austin, hundreds of white settlers migrated to the region. They called the area "Texas."

Below: Revolting against Mexico's president, Santa Anna, a band of 187 Texians defied a Mexican army of thousands for 12 days. All of the men were killed, and "Remember the Alamo!" became a rallying cry for the Texian settlers.

President John Quincy Adams, who had been elected in 1824, tried to buy Texas from Mexico, but he was refused. After his election in 1828, President Jackson also tried to buy Texas. Again, Mexico refused.

By 1834, so many "Anglos" had moved into the region that they outnumbered the Spanish Mexicans 4 to 1. Most of these white settlers refused to obey Mexican laws about slavery and refused to convert to the Catholic religion. Increasingly, the 20,000 white colonists regarded themselves as "Texians" rather than as Mexican subjects. General Antonio López de Santa Anna, who had been elected Mexico's president in 1833, was increasingly disturbed by the large numbers of white settlers, and he was determined to take control of the Texians. Under a new constitution, he took away any special privileges in Texas and forbade additional settlers from coming into the area.

Furious over these changes, the Texians declared their independence, knowing that a showdown was inevitable. Santa Anna led about 2,000 troops against the rebellious Texians. He quickly took control of San Antonio but was not able to capture the Alamo, an old Spanish mission where less than 190 Texians were determined to make a stand.

After a siege of twelve days, Santa Anna's troops stormed the fort. All of the Texas settlers were killed. A few weeks later, Santa Anna ordered the execution of 350 Texians being held at Goliad. These two incidents inspired the Texians. Two months later, Sam Houston led eight hundred men against Santa Anna at the Battle of San Jacinto. With cries of "Remember the Alamo" and "Remember Goliad" ringing in the air, the Texians defeated Santa Anna's army and gained Texas's independence from Mexico.

The people of Texas formed the Republic of Texas, also known as the Lone Star Republic. They wanted to become part of the United States as quickly as possible. However, because slavery was allowed in Texas, it was not until December 1845 that it was annexed (added on) and became the twenty-eighth state in the United States.

The Mexican-American War

After the annexation of Texas, Mexico angrily cut off all diplomatic ties with the United States. To add insult to injury, U.S. officials demanded that the Rio Grande be the southern border of Texas. As skirmishes (minor, short-term battles) broke out, President James Polk offered to buy California and New

Below: Sam Houston led the Texian forces after the Alamo and Goliad. Bottom: "News from the Mexican War Front" shows how interested people were in the war.

Top: The Battle of Chapultepec Castle was the last battle of the Mexican-American War. Above: In the war, General Zachary Taylor won major victories at Monterrey and Buena Vista.

Mexico and to take on Mexico's debt in order to keep the Rio Grande as the border. Mexico's response was an invasion of Texas.

Polk sent General Zachary Taylor and 3,500 troops to observe the happenings along the Rio Grande. After several of Taylor's men were killed in what some called a staged provocation of the small Mexican army, Polk asked Congress to declare war on Mexico.

The first time the two nations met was at Palo Alto, and the battle provided an indication of what was to come. Taylor, called "Old Rough and Ready" by his troops, easily defeated a force twice his size. Then in a follow-up campaign, 1,700 U.S. troops defeated a Mexican force of 4,500. American losses in both battles were 50 men; Mexican losses totaled more than 1,000.

In September 1847, after six months of hard fighting and as the war drew to a close, General Winfield Scott led 7,000 troops to Mexico City. There they were met by about 1,100 Mexican troops and a small group of cadets who attended the military academy at Chapultepec Castle. Ordered by their commandant to leave, the cadets—boys between the

As American soldiers marched across the dry, dusty land, they were covered with a thin white film that resembled Mexican adobe. The Mexican soldiers nicknamed the American troops "dobies" or "doughboys." That name stuck for the next one hundred years.

ages of 13 and 17—instead joined the battle. One of the cadets, Juan Escutia, died clutching the Mexican flag to keep it away from American troops. In Mexican history, these cadets are referred to as "Los Niños Heroes," or the boy heroes of Chapultepec. The event is lovingly commemorated by citizens of Mexico each September 13.

After American forces took Mexico City, the two countries signed the Treaty of Guadalupe Hidalgo. The treaty gave the United States more than 500,000 square miles of territory, which today includes California, Nevada, Utah, Arizona, most of New Mexico, and parts of Wyoming and Colorado. Mexico agreed to drop its claims on Texas lands at the Rio Grande. In turn, Polk agreed to pay Mexico $18.25 million, about 20 percent less than he had originally offered for the land. More than 112,000 Americans fought in the war, including over 2,100 Georgians. Although over 1,500 soldiers died in battle, more than 12,000 American soldiers died from diseases and accidents.

In 1853, through the Gadsden Purchase, the United States obtained the southern part of New Mexico for $10 million. With that purchase, the country's continental boundaries ran from coast to coast.

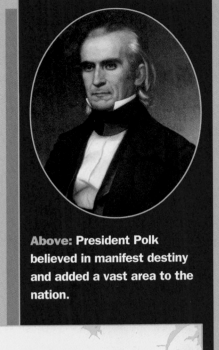

Above: President Polk believed in manifest destiny and added a vast area to the nation.

Oregon

Another land area wanted by the United States was the Oregon Territory. This region was west of the Rocky Mountains and north of California. It stretched northward to 54° 40' north latitude, which today is British Columbia's northern border. Great Britain and the United States had an ongoing dispute over the location of the boundary line between Canada and the United States. Americans claimed it should be drawn at 54° 40' north latitude. The British disagreed, and war was a possibility.

In a 1818 treaty, the United States and Great Britain had set the boundary between the United States and Canada at the 49th parallel (49° north latitude) westward from the Lake of the Woods (in Minnesota) to the Continental Divide. (The *Continental Divide* is a series of mountain ridges from Alaska to Mexico that divides the areas drained by different river systems.) After many negotiations, the two countries agreed to split the Oregon Territory by extending the border along the 49th parallel to the Pacific coast.

California

When the Mexican-American War was over, America's borders stretched from the Atlantic to the Pacific. Thousands of pioneers heeded Horace Greeley's advice of "Go west, young man" and moved into the new territories. Their reasons for moving west were many. Some wanted adventure; some were

**Map 30
Expansion of the United States**

Map Skill What states were included—in total or in part—in the Oregon Territory?

Above: Those who came to mine for California's gold were called "forty-niners."

It's Your Turn

1. What was the concept of *manifest destiny*?
2. Did Santa Anna have reason to be angry with the Texians? How would your life be different today if Texas had remained a part of Mexico?
3. What boundary dispute was reflected by the campaign slogan "54-40 or fight"?

looking for riches. Many wanted new lands for farming, mining, or trapping. Some, such as the Mormons, were escaping religious persecution; others just wanted to escape the overcrowded cities of the East.

The Oregon and Santa Fe trails were the favored routes west. Settlers rode months in covered wagons across barren and hostile lands facing Indian attacks, severe weather, the harsh Rocky Mountains, and frontier hardships. Many died along the way and were buried beneath the hardpacked trails. But none of these hardships stopped thousands from leaving hearth and home once they heard the word *gold*.

In 1829, gold had been discovered in Dahlonega, creating the country's first gold rush. Twenty years later, an even greater gold rush took place. In January 1848, John Marshall was building a lumber mill for John Sutter on California's American Fork River. He discovered something shiny in the river. Marshall had discovered the gold in the California hills. The two men tried to keep the discovery secret, but word got out. In December 1848, President James Polk confirmed the presence of gold, and a national stampede toward California got underway. People traveled in wagon trails, on horseback, and on foot to reach the gold fields. They came not just from the eastern United States but also by ship around the Cape of Good Horn and by mule trains from Panama. Mining camps sprang up overnight as over 80,000 people rushed into California. Between 1848 and 1850, the population of the area increased tenfold. Many who traveled west in search of riches never found any gold, but they stayed to settle the frontier territory trapping, ranching, and farming.

Deepening Divisions

Section Preview

As you read, look for:
• the differences between North and South during the antebellum period,
• southern class structure,
• slavery and the compromises made in the 1800s,
• differences between the economies of the North and South, and,
• vocabulary terms: states' rights, yeoman farmer, overseer, abolition, free state, slave state, Missouri Compromise, sectionalism, Compromise of 1850, Kansas-Nebraska Act, popular sovereignty, and free soiler.

During the antebellum period, the nation was basically divided into four sections. Among these four sections were political, economic, social, and cultural differences as well as some specific cause-and-effect events.

While the western territorial boundaries were expanding, differences between the other sections of the country were intensifying, particularly between the North and the South. Look at Figure 18 on page 216 to get an idea of how these differences eventually led to war.

States' Rights

Probably the simplest or at least the clearest difference between the North and South involved the concept of states' rights. **States' rights** is the belief that the state's interests should take precedence over the interests of the national government.

Northern states believed that, in order for the United States to function as one Union, political decisions should be made that would benefit the entire country. They believed that all states should abide by laws made by Congress, signed by the president, or decreed by the courts.

Southern states, on the other hand, believed deeply in the idea of states' rights. They thought that states had the right to govern themselves and to decide what would be best for their own needs and situation. They believed that politicians from a state like Maine or New York could not possibly understand or care about South Carolina or Georgia.

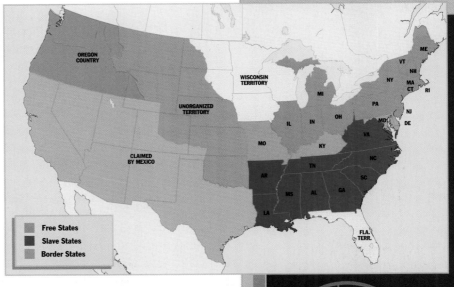

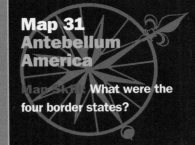

Map 31 Antebellum America

Map Skills: What were the four border states?

Class Structure

As Figure 18 indicates, class structure in the North was generally based on wealth. That wealth allowed people to move upward from one social class to another. In the South, however, the social structure was based more on class and, even though that included money, being "born into the right family." Southern class differences were quite rigid, and it was far more difficult to move upward from one group to another.

Although there had been a highly defined social structure in America since its beginnings, it became even more rigid during the antebellum era. Georgia's social structure mirrored that of the other southern states.

Figure 18   North-South Differences

Issue	North	South
Slavery	Wanted to abolish slavery.	Supported slavery.
States' rights	Believed in a strong national government.	Believed that states had the right to rule themselves.
Economy	Based on factories, mining, banks, stores, and railroads.	Based on agriculture, including cotton, tobacco, and rice. Cotton was shipped north to make cloth and thread.
Tariffs	Favored high tariffs on goods from other countries so goods manufactured in North cost less and would outsell foreign goods.	Favored low tariffs because they bought so many goods from other countries.
Culture	Had a number of large cities offering museums, opera, lectures, theaters.	Had few large cities other than Richmond, Charleston, Savannah, Augusta.
Education	Many private schools, including church-sponsored schools, accepted both boys and girls. Some public schools were open to both. Private universities such as Brown, Harvard, Yale were opening.	No formal educational system in the South. Private tutors or school abroad were options for upper class. Some community schools but teachers were not usually trained. Some state-chartered universities such as University of Georgia, University of North Carolina, and some private schools such as Suwanee (University of the South).
Sectionalism	Northern states believed that their stand against slavery and their concerns over tariffs, culture and lifestyle made them the favored, and therefore best, section of the country.	Southern states believed that their stand on slavery was just, their concerns over tariffs were fair, and their culture and lifestyle were to be treasured. They believed in the rights of states to determine their own destiny. They knew their section of the country was best.

Planters

Planters were divided into two categories—large and small. Owners of large plantations were those who owned over fifty slaves and over one thousand acres of land. By 1860, although they represented less than 1 percent of white families, planters were the wealthiest people in the United States. Their lives were filled with luxury in magnificently built mansions.

Planters and their families took part in parties, dance balls, picnics, rides in the country, horse races, fine dining with elegant wines, and week-long house parties. Furniture was imported from Great Britain or specially made for their mansions. Fine day clothes were imported or hand-sewn, and evening dress was most elegant. Each household member, from newborn to master of the plantation, had a slave who served his or her needs—from helping to bathe and dress them, to providing hair dressings or make-up, to bringing refreshments. There were even slaves, usually youngsters, who stood near dining tables and waved large fans during meals and slaves who nursed newborns.

Owners of small plantations owned between twenty and forty-nine slaves and between one hundred and one thousand acres. They made up about 3 percent of the white southern families. They controlled most of the wealth in the South and produced most of its political leaders. Their homes, although not as lavish as the larger plantation homes, were still elegant. In the larger cities, like Athens, Augusta, Macon, and Savannah, their favorite entertainments were theaters, trading shows, and lectures.

Above: The dining room of the Dickey House, built in 1840, is a typical plantation home. It was moved to Stone Mountain Park in 1961.

Farmers with Slaves

Farmers who owned fewer than twenty slaves were about 20 percent of the southern whites. Most of these farmers owned five or fewer slaves. They

**Figure 19
Southern Social
Ladder**

- Planters large and small
- Farmers with Slaves
- Merchants and People of "Letters"
- Yeoman Farmers and Poor Whites
- Free Blacks
- Slaves

made up the small middle class around towns and cities. The head of the household took a direct, day-to-day approach to running the farm. Homes were comfortable but not nearly the size of plantation mansions. Women of the house usually worked side-by-side with a household servant. Parties were only held around holidays and special occasions and included close family and friends. Food and clothes were simpler although adequate, and there was little intermingling with the planter class.

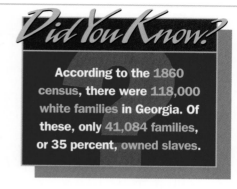

Merchants and "People of Letters"

Members of this class were primarily located in towns and cities. The group included cotton brokers, merchants, teachers, doctors, ministers, newspaper publishers, and lawyers. They made up about 1-2 percent of the population of a city. Many merchants were wealthy and lived in fine brick homes with gardens. They were usually quite knowledgeable about the workings of their city or town. They tended to socialize among their own group and enjoyed a very good life.

Within the merchant group were the *artisans*, people who depended on their own talents and recognition. Artisans kept to themselves within their social class. Some artisans, such as carpenters, bricklayers, millwrights (those who put up mills), saddlers, shoemakers, and milliners were considered to be in the same class as yeoman farmers. Others, such as furniture designers and makers, landscapers, and portrait painters were in the same social class as merchants.

Yeoman Farmers and Poor Whites

Yeoman farmers were by far the largest group of white southerners, making up about 75 percent of the white population. These were independent farmers who often lived from season to season. Many were *subsistence farmers*, who literally lived off the land with almost no cash money. What they needed, they grew or made or got by trading their own goods or homemade products. Overseers (persons hired to manage slaves on a day-to-day basis) were usually considered part of this class. Some of the "better off" yeoman farmers did have a few slaves, but the majority scrambled just to eke out a living.

Life was very hard, and homes were usually unpainted wood cabins or even shacks. Food consisted of what could be raised, traded, or hunted. Their work days ran from "sun up to sun down," and children also worked. Many children ran about barefoot and usually had only two outfits. Leisure time was largely a daydream.

Poor whites were the poorest yeoman farmers and might be squatters, day laborers, or those who simply wandered from place to place seeking jobs,

food, and clothes. This group included those known primarily as "white trash." They seldom worked and depended upon others for survival.

Free Blacks

Free blacks included farmers, day laborers, artisans, or tenant farmers; they were concentrated in the upper South in Maryland and Virginia. A few free blacks owned slaves and small plantations or large farms, but they could not move in the same social circles as their white counterparts. Free blacks who lived in the South were about 6 percent of the total free black population of 500,000.

Although free in name, they were denied most citizenship rights, and in only two northern states did they have the right to vote. They could not lay claim to public land, travel abroad, or even travel freely in the United States without a pass. In most places, they could not get an education. And, regardless of the state, they were relegated to segregated neighborhoods. In the South, free blacks primarily socialized only with each other.

Slaves

Slaves were about 4 million of the total black population in the country in the 1860s. By far, the majority lived in the South, and by 1860, about 11.5 percent of the slaves lived in Georgia.

There were classes of slaves, which, on some plantations, were as rigid as the class structure among whites. Skin color made a difference in the slave social structure. Slaves with lighter complexions often had positions inside the plantation house, which meant better clothes or hand-me-downs, food, and huts.

Did You Know?

In 1860, there were 3,500 free blacks living in Georgia.

**Figure 20
Slaves' Social Ladder**

Butler or manservant

Coach Driver/ Doorman

Ladies Maid and Dresser

Cook

Household Maids

Slave Driver

Field Hands

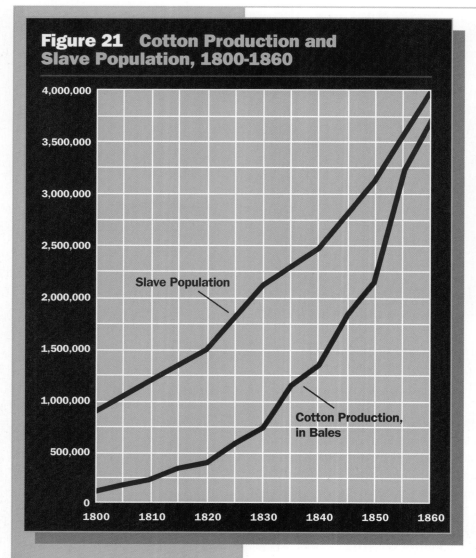

Figure 21 Cotton Production and Slave Population, 1800–1860

Slave Population

Cotton Production, in Bales

The Issue of Slavery

The most divisive issue that led to the Civil War was the question of slavery. Did one man have the right to own another? In order to answer that question, let us first look back in history.

Much of the antebellum period was about "cause and effect," the concept that for each event or thing that happens, there is a *cause*. In turn, each cause leads to a result, or *effect*. Then, that result can cause another event, resulting in a chain reaction of cause-and-effect relationships. Several events from the past directly impacted the antebellum period.

By 1800, the South was stagnant (not growing or changing) both in terms of population growth and agriculture. Tobacco had depleted the soil in Virginia and North Carolina. Rice could only be grown in the coastal areas of South Carolina and Georgia. And cotton was not cost effective. But Eli Whitney's cotton gin greatly increased the profits of growing cotton in the South. In turn, that led to a dramatic increase in the numbers of slaves needed to cultivate "King Cotton." By 1860, the lower South, which became known as the "Cotton Kingdom," produced most of the world's supply of cotton and accounted for over 50 percent of America's exports.

Abolitionists

In the 1820s, a second "Great Awakening" swept the country. One result of this religious revival was increased and interracial support for abolition. Abolition was the movement to do away with slavery.

Many northern whites, some southern whites, and free blacks worked to get rid of slavery. These abolitionists made speeches, wrote books and articles, and offered their homes as safe houses for runaway

When *Uncle Tom's Cabin* was published in 1852, it sold more than one million copies in less than two years. This was a huge number of books, considering not only the population of the country at the time but also the number of people who could read.

Spotlight on the Economy

The Cost of Slavery

It is clear that the institution of slavery damaged the overall economy of the South throughout most of the 1800s. In the 1800s, the U.S. economy was changing. The North, which had an economy based on manufacturing, benefitted from new mechanical inventions and the system of interchangeable parts. The North relied on free labor, workers who earned wages and spent those wages in the communities where they lived and worked. As workers earned more, they spent more on goods and products. This cycle of earning and buying strengthened the economy of the Northeast.

The South remained an agricultural economy focusing on two main products—food and cotton. On the large cotton plantations (those having over fifty slaves) about 40 percent of the crop value came from food production. But southern cotton was still the nation's number one export. The cotton was sold to northern and European markets. As long as the demand for cotton remained high, the prices of cotton remained high and provided incentives for southern plantation owners to continue to plant cotton.

Cotton was labor intensive, requiring large groups of workers who worked in "gangs" or "teams." This gave plantation owners an incentive to continue to use slave labor. By 1860, there were about 4 million slaves in the South, although as many as one-half of all farms in the South had no slaves at all. The southern plantation owners who did use slave labor had much of their personal wealth tied up in slaves. By 1860, almost 60 percent of the agricultural wealth of the Deep South was in slaves, and slave prices had risen steadily throughout the early 1800s. The owner of a plantation with fifty slaves could have as much as $80,000 invested in slave workers. These workers, of

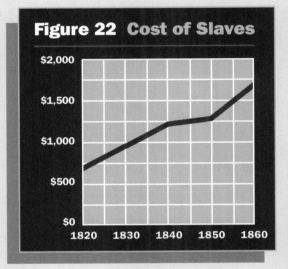

Figure 22 Cost of Slaves

course, produced children who were also slaves to their parents' master. And, of course, plantation owners "invested" additional funds in feeding, clothing, and housing their slaves.

With so much invested in slaves, the large slave owners had little incentive to invest in permanent community improvements such as city infrastructures, transportation systems, public schools, and community health facilities. The plantations did not need local markets for their goods, local communities for free workers or laborers, or urban areas. This lack of investment in the South outside of the large farms or plantations was a serious cost of slavery.

Another cost of slavery was the lack of emphasis southern leaders (large land owners and politically influential plantation owners) placed on investments in technology and mechanized agriculture. As the costs of owning slaves rose, southern farming would have been more profitable with the use of machines and motivated free labor. However, neither was available in an area that had not encouraged either.

Slavery, as an institution, was profitable only for the largest slave owners. Since at least 80 percent of the adult population of the South were free laborers and did not own slaves, slavery was not profitable for the South as a region. The economy of the South was less prosperous overall because of the institution of slavery.

Historians have estimated that the dollar value of the labor produced by slaves in the South between 1790 and 1860 ranged from $7 billion to $40 billion. Without question, that labor would have produced much more for the South had it been the product of free laborers motivated to work hard, to improve themselves, their lives, and their communities.

slaves. In 1831, white abolitionist William Lloyd Garrison published the first issue of his antislavery newspaper *The Liberator*. In *Uncle Tom's Cabin*, Harriet Beecher Stowe wrote about slaves as individuals rather than as a group. Although Stowe, who grew up in Connecticut, had seen slaves only once when visiting in Kentucky, her book described some of the worst things about slavery and the fugitive slave laws. The book was a huge success, and the information in it caused northerners to like slavery less and abolition more.

The best-known black abolitionist was Frederick Douglass, a former slave, who published a newspaper called the *North Star*. Douglass was also a spirited orator (speaker) and traveled around the country describing the evils of slavery.

But the abolitionist movement had a backlash in the South. In the 1820s, Charles Fitzhugh published *Positive Good Thesis of Slavery* in which he characterized slavery as an obligation of whites to feed, clothe, and provide church instruction to slaves. The result was that many southerners actually believed that enslavement was a favor.

Above: Frederick Douglass, born a slave, was a leader in the abolitionist movement.

The Missouri Compromise

In 1819, the United States had twenty-two states. Eleven were slave states (states that did allow slavery), and eleven were free states (states that did not allow slavery). This meant that, in the Senate, there was an equal number of senators from slave states and from free states. In the House of Representatives, the free states had more representatives than the slave states.

In 1819, the territory of Missouri applied for statehood as a slave state. After a great deal of debate, Congress adopted the Missouri Compromise in 1820. Maine entered the Union as a free state, and Missouri entered as a slave state. The measure also prohibited slavery north of 36°20' latitude, which was the southern border of Missouri. This included the Louisiana Territory lands west of Missouri. This compromise kept a balance of power between the free states and slave states in the Senate and provided a temporary solution to the slavery question.

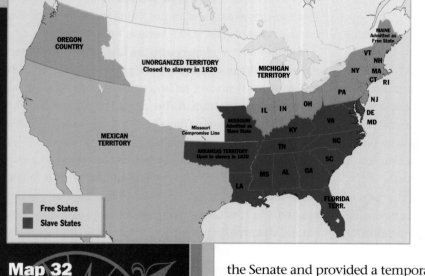

Map 32
The Missouri Compromise

Map Skill: Where were all of the free states located?

In 1836, the House of Representatives adopted a "gag rule" that placed all antislavery petitions "on the table" (no additional action would be taken). The rule so angered former President John Quincy Adams, who was a congressman from Massachusetts, that he fought vigorously to rally northern support. As a result, in one late session, 200,000 antislavery petitions flooded Washington. The rule was rescinded in 1844. but it had accomplished its purpose—it kept blacks as slaves without legislative intervention.

The *Dred Scott* Decision

In 1834, Dred Scott, a slave, was taken by his owner from the slave state of Missouri to the free state of Illinois. Later they went to Wisconsin, another free state. When Scott and his master returned to Missouri, Scott filed a lawsuit claiming he was free since he had lived in a free state.

Abolitionists from the North raised enough money to take the case to the U.S. Supreme Court. In March 1857, the Supreme Court ruled on the case. The justices said Scott could not sue because he was a slave, and slaves were not citizens. The Court also said Congress had no right to stop slavery in territories. The *Dred Scott* decision further divided the North and South and pushed them closer to war.

Sectionalism

As the chart on the differences between the North and South indicated, sectionalism was fast becoming a national issue. Sectionalism is the belief by the people in a given region or area that their ideas and interests are better and more important than those of another region or area. As the country expanded westward, it meant that the slavery question had to be answered. Both Congress and the courts tried.

Above: In 1846, Dred Scott filed suit for his freedom.

The Compromise of 1850

After gold was discovered in California, people from all over the world traveled there dreaming of riches. By late 1849, the population of California was over 100,000, enough to ask for statehood.

In 1850, there were fifteen slave states and fifteen free states. California's constitution did not allow slavery. If California became a state, the balance in the Senate between slave states and free states would change. For eight months, what was later called "The Great Debate" raged as Congress tried to agree on what to do about California.

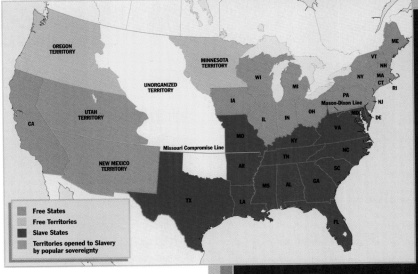

Free States
Free Territories
Slave States
Territories opened to Slavery by popular sovereignty

**Map 33
The Compromise of 1850**

Map Skill: According to the Compromise of 1850, should the Utah Territory have been slave or free?

Seeing that these hotly debated issues might disrupt the Union, Senator Henry Clay of Kentucky proposed a compromise bill in early 1850. Strong leaders on both sides opposed certain parts of the bill. Senator John C. Calhoun of South Carolina would not accept any limits on slavery. President Zachary Taylor would not sign any bill that tied California statehood to other issues. It looked as though compromise was dead and the Union in danger. Instead, death took both men, Calhoun in March and Taylor in July. The new president, Millard Fillmore, favored the compromise.

Above: Kentucky Senator Henry Clay is seen here urging his colleagues to accept the Compromise of 1850 to preserve the Union.

Figure 23 The Compromise of 1850

Benefits for the North

- California came into the Union as a free state.

- Slave trading was ended in the District of Columbia.

- Texas gave up its idea of annexing New Mexico, thus taking that territory away from a slave state.

Benefits for the South

- The territories of New Mexico and Utah would determine whether they wanted to be slave or free.

- The residents of the District of Columbia could keep the slaves they already had.

- Congress would pass a law (the Fugitive Slave Act) stating that slaves who ran away to free states would be returned to their owners.

Clay's **Compromise of 1850** was thus passed by Congress. The compromise offered something to please both North and South (see Figure 23).

Kansas-Nebraska Act

The slavery issue, however, would not die. As more people moved into the grassy plains west of Missouri and Iowa, there was a need for a territorial government. In 1854, Stephen Douglas of Illinois brought about passage of the **Kansas-Nebraska Act**, which created the territories of Kansas and Nebraska and which contained a clause on popular sovereignty. **Popular sovereignty** meant that when a territory asked for statehood, the people of a territory could vote on whether they wanted to be a free state or slave state. Northerners were angry because this law changed the Missouri Compromise, which did not permit slavery north of Missouri's southern boundary.

Did You Know?

There was so much **violence** in **Kansas** between the proslavery **people and the free soilers that the territory was called "Bleeding Kansas."**

Most people in the new territories belonged to one of two groups: proslavery or free soil. **Free soilers** were against slavery and also wanted land to be given to western settlers for farming. After Congress passed the Kansas-Nebraska Act, bloody fights broke out between proslavery and free soil groups. Abolitionists in other states promised to send antislavery

Below: Proslavery "border ruffians" from Missouri on their way to Kansas before the first territorial election in 1855. They took over the polls, prevented free soilers from voting, and ensured the election of a proslavery legislature.

Above: The Butler Plantation, a 19th-century rice plantation on the Altamaha River near Darien. The rice fields used a system of dikes and canals designed by engineers from Holland. The chimney is for a steam-driven rice mill. The plantation was owned by Pierce Butler of Philadelphia, who was married to the famous English actress Fannie Kemble. After a visit here in 1839-40, she wrote "Journal of a Residence on a Georgia Plantation," which, through its depiction of slavery, was believed to have influenced England against the Confederacy.

settlers with guns into Kansas. Missouri proslavery people promised to send men across the border to fight for slavery. When Congress rejected Kansas's bid for statehood, southerners again realized that northern votes alone could keep slave states from the Union.

Economic Considerations

In addition to slavery and sectional differences, there were striking economic contrasts between the North and the South, including the major sources of their wealth. Because of these vastly different sources, the North and the South also disagreed on trade policies and restraints.

Agriculture Versus Industry

The economy of the North was based on industry. A cold climate and short growing season in the New England states meant there was little profit in farming. Northerners worked in factories, mines, banks, stores, and on railroads. The railroad system carried their industrial products to other parts of the country.

The South, on the other hand, depended on agriculture. Cotton and tobacco were the two main crops, but there were also rice plantations on the Georgia and South Carolina coasts. Even though cotton was "king" in the South, southerners shipped most of it to northern states where mills made thread and cloth. In 1850, there were 564 mills in New England. These mills employed 61,893 workers and had a value of over $58 million, In the South, there were only 166 mills, with 10,043 workers and a value of $7.25 million.

In fact, the antebellum South manufactured only 10 percent of the nation's goods. Few farmers and planters were interested in factories.

Tariffs

Tariffs, or taxes on imported goods, were another source of conflict between the North and the South. Northern states wanted foreign countries that shipped goods to the United States to pay high tariffs. With high tariffs, items made in the North would cost less than imported ones. For example, a suit made and sold in Boston might cost $50. With an import tax of $20, an identical suit made in Great Britain and sold in Boston might cost $70. Customers would more likely buy the American-made suit.

Southern states had fewer factories and, therefore, bought many manufactured goods from foreign countries. Southerners did not want the prices they paid on imported goods made higher by tariffs.

In 1832, South Carolina threatened to secede from the Union because a new tariff was too high. South Carolinians began to arm themselves and hold practice drills. President Andrew Jackson asked Congress to allow him to take an army into South Carolina and force them to accept the tariff. Instead, Congress passed a compromise tariff law, which reduced the tariff over a ten-year period. The compromise pleased South Carolinians, and their protests ended.

The differences over tariffs became worse when a depression, known as the Panic of 1857, hit the country. Before that time, many northern industrialists built their factories with borrowed money. Nearly five thousand of them went bankrupt during the Panic of 1857. The factory owners asked Congress to pass higher tariffs to stop the British from shipping goods to the United States. Because there were so few factories in the South, the depression did not hurt southerners as badly. Their representatives, therefore, refused to support higher tariffs. The debates that followed further damaged feelings between the North and South.

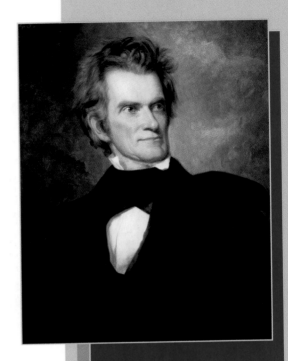

Above: Vice President John C. Calhoun of South Carolina strongly opposed the tariff Congress passed in 1828. He supported states' rights and believed that the states had a right to nullify any federal law that they thought was unconstitutional. In 1832, he resigned the vice presidency to take a seat in the U.S. Senate where he believed he could better help southern interests.

It's Your Turn

1. What is your opinion of states' rights? Support your opinion with some factual information.
2. Knowing what you know about the rigid social ladder of antebellum society, in which social class would you have been most comfortable? Explain your response.
3. Why was the lower South called the "Cotton Kingdom"?
4. Why was the Compromise of 1850 so important?
5. On what was the economy of the North based?
6. What percent of the nation's industrial goods were manufactured in the South?

Slavery as a Way of Life

As you have read, the slavery issue had been emotionally charged for some time. But that did little to make daily life for slaves more bearable.

Daily Life for Slaves

While the arguments over slavery intensified, the daily lives of slaves became even more harsh. Most slaves who worked on plantations lived in one-room huts with fireplaces for heating and cooking. They had little furniture—perhaps a table, some chairs, and pallets to sleep on. Slave housing was poorly built with inferior materials or with timber and stone found nearby. The house usually had stick-and-dirt chimneys, one door, and one window without glass. These slave huts were often small, crowded, and smoky. Some slaveholders did provide sturdier housing for their workers, but this was more the exception than the rule.

Slaves wore clothing made from materials that would last a long time. Usually there was only one set of clothing for a slave—heavy pants or skirts, shirts or blouses that rarely fit, along with wide-brimmed hats, heavy-duty

Section Preview

As you read, look for:
• daily life for slaves in Georgia,
• how slaves fought back against slavery, and
• vocabulary terms: driver, slave code, arsenal, and underground railroad.

Below: Slave housing offered only the most basic shelter and furnishings. Visitors can see these reconstructed slave cabins at Stone Mountain Park.

shoes, socks or stockings, and under-garments. Slaves frequently worked barefoot in the fields. House slaves fared better and often were given clothes that members of the planta-tion family no longer wore.

Slaves' diet usually consisted of fatback, molasses, and corn bread. On some plantations, slaves could have a vegetable garden and fish in streams and ponds. Sometimes, plantation owners gave the slaves rabbits, opossums, squirrels, or other small game they had killed.

Work Routines

The jobs done by slaves varied according to the crops grown in dif-ferent parts of the state. Those who worked for rice planters were said to have the "hardest work" that slaves could have. The slaves worked long hours in flooded, swampy fields and were bent over most of the time. Each was expected to produce four or five barrels of rice a season. (A barrel weighed about 500 pounds.) It took two acres of land to produce the four or five barrels.

Cotton and tobacco were equally demanding crops. Slaves spent many hours in the hot summer sun "chopping cotton" to remove the never-end-ing weeds. From August to November, slaves had to pick the cotton by hand, stooping over each plant. Sometimes there were as many as six pickings dur-ing the season, because the cotton ripened gradually instead of all at once.

Field hands worked in the cotton, tobacco, or rice fields six days a week. They started before the sun came up and stayed until sundown. When it was time to harvest the crops, both adults and children had a set amount to bring in each day. If a slave did not harvest enough, the owner or overseer might punish him or her. Owners and overseers always watched slaves to make sure they stayed busy.

Besides working in the fields, the slaves also cut down and sawed trees, rolled logs, and cleared vines and underbrush. They loaded crops on vessels, repaired ditches, and built dikes. Anytime the overseer was displeased in any way, a lashing on

Did You Know?

Rice is still grown in Georgia at the Maryfield Plantation in Camden County.

Above: Cotton had to be picked by hand, as illustrated in this engraving entitled "Picking Cotton on the Coast." There could be as many as six pickings during the season.

a bare back was the likely punishment. Frequently, **drivers** (older slaves the plantation owner thought were loyal) were also used to supervise the field hands.

Slave women worked just as hard as slave men. When not working in the fields, they spent time spinning, sewing, weaving, preparing food, and minding children. Even the children worked, sometimes starting as young as five years old. They shooed chickens out of the garden and flies off the table. The children carried water to the workers in the field, gathered nuts and berries, and collected kindling for fires. They continued working until they were either too old or too sick to be of any use in the fields or the "big house."

Slave Families

Given the harshness of their lives, the black family proved remarkably strong. The slave community extended far beyond a particular plantation. Slaves who could not find marriage partners on their own plantations often found them on other plantations. Masters encouraged slave women to marry men on adjoining farms or plantations because any children that came from such a union became the property of the woman's master.

Unfortunately, the law did not recognize slave marriages. Even though many masters tried not to separate black families, that tragedy often happened. Changes in a master's life made slaves especially vulnerable. Marriage, death, or relocation in the slaveholder's family were the greatest threats to a slave family's stability. Planters often made presents of slaves to newly married children. In their wills, planters divided slaves among white family members. Slaves were also sold to pay off debts or to remove black troublemakers.

Religion and Education

Religion played a key role in the lives of slaves. During the Great Revival of the early 1800s, most blacks—free and slave—converted to Christianity.

Many large plantations had a church where both slaves and the plantation family attended services on Sunday mornings. The white ministers of these churches gave sermons on the theme "Servants, obey your masters." In the slave quarters, black preachers delivered a far different message. Here, and wherever slaves were allowed to have church meetings of their own, the black preachers voiced a strong desire for freedom and justice.

Spiritual songs were an important part of slave life. Slaves sang them at church, home, and work. The words gave them comfort and spoke of faith in God and belief in freedom. Spirituals such as "Go Down Moses," "Swing

Below: During the early 1800s, black preachers often delivered sermons to mixed audiences. Bottom: These slaves are waiting to be sold at a slave auction.

Low Sweet Chariot," "Nobody Knows the Trouble I See," and others all spoke of the need for comfort. Some songs were written to send a message. For example, "Follow the Drinking Gourd" gave directions for the underground railroad. The song "Michael, Row the Boat Ashore" was also a song about slavery and escape.

Education was almost nonexistent for most slaves. It was against the law for a slave owner to teach any slave to read or write. Some owners, however, recognized that it was useful to have slaves who could read well enough to distinguish labels on barrels of foodstuffs or to be able to write simple messages. In these instances, the slave owner or his wife used the Bible to teach their slaves the basics of reading and writing. However, the slaveholders also feared that slaves who could read and write might also use their talents to stir up discontent among other slaves and lead to uprisings.

Above: Nat Turner, a slave preacher from Virginia, believed God wanted him to end slavery in America. In 1831, he led a revolt that resulted in the deaths of over fifty whites and numerous slaves. Turner was captured and hanged.

Rules and Rebellions

Some slaves fought their enslavement. In 1800, Gabriel Prosser gathered as many as 1,000 slaves in Richmond, Virginia, and planned to carry out the largest slave revolt in U.S. history. Betrayed by two slaves, word of the rebellion was passed to slave owners. Prosser did not know he had been betrayed, but a severe thunderstorm stopped the rebellion. Prosser was arrested and executed for his plans.

In 1822, free black carpenter Denmark Vesey's failed slave rebellion involved over 5,000 blacks in Charleston, South Carolina. As a side effect of that incident, the eminent South Carolina A.M.E. leader Morris Brown (for whom one of our colleges in Atlanta is named) was named as a suspect in the rebellion. He moved north, where he later succeeded Richard Allen as bishop of the A.M.E. Church.

In 1831, Nat Turner led the bloodiest slave revolt in American history in Virginia. Between fifty-seven and eighty-five people were killed. After Nat Turner's insurrection in 1831, strict laws were passed throughout the South to curtail slave movements, meetings, and efforts to learn to read and write. These laws applied to both slaves and freed blacks. The latter were considered a threat because they might help educate slaves or help them escape.

It was hard for a group of slaves on one farm to get messages to groups in other places. When slaves left their plantation, they either went with the owner or overseer or had to have a pass. Because passes stated where slaves could go and when they must be back, secret meetings were almost impossible. In addition, the fugitive slave laws required that runaway slaves be returned to their masters.

By 1833, another literary law in Georgia provided that any teaching of people of color would result in fines and public whippings. That same year, an employment law prohibited people of color from working in any job that even involved reading or writing. That law, and similar restrictions throughout the South, was passed to cut down on the number of runaway slaves who moved into large cities and towns and use forged papers to get jobs as free blacks. A few years later the job prohibition extended to drug stores and by 1845, Georgians were prohibited from making any contact with black mechanics.

Other laws, called slave codes, took away nearly all the rights of slaves. It was against the law for them to testify against whites, show disrespect to white persons, make any type of contact, hit a white, or carry a weapon. On some plantations, overseers counted hoes, pitchforks, and shovels at the end of the day so they could not be kept for use as weapons. Slaves had little time to talk together. They were watched every day except Sundays, and on holidays like Christmas, New Year's Day, and the Fourth of July. Even some free blacks who owned slaves kept a careful eye on them.

Above: John Brown was a fiery abolitionist. He is best known for his campaigns on behalf of free soilers in Missouri and Kansas and his attack on the federal arsenal at Harpers Ferry. He was tried and convicted of treason for his raid on Harpers Ferry. His death made him a martyr to many northerners.

Did You Know?

One of John Brown's prisoners was Lewis Washington, the great-grandnephew of George Washington. Brown took him prisoner in order to obtain a sword that had been given to George Washington by Frederick the Great of Russia and inscribed "From the oldest general in the world to the greatest."

Even with additional laws and restrictions, there were still instances of rebellion on plantations. Actions such as breaking farm equipment, pulling down fences, damaging boats, ruining clothing, and setting fires to barns or stables were gestures of rebellion. So was careless work in fields. While such rebellion did not end slavery, it did add a sense of purpose to a slave's endless drudgery and feelings of hopelessness.

Another incident added to the fears of slave owners. White abolitionist John Brown hated slavery. In 1859, he decided to try to help slaves in the South become free of their owners. To do this, Brown needed guns and ammunition.

Brown led a party of twenty-one men, blacks as well as whites, in a raid on the federal **arsenal** (arms storehouse) at Harpers Ferry, Virginia (now in West Virginia). They made prisoners of a number of prominent citizens. Then Brown and his men took over the building where the guns were stored.

Within twenty-four hours, troops led by Colonel Robert E. Lee had captured Brown. Two months later, the state of Virginia tried Brown for treason and sentenced him to be hanged. Not long before he died, Brown wrote to his family and said he was as content "to die for God's eternal truth on the scaffold as in any other way."

Southerners thought John Brown was a murderer, and they were afraid others would try to lead slaves to rise up against owners. Many northerners opposed Brown's tactics but they saw Brown as a hero. Henry Wadsworth Longfellow wrote, "This will be a great day in our history, the date of a new revolution. . . . As I write, they are leading old John Brown to execution. . . . This is sowing the wind to reap the whirlwind which will come soon. . . ." Longfellow was so right.

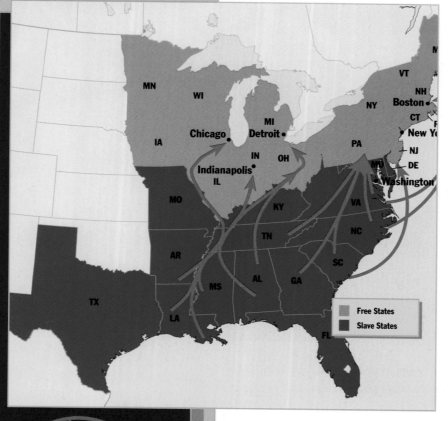

**Map 34
The Underground
Railroad**

Map Skill: Through which free states did most of the routes run?

Riding the Underground Railroad

As abolitionists did what they could to end slavery, other groups took a different approach by helping slaves escape. They helped slaves flee the South and travel to selected northern states or to Canada. One of the most notable groups was a mixture of whites and blacks who operated the **underground railroad**.

The underground railroad was responsible for helping thousands of slaves escape into freedom. But it was not easy. Technically, the underground railroad was a network of roads, houses, river crossings, boats and wagons, woods and streams that provided a trail of flight. Trips, by horse-drawn carts, carriages, or even a real rail car, could take weeks or even months. Stops along the way were called *stations* where a lantern or a candle in a window meant warmth, a hot meal, or even a change of clothes at the homes of station masters. Underground railroad workers also gave directions and help for the next leg of the journey, while conductors led groups to freedom. According to some reports, even quilts hanging on a line could provide instructions

Sojourner Truth

Isabella Baumfree was born a slave in New York around 1797. She was freed in 1827 when New York abolished slavery. She moved to New York City and worked as a housekeeper, spending her spare time in religious instruction and prayer at a white Methodist Church. Later, she joined the A.M.E. Church. After about fifteen years, she emerged a "remade woman" and became a traveling preacher, taking on the name "Sojourner Truth."

With little more than the clothes she wore, Sojourner walked throughout Long Island, New York, and Connecticut sharing her beliefs with all she met. This six-foot-tall, deep-voiced woman was said to bring an audience to tears with her stories and teachings. In 1843, she went to live at the Northhampton Association of Education and Industry in Florence, Massachusetts, which was dedicated to the abolition of slavery, equality, and the betterment of society. She worked alongside William Lloyd Garrison, publisher of *The Liberator*, and influential abolitionist Frederick Douglass. Douglass referred to Sojourner Truth as "a strange compound of wit and wisdom, of wild enthusiasm, and flintlike common sense."

Her published memoirs, *The Narrative of Sojourner Truth: A Northern Slave*, made her a popular speaker on the anti-slavery and woman's rights lecture circuits. For ten years, she mesmerized audiences with her speeches, and none was more famous than her "Ain't I a Woman?" speech, which was delivered before a woman's rights convention in Akron, Ohio, in 1851.

Truth moved to Battle Creek, Michigan, where she lived and continued her abolitionist work. She traveled to Washington, D.C., during the Civil War years, meeting twice with President Lincoln and once with President Grant. According to reports, during the meetings with Lincoln she begged him to allow black soldiers to fight on the Union side in the war.

After the Emancipation Proclamation was issued, Sojourner Truth moved to Washington where, in her late 60s she worked tirelessly with former slaves through the National Freedmen's Relief Association and the Freedman's

Above: Sojourner Truth, an extraordinary woman.

Bureau. She also spoke constantly about the promise of the government to grant free lands in Kansas, but this goal was never met. However, many former southern slaves known as *Exodusters*, did move to Kansas in 1879, an action she applauded and in which she assisted. She believed that property ownership and education were the two keys to the advancement of blacks.

Finally, in 1882, at the age of 83, she was forced to give up her preaching and teaching. She retired to Battle Creek, where she lived with her daughter until her death three years later. She is remembered as one of the notable women in our nation's history.

through different patterns, although recent historians have doubts about that.

Before 1850, escaped slaves were safe when they reached such cities as Philadelphia, Cincinnati, New York, or Boston. But after the Fugitive Slave Act was passed, slave trackers could go into these cities, capture the escaped slaves, and return them to their owners in the South. The underground railroad then extended its line into Canada.

Although there were white abolitionist conductors, such as James Fairfield who posed as a slave trader and traveled into the Deep South, perhaps the best known conductor was ex-slave Harriet Tubman. She was named "Moses" and, like the Biblical figure, she brought her people—more than three hundred—out of bondage and into the promised land.

It's Your Turn

1. Why would religion have been so important in the life of a slave?
2. Why did the southern slaves pass slave codes?
3. Based on your reading, sketch a portrait of slave life.

Antebellum Georgia

Section Preview

As you read, look for:
• Georgia's antebellum economy,
• Georgia's antebellum political leaders, and
• vocabulary term: Know Nothing party.

As you learned in the last chapter, during the early part of the antebellum period, Georgians worked hard to remove Native Americans from the state in order to obtain their land. After that was accomplished, the citizens of the state turned their full attention to other interests.

Georgia's Economy

The backbone of Georgia's economy was agriculture. By 1860, there were 68,000 farms in the state, and cotton was the main crop. The farms produced 700,000 bales of cotton in 1860. This was a 115 percent increase from 1839. Most of Georgia's farms were less than one hundred acres. Only 3,500 farms had five hundred acres or more and could be called plantations. Because the land itself did not cost much, a plantation owner's worth was largely measured by the number of slaves he owned. Only 236 Georgians owned more than 100 slaves, and 60 percent had no slaves at all.

Just before the Civil War, half of Georgia's total wealth, or $400 million, was in slaves. In 1845, a good field hand cost $600; by 1860, the price had risen to $1,800. In major slave markets, such as those in Augusta, Louisville, Macon, or Savannah, the value of a slave was determined by the cost of a pound of cotton. A planter had to sell 16,500 pounds of processed cotton to buy such a slave, and he bought the slave to increase his cotton production.

Most manufacturing in Georgia grew out of agriculture. The state had about 40 cotton mills in the area where cotton was grown. There were also a few tanneries, shoe factories, iron foundries, grist mills, and brick and pottery factories. All told, Georgia had 1,890 factories by 1860 with a value of about $11 million. Even so, Georgia's industrial base was far smaller than that of a comparable northern state.

Below: The first train to arrive in Terminus had to be pulled into town by sixteen mules hitched to a wagon.

Of Special Interest

A Discovery

In 1842, John Tyler was president, the question of Texas becoming a state was still being debated in Congress, and the Civil War was nineteen years away. There was, however, one thing on which all Americans could agree—the mere mention of the word *surgery* instantly brought feelings of horror. In those days, surgeons were known for their speed in operating. A good surgeon could amputate a leg in ninety seconds. Why was that important? Because, in those days, patients were awake during the entire surgery!

Before any surgery was started, patients were given several swallows of alcohol or opiates (pain-killing drugs). Physicians' assistants stood over the patients holding down their legs and arms. Some patients were simply knocked unconscious. Many men, women, and children died from infections rather than face surgery. Who could blame them? But in 1842, 27-year-old physician Dr. Crawford W. Long, who had been born in Danielsville, Georgia, began the process of freeing people from the excruciating pain of surgery's knife.

Dr. Long entered Franklin College (later the University of Georgia) when he was only fourteen. After training at Transylvania University and the University of Pennsylvania and interning in New York, the young doctor returned to Georgia to set up his medical practice in Jefferson. After observing how people at parties reacted to taking ether,

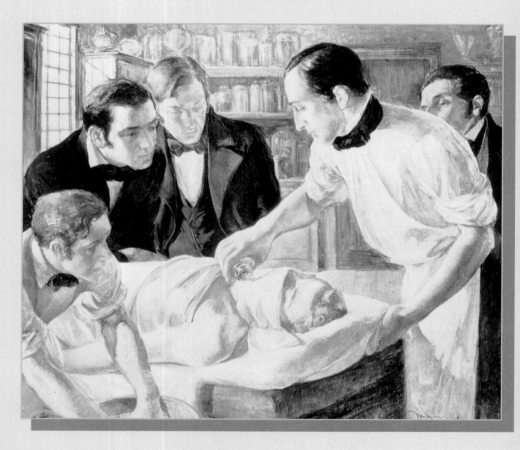

Above: In 1842, Dr. Crawford Long operated on James Venable and used ether to make him unconscious. Venable felt no pain during the operation. Dr. Long continued to use perform other surgeries using either.

he decided to conduct some experiments with sulfuric ether. One day, James Venable asked Dr. Long to remove a painful cyst, or tumor, on his neck. Dr. Long decided to use ether on his patient as an anesthetic. It worked!

Although Dr. Long was excited about his discovery, he failed to publish his findings. As a result, Dr. William Morton, who publically demonstrated the use of ether in tooth extractions, was given credit for discovering the anesthesia. But we in Georgia know, don't we!

Education

Education was not an important element in the life of most antebellum Georgians. The sons of some wealthy planters had tutors (private teachers) in their homes or went to private academies. However, most Georgians had little education.

In 1850, about 20 percent of Georgia's whites could not read or write. About half of Georgia's children were black and did not go to school at all. In 1858, the state legislature, using income from the state-owned Western and Atlantic Railroad, set aside $100,000 to begin free schools. But before plans were finished, the Civil War started and education was put aside.

There were other developments in the field of education during the 1850s. In 1851, Georgia Military Institute was founded in Marietta. In the same year, the Georgia Academy for the Blind was begun in Macon. Later, in 1859, Joseph Lumpkin and Thomas Cobb founded Georgia's first law school in Athens.

Religion

Like many others in the South, Georgians were caught up in the Great Revival movement of the early 1800s. Religious revivals, often in the form of camp meetings, were popular, especially among Methodists. Sometimes people came from miles away and camped while attending a two- or three-day meeting. Often, the camp meetings lasted for a week or longer.

Top and above: The Stewart County Academy at Westville. Visitors can see what school was like in the 1850s.

On the Road Again

Westville

The idea for Westville came from former history professor and college president John Ward West. The reconstructed Westville was first brought to life in 1968. Today, you can get a feel for life in the 1800s by wandering through over thirty-five structures such as the blacksmith shop, country doctor's office, cotton gin, churches, cabinet shop, and shoe-making workroom. You can also visit the log cabin homes of the early residents and see the "showplace" homes where the town's wealthier citizens lived. And be sure to see the old school house. You will find it very different from your classroom.

Another unique aspect of a trip to Westville is a tour of an 1854 Chattahoochee County courthouse, which was moved into Westville in 1975 to save the historic structure. It is the only antebellum wood-frame county courthouse in our state that has not undergone structural changes. It fea-

Above: Westville is a living history village. The buildings were all built before 1850. This is a merchant's house.

tures entrances on all sides, twin stairways to the second floor courtroom, and original courthouse furnishings. Because of this courthouse, Westville is on Georgia's Historic Courthouse Tour.

During a visit to Westville, you will find the townspeople going about their business on the dirt streets. You can ask them questions about life in the 1800s, and you can observe the craftspeople as they show you how to cobble shoes, make candles or furniture, or cook biscuits.

On July 4, the people of Westville celebrate as people did in the mid-1800s. There is a fall festival to celebrate the harvest season and a spring festival when the restored nineteenth-century town is in full bloom.

Top left: Townspeople practice traditional skills. This is the blacksmith. **Top right:** The potter uses local clay. **Above left:** The store for Johann G. Singer Boots and Shoes. **Above right:** This basketmaker displays his skills. **Left:** The Chattahoochee County courthouse occupies a special place on the town square.

During the 1850s, church membership grew in Georgia; by 1860, there were 2,393 churches in the state. In the South, Georgia was second only to Virginia in the number of churches. Methodist and Baptist were the two largest denominations, but the Episcopal, Catholic, and Presbyterian churches also grew during this period. Jews, one of colonial Georgia's earliest religious groups, were few in number, but they added to the state's religious diversity. There were a few segregated churches, but slaves usually attended the same churches as their masters.

Slavery caused great divisiveness among some denominations. Methodists in the South pulled out of their national organization and formed the Methodist Episcopal Church. In 1845, southern Baptists met in Augusta to form the Southern Baptist Convention. Baptists in the South left the American Baptist Union when its foreign mission board would not accept slave owners as missionaries.

Georgia Politics

It was hard to keep up with political changes in Georgia during the antebellum period. In the 1840s, the two major political parties were the Democrats and the Whigs.

Democrats supported states' rights and took a strong stand for slavery. Their leaders were Herschel V. Johnson, Joseph E. Brown, and U.S. Congressman Howell Cobb.

Below: The Old Governor's Mansion in Milledgeville was home to eight of Georgia's governors from 1839 to 1868. **Bottom:** The Old Capitol Building sits on the highest point in Milledgeville. Today it is part of Georgia Military College.

By the Side of the Road

As you visit historic sites in Georgia, be sure to travel to Washington in Wilkes County where several historical markers identify places of interest. One marker describes the home of Robert Toombs and is located at 216 East Robert Toombs Avenue in Washington. Toombs bought the home in 1837.

HOME OF
ROBERT TOOMBS

This was the home of Robert Toombs — planter, lawyer, and distinguished Southern statesman. Born July 2, 1810, Robert Toombs was educated at Franklin College, Georgia, at Union College, New York, and at the University of Virginia. He was a member of the Georgia House of Representatives, 1837-1840, 1842-1845; of the United States House of Representatives, 1845-1853; of the United States Senate from 1853 until his resignation in 1861. He served as Secretary of State, C.S.A., resigning to become a Brigadier General in the Confederate Army. He was a member of the Constitutional Convention in 1877.

Robert Toombs died in this house on December 15, 1885, an "Unreconstructed Rebel." After his death this became the home of his devoted niece, Mrs. Frank Colley.

This marker replaces one erected by the Children of the Confederacy of Georgia in June, 1941.

GEORGIA HISTORICAL COMMISSION

Whigs were mostly members of the upper social classes. They favored a moderate protective tariff and federal help for the South. Robert Toombs and Alexander H. Stephens, both congressmen from Georgia, led the Whigs.

Although there was little real difference in what the two parties believed, each wanted to govern the state. During the 1840s, most governors were Democrats, while most members of the legislature were Whigs. In larger Georgia towns, there were two newspapers: one for Democrats and one for Whigs.

The 1850s brought about a change for both parties. Many Georgians did not like the Compromise of 1850. However, Democrat Cobb and Whigs Stephens and Toombs asked the citizens of Georgia to accept it. All three had strongly supported the measure in the U.S. Congress. In part because of the persuasiveness of these congressmen, the "Georgia Platform" supporting the compromise was adopted at a convention held in the

Did You Know?

Howell Cobb was the Speaker of the U.S. House of Representatives in 1849 and 1850.

Above: As governor of Georgia from 1851 to 1853, Howell Cobb approved the leasing of the state-owned Western and Atlantic Railroad and worked for increased state funding for education.

state capital of Milledgeville. It was clear even to those Georgians who did not approve of it that the compromise was necessary if the state were to stay in the Union.

Not long after the platform was adopted, some Georgians formed the Constitutional Union party. Howell Cobb, an Athens lawyer who had been a Democrat, joined the new party along with former Whigs Stephens and Toombs. Cobb was elected governor in 1851. While he was in office, Cobb encouraged the growth of Georgia's railroad system and state support for schools.

At the same time, Joseph E. Brown, Herschel V. Johnson, and C. B. Strong gathered together some Georgians who did not agree with the Compromise of 1850. This group formed the States' Rights party. The party did not want to leave the Union, but its members thought southern states should not accept the Compromise until Congress agreed to protect slavery and states' rights.

The Constitutional Union party broke up in August 1852. It had done what it set out to do: get Georgians to accept the Compromise of 1850. Toombs and Stephens joined the Democrats, while other Whigs joined the Know Nothing party. The Know Nothing party did not want immigrants to become citizens or anyone not born in the United States to hold political office. It was a secret group whose members answered questions with, "I don't know," thus the name Know-Nothing.

After all the changes, the Democrats became the leading party. In 1856, James Buchanan, the Democratic presidential candidate, carried Georgia with no trouble. The next year, Democrat Joseph E. Brown became governor. Brown believed in states' rights and was also a good manager. He brought about railroad reforms and used money from state-owned railroads to begin a common school fund for public education. Brown was re-elected in 1859, and he served two more terms during the Civil War.

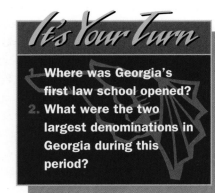

It's Your Turn

1. Where was Georgia's first law school opened?
2. What were the two largest denominations in Georgia during this period?

The Election of 1860

Section Preview

As you read, look for:
- the birth of the Republican party,
- the election of 1860,
- the steps leading to Georgia's secession, and
- vocabulary terms: Republican party, platform, secession, ordinance, and Confederate States of America.

By 1860, the division between the North and the South had become sharper on a number of major issues, and the outlook for reconciling those difference was poor. In addition to the other problems that separated the North and South, new events on the national scene increased the tensions between the two sections. Chief among these was the rise of a new national party and the election of 1860.

The Rise of the Republican Party

Up to this time, the major parties had been national ones. But this was soon to change. Just as it had in Georgia, the Whig party began to break up nationally after the election of 1852. The northern wing of the party had become more antislavery and was less willing to compromise with the southern wing to keep internal peace.

The result was the creation in 1854 of a new political party—one that existed only in the free states. This new party was called the Republican party. It grew quickly, drawing antislavery Whigs and Democrats as members. In 1856, the Republicans nominated Savannah-born John C. Fremont for president on a platform that opposed the spread of slavery. (A platform is a statement of the principles and policies the party supports.) Democrat James Buchanan won, but Fremont managed to get 1.3 million votes.

The Election of 1860

When the Democrats met in Charleston, South Carolina, for the national convention in 1860, a fight over the party platform brought matters to a head. The supporters of Stephen A. Douglas of Illinois controlled the platform committee. They wanted to campaign on the issue of popular sovereignty. Southern Democrats did not agree and believed slavery should be allowed in all the territories. The two groups split over the issue. Northern Democrats nominated Stephen Douglas for president. Southern Democrats met separately in Baltimore and nominated Vice President John Breckenridge of Kentucky for president. Whigs from the border states also met in Baltimore to form the Constitutional Union party. They supported the Union and named John Bell of Tennessee as their presidential candidate.

At the same time, the Republicans met in Chicago, where they nominated Abraham Lincoln of Illinois. The Republican platform was not just against

Above: This photograph of Abraham Lincoln was taken in 1860, before he was elected president.

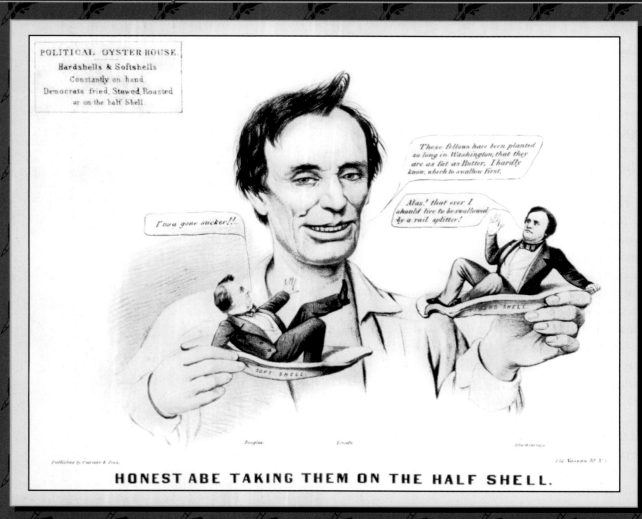

HONEST ABE TAKING THEM ON THE HALF SHELL.

In this 1860 political cartoon, Republican nominee Lincoln is shown in a "Political Oyster House," preparing to swallow two of his Democratic opponents for the presidency—Douglas (left) and Breckinridge (right).

slavery, although the party said it would not try to end slavery in the slave states. It also supported a protective tariff, proposed a plan to give free western land to settlers, and called for the construction of a transcontinental railroad with one end in the North. None of these measures would benefit the South. The Republican party and its presidential candidate, Abraham Lincoln, appeared to be against everything southerners wanted.

The election amounted to a revolution in politics. For the first time, a party getting votes from only one section of the nation won the election. Abraham Lincoln received 1.9 million votes (a minority of the votes cast) and was elected president. Almost all of Lincoln's electoral votes were from the free states. He won without receiving a single electoral vote from the states in the South.

Georgia Reacts to Lincoln's Election

After Lincoln's election, talk of se-cession (the act of pulling out of the Union) and war swirled around every barbecue, quilting bee, and picnic. Wherever Georgians gathered in a group, passionate debates took place. For eighty-four years, the nation had lived with the concept of a union of all states. Now southerners had to deal with questions over the conflict between states' rights and Union rights. Could they believe in the concept of the Union while maintaining a state's right to pass laws for the good of that state rather than to accept laws forced on it by the federal government? There was no easy answer to the question. Georgians were, for the most part, for the Union; however, they were even more strongly for states' rights. Now they were suddenly forced to make a choice, and many households in Georgia found themselves in the midst of a bitter split.

The Call to the Legislators

Immediately after Lincoln's election, Georgia's Democratic governor, Joseph E. Brown, called a legislative session to determine whether a special convention should be held to decide the question of secession. The special session could also suggest that Georgia bide its time and see what South Carolina did. The legislative chamber was buzzing with activity as arguments resounded off the walls and memos and notes were passed back and forth. Speakers rose in quick succession to argue their views. Alexander Stephens of Crawfordville was especially stirring with his arguments against seceding.

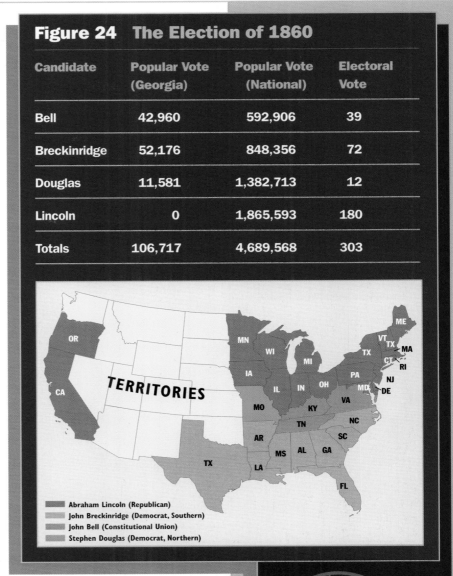

Figure 24 The Election of 1860

Candidate	Popular Vote (Georgia)	Popular Vote (National)	Electoral Vote
Bell	42,960	592,906	39
Breckinridge	52,176	848,356	72
Douglas	11,581	1,382,713	12
Lincoln	0	1,865,593	180
Totals	106,717	4,689,568	303

Abraham Lincoln (Republican)
John Breckinridge (Democrat, Southern)
John Bell (Constitutional Union)
Stephen Douglas (Democrat, Northern)

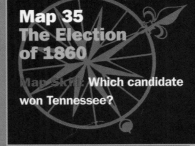

**Map 35
The Election
of 1860**

Map Skill: Which candidate won Tennessee?

Did You Know?

Abraham Lincoln **received** only 16,388 votes **from the** slave states.

The first question that presents itself is, shall the people of Georgia secede from the Union in consequence of the election of Mr. Lincoln to the Presidency of the United States. My countrymen, I tell you frankly, candidly, and earnestly, that I do not think they ought.

In my judgment, the election of no man, constitutionally chosen to that high office, is sufficient cause to justify any State to separate from the Union. It ought to stand by and aid still in maintaining the Constitution of the country. . . .

Whatever fate is to befall this country, let it never be laid to the charge of the people of the South, and especially the people of Georgia, that we were untrue to our national engagements. Let the fault and the wrong rest upon others. If all our hopes are to be blasted, if the Republic is to go down, let us be found to the last moment standing on the deck with the Constitution of the United States waving over heads.

Stephens's speech was interrupted many times by Robert Toombs, who along with Thomas Cobb, strongly supported immediate secession. Other conservative legislators, however, loudly applauded Stephens's pleas for caution. But his eloquence was no match for the fiery leadership of Toombs, Cobb, and Governor Brown. On November 21, 1860, Governor Brown called for a secession convention.

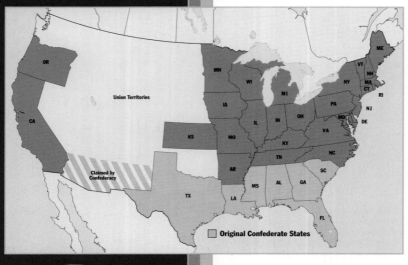

Original Confederate States

Map 36
The Original
Confederate States

Map Skill: What can you say about the location of these seven states?

Top: Governor Joseph E. Brown favored secession and used his terms as governor to prepare the state for war.

South Carolina Secedes

Other southerners, convinced that, with the election of Lincoln, Congress would not allow slavery in the territories, were also calling for action. South Carolinians had repeatedly said that they would secede if Lincoln won the presidency. In December 1860, South Carolina held a secession convention. On December 20, 1860, a little more than a month after Lincoln's election, South Carolina left the Union. Soon after, extremists in every other southern state were loudly yelling for their states to follow South Carolina's lead.

Most Georgians supported South Carolina's action. On January 16, 1861, the special convention requested by Governor Brown was held in Milledgeville. When Eugenius Nisbet proposed a secession ordinance (bill) to the 297 delegates, 208 voted in favor. On January 19, 1861, Georgia was declared an independent republic with the following words: "The people of Georgia, having dissolved their political connection with the Government of the United States of America, present to their confederates and the world, the causes which have led to the separation."

By February 1, 1861, Florida, Alabama, Mississippi, Louisiana, and Texas had also voted to secede from the Union. On February 4, 1861, delegates from each of these states met in Montgomery, Alabama, and formed a new nation called the Confederate States of America. Jefferson Davis of Mississippi was elected president, and Robert Toombs of Georgia was chosen secretary of state. Georgian Alexander Stephens, who had argued so passionately against secession, was named vice president.

War was only two months away.

It's Your Turn

1. Why were southerners against Lincoln's election to the presidency?
2. What was the name the seceding states gave to their new nation? Which states made up the group?
3. Why was Georgia's Alexander Stephens so against seceding and why do you think he was elected vice president of the new group of states?

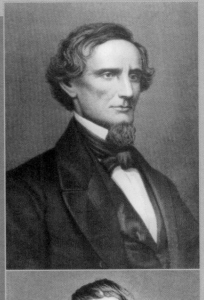

A Final Note

Historians all agree that slavery, sectionalism, and states' rights led to the first and only war within our nation's boundaries. But, there was also another underlying feeling for both sections—a sense of loyalty. One of your Georgia character words, **loyalty** means a person's devotion or feeling of attachment to a person, group, or idea. You have read that most southerners of this period did not own slaves. In addition, some were very much opposed to slavery. Even so, southerners were intensely loyal to their region. When it became apparent that South Carolina would secede from the Union, southerners chose to fight alongside, and die for their friends, neighbors, and strangers.

What are some things or people to whom you feel loyal? Make a list of these ideas or people and beside each, indicate why you are loyal to them. In what ways are you loyal to your school? Be specific. Can loyalty be taken too far? Give at least four examples.

Chapter Summary

- During the antebellum period, the United States followed a doctrine of manifest destiny, expanding its boundaries from ocean to ocean.

- As the antebellum period drew to a close, differences between the North and South intensified.

- The issue that aroused the strongest passions was slavery.

- The daily life of slaves was one of hard work and harsh treatment.

- Several slave revolts were attempted, but none were successful.

- Other issues that divided North and South were sectionalism, economic considerations, cultural differences, and states' rights.

- Finally, national events, especially the election of Abraham Lincoln, caused southern states, including Georgia, to secede from the Union and form the Confederate States of America.

Top: As a senator, Jefferson Davis worked to keep the Union together. He resigned from the Senate in January 1861 and was elected president of the Confederacy one month later. **Above:** Many southerners opposed Alexander Stephens's election as vice president of the Confederacy since he had spoken against secession.

Chapter Review

Reviewing People, Places, and Terms

Match each word or phrase with the correct definition below.

antebellum

driver

overseer

platform

slave code

1. A person responsible for seeing that slaves performed their assigned tasks

2. A set of laws that defined what slaves could or could not do

3. The period before the Civil War

4. A slave placed in charge of a group of slaves

5. A statement of the principles and policies that a political party supports

Understanding the Facts

1. What $10 million purchase completed the physical boundaries of the United States from ocean to ocean?

2. What border dispute led to the Mexican-American War?

3. What abolitionist published the newspaper called *The Liberator*?

4. How many free states were there in 1850?

5. What was meant by the term *popular sovereignty*?

6. In what ways might slaves have learned to read in spite of the conditions that existed at the time?

7. Why did southerners not want higher tariffs?

8. In what year was the Republican party created?

9. Besides slavery, what were the major issues dividing North and South?

Developing Critical Thinking

1. How does social mobility in the South today compare with the social mobility of the antebellum period?

2. How do you think the diets of slaves affected them?

3. If rice, cotton, and tobacco were so difficult for slaves to produce, why do you think slave owners wanted to grow these crops?

4. Why do you think the slave codes were so effective in keeping blacks enslaved?

Checking It Out

1. A *maverick* is a person who stands apart from the crowd or goes her or his own way. The word came from Texas cattleman Samuel A. Maverick, who ranched in San Antonio in the 1840s. Check it out and find out why he became a maverick's Maverick!

2. During the California gold rush, Levi Strauss planned to sell tents and wagon covers to the prospectors. When they were not interested in his tents, he decided to make pants out of the canvas he had. Research to find out more about this German immigrant and the product he created.

Writing Across the Curriculum

1. Prepare a report on the history and operation of the underground railroad, which helped slaves escape to free states and Canada.

2. Write a news article about one of the slave rebellions described in the text. Be sure to use the five *W*'s and *H*: *who, what, when, where, why*, and *how*.

Exploring Technology

1. In 1841, the U.S. Supreme Court ruled that rebellious Africans on board the slave ship *Amistad* were free, not slaves. Using the Internet, research the *Amistad* incident and tell the story of what happened on board the ship.

2. Few events from the past have created as much current interest as the Donner Party, which, in 2003, was verified through an archaeological dig. If you want to learn exactly what happened to this small group of freezing and starving settlers and you do not mind grizzly stories, use your favorite search engine to research the Donner Party and answer the following questions: In your opinion, were members of the group justified in what they did? How do you think they felt afterward?

3. The Mormon Trail and the settlers who traveled it were different from the other explorers in that they were escaping religious persecution. Using the Internet, find out why they traveled to Utah and read about the "hand carts" used by later Mormons making the trip. Using your geography and math skills, determine how far these hand-cart settlers had to walk.

Applying Your Skills

1. Draw two pictures that represent the differences between the North and the South during the antebellum era.

2. About how many slaves lived in Georgia in 1860?

Photo Question

To which social class do you think the owner of this house would have belonged?

Chapter 8
1860–1865

The Civil War, A Nation in Conflict

While Abraham Lincoln was on his way to be inaugurated as the nation's sixteenth president, he learned that Jefferson Davis had been chosen as the president of the Confederate States of America. Georgia's Alexander Stephens had been chosen as vice president.

It was February 18, 1861, in Montgomery, Alabama, the selected capital of the Confederacy. Davis was introduced to cheering crowds by William Yancey, who proclaimed "The man and the hour have met. Prosperity, honor, and victory await his administration." Amidst yells, the singing of "Dixie," and booming cannons, southerners who were there and those who later heard the retelling were convinced that Yancey's words were true. Although the crowd's vision of the future was never realized, one thing was certain—these two presidents determined a course of history debated even to this day.

Above: A statue of Jefferson Davis stands where he was inaugurated. Opposite page: This monument honors the Georgia troops who fought at Chickamauga.

Signs of the Times 1860-1865

Population: Population: 34.3 million—26.2 million in the Union and 8.1 million in Confederacy (of which 4 million were slaves)

Life Expectancy: 41.8 years

Costs of Living: Eggs were as much as $6 a dozen and bacon was $0.15 a pound; the price of both rose 75 percent during the war. A plate of beans, potatoes, corned beef, bread, and cup of coffee was $0.15 in the North; by the end of the war, it was impossible to buy that in the South.

Music: Songs of the period included "John Brown's Body," "Beautiful Dreamer," "Dixieland" (Dixie), "Battle Hymn of the Republic," "Tenting Tonight," "The Bonnie Blue Flag," "Marching Through Georgia," and "When Johnny Comes Marching Home."

Fads/Fashions: In the early days of the war, people gathered for a picnic on a hilltop overlooking battles and watched as they unfolded. Women's fashions changed drastically when Ebenezer Butterick invented the first paper dress patterns sold in the United States.

Wages/Salary: In the Union army, privates earned $13-$16 a month, second lieutenants $105.50 a month, colonels averaged $212 monthly, and generals made from $315 to $758 a month. In the Confederate army, privates earned $11-$18 a month, colonels $195-$210 month, and generals about $14 less a month than their Union counterparts.

Art/Architecture: Congress commissioned German American artist Emanual Leutze to paint a mural for the staircase in the U.S. Capitol. Photographer Mathew Brady began a photographic record of the Civil War. The Metropolitan Museum was founded in New York City.

Literature: Henry Wadsworth Longfellow published *Tales of a Wayside Inn*, which included "Paul Revere's Ride." Mary Mapes Dodge published *Hans Brinker and the Silver Skates*. Walt Whitman published *Drum Taps*, a collection of Civil War poems.

Leisure Time: Croquet was brought from England and became a big hit. Boxing continued to be enjoyed during wartime. In 1863, Joe Coburn won the American Boxing Championship after a 63-round event. Roller skating was introduced.

Science/Inventions: Telegraph wires stretched from New York to San Francisco making coast-to-coast communication possible but bringing an end to the Pony Express. Eberhard Faber opened a factory in New York to mass produce pencils. Gail Borden patented a process to concentrate orange juice.

Education: Elizabeth Peabody established the first kindergarten in Boston. Vassar became the first women's college with facilities equal to men's colleges. The Morrill Act authorized land grants to the states for agriculture and industry colleges, which included the University of Georgia.

Religion: "In God We Trust" appeared on a U.S. coin (the two-cent piece) for the first time. Olympia Brown entered St. Lawrence University and became the first woman to study theology beside men.

Transportation: American balloonist Thaddeus Lowe traveled a record distance from Cincinnati to South Carolina's coast in only nine hours. The Pennsylvania Railroad began using steel for rails. George Pullman built the "Pullman Car," a railroad sleeping car.

Figure 25 Timeline: 1861–1865

1861
Fort Pulaski taken by Confederate troops

1862
Fort Pulaski recaptured by federal troops

1863
Federal forces defeated at Battle of Chickamauga

1864
Atlanta captured and burned
Sherman began March to the Sea
Savannah surrendered

1865
Jefferson Davis captured near Irwinville

1861   1862   1863   1864   1865

1861
Civil War started with capture of Fort Sumter
First transcontinental telegraph message sent
Yale awarded first Ph.D. degrees in the nation

1862
Homestead Act signed
Battle of the *Monitor* and the *Merrimack*

1863
Emancipation Proclamation became effective
Thanksgiving declared a national holiday
First Medal of Honor awarded

1864
Lincoln re-elected
Arlington National Cemetery established

1865
Lee surrendered at Appomattox Courthouse
Stetson hat introduced

The Road to War

Section Preview

As you read, look for:
- the event that began the Civil War,
- the advantages and disadvantages of the North and the South,
- wartime strategies, and
- vocabulary terms: conscription, strategy, blockade, ironclad, blockade runner, and King Cotton diplomacy.

Flanked by General Winfield Scott, and under the watchful protection of military troops and squads of riflemen atop government buildings surrounding the capital, a serious Abraham Lincoln walked up the steps of the U.S. Capitol to take his oath of office. It was a bright and warm March 4, 1861.

Later, as Lincoln rose to deliver his inaugural address, it was with the full knowledge that seven southern states had left the Union in protest of his election and their belief in a state's right to secede. He knew that the speech he was about to deliver was crucially important. For weeks, he had studied a variety of historic documents, looking for wisdom. Historical records indicate that Lincoln still thought he could prevent war.

President Lincoln pleaded for the preservation of the Union and promised that Union forces would not be used to maintain the Union. He also promised the South that he would not interfere with slavery in those states where it already existed. Lincoln ended his address with these words:

In your hands, my dissatisfied fellow-countrymen, and not in mine is the momentous issue of civil war. The Government will not assail you. You can have no conflict without being yourselves the aggressors. You have no oath registered in heaven to destroy the Government, while I shall have the most solemn one to "preserve, protect, and defend it."

I am loath to close. We are not enemies, but friends. We must not be enemies. Though passion may have strained, it must not break our bonds of affection. The mystic chords of memory, stretching from every battlefield and patriot grave to every living heart and hearthstone, all over this broad land, will yet swell the chorus of the Union, when again touched, as surely they will be, by the better angels of our nature.

Fort Sumter—The Start of the War

Within weeks of Lincoln's stirring address, the South gave him their answer. Confederate forces captured all but four federal garrisons in the South, including Fort Pulaski in Savannah. The only southern garrisons left under Union control were Forts Jefferson, Pickens, and Taylor in Florida

Above: General P. G. T. Beauregard commanded the Confederate forces that fired the first shot of the Civil War—against Fort Sumter. Left: John Ross Key painted this view of "The Bombardment of Fort Sumter."

Did You Know?

During the bombardment of Fort Sumter, men and women of wealth and position watched from the Battery, an embankment across the harbor from the fort.

and Fort Sumter in South Carolina. It was Fort Sumter in Charleston harbor that forced Lincoln's hand.

Lincoln received word that the fort was low on ammunition and provisions and needed to be resupplied. Tensions between the North and the South were very high. Lincoln did not want to worsen the situation, but he was commander-in-chief and he had promised that he would not give up control of federal territory. He agreed to send the supplies and additional troops requested by Major Robert Anderson, the Union commander.

On April 10, 1861, as Major Anderson waited for additional men and supplies, the new Confederate government directed Brigadier General P. G.T. Beauregard to demand the surrender of Fort Sumter. Anderson refused. His eighty-five soldiers and forty-three laborers prepared to fight with the fort's forty-eight cannons.

At 4:30 a.m on April 12, Confederate forces opened fire on Fort Sumter. Thirty-six hours later, a white flag waved over the fort. Major Anderson formally surrendered the fort on April 13 and left for New York, where he and his men were welcomed as heroes. The Confederacy had won its first skirmish of the war, and the war had officially begun.

After the firing on Fort Sumter, both North and South increased their preparations for war. Arkansas, Tennessee, North Carolina, and Virginia seceded and joined the Confederacy, bringing the number of seceded states to eleven. The capital of the new Confederacy moved from Montgomery, Alabama, to Richmond, Virginia.

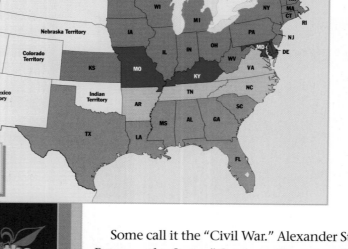

**Map 37
The Union and the Confederacy**

Map Skill **How many states remained in the Union?**

Some call it the "Civil War." Alexander Stephens coined the phrase "War Between the States." Some southerners called it the "War of Northern Aggression." It has also been referred to as the "Brother's War" and the "Children's Crusade," because so many youngsters your age were involved in the fighting. Whichever name is used, it was brother against brother or father against son on blood-soaked battlefields. Before it was over, battles were fought at 10,000 sites on U.S. soil, seven future U.S. presidents took up arms, slavery was abolished, and over 620,000 Americans died.

Raising Armies

When Lincoln heard of the fall of Fort Sumter, he called on the remaining Union garrisons to send 75,000 troops to put down the rebellion and protect Washington. From that point on, every few months, both governments called for volunteers. At first, most men joined voluntarily. Later, men

In this political cartoon, Lady Liberty fights off Copperhead leaders. The *Copperheads* were a group of northerners who opposed the Civil War. This cartoon shows them as dangerous to the Union. In fact, articles in Copperhead newspapers helped stir up the New York draft riots.

received cash awards or bounties for signing up. There were even "bounty jumpers," men who took the bounty to join the army and who then deserted, changed their names, joined a different regiment, and collected another bounty. In other instances, men paid someone else (usually from a family in need of money) to take their place.

By 1862, the Confederate Congress approved conscription, or the drafting of men to serve in the army. The U.S. Congress did the same thing in 1863. Never before in the nation's short history had men been forced by a government to go into battle. Many on both sides disagreed with the draft. In July 1863, draft riots broke out in New York City.

Above: Riots broke out in New York over the draft.

A Matter of Resources

Conditions in the North and the South were very different. In 1860, the U.S. population was about 31 million. Of that number, 22 million lived in the North. Only 9 million lived in the South, 3.5 million of whom were slaves. That left about 6 million whites, a number that included women, children, the old, and the ill. The South actually had only about 800,000 men between the ages of 15 and 50 to fill its army. Just raising an army was a huge task for the South.

The North had over 100,000 factories employing 1.1 million workers. The South had only 20,000 factories employing 100,000 workers. By 1862, the South could not supply any of the basic materials needed to fight a modern war: blankets, arms, food, clothes, boots, medical supplies, and the like.

The North also had the advantage in transportation. In 1860, there were about 31,000 miles of railroad track in the country. The North's 22,000 miles connected all of the major cities and had been built to carry heavy industrial machinery. The South's 9,000 miles of rail had been built to move farm products and cotton; the rails were too light to carry troop trains and heavy equipment effectively. By the end of the war, the South's rail system was virtually unusable.

Other advantages of the North included the fact that it had 67 percent of all the farms in the United States and 75 percent of the wealth of the country. The North had a monetary system in place; the South had to create one. Finally, the North had an army, a navy, and an experienced government.

The Confederacy did, however, have some advantages. Many of the best military leaders in the United States were southerners. For the most part, the war was fought in the South. People fight harder when they are defending their homes. Southern soldiers were fighting on "familiar" territory and were more likely to have experience riding horses on long journeys and firing weapons. Southerners also had a cause—independence—for which they could fight.

Wartime Strategies

After Fort Sumter, both Union and Confederate political and military leaders developed strategies (plans) for winning the war. Sometimes the plans worked; at other times, they did not. Over the course of the war, the strategies shifted as advances or setbacks caused changes.

At first, the Union strategy was to blockade, or obstruct, all Confederate ports. A blockade would prevent the South from selling its cotton abroad and importing needed war equipment and supplies from foreign nations. Early in the war, 26 Union ships steamed up and down the coast to prevent ships from moving into or out of southern harbors. Later, the North spent

Above: During the Mexican-American War, General Winfield Scott wrote that Robert E. Lee was "the very best soldier I ever saw in the field." Lee turned down the opportunity to command Union forces during the war.

Did You Know?

In 1863, the U.S. Congress enacted the nation's first income tax to finance the war. It was eliminated in 1872.

Spotlight on the Economy

Economy of the North and the South

As both the North and the South prepared for war after the fall of Fort Sumter, it may be difficult to understand how the South ever thought it could win a war against so strong a foe or that it thought the war would be brief. Examine the information in Figure 26. What do you think?

Even a brief examination of the figures is enough to know that the Union far surpassed the newly formed Confederacy in all but a few areas such as cotton production. The Confederacy had fewer and smaller banks than the North, and most of the South's capital was invested in slaves and land. As a result, the South had much smaller assets in banks and in individual hands. Although the Confederacy seized monies in federal mints located in the South, that provided only about $1 million.

Because both sides needed cash to pay their armies, both sides issued paper money and treasury notes, causing rampant inflation (a general increase in the prices of goods and services over time) in both North and South.

In terms of money alone, the Civil War cost the U.S. government about $6 billion. By 1910, after benefits were paid to veterans and their widows, that cost estimate soared to $11.5 billion. Although southern records were mostly destroyed, estimates place southern expenditures for the war at a little over $4 billion.

Figure 26 Resources: North versus South

	North (23 states)	South (11 states)
Overall population	22 million people	9 million people (3.5 to 4 million were slaves)
Men of combat age	4 million	.8 million
Military forces	Trained army and navy	None
Factories	100,000 with 1.1 million workers	20,000 with 100,000 workers
Miles of railroad track	22,000	9,000
Railroad equipment	96 percent of nation's supply	4 percent of nation's supply
Banks/Funds	81 percent of nation's deposits	19 percent of nation's deposits
Gold	$56 million	None
Farms	67 percent of nation's total	33 percent of nation's total
Agriculture/Grain	64 percent of nation's supply	36 percent of nation's supply
Number of draft animals (horses, mules, oxen)	4.6 million	2.6 million

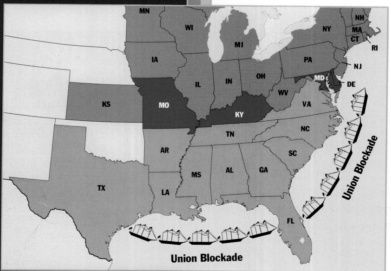

Union Blockade

Map 38
The Union Blockade

Map Skill: Why did the blockade not extend around Florida?

Top: Blockade ships can be seen outside Charleston harbor.

millions of dollars to build more ships, 74 of which were **ironclads** (armored ships). However, Union vessels were no match for the **blockade runners**, mostly private ships that slipped around the blockade and sped into and out of the blocked ports. There were over 650 private blockade runners during 1861; 9 out of every 10 blockade runners were able to run past the federal ships and sail into open waters. Before the Confederacy surrendered, it is estimated that 6,000 vessels carrying clothes, medicines, ammunition, and supplies worth $200 million made it through the federal blockade.

Blockade running was very profitable. Captains were paid $5,000 for each trip; the ship's pilots earned $3,500. Many ship owners and speculators made millions during the war. They slipped past federal ships to deliver cotton to British markets at large profits. In Great Britain, the blockade runners purchased military supplies, food, and medical supplies and returned to sell these essentials to the Confederacy for yet another huge profit. As the war progressed, however, it became more and more difficult for blockade runners to get past federal ships.

A second Union strategy was to capture the Mississippi River and split the Confederacy in half leaving Texas, Arkansas, and Louisiana stranded. This strategy was known as the "Anaconda Plan" because, if successful, it would squeeze the Confederacy to death just like the giant anaconda snake squeezes its prey to death.

Still later, Union generals decided that the capture of the Confederate capital of Richmond could end the war. That strategy failed, however, as General Robert E. Lee held off Union troops from the doors of Richmond for several years.

In 1864 and 1865, Union Generals Ulysses S. Grant and William T. Sherman developed a strategy that ensured victory for the North. Their plan was twofold: (1) to destroy Confederate armies on the battlefields and (2) to lay waste to the land so that southern civilians would stop supporting the war. One result of this plan was Sherman's devastating march through Georgia.

The Confederate leaders also had strategies for winning the war. On land, they hoped to wear down the invading Union armies. They believed that rising casualties would weaken northerners' support for the war. At sea, the Confederates wanted to make sure the Union blockade did not work. The Confederate Navy used swift *raiders* (fast, lightly armed ships) to capture Union merchant ships and draw the Union Navy away from their blockade duties. In coastal waters, the Confederates used ironclads and even a submarine to sink the Union's wooden ships and to open southern ports for trade with other nations. Confederate leaders knew it was essential to keep ports open and able to trade with foreign markets.

The South's political strategy was known as **King Cotton diplomacy**. Southern leaders believed that the British and French textile mills needed the South's cotton to keep running. The Confederacy believed that if it stopped selling cotton abroad for a time, France and Great Britain would be forced to help the South break the blockades to get the cotton they needed. However, the North put pressure on France and Great Britain and those two nations switched to cotton grown in Egypt.

Above: Union General Ulysses S. Grant, with the help of General Sherman, developed the strategy that eventually won the war for the North.

It's Your Turn

1. Which Georgian was named vice president of the Confederacy?
2. Identify five areas in which the Union's resources outweighed the Confederacy's.
3. What was the purpose of the Union blockades?
4. Why was the North's strategy known as the Anaconda Plan?
5. Why was the South's strategy called King Cotton diplomacy?

The Great Locomotive Chase

In the spring of 1862, Marietta played host to many strangers. One was Kentuckian James Andrews. But Andrews was no Confederate sympathizer.

On the morning of April 12, 1862, Andrews boarded the *General*, a train owned by the Western and Atlantic Railroad that carried both passengers and war supplies from Atlanta to Confederate troops in Tennessee. Also boarding the train were nineteen young men who, though dressed in civilian clothes, were really Union soldiers.

The train stopped for breakfast at Big Shanty station. Conductor William Fuller and his crew were eating breakfast when they heard a familiar sound—the noise of the *General* and three boxcars pulling out of the station! Stunned, Fuller and his crew raced out the door and began running after the train.

James Andrews and the men with him on the train were Union spies who had carefully planned the raid. The raiders chose to make their move at Big Shanty station because it had no telegraph. Their intent was to head north to Huntsville to meet Union General Mitchel and then move on to Chattanooga. Along the way, they would cut telegraph lines, burn bridges, and destroy railroad tracks. What they did not count on was the spirit and determination of Fuller and his crew, who took the theft as a personal affront.

After running on the tracks for two miles, Fuller and his men found a platform handcar. They pushed themselves along the tracks, picking up two more men to help them. They came upon the switch engine *Yonah*, which they commandeered. At Kingston, they picked up the *William F. Smith,* only to abandon

when the Union raiders saw an incredible sight. The mighty *Texas*, without any cars, was barreling down the railroad tracks—in reverse.

Andrews' raiders were now filled with fear. The law was very clear about the sentencing of spies. The raiders first tried unsuccessfully to pry up rails. Next they tossed crossties on the tracks to stop their pursuers. Then they released two boxcars, but the *Texas* pushed them aside.

As they approached the wooden bridge over the Oostanaula River, Andrews set fire to the last boxcar, hoping that it would burn the bridge and stop the *Texas*. But the bridge was too wet from rains the previous day to burn. Again, the *Texas* pushed aside the burning boxcar and continued its chase.

The race finally ended near Ringgold Gap, eighteen miles south of Chattanooga, when the *General* ran out of steam. The raiders fled but were rounded up within two weeks. Two months later, James Andrews and seven of his men were court-martialed and hanged in Atlanta. The remaining men were sent to Confederate prisons.

After the war, some of Andrews Raiders received the Medal of Honor. However, because Andrews was not in the military, he did not.

Today, the *General* can be seen at the Kennesaw Civil War Museum in Kennesaw. The *Texas* is on display at the Cyclorama in Atlanta.

Above: The *General* in Kennesaw. Opposite page, above: The *Texas* gives chase. Opposite page, below: James Andrews. Below: The locomotive thieves escape after the train runs out of fuel.

it because the Union raiders had removed tracks. Finally, after still another foot pursuit, the weary but angry band of men met an engine named *Texas* headed south from Adairsville. They quickly climbed aboard and continued the pursuit.

The *General*, which had been slowed because of southbound train traffic, was north of Calhoun

The War on the Battlefield

Section Preview

As you read, look for:
- ten major battles of the Civil War,
- the battles in Georgia during the Chickamauga and Atlanta campaigns, and
- vocabulary term: Emancipation Proclamation.

Did You Know?

The Confederates generally named battles for the nearest town or community. The Union named battles for the nearest body of water.

Today's modern warfare involves long-range guns and "smart" bombs guided by computers. It is hard to imagine Civil War battles where long lines of hundreds of men faced each other separated by only 1,000 yards or less. Those lines were often two or three men deep; the front line fired at opposing troops while the lines behind them reloaded. Cannon fire hitting the line killed four or five soldiers at a time, but the line quickly filled in and gunfire continued.

By far, the most frightening part of the battle line was the moment when the commanding officer raised his sword and shouted the word "Charge." Suddenly, hundreds or thousands of screaming men ran furiously forward over open fields, jumping over fences or streams, firing as they ran and with bayonets leveled at the opposing line. The ensuing battle was hand-to-hand combat.

The noise could be deafening with cannons roaring from both sides, musket fire ripping through the air, orders shouted down the line, war yells bouncing about the countryside, and the screams of wounded and dying men.

Figure 27 Ten Major Civil War Battles

Battle	Date	Confederate Commanders	Confederate Strength
Fort Donelson, Tennessee	Feb. 13-16, 1862	John B. Floyd, Simon B. Buckner	21,000 men
Shiloh, Tennessee	Apr. 6-7, 1862	A. S. Johnston, P. G. T. Beauregard	40,335 men
Second Manassas, Virginia	Aug. 29-30, 1862	Robert E. Lee	48,527 men
Antietam, Maryland	Sept. 17, 1862	Robert E. Lee	51,844 men
Stone's River, Tennessee	Dec. 31, 1862	Braxton Bragg	37,739 men
Chancellorsville, Virginia	May 1-4, 1863	Robert E. Lee	60,892 men
Gettysburg, Pennsylvania	July 1-3, 1863	Robert E. Lee	75,000 men
Chickamauga, Georgia	Sept. 19-20, 1863	Braxton Bragg	66,326 men
The Wilderness, Virginia	May 5-7, 1864	Robert E. Lee	61,025 men
Spotsylvania, Virginia	May 8-19, 1864	Robert E. Lee	50,000 men

Major Battles of the War

The Civil War, which so many thought would neither last long nor disrupt many lives, proved to be exceptionally costly both in economic and human terms. During its course, some of the bloodiest battles in U.S. history were waged, battles that often pitted brother against brother and neighbor against neighbor.

At the first Battle of Manassas (the first Battle of Bull Run), Georgia's 21st Regiment lost 184 of its 242 men, almost 76 percent of its troops. This alarmed those who had thought the Yanks would be easily defeated.

Information about the major battles of the war appears in Figure 27.

By far, the majority of battles and skirmishes during the Civil War were fought on southern soil. Virginia was the site of the most battles, followed by Tennessee and Georgia.

Freeing the Slaves

On September 22, 1862, five days after the Battle of Antietam, President Lincoln issued the Emancipation Proclamation, a document ultimately

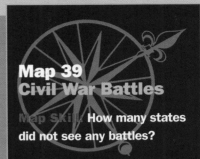

**Map 39
Civil War Battles**

Map Skill: How many states did not see any battles?

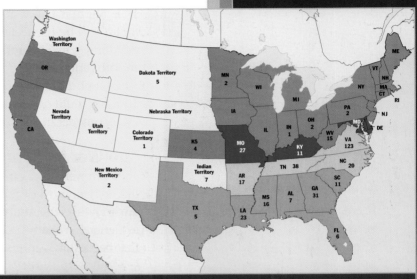

Union Commanders	Union Strength	Outcome	Casualties
Ulysses S. Grant	27,000 men	Union victory	19,455 (2,832 Union; 16,623 Confederate)
Ulysses S. Grant	62,682 men	Union victory	23,741 (13,047 Union; 10,694 Confederate)
John Pope	75,696 men	Confederate victory	25,251 (16,054 Union; 9,197 Confederate)
George B. McClellan	75,316 men	Union victory	26,134 (12,410 Union; 13,724 Confederate)
William S. Rosecrans	41,400 men	Union victory	24,645 (12,906 Union; 11,739 Confederate)
Joseph Hooker	133,868 men	Confederate victory	30,099 (17,278 Union; 12,821 Confederate)
George G. Meade	82,289 men	Union victory	51,112 (23,048 Union; 28,064 Confederate)
William Rosecrans	58,222 men	Confederate victory	34,624 (16,170 Union; 18,454 Confederate)
Ulysses S. Grant	101,895 men	No victor	25,416 (17,666 Union; 7,750 Confederate)
Ulysses S. Grant	83,000 men	Confederate victory	27,399 (18,399 Union; 9,000 Confederate)

affecting 4 million slaves in the United States. Lincoln wanted the Confederate states to end the war, return to the Union, and end 244 years of slavery. In this now famous document, Lincoln stated that unless the South surrendered by January 1, 1863, "all slaves in states or districts in rebellion against the United States will be thenceforth and forever free." For three months and nine days after the Proclamation was issued, the South faced a choice. If it surrendered, slavery would continue in the South. If it did not surrender, the institution of slavery would end. The Confederate leaders chose to continue to fight.

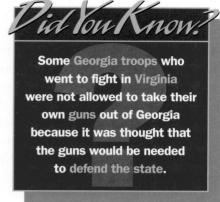

The War in Georgia

There were over one hundred Civil War battles and skirmishes in Georgia; most of them, ninety-two, were in 1864 during what are known as the Atlanta Campaign and the Savannah Campaign as General William T. Sherman led his March through Georgia. The first battles on Georgia soil, however, took place in 1862.

On April 6-7, 1862, while most of the Confederate forces were concentrated in Virginia, two areas of Georgia's coast were suffer-

ing their first major attacks—Tybee Island and Fort Pulaski, both located just east of Savannah.

Fort Pulaski, finished in 1847, was an important coastal defense site. It was named for Revolutionary War hero Count Casimir Pulaski. The fort was made of brick, and most thought it was strong enough to withstand any attacks. On January 3, 1861, Confederate forces had overrun the federal fort and captured it. Inside, they dug trenches and put down heavy pieces of wood to support their cannons.

In early April 1862, Union forces took Tybee Island, which was only a mile across the Savannah River from Fort Pulaski. They called on the fort's 25-year-old commander, Colonel Charles Olmstead, and his 385 men to surrender the fort back to Union control. Olmstead refused, and Union forces began firing on the fort at 8:00 a.m. on April 10. After a day and a half of cannon fire, the fort's brick walls were falling down, and Olmstead was forced to surrender. In a letter to his wife, the young Confederate commander wrote, "I feel that I have done my duty, my whole duty, that I have been forced to yield only to [the] superior might of metal. Guns such as have never before been brought to bear against any fortification have overpowered me, but I trust to history to keep my name untarnished." The guns to which Olmstead referred were rifled cannons, which were first used in modern warfare at Fort Pulaski. The Battle of Fort Pulaski was the only battle fought in Georgia during 1862. However, before the war was over, more than thirty battles were fought on Georgia's soil. Some of those battles are listed in Figure 28. A look at two of the battles—Chickamauga and Atlanta—offers insight into the Union's defeat of the South.

Top: Park rangers at Fort Pulaski demonstrate firing of the cannon. Above: Brotherton Cabin is the site of the Confederate break-through on the second day of the Battle of Chickamauga.

The Battle of Chickamauga

In late 1863, Union forces moved against the major railroad center in Chattanooga, Tennessee, just across the Georgia line. On September 19-20, Union General Rosecrans led his troops against Confederate General Braxton Bragg seven miles south of Chattanooga at Chickamauga Creek. Bragg's army

Figure 28 Civil War Battles in Georgia

Battle	Date	Union Commanders
Fort Pulaski, Chatham County	April 10-11, 1862	David Hunter
Fort McAllister I, Bryan County	March 3, 1863	P. Drayton
Davis's Cross Roads, Dade and Walker counties	September 10-11, 1863	James Negley
Chickamauga, Catoosa and Walker counties	September 18-20, 1863	William S. Rosecrans
Ringgold Gap, Catoosa County	November 27, 1863	Joseph Hooker
Dalton I, Whitfield County	February 22-27, 1864	George H. Thomas
Rocky Face Ridge, Whitfield County	May 7-13, 1864	William T. Sherman
Resaca,Gordon and Whitfield counties	May 13-15, 1864	William T. Sherman
Adairsville, Bartow and Gordon counties	May 17, 1864	William T. Sherman
New Hope Church, Paulding County	May 25-26, 1864	William T. Sherman
Dallas, Paulding County	May 26-June 1, 1864	William T. Sherman
Pickett's Mill, Paulding County	May 27, 1864	Oliver Otis Howard
Marietta (I, II, III, IV), Cobb County	June 9-July 3, 1864	William T. Sherman
Kolb's Farm, Cobb County	June 22, 1864	John M. Schofield
Kennesaw Mountain, Cobb County	June 27, 1864	William T. Sherman
Peachtree Creek, Fulton County	July 20, 1864	George H. Thomas
Atlanta, Fulton County	July 22, 1864	William T. Sherman
Ezra Church, Fulton County	July 28, 1864	Oliver O. Howard
Utoy Creek, Fulton County	August 5-7, 1864	John M. Schofield
Dalton II, Whitfield County	August 14-15, 1864	James B. Steedman
Lovejoy's Station, Clayton County	August 20, 1864	H. Judson Kilpatrick
Jonesboro, Clayton County	August 31 - September 1, 1864	William T. Sherman
Allatoona, Bartow County	October 5, 1864	John M. Corse
Griswoldville, Jones and Twiggs counties	November 22, 1864	Charles C. Walcutt
Buck Head Creek, Jenkins County	November 28, 1864	H. Judson Kilpatrick
Waynesborough, Burke County	December 4, 1864	H. Judson Kilpatrick
Fort McAllister II, Bryan County	December 13, 1864	William B. Hazen

In June 1864, Sherman attacked Johnston's troops at Kennesaw Mountain but lost that battle.

Jefferson Davis, president of the Confederacy, disagreed with Johnston's strategies and wanted Sherman's troops attacked head-on. Davis replaced Johnston with General John Bell Hood. In July, Hood led his troops in an attack on Sherman, losing over 11,000 men in two days. The two armies continued to fight during July until Hood concentrated his troops within the city of Atlanta. The main battle of Atlanta was on July 22. Hood hoped Sherman would follow him into the city so that he could attack Sherman's army on the left flank and rear guard. However, the attacks did not succeed.

The two armies fought for the rest of July and August until Hood finally left the city on September 1 after the citizens evacuated Atlanta. The next day, the Union army moved into Atlanta and took over its railroads and factories. The soldiers stayed until November 15 when, about three o'clock in the afternoon, they set fire to the city. On November 16, Sherman's army left Atlanta in flames and began their infamous "March to the Sea."

Top: Although Sherman lost the battle at Kennesaw Mountain, that did not stop him from pushing on toward Atlanta. Above: Sherman's and Hood's armies fought for over a month in and around Atlanta before Hood finally evacuated the city. The Atlanta Cyclorama has a 358-foot painting of the battle.

Sherman's March to the Sea

Sherman's army moved quickly through the state heading from Atlanta to Savannah, burning everything in a path sixty miles wide on the three-hundred mile trek to the coast. On his way from Atlanta to Savannah, Sherman destroyed all military targets and the civilian economic system (farms, homes, towns, railroads, bridges, roads) that supported the Confederate military. The move took over two months and left a large area of the state totally destroyed. In response to criticism of the destruction, Sherman reportedly said, "If the people [of Georgia] raise a howl against my barbarity and cruelty, I will answer that war is war and not popularity seeking." Estimates of the damage from Sherman's March to the Sea were as high as $100 million.

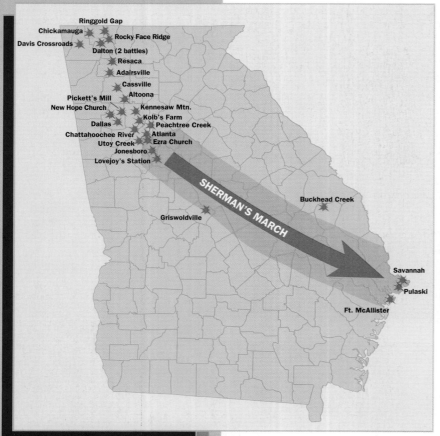

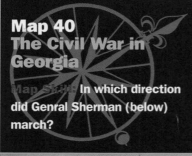

Map 40
The Civil War in Georgia

Map Skill: In which direction did General Sherman (below) march?

On December 22, 1864, Sherman sent a wire to President Lincoln: "I beg to present you as a Christmas gift the City of Savannah with one hundred fifty heavy guns, plenty of ammunition, also about twenty-five thousand bales of cotton." The next day, Union troops took over Savannah. Interestingly enough, Sherman did not burn Savannah. He knew that there was a treasure to be saved in Savannah, a treasure the Union Army needed. Since the city had been cut off by the naval blockade, bales of cotton had been accumulating in the warehouses and on the docks. Sherman quickly had it loaded, shipped to the North, and sold for a reported $28 million.

When Savannah surrendered, Sherman had effectively divided the upper and lower Confederacy, cutting Robert E. Lee off from the vital supplies needed to continue the Southern war effort and ending the war in Georgia. The main concern of those who remained in Georgia was finding food and shelter. The factories, rail lines, mills, plantations, and farm fields lay around them in ruins.

The Final Battles of the War

On January 13, 1865, the North captured Fort Fisher in North Carolina and closed the last Confederate blockade-running port. In Virginia, Lee's troops continued to fight Grant's army, which was over twice the size of the remaining Confederate force. On March 2, Lee asked to meet with Grant to talk about ending the war. President Lincoln refused to allow the meeting unless the South surrendered.

Lee tried one final time to push Union troops back from Petersburg, Virginia. He failed. Before he could reach the remaining Confederate forces in North Carolina, Union troops cut off his retreat. President Jefferson Davis knew the war was near its end. He left Richmond and went to Danville, Virginia, to avoid capture. He was eventually captured near Irwinville, Georgia.

On April 9, 1865, General Lee surrendered to General Grant at Appomattox Court House in Virginia. While there were still a few skirmishes in North Carolina, the Civil War was officially over.

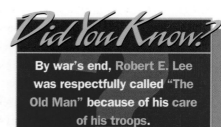

Did You Know?

By war's end, Robert E. Lee was respectfully called "The Old Man" because of his care of his troops.

By the Side of the Road

In 1862, local housebuilder and mechanic John Gilleland from Athens had an idea for a double-barreled cannon that would fire two cannonballs connected with a chain. After it was cast, Gilleland's cannon was taken for its first test. Unfortunately, the two balls did not fire at exactly the same time. The chain connecting them broke, and each cannonball followed an erratic course. One killed a cow, and the other hit a chimney on a cabin. Although Gilleland was convinced that his cannon was a success, he could not convince anyone else. The cannon was returned to Athens, where it was used as a signal gun. Today, the only known specimen of a double-barreled cannon stands on the grounds of City Hall in Athens.

THE ATHENS DOUBLE-BARRELLED CANNON

This cannon, the only known one of its kind, was designed by Mr. John Gilleland, a private in the "Mitchell Thunderbolts," an elite "home guard" unit of business and professional men ineligible because of age or disability for service in the Confederate army. Cast in the Athens foundry, it was intended to fire simultaneously two balls connected by a chain which would "mow down the enemy somewhat as a scythe cuts wheat." It failed for lack of a means of firing both barrels at the exact instant.

It was tested in a field on the Newton's Bridge road against a target of upright poles. With both balls rammed home and the chain dangling from the twin muzzles, the piece was fired; but the lack of precise simultaneity caused uneven explosion of the propelling charges, which snapped the chain and gave each ball an erratic and unpredictable trajectory.

Lacking a workable firing device, the gun was a failure. It was presented to the City of Athens where, for almost a century, it has been preserved as an object of curiosity, and where it performed sturdy service for many years in celebrating political victories.

Civil War Prisons

A particularly dark side of the Civil War was the way prisoners of both sides were treated by their captors. At first, each side routinely exchanged prisoners. However, in 1864, after an incident in which northern black military prisoners were reported to have been killed by their Confederate captors, General Grant stopped exchanging prisoners with the South. This kept the Confederacy from getting back men needed for the army. It also made military prisons overflow.

One of the Confederate prisons for Union soldiers was in Andersonville, Georgia. The prison was dirty; the only shelter was whatever the prisoners could put together; and there was not enough food, water, or medical supplies. Much of the available water was contaminated. The prison was always crowded beyond reason. During the fifteen months Andersonville operated, almost 13,000 Union prisoners died.

Stories of the conditions at Andersonville were so bad that the Confederate War Department had a medical team look at the prison. The team recommended moving the soldiers to better places. Although records indicate

Below: The Andersonville National Historic Site is also home to the National Prisoner of War Museum. Opened in 1998, it is dedicated to the men and women of this country who have suffered captivity. Bottom: This monument to the Iowa dead is in the Andersonville National Cemetery.

Andersonville's commander, Captain Henry Wirz, tried to improve conditions at the prison, he was executed in 1865 for "excessive cruelty." Today, Andersonville is a national cemetery where 13,700 Union dead are buried.

Although conditions at Andersonville Prison were horrible, the problems in prison camps were not limited to the South. Over 26,000 southerners died in northern camps such as Point Lookout, Maryland, and Camp Douglas, Illinois.

One Union prison was located at Elmira, New York. Before the war's end, one-fourth of the 12,123 Confederate prisoners at Elmira died. The prisoners faced malnutrition, exposure to the cold, and poor medical conditions. A man gnawing on a meat bone was envied by those about him. Broken arms and legs often were not tended. Prisoners, unaccustomed to the severe cold of New York winters, were often made to stand at attention barefooted on the snowy, ice-cold grounds. During summer months, prisoners were often made to stand for days in a sweat box seven feet high, twenty inches wide, and twelve inches deep without food, water, or ventilation.

Neither the North nor the South had foreseen the problems that would be caused by large numbers of prisoners over a prolonged war period. They had not planned how to house and feed and care for thousands of military prisoners, and they were unable to do so.

It's Your Turn

1. What was the first battle of the Civil War that took place on Georgia soil?
2. Could the Confederacy have maintained slavery even after the war was underway?
3. Why did General Sherman attack the civilian infrastructure between Atlanta and Savannah?
4. What military mistake cost Southern forces the initiative after the Battle of Chickamauga?
5. Who was executed for "excessive cruelty" at Andersonville Prison? Was that action justified?

Life for the Civil War Soldier

Section Preview

As you read, look for:
- the life of common soldiers during the war,
- the roles played by blacks and Latinos in the war, and
- vocabulary terms: **rations** and **sutler wagon.**

Historians often write about the big battles and the great generals. The lives of ordinary soldiers, however, give a truer picture of war. Although they sometimes spoke with different accents and represented different governments, the soldiers—nicknamed "Johnny Reb" and "Billy Yank"—were very much alike. Most were under the age of twenty-one. Over 250,000 were sixteen years old or younger, and some were as young as ten. The majority of the soldiers came from the lower economic groups and knew nothing about war. In many cases, young men joined simply to escape the boredom of farm life and to seek adventures away from home. Too soon they faced a very different reality.

Daily Rations

From the beginning of the war, northern troops generally ate better than their southern counterparts. Union records from 1864 indicate that the basic daily rations (portions of food) in ounces for Union soldiers were: "20-beef; 18-flour; 2.56-dried beans; 1.6-green coffee; 2.4- sugar; .64- salt." They also received small amounts of pepper, yeast powder, soap, candles, and

Below: These re-enactors are dressed in Confederate uniforms. Re-enactors are those who recreate or perform certain actions, particularly Civil War battles.

vinegar. Similar records for the Army of Northern Virginia in 1863 listed rations for 100 Confederate soldiers over a thirty-day period. Each day, they had to share "1/4 pound of bacon, 18 oz. flour, 10 lbs. rice, and small amounts of peas and dried fruits when they could be obtained." As the war progressed, food became even more scarce for the Confederates.

Soldiers from both North and South had to depend on food found in the woods or taken from farms. The term favored by the soldiers was "liberating" chickens, hogs, pies, and eggs. For soldiers with money, hunger pangs could be eased by a visit to the sutler wagons. Though not a part of the military, **sutler wagons** followed behind the troops and were packed with food, razors, writing papers and pens, sewing needles, and other goods. Prices, especially those for food, were often double or triple the item's normal cost. A dozen eggs, for example, could set the soldier back $6, which is expensive even by today's standards but which was a small fortune to a soldier in Civil War days.

By far the most valuable item, particularly during the summer, was water. Many men on both sides of the battles were felled not by bullets or cannon fire, but by dehydration (lack of water).

Supplies

During the early days of the war, it was often impossible to tell which side a soldier represented because uniforms were so seldom alike. The battlefields were a hodgepodge of colorful, often homespun, shirts, jackets, and trousers with a variety of hats including those made of straw. One regiment even marched off to battle in kilts. In one instance, Union soldiers let a group of men in blue jackets into their line, thinking they were friendly forces. By the time they discovered their mistake, the Confederate unit in blue had overrun the Union troops.

After a few months, Confederate soldiers dressed in double-breasted, hip-length coats and gray pants. Many of the Confederate officers started off wearing elaborate gold

Top: Sutlers usually set up tents or wagons at encampments. Men often met at the sutler wagon in the evenings for conversation and companionship. **Above:** This soldier has just "liberated" an ear of corn from a farmer's field.

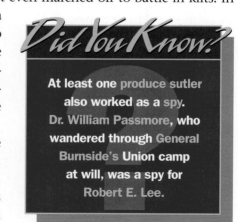

Did You Know?

At least one produce sutler also worked as a spy. Dr. William Passmore, who wandered through General Burnside's Union camp at will, was a spy for Robert E. Lee.

braided uniforms made by hometown tailors or slaves. But without factories to mass produce uniforms, as the North had, those officers' fancy clothes quickly gave way to a more practical homespun outfit. The hip-length coats were quickly replaced by short-waisted, single-breasted jackets. Each branch of the army had a different trim on its uniforms, and officers wore brass buttons to designate their branch of service. The uniforms of Union soldiers were blue, but the trim was much the same as the Confederate's. These troops also wore caps and hats with branch insignia in appropriate colors.

As the war dragged on, few Confederate soldiers dressed in gray uniforms. Most wore clothing made at home and sent by family and friends. Replacement uniforms became a luxury the Confederacy could not afford. By the war's end, most returned to their homes in little more than rags.

Boots and shoes quickly wore out from days of marching on hot dusty roads in the summer or in ice and cold rains in the winter. Again, replacements were hard to find, and more than one Confederate soldier chose to march barefoot.

Soldiers had knapsacks in which they carried their writing paper, pictures, books, and toiletries. However, the soldiers found the knapsacks hard to hold onto and soon lost them. Instead, they wrapped personal items in a blanket and carried them in a tent canvas. They also carried a musket and a leather box for ammunition. On their belts, they fastened a cap box, a bayonet in its sheath, a sewing kit, and their mess equipment (a knife, fork, spoon, cup, and, sometimes, a light cooking skillet). Together, all of these items weighed about forty or fifty pounds. The longer a soldier stayed in the army, the more likely he was to leave behind everything he could do without.

At the beginning of the war, Union soldiers were issued single shot, muzzle-loading, .54 caliber rifles. Later, those rifles were replaced with the forty-inch barrel Springfield rifles. Confederates depended on foreign weapons or

Below: This illustration shows Confederate uniforms around 1862. Bottom: Precise lines rarely lasted long when the soldiers were on the march.

those bought at local arsenals. Some soldiers went into the early skirmishes of the war with little more than their hunting rifles. When the foreign rifles were damaged or broken, there were no replacements. Southern soldiers quickly learned to scan the battlefield after the fighting was over and pick up the rifles of their fallen opponents.

Infantry soldiers on both sides of the conflict carried long fighting blades, but these were mainly for appearance. Most of the swords became wartime souvenirs.

Camp Life

It may seem strange to think of soldiers getting bored during a war, but actual battles took up very little time. A far greater amount of time was spent marching to the next battle site. Each man had to find ways of making the long nights pass more quickly. Oftentimes, soldiers played jokes on each other. For example, in winter months, a favorite joke was to steal the bugler's bugle and fill the horn with water. In the morning when the bugler rose to sound revelry, he found a bugle frozen solid with ice that had to be thawed out before he could blow it.

Around camp, soldiers on both sides passed the time sitting around and talking about good times at home, grumbling about a particular officer, or bragging about which side was bravest. Some wrote letters home or spent their time reading and rereading the last mail they had received. The men also played games such as checkers, chess, backgammon, and dominoes and games of chance, such as poker. Having their pictures taken was another popular pastime and, for a mere 50 cents, a soldier could purchase a picture

Did You Know?

Military mail was not censored during the Civil War. Letters spoke not only of love and missing family, but also detailed military information, plans, and maneuvers.

Below: These re-enactors have recreated a typical camp scene. How different is this from what you have seen in the movies?

of a "pin-up girl," a woman whose neck and arms were uncovered.

Almost everyone—from General Grant to the lowest-ranking private—whittled. They used soup bones, wood, or soft lead and made figures of people, animals, combat shields, badges, sinkers for fishing, or even uniform buttons. Another favorite activity was singing. As soon as a soldier took out his concertina (similar to a small accordion), men would gather around and begin to sing popular wartime songs or songs of home. Others would join in a makeshift band with wooden clappers, a Jew's harp, and wooden fife. Baseball games were often formed, and several games might be going on at one time in the camp.

Another important pastime was prayer and camp meetings. At the beginning of the war, each regiment had a chaplain. As the war wore on, groups had to share. In most camps, there were daily preaching sessions or prayer services in the evening. Soldiers had their own prayer books, and many carried their own Bibles.

During the hard winter months, there was much less fighting and men lived in wooden huts they built themselves. When spring came, they tore down the huts and used the wood for firewood. In better weather, they lived in 4-8 man tents or slept directly under the sky.

Above: Chaplains were assigned to regiments of both armies. A "great revival" took place in the Confederate army in 1863, and camp meetings were commonplace.

Blacks in the Civil War

Some 178,985 enlisted men and 7,122 officers served in black regiments during the Civil War. Union General David Hunter first organized black troops in 1862 but found little support from the War Department. More than any other thing, it was the 54th Massachusetts Volunteers that led to the idea of using "Negro troops" in battle. Up to that time, most black troops built defenses, manned garrisons, and helped maintain army camps. Others served as nurses, servants, cooks, and spies.

At the end of March 1862, the first black volunteer regiment began training at Readville Camp in Massachusetts. Robert G. Shaw, the 26-year-old son of an influential abolitionist, was named commander of the regiment. The group was mostly made up of freed blacks from Massachusetts and Pennsylvania and included Lewis and Charles Douglass, sons of Frederick Douglass.

The regiment saw its first action on James Island near Hilton Head, South Carolina, on June 3, 1863. They demonstrated such courage that Shaw volunteered to lead them on a charge at Fort Wagner near Charleston, a charge many considered a suicide mission.

On July 18, 1863, Shaw, with sword drawn, yelled "Onward, 54th" and led his men into a tremendous barrage of cannon fire. Shaw was wounded,

Above: Members of the 54th Massachusetts Infantry led the charge on Fort Wagner. The brigade scaled the parapet but after brutal hand-to-hand combat were driven out.

Did You Know?

Ultimately, the 54th Massachusetts Volunteers had a Georgia connection. The movie *Glory*, depicting the historic battle by that regiment, was filmed in Savannah, McDonough, and Jekyll Island.

but his men forged ahead over the last sand dune and met the Confederates in hand-to-hand combat. Over one-half of the regiment (281 men including Shaw) were killed or injured in the unsuccessful assault. Union forces eventually gave up trying to take Fort Wagner. But President Lincoln and members of Congress were so impressed by the exploits of the 54th Massachusetts Volunteers that other black groups were given the opportunity to fight in combat rather than serve behind the lines in support roles.

By October 1863, there were fifty-eight black regiments in the Union Army. These soldiers, about 3,500 of whom were from Georgia, took part in over 450 battles and skirmishes.

On March 13, 1865, Confederate President Jefferson Davis signed the Negro Soldier Law, which allowed slaves to enlist in the Confederate Army. A few blacks enlisted in Richmond, but before a black regiment could be organized, Richmond had fallen to Union forces and the Civil War was drawing to an end.

Latinos in the Civil War

Before the Civil War, immigrants flooded into the United States from such countries as China, Sweden, Germany, Italy, Russia, Canada, Cuba, Brazil, and Ireland. Federal recruiters met many immigrants in New York and offered them money to join the Union Army. Many joined for the cash, although they had little idea what the war was all about. One immigrant group were Latinos from Spain and Latin America.

There were entire Latino battalions from California, Louisiana, Arizona, Texas, and New Mexico. Although many individuals received commendations or recognitions for bravery, some were national heroes. One was David Farragut, who became the first U.S. Navy admiral and who was responsible for the successful blockade of the South.

When the Civil War broke out, Farragut reluctantly left his home and friends in Virginia and moved to New York. When he captured New Orleans after a fierce battle, President Lincoln appointed him rear admiral, the highest rank in the Navy. Farragut continued to capture port cities until only one major southern port remained—Mobile Bay in Alabama. In January 1864, Farragut conducted one of the most daring naval battles of the war. When it was over, he had captured the last Gulf Coast port under Confederate control. For all practical purposes, the victory ended the Civil War and made Farragut into a national hero. In the spring of 1868, politicians tried to talk the famous admiral into running for president. He refused, saying that he was best trained for war, not politics.

Other Latinos remembered from the Civil War include Loreta Velazquez, who disguised herself as a man and joined her Confederate husband in combat. She fought gallantly maintaining her disguise in several battles, including the Battle of Fort Donelson and the Battle of Shiloh. She also served as a spy for the Confederacy.

Below: When the smoke from the Battle of Mobile became too thick, Admiral Farragut climbed the rigging to get a better view. Mobile fell to Farragut's forces in one of the most decisive naval victories of the Civil War.

In April 1861 Laredo, Texas, businessman Santos Benavides (whose great, great grandfather had originally settled Laredo) formed the Benavides Regiment and drove a Union force out of the small Texas town of Carrizo. In 1863, he was promoted to colonel, making him one of the highest-ranking Latinos in the Confederacy. Benavides also stopped local revolts against the Texas Confederate government, defended Laredo against the Union 1st Texas Cavalry, and drove the Union forces out of Brownsville.

On the Union side was Rafael Chacon, a former Mexican soldier during the Mexican-American War. In 1861, the 28-year-old was made captain of an almost totally Spanish-speaking regiment under the command of famous frontiersman Kit Carson. In February 1862, three thousand Confederate troops under the command of General Henry Sibley neared Fort Craig, in New Mexico Territory. Confederate troops hoped to capture New Mexico since it led to the California and Colorado gold fields. Chacon and his men harassed the Confederate troops and forced Sibley's men to retreat away from the fort. A few days later, the real battle began at Valverde. During the battle, Chacon led an assault deep into enemy lines. When Union comrades called for a retreat, Chacon's regiment was the last to cross back to safety. This battle was the westernmost engagement of the Civil War. Although it was a Confederate victory, the southern troops were weakened by casualties and defeated a month later at the Battle of Glorieta Pass.

Lieutenant Colonel Manuel Chaves, nicknamed El Lioncita (the Little Lion) was in charge of the First New Mexico Volunteers. He also fought at the Battle of Valverde. But it was at Glorieta Pass that Chaves's scouting skills came into play. He led the Union troops through 16 miles of mountain wilderness to a point right on top of Sibley's Confederate base camp, which was filled with all the supplies needed to keep the army traveling toward the gold fields. After a short battle, the camp was destroyed and the Confederates were forced to retreat back into Texas, giving up their dream of capturing the western gold fields. Although the Battle of Glorieta Pass did not result in major casualties, it was a turning point and is sometimes referred to as the "Gettysburg of the West."

It's Your Turn

1. What were the common nicknames for the Union and Confederate soldiers?
2. What were the sutler wagons that followed the armies from camp to camp? Do you think it was "right" to sell items for such highly inflated prices? Why or why not?
3. Why do you think the Union soldiers were better dressed and better armed than their southern counterparts?
4. Describe some of the activities soldiers used while in camp for their own entertainment and amusement.
5. What part did David Farragut play in the Civil War?

Federico Cavada

For all of its controversy, the American Civil War produced many courageous and heroic individuals. Thomas "Stonewall" Jackson, George Meade, Robert E. Lee, Joshua Chamberlain, George Pickett, Robert Gould Shaw, and Ulysses S. Grant were officers, but ordinary soldiers like Daniel Crotty and civilians such as Clara Barton were also heroes.

Another hero was a Latino named Federico Cavada, who combined courage (the character word for this chapter) with natural artistic and professional talents. Federico Cavada's family had immigrated from Cuba to Philadelphia. An engineer and hot air balloonist, 30-year-old Cavada volunteered to fight for his new country the day before the Battle of Bull Run (Battle of Manassas).

Above: Federico Cavada was an artist, soldier, author, diplomat, and a leader in the fight for Cuban independence.

sylvania Historical Society and is called "The Battle of Marye's Heights."

During the Battle of Gettysburg in 1863, Cavada was captured and spent the rest of the war at Libby Concentration Camp in Richmond. Even there, Cavada continued to use his talents to sketch and write about prison life. The result was a publication called *Libby Life*. Released from prison in March 1864, Cavada returned to the army and served under the command of his good friend General David Birney, who was killed during Grant's Wilderness Campaign. Saddened by his friend's death, Cavada wrote the poem "Burney's Grave," a touching account of his friend's bravery and the horror of war.

After the war ended, Cavada returned to Cuba as a U.S. diplomat. After three years of service,

He was quickly given the rank of captain in the Union Army and given an assignment to match his unusual talents. He became part of a group nicknamed "the eyes of the Army of the Potomac." Cavada, an excellent artist, flew above the battlefields in a balloon and sketched the scenes below. This helped federal forces coordinate responses to Confederate troop movements. An excellent horseman, Cavada also joined the cavalry and fought in a number of battles including Antietam and Fredericksburg. For his courage, he was promoted to the rank of lieutenant colonel. He later used his artistic ability to paint a scene from the Battle of Fredericksburg that now hangs in the Penn-

he resigned and used his military experience to form a training camp for Cuban soldiers involved in a war with Spain for independence. He introduced guerilla warfare tactics and in 1870, he became commander-in-chief of the Cuban Revolutionary Army. A year later, he was captured by Spanish forces when he refused to leave a wounded friend to escape into the mountains.

Cavada was scheduled for execution. The U.S. tried to intervene, and many former Civil War comrades, including President Ulysses S. Grant, begged the Spanish government to call off his execution. However, he was executed by a firing squad the day after his capture.

Section Preview

As you read, look for:
• the life of civilians during the war.

Did You Know?

There was such a shortage of coal during the war that southerners mixed coal dust, sawdust, sand, and wet clay for fuel.

Life During the Civil War

While the leaders of both sides planned strategies and waged battles, others in the North and the South made their own contributions to the war effort. Both northern and southern communities endured hardships during the Civil War, and the civilians at home suffered no matter which side of the conflict they were on.

In 1863, the South had to import everything from a hairpin to a tooth-pick, from a cradle to a coffin. Southerners found it difficult to get such farm supplies as seed, horse harnesses, ropes, and water tubs. The cost of feed for the animals and salt to cure, or preserve, meat was high. Household items, such as soap, candles, and matches were hard to come by. People often went without oil or gas for lighting and wood or coal for heating. There were not enough medical supplies for the civilians or the army. Many of the rail lines were inoperable because there were no tracks to replace war-damaged lines. There was a severe lack of replacement parts for manufacturing machinery. The few manufacturing facilities in the South were not functional as the war wore on. Life in Georgia, as in all southern states, became very difficult.

Bread riots broke out in Richmond, Virginia. It was almost impossible to get items such as coffee or sugar. People used molasses as a sweetener instead of sugar. When they had no more coffee, people made drinks from chicory, peanuts, okra seed, and sweet potatoes. Many southerners used food items they had never tried before. Some ate mule meat and rats.

Women made clothing from curtains or carpets. Shoes were made from horsehide, deerskin, pigskin, and, sometimes, book covers. When they could not find the right kind of paper, some publishers used multicolored or patterned wallpaper for newsprint.

Prices in the South shot up, and money became worth less and less. Salt, which had cost a penny a pound before the war, rose to 50 cents a pound. Flour jumped to $200 a barrel. Dress shoes cost as much as $100. People began

Above: In Union-occupied towns, southern women were sometimes reduced to asking the soldiers for food.

to barter items. According to one news report, a woman traded a $600 hat for five turkeys. Newspaper ads with barter requests were common.

There were not enough teachers or books to keep most schools open. Soldiers needed the ammunition and horses, so there were few hunts or races. Some communities tried to raise money for the war with talent shows, musicals, or even road shows. The admission price of one such show in Uniontown, Alabama, was $2 or "one pair of socks."

Neighbors and friends still visited each other, but the gatherings were no longer carefree parties. Southern women, trying to keep up family farms, did not always look forward to getting mail. They knew any letter might bring news of an injured or dead husband, son, or brother.

Women in the Civil War

Women played a variety of roles in the war. They ran family farms or worked in factories, jobs traditionally held by men before the war. According to some reports, about four hundred women disguised themselves as men and fought as soldiers. On more than one occasion, women acted as spies and Army scouts for both Union and Confederate troops; others served in the army as stewardesses, laundresses, and nurses. When the Confederate Army in Tennessee was desperate for ammunition, ladies in Augusta were called into the Powder Works Gunpowder Plant to help produce 75,000 cartridges a day. Thousands of women worked as paid or unpaid volunteers, and some were placed in positions of major importance.

Thirty-nine-year-old Phoebe Pember of Savannah was in charge of housekeeping and patient diet at one of the divisions of Richmond's Chimborazo Hospital. During the war, 15,000 patients were under her direct care. Sally Tompkins ran a southern military hospital and was made a captain by Jefferson Davis, the only woman to receive an officer's rank in the Confederate Army. Dorothea Dix, who was known for her tireless campaign on behalf of the mentally ill, was head of the Union's Nursing Corps. Clara Barton was a Union Army nurse supervisor. After the war, she used her field-hospital experiences to found the American Red Cross in 1881.

Other women, such as Mary Boykin Chesnut of South Carolina, used their literary talents to record the drama of the Civil War. Chesnut's *A Diary from Dixie* was a shortened version of a 400,000-word manuscript about life

Above: Clara Barton also helped with the efforts to identify 13,000 unknown Union dead at the Andersonville prisoner-of-war camp.

during the period. Abolitionists such as Elizabeth Cady Stanton and Susan B. Anthony not only promoted the abolition of slavery but worked to obtain equal rights and suffrage for women.

Women helped in the war effort in a very important way by simply keeping in touch with husbands, sons, brothers, and friends. By some accounts, close to 150,000 letters were sent out from Union postal offices each day. Although southern mail took far longer, the same support was given to Confederate troops.

Occasionally, women supported the war effort in a less-than-dignified fashion. When New Orleans was occupied by Union soldiers, women cast hateful glances at the soldiers as they passed by. They sang Confederate songs in loud voices and even spit on Union troops. One woman even emptied a bed chamber pot out a window on the head of Admiral David Farragut. Shortly thereafter, Union officials passed the "Woman's Order," which made it a crime to treat soldiers in an undignified manner.

Most women, however, were content to help the war effort by keeping home and hearth going, by making clothes and bandages for soldiers, or filling the more traditional role of nursing the wounded.

Young People During the Civil War

During the Civil War, life for young people in the North did not change too drastically. They still attended school from 8 to 5, but the teachers were female. Male teachers had left for the battlefields. Students returned home for "dinner" as the midday meal, and they might have even taken a nap before returning to school for afternoon classes. Immigrant children, however, probably worked in a factory instead of attending school.

Children still had chores at home. Girls sewed and knitted for the men in their fathers' regiments. Boys hauled potatoes and onions to maintain a diet that would prevent scurvy. Many sawed wood for the family's fireplaces and cooking stoves. Those who lived on farms worked much longer hours feeding the animals and helping out during harvests.

In the South, children's lives were very different. There had been few public schools before the war, and none really operated during the war. Only wealthy children with private tutors were schooled during the war years.

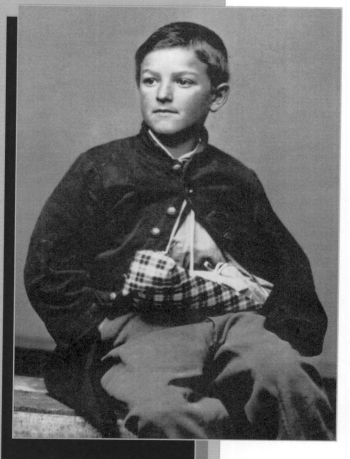

Above: Twelve-year-old drummer boy William Black is considered to be the youngest wounded soldier in the Civil War.

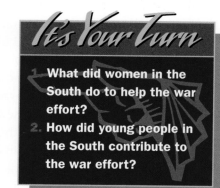

It's Your Turn

1. What did women in the South do to help the war effort?
2. How did young people in the South contribute to the war effort?

With most of the men away, children had to help maintain homes and farms and take care of younger brothers and sisters. Mealtimes were not much of a treat as food became quite scarce in most areas of the South.

Because of the blockade, replacement items were hard to come by. Clothes and shoes were patched and not replaced when they wore out. Recreational sports such as fishing and hunting were now essential to provide food for the family.

Many young boys, however, went off to war. In the Union Army, there were thousands of soldiers between the ages of fourteen and sixteen. Over three hundred soldiers were age thirteen or younger, and some were as young as ten. Confederate Army records were not as well maintained, but it is assumed that boys as young as age 10 served as soldiers.

A Final Note

The Civil War cost our nation much more than the devastation and destruction of the towns and lands upon which battles were fought. It cost much more than the emotional heartache of a war that split our nation in half for five bloody years.

Over 620,000 soldiers died in the Civil War. About one-third of those men died on the battlefield, but most died from diseases, wounds, or the hardships of military prisons. On both sides of the tragic conflict, some of the men fought out of a sense of loyalty and duty; others fought from a sense of adventure. Neither the North nor the South was ever the same again. The healing of emotional wounds took far longer than the war itself. In the end, all that remained was the challenge of rebuilding a nation that had been devastated by the internal strife.

Chapter Summary

- The Civil War had many outstanding leaders from both North and South, but the two men who led the governments of that time were President Jefferson Davis of the Confederate States of America and United States President Abraham Lincoln.
- Hostilities actually began with the firing on Fort Sumter by Confederate troops on April 12, 1861.
- Most of the battles of the war took place on southern soil, so most of the damage to civilian areas occurred in the South.
- Northern strategies during the war included a blockade of southern ports to prevent trade with other nations, the Anaconda Plan to squeeze the Confederacy in half, the capture of the Confederate capital, and the plan by Generals Grant and Sherman to destroy the Confederate armies while, at the same time, destroying the civilian areas to end civilian support for the war effort.
- The South's primary strategy was called King Cotton diplomacy. The Confederacy hoped that British and French businesses would need its cotton and would maintain trade with the South, providing money, supplies, and munitions to help the South win the war.
- There were over one hundred Civil War battles fought in Georgia with most, ninety-two, coming in 1864. The two major Union campaigns of that year were the Atlanta Campaign, which led to the fall and burning of Atlanta in November 1864, and the Savannah Campaign, which included Sherman's infamous March to the Sea and ended in December 1864 with the surrender of Savannah.
- Lincoln's Emancipation Proclamation, issued in September 1862, promised to allow slavery in states where it already existed if the South would end the war. The South chose to continue to fight.
- Neither the North nor the South were capable of handling the large numbers of prisoners of war during the four-year period. As a result, Civil War prisons were generally inhumane. There were stories of abuse, starvation, and mistreatment in prisons of both the North and the South.
- Lives of the soldiers for both the Union and the Confederacy were very similar although southern troops suffered far more from a lack of supplies, rations, and ammunition than did northern troops.
- Participants in the Civil War included people from all walks of life, and all ethnic groups in the United States with outstanding contributions from women, children, Latinos, and blacks.
- Over 620,000 Americans died in the Civil War, and total costs to the North and South in financial terms exceeded $15 billion.

ChapterReview

Reviewing People, Places, and Terms

Write a sentence explain the importance of each of the following people or places to U.S. history during the Civil War period.

1. Atlanta
2. Clara Barton
3. Chickamauga
4. Fort Pulaski
5. Ulysses S. Grant
6. John Bell Hood
7. Joseph E. Johnston
8. Robert E. Lee
9. Abraham Lincoln
10. Charles Olmstead
11. Savannah

Understanding the Facts

1. What stand did Lincoln take on slavery in his inaugural address?

2. Which battle signaled the start of the Civil War?

3. Describe the different strategies for winning the war.

4. Why did President Jefferson Davis replace General Joseph E. Johnston with General John Bell Hood? What happened in the battle after that change of command?

5. What were the two major campaigns fought in Georgia in 1864?

6. What impact did the fall of Georgia to Union troops have on the war?

7. Which battle ended hostilities in the western territories in the war?

Developing Critical Thinking

1. What do you think was the greatest factor in the Confederacy's defeat?

2. One person called the Civil War "a rich man's war and a poor man's fight." What do you think that meant?

3. Was General Sherman's "seared earth" plan really necessary? What did it accomplish?

Checking It Out

1. No battle in our history involved more casualties than the Battle of Gettysburg. But the huge task of moving so many men (75,000 Union troops and 82,289 Confederate troops) to the battle site is one aspect that many history students do not consider. Research that battle. Identify at least ten factors that would make the movement of troops into battle positions so difficult.

2. Most of the battles described in this chapter were land battles, but sea power played an important part in the war. Research the role of sea power for both Union and Confederate forces. Why did so many blockade runners manage to get through the Union blockades? What role did sea vessels play in transporting men, supplies, and munitions for both armies? What was the importance of rivers in the war, especially the larger rivers such as the Mississippi? Look too at the battle between the *Monitor* and the *Merrimac.*

3. Jefferson Davis proposed the creation of a camel-mounted cavalry to patrol the southwestern desert. Check out Civil War facts in your media center or on the Internet and see if his idea came to pass.

Writing Across the Curriculum

1. Most of the battles that took place in Georgia occurred in 1864 as a part of the Atlanta Campaign and the Savannah Campaign. Select the battles that took place nearest your home and research at least one of those battles. Prepare a short report on the location, the commanders of both sides, the number of troops, the number of casualties, the battle's outcome, and the strategies involved in the battle.

2. Few resources are more valuable to a historian than primary resources, such as letters that have been saved from soldiers to their families or from commanders to their leaders. Pretend that you are a 15-year-old soldier on the lines at the Battle of Resaca. Write a letter to a friend describing your daily activities, your food and supplies, life in your camp, and the battle in which you have just taken part.

Exploring Technology

1. Use your favorite search engine to research the lives of any three of the following Civil War leaders—Robert E. Lee, Ulysses S. Grant, William T. Sherman, Raphael Semmes, David Farragut, Philip Sheridan, J. E. B. Stuart, Joseph Johnston, George McClellan, Thomas "Stonewall" Jackson, James Longstreet, Joshua Chamberlain, George Pickett, Nathan Bedford Forrest, Governor Joseph E. Brown, John Bell Hood. Determine the following facts:

   a. What attributes or character traits did they have in common?

   b. What did they do before the war? How did that help them in their military careers or in battles?

   c. Did they share any common experiences before or after the war? Explain.

d. What military role did they play in the war?

e. How were they viewed by their men?

f. How does history portray them?

2. Use your Internet research skills to find out who Quantrill's Raiders were and for what were they most known.

3. The Massacre at Fort Pillow has long been a source of controversy. Use your Internet skills to find at least four different accounts and determine the following information:

   a. Did Nathan Bedford Forrest order the killing or wounding of 70 percent of the "coloured troops" and 43 percent of the "white troops"?

   b. In your opinion, what caused the massacre? List as many elements as you can.

   c. Do you think that the results of the investigation were correct? Why or why not?

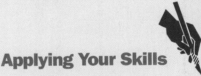

Applying Your Skills

1. Canned foods were a new thing resulting from wartime needs. New canned items included Underwood deviled ham, Borden's condensed milk, Van Camp pork & beans, Lea & Perrins worcestershire sauce, and McIhenny's tabasco sauce. The next time the family goes grocery shopping, go with them and see if you can find any of those items on the shelves. Or, just check the kitchen shelves or pantry in your home.

2. On a county map of Georgia, mark the locations of the battles that took place in Georgia. Show which campaign each battle was a part of by color-coding the map. As you prepare the legend for your map, list the year and date for each battle and the major commanders involved in each battle.

3. Did you know that an estimated 3,530 Native Americans fought for the Union in the Civil War? About 1,018 of those troops were killed. What percentage of Indians fighting in the Union were killed?

A New Spirit

I n the South, the period following the Civil War was a time for rebuilding homes, towns, businesses, farms, government, and —yes— lives and hearts. With leadership from men and women like Hoke Smith, Rebecca Felton, and Henry W. Grady, Georgia recovered physically. Rebuilding lives and hearts, however, was more difficult. While groups like the Freedman's Bureau worked on changing lives, other people and groups, including the Bourbons, Tom Watson, and the Ku Klux Klan, worked just as hard to maintain "Old South" ways.

This was also an era of progressive ideals that demanded reform. Suffrage for women, improvements for workers, temperance, prison reform, educational reforms, equality and freedom from discrimination for African Americans were all important goals for reformers.

After the turn of the century, reform took a backseat to World War I. That was followed by the carefree ways of the "Roaring Twenties." But the levity of the twenties disappeared in 1929 with the crash of the stock market. Suddenly, the nation and Georgia were swept into an economic depression.

President Franklin Delano Roosevelt and his New Deal policies helped ease the pain of the depression. But it was World War II that actually set America and Georgia back on their feet. What had once been an agricultural state with little industry became a leader in business and industry. Another result of the war effort was that military bases and installations spread throughout the state.

Left: The Madison-Morgan Cultural Center is housed in a red brick building that was erected in 1895 as one of the first graded public schools in the South. **Right:** This is a restored classroom of the period in the Cultural Center.

Chapter 9

1866–1889

Reconstruction and the New South

Georgians, and other southerners, had to deal with three basic questions in the aftermath of the war: (1) What would be done with 4 million newly freed slaves? (2) How could sectional differences and emotional war wounds be healed so that the nation could be reunited? (3) How could the South, which had suffered most of the war damage, resurrect itself and its economy? In addition to those questions, southerners had yet to find out what type of treatment the defeated Confederacy would receive from the victorious Union.

Left: This depot, reconstructed at the Georgia Agrirama in Tifton, was originally built in Montezuma and belonged to the Atlanta, Birmingham and Atlantic Railroad. After the Civil War, the railroads in the South had to be almost completely rebuilt. They were critical to the economic recovery of Georgia and the South.

Signs of the Times 1865-1889

Population: 1,184,109 in 1870; 1,542,180 in 1880

Life Expectancy: 44 years in 1870, but 39.4 years in 1880

Costs of Living: It varied, depending on the section of country: Rent averaged $10-$25 a month; food, lights, and fuel averaged $40 a month

Wages/Salaries: In the mid-1870s, a school teacher might earn $360 a year, a factory worker, $500, a farm worker, $180, a cowboy, $480, a bank clerk $1,800, a policeman $600-$900, and a reporter, $1,040.

Art/Architecture: Artist Winslow Homer, known for his ocean scenes, painted "Prisoners for the Front," "Fog Warning," and "The Life Line." Frederick Remington became famous for his paintings of the American West. The "Shingle" architectural style was introduced for houses.

Music: Showboats and vaudeville musical reviews reappeared. Popular songs of the period included "Silver Threads Among the Gold," "I've Been Working on the Railroad," "Clementine," "My Wild Irish Rose," and " Sweet Rosie O'Grady." John Philip Sousa popularized such march songs as "The Stars and Stripes Forever" and "Semper Fidelis."

Literature: Louisa Mae Alcott published *Little Women* and *Little Men*. Mark Twain published *The Adventures of Tom Sawyer*, *Life on the Mississippi*, *The Prince and the Pauper*, and *The Adventures of Huckleberry Finn*. Sidney Lanier published "Corn," about farming in the old South, and "The Symphony," about the industrial North. Joel Chandler Harris wrote *Uncle Remus: His Songs and Sayings* using black dialect.

Fads/Fashions: The popularity of bicycling enabled women to give up long-skirted, heavy Victorian attire and use long hose and balloon below-the -knee trousers. Zippers were invented by Whitcomb Judson. Louis Tiffany opened his glass factory and his incredible lamp designs became fads among the wealthy.

Religion: In 1872, Charles Russell organized Jehovah's Witnesses. Mary Baker Eddy published *Science and Health*, the beginning of Christian Science. The American branch of the Salvation Army was founded in Philadelphia. The Knights of Columbus, a fraternal organization of Catholic men, was formed. Billy Sunday began his evangelistic career.

Transportation: Andrew Hallidie, a California engineer, invented the cable car for San Francisco. John Montgomery began air travel by launching a glider from a 300-foot hill; it flew 600 feet. Pullman Car Company constructed an electric locomotive for hauling freight.

Science/Inventions: Inventions of the period include an electric voting machine, mimeograph machine, phonograph, incandescent lamp, air brakes, typewriter, adding machine, and fountain pen. Alexander Graham Bell invented the telephone; his first words in the first call were "Mr. Watson, come here. I want you." Saccharin (500 times stronger than sugar) was discovered.

Education: Howard University was founded in Washington, D.C. The first school of nursing opened in 1873 in New York at Bellevue Hospital. Booker T. Washington became president of the school that was to become Tuskegee Institute. The first state-supported women's college was chartered— Mississippi State College for Women.

Leisure Time: Basketball and ice hockey were introduced. The first running of the Belmont Stakes and Kentucky Derby horse races took place. The first annual indoor track and field meet was held by the New York Athletic Club. The first professional baseball team was formed—the Cincinnati Red Stockings. The first intercollegiate football game was played with Rutgers beating Princeton 6 to 4.

Figure 29 Timeline: 1865–1890

1865
Georgia adopted new constitution and ratified 13th Amendment

1867
Georgia put under military rule; Atlanta University granted charter

1868
Atlanta named capital; Georgia adopted new constitution and ratified 14th Amendment

1869
Georgia Act passed; State returned to military control

1870
15th Amendment ratified; Georgia readmitted to Union

1872
Grange chapter founded in state

1874
State Department of Agriculture established

1877
New state constitution adopted; Atlanta named permanent capital

1881
International Cotton Exposition held in Atlanta

1887
Bauxite discovered in Georgia

1865   1870   1875   1880   1885   1890

1875
Congress passed Civil Rights Act

1889
Johnstown flood

1878
Yellow fever epidemic swept through South killing 14,000

1886
Statue of Liberty, a gift from France, dedicated in New York Harbor

1867
Grange founded

1881
Clara Barton established National Red Cross

1883
Supreme Court struck down Civil Rights Act of 1865

1865
Lincoln assassinated

Section Preview

As you read, look for:
- the purpose of the Freedmen's Bureau,
- the presidential plans for Reconstruction, and
- vocabulary terms: freedmen, Freedmen's Bureau, Reconstruction, disfranchise, Thirteenth Amendment, and nullify.

Lincoln and Reconstruction

The Georgia to which the war-weary Confederate soldiers returned was not as they had left it. Fields lay in ruins. Most houses were badly run down or had been destroyed. Railroad tracks lay twisted, bridges had been burned, cotton mills and factories were closed or burned. There was not enough food, and many people were starving. Many banks had closed their doors. The Confederacy had a war debt of over $700 million, and Georgia faced a debt of $20 million.

Of the 125,000 Georgians who fought in the war, 25,000 did not return home due to battle deaths and diseases. Many others could not work because of their injuries. For most white Georgians, there were new struggles each day just to eat. Life was no better for the men, women, and children freed from slavery.

The Freedmen

The thousands of freedmen (former slaves) faced great hardships. Homeless, uneducated, and free for first time in their lives, the freedmen had little more than the clothes on their backs. Many went from place to place looking for food, shelter, and work. Some traveled just to demonstrate that they

Below: After the war, many northerners came South and established schools to teach the freedmen to read and write.

By the Side of the Road

Founded in 1773, Springfield Baptist Church is the oldest African American church in the United States. It was also the only Baptist Church in Augusta until 1820 and the only black church until 1840. The church building itself, built in 1801, is the oldest surviving church building in Augusta and one of the oldest in Georgia. But Springfield Baptist Church is also significant for other reasons.

On January 10, 1866, thirty-eight African Americans from eleven Georgia counties met at the church and prepared a petition to the Georgia legislature asking for inclusion on juries, civil treatment on railroads, and the right to vote. Before adjourning, the men established the Georgia Equal Rights Association, which later became the Republican party in Georgia.

In 1867, the Augusta Baptist Institute opened at the church with thirty-seven students. In 1870, the Institute moved to Atlanta and was renamed Morehouse College.

SPRINGFIELD BAPTIST CHURCH
BIRTHPLACE OF MOREHOUSE COLLEGE

This building, which was erected in 1801 by Augusta's first Methodist Society, was moved to this location in 1844 to become the home of the Springfield Baptist Church.

Organized in 1787 by Jesse Peters, the Springfield Baptist Church is the oldest independent African-American Church in the nation. This church helped bridge the transition between slavery and free citizenship and has stood as a focus for black community life.

This church building is the major landmark remaining from the early free-black community of Springfield. The original structure was moved to the rear of the lot when the new brick church was built in 1897. Springfield Church helped to establish many black institutions.

In 1867, Morehouse College, the nation's only all-male, historically black undergraduate institution, was founded in the basement of Springfield Baptist Church as Augusta Institute by William Jefferson White, as requested by Richard Coulter and Edmund Turney, while Henry Watts was serving as pastor. The school moved to Atlanta in 1879 and was renamed Morehouse College in 1913. This marker unveiled February 16, 1992, commemorates the 125th anniversary of Morehouse College's founding.

could. Others searched for spouses, children, other family members, or friends who had been sold away from them during slavery.

Because the Civil War destroyed the master-slave relationship, a new relationship had to be developed between the two races. That would not be easy. Former slaves feared that their old masters would try to re-enslave them. Most whites found it difficult to accept former slaves as free persons, nor would they accept them as equals.

The Freedmen's Bureau

In an effort to help the struggling freedmen, the United States government established the Bureau of Refugees, Freedmen, and Abandoned Lands

Did You Know?

Some historians estimate that Georgia lost 75 percent of its former material wealth.

Figure 30 Typical Loyalty Oath

I, _____, of the County of _____, State of Georgia, do solemnly swear or affirm, in the presence of Almighty God, that I will henceforth faithfully support and defend the Constitution of the United States and the Union faithfully of the States thereunder, and that I will in like manner, abide by and faithfully support all laws and proclamations which have been made during the existing rebellion with reference to the emancipation of slaves—So help me, God.

Above: It has been said that the presidency ages the people who hold that office. This photograph of President Abraham Lincoln was taken in 1865. Compare this photograph of Lincoln with the photograph on page 245, taken just five years earlier.

in March 1865. Its first commissioner was Union General Oliver O. Howard, who later founded Howard University in Washington, D.C. The original purpose of the agency, which soon became known as the Freedmen's Bureau, was to help both former slaves and poor whites cope with their everyday problems by offering them clothing, food, and other necessities.

After a while, the bureau's focus changed; it became concerned mainly with helping the freedmen adjust to their new circumstances. An important focus was education. The bureau set up over 4,000 primary schools, 64 industrial schools, and 74 teacher-training institutions for young African Americans in addition to spending over $400,000 to help establish teacher-training centers.

Northerners and missionary societies helped by sending both money and teachers. In 1867, the American Missionary Association sponsored the chartering of Georgia's Atlanta University. The American Baptist Home Mission society organized Morehouse College in Augusta. Morehouse, which moved to Atlanta in 1870, is still in operation today. A third Georgia Reconstruction-era school was Clark College in Atlanta, which first opened as a school for children. By 1877, it had become a college.

Lincoln's Plan for Reconstruction

During the closing days of the war, President Lincoln developed a plan to rebuild the South and restore the southern states to the Union as quickly and easily as possible. The process was known as Reconstruction. Lincoln's plan had two simple steps: (1) All southerners, except for high-ranking Confederate civil and military leaders, would be pardoned after taking an oath of allegiance to the United States; and (2) when 10 percent of the voters in each state had taken the oath of loyalty, the state would be permitted to form a legal government and rejoin the Union.

It soon became apparent that Congress and many northerners thought that the South should be punished. They believed that those Confederate states that seceded should be treated like a conquered country. In 1864, Congress passed the Wade-Davis Bill, which Lincoln saw as an attempt to punish the South for the actions of the seces-

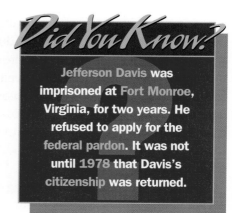

Did You Know?

Jefferson Davis was imprisoned at Fort Monroe, Virginia, for two years. He refused to apply for the federal pardon. It was not until 1978 that Davis's citizenship was returned.

sionists. Lincoln did not sign the bill into law; he let it die quietly. This action signaled that there would be a fight over Reconstruction. Lincoln, however, was not part of that fight.

The Assassination of President Lincoln

On Good Friday, April 14, 1865, Lincoln and his wife accompanied friends to Ford's Theatre to see an English play, *Our American Cousin*. The play was nearly over when John Wilkes Booth, an actor who was a southern sympathizer, entered Lincoln's theater box. At 10:15 p.m., timing his action with the play's biggest laugh, Booth shot the president in the back of the head. Booth leapt from the box and slipped out of Washington without getting caught. He was cornered and shot two weeks later.

The wounded president was taken to a boarding house across the street from the theater. Lincoln died the next morning. As it turned out, Booth probably did more harm to the South than good. Lincoln was no longer around to keep the radical Republicans (those who wanted to punish the South) in check.

Above: As president, Andrew Johnson decided to carry out Lincoln's moderate plan for Reconstruction.

Johnson Tackles Reconstruction

Lincoln's assassination took place before his plan for Reconstruction went into effect. Upon Lincoln's death, Vice President Andrew Johnson, a North Carolinian, became the nation's seventeenth president. Soon after taking office, he took on the responsibility for returning the former Confederate states to the Union.

Johnson's Reconstruction plan was much like Lincoln's plan except that Johnson expanded the groups of southerners not granted a general pardon. Those who had owned property worth more than $20,000 or those who had held high civil or military positions had to apply directly to the president for a pardon.

At first, some of the radicals were willing to work with Johnson because they approved of his plan to offer a reward for the arrest of Jefferson Davis. But after Davis was captured and imprisoned, the radicals turned their attention back to the president's plan and began to disagree with it. They were afraid that the freedmen would be **disfranchised** (have their voting rights taken away). They also thought that the South deserved a greater punishment than Johnson's plan provided.

After some pressure, President Johnson added several more requirements. First, the southern states had to approve the **Thirteenth Amendment**, which made slavery illegal. Second, the southern states had to **nullify** (declare invalid) their ordinances of secession. Third, the southern states had to promise not to repay the individuals and institutions that had helped finance the Confederacy.

Figure 31 The Thirteenth Amendment to the U.S. Constitution

Section 1. Neither slavery nor involuntary servitude, except as a punishment for crime whereof the party shall have been duly convicted, shall exist within the United States, or any place subject to their jurisdiction.

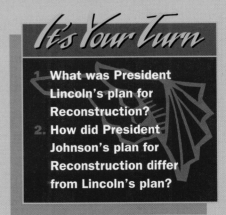

It's Your Turn

1. What was President Lincoln's plan for Reconstruction?
2. How did President Johnson's plan for Reconstruction differ from Lincoln's plan?

Reconstruction in Georgia

In June 1865, President Johnson appointed James Johnson, an attorney from Columbus, as provisional (temporary) governor of Georgia because the president remembered that Johnson had opposed succession as a state congressman. Six months after Lee's surrender at Appomattox, the president directed Governor Johnson to hold a constitutional convention in Milledgeville, Georgia's capital.

The Constitutional Convention of 1865

The convention repealed the ordinance of secession and voted to abolish slavery. The delegates wrote a new constitution that, although quite similar to the constitution of 1861, was acceptable to the president.

In November, the state elected Charles Jenkins as governor. Jenkins, who was the only candidate, was a Unionist judge from Augusta. In the following months, the legislature met and formally ratified the Thirteenth Amendment. In December 1865, after President Johnson removed the provisional governor, the state inaugurated Jenkins.

The Georgia General Assembly met in January 1866 and elected two U.S. senators—Alexander Stephens, former vice president of the Confederacy, and Herschel Johnson. The General Assembly also voted to extend civil rights to the freedmen. However, like other southern states, Georgia limited those rights using, in part, a system of Black Codes.

Black Codes

Although the Thirteenth Amendment abolished slavery, it did not abolish discrimination (unfair treatment of a person or group because of prejudice). By 1865, most of the southern states, including Georgia, had passed a number of laws known as Black Codes, which were designed to restrict the rights of the freedmen. The codes included regulations that controlled the types of employment freedmen could have, permitted whipping as punishment, and established labor periods from sunrise to sunset, six days a week. Because these codes permitted the imprisonment of jobless blacks, freedmen were forced to take whatever jobs they could find regardless

Above: James Johnson, a pro-Union Georgian, became provisional governor in June 1865. He served until December 1865.

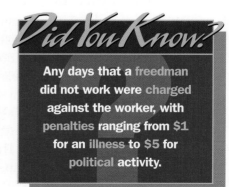

Did You Know?

Any days that a freedman did not work were charged against the worker, with penalties ranging from $1 for an illness to $5 for political activity.

of low wages or other conditions. Although the Freedmen's Bureau recommended wages of $144 a year, plus food and shelter, most workers were paid between $50 and $100 per year.

Other sections of the Black Codes did not allow freedmen to vote, to serve on juries, or to testify in court against whites. The codes also declared marriage between the races illegal.

Even with the codes, Georgia had done what President Johnson's plan required, and it was ready to re-enter the Union. But President Johnson no longer had the influence he once had. The more radical groups in Congress were now in charge of Reconstruction.

Congressional Reconstruction

Reaction to the Black Codes was fairly swift. Congress, overriding a presidential veto, passed the Civil Rights Act of 1866. This law not only extended citizenship to African Americans, it also gave the federal government the right and responsibility to intervene any time civil rights were taken away from the newly freed men and women. To ensure this, Congress passed the **Fourteenth Amendment**, which granted citizenship to the freedmen and forbade any state from denying anyone the "equal protection of the law."

Figure 32 Excerpt from the Fourteenth Amendment to the U.S. Constitution

Section 1. All persons born or naturalized in the United States and subject to the jurisdiction thereof, are citizens of the United States and of the State wherein they reside. No State shall make or enforce any law which shall abridge the privileges or immunities of citizens of the United States; nor shall any State deprive any person of life, liberty, or property, without due process of law; nor deny to any person within its jurisdiction the equal protection of the laws.

That same year, the radical Republicans gained control of both houses of Congress. They maintained that the southern states were not "adequately reconstructed" and must ratify the Fourteenth Amendment before they could rejoin the Union. One radical, Thaddeus Stevens, wanted to punish the South even more by breaking up all of the plantations and providing every farm slave with "forty acres and a mule." But the Republicans, who valued personal property, refused to seriously consider his plan.

When all of the southern states except Tennessee refused to ratify the Fourteenth Amendment, Congress acted quickly to invalidate the state governments and re-establish military rule in March 1867. Each state was assigned to a region under the command of a federal general. Georgia, Alabama, and Florida were placed in the Third Military District, governed by General John Pope. One of Pope's first tasks was to register all eligible male voters—black and white—who swore allegiance to the United States.

States were directed to hold constitutional conventions whose delegates were elected by adult males. Each convention was to draft a new constitution that extended the right to vote to African Americans. States were also required to have their citizens ratify the new constitutions and the Fourteenth Amendment. Until that was completed, the southern states remained under military supervision.

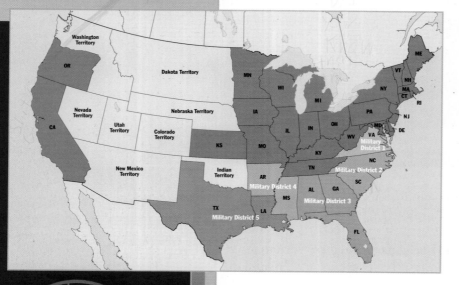

Map 41 Military Reconstruction Districts

Map Skill: Which two states made up the largest district?

Did You Know?

Scalawag is a term that means "scoundrel" or "worthless rascal."

The Constitutional Convention of 1867

During the fall of 1867, Georgians held an election to determine if there should be a constitutional convention and, if so, who should be selected as delegates. For African American males, it was the first time they were allowed to vote in Georgia. Voters agreed to hold the convention, and they elected 169 delegates. Twelve of the delegates were conservative whites, and nine were carpetbaggers. Carpetbaggers were northerners who moved south after the war. Southerners claimed that they came with all of their possessions in a bag made of carpet material. Thirty-six of the delegates were African Americans. Most of the delegates were scalawags, a term used to describe southerners who supported the Republicans.

The convention proved to be a fiery one from the outset. As delegates gathered in Milledgeville, the African American delegates were refused rooms at the local hotels. General Pope then ordered that the convention be moved from Milledgeville to Atlanta, a move that led to the city becoming the state's permanent capital.

Despite the conflicts of the convention, much was accomplished. The delegates wrote a new constitution that gave civil rights to all of the state's citizens, approved free public education for all children, and allowed married women to control their own property (the first state to do so).

Georgia voters approved the new constitution in April 1868 and elected Republican Rufus Bullock governor. For a second time, Georgia had met the requirements for re-admission to the Union, and federal troops left the state. As you will see, however, they returned shortly.

African Americans in Politics

In 1867, African Americans voted for the first time in Georgia. In 1868, they helped elect a Republican governor. They also helped elect twenty-nine African Americans to the Georgia house of representatives and three African Americans to the Georgia senate. Some of those elected were Tunis G. Campbell, Jr., Henry McNeal Turner, and Aaron A. Bradley. However, all of these men were expelled in September 1868 on the grounds that although the constitution had given them the right to vote, it did not specifically give them the right to hold political office.

During Reconstruction, African Americans formed the largest group of southern Republicans, and thousands voted in the new elections to help keep Republicans in power. By the same token, Republican carpetbaggers, along with some agents and many volunteers of the Freedmen's Bureau, worked hard to make African Americans part of the political scene. Hiram Revels and Blanche Bruce of Mississippi were the first African Americans to serve as U.S. senators. Others served in the U.S. House of Representatives and state legislatures.

Realizing political empowerment (the ability to bring about change) for the first time, thousands joined the Union League, which had become the freedmen's political organization. From church meetings to picnics and family gatherings, politics became "the" topic of discussion and debate.

Above: Reverend Henry McNeal Turner was one of the first African Americans elected to the Georgia General Assembly.

Ku Klux Klan

During this same time period, the Ku Klux Klan became a force in Georgia. The Klan, as it was called, was one of several secret organizations that tried to keep freedmen from exercising their new civil rights. The group began in Pulaski, Tennessee, in 1865 as a social club for returning soldiers. However, it quickly changed into a force of terror. Its members dressed in robes and hoods so no one would recognize them. They terrorized and intimidated African Americans to keep them from voting and, by doing so, to return control of the state to the Democrats. There were numerous reports of beatings, whippings, and murders.

Above: Early members of the Ku Klux Klan used robes and hoods as disguises and to appear more frightful to those they wanted to scare.

Figure 33 Fifteenth Amendment to the U.S. Constitution

Section 1. The right of citizens of the United States to vote shall not be denied or abridged by the United States or by any state on account of race, color, or previous condition of servitude.

Freedmen who were not frightened away from the polls were carefully watched. Those voting Republican lay awake at night listening for the sounds of horses indicating the Klan was nearby. All knew that the price for suffrage (voting rights) could be death. Hostilities between whites and African Americans increased, and there were many incidents of racial conflict.

The Georgia Act

Ku Klux Klan activities were increasing throughout the state, and there was evidence that the group had prevented many African Americans from voting in the 1868 presidential election. Governor Bullock appealed to the federal government for help. Congress responded by passing the Georgia Act in December 1869. This law returned Georgia to military control for the third time. General Alfred Terry became Georgia's new military commander, and Rufus Bullock became the provisional governor.

Earlier in the year, Congress had passed the Fifteenth Amendment to the U.S. Constitution, which gave all male citizens the right to vote. In addition to returning Georgia to federal military control, the Georgia Act required that the state ratify the Fifteenth Amendment before it could return to the Union.

Reconstruction Ends in Georgia

The Georgia supreme court ruled that blacks were eligible to hold office. When the General Assembly met in January 1870, it reseated the African American representatives who had been expelled from the General Assembly in September 1868. The legislature again approved the Fourteenth Amendment and ratified the Fifteenth Amendment.

Georgia was readmitted to the Union in July 1870. Senators Joshua Hill and H. V. M. Miller, elected in 1868, were seated in Congress. For Georgia, Reconstruction was officially over.

There was one final political note to the end of Reconstruction. In the December 1870 election, the Democrats regained control of both houses of the Georgia General Assembly. Governor Bullock, a Republican, knew the General Assembly would impeach him (bring charges against a public official while that person is still in office) when it met in November 1871. Rather than face impeachment, Bullock resigned. Secretly,

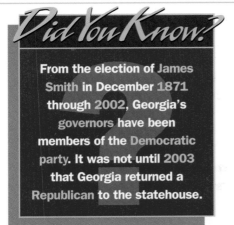
he swore in as governor Benjamin Conley, who had been president of the senate during the last legislative session. Conley served as governor for only two months before the General Assembly ordered a special election. In December, Democrat James M. Smith, former speaker of the house of representatives and a lawyer from Columbus, ran unopposed for the office of governor. Smith was inaugurated on January 12, 1872.

Economic Reconstruction

Georgia was still an agricultural region during Reconstruction. With the end of the large plantation system came the beginning of a new way of farming.

Sharecropping and Tenant Farming

Planters and farmers needed laborers to work on their land. And there were many former slaves, as well as some landless whites, who needed jobs. Workers who had nothing but their labor to offer often resorted to sharecropping. Under this system, the landowners provided land, a house, farming tools and animals, seed, and fertilizer. The workers agreed to give the owner a share of the harvest. Until the workers sold their crop, the owners often let them have food, medicine, clothing, and other supplies at high prices on credit. Credit is the ability to buy something now and pay for it later or over a period of time.

For many, this credit was their undoing. After selling the crop and paying the bills, the typical sharecropper had little, if any, cash left. Because few sharecroppers could read or count, the planter or the store owner could easily cheat them, and many did. Year after year, sharecroppers were in debt. They had little hope they could ever save enough to buy their own land and equipment.

Tenant farming was similar to sharecropping. The main difference was that tenants usually owned some agricultural equipment and farm animals, such as mules. They also bought their own seed and fertilizer. At the end of the year, tenant farmers either paid the landowner a set amount of cash or an agreed-upon share

Below: The Georgia Agrirama in Tifton is a living history center. This man demonstrates the work a farmer of the late 1800s would do. Here he is raking burned corn stubs. What tool is he using?

Top and above: This is the farmhouse of a subsistence farmer on display at the Georgia Agrirama. In the late 1800s, the kitchen was in a separate building because of fire danger from the mud-and-stick chimneys.

of the crop. Because tenant farmers owned more than sharecroppers, they usually made a small profit. However, the lives of both groups were very hard. The tenant farming and sharecropping systems allowed landowners to keep their farms in operation without having to spend money for labor.

On the surface, it would seem that landowners who used tenants and sharecroppers made a profit while taking few risks. However, many landowners who did not have the money to buy the needed seed, fertilizer, and tools borrowed the money and used the crops to back up the loan. Interest on such loans was often more than the crops were worth. Because bankers expected farmers to grow cotton or tobacco year after year, the soil was eventually ruined. In time, many landowners in the South, like the sharecroppers and tenants who worked their land, became poorer each year.

At the end of Reconstruction, cotton was again the most important crop in most of Georgia. The coastal region, however, never regained its prewar position in either cotton or rice production. Fortunately, that region turned to other natural resources to reclaim its economic power.

Business, Industry, Railroads, and Shipping

Increasing cotton production brought industry to some parts of Georgia. Northern investors put money into building textile mills. Slowly, banks began to reopen and were able to loan money to merchants and businessmen.

By the late 1860s, dry goods stores, shops, and hotels were again in business. Atlanta, almost completely destroyed during the war, rebuilt and grew rapidly after it became the state capital.

Railroads, which were necessary to the success of Georgia's economy, expanded during this time. At the end of the Civil War, only the state-owned Western and Atlantic Railroad was still in operation. Union soldiers had kept

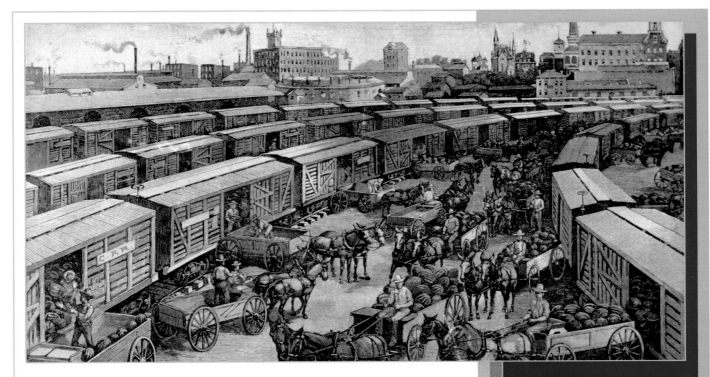

Above: Railroads played an important part in Atlanta's rebirth after the Civil War. This scene shows watermelons being loaded into boxcars for shipment north.

it up to transport troops and equipment. In the eight years immediately following the war, rail companies laid 840 miles of track in Georgia. Rail lines began to compete with each other.

Shipping companies also took on new life. Savannah again became the major port for exporting cotton, and Brunswick was a close second. Even with the growth of banks, rail lines, and shipping companies, economic reconstruction was slow. There was a common saying of the period, "We're eating the long corn now!" The saying meant that the family was financially well off. It would be another sixty-five years before many in the state could claim the long corn, but at least the seeds were planted for Georgia's future.

It's Your Turn

1. How did Black Codes restrict the freedmen?
2. Why do you think the majority of southern states refused to ratify the Fourteenth Amendment to the U.S. Constitution?
3. Do you think the constitutional convention of 1867 was a failure, a success, or both? Explain your answer.
4. If you had been a freedmen in this period, would you have gone to the polls to vote? Why or why not?
5. Was Georgia, and the rest of the South, "adequately reconstructed"? What would you have done differently if you had been in charge of Reconstruction?
6. What was the difference between a sharecropper and a tenant farmer?

A City Rises From the Ashes

At the beginning of Reconstruction, Atlanta literally had to rebuild itself from the ashes. When Sherman's troops moved out of Atlanta on their infamous March to the Sea, they left the city virtually destroyed. But the city had a proud past and the heart to rebuild for a proud future.

Atlanta had begun in 1837 when a railroad engineer, Stephen Long, surveyed the best route for the Georgia State Railroad. He wrote that a collection of shacks known as the terminus (end) might be "a good location for one tavern, a blacksmith shops, a grocery store and nothing else."

Below: By 1860, Atlanta had a population of 9,500 and was Georgia's fourth largest city, behind Savannah, Augusta, and Columbus. It was dubbed the "Gate City of the South" for its increasing importance as a rail center.

By 1842, the railroad lines into Terminus had grown, and it was home to almost thirty people. In that year, the community was renamed Marthasville, in honor of Governor Lumpkin's daughter.

Because freight shipped to the city was marked "Atlanta" (a feminine form of the word *Atlantic* in Atlantic and Pacific Railroad), the town was called Atlanta by railroad officials and crews. Soon the name Marthasville was discarded, and the state issued a municipal charter for the city to be named Atlanta.

At the beginning of the Civil War, Atlanta was Georgia's fourth largest city, with a population of over 9,500. Only Savannah, Augusta, and Columbus were larger. During the war, Atlanta grew even more in population and importance as the South's center for communications and supplies.

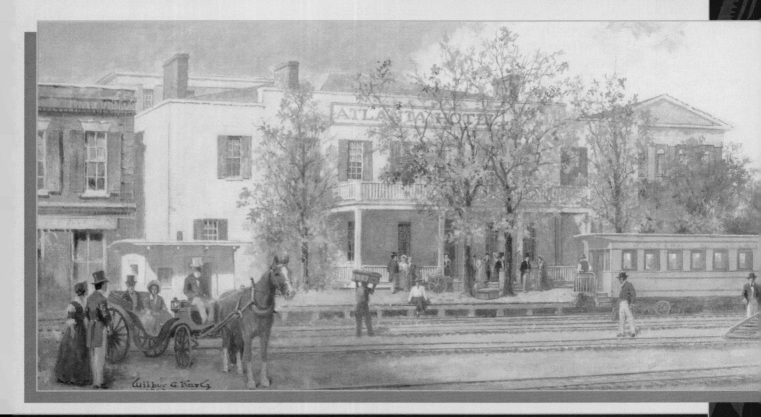

About fifty families had remained in the city after its burning. Joined by others, they worked throughout the Reconstruction period to rebuild the city. It rose out of the ashes like a *phoenix*, a mythical Arabian bird said to periodically burn itself to death and emerge from the ashes as a new phoenix. The phoenix became the center of the city's seal and depicted a spirit born out of necessity.

The city grew rapidly during Reconstruction and the New South era, both commercially and politically. When it became the capital in 1868, its continued rise was assured and its role in the New South gave it national prominence. By the dawn of the twenty-first century, Atlanta had a population of over 4 million, national recognition as a center of business and commerce, and a place among the world's great cities. Quite an accomplishment for a town that had to rebuild from ashes!

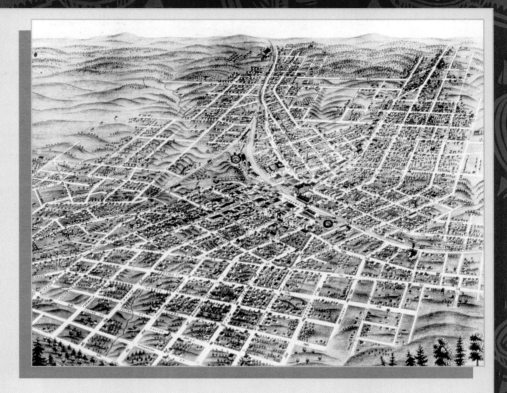

Above: This bird's-eye view of Atlanta, prepared by Albert Ruger, illustrates the rebuilding of the city following the Civil War. By 1868, Atlanta had replaced Milledgeville as the state's capital.

Section Preview

As you read, look for:
• the Bourbon Triumvirate,
• reform efforts by William and Rebecca Latimer Felton,
• the convict lease system, and
• vocabulary terms: Redemption, white supremacy, Bourbon Triumvirate, ally, temperance, and convict lease system.

Section 3
Georgia's Redemption Years

Georgia's Redemption period followed its Reconstruction period. During the Redemption period, the state struggled to overcome the hardships that Reconstruction had brought to the state and a faltering economy. The redeemers also wanted to take back the control of the state government from the Republicans.

The Bourbon Triumvirate

When Reconstruction was finally over and it was time to "redeem" the state from the hardships it had fared, the job fell primarily to three Democrats—Joseph E. Brown, Alfred H. Colquitt, and John B. Gordon. All of these leaders wanted stronger economic ties with the industrial North in order to expand Georgia's economy. They also wanted to keep many old southern traditions including white supremacy (the belief that the white race is superior to any other race). Brown, Colquitt, and Gordon were active in Georgia politics from 1872 to 1890, but their influence carried over well into the twentieth century.

The three Georgia leaders were called the Bourbon Triumvirate. *Bourbon* was the name of a castle and territory in France, as well as a line of French kings who ruled for over two hundred years. *Triumvirate* refers to a ruling body of three. Although the background of each man was different, politics and power drew them together.

Joseph E. Brown

Joseph E. Brown, the oldest member of the triumvirate, was born in South Carolina but grew up in Union County in the North Georgia mountains. After graduating from Yale Law School in 1846, Brown opened a law office in Canton, Georgia. He was elected to the state sen-

Below: Joseph E. Brown was the only man to have been elected governor of Georgia four times.

ate in 1849 and served there until 1855, when he became a judge for the Blue Ridge Judicial Circuit.

In 1857, Brown was elected Georgia's governor. He became a popular "states' rights" governor and was re-elected to two more terms.

Governor Brown guided the state through the difficult war years and was re-elected to a fourth term. When Reconstruction began, Brown lost much of his popularity by asking Georgians to go along with radical Reconstruction policies. He believed this would shorten Reconstruction. Brown remained in office until June 1865, when federal officials took over Reconstruction. Governor Rufus Bullock appointed Brown chief justice of the Georgia supreme court. He served there two years before resigning to head a company that leased the Western and Atlantic Railroad.

In 1880, he re-entered politics. When John Gordon resigned from the U.S. Senate, Governor Colquitt appointed Brown to Gordon's Senate seat. Brown stayed in the Senate until 1891. During his retirement years, Brown continued his public service in education. He was a trustee of the University of Georgia for thirty-two years and president of the Atlanta Board of Education.

Did You Know?

In 1877, Georgia voters chose Atlanta to be the permanent state capital. The vote was 99,147 to 55,201.

Above: In 1876, Alfred Holt Colquitt became governor of Georgia by the largest majority in state history up to that time.

Alfred H. Colquitt

Born April 20, 1824, in Walton County, Alfred H. Colquitt was the son of U.S. Senator Walter Colquitt, for whom Colquitt County is named. After graduating from Princeton University, he fought in the Mexican War. He was twenty-five when he entered Georgia politics, joining Joseph E. Brown in the state senate in 1849. The two developed a political bond that lasted for the next forty-four years. Before the Civil War, Colquitt served in Congress and at Georgia's secession convention. During the war years, he was an able military leader and rose to the rank of major general.

Colquitt was elected governor in 1876. Around that time, several thousand friends asked for about thirty open government jobs. Those who did not get one of the jobs tried to turn voters against Colquitt. There also were rumors that Colquitt had been involved in illegal dealings with the Northeastern Railroad. Colquitt himself called for an investigation, hoping to end the scandal.

A legislative committee found Colquitt innocent of the charges, although other members of Georgia's executive branch were found guilty. Colquitt was re-elected and served until 1882. During his administration, the state's debt was reduced and, in 1877, a new state constitution was approved. The 1877 constitution was not rewritten until 1945.

Colquitt was elected to the U.S. Senate in 1883 and 1888. He died in March 1894, three months after the death of his political ally (one who shares a common cause) Joseph E. Brown.

John B. Gordon

John B. Gordon, the third member of the Bourbon Triumvirate, was the son of a minister. He was born in 1832 in Upson County and attended the University of Georgia.

Gordon worked for a while as a newspaper correspondent, then as manager of a coal mine in Dade County. When the Civil War broke out, Gordon proved an able leader. He fought in many major battles and was one of three Georgia officers who reached the rank of lieutenant general. Gordon's wife often traveled with him and occasionally followed him into battle. After the war, Gordon wrote a book, titled *Reminiscences,* and became a popular speaker across the nation.

In 1872, Gordon defeated Alexander Stephens to become Georgia's U.S. senator. In 1880, he resigned from the Senate and accepted a position with one of the railroads. In 1886, he began the first of his two terms as governor of Georgia. While governor, Gordon reduced the state's debt and brought new industry into the area.

He returned to the U.S. Senate in 1891 and served until 1897. Gordon College in Barnesville is named for him.

The Decline of the Bourbon Triumvirate

Leaders such as Gordon, Colquitt, and Brown, along with men like the fiery segregationist Robert Toombs, helped carry Georgia through economic reconstruction as they lowered taxes, reduced the war debts, and expanded business and industry. However, they were criticized for accomplishing little to help the poor, improve education, reform factory working conditions, improve mental hospitals, or improve the lives of convicts. As a matter of fact, they profited personally from the use of prison labor.

By the end of Reconstruction, the influence of the Republican party had almost ended completely, and Democrats took over state politics. However, not all Georgians agreed with the beliefs or practices of the Bourbon Triumvirate or the Democrats who controlled state politics.

The Feltons Challenge the Bourbons

A new group calling themselves Independent Democrats was slowly gaining recognition. They started in the Seventh Congressional District of North Georgia in Cartersville. One of the group's leaders was William Felton, a doctor, farmer, Methodist preacher, and public speaker. His wife Rebecca worked with him to support political causes. The two used their family-owned news-

Above: John B. Gordon served as Georgia's U.S. senator from 1873 to 1880 and from 1891 to 1897 and as governor from 1886 to 1890.

paper, *The Cartersville Courant,* to attack the Bourbons. They traveled the state arguing that the leaders of the Democratic party in Georgia were ignoring the poor and the lower middle class.

Just like her husband, Rebecca Latimer Felton was a tireless worker for fairness and justice and was deeply involved with many causes. She was a leader in the suffrage and **temperance** (antialcohol) movements. Long before the early 1900s, when women began to push for equal rights, Rebecca Latimer Felton was publicly active. Moreover, she had a platform from which to publish her views. In 1889, Hoke Smith, publisher of the *Atlanta Journal,* asked her to be a columnist. She was a popular writer, and she continued to share her ideals and influence through the newspaper for the next forty-one years.

One particular issue over which the Feltons clashed with the Bourbon Triumvirate was the convict lease system.

The Convict Lease System

One of the most serious problems facing Georgia during the Redemption era was the treatment of prisoners. Many prisons were destroyed during the Civil War. After the war, the lack of jobs led to an increase in crime. The state had to decide what to do with the added prison population, of which nearly 90 percent were blacks. One solution was the **convict lease system**. Under this plan, prisoners were leased (hired out) to people who provided them with housing and food in exchange for labor.

Above: Rebecca Latimer Felton and her husband William H. Felton were reformers who helped to end the influence of the Bourbon Triumvirate.

When the convict lease system began in 1866, the prisoners were used to complete public works projects, such as rebuilding roads destroyed during the war. But by 1879, injustices began to show in the program. Most of the prisoners were leased to one of three large companies. (Two of these companies were owned by Bourbons Joseph E. Brown and John B. Gordon.) Each of the companies agreed to pay the state $25,000 a year, no matter how many convicts it used. The work the convicts did ranged from clearing land and farming to mining coal and building railroads.

Companies who leased convicts agreed to provide medical care, to allow prisoners to rest on Sundays, and to see that the prisoners had adequate housing and clothing.

This political cartoon, entitled the "Great Acrobatic Feat of Rutherford B. Hayes," refers to the disputed 1876 presidential election. Democrat Samuel Tilden won the popular vote. The results in three southern states, which were still under military Reconstruction, were questioned. Amidst allegations of fraud, the electoral votes of those states went to Republican Rutherford B. Hayes, giving him the victory.

However, these rules were widely ignored. All too often the prisoners received no clothes, no medical care, and little food. Some companies literally worked the prisoners to death and then simply leased more.

Prisoners were not the only ones to suffer from the lease system. Paid laborers lost out on the jobs convicts did. They had to compete for a limited number of available jobs, most of which paid very low wages. This increased the large number of poor and unemployed.

In 1880, a special legislative committee was formed to look into the handling of leased prisoners, but few changes were made. Although William and Rebecca Felton continued to demand reforms, it was not until 1897 that the convict lease law was changed.

Much later, a commission appointed to study the convict lease system created state run prison farms where young male offenders and old or sick inmates, at least, were separated from other prisoners. The commission also established a separate prison farm for females.

Dr. Felton Elected to Congress

In 1874, Dr. Felton was elected to Congress and served there until 1880. In 1880, he became a member of the Georgia General Assembly. While in the legislature, Felton pushed for improvements in education, prison reform, and limits on alcohol traffic in the state. Because of the work of the Feltons, the roots of the Populist Movement were planted in the state.

Did You Know?

In 1997, Rebecca Latimer Felton was named as one of Georgia's Women of Achievement.

It's Your Turn

1. What tradition did the Bourbon Triumvirate want to keep? Why do you think they favored keeping that tradition?
2. How do the two key terms used in the chapter, *Redemption* and *Reconstruction*, differ? In what ways are the two the same?
3. In what ways do you think the convict lease program was wrong? From your observations and research, are there elements of the convict lease system still being practiced in Georgia today? Explain.

The New South

While the Bourbon Triumvirate was controlling the political arena in the state, Henry W. Grady, the leading journalist of the time and a brilliant orator, was leading another movement that would bring much change to Georgia. In 1874, Grady, writing in the *Atlanta Daily Herald*, described the need for a New South, a South that would become much more like the industrialized North.

The Athens native became managing editor of another Atlanta newspaper, the *Atlanta Constitution*. During his brief but brilliant career, Grady made many speeches in Georgia and across the country especially in northern states. He also published many articles that described a South that could compete economically with its northern neighbors.

Grady also wanted to improve race relations in the state and was primarily concerned with seeing what he described as "a South, the home of 50

Section Preview

As you read, look for:
* improvements to education,
* important Georgia writers,
* farmers' organizations, and
* vocabulary terms: New South, normal school, segregate, Grange, Farmers' Alliance, and co-op.

Above: This statue of Henry W. Grady is at the corner of Marietta and Forsyth streets in Atlanta. Grady coined the term "The New South."

Henry W. Grady,
the South's Best Salesman

Known as the "voice of the New South," Henry Woodfin Grady was born in 1850, the son of a prominent Athens family. He graduated from the University of Georgia and attended two years of law school at the University of Virginia. Returning to Georgia, he married his childhood sweetheart and the two settled in Rome, where Henry began working for the *Rome Courier*. His writing skills caught the attention of editors at *The New York Herald*, and he was hired as their southern correspondent headquartered in Atlanta.

In 1880, Grady became managing editor of the *Atlanta Constitution*. He quickly became known for his insightful, timely, and sometimes controversial editorials. Grady visited northern cities and spoke frequently about the "New South." In one of his most famous speeches, he spoke about the need for industry in Georgia:

Above: Henry Woodfin Grady

I attended a funeral in a Georgia county. It was a poor one-gallused fellow. They buried him in the midst of a marble quarry; they cut through solid marble to make his grave; yet the little tombstone they put above him was from Vermont. They buried him in the midst of a pine forest, but his pine coffin was imported from Cincinnati. They buried him within touch of an iron mine, but the nails in his coffin and the iron in the shovel that dug his grave were from Pittsburgh. They buried him near the best sheep-grazing country in the world, yet the wool in the coffin bands was brought from the North. They buried him in a New York coat, a Boston pair of shoes, a pair of breeches from Chicago, and a shirt from Cincinnati. Georgia furnished only the corpse and a hole in the ground.

In the speech, Grady also said that the southern economy was growing as agriculture was replaced by industry, particularly textile mills, coal and iron ore mining, and tobacco factories. He praised the new practices that made farming more productive. He also pointed out that race relations in the South were changing and that African Americans had become partners in developing this "New South."

Grady's ability to sell the concept of a "New South" helped bring jobs, recognition, and investments to the recovering Georgia economy. He consistently backed up his words with actions. He was one of the principal planners for Atlanta's 1881 International Cotton Exposition, which was designed to show off the South's new industries. As a creative journalist and part-owner of the newspaper, he introduced new technology, used the "interview process" in news stories, and increased circulation from 10,000 to over 140,000, making the *Atlanta Constitution* one of the most widely read newspapers in the nation.

Of more lasting importance, he worked to establish the Georgia Institute of Technology (Georgia Tech), and he helped raise funds to develop the Young Men's Christian Association building in Atlanta.

During a Boston speaking engagement in 1889, the 39-year-old Grady caught pneumonia and later died. Even with his numerous accomplishments, we can only wonder what else this man of journalistic influence might have done.

millions of people; her cities vast hives of industry; her countrysides the treasures from which their resources are drawn; her streams vocal with whirring spindles."

Nor was Grady the only spokesman for this move toward change and industrialization. Antebellum politician Benjamin Hill began working to lift Georgia into new times and new thoughts. He encouraged the use of more efficient agricultural techniques and improvements in education. Hill remarked that "Times change; issues change; and we should adapt ourselves to them if we prosper." But the hopes and dreams of both Hill and Grady would not be easy to fulfill.

Education in the New South Era

Georgia's 1868 constitution had called for "free public education for all children of the state." The state established a system of public instruction in 1870 but did not fund it until 1871. Over 49,000 students enrolled, and the state agreed to spend $175,000 a year.

In 1872, Dr. Gustavus James Orr was named state school commissioner. His efforts focused on improving state funding for schools and providing equal treatment for African American students.

When Orr passed away in 1887, Sandersville attorney James S. Hook became state school commissioner. Tax monies for schools increased so that by 1893, almost $700,000 was being spent on public schools. Still, teachers made little more than farm laborers.

By 1895, due largely to efforts of local newspapers such as the *Atlanta Constitution* and the *Augusta Chronicle*, $100,000 a year was raised for school buildings. Most of the money came from local communities.

Below: This costumed interpreter is a teacher in a one-room school at the Georgia Agrirama in Tifton. Bottom: Copy of *McGuffey's First Eclectic Reader*, which was first published in 1838.

The Three-Month School Year

The three-month school year (a school term of three months) met two important needs. It enabled children to both get a public school education and work either in the factories or mills. It also offset the difference between the need for teachers and the availability of them.

Above: This photograph of the sixth graders at the Calhoun School in Atlanta was taken in 1896. Compare the clothing of these students with your classmates'.

The three-month school year was held at different times in different counties. Because of this, it was possible for teachers to teach in more than one county. In addition, this flexibility took into consideration the different work needs of the students.

Each local district decided where school would be held. In one rural county, the citizens used a building "good enough to winter a cow." In another, forty or fifty children crowded into a building with sawmill slabs for seats. Restrooms were outdoors, and drinking water was in buckets. Some schools had a hand bell. In others, teachers hit the door with a stick to call children to class.

Teacher Training

In 1870, local school commissioners made up tests for people who wanted to teach. In most cases, a passing grade was 70. The tests covered such subjects as orthography (spelling), reading, writing, English grammar, and geography. Sometimes, when a county needed teachers, the tests were no more than a spur-of-the-moment, question-and-answer session between the school officials and the potential teachers. Very few teachers had been to college. Most finished common school, then took the teacher's test.

In 1870, Georgia tried to start a **normal school** (teacher-training school). The legislature agreed to pay $6,000 a year if Peabody Normal School would move from Nashville to Georgia. Peabody, however, rejected the proposal.

While state school commissioner, Dr. Orr worked with Atlanta University to train black teachers; beginning in 1874, the General Assembly paid the university $8,000 a year in return for the teacher-training program. On its part, Atlanta University agreed to admit, free of tuition, as many black students as there were members in the Georgia house of representatives.

In 1882, the legislature set aside funds to send 252 teachers (154 white and 98 black) to a one-month training institute in either Americus, Milledgeville, or Toccoa. There were 6,128 teachers instructing 243,000 Georgia school children at that time. These institutes were the state's first efforts to improve the skills of teachers.

Education Takes a Giant Step Backward

The 1877 Georgia constitution limited public education to elementary school. Again, most Georgians believed that education beyond eighth grade was not particularly useful, especially when a teenager's time could be better spent at work. They also felt that too much schooling might cause teenagers to be dissatisfied with their lot in life and, worse of all, to long for a much better one.

The constitution of 1877 also called for segregated schools. (To segregate is to separate by race.) From then until the 1950s, African American students were left to be schooled, for the most part, in second-rate school buildings, to be given outdated materials and equipment, and to be taught by teachers who were often underpaid.

Below: Needwood School, near Darien, a one-room black school used from 1907 until the 1960s.

Spotlight on the Economy

The Development of Industries in Georgia

In the late 1800s, much of Georgia was still mainly agricultural. But Henry Grady's dream of a New South based on business and industry was, in part, coming to pass. The expanding railroads were important to the development and growth of industries that used the network of railroad lines to transport their products. Among the emerging new industries were those dealing with textiles, forest products, and mining.

One of the state's first industries was textiles (woven materials). Textile mills used raw materials, such as cotton or wool, to produce textile for clothing, bed sheets, blankets, and carpets. Once begun, Georgia's textile industry grew steadily. The main manufacturing centers were located along the Fall Line in Augusta, Columbus, and Macon. There, major rivers provided water power. There were also mills in smaller towns. By 1890, Georgia's textile industry produced over $12.5 million worth of goods.

Below: In the late 1800s, northerners invested in southern textile mills. Women provided much of the cheap labor.

Georgia's rich acres of timberlands provided another major source of industrial growth. Trees from the forests were turned into lumber that was used to replace buildings destroyed in the war and to build new factories, mills, and housing for those who worked in them. The forests furnished the raw materials that wound up in a variety of products, from furniture to the naval stores (turpentine, rosin, tar, and pitch) used in shipbuilding to pulp and paper.

Georgia's forests not only provided raw materials; they also created work. Sawmills, often the center of new communities, were needed to convert the raw lumber into boards. Railroads were improved or extended to transport the materials to customers both within the state and elsewhere. Factories were built to manufacture furniture and other household items. Mills were constructed to produce paper and pulp products.

The state's mineral resources also spurred new or expanded industries. Georgia's rich stores of kaolin (a white clay used in the manufacture of paper and other products), gold, coal, and iron led to a growth in the mining industry. Mining for bauxite, a mineral used in the manufacture of

Top: This steam-powered sawmill from the 1890s still works. It can be seen at Georgia Agrirama. Above: Businesses grew up near the railroads, which provided transportation routes for both raw materials in and finished products out.

aluminum, increased after the development of an inexpensive method of converting bauxite into the metal.

Together, textiles, forest products, and mining led Georgia's economy out of Reconstruction and Redemption and into a new era.

Below: Joel Chandler Harris on the front porch of his home, Wren's Nest, where he did much of his writing. **Opposite page, top:** Georgia's best known poet, Sidney Lanier. **Opposite page, middle:** A postcard of Lanier's boyhood home in Macon. **Opposite page, below:** Charles Henry Smith, better known as Bill Arp.

The Arts of the New South Era

During this period of our history, young people your age were reading such favorites as *Hans Brinker and the Silver Skates, Little Women, Little Men, The Adventures of Tom Sawyer*, and *Huckleberry Finn*. Georgia was the birthplace of several widely read authors.

Joel Chandler Harris

One of the New South's most famous authors was Georgia-born Joel Chandler Harris from Eatonton (Putman County). Chandler was known as a humorist. He began writing stories about his southern past that came not from plantation verandas or magnolia covered lawns, but from slave cabins, cotton fields, and briar patches. His most famous book, *Uncle Remus: His Songs and Sayings*, was published in 1880 and later expanded into two volumes. Written primarily in dialect, these were fables based on African folklore. Called "trickster tales," they told stories of survival and morals using animals who tricked those around them.

He also wrote six children's books, several novels, and other major collections. In addition, over his twenty-five years with the *Atlanta Constitution*, Harris wrote many editorials dealing with southern race problems.

His death in 1908 at the age of 59 left a void in southern literature. Today, his Atlanta home, "Wren's Nest," is a museum open to the public.

Sidney Lanier

Poet Sidney Lanier was a native of Macon. Born in 1842, Lanier was a gifted musician even as a small child. He graduated from Oglethorpe University in Midway at the age of fourteen and became a tutor. With his brother, Lanier enlisted in the Confederate Army in 1861. He was captured while running a blockade off the coast of Wilmington, North Carolina, and placed in an army prison at Point Lookout, Maryland. While there, he became ill with tuberculosis. He was released after only five months in prison and, with a friend, walked most of the way back to Macon.

Lanier moved frequently after the war looking for a climate that would be good for his health. In 1873, he moved to Baltimore, where he played first flute in the Peabody Symphony and became a teacher at Johns Hopkins University. It was in Baltimore that he had his first real success as a writer. Among his works are "Evening Song," "The Song of the Chattahoochee," "The Marshes of Glynn," and, one of his most famous poems, "Sunrise." His poems on the Reconstruction experiences of Georgia include "Night and Day" and "The Raven Days."

Lanier died in 1881 in Lynn, North Carolina. His vivid and realistic descriptions of the Georgia coastal area made him one of America's most successful poets of the century.

Charles Henry Smith (Bill Arp)

Charles Henry Smith was a humorist who wrote for the *Atlanta Constitution*. A native of Lawrenceville, Smith attended Franklin College (now the University of Georgia). He served in the Confederate Army until he was sent home on a medical discharge in 1863. In 1865, Smith was elected to the state senate. In 1867, he was elected mayor of Rome, where he and his family lived. For a while, Smith worked as a journalist for the *Rome Courier* and then for the competing newspaper, the *Rome Commercial*. In 1877, he and his wife moved to a farm near Cartersville. Smith wrote articles to the *Atlanta Constitution* to add to his farm income.

By the time of his death in 1903, Smith had written 1,250 articles for the *Constitution* and many of those had been reprinted by newspapers across the nation. The "Bill Arp Letters" were satirical letters that were supposedly written by Bill Arp, a simple Georgia cracker with little education. The early letters were written in a deep-southern backwoods dialect. Writers use satire to make fun of something or someone in order to make changes. While the issues and personalities changed over the years, Smith's use of satire did not. Under the pen name Bill Arp, Smith continued to make fun of politics, politicians, and businessmen.

Agriculture in the New South Era

When the United States was formed, farm families made up most of the population. As the country grew, so did the need for farm products. To produce needed crops, farmers had to be willing to work hard and take risks. Weather, insects, plant diseases, bank loan interest, shipping costs, and market prices were all beyond the farmers' control.

The Grange

In 1866, a clerk in the Bureau of Agriculture toured the South and found farmers discouraged, tired, and often without enough money. The next year he formed the "Patrons of Husbandry," which soon became known as the Grange. *Grange* is a word that means a farm and its buildings. At first, Grange meetings were mostly social—dances, informal get-togethers, or speakers who shared the newest farming techniques and equipment improvements.

After the early 1870s, crop prices began to drop drastically. By the 1880s, after paying the landowner, a small Georgia sharecropper might not make more than $130 for his cotton crop—a year's work. Banks loaned farmers less money, and, as a result, many farmers were forced into bankruptcy.

As economic conditions worsened, the Grange became more political. In 1872, Granges began organizing and meeting in Georgia. By 1875, there were 18,000 members of Georgia's local Grange chapters and about 750,000 members in the nation. Georgia's Grange put enough pressure on the state legislature to force the formation of a state department of agriculture in 1874, making Georgia the first state in the nation to have a government agency concerned entirely with farming.

Above: The "Gift of the Grangers" poster depicts the contributions farmers make to the nation's welfare.

The Farmers' Alliance

During the late 1870s and early 1880s, the Farmers' Alliance was formed. There was one large group in the Northwest and another in the South. Like the Grange, the Alliance began as a social organization. However, many of the

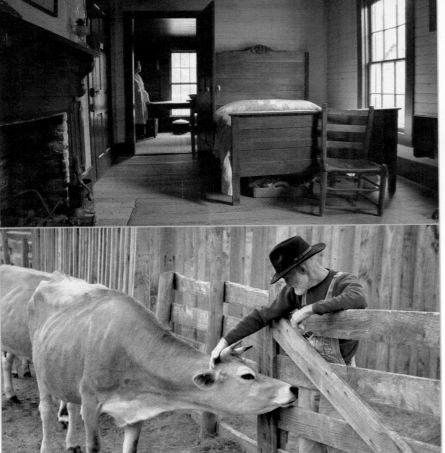

Above, left, and below: One area at the Georgia Agrirama at Tifton is a "progressive" farmstead. The progressive farmhouse is larger, better furnished, and has more modern conveniences. One convenience was a stove for cooking. The girls' bedroom was next to the kitchen because the girls were the first up to start breakfast. Having the kitchen and dining room within the main house was also a new development.

On the Road Again

The St. Simons Island Lighthouse

One of the most notable landmarks along the Georgia coast is the lighthouse at St. Simons Island. The original building was built in 1810 of tabby—a mixture of sand, oyster shells, water, and lime. During the Civil War, Confederate forces burned it to prevent the Union Army from using it as an entry point to the Georgia coast.

A new lighthouse was started in 1867. Although some of the workers, along with the well-known Georgia architect Charles Cluskey, died from malaria during the rebuilding, the grey brick lighthouse and keeper's cottage were completed in 1871. The lighthouse continues to function today, and visitors are welcome to visit and take a step back into Georgia's coastal history. Before you go, you might want to know about an incident that happened there. In 1880, the lighthouse keeper and his assistant, Frederick Osbourne, had a heated argument that resulted in Osbourne's death. According to local lore, you might just hear Osbourne's footsteps in the tower if you listen carefully.

local alliances formed cooperative buying stores, or co-ops. The co-ops purchased goods and equipment directly from producers, which enabled farmers to buy seed, fertilizer, and farm tools at lower prices.

Farmers' Alliance leaders worked against high railroad freight rates and high interest rates charged by banks for farm loans. The Alliance wanted to change the federal government's money policy. The government had followed a "tight" money policy since the Civil War; that is, the government limited the amount of money in circulation and measured the money against the value of gold it had. The Alliance believed this policy caused prices for crops and other goods to fall. The policy also limited the amount of credit available to farmers. The Alliance wanted the federal government to issue more paper money and to circulate silver coins.

During the coming years, this small group would grow into a political party called the Populist party and would support changes that continue to impact our lives today.

A Final Note

In a strange way, much of Reconstruction and the New South era was about gaining self-respect. For the newly freed men and women, it meant openly demonstrating a pride

It's Your Turn

1. When did Georgia first have state-funded schools?
2. What is a normal school?
3. When did the state constitution call for segregated schools?
4. Who was Charles H. Smith?
5. Why was the Farmers' Alliance formed?

that they had always felt during slavery, but that they were forced to hide. And, for the first time, additional self-respect resulted from their newly acquired political power and influence.

For the sharecropper and tenant farmer, it meant maintaining an "inner" self-respect in the face of crushing poverty. For the "New South," it meant trying to repair the southern economic dignity and self-sufficiency that were destroyed by the war.

As you read through the chapter, identify at least five events or individuals who demonstrated self-respect. Also describe five positive ways you can show dignified pride and self-respect as you go about your daily life.

Chapter Summary

- The period right after the Civil War was called Reconstruction, as the southern states began rebuilding and underwent the steps required to rejoin the Union.

- During Reconstruction, Congress passed and, required all of the returning Confederate states to ratify, the Thirteenth (abolishing slavery), Fourteenth (granting citizenship to the freedmen and guaranteeing equal protection under the law), and Fifteenth (guaranteeing the right to vote) amendments to the U.S. Constitution.

- During Reconstruction, most southern states enacted Black Codes, laws aimed at restricting the rights of the freedmen.

- During Reconstruction, Georgia fell under federal military rule three separate times before finally gaining readmission to the Union in 1870.

- Georgia rewrote its constitution in 1865 and in 1867.

- As agriculture struggled to recover, two new types of farming became common—tenant farming and sharecropping.

- The years immediately following the Reconstruction period are known as the Redemption years, during which the state had to recover from the hardships of Reconstruction.

- Three men, known as the Bourbon Triumvirate, led Georgia during this period—Joseph E. Brown, Alfred H. Colquitt, John B. Gordon. Business and industry began to grow under the Bourbon Triumvirate, and the Democratic party ruled the state.

- Challengers to the Bourbons included the Feltons, who worked for, among other things, prison reforms.

- Journalist Henry W. Grady, editor of the *Atlanta Constitution*, coined the phrase "New South" to describe a state striving to develop business and industry to rival the North.

- Georgia developed a state-funded public education system.

- As agricultural profits declined and rural powers lessened, farmers organized into groups such as the Grange and the Farmers' Alliance.

Above: The farms are popular attractions at the Georgia Agrirama. Here visitors check out the new pigs.

Chapter Review

Reviewing People, Places, and Terms

Use the following terms in complete sentences that show how each term relates to this period of Georgia's history.

1. Black Codes

2. Bourbon Triumvirate

3. discrimination

4. disfranchise

5. Freedmen's Bureau

6. free public schools

7. Henry W. Grady

8. Joel Chandler Harris

9. Reconstruction

10. Redemption era

11. sharecropping

Understanding the Facts

1. What rights were provided by the Thirteenth, Fourteenth, and Fifteenth amendments to the U.S. Constitution?

2. What was the difference between carpetbaggers and scalawags?

3. Why did Georgia fall under military rule three times before finally being re-admitted to the Union in 1870?

4. What were the weaknesses of the convict lease system?

5. In what year did Georgia first begin formal teacher education?

6. What was the first major industry to expand in Georgia after the war?

7. What is the "tight money policy" implemented after Reconstruction?

Developing Critical Thinking

1. In what ways do you think Lincoln's assassination impacted Reconstruction?

2. What did blacks *not* gain during Reconstruction? Explain your answer.

3. What were the major accomplishments of Reconstruction? The major failures?

4. Identify some of the reasons that made Georgia's economic recovery after the Civil War so difficult.

5. The ouster of the Republicans after Reconstruction and the dominance of the Democratic party for the next hundred years made Georgia a one-party state. What do you think are the advantages of having a two-party state government, or do you think there are advantages in retaining a single-party dominance in politics?

6. You have read about Rebecca Latimer Felton. If you had to describe her to a friend, what are three terms you would use to explain her character?

Checking It Out

1. During Reconstruction, African Americans gained a political voice in Georgia for the first

time. Tunis G. Campbell, Henry McNeal Turner, Aaron A. Bradley, and William Finch were key leaders. Choose one of these men and learn more about him. Share your findings with the class.

2. Use your research skills to learn more about sharecropping or tenant farming. How long was sharecropping used in Georgia? Try to find a copy of an agreement between a landowner and a sharecropper.

Writing Across the Curriculum

1. Pretend you are a Confederate soldier returning home in 1865 from the war after four years of being away. Write a letter to a friend in another state describing how things have changed in Georgia since you were last home.

2. Jefferson Davis's citizenship was not restored until 1978. Prepare a short report on why this was so.

3. Some historians argue that a weakness of the federal government's Reconstruction plan was that it failed to guarantee land grants to former slaves. In a short paragraph, argue either for or against land grants for former slaves as a condition of Rreconstruction.

4. Re-examine the speech of Henry W. Grady on page 318. He told the story about a funeral for a Georgian. What was the point he wanted that story to reinforce? We often use stories to make points or teach lessons. Write a short story, one page in length, that teaches a lesson using an experience from your own background. Briefly identify the lesson point on the back side of the page and let your classmates guess your point from hearing the story.

Exploring Technology

1. Use your Internet research skills to read about the *Mary Celeste*, which sailed for New York but which was found, in 1872, abandoned in the Atlantic. The captain, his wife and daughter, and a crew of eight had vanished. Read at least four accounts of the mystery and prepare a hypothesis about what you think must have happened to the *Mary Celeste*.

2. One of the most influential journalists of the period was cartoonist Thomas Nast. His cartoons were so influential that he was once offered $500,000 to leave the city of New York in order to stop his editorial cartoons about Boss Tweed. Research Thomas Nast and his career. Research Nast's drawings of the Republican and Democratic party symbols – the elephant and the donkey. Why do you think he chose those two animals as the symbols? Finally, examine two other cartoon areas which made him equally famous—Santa Claus and Uncle Sam. View each cartoon and explain why his version is still used today.

Applying Your Skills

1. Using a Venn diagram, compare and contrast President Johnson's view of Reconstruction with the view of the radical Republicans.

2. Using a Venn diagram, compare and contrast sharecropping and tenant farming using more detailed information than is provided in your textbook. You will have to use your research skills to obtain that information.

Chapter 10

1889–1919

The Progressive Era

By the end of the nineteenth century, the United States had become the world's leading industrial nation, providing over one-third of the world's manufacturing goods and services. At the same time, great wealth became concentrated in the hands of a few business leaders. But while some became rich, others sank into poverty. Many saw the need for improvements in social justice and the regulation of businesses. During this time, Georgia and Georgians played a significant role in the nation's development.

Left: During the late 1800s, Thomasville was a popular resort for wealthy northerners. The Lapham-Patterson House was built in 1884 in Thomasville by Chicago industrialist C. W. Lapham as a winter retreat.

Signs of the Times
1889-1919

Population: 92.5 million in 1910

Life Expectancy: In 1900, women could expect to live 47.3 years; by 1919, that was 51.8 years. In 1900, men could expect to live 46.3 years; in 1919, that was 48.4 years.

Costs of Living: The average annual salary ranged from $400 a year at the beginning of the period to about $750 a year at the end of the period. In 1902, sugar cost $0.04 a pound, eggs were $0.14 a dozen, and coffee was $0.15 a pound. Sears offered a baseball for $0.55, a 100-piece set of china for under $6.00, and a wood-and-coal stove for less than $15.00.

Music: Hit songs of the period included "Sweet Adeline," "Bill Bailey Won't You Please Come Home," "Danny Boy," "Swing Low, Sweet Chariot," "In the Good Old Summertime," "Lift Every Voice and Sing," "Waiting for the Robert E. Lee," and "I'll Walk Alone."

Art/Architecture: The first skyscraper in New York was the 21-story Flatiron Building, finished in 1902. People could buy homes as well as furnishings from the Sears Company's *Book of Modern Homes and Building Plans*. Norman Rockwell painted his first cover for the *Saturday Evening Post* in 1916.

Literature: Books published during this period included *The Virginian* by Owen Wister, *The Wonderful World of Oz* by L. Frank Baum, *Tarzan of the Apes* by Edgar Rice Burroughs, Rudyard Kipling's *Captains Courageous*, Alice Rice's *Mrs. Wiggs of the Cabbage Patch*, and Jack London's *White Fang*, *The Call of the Wild*, and *The Sea Wolf*.

Leisure Time: Basketball and ice hockey were introduced. The first running of the Belmont Stakes and Kentucky Derby horse races took place. The first annual indoor track and field meet was held by the New York Athletic Club. The first professional baseball team was formed—the Cincinnati Red Stockings. The first intercollegiate football game was played with Rutgers beating Princeton 6 to 4.

Fads/Fashions: Hit toys of the period included erector sets, tinker toys, Lincoln logs, teddy bears, and Ouija boards. Dance crazes included the fox trot and the tango. Lightweight, cotton knit shirts became popular for men. Women wore corsets and narrow skirts. Skirts grew shorter to allow them to step into trolleys and automobiles.

Science/Inventions: Michael Owens invented a bottle-making machine. Kodak produced the first box camera for mass use. Electric washing machines were introduced in 1910. Western Union invented a jamming device for interfering with wartime enemy radio signals. The first moving assembly line began in 1914 at Ford Motor Company.

Education: John Dewey wrote *The School and Society*, arguing that education begins with actual experiences rather than learned traditional subjects. Maria Montessori became known for new teaching methods. Waves of immigrants caused overcrowding in schools at all levels.

Religion: "Blue laws," which prohibited sports events on Sundays, were common. The Gideon Association was founded by traveling salesmen in 1899. It began placing Gideon Bibles in hotels in 1908.

Transportation: In 1908, when Ford introduced the "Model T," it cost $850. Ocean liners were popular as new floating hotels, but the *Titanic* sank during this era. The Wright Brothers made their famous flight at Kitty Hawk. The first cross-country auto trip took 52 days in a Packard. New York began subway service. Airmail service began coast to coast.

Figure 34 Timeline: 1890–1920

1918
Georgia ratified Eighteenth Amendment (prohibition)

1900
Prison farm established near Milledgeville

1901
Federal penitentiary built near Atlanta

1898
Unsuccessful strike at Columbia Textile Mill

1895
International and Cotton States Exposition held in Atlanta

1902
Martha Berry Schools for mountain children established

1908
Chain gangs instituted

1910
Girl Scouts of America founded by Juliette Low of Savannah

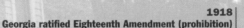

1890	1895	1900	1905	1910	1915	1920

1896
Plessy v. Ferguson

1914
World War I began

1893
A hurricane killed over 1,000 in Savannah

1918
World War I ended

1890
Sherman Anti-Trust Act

1920
Nineteenth Amendment ratified

The Progressive Movement

Section Preview

As you read, look for:
• the purpose of the progressive movement,
• the muckrakers,
• the major areas for which progressives wanted reforms, and
• vocabulary terms: progressive movement, muckraker, chain gang, labor union, strike, sweatshop, prohibition, Eighteenth Amendment, suffragette, and Nineteenth Amendment.

During the late 1800s and early 1900s, the progressive movement swept the country. Progressives believed that government—local, state, and national—was best equipped to correct the ills of society. They had faith in the idea of *progress*, the belief that humans could keep improving society to make it better and better.

The progressive movement was actually a series of movements. It worked to reform society in three main ways. (1) Progressives wanted government to fight poverty and improve the living conditions of its citizens. Progressives worked hard to reform prisons, improve working conditions, outlaw alcohol, and extend voting rights to women. (2) Progressives wanted to break up large corporations and regulate business. They hoped to decrease corporations' voice in government. (3) Progressives wanted voters to have more influence in government. They believed that people could improve society if they only had a greater voice. Strangely, however, progressives also justified the disfranchisement of African Americans on the ground that the black vote could be bought.

The reform movements were largely due to changes in industry and agriculture. Many people left farms to work in manufacturing plants in the cities. Overcrowding often resulted in slum conditions. Books, newspapers, and magazines such as *Collier's*, *McClure's*, and *Everybody's* printed stories about dishonesty in business, corruption in government and politics, and the horrors of being poor. In a 1906 speech, Theodore Roosevelt said these writers "raked filth for their reports." From then on, writers who wrote about the problems of American life in the early twentieth century were called muckrakers.

One of the most famous muckrakers was Upton Sinclair. His novel *The Jungle* described the horrible working conditions at Chicago's meat-packing plants. As a result of this book, Congress passed the 1907 Meat Inspection Act, which required federal inspection of meat-packing plants. Ida Tarbell and Henry Demerest wrote of the greed and power plays of the Standard Oil Company and tycoon John D. Rockefeller. In his books *The Shame of the Cities* and *Tweed Days in St. Louis*, Lincoln Steffens described the corruption of many city governments. Jacob Riis, an immigrant from Denmark, wrote of life in the slums of New York in *How the Other Half Lives*. *The Bitter Cry of the Children* by John Spargo told of the ugly conditions in factories where young children worked 12-hour days for pennies.

Inventions of the late 1800s and early 1900s made it easier for reformers to spread the word about conditions they felt needed correction. Reformers now had at their disposal typewriters, telephones, and wireless telegraph. All of these were put to use to deliver the calls for reform quickly across the country.

Prison Reform

As you learned in Chapter 9, Georgia, as well as some other southern states, had a convict lease system. A special legislative committee formed in 1880 to look into the handling of leased prisoners, but major changes were not made until 1897. At that time, a prison farm was established to separate young offenders and old or sick inmates from other prisoners. The farm, located near Milledgeville, was built in 1900. On the farm, prisoners grew their own food and built and kept up their living quarters. Another prison was set aside for females. In 1910, a large federal penitentiary was built in nearby Atlanta.

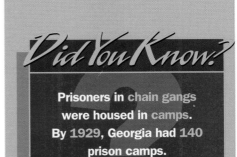

Chain Gangs Replace Convict Lease System

Georgia's Rebecca Latimer Felton worked hard to bring about reform in the state's prison system. As a columnist for the *Atlanta Journal*, she spoke out against abuses started by the Bourbon Redeemers.

In 1908, the convict lease system was eliminated completely and replaced with county work camps or chain gangs. Prisoners in chain gangs wore distinctive black-and-white-striped uniforms and were chained at their wrists and ankles so they could not escape. The work they did was hard, and whippings were common. There was no training or any other effort to prepare them for life after they had served their prison sentences. Housing, sanitary conditions, and the quality of food were often poor.

Above: The chain gang is building a road near Atlanta. Opposite page above: Jacob Riis was a police reporter when he set out to document some of the misery he had seen on the streets of New York. Opposite page below: Riis took this photograph of young children sleeping on the streets of New York.

Juvenile Court System

Georgia's ways of dealing with criminals did not improve greatly until the early 1940s, when modern equipment replaced chain gang workers. However, one positive change was made during the Progressive Era. In 1915, at the urging of social reformers, the Georgia General Assembly created the juvenile court system. For the first time, young offenders were tried and punished differently from adults.

Labor Reforms

In 1900, unskilled employees in factories and manufacturing plants were earning ten cents an hour and working twelve-hour days. Many of these workers were children. Across the nation, weekly pay was less than $10. Workers could hardly provide for their families and had little hope of things getting better.

Labor Unions

Factories were often unsafe, and job-related accidents and deaths were common in both factories and mines. People who tried to form labor unions were often punished or fired. A labor union is an organization of workers formed to improve their wages, benefits, and working conditions. One labor union, the American Federation of Labor (AFL), was successful in organizing workers in the late 1800s.

During the Progressive Era, Georgians, like most other southerners, did not support unions. Often, industries were locally owned, and workers lived in the community. They attended church, social activities, and ball games with the factory, mill, or mine owners. In Georgia's mill towns, the homes of many workers and many of the town stores belonged to mill owners. Most workers thought that if they caused trouble or took part in unions, they would lose their jobs and the houses in which they lived.

In 1898, Prince W. Greene organized workers at the Columbus Textile Mill and led them in a strike against the company. A strike is a work stoppage in protest over some grievance. This strike and efforts by workers in Atlanta and Augusta to promote membership in the National Union of Textile Workers, part of the AFL, were not successful. By the early 1900s, while unions were gaining influence in other parts of the country, attempts to form unions ended in Georgia.

Above: This young girl, working at a textile mill in Macon before child labor laws were passed, was so small she had to climb up on the spinning frame to mend the broken thread.

Child Labor Laws

In 1900, over one million children under the age of sixteen worked thirteen or more hours a day in northern sweatshops (factories with especially harsh working conditions) or in southern cotton fields and textile plants. Most made only a few cents an hour. Child labor reform, however, was slow. Over time, state legislatures, including Georgia's, set minimum wages for children. Other laws required school attendance and forbade children working in dangerous places, such as around fast-moving machines or in some types of mining. However, it was the 1930s before there was adequate legal protection for child workers.

The Temperance Movement

Ever since colonial days, groups had tried to end the production and use of alcoholic beverages. In 1873, some women in Hillsboro, Ohio, heard a lecture by a health authority and began a crusade to close the town's saloons. The campaign spread to other communities, and within two months twenty states had become "dry" (alcohol-free) without any laws being passed.

By November 1874, women from seventeen states had gathered in Cleveland, Ohio, and formed a permanent organization against the use of alcoholic beverages. It was called the Women's Christian Temperance Union (WCTU). Led by Frances Willard, the WCTU grew rapidly. In 1893, a second group, called the Anti-Saloon League, formed to force saloons to close.

Carrie Nation

One of the most colorful people in the temperance movement was Carrie Nation. On June 7, 1900, the 6-foot-tall woman entered Dobson's Saloon in Kiowa, Kansas. Armed with rocks, she took careful aim at the bottles behind the bar.

Within minutes, the floor was covered with broken glass. Looking at the speechless bar owner, Nation is reported to have said, "Now, Mr. Dobson, I have finished! God be with you." She walked out of the bar and, with a buggy load of rocks, went down the street and wrecked two other saloons. Mrs. Nation demanded that the sheriff arrest her, but the shocked lawman just asked her to leave town quickly.

As president of the local WCTU, Nation then started a series of raids on saloons in Topeka and Wichita. For those, she carried a hatchet in one hand and a Bible in the other. Her "hatchetations" continued in other parts of Kansas and in such cities as New York, Washington, and San Francisco. Nation was arrested more than thirty times. She raised money to pay her fines by making speeches and selling tiny silver hatchets as souvenirs.

Georgia Women Speak Out

About the same time, Georgia reformer Mary Harris Armor was also speaking against "demon rum." She was a skillful speaker and fundraiser for the temperance movement. Armor spoke to conventions in Boston, London, Glasgow, and Toronto. During World War I, President Woodrow Wilson asked her to be the U.S. representative to the World Congress on Alcoholism in Milan, Italy.

Armor and Rebecca Latimer Felton joined hundreds of Georgia women in the WCTU. As the movement grew stronger, temperance leaders persuaded the Georgia General Assembly to outlaw the sale of liquor in areas near schools and churches. This was followed by laws that called for each county to decide if it wanted to be "wet" (to allow alcohol) or "dry" (to ban alcohol).

Georgia Bans the Use of Alcohol

By 1881, forty-eight Georgia counties had banned the sale of alcohol. A state temperance conference was held in Atlanta in July 1881 during which

Top: Standing at nearly 6 feet tall and weighing 180 pounds, Carrie Nation was an imposing figure. Wielding a hatchet, she was downright frightful. **Above:** This 1874 temperance poster by Currier & Ives is titled "Women's Holy War."

Above: This 1908 cartoon shows "Carrie Nation cadets" marching through Georgia.

the attendees committed themselves to making the entire state dry. By 1885, prohibition (the banning of alcohol) was one of the main topics of conversation in churches, political meetings, and at many dinner tables. Ninety-one counties had voted to go dry.

In 1887, however, the tide started to turn against prohibition. Businesses that depended on the sale of alcohol formed an antiprohibition group, and temperance forces in Fulton County lost. By the end of 1888, twenty-seven counties were again wet.

Prohibitionists tried to get rid of distilleries (places where alcohol is made); in 1900, there were 135 of them in the state. But the distilleries paid taxes and provided $150,000 for education in the state. In 1907, with the support of Governor Hoke Smith, the legislature passed a law prohibiting alcohol. The law was hard to enforce, however, and saloons selling "near beer'" began to open. Soon, they were selling liquor, and officers of the law paid little attention. Individuals could also buy liquor outside the state and bring it into Georgia. It was not long until the loading platforms at railroad stations were filled with boxes of liquor.

In 1913, the U.S. Congress passed a law making it illegal for railroads to carry alcohol into dry states. Nevertheless, the near-beer saloons and clubs that kept liquor on hand for members grew in number. In 1914, Georgians elected Nathaniel E. Harris as governor. Harris called a special legislative session and pushed through a bill to close the near-beer saloons and private clubs. By 1919, it was illegal for a Georgian to have any alcoholic beverage at all.

Also in 1919, the states ratified the Eighteenth Amendment to the Constitution. This amendment prohibited the manufacture, sale, and transportation of "intoxicating beverages." For the next fourteen years, the nation was legally dry. Carrie Nation could put away her hatchet.

Woman's Suffrage

In the late 1700s and early 1800s, there had been little difference between the roles of men and women. Women who moved west with their families were equal pioneers with their husbands. In the industrialized North, factory jobs and teaching positions were filled by both men and women. However, by 1830, "a woman's place was in the home." Married women had few chances to earn money, and what they had was controlled by their husbands. There was little hope that a woman could be a political or business leader.

In July 1848, Lucretia Mott, Elizabeth Cady Stanton, and three other women met at the Stanton home in Seneca Falls, New York, and decided to get others involved in the cause of women's rights. On July 19, more than

American Spotlight

Juliette Gordon Low

Juliette Magill Kinzie Gordon, "Daisy" to her friends, was born on Halloween in 1860. She was an adventurous child who rarely held back her opinions. When she was four, she met Union General O. O. Howard and commented on how he lost his arm, "Well, I shouldn't wonder if my papa did it. He has shot lots of Yankees."

As a young woman, she traveled throughout the United States and Europe where she loved introducing her European friends to Southern favorites like grits, sweet potatoes, and cucumber pickles. In 1886, Daisy married a British cotton heir, William "Willie" MacKay Low. Although the couple settled at the family home in Lafayette Square, they spent most of their time in England, where she made many friends in British society. Although she enjoyed her life of travel and leisure, all was not well in her marriage. In 1904, Willie left Daisy, much to the horror of Savannah society. Before the divorce was final, Willie died.

During the next few years, Daisy traveled. She wrote, "I am just an idle woman of the world with no real work or duties." That, however, was about to change. In 1911, she was introduced to Lord Robert Baden-Powell, who had founded the British Boy Scouts. She began working with the Girl Guides, which was led by Baden-Powell's sister Agnes. Low set up a group at her Scotland estate and two troops in England. Daisy, who had been somewhat of a tomboy in her youth, enjoyed working with the girls and found a new sense of direction.

Above: Juliette Gordon Low was named a Georgia Woman of Achievement in 1992. **Below:** Low presents a scout with a Golden Eaglet.

When she returned to Savannah, she phoned a friend and said, "Come right over. I've got something for the girls of Savannah and all America and all the world and we're going to start it tonight!" On March 12, 1912, the first Girl Guide Patrol, or troop, was founded with her namesake and niece as its first member.

The following year, the Guides became the Girl Scouts. Low committed herself, her time and money, and her friends' money to helping young girls come into their own. Through her efforts, the organization gained national and international recognition. She helped develop the Girl Scout Handbook, *How Girls Can Help Their Country*, and was instrumental in organizing the first World Girl Scout Camp in the United States in 1926. In 1927, Juliette Gordon Low died from cancer. She was buried in the scouting uniform of which she was so proud.

three hundred people, including black publisher Frederick Douglass, gathered in the Seneca Falls Methodist Church. The group talked about a variety of subjects including property rights, divorce laws, and voting rights. As word of the convention spread, thousands of women joined the movement to demand that the right to vote be given to women and blacks.

The Fifteenth Amendment, ratified in 1870, had given black men the right to vote, but did nothing for women. The suffragettes, as those fighting for women's right to vote were called, felt they were getting somewhere when, in 1869, the Territory of Wyoming gave women the right to vote. When the territory applied for statehood, some Congressmen asked them to change the suffrage law. Wyoming leaders wired their answer: "We will remain out of the Union 100 years rather than come in without the women." In 1890, it became the first "women's suffrage state." By 1900, women could also vote in Utah, Colorado, and Idaho.

In 1914, W. G. Raoul, Mary Raoul, and Emily MacDougald formed Georgia's Equal Suffrage party to gain support for the Nineteenth Amendment giving women the right to vote. Within one year, the group had grown to over 2,000 members. In November 1915, the group marched in Atlanta's annual Harvest Festival parade. However, their assigned place in the parade

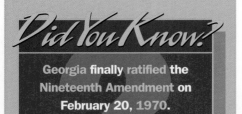

Did You Know?

Georgia finally ratified the Nineteenth Amendment on February 20, 1970.

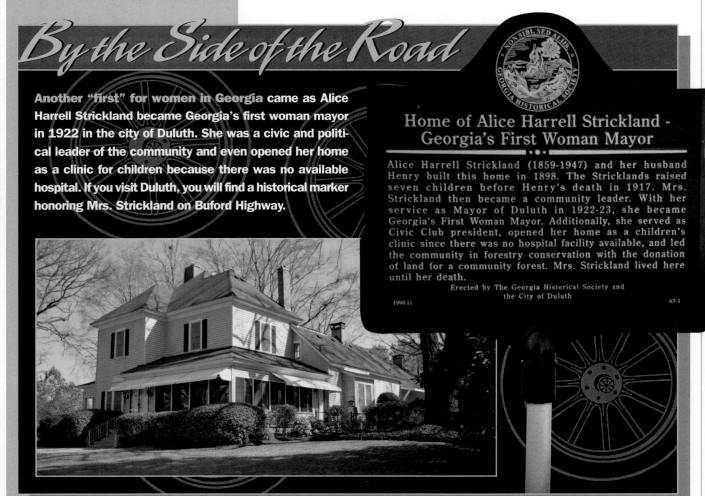

By the Side of the Road

Another "first" for women in Georgia came as Alice Harrell Strickland became Georgia's first woman mayor in 1922 in the city of Duluth. She was a civic and political leader of the community and even opened her home as a clinic for children because there was no available hospital. If you visit Duluth, you will find a historical marker honoring Mrs. Strickland on Buford Highway.

Home of Alice Harrell Strickland - Georgia's First Woman Mayor

Alice Harrell Strickland (1859-1947) and her husband Henry built this home in 1898. The Stricklands raised seven children before Henry's death in 1917. Mrs. Strickland then became a community leader. With her service as Mayor of Duluth in 1922-23, she became Georgia's First Woman Mayor. Additionally, she served as Civic Club president, opened her home as a children's clinic since there was no hospital facility available, and led the community in forestry conservation with the donation of land for a community forest. Mrs. Strickland lived here until her death.

Erected by The Georgia Historical Society and the City of Duluth

1999.11   67-1

indicated the support they had among the politicians—they marched at the end of the parade behind the city trash carts.

Thirty-six states had to ratify the Nineteenth Amendment for it to become law. On Wednesday, August 18, 1920, the Tennessee legislature met to consider the amendment and gave it the final ratifying vote needed to make it the law of the land. Georgia was one of five states that did not ratify the amendment. Suffragette Rebecca Felton said, "It is embarrassing to apologize for the ignorance and stupidity of the state legislature." Without Georgia's help, women received the right to vote in 1920.

It's Your Turn

1. What prison method replaced the convict lease system?
2. What did the juvenile court system accomplish?
3. Why do you suppose many Georgians did not support labor unions?
4. What did the Eighteenth Amendment to the U.S. Constitution prohibit?
5. Which amendment gave women the right to vote?

Berry College

In Rome, sixty-five miles northwest of Atlanta and sixty-five miles south of Chattanooga, sits Berry College, in the midst of 28,000 acres of rolling hills. Berry is one of the largest college campuses in the world, and it has certainly fulfilled its founder's vision of making "beauty a part of education." In 2004, *U.S. News & World Report* ranked Berry College as the No. 2 undergraduate comprehensive college in the South. That is quite an honor for the 104-year-old school founded by Martha McChesney Berry.

Martha was born into wealth and social prestige near Rome on October 7, 1866. From Oak Hill, the family plantation, Martha often helped her father deliver food and cloth-

Above: The overshot waterwheel at the Old Mill on the Mountain Campus is one of the largest in the world, measuring 42 feet in diameter. Opposite page, above: Martha Berry shown here writing at her desk. Opposite page, below: Clara Hall (foreground) and Ford Hall (right), two of the buildings on the Berry College Campus.

ing to the poor. At an early age, she understood the feeling of satisfaction that comes from helping others.

Berry's study, where she liked to write, was a log cabin on the plantation. One Sunday afternoon, three boys in ragged overalls were playing outside the study. Martha asked them to come in, gave them apples, and told them Bible stories. The next Sunday, the boys brought their brothers and sisters. Soon, parents came for Berry's weekly "Sunday School." When the group outgrew the cabin, they moved to an old church building at Possum Trot. When there were too many people to get in that building, Berry began other Sunday Schools in nearby communities. In addition to sharing Bible stories, Martha taught reading, singing, and good health practices. The people of the area called Martha Berry the "Sunday Lady of Possum Trot."

In 1901, Berry used $1,000 of her own money and 83 acres of land to establish a school. She built a small school-

house across the road from her home. The next year, a dormitory was added. There was no tuition, but each student worked. They grew vegetables, raised cattle, and helped build roads and other school structures as needed. Berry called the entrance to the school the "Gate of Opportunity." Here, poor young boys of the mountain area learned to read, write, and do arithmetic. They also got job training that would help them find work when school days were over. From its beginnings, Martha Berry's mission was to integrate head, heart, and hand, and she chose as the school's motto "Not to be ministered unto, but to minister." She promised "to give her students to America, strong of heart, mind, and soul."

Like the Sunday classes, the school quickly became overcrowded. Berry asked for and got help from some of America's wealthiest businessmen. In 1909, she started a girls' division of the school and renamed it The Berry Schools. In 1926, Berry opened Berry Junior College to train teachers. By 1932, the small college had become a four-year institution.

On February 27, 1942, Martha McChesney Berry died at St. Joseph's Hospital in Atlanta. In her book about Miss Berry, Georgia author Joyce Blackburn calls her "A woman of courgeous spirit and bold dreams."

Southern Politics in Action

A bridge between the New South era and the Progressive era was a grassroots political movement called populism. As big business continued to dominate America's economy, a growing group of poor farmers and hourly wage workers demanded to be heard.

The People's Party

The term *populism* refers to a political doctrine "that supports the rights and powers of the common people in their struggle with the privileged elite." At the end of the Reconstruction period, two organizations formed to help farmers—the Grange and the Farmers' Alliance.

The Alliance's political influence grew along with its membership. In 1890, forty-five "Alliancemen" were elected to Congress. Alliance-backed men became governors in several southern states. Encouraged, the Alliance talked about selecting the president of the United States in the 1892 election.

Members of labor organizations joined with the Alliance to form a new political party in 1891. They named it the People's party, but it was usually called the Populist party. The first Populist party nominating convention met in Omaha, Nebraska, in July 1892. The platform contained many "futuristic" reforms including an eight-hour workday, a graduated income tax, restrictions on immigration, and government ownership of railroads and telephone and telegraph services. The platform also called for the "free" or unlimited coinage of silver into dollars, the direct election of U.S. senators, a reduction of tariffs, and finally, the use of the Australian ballot. An Australian ballot is printed by the government (rather than by a political party), distributed at voting places, and collected there in sealed boxes so that the votes are kept secret.

The Populist candidate for president in the 1892 election was James B. Weaver. Although Weaver lost to Democrat Grover Cleveland, he received over a million popular votes and twenty-two electoral votes. But by courting African American votes, the Populists lost much of their support in the South. Nevertheless, the party's platform of reform paved the way for future changes.

Georgia's Best-Known Populist

A controversial national leader of the Populist party was Thomson native Tom Watson. As a young man, the slim, red-haired Watson had been an excellent student who loved to write essays and poems. He had to drop out

Section Preview

As you read, look for:
• the Populist party,
• legislation introduced by Georgia politicians, and
• vocabulary terms: Populist party, Australian ballot, Rural Free Delivery bill, poll, Smith-Lever Act, Agricultural Extension Service, Smith-Hughes Act, county unit system, and plurality.

Above: During the 1880s and 1890s, Tom Watson of Thomson supported the interests of the poor farmers of the state.

of Mercer University when his father went bankrupt during the economic panic of 1873. Nevertheless, Watson taught school and studied law until he passed the state bar exam in 1877, at the age of twenty-one. As a criminal lawyer, Watson was known for his "down-to-earth" style of defense.

In 1882, he was elected to the General Assembly. Even though he became wealthy, Watson was concerned about Georgia's poor and struggling farmers. Early in his career, he was the first native southern politician to be concerned about African American farmers, many of whom were tenant farmers or share-croppers. He realized that agrarian reform was possible if the two races came together politically. With the backing of the Farmers' Alliance, Watson was elected to Congress in 1890 as a Democrat. He represented the 10th Congressional District, which stretched from Augusta west across the state.

A year later, Watson switched political sides and spoke for the causes of the Populist party. In one of his many congressional speeches for farmers, Watson declared, "Before I give up this fight, I will stay here 'til the ants tote me out of the keyhole."

Watson Introduces Rural Free Delivery Bill

Watson represented Georgia in the U.S. House of Representatives for only two years. However, he gained a place in congressional history by introducing the **Rural Free Delivery (RFD) bill**, which required the U.S. postmaster general to find a way to deliver mail to rural homes free of charge. It took several years to put the system into action in rural areas. However, because of Watson's bill, farm families no longer had to travel to the nearest post office for their mail. The first official RFD route in Georgia was in Warren County.

Below: Until the RFD system went into effect, a farmer might not pick up mail for days, weeks, or even months until a trip into town for supplies, food, or equipment was also scheduled.

Watson was known all over the country because of the RFD bill and his support of farmers. In 1892, the Democrat-turned-Populist became a candidate for re-election from the 10th District. However, the state's Democratic party wanted Watson out of Georgia politics. Because he had no organized support, Watson appealed to African American farmers to return him to Congress. By election day, there were reports of vote buying, physical attacks, and attempts to frighten African Americans to prevent their voting. When the polls (voting places) closed and the votes were counted, Watson had lost. Had it not been for the large number of votes cast in Augusta (Richmond County), Watson would have won re-election. Interestingly, the total vote count was twice the number of registered voters!

Watson ran for Congress again in 1894 and was again defeated. He returned to his home, Hickory Hill, near Thomson, to influence politics through the power of the press. He began two magazines—*The Weekly Jeffersonian* and the monthly *Watson's Jeffersonian.*

In 1896, Watson was the Populist party's nominee for vice president; in 1904, he was the party's nominee for president. He lost both elections. In 1905, Watson returned to the Democratic party, but his stand on civil rights had changed significantly. Fifteen years earlier, Watson had asked for African American votes. Now, he opposed all minority rights, including those for African Americans, Catholics, and Jews. In 1920, Watson ran against Hoke Smith for the U.S. Senate and won. Two years later, he died in Washington, D.C.

Georgia's Progressive-Era Governors

In 1906, two newspaper men ran against each other for the office of governor. Clarke Howell, publisher of the *Atlanta Constitution*, ran as a conservative Democrat. His opponent was attorney Hoke Smith, owner of the *Atlanta Evening Journal* (today's *Atlanta Journal*). Smith was a reform candidate. He promised that corporations and private railroad companies would no longer have any power in state government.

Both of the candidates ran as conservative white supremacists. Populist Tom Watson agreed to support Smith's campaign if Smith would support a law to disfranchise African Americans. A statement in the black-owned *Savannah Tribune* read: "God help the civilization and future of the Democratic white man if Hoke Smith represents his ideas." Nevertheless, Smith won by a landslide. His election was seen as a victory for both the state's reformers and its farmers. Smith gained farm support by promising to take political power away from the cities and return it to the rural areas. After Smith's election, rural Georgia remained the principal power base of state politics for the next fifty-six years.

"Little Joe" Brown Elected

In the 1908 governor's election, Joseph M. Brown defeated Hoke Smith. Brown, the son of Civil War Governor Joseph E. Brown, was called "Little

Joe." He used a 1907 economic depression to blame Smith for Georgia's problems. One of Brown's slogans was "Hoke and Hunger; Brown and Bread."

Another reason for Smith's defeat was that Tom Watson changed his support to Brown. Watson's friend Arthur Glover had been convicted of murdering a woman in Augusta and sentenced to be hanged. Watson asked Governor Smith to change the sentence to life in prison. Smith refused, and Watson withdrew his support.

Smith Re-elected

Hoke Smith was again elected governor in 1910. He still believed in white supremacy and supported antiblack laws. Under his leadership, the Georgia General Assembly passed a constitutional amendment that said a person had to own property and be able to read in order to vote. As a result, most African Americans and many poor whites were removed from the voter rolls.

At the same time, there were also positive changes during Smith's two terms in office. The Railroad Commission became responsible for the regulation of gas lines, electric power companies, and trolley cars. Public schools received better funding, and child labor laws changed. Smith worked with the legislature to regulate lobbying groups and to place limits on campaign contributions.

In 1911, the Georgia General Assembly named Hoke Smith to succeed Joseph M. Terrell in the U.S. Senate. Smith served in the Senate until 1921, where he was responsible for two major pieces of legislation: the Smith-Lever Act and the Smith-Hughes Act. The 1914 Smith-Lever Act created the Agricultural Extension Service, which gave matching federal funds to states that spent money to teach young people better farming methods. The Smith-Hughes Act helped establish vocational programs in public schools across the nation. The Act also set up a federal board for vocational education to help states plan and carry out vocational training goals. By the 1920s, young people were being trained in trades, agriculture, and home economics as a result of Smith's legislation.

The County Unit System

The 1917 Neill Primary Act established a county unit system for political primaries. At that time, the Democratic party was the only active political party in the state. This meant the

Figure 35
Provisions of Neill Primary Act

1. Primary elections for major offices—governor, U.S. senators, justices of the supreme court, court of appeals judges, and statehouse offices—would be held on the second Wednesday in September in the years of general elections.

2. Candidates who received the largest popular vote in a county would "carry that county" and receive all of the county's unit votes.

3. County unit votes would be determined by the number of lower house representatives in the General Assembly, with counties receiving two unit votes per representative.

4. If there was a tie between two candidates in a county's primary election, the unit votes for that county would be split.

5. A majority of the county unit votes would be required to nominate a candidate for governor or for the U.S. Senate. If there was a tie, the candidate who received the most popular votes would be nominated.

6. For all other offices, a tie would result in a second primary election, allowing the top two county unit winners to run against each other again.

7. A plurality (the margin of victory for the winner over the nearest rival) of county unit votes was required to elect an individual in any race except those for governor and the U.S. Senate.

Right: The county unit system gave rural areas, such as Murray County (county seat Chatsworth), considerable political power when united with other rural areas.

Figure 36 Eight Most Populous Counties, 1920

	County	Population
1.	Fulton County	232,606
2.	Chatham County	100,032
3.	Bibb County	71,304
4.	Richmond County	63,692
5.	Muscogee County	44,195
6.	DeKalb County	44,051
7.	Floyd County	39,841
8.	Laurens County	39,605

outcome of primary elections and general elections were usually the same. Because that was true, the county unit system, in fact, affected both elections.

Under the county unit system, the 8 most populated counties had 6 county unit votes each (total, 48). The next 30 counties had 4 county unit votes each (total, 120), and the remaining 121 counties had 2 county unit votes each (total, 242). The 38 largest counties had two-thirds of Georgia's voters, but the other 121 counties together could decide a state election.

Those who opposed the county unit system pointed out that people were elected to office without a majority of the state's popular vote. Those who supported it said the system allowed small, less-populated counties to have the same power and influence as larger ones. The county unit system was in effect until 1962, when it was declared unconstitutional.

It's Your Turn

1. What farmers' organization joined with labor organizations to form the Populist party?
2. What reform supported by the Populist party was eventually implemented and is still in use today?
3. What act created the Agricultural Extension Service?
4. What were the reasons people opposed the county unit system?
5. What were the reasons people supported the county unit system?

Section 3

The Continuing Fight for Civil Rights

Civil rights are the rights that a person has simply because he or she is a citizen. There is no single listing of these rights, but most people include the following: freedom of speech, freedom of religion and the press, the right to assemble and petition the government, the right to privacy, protection by due process of law, a trial by a jury of one's peers (equals), property ownership, voting (if qualified), access to jobs, and the ability to travel wherever one wishes inside the country. Over the years, many laws relating to these laws have been passed. However, having a law does not always mean it will be enforced.

During the late 1800s and early 1900s, the concept of white supremacy was popular not only in the South, but also in other areas of the western world. During Reconstruction and the New South era, most whites and many African Americans accepted racial segregation as a natural way of life unofficially protected by Jim Crow laws.

Separate But Equal

Jim Crow laws were passed to establish "separate-but-equal" facilities for whites and for blacks. The laws resulted in separate restrooms, water fountains, railroad cars, waiting rooms, lodging facilities, dining areas, and schools. In 1889, the Georgia General Assembly segregated a number of

Section Preview

As you read, look for:
- methods used to enforce segregation,
- important African American leaders of the period,
- African American organizations,
- the Leo Frank case, and
- **vocabulary terms:** civil rights, Jim Crow laws, injunction, Atlanta Compromise speech, lynching, Back-to-Africa movement, grandfather clause, poll tax, gerrymander, martial law, National Association for the Advancement of Colored People, and National Urban League.

Below: During this period, African Americans in the South had few economic options. These are servants.

public facilities including theaters, prison camps, water fountains, and restrooms. Although facilities for African Americans were separate, they were rarely equal to those set aside for whites. African Americans protested the Jim Crow laws in public meetings throughout the nation. Georgia's Henry McNeal Turner, a bishop of the African Methodist Episcopal Church, called the new civil rights laws and the segregation that followed as a result of them "barbarous."

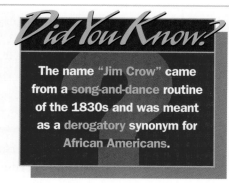

Plessy v. Ferguson

A U.S. Supreme Court decision in *Plessy v. Ferguson* opened the door for even more Jim Crow laws. In actual practice, the decision in *Plessy v. Ferguson* made segregation the law of the land until 1954.

In 1892, Homer Plessy bought a train ticket from New Orleans to Covington, Louisiana. Because he was seven-eighths white and one-eighth black, he took a seat in the "whites only" car. When he refused to move, he was arrested under the "Jim Crow Car Act of 1890," which required separate-but-equal accommodations for whites and blacks on railroad cars.

Plessy staged the incident to test the constitutionality of the 1890 law. In 1896, the U.S. Supreme Court heard the case and, by a 7-1 vote, upheld the law. A southerner, Justice John Marshall Harlan, cast the single dissenting vote. Harlan argued: "Our Constitution is color-blind, and neither knows nor tolerates classes among citizens. In respect of civil rights, all citizens are equal before the law."

Plessy v. Ferguson gave states the right to control social discrimination and to promote segregation of the races. Throughout the South, numerous laws forced blacks to use separate facilities such as parks and public transportation. Schools soon followed.

Above: Supreme Court Justice John Marshall Harlan is probably best known for his eloquent dissent in the 1896 case, *Plessy v. Ferguson*.

Cummings v. Richmond County Board of Education

Plessy was soon tested when a case originating in Augusta made its way to the U.S. Supreme Court. Until 1899, Richmond County had the only public high school in Georgia for descendants of enslaved Africans. The school board, supposedly for "purely economic reasons," closed the school, which served 60 high school students, and opened it as an elementary school for 300 students. Three parents sued the school board based on the *Plessy* law that ensured separate-but-equal facilities. They filed for an injunction (a court order stating that something must or must not be done) to close the white public high school until another high school was opened for African American students. The lower court agreed, but the Georgia Supreme Court overturned that ruling.

The case reached the U.S. Supreme Court in December 1899. The court ruled that (1) African American students had the right to be educated only until the eighth grade, (2) closing the white high school did not relate to the equal rights granted by the Fourteenth Amendment, and (3) the use of funds to open the elementary school and close the high school was a state issue.

On a final note, Justice Harlan, the same justice who had written the dissenting opinion in *Plessy*, wrote the ruling opinion in *Cummings*. In it, he wrote, "Georgia had the right to create 'separate but equal' schools." It was not until 1954 with the *Brown v. Board of Education* ruling that segregated schools became unlawful.

Booker T. Washington

Booker T. Washington was one of the outstanding civil rights leaders of the period. He was the president of Tuskegee Institute in Alabama and had worked hard to establish the school. Washington believed that, for African Americans, economic independence was the only road to social and political equality. He spoke throughout the United States and Europe, but one of his most famous speeches was given in Atlanta on September 18, 1895.

Visitors from all over the nation were there for the opening of the Cotton States and International Exposition. A racially mixed crowd heard the opening-day speeches in Exposition Hall. After several remarks by industrialists and politicians, Washington was introduced. What he said that day shaped race relations and strongly influenced black leadership for the next twenty years. Washington, a tall, muscular man with a strong, clear voice, began to speak:

Above: From 1895 to 1915, Booker T. Washington was the most powerful and influential African American in the United States. He was a forceful speaker, a skilled politician, and an advisor to presidents.

A ship lost at sea for many days suddenly sighted a friendly vessel. From the mast of the unfortunate vessel was seen a signal, "Water, water; we die of thirst!" The answer from the friendly vessel at once came back, "Cast down your bucket where you are." A second time the signal "Water, water; send us water!" ran up from the distressed vessel, and was answered, "Cast down your bucket where you are!" A third and fourth signal for water was answered, "Cast down your bucket where you are."

The captain of the distressed vessel, at last heeding the injunction, cast down his bucket and it came up full of fresh, sparkling water from the mouth of the Amazon River. To those of my race who depend on bettering their condition in a foreign land or who underestimate the importance of cultivating friendly relations with the southern white man, who is their next door neighbor, I would say: "Cast down your bucket where you are. . . ."

To whites, Washington offered the same advice:

Cast down your bucket . . . among the eight millions of Negroes . . . who have, without strikes and labor wars, tilled your fields, cleared your forests, builded your railroads and cities . . . the most patient, faithful, law-abiding, and unresentful people that the world has seen.

Suddenly, Washington flung his hand up, the fingers held apart and said:

In all things that are purely social, we can be as separate as the fingers. . .

He then balled up his fingers into a fist and continued:

yet one as the hand in all things essential to mutual progress.

The crowd in Exposition Hall went wild. People cheered and waved handkerchiefs. Loud applause interrupted the speech. After the shouts finally died down, Washington addressed the problems of social equality:

The wisest among my race understand that the agitation of questions of social equality is the extremist folly, and that progress in the enjoyment of all the privileges that will come to us must be the result of severe and constant struggle rather than of artificial forcing. . . .

No race that has anything to contribute to the markets of the world is long in any degree ostracized. It is important and right that all privileges of the law be ours, but it is vastly more important that we be prepared for the exercise of those privileges. The opportunity to earn a dollar in a factory just now is worth infinitely more than the opportunity to spend a dollar in an opera house.

When Washington made his comments on social equality, he believed in them from a practical and realistic point of view that reflected the time. His speech became known as the **Atlanta Compromise speech**, because it proposed that blacks and whites should agree to benefit from each other.

Above: Booker T. Washington was an extraordinary orator and a supporter of black self-improvement.

W. E. B. Dubois

Atlanta University Professor William Edward Burghardt DuBois (pronounced Du Boyce) did not agree with Booker T. Washington.

In Atlanta, Dr. DuBois taught economics and political science. At first, he thought truth and knowledge would help different races understand and accept each other. DuBois wanted social and political integration, as well as higher education for 10 percent—what he called a "Talented Tenth"—of the African American population. He believed this group could become leaders for all other African Americans.

However, the late 1800s were a time of extreme racial unrest. Between 1884 and 1918, there were over 2,500 reported **lynchings** (illegal hangings, usually by mobs) or burnings at the stake of African Americans in the United States. DuBois described each death by lynching as "a scar upon my soul." He decided that knowledge and truth alone were not enough. There must also be action if African Americans and whites were to understand and accept each other.

After Booker T. Washington made his famous Atlanta Compromise speech, differences in their approaches to racial problems caused a split between Washington and DuBois. DuBois did not like what he called the "Tuskegee Machine," referring to Washington's support at the school he had helped found. He thought Washington was making social, political, and economic decisions that affected all blacks. DuBois also disagreed with Washington's idea that blacks who became economically successful and waited long enough would see race relations improve. In his book *The Souls of Black Folk*, DuBois wrote:

Manly self-respect is worth more than land and houses, and . . . a people who voluntarily surrender such respect, or cease striving for it, are not worth criticizing.

DuBois concluded:

So far as Mr. Washington preaches Thrift, Patience, and Industrial Training for the masses, we must hold up his hands and strive with him. . . . But, as far as Mr. Washington apologizes for injustices, North or South, does not rightly value the privilege and duty of voting, belittles the emasculating effects of caste distinctions, and opposes the higher training and ambition of our brighter minds,—as far as he, the South or the Nation, does this—we must unceasingly and firmly oppose them.

Above: The originator of the "Talented Tenth" philosophy, Dr. W. E. B. DuBois had a far different view of black progress than did Booker T. Washington. After reading the opinions of both men, what is your view of their philosophies?

Above: John Hope was an important educator and leader of African Americans in the early 1900s. In this photograph, he is seen with his wife Lugenia and sons Edward and John Jr.

John Hope

Another important leader in our state during this time was John Hope. Hope was born in Augusta, on June 2, 1868, to a white father and a black mother. During early childhood, he was treated as the son of a plantation owner. However, his father died when John was eight; afterwards, he had neither money nor social acceptance. Although he could have made things a bit easier by passing as a white person, he was proud of his African American heritage.

Hope attended Augusta public schools and, in 1886, went to Worchester Academy in Massachusetts. He graduated from Brown University and taught at Roger Williams University in Nashville from 1894 to 1898. He then joined the faculty of Atlanta Baptist College (which was renamed Morehouse in 1913). Hope became the school's first black president in 1906. In 1929, he was chosen to be president of Atlanta University.

Hope worked for social equality all his adult life. He heard Booker T. Washington's Atlanta Compromise speech in 1895 but did not share his views. Speaking to a debating society in 1896, Hope said:

If we are not striving for equality, in heaven's name, for what are we living? . . . Now catch your breath, for I am going to use an adjective. I am going to say we demand social equality!

While Hope was at Atlanta Baptist College, he became close friends with W. E. B. DuBois, who was then on the faculty at Atlanta University. He was

the only college president at the 1909 protest meeting in New York that resulted in the founding of the NAACP. During the Atlanta race riot, Hope was an active civic leader who worked to restore calm to his city.

John Hope was president of the National Association of Teachers of Colored Schools and a leader in the Association for the Study of Negro Life and History. He gained international recognition for his work with the YMCA. Under Hope's leadership, Morehouse, Spelman, Morris Brown, and Clark colleges, Gannon Theological Seminary, and Atlanta University formed the Atlanta University Center.

John Hope's wife, Lugenia, was a "mover and shaker" as well as a well-known civic leader. She organized the Neighborhood Union, which offered vocational classes for children, a health center, and clubs for boys and girls. The Neighborhood Union also provided financial aid for needy families and pressured city leaders to improve roads, lighting, and sanitation in the African American neighborhoods of Atlanta.

A Loss of Voting Rights

By 1900, almost 12 percent of the African Americans in the nation lived in Georgia, making up about 47 percent of the state's population. More and more, however, these citizens found themselves pushed aside and without political power. African American leaders began to speak out, but law after law was passed with the sole purpose of keeping them from voting.

In 1908, Georgia followed other southern states and enacted a grandfather clause. The clause stated that only those men whose fathers or grandfathers had been eligible to vote in 1867 were eligible to vote. Because few African Americans were able to vote in 1867, the grandfather clause kept most of Georgia's African Americans from voting.

Even those who could pass the standards of the grandfather clause faced problems at the voting booth. The state and local areas passed a series of additional qualifications for voting. Voters had to own property, pay a poll tax (a tax to be able to vote), and pass literacy tests. Because the literacy tests were not standard, the questions could—and did—contain almost anything the voting clerk thought would stump the potential

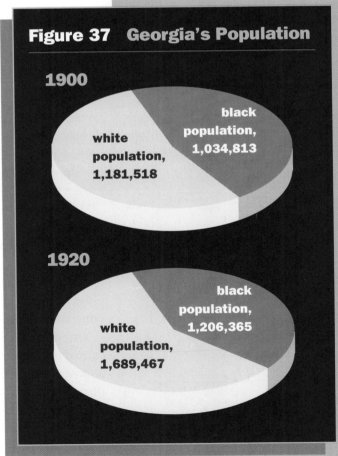

Figure 37   Georgia's Population

1900

white population, 1,181,518

black population, 1,034,813

1920

white population, 1,689,467

black population, 1,206,365

In 1812, this political cartoon appeared in the Boston *Weekly Messenger* depicting the odd shape of a voting district created by Massachusetts Governor Elbridge Gerry to gain political advantage for his party. The cartoonist called it a "Gerry-mander."

voter. One story—that may or may not be true—told of an African American teacher with a degree from Harvard University who tried to register to vote in a southern state after 1908. The voting clerk had the teacher read parts of the U.S. Constitution and pages from several books. He then had the teacher read in Latin, French, German, and Spanish—all of which he did successfully. Finally, the frustrated clerk held up a page of Chinese characters and asked, "What does this mean?" The teacher responded, "It means that you do not want me to vote."

Southern politicians also used gerrymandering to prevent African Americans from voting. To **gerrymander** means to draw up an election district in such a way that it benefits a certain group. A district can be drawn up to benefit racial groups, a political party, or any other special interest. Gerrymandering was first used in 1812 in Massachusetts by Governor Elbridge Gerry. Gerry created a voting district that was shaped like a salamander, hence, the term *gerrymandering*. In Georgia and throughout the South, voting districts were drawn specifically to weaken African American voting power.

Race Riots in Atlanta

The year 1906 was a memorable year in Atlanta's history. While Georgia's politicians worked for political control, Atlanta experienced one of the worst race riots in the nation's history. Some thought the riot came about because men like Tom Watson spread racial fears. Others believed that Hoke Smith had used racial fears to gain votes during the gubernatorial campaign of that year. Still others blamed Atlanta newspapers, which printed story after story of African American violence against whites.

On the afternoon of Saturday, September 22, local newspaper headlines carried false reports of black assaults. By 9 p.m., a crowd of over 5,000 whites and African Americans had gathered on Decatur Street. Some accounts reported that thousands of whites brought guns and began to roam through the downtown area. Fears grew, and the attacks became real.

The riot lasted two days. Martial law was declared before the city once again became calm. (**Martial law** occurs when military forces are used to maintain order because civilian forces will not or cannot maintain order.) The cost in human life was high. At least eighteen African Americans and three whites were killed; hundreds of people were injured. The value of property destroyed was also high, but it could not be accurately estimated.

African Americans Organize

In the early 1900s, there were periods of racial unrest in cities across the country. The unrest led African Americans to look for new ways to achieve equality, including forming new organizations.

The NAACP

In 1909, Oswald Garrison Villard, grandson of the abolitionist William Lloyd Garrison, asked white liberals to join with the Niagara Movement (a group of black educators and professional men) to form a new organization. This new group became known as the National Association for the Advancement of Colored People (NAACP).

The goal of the NAACP was to work for the rights of African Americans. W. E. B. DuBois left Atlanta University to live in New York and edit *The Crisis*, a monthly NAACP publication. In his column, "As The Crow Flies," DuBois used humor and wit to support protest. NAACP chapters were organized all over the country, and, during World War I, the organization became strong in Georgia. Soon other groups were organized to help in the struggle for equality.

LES « LYNCHAGES » AUX ÉTATS-UNIS
Massacre de nègres à Atlanta (Georgie)

The National Urban League

The National Urban League was formed in 1910. The interracial group worked to solve social problems facing African Americans who lived in the cities. During this period, many African Americans moved from the rural South to cities in the North. They were looking for better jobs and less racial segregation. The National Urban League was able to help them deal with the problems of living in the cities and to make the adjustment to city life easier.

The Trial of Leo Frank

Georgia suffered a civil rights setback with a court case that attracted national attention and that resulted in the rebirth of the Ku Klux Klan. On August 17, 1915, Leo M. Frank was lynched in Marietta.

The 29-year-old Frank was from Brooklyn and had been the superintendent of the National Pencil Company factory in Atlanta for five years. On April 26, 1913, he was charged with the murder of Mary Phagan, a 14-year-old employee. The trial that followed was one of the most debated in Georgia's history. Although there was little evidence, Frank was convicted and sentenced to death, largely because of the testimony of Jim Conley, the factory's African American janitor. Because Conley was also a suspect, his testimony normally would not have been heard. However, these were not normal times. Frank was Jewish, and during that time, many people disliked Jews.

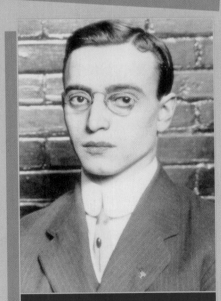

Top: This French newspaper carried a front-page story of the Atlanta race riot. **Above:** The trial of Leo Frank showed the degree of racial and religious intolerance during this era.

Above: This picture of a Ku Klux Klan rally was taken at Stone Mountain in 1921. Between 1920 and 1923, Ku Klux Klan membership nationwide grew from 5,000 to several million members.

This Dosent Belong to you!

Frank's lawyers appealed the case to the state supreme court. Georgia Governor John Slaton was under pressure to pardon Frank. The day before his term of office ended in June 1915, Slaton changed Frank's sentence from death to life imprisonment. In his magazine, *The Weekly Jeffersonian*, Tom Watson led a public outcry against Slaton's action. He even called on the people to take matters into their own hands. The anger directed at Slaton because of his change of Frank's sentence led him to leave the state.

Two months after the sentence change, twenty-five armed men walked into the state penitentiary in Milledgeville and took Frank from his prison cell. They drove to Marietta, the home of Mary Phagan, and hanged Frank from a tree. The next day, about 15,000 curious people filed by Frank's open casket in an Atlanta mortuary. Pictures of Frank's hanging body were sold, and "The Ballad of Mary Phagan" became popular.

The ~~Klan~~ Bullshit Is Reborn

In July 1915, amid the anti-Jewish feelings and continuing racial unrest of the Leo Frank case, the Ku Klux Klan received a charter from the Fulton County Superior Court. On Thanksgiving night 1915, Atlanta preacher and salesman William Simmons and thirty-four others climbed to the top of Stone Mountain near Atlanta. There, the group, which called itself the Knights of Mary Phagan, lit torches as they circled a burning cross. The Ku Klux Klan was reborn in Georgia and elsewhere in the country.

Did You Know?

Seventy-one years after Leo Frank was hanged, the Georgia Board of Pardons and Paroles issued Leo Frank a pardon. The pardon, however, was based on the state's failure to protect him while in custody; it did not officially absolve him of the crime.

It's Your Turn

1. What did *Plessy v. Ferguson* accomplish?
2. What did *Cummings v. Richmond County Board of Education* accomplish?
3. What did Booker T. Washington propose in his Atlanta Compromise speech?
4. How did poll taxes and literacy tests prevent many African Americans from voting?

Section 4

Business in Georgia

In 1895, Atlanta was host to 800,000 visitors during the three-month-long Cotton States and International Exposition. This exhibition was a way to showcase the economic recovery of the South (in which cotton played a large role), to highlight the region's natural resources, and to lure northern investors. At the 6,000 exhibits of the Exposition, visitors saw new machinery and learned how cotton was made into marketable products.

Section Preview

As you read, look for:
- three businesses that developed during this period and
- vocabulary term: scrip.

Did You Know?

John Philip Sousa wrote the "King Cotton March" in 1895 for the Cotton States and International Exposition. Sousa's band played at the exposition for three weeks. The march was one of Sousa's personal favorites, and it has become one of his most popular.

Left: Between 1881 and 1895, Atlanta was host to three expositions. One was the Cotton States and International Exposition in 1895. In 1887, the Piedmont Exposition brought 200,000 visitors to Atlanta, including President Grover Cleveland. This special newspaper supplement celebrates President Cleveland's visit.

This period also saw the rise of many new businesses and a new breed of business people to run them. Among these were three Atlanta institutions—Rich's Department Store, Coca-Cola, and Atlanta Mutual Life.

Rich's

In 1867, a young businessman named Morris Rich moved to Atlanta and opened a small store. In 1881, Rich and his brothers opened a new and bigger store on Whitehall Street. The inside of the building was decorated in black and gold, and it featured Atlanta's first plate glass store windows. In 1924, the store moved to the corner of Broad and Alabama streets in the heart of downtown Atlanta. There it became an Atlanta institution.

Rich's became "the" place to shop in Georgia. Memories of the downtown Rich's will forever be associated with the Pink Pig, the lighting of the Christmas Tree on Thanksgiving night, and Hanukkah holidays. The store with a "heart" will also be remembered for taking farmers' produce in payment for merchandise and for accepting teachers' **scrip** (paper money that is not legal currency) during the Great Depression.

As suburban malls and shopping centers replaced downtown megastores, Rich's expanded through the metro-Atlanta area and in the Southeast. But it was the downtown store, which closed in 1991, that made the Rich's legend. There shoppers wore hats and gloves to shop and have lunch in the tearoom.

Above: Hungarian immigrant Morris Rich was typical of the entrepreneurs who, through diligence and hard work, built prosperous businesses in Atlanta. Right: The small 1867 store of Morris Rich rapidly grew into one of Atlanta's shopping institutions.

Spotlight on the Economy

New Forms of Doing Business

As America's businesses grew, they required capital (money) to carry on business, build and expand factories, develop and install equipment, and hire and pay workers. Most businessmen needed outside financial help from people called *investors*. As a result, a new type of business structure called the corporation was developed. Corporations can sell shares of *stock* in their business to investors to raise the capital needed to operate or expand. People who invest in these corporations are called *stockholders*, and they receive a share of the corporations' profits called *dividends*.

To operate, corporations must receive a license from the state called a *charter*. Corporations are defined as being separate from the people who own them (stockholders). Legally, corporations operate almost like people. They can make deals, sign contracts, buy and sell property, or take legal action in court.

Our economy is based on the free enterprise system in which businesses compete for customers. In the 1880s and 1890, some businessmen within the same industry began to work together to control the prices of raw materials and supplies and the prices of manufactured goods. These efforts to stabilize the economy also reduced or eliminated competition.

Some businesses merged into trusts. In a trust, major stockholders of several companies within an industry pool their shares of stock and place them under the control

Above: John D. Rockefeller, one of the founders of the Standard Oil Company.

of a group of *trustees* who run all of the companies in the trust as though they were really just one company. Trusts not only had the power to corner all of the raw materials, to make special deals with banks for financing and with railroads for shipping, but they also had the power to run smaller companies out of business. They could undercut prices of smaller companies until those companies failed, then the trust could raise its prices to recover the profits lost. They could all but eliminate any competition within an industry.

Standard Oil Company became the nation's first trust in 1882 and soon controlled over 90 percent of the nation's refining capacity. Its main stockholder, John D. Rockefeller, amassed a fortune of more than $800 million by 1892.

Trusts led to monopolies, in which one company (or trust) controls an entire industry. These monopolies set and controlled prices for consumers as well as prices for those industries who sold to monopolies. Leaders of these monopolies gained not only great financial wealth but also great political power.

By 1890, there were so many trusts that Congress passed the Sherman Antitrust Act of 1890. But it was largely unenforced until President Theodore Roosevelt convinced Congress to support his "trust-busting efforts" in 1903. Under Roosevelt, the Department of Justice filed more trust-busting lawsuits against corporations than had been filed in all previous administrations.

Coca-Cola—The Headache that Created a Fortune

During the period of root beer, ice cream sodas, and ginger ale, two new soft drinks were added for America's taste buds. In 1898, in New Bern, North Carolina, pharmacist Caleb Bradham invented a soda called "Brad's Drink," which soon changed its name to "Pepsi." However, a few years before that, an Atlanta pharmacist, working in his own backyard, invented a soda that impacted not just Georgia, but the world.

Atlanta druggist John Styth Pemberton mixed and sold medicines such as Globe of Flower Cough Syrup and Triplex Liver Pills. The most popular of "Doc" Pemberton's mixtures was a tonic called "French Wine Coca," a syrup that included a considerable amount of alcohol. To keep up with the demand for his "Delightful Nerve Tonic and Stimulant That Never Intoxicates," Pemberton built a small chemical plant for $160.

In 1885, the temperance movement swept across most of the country. Pemberton began looking for a way to remove the alcohol from his tonic and still have its good taste. He put a three-legged, thirty-gallon, brass stirring kettle over a fire and started work on a new recipe. He named his new tonic "Coca-Cola" after its two main ingredients—the coca plant and the kola nut. The tonic was put into pint beer bottles, labeled the "Intellectual Beverage and Temperance Drink," and sold for twenty-five cents in several Atlanta drugstores.

Willis Venable was the soda fountain man at Jacob's Pharmacy. One day, a customer came in with a severe headache. He bought Coca-Cola syrup and asked Venable to mix some with water so he could take it immediately. The tap water faucet was at the other end of the counter, so Venable suggested soda water instead of plain water. The customer agreed and, after drinking the mixture, said it was much better than with plain water. Within weeks, several other drugstores began mixing the medicine with soda water rather than tap water. Within a year, production had grown from 25 to 1,049 gallons.

In July 1887, Pemberton's health began to fail. He needed money, so he sold Venable a two-thirds interest in his company. Equipment, supplies, and advertising items were moved from Pemberton's home to

Top: After the Civil War, pharmacist John S. Pemberton settled in Atlanta and began distributing his popular "nerve tonic." Above: Pemberton concocted the formula for Coca-Cola in the backyard of his home in Atlanta.

Did You Know?

Only a small handful of executives and chemists at Coca-Cola know the exact formula for the soft drink, and those executives are never allowed to all fly together to events or functions.

THE COCA-COLA GIRL

DRINK
DELICIOUS
Coca-Cola

the basement of Jacob's Pharmacy. Pemberton died penniless in August 1888. But before his death, a Villa Rica native and druggist named Asa Candler bought all the Coca-Cola stock for $2,300.

By 1892, the drink had become so popular that Candler sold his drugstore and formed the Coca-Cola Company. Candler became a wealthy man. He donated some of that wealth to establish Emory University and Hospital. He also served as mayor of Atlanta for several years without pay.

In 1919, after the death of his wife, Candler sold the company to Atlanta businessman Ernest Woodruff for $25 million. At that time, it was the largest business deal ever made in the South. In 1923, Ernest Woodruff's son Robert became president. Robert Woodruff led the company into a multibillion-dollar international business.

Woodruff continued the clever marketing policies that had been begun earlier. The beverage's uniquely shaped green bottle and its wholesome advertisements were everywhere, both in this country and abroad. He built bottling plants in Europe during World War II. This gave American soldiers

An Ecological Georgia Victory

Copper was first used 10,000 years ago as jewelry. Today, it is used as money, in watches and clocks, in printing, in shipping and rail travel, food preparation, and so on. But it must be smelted, or processed, and that is where the problem started for several Georgia communities. When copper is smelted, sulfur dioxide is formed. If you have ever smelled sulphur dioxide, you do not soon forget the stench. Neither did the people who lived in the Hiawassee, Ellijay, or Cleveland areas in the 1870s.

The 60,000-acre copper basin lies across the Georgia state line in Polk County, Tennessee. From the time copper was first mined there in 1848, Georgia was a part of the story. A rail line ran from the Ducktown mining company there to Marietta.

After the Civil War, the mining companies stripped the land around the basin of the timber they needed for the smelting furnaces. Mine officials started buying timber from Georgia's Fannin County and floated the logs along the Oconee River. By 1878, some 50 square miles around Fannin County had been stripped of all trees. With no trees, the topsoil was lost, along with all vegetation and animal life. In addition, the sulfur and noxious fumes were killing the apple orchards and making people in the area physically ill.

Efforts by the copper company to build 325-foot-tall smoke stacks to disperse the gases made matters worse. The state of Georgia sued on behalf of its North Georgia citizens. By 1907, the case reached the U.S. Supreme Court. In 1915, the decision came down with Chief Justice Oliver Wendell Holmes delivering the majority opinion. Justice Holmes wrote,

Above: This abandoned pit mine near Ducktown is an example of the devastation left behind as natural resources are removed. **Below:** Chief Justice Oliver Wendell Holmes delivered the majority opinion in *Georgia v. Tennessee Copper Co. and Ducktown Sulphur, Copper & Iron Co.*

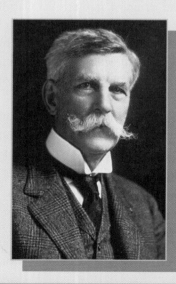

It is a fair and reasonable demand on the part of a sovereign that the air over its territory should not be polluted on a great scale by sulphurous acid gas, that the forests on its mountains should not be further destroyed or threatened by the act of persons beyond its control, that the crops and orchards on its hills should not be endangered.

The court's decision forced the Tennessee Copper Company and the Ducktown Sulphur, Copper, and Iron Company to reduce the amount of pollution in the air. They also had to submit to inspections from a court-approved professor from Vanderbilt University. Its decision set the stage for future Georgia air quality control fights.

a little touch of home, and Europeans began to enjoy the American "pause that refreshes."

Like Asa Candler, Robert Woodruff gave money to worthy causes. His gifts included $105 million worth of Coca-Cola stock to Emory University. For many years, this remained one of the largest single gifts in American history.

Today, Coca-Cola products are enjoyed around the world by over 470 million people each day. What was begun by "Doc" Pemberton, soda fountain man Willis Venable, and the customer with a headache has mushroomed into a giant international company with annual sales in the billions of dollars.

Atlanta Mutual Insurance Company

Another business giant of the Progressive Era was Alonzo Herndon. In 1858, Herndon was born a slave on a Walton County plantation. He grew up in Social Circle. After the Civil War, he worked for his former master for a short time at a salary of $25 a year.

Herndon learned to be a barber and moved to Jonesboro to open his own barber shop. Thinking that business would be better in Atlanta, he moved there and worked in a barber shop. Within six months, he owned a half interest in the business. By the early 1900s, he had opened three new shops for white customers. Herndon began buying property, and he soon owned a block of office buildings on Auburn Avenue and a hundred rental houses.

In 1905, Herndon bought a small insurance company for $140. He knew little about insurance, so he hired African American college graduates to run the Atlanta Mutual Insurance Company.

Herndon was still president of his insurance company when he died in 1927; his son Norris took over. That company is now the Atlanta Life Insurance Company. One of the largest African American-owned businesses in the United States, Atlanta Life has a net worth of over $200 million and operations in seventeen states. Perhaps the secret of Herndon's success in business was best explained when he said, "Some of us sit and wait for opportunity when it is always with us."

Above: Alonzo Franklin Herndon was one of the most astute businessmen of his time. Through hard work, Herndon built a business empire worth millions of dollars.

It's Your Turn

1. Why do you think Rich's was successful as a "downtown" Atlanta institution?
2. How did a man's headache prove the start of the international Coca-Cola Company?
3. What business did Alonzo Herndon found?

The Jekyll Island Club

In Chapter 1, you learned that Jekyll Island is a barrier island off the coast of Georgia near Brunswick. The island had long been known for its isolated beauty and mild climate. As winter hit the northern cities or when the daily business routine of the nation's leading industrialists became too hectic, yachts and private trains from Boston, New York, Chicago, and Philadelphia converged on the exclusive winter retreat and the Jekyll Island Club.

Hunting was a favored pastime for both men and women. To add to the wild game already on the island, pheasants were shipped from England, and quail, turkey, and deer were brought from Virginia. By 1919, however, the hunting grounds had given way to golf courses and tennis courts.

At the end of the day, as the sun set over the marshes and waterways, families retreated to their elaborate 18- to 24-room "cottages" to dress for dinner. The Victorian-styled Clubhouse (which today is a full-service hotel) had fifteen-

Above: Moss Cottage, built in 1896, was the home of George Henry Macy, president of the Union Pacific Tea Company.

foot ceilings, a columned dining room, and carved oak woodwork. Guests enjoyed the freshest seafood, game, and beef; the finest wines; and the most tempting pastries.

As the women admired each other's fashions and discussed social events and plans, the men withdrew for brandy and cigars and talked business and politics. They discussed the state of the nation's economy, which, for the most part, they personally controlled. They determined which politicians were deserving of their favors and support, and they shared ideas about America's future.

The next day was another whirlwind of activities with carriage rides around the grounds, games and sports, ponies on the beach, and lawn parties before preparations for a big costume ball scheduled for that evening. Such were the lives of the rich and famous in the late nineteenth century.

As word spread about the Jekyll Island Club and all of the attractions available in the area, other business and industrial giants built second homes along Georgia's coastline. Cumberland Island, near St. Marys, was one favorite. Another popular Georgia retreat for northern millionaires escaping the cold weather was Thomasville, in Thomas County. Thomasville was the southernmost rail terminus at the time, and many who came to visit ended up staying in the gracious and pleasant town.

We can only guess at the number of business transactions, marriage and social contracts, and political alliances forged at these three grand Georgia winter retreats.

Below: The National Trust for Historic Preservation named the Jekyll Island Clubhouse a National Historic Landmark in 1978 and a Historic Hotel of America.

World War I

Section Preview

As you read, look for:
• the reasons why the United States entered World War I,
• the ways in which Georgians contributed to the war effort, and
• vocabulary terms: World War I, neutral, propaganda, and armistice.

In August 1914, World War I broke out in Europe. President Woodrow Wilson, who had been elected in 1912, declared America a neutral nation. In other words, the United States would not take sides between the *Central Powers* led by Germany and Austria-Hungary and the *Allied Powers* led by France, Great Britain, and Russia.

Some Georgians, however, did take sides. They volunteered to fight for the French and British, serving as aviators, soldiers, ambulance drivers, and nurses. Some joined with other Americans and flew with the Lafayette Escadrille, a squadron of American aviators who fought for France. Another American who fought for France was Eugene Jacques Bullard.

Eugene Jacques Bullard

The first African American combat pilot was a Columbus native, Eugene Jacques Bullard. Bullard's grandfather had been a slave, and his father spoke often of countries where whites and blacks were treated as equals—countries such as France. Bullard's childhood dream was to live in France.

At 18, Bullard hitchhiked from Georgia to Virginia, where he stowed away on a ship headed for Scotland. Once there, Bullard made his way through England and into France. When the war broke out in 1914, he enlisted in the French Foreign Legion. Later, he transferred to a regular unit of the French army and was wounded twice in combat. Declared disabled by the army, Bullard applied for pilot training with the French Air Service in 1916. He became a decorated fighter pilot, flying over twenty combat missions against the Germans. He was wounded several times before being discharged again.

When the United States entered the war in 1917, Bullard volunteered his services to the Army Air Force. When his offer was rejected, he remained with the French forces. Bullard stayed in France after the war. During World War II, he worked as a member of the French underground. Bullard earned many decorations for valor in his military career in France including the Croix de Guerre and the Legion d'Honneur, France's highest medal for heroism.

Bullard returned to the United States at age forty having spent all of his adult life in France. First Lady Eleanor Roosevelt heard of Bullard's experiences and saluted his courage saying, "He dreamed of better places and conditions . . . he went to better places and conditions."

Above: Because of his exploits during World War I and II, French President Charles de Gaulle called Eugene Jacques Bullard a French hero.

The United States Enters the War

President Wilson hoped to keep the United States neutral and had based his 1916 re-election campaign on the slogan, "He kept us out of war." But a series of actions by Germany led him to ask Congress to declare war on Germany in April 1917. When President Wilson spoke to Congress, he asked Americans to fight a war "to make the world safe for democracy."

At the start of World War I, the United States was neutral. By international law, that meant the United States could trade with both warring sides. This was called "freedom of the seas." The British tried to stop neutral countries' trade with Germany by mining the North Sea with explosives. Germany used its submarines to sink ships trading with the British.

In May 1915, a German submarine sank the British ocean liner *Lusitania* off Ireland. Among the hundreds killed were 128 Americans. President Wilson warned Germany not to continue to violate international law, which required warships to provide for the safety of the passengers and crews of trading ships they sank. Germany apologized and stopped the submarine warfare for fear that the United States would enter the war.

Meanwhile, the United States became more committed to the Allies, who depended on the United States for food and war supplies. The British bombarded America with anti-German **propaganda** (information that is spread for the purpose of promoting some cause). Americans believed the propaganda, especially after German spies tried to sabotage American industry. Congress began preparing for war.

In early 1917, Germany resumed its submarine attacks, and in March 1917 German submarines sank several American ships. Meanwhile, the British intercepted and decoded a secret radio message from Germany to Mexico. In this so-called Zimmermann telegram, Germany urged Mexico to attack the United States in return for regaining the southwestern United States. This was the final blow. President Wilson asked Congress to declare war.

Top: This captured German submarine crew is on its way to a POW camp at Fort McPherson. Above: American infantrymen of the Second Division fighting in France.

Georgia and World War I

When the United States declared war, between 85,000 and 100,000 of Georgia's citizens joined the armed forces. Soldiers came from other states to be trained at military posts located throughout the state, including Camp Benning, Fort McPherson, and Camp Gordon.

Camp Benning was opened in 1917 as a result of orders from General John Pershing, the leader of the American armed forces. Located near Columbus, Camp Benning trained infantry troops. Named in honor of Confederate General Henry Benning, it became Fort Benning in 1922. During the war, a German submarine crew was imprisoned at Fort McPherson, which was just outside of Atlanta. Camp Gordon (later renamed Fort Gordon) is located outside of Augusta. These and other military installations were a major factor in the state's economy.

Georgians contributed to the war effort in other ways. Textile mills made fabric for military uniforms. Railroads carried arms, ammunition, and soldiers to ports where ships waited to sail for Europe. Farmers grew more food crops, tobacco, and livestock. Many town residents planted "victory gardens" to raise their own vegetables so there would be more food for the military. Women volunteered to work for the Red Cross, to welcome soldiers, to knit, and to help sell bonds. However, Georgia's most important contribution was the three thousand young people from all over the state who died in an effort to "make the world safe for democracy."

The entry of the United States into the war and the vast amounts of personnel, supplies, and equipment it was able to contribute helped to defeat the Central Powers. On November 11, 1918, the war officially ended when both sides signed an armistice (an agreement to stop fighting). For years afterward, Georgia and the rest of the nation rang church bells and held ceremonies at the 11th hour on the 11th day of the 11th month to commemorate victory and peace.

Atlanta Fire

On May 21, 1917, Atlanta's attention was briefly drawn away from the war by a local event. Early that morning, many residents were told to collect water they might need for the day because the city's water supply was to be off for a while. When a fire broke out in the west end of town, firemen had little water to put it out. Over the next 10-12 hours, more than seventy city blocks were destroyed.

Dry weather and wooden houses built close together made it easy for the fire to spread. About 1,900 houses and 1,553 other buildings were destroyed; between 6,000 and 10,000 people were left homeless.

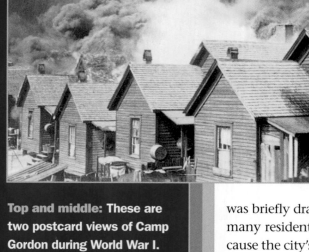

Top and middle: These are two postcard views of Camp Gordon during World War I. Bottom: Although as many as 10,000 people were left homeless, no one was killed in the 1917 Atlanta fire.

A Final Note

The term *generosity* refers to the act of being kindly, charitable, open-handed, and giving. You can show your generosity by giving money to those in need or to a cause in which you believe. You can also be generous with your time in helping others, with your words by sharing positive comments or knowledge, or just by sharing your talents whether they range from baking cookies to playing the piano to sketching pictures.

This chapter includes a look at some famous Americans and Georgians who shared their generosity with those around them. Choose two individuals from the chapter and, for each one, list three ways that these people showed their generous nature.

Chapter Summary

- Muckrakers was the term applied to reform-minded journalists and writers of this period.

- The Progressive Era was a time of great cultural, social, economic, and political changes.

- Social changes included prison reforms, labor reforms, the temperance movement and prohibition, women's suffrage, and civil rights struggles.

- Economic changes included the development of the corporation, the growth of trusts and monopolies, and later efforts to limit trusts and monopolies.

- Political changes included the growth of the Populist party, the use of the Australian ballot, and establishment of Georgia's county unit system, which gave great influence to rural politicians.

- The nation ratified the Eighteenth (prohibition) and Nineteenth (suffrage for women) amendments to the U.S. Constitution.

- During this period, African Americans struggled against discrimination and the passage of laws that segregated public facilities and prevented them from voting.

- Georgian Tom Watson, who represented the state in the U.S. House of Representatives, sponsored the Rural Free Delivery bill, which required the U.S. Post Office to deliver mail to rural areas.

- Georgian Hoke Smith, while serving in the U.S. Senate, sponsored legislation creating the Agricultural Extension Service and vocational education programs in public schools.

- Coca-Cola, one of the world's largest corporations, was founded in Atlanta.

- After several years of neutrality, the United States entered World War I on the side of the Allied Powers. Georgia's military installations expanded during the war, which ended in 1918.

It's Your Turn

1. When did the United States enter World War I?

2. Describe at least four ways Georgians contributed to the victory in World War I.

3. Do you think World War I did "make the world safe for democracy"? Why or why not?

Chapter Review

Reviewing People, Places and Terms

Use the following names or terms in a sentence about this period of Georgia's history.

1. armistice
2. Asa Candler
3. civil rights
4. corporation
5. John Hope
6. Jim Crow laws
7. labor union
8. martial law
9. prohibition
10. suffragette

Understanding the Facts

1. Name the three areas in which progressives worked for reforms.
2. Describe two major prison reforms of this era. Are those reforms still in place today?
3. What was the mission of the WCTU?
4. Who were Georgia's leaders against "demon rum"?
5. What were four reforms sought by the Populist party?
6. For what legislation is Thomas Watson best remembered?
7. What were the results of the Smith-Lever Act and the Smith-Hughes Act? How did this federal legislation help Georgia's citizens?

8. How did the county unit system work in Georgia? What did it accomplish?
9. Explain the major conflict between civil rights leaders Booker T. Washington and W. E. B. DuBois.
10. Which U.S. Supreme Court cases of this era reinforced segregation in the nation and in Georgia's schools?
11. What were three strategies used by white supremacists to minimize African American voting powers?
12. What were two of the events that forced the United States into World War I?

Developing Critical Thinking

1. Today, many colleges have forbidden or are considering forbidding alcohol on campus to curtail students' "binge" drinking. Do you think this is a good idea?
2. Why do you think Americans took so long to give women the vote?
3. The United States was officially neutral when World War I broke out, yet Americans could not help but take sides in the war because so many citizens were recent immigrants from Europe. How do you think our immigration patterns influenced our decision-making skills during the period leading up to our entry into the war? How does our diverse, multicultural population influence our political decision-making today? In your opinion, is this influence a good thing or a bad thing? Why?

Checking It Out

1. After the success of the movie *Titanic*, you probably think that you know all there is to know about the sinking of the famous ship. Use your research skills to check it out. Could the catastrophe have been avoided? How? Who were some of the rich and famous people aboard the ship on that fateful evening? How many fatalities were there? How many survivors?

2. In 2004, Berry College in Rome was selected as the nation's No. 2 comprehensive undergraduate college in the South. Use your research skills to find out who was No. 1. Then use a Venn diagram to compare and contrast the two schools. Do you agree with the magazine's ranking? Why or why not?

3. Average salaries in 1892 were quite different than average salaries today. For each of the following job categories, use your research skills to locate a modern-day salary equivalent. Then calculate the percentage of increase in salary for each category. (1) Factory worker, 1892 salary $446; (2) Miner, 1892 wages $393; (3) Clerk, 1892 salary $885; (4) Schoolteacher, 1892 salary $270.

Writing Across the Curriculum

1. The progressives wanted to reform society in the late 1800s and early 1900s. Write a paragraph describing some aspect of society that you would like to reform today.

2. Write an editorial that might have appeared in an Atlanta newspaper following Booker T. Washington's speech at the Cotton States and International Exposition.

Exploring Technology

1. There were many technical advancements during this era, far more than can be listed under the Signs of the Times. Go to Internet site www.enchantedlearning.com/inventors/ to find out about ten inventions or discoveries of the period. Prepare a chart that lists information for each invention or discovery you find.

2. During World War I, propaganda consisted of cartoons, patriotic photographs, patriotic slogans, and posters. Use an Internet search engine to look at some of the World War I posters supporting bonds, victory gardens, war savings stamps, saving food, and volunteering. What appeals do these posters use?

Applying Your Skills

1. Try your hand at developing a series of posters for today's citizens of Georgia. Try to enlist their support in any project your school plans or in any community improvement effort.

2. Find three newspaper articles that deal with the issue of civil rights in today's society.

3. Draw a political cartoon that deals with one of the issues discussed in this chapter.

Picture Question

This statue of Georgia's best-known populist stands at the main entrance of the Georgia State Capitol in Atlanta. Who is he?

Chapter 11

1920–1945

Flappers, Depression, and Global War

his chapter covers only a twenty-five-year period, but this was one of Georgia's and America's most eventful times. "Calamity Jane," a huge heavy artillery gun on wheels, fired the final shots of World War I at 10:59 a.m. on November 11, 1918. The "war to end all wars" was over. President Wilson wrote, "Everything for which America has fought has been accomplished. It will now be our fortunate duty to assist by example, by sober, friendly counsel, and by material aid, in the establishment of just democracy throughout the world." America was at peace, and the party was about to begin.

Left: Democratic presidential candidate Franklin Delano Roosevelt campaigns in Atlanta in 1932. His wife Eleanor is sitting on the right side of the car.

Signs of the Times 1920-1945

Population: 131.6 million in 1940

Life Expectancy: In 1920, Male 53.6 and Female 54.6; in 1940, Male 60.8 and Female 68.2

Costs of Living: During the Depression, milk was $0.14 a quart, bread was $0.09 a loaf, flour was $0.39 a pound, coffee was $0.46 a pound, eggs were $0.15 a dozen, and 10 pounds of sugar cost $0.43. A new house cost $7,146. A new car cost $610, and gas was $0.10 a gallon.

Wages: The average annual salary in 1920 was $2,160 but only $1,973 in 1930. In 1920, a teacher's salary was $970; in 1940, it was $1,441. The minimum wage in the 1940s was $0.43 an hour.

Art/Architecture: Important artists of the period included Willem de Kooning, Georgia O'Keeffe, Thomas Hart Benton, Edward Hopper, Grant Wood, N. C. Wyeth, Jackson Pollock, Piet Mondarian, and Andrew Wyeth. Skyscrapers erected during this period included the Woolworth Building and the Empire State Building in New York and the Wrigley Building in Chicago. U.S. Army Engineers completed the five-sided Pentagon Building.

Music: The music of the 1920s featured jazz, the blues, and sentimental ballads. The 1930s was the big band era. Big bands gave way to rhythm and blues. Hit songs included "I'm Just Wild About Harry," "California Here I Come," and "Second Hand Rose." Hit singers included Frank Sinatra, Dinah Shore, Kate Smith, Bing Crosby, Perry Como, Billie Holiday, and Ella Fitzgerald.

Fads/Fashions: Popularity of radio boomed, and television began to expand late in the era. Dance marathons were popular; popular dances were the Charleston, black bottom, shimmy, and jitterbug. The board game "Monopoly" was invented. Women began wearing knee-length skirts. Ready-to-wear fashions became popular. Zippers became common in clothes. Hats were mandatory for men. Women's nylon stockings were first marketed in 1939.

Literature: Books published during the period included Dr. Benjamin Spock's *Common Sense Book of Baby and Child Care*, Dashiell Hammett's *The Maltese Falcon*, Pearl Buck's *The Good Earth*, John Steinbeck's *The Grapes of Wrath*, Marjorie Kinnan Rawlings's *The Yearling*, Margaret Mitchell's *Gone With the Wind*, Richard Wright's *Native Son*, and E. B. White's *Stuart Little*. Leading poets of the era included e. e. cummings, Carl Sandburg, Edna St. Vincent Millay, Langston Hughes, and Robert Frost.

Religion: The American Lutheran Church formed in 1930 in Toledo, Ohio. The International Bible Students Association became Jehovah's Witnesses in 1931. The U.S. Supreme Court ruled in 1943 that schoolchildren could not be required to salute the flag in school if their religion prohibited it.

Science: The bulldozer was invented in 1923. RCA licensed NBC as the first nationwide entertainment network in 1926; CBS was organized in 1927. The nation's first planetarium opened in Chicago in 1930. DuPont marketed the first nylon product—a toothbrush. Aerosol spray cans were introduced. Computers were developed in 1945; the digital computer named ENIAC weighed 30 tons and stood two stories high.

Education: At the height of the depression in 1933, some 2,000 rural schools closed, 200,000 teachers were out of work, and about 2.3 million children were out of school. The concept of junior high schools spread across the nation in the 1920s. National Spelling Bee began in 1925, sponsored by the Louisville *Courier-Journal*.

Transportation: The first coast-to-coast bus line, Yelloway Bus Line, offered service from New York to Los Angeles, a 5-day, 14-hour trip. Charles Lindbergh made the first nonstop transatlantic airplane flight. Amelia Earhart became the first woman to fly alone across the Atlantic in 1932. She disappeared on a flight across the Pacific in 1937. The *Queen Mary* arrived in New York on its maiden voyage. Golden Gate Bridge in San Francisco opened.

Leisure Time: The movie *Gone With the Wind* premiered in Atlanta, and Margaret Mitchell won a Pulitzer Prize for her novel. Eight Chicago White Sox players were accused of "fixing" the World Series; they were found not guilty but banned from baseball. Baseball Hall of Fame established in Cooperstown, New York. The first Winter Olympic Games were held the in U.S. in Lake Placid, New York in 1932. Bobby Jones developed the Augusta National Golf Club, which opened for play in 1933.

Figure 38 Timeline: 1920–1945

1922 Rebecca Latimer Felton appointed to U.S. Senate WSB radio went on air	**1924** Drought hit state	**1937** Margaret Mitchell won Pulitzer Prize for *Gone With the Wind*	**1939** *Gone With the Wind* movie premiered in Atlanta	
	1931 Paved highway opened from Atlanta to Brunswick	**1932** State government reorganized into 17 agencies		**1943** Georgia first state to allow 18-year-olds to vote

1920   1925   1930   1935   1940   1945

	1929 Stock market crashed	**1934** Textile workers strike		**1945** World War II ended
	1932 Franklin Roosevelt elected president	**1939** World War II broke out in Europe		President Roosevelt died at Warm Springs
	1933 CCC and TVA created	**1941** U.S. entered World War II after attack on Pearl Harbor		

The Roaring Twenties

Section Preview

As you read, look for:
• Georgia's first two female legislators,
• new forms of music,
• problems in agriculture, and
• vocabulary terms: jazz, the blues, boll weevil, and Great Migration.

When the peace treaty ending World War I was signed, people throughout the nation were ready to celebrate the end of rationing, the end of worry about loved ones overseas, the end of sadness associated with a deadly world-wide flu epidemic, and the end of hard times associated with the war. In his presidential campaign, President Warren Harding had promised to return the country to normalcy, and that is exactly what he tried to do. But the normalcy of the past was going to take a big left turn.

The New Woman

On August 26, 1920, the Nineteenth Amendment was ratified, giving women the right to vote. Suddenly, women felt a new sense of equality and a new freedom of expression. Many who had stepped into the labor force during the war years wanted to continue working.

The idea of femininity changed drastically. Out were tight corsets and long petticoats. In were knee-length, free-moving dresses that exposed women's legs and arms. Out was the long hair put up in buns or braids; in was a short, bobbed, boyish hair style. Out was the natural look; in was make-up such as lipstick and rouge. Out was the demure, modest, and well-behaved matron. In was the young woman who drank, smoked, and danced all night without a chaperone. And times would never again be the same. Many of the females of the 1920s proudly took on the label *flappers*. The term was first used in Great Britain after World War I to describe young girls between childhood and adulthood. But writer and publisher H. L. Mencken described the flapper as "a somewhat foolish girl, full of wild surmises and inclined to revolt against the precepts and admonitions of her elders."

The Nineteenth Amendment also opened the doors for women to run for political office. In 1922, two women became the first female legislators in the Georgia house of representatives—Bessie Kempton Crowell from Fulton County and Viola Ross Napier from Bibb County.

In that same year, Rebecca Latimer Felton was honored when Governor Thomas Hardwick appointed her to fill the U.S. Senate seat of Tom Watson, who had died in office. Felton's appointment was an acknowledgment of her outstanding reform work and efforts supporting the suffrage movement. Since the Senate was not in session at the time of her appointment, Felton was not officially sworn in to her new office. Nor did she really serve time in Congress; Walter F. George was elected to the Senate seat in a special election. But when the Senate reconvened, the 87-year-old Felton was sworn in for a day, making her the first woman to serve in the U.S. Senate.

Music

Thousands of clubs called *speakeasies* opened across the country, and most were well stocked with illegal liquor. Often, the music that was played in those clubs was a unique African American contribution known as jazz. Jazz was different from traditional music styles because it relied on improvisation. That is, jazz was "on the spur of the moment"; it did not follow written notes. Although jazz had been around for a long time, it burst onto the national stage during the 1920s. Musicians such as Duke Ellington and Louis Armstrong played at jazz clubs, which opened up around the country. The most famous club was the Cotton Club in Harlem, which was packed each night with black and white audiences.

The blues was another popular music of the period. Blues music was based on black folk music. Georgia's own Ma Rainey became known as the "Mother of the Blues," and she recorded about one hundred songs between 1923 and 1928. Her songs usually spoke of lost love, loneliness, poverty, and jealousy. Another popular blues singer of the period was Bessie Smith.

An African American musical, "Runnin Wild," featured a dance that swept the nation and became synonymous with the period—the Charleston.

The Art of Politics

Rebecca Latimer Felton was the first woman to serve in the U.S. Senate. Mrs. Felton was also the senator who, having served one day, served the shortest term and was the oldest senator, at age 87, at the time of her swearing-in.

Did You Know?

The music of the era also led to a new craze—dance marathons. One marathon held at Madison Square Garden in 1928 lasted 481 hours. Ninety-one couples took part.

Above: The bob hairstyle was popular in the 1920s.
Opposite page: Women's fashions of the 1920s reflected social changes.

Crime

There was a dark note to the Roaring Twenties, as the period was called. The prohibition of the 1920s gave rise to organized gangs in large cities such as Chicago and New York. These gangsters made millions by supplying illegal liquor to speakeasies and other private clubs. The public followed the misdeeds of such mobsters as Scarface Al Capone, "Bugs" Moran, Baby Face Nelson, and Frank Nitty.

Capone, dubbed Chicago's "Public Enemy No. 1," was finally arrested and convicted of tax evasion. Capone spent one year in the Atlanta federal penitentiary before he was transferred to Alcatraz.

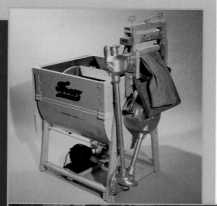

Life in the Roaring Twenties

After the war years, life was good. A trip to the doctor's office was only $5, and for an extra dollar or two the doctor would come to your home. Many things came right to the front door—milk, butter and cream, ice, and even fresh vegetables. Vegetable deliveries were short lived, however. In 1926, a man named Clarence Birdseye perfected a method for freezing and packaging foods. His process freed women from the chore of buying fresh foods every day and from having to cook everything from scratch.

Little by little, life was becoming more convenient. Electricity became more widely available, and electric appliances became more common. For example, in 1927, the first pop-up toaster was introduced. Gas ranges replaced wood and coal stoves. Convenience foods began to appear. Quick-cooking rolled oats, pancake mix, and canned goods (everything from tuna to pineapple) were available. By the end of the decade, families could buy presliced bread. Gerber's baby foods first went on the market in 1928.

In November 1920, radio station KDKA started broadcasting in Pittsburgh, and it changed America forever. One year later, Americans spent $10 million on radio sets and parts. Families gathered around the radio to listen to baseball games, news reports, and favored programs such as "The Grand Ole Opry." In 1922, WSB radio in Atlanta joined the ever growing number of stations throughout the country. Those tuned in heard a jazz rendition of the "Light Cavalry Overture." The station became known as the "Voice of the South." In 1923, WRAB radio was licensed in Savannah, and in 1924 radio station WDBA was li-

Top : This is an early washing machine. Center: These flappers of the 1920s are dancing the Charleston. Bottom: The two items in the background are early radios. The disks in the foreground are 78rpm records.

Did You Know?

The call letters for radio station WSB in Atlanta reportedly stood for "Welcome South Brother."

censed in Columbus. The radio stations linked Americans to each other and to the world more than ever before.

Movies were a favorite pastime. In 1927, the first talking motion picture, *The Jazz Singer* with Al Jolson, hit theaters. Children and adults were enthralled just a year later when Walt Disney's first talking cartoon, "Steamboat Willie," appeared. It introduced a new American movie hero—Mickey Mouse.

The Destruction of King Cotton

For many Georgians, the twenties were not a time of abundance. A small, grayish, long-snouted beetle, the boll weevil, was destroying the primary source of income for many Georgia farmers: cotton. The boll weevil had come from Mexico, moved through Texas, and into the southern states in the 1890s. The beetles hatch in the yellow flower of the cotton plant. As the flower becomes a boll (the place were the fibers are formed), the larvae feeds on the growing white, fluffy cotton, making it useless.

The boll weevil appeared in southwest Georgia in 1915 and quickly spread across the state, destroying thousands of acres of Georgia's major agricultural crop. By 1923, cotton production had dropped to 600,000 bales from a high of 2.8 million bales in 1914. The postwar price was only fifteen to seventeen cents a pound.

In 1924, Georgia farmers were hit with another natural disaster—a major drought. The sun-baked fields slowed down the destruction of the boll weevil, but the drought ruined most of Georgia's other crops. Over 375,000 farm workers left Georgia between 1920 and 1925. The number of working farms fell from 310,132 to 249,095.

When farms failed, banks that had loaned the farmers money took huge losses. Many farm-related businesses closed. Georgia was in a deep depression.

The Great Migration

While parts of the nation were living it up during the Roaring Twenties, an agricultural depression led many tenant farmers to leave the South and migrate north looking for work. Black farmers, in particular, moved to northern industrial cities such as Chicago and Detroit, hoping to find work in factories and assembly plants. This movement of southern blacks, which lasted until the 1960s, was called the Great Migration.

In the South, most well-paying jobs went to whites. Better jobs and higher pay were available in the North. In fact, many northern companies actively recruited African Americans for jobs.

There were other reasons for the migration. Southern states restricted voting rights, while the North offered the hope of full citizenship rights. Public

Above: These young African American men from the South moved north and found work in shipyards, meat-packing plants and steel mills.

Wy are trey holding american Flags???

schools for African Americans in much of the South were poor, and the North offered more educational opportunities. Health care was better in the North. In addition, segregation in the South kept African Americans from hotels, restaurants, and recreation areas, while the North offered open access to these facilities.

Because they did not have enough money to move everyone at once, African American and poor white families first sent their young men to get jobs. Most were unskilled and found work in the meat-packing plants, shipyards, and steel mills. When they had saved enough money, they sent for the rest of their families. The African Americans generally improved their lives by moving north. But they were also crowded into segregated housing in overpopulated cities and faced a different type of prejudice than they had known in the South.

The Klan Strengthens

In Chapter 10, you learned that the Ku Klux Klan was reborn in Atlanta in 1915. The Klan's targets included not only African Americans but also Jews, Catholics, and immigrants. Talk of "returning America to traditional values and morals" and a "patriotism of traditional America" gained the group new members. Not only did membership increase in numbers, it also increased in stature as doctors, lawyers, judges, businessmen, and even ministers joined.

During the 1920s, the Klan gained a foothold in the Midwest and the Southwest. By 1922, the Klan had branches in all forty-eight states. In 1925, forty thousand costumed and hooded Klansmen marched past the White

Below: The Ku Klux Klan was not just a force in the South. This march took place in Washington, D.C., in 1926.

GEORGIA'S PIONEER AVIATOR
BEN T. EPPS
—1888~1937—

Ben T. Epps - Georgia's First in Flight - designed, built and in 1907 flew the first airplane in the State of Georgia. He was born in Oconee County, educated in Clarke County, and attended Georgia Tech. A self-taught aviator, aircraft designer, and builder, Epps built the 1907 Monoplane in his shop on Washington Street in Athens and designed and flew new airplanes in 1909, 1911, 1916, 1924, and 1930. The 1924 Epps Monoplane weighed only 350 pounds, had a wingspan of 25 feet, and was powered by a two-cylinder motorcycle engine. Designed for the average man, easy to fly, and inexpensive to operate, it would get 25 miles per gallon at 60 miles per hour.
Epps began operation of an airport at this location in 1917, and operated a flying service for the next 20 years. In 1937, he died of injuries incurred here after engine failure and the crash of his light biplane on take-off.

GEORGIA HISTORIC MARKER

A native of Oconee County, Ben Epps is known as the "father of aviation in Georgia." The first Georgian to build and fly an airplane. Epps was fascinated by the stories of the Wright brothers' experiments. One of the models he designed was a light monoplane (a plane with one wing) that he hoped would make flying economically available to the average person. You can learn about Ben Epps when you visit his home in Athens and see the historical marker beside the Athens-Clarke County Airport.

House. Only rain prevented them from burning a cross beside the Washington Monument. The Klan also gained political influence, and five U.S. Senators elected in the 1920s were open members of the Klan. One member, who later recanted his membership, became a Supreme Court justice.

Race riots broke out in many parts of the country in the early and mid-1920s. In some places, the Klan even became an organized part of local law enforcement.

Scandals within the Klan leadership in the late 1920s led to a decline in membership throughout the country. People began to see the relationship between the Klan and racial terrorism. By the time the Depression hit, the Klan had lost most of its national power.

A Special Day

In 1919, a wealthy hotel businessman announced a prize of $25,000 to the first person who flew nonstop from New York to Paris, France, or from Paris to New York. In May 1927, three pilots in the United States were poised to make the attempt. One was a tall, lean, quiet, boyish pilot who had flown mail out of St. Louis. In fact, he named his plane the "Spirit of St. Louis." He was 25-year-old Charles Lindbergh, and he tackled the 3,600-mile transatlantic trip alone.

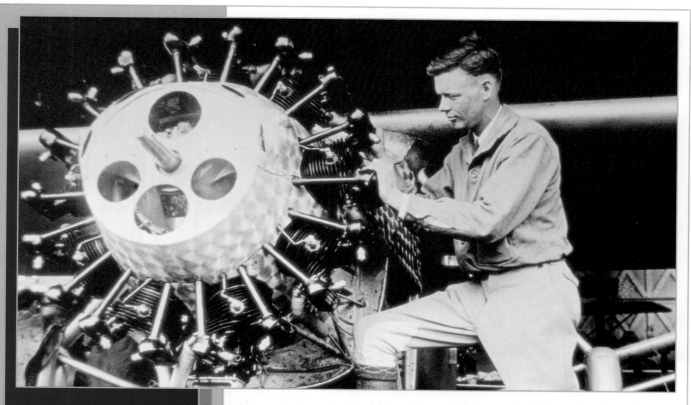

Above: Charles Lindbergh checks the engine of his plane, the "Spirit of St. Louis," before his record-breaking flight to France. Because he was a lone pilot in a single-engine plane, he was nick-named the "Lone Eagle."

Lindbergh flew without the help of navigational or weather instruments, using only landmarks to guide him. He took with him a bag of sandwiches and a quart of water, along with a rubber raft in case he had to ditch in the ocean. Lindbergh took off on a misty Friday morning, May 20, 1927, at 8:00 a.m., from Long Island, New York. The public followed his progress, staying glued to their radio sets.

The trip took 33½ hours. Upon his arrival in France, Lindbergh became an instant hero. Songs were written about him, including one called "Lucky Lindy." Wherever he went, crowds of people gathered to see him. In October 1927, six months after his historic flight, Lindbergh flew into Atlanta, where he was welcomed by over 20,000 admirers. Soon afterward, a street in the city was named Lindbergh Drive in honor of the "Lone Eagle."

Did You Know?

In 1927, Charles Lindbergh was the first person honored as *Time* magazine's "Man of the Year."

It's Your Turn

1. Who were the first female members of the Georgia General Assembly?
2. Who was the "Mother of Blues"?
3. What two factors led to Georgia's agricultural problems during the Roaring Twenties?
4. How does the Great Migration pattern of sending young men to find work and then moving families to join them repeat itself today with immigration patterns in the United States?

The Great Depression

Buck Rogers first appeared in comic strips and wax milk cartons were used for the first time. It was the year Wyatt Earp died, but it was also the year Martin Luther King, Jr., was born. Georgian Bobby Jones won the U.S. Open Golf Championship, and Royston resident Ty Cobb continued to display unparalleled baseball talents. Despite these highlights, 1929 is most remembered as the "boom that went bust!"

The Bottom Drops Out

People thought that the good times of the Roaring Twenties would last forever. Few realized its end would be so drastic. In March 1929, right after President Herbert Hoover was inaugurated, the Federal Reserve Board began meeting daily. In March, a series of "mini-crashes" had occurred in the stock market, the place where shares of ownership in corporations (stock) are bought and sold. Each time, the economy recovered. Summer seemed to bring back the good times—until the day after Labor Day. Then, the roller coaster started.

It was Thursday morning, October 24, 1929. With the opening bell of the stock exchange, the ticker tape machines began running. Investors tried to sell their stocks at any price. Screams of "Sell, Sell, Sell" could be heard all over New York's Wall Street. By noon, police were called in to handle the growing crowd. The lunch break seemed to slow things down a bit, and there

Below: Mounted police had to be called in to control the crowd on Wall Street on "Black Tuesday."

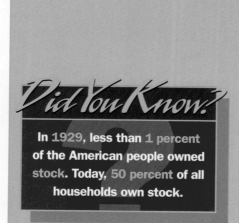

Above: This is a caricature (an exaggerated drawing) of President Herbert Hoover. The president tried but was unable to stimulate the American economy.

was even a small rebound that carried over into Friday. Everyone was relieved when the weekend arrived and the market closed.

On Monday, it became clear that things were not getting better. Panic set in as people all over the country began trading anew. Unlike the previous week, this trading was not a recovery. On Tuesday, October 29, 1929, a day known as "Black Tuesday," the stock market "crashed." By the end of that day, millions of Americans had lost everything they had.

With each day that passed, the country went deeper and deeper into an economic downturn, which today we call the Great Depression. By the end of the year, the value of stocks on the stock market had fallen $40 billion. A share of U.S. Steel that had been selling for $262 had dropped to $22, a 92 percent decrease. Montgomery Ward stock prices sank from $138 to $4 a share, a 97 percent decrease. Many stocks dropped to a penny or less a share.

Causes of the Depression

What caused the Great Depression? One cause was that the people of the United States had borrowed more money than they could afford to repay. This hurt the banks that had loaned the money and the businesses waiting for their payments. Businesses that did not get paid had to lay off workers.

Many factories had produced more goods than they could sell. When the demand for the goods fell, the businesses had to slow production until the surpluses were gone. Farmers were also guilty of overproduction. For several seasons, the farmers had produced surplus crops, causing prices to decline steadily. After World War I, European farmers began raising crops again; that added to the worldwide overproduction. The decline in farm income meant farmers could not repay their debts or buy goods from suppliers.

After World War I, Americans wanted to trade with other nations. But the United States and other nations had enacted tariffs. The high tariffs made it difficult for other countries to sell their goods in the United States to get money with which to repay wartime loans and buy American products.

Speculation in the stock market also helped cause the Great Depression. During the 1920s, most people bought stock and paid only a portion of the cost of the stock at the time of the purchase. Even though the stock was not completely paid for, the investor had the right to sell it. If the stock price had gone up, the investor sold the stock and made enough to finish paying for the stock. This practice forced the price of stocks up, making them higher than what they were really worth.

Many banks had purchased large amounts of stock. When the market crashed, the banks lost a lot of money. When depositors learned this, there were runs on the banks. When too many people withdraw their money from a bank, the bank collapses; everyone loses.

One final cause was the laissez-faire attitude of the American people and of American government and business leaders. Almost every government official believed the economy itself, not the government, would work out any problems. President Hoover did what any other politician of the time would have done—nothing. Hoover kept telling the American people that "prosperity is just around the corner." But prosperity was *not* just around the corner.

Living Through the Depression

By 1932, unemployment in the nation had reached 13 million; 1 out of 4 Americans was unemployed. Men who had once managed large corporations were walking the streets looking for any type of work or were standing on street corners selling apples.

Over 9,000 banks closed their doors. Millions lost their savings and their cash. In 1931 alone, 31 banks failed in Georgia.

People were forced out of their homes, and many lived in shacks made of collected junk. Such "neighborhoods" were called "Hoovervilles" for the president who was powerless to help. Many people were literally starving and were saved only by soup kitchens set up by the government or charities. Barter became a common practice, particularly in the South.

Education suffered tremendously during the depression. With little cash and few taxes, many schools were forced to close or to shorten schedules. Salaries were cut, and teachers making $40-$50 a month considered themselves lucky.

Because Georgia was already in an economic depression when the stock market crashed, Georgians did not immediately feel the impact of "Black Tuesday." However, between 1929 and 1932, an average farmer's income dropped from $206 a year to $83; cotton prices fell to $0.05 a pound.

During the depression, most Georgians were challenged simply by trying to meet their everyday needs. Many workers in the state lost their jobs, resulting in great suffering and despair. Children of the unemployed often did

Below: Collie Smith of Carroll County reads the *Progressive Farmer*. Bottom: This is a one-room, one-teacher school for African American children in Veazy.

not go to school because they had no shoes or proper clothes. Families went hungry, with many living for weeks on a single food like cornmeal or rice.

State services suffered. Many rural children did not get an education. There was no money for health care and highway construction. The economic advances of the previous several decades were stopped dead in their tracks.

But there were some bright spots. In 1930, plane service from Atlanta to New York was introduced and strengthened business ties between the "Empire State of the South" and the nation's center of commerce. Another major transportation feat of the period was the completion of the highway from Atlanta to Brunswick. Finally, Georgians could travel to most of the state's cities on paved roads. One of those roads led to Augusta.

In 1931, world class amateur golfer Bobby Jones, a native of Atlanta, announced his intentions to build a golf course in Augusta. That golf club, Augusta National, opened in 1933. Today, it is home to one of the world's four major golf tournaments—the Masters.

Above: Bobby Jones, born in Atlanta, is considered the greatest golfer in the history of the game.

It's Your Turn

1. What happened on "Black Tuesday"?
2. Explain the laissez-faire attitude of the American government toward the economy.
3. Do you think President Hoover should have done more to end the Great Depression? Why or why not?

Easing the Burden

President Herbert Hoover was the first president to use the power of the federal government to help the economy recover. In one program designed to help farmers, the government bought large amounts of cotton, wheat, and other commodities (crops). This, it was believed, would cause farm prices to rise. The government would then sell its commodities on the market later, after the prices had risen. However, the government bought too little of the commodities, and the plan did not work. Hoover did use the government's stored wheat and cotton to provide flour and cloth for the needy.

President Hoover approved a program that loaned federal money to needy businesses. He also supported public works projects, such as the building of post offices, parks, courthouses, and roads. These projects put many unemployed men back to work. With Hoover's urging, the government loaned money to the states for their own public works projects. Hoover's programs helped, but they did not end the depression or provide enough help for the poor.

Besides the federal and state governments, many local agencies also helped. The most effective were the Red Cross and the Salvation Army. Hospitals provided free lunches for the needy. Local governments provided free lunches for needy children and paid men low wages to sweep streets, plant trees, drain swamps, cut firewood, and plant gardens. Still, public and private efforts to provide relief (money and goods given to people in special need) were not enough. What was needed was a program that coordinated efforts at all levels.

The New Deal

Section Preview

As you read, look for:
* New Deal programs,
* New Deal programs in Georgia,
* Georgia's governors, and
* vocabulary terms: New Deal, minimum wage, stretch out, collective bargaining, rural electrification, subsidy, and integrate.

In 1932, President Hoover ran for re-election. His opponent was Governor Franklin D. Roosevelt of New York. When Roosevelt accepted his party's nomination, he told the audience, "I pledge you, I pledge myself, to a new deal for the American people." Campaigning was difficult at times, because Roosevelt had been struck with polio in 1921, and his legs were paralyzed. He wore steel leg braces, but most people did not know about his paralysis. However, his spirits were high as he campaigned for the presidency, and he became very popular with the American people.

Roosevelt won the election. In his inaugural address, Roosevelt said:

We are stricken by no plague of locusts. Compared with the perils which our forefathers conquered because they believed and were not afraid, we have still much to be thankful for. Nature still offers her bounty and human efforts have multiplied it. Plenty is at our doorstep. . . .

His speech and his natural optimism won the people's confidence. They believed Roosevelt would try new ways to end the depression, which was, by then, felt all over the world. When Roosevelt took office on March 4, 1933, he took steps to fulfil his promise of "a new deal for the American people."

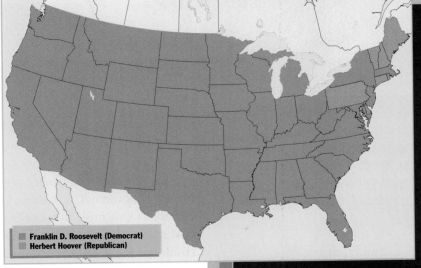

Franklin D. Roosevelt (Democrat)
Herbert Hoover (Republican)

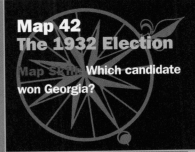

**Map 42
The 1932 Election**

Map Skill: Which candidate won Georgia?

Roosevelt had no clear idea of how to deal with the depression. He gathered a group of advisers from all over the country; they became known as the "brain trust." With their help and at Roosevelt's urging, Congress passed a series of laws that came to be known as the New Deal. The purpose of these laws was to bring about economic recovery, relieve the suffering of the unemployed, reform defects in the economy, and improve society.

The first objective of the New Deal was economic recovery. The day after his inauguration, Roosevelt closed all banks until each could be investigated for soundness. The sound banks were allowed to re-open. The government loaned money to others to reopen. This action went a long way in helping the citizens regain faith in America's banking system. Other economic recovery programs were designed to help farmers and manufacturers.

A number of New Deal programs were designed to help the unemployed. The New Deal tried to correct weaknesses in the economy that may have added to the depression. Finally, the New Deal went beyond trying to solve

the problems of the depression by trying to improve people's lives.

Congress implemented so many programs that the New Deal agencies became known by their initials. There were so many agencies that Roosevelt's administration was called "government by alphabet." Figure 39 lists a number of the New Deal programs, many of which are still in place.

Although some of Roosevelt's New Deal programs worked better than others, together they provided the nation with the chance for recovery that it so desperately needed. The New Deal did not end unemployment, and it did not bring the depression to a halt. But it paved the way for recovery, and it showed Americans that they could believe in government again.

Above: This 1934 cartoon pokes fun at President Roosevelt and the many "alphabet" agencies created under the New Deal.

Georgia and the New Deal

One of the president's New Deal programs that did not work was the National Industrial Recovery Act (NIRA). It was designed to help workers by setting minimum wages, permitting them to organize unions, and allowing factories to cut back on production. (A **minimum wage** is the least amount an employer can pay an employee for a certain number of hours worked.) In Georgia, this legislation mainly affected the textile industry. Although labor unions had been active in the North for many years, most manufacturers in the South had forbidden unions, and workers were not allowed to even discuss them. Those who did were often fired for being "trouble makers."

Roosevelt's NIRA posed a major threat to mill owners, and it did not take long for trouble to break out. Mill owners began using the **stretch out**, a practice requiring workers to tend more machines. Under this practice, workers had to do the same

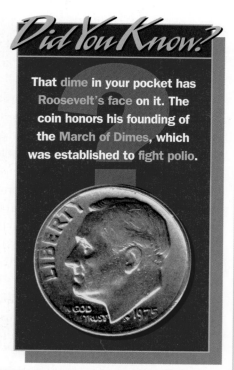

Did You Know?

That **dime** in your pocket has **Roosevelt's face** on it. The coin honors his founding of the **March of Dimes**, which **was established to** fight polio.

Figure 39 New Deal Programs and Legislation

Program/Legislation	Date	Purpose
Tennessee Valley Authority (TVA)	1933	Built dams on the Tennessee River to control flooding and generate electricity. Three north Georgia lakes are now a part of the TVA.
Public Works Administration (PWA)	1933	Put people to work building roads, buildings, and other public works projects.
Federal Deposit Insurance Corporation (FDIC)	1933	Insured individual savings accounts so that people did not lose their money if banks failed or closed their doors.
Federal Emergency Relief Administration (FERA)	1933	Provided federal funds for state and community relief efforts.
Civil Works Administration (CWA)	1933	Provided temporary federal jobs for the unemployed.
Civilian Conservation Corps (CCC)	1933	Provided jobs for young single men building forest trails and roads, planting trees to reforest the land and control flooding, and building parks.
Federal Housing Administration (FHA)	1934	Insured home loans for low-income families.
Securities and Exchange Commission (SEC)	1934	Regulated stocks and gave stock information.
Social Security Administration (SSA)	1935	Created a system for retirement and unemployment insurance.
Works Progress Administration (WPA)	1935	Employed out-of-work Americans to repair roads, build or repair bridges, paint murals, write guidebooks, put on plays and musical performances, and create statues in parks.
National Labor Relations Act	1935	Guaranteed the right of employees to organize and to bargain collectively with their employers. Created the National Labor Relations Board to hear unfair labor practices.
National Youth Administration (NYA)	1935	Provided job training and part-time work for college students.
Fair Labor Standards Act	1938	Established a maximum workweek and a minimum wage, prohibited child labor in certain industries, and set a minimum age for child workers.

amount of work in an 8-hour shift that they had previously done in a 12-hour shift. It was a brutal, if not impossible, schedule and clearly against the intent of the law.

In August 1934, textile workers all over the South joined in a strike called by the Textile Workers of America union. Workers immediately left their jobs and went into the streets of cities such as Macon, where 3,500 mill workers protested their treatment. Across Georgia, some 45,000 union workers took part, a large portion of the 60,000 mill hands in the state. Groups of striking workers, called "flying squadrons," traveled from mill to mill stirring up workers and closing down production. At one point, things were so bad that Governor Eugene Talmadge called out the National Guard and had thousands of workers arrested.

For many mill workers, however, the strike caused financial hardships. On September 22, the union called off the strike. Although mill workers returned to their jobs, many things were never the same. Feuds between strikers and nonstrikers increased. Some union activists were blacklisted and unable to find work. Workers were forced to leave their mill homes. The failed strike and the hardships that followed made an impression on Georgia workers that lasted for years.

In 1935, the U.S. Supreme Court declared the NIRA unconstitutional. To replace it, Congress quickly passed several laws to protect workers. The Wagner Act of 1935 guaranteed workers the right of **collective bargaining**, discussions between a union and employer to determine such things as working conditions and employees' wages, hours, and benefits. It also outlawed many unfair labor practices (such as firing union members) and established a board to enforce the law. Congress hoped workers would organize for higher wages. With higher wages, workers could buy more consumer goods and help the economy recover.

One New Deal program was more popular in Georgia and is still enjoyed today. As a result of the TVA, we now have Blue Ridge Lake (which was actually created in 1925), Lake Chatuge, and Lake Nottely.

The Civilian Conservation Corps (CCC) was popular in Georgia in part because of its work at Camp Brumby with the Kennesaw Mountain National Battlefield Park. The CCC also built many of the facilities at Roosevelt State

**Map 43
Georgia's TVA Lakes**

Map Skills In which counties are these lakes located?

Top: Lake Chatuge is an important part of the TVA's system for flood control and electricity generation.

Park in Pine Mountain. Other CCC projects in Georgia included construction of sewer projects in many of the state's cities; flood control and drainage projects such as Tybee Island's seawall; recreational facilities such as ball fields, band stands, and theaters throughout the state; and a host of municipal facilities such as Augusta's Savannah River Levee, Atlanta's Municipal Auditorium, St. Simons' airport, Macon's airport, Stewart County's courthouse and jail, and renovations of Dalton's city hall. The CCC also worked to build, expand, or improve schools and hospitals throughout the state. For example, much of the work on Grady Hospital in Atlanta was done by the CCC.

Rural electrification was an important New Deal program. In the 1920s, power companies mainly ran lines to towns and cities. Because the rural population was spread out, power lines were expensive to build and maintain. The Rural Electrification Authority (REA) reportedly was a result of President Roosevelt's first night at Warm Springs, Georgia. He was sitting on the porch of his small cottage, trying to catch a breeze on a hot, sultry summer night. He noticed that no lights were showing from neighboring farms. When he received his electrical bill at the end of the month, he saw that it was many times higher than what he paid at his mansion in Hyde Park, New York. Roosevelt never forgot that night, and on May 11, 1935, he signed into law the act creating the REA. The REA loaned over $300 million to farmers' cooperatives to help them extend their own power lines and buy power wholesale. This program was one on the most important and far-reaching of the New Deal programs. By 1940, a significant percentage of farmers in Georgia and other parts of the nation had electricity. Electric water pumps, lights, milking machines, and appliances made farm life much easier.

Above: More than 3 million young men earned a dollar a day from jobs with the Civilian Conservation Corps.

Did You Know?

Workers in the CCC made $30 per month. They were expected to send most of that money home to their families.

African Americans During the New Deal

Although most African Americans supported Roosevelt's candidacy for president, they did not, as a whole, make great gains under the New Deal. For example, under the Agricultural Adjustment Act, farm **subsidies** (grants of money from the government) went to property owners rather than to the tenant farmers, who were predominantly black. The Social Security Act was not designed to provide an income for farm and household workers, so African Americans working at those jobs were not covered.

When the WPA and other federal employment programs were organized, President Roosevelt ordered state relief officials "not to discriminate . . . because of race or religion or politics." Despite a lack of support from Governor Eugene Talmadge, those responsible for New Deal programs in Georgia made every effort to equally distribute WPA programs.

Several prominent African Americans were instrumental in leading

Did You Know?

On February 17, 1930, the folk drama *Heaven Bound* was first performed at the Big Bethel AME Church. The performances were so popular that it has been repeated hundreds of times over the years. Today it is still a tradition.

the New Deal programs. Clark Foreman, a staff member at the Office of the Secretary of the Interior, brought qualified African Americans into government agencies and investigated complaints about racial discrimination. Robert Weaver started his government career during the New Deal and later, in the 1960s, became the first head of the Department of Housing and Urban Development. William Hastie was the assistant solicitor (lawyer) for the Department of the Interior. In 1937, he became the first African American federal judge. Educator Mary McLeod Bethune was appointed to an advisory committee for the NYA. She made sure that African Americans received a fair share of federal funds to provide jobs for young people. Those four influential African Americans made up what some called Roosevelt's "Black Cabinet."

Above: Mary McLeod Bethune was perhaps the most prominent African American to serve in the government during the New Deal. In the glass behind her, you can just see a portrait of President Roosevelt. **Left:** William Hastie was a lawyer, federal judge, law professor, law school dean, and governor of the Virgin Islands.

Above: This 1939 photograph shows some of the governors who served Georgia from 1911 to 1941. They are, left to right, Ed Rivers, Eugene Talmadge, Richard B. Russell, Jr., Clifford Walker, Thomas Hardwick, Hugh Dorsey, and John Slaton.

Georgia's New Deal Governors

The depression years brought new leadership to Georgia. Like the people in the rest of the nation, Georgians based their hopes for a better future on this new leadership.

Richard Russell, Jr.

On June 27, 1931, Winder resident Richard Russell, Jr., succeeded Lamartine Hardman as governor. Administering the oath of office was his father, Georgia Supreme Court Chief Justice Richard B. Russell, Sr.

Richard B. Russell, Jr., used his experience as a former member and speaker of the Georgia house of representatives to make some needed changes. One of his first acts was to combine 102 state offices into 17 agencies. In an equally daring political move, he combined the boards of trustees of state colleges and universities into one governing group—the Board of Regents of the University System of Georgia. During the creation of the new system, some colleges were closed while others were combined. Russell appointed Hughes Spalding, an Atlanta lawyer, as the first chairman of the board of regents.

Russell tried to run the state like a successful business. His approach eased some of the problems brought on by the depression. In 1932, Governor

Russell was elected to the U.S. Senate, where he served for the next thirty-eight years. Russell favored national military preparedness and states' rights. He served on the powerful Senate Appropriations Committee, which was responsible for funding government programs. He became a respected advisor to six United States presidents and, when he served as president pro tempore of the Senate, he was third in line for the presidency.

Eugene Talmadge

State government changed greatly when Eugene Talmadge became governor in 1933. The Forsyth farmer, lawyer, and sawmill owner had been elected commissioner of agriculture in 1926 and had served three years in that position. Talmadge was a dramatic politician in the style of Tom Watson. He often compared himself with Watson, especially when trying to get the support of rural voters. You may have heard the expression that politicians "stumped the state" giving speeches to voters. Talmadge actually took a stump with him, a sawed off section of an oak, two feet high and three feet in diameter. He put it in the middle of the crowd, stood on it, and delivered fiery speeches. He often told rural Georgia voters that they had three friends – Sears Roebuck, God Almighty, and Eugene Herman Talmadge.

Talmadge was a conservative white supremacist who did not like federal government intervention or government debts. He especially disliked relief efforts, public welfare, and federal assistance programs. After becoming governor, he tried to rid the state of New Deal programs. He used federal funds to build highways more often than to help the unemployed. He reduced property taxes, utility rates, and some license fees.

Talmadge was elected to a second term in 1934 by a landslide. Officials who disagreed with Talmadge were fired and replaced with his supporters. Once, Talmadge ordered the highway commissioner to reduce spending or resign. The commissioner refused. Talmadge called in the National Guard, declared martial law, and had the commissioner physically removed from his office. A Talmadge supporter was named as the new commissioner. When Talmadge refused to follow federal New Deal regulations, the federal government took over New Deal programs in Georgia.

In 1934, during the state's worst textile strike, the governor declared martial law again and used the National Guard to arrest strikers. However, Talmadge's political power plays did not change the fact that Georgia law would not allow him to serve more than two consecutive terms. Because he could not run for governor, Talmadge ran for the U.S. Senate in 1936 against Richard Russell and was soundly defeated.

Top: As governor, Richard Russell, Jr., reorganized state government. Above: Eugene Talmadge was a master at campaigning on the "stump."

Eurith Rivers

Talmadge's hand-picked successor for governor, Charles Redwine, was beaten by Lanier County resident Eurith "Ed" Rivers. A former newspaperman and speaker of the Georgia house of representatives, Rivers supported President Roosevelt's New Deal programs. He also supported and gained passage of constitutional amendments granting health services for all Georgians, old age pensions, teacher pay raises, a seven-month school year, homestead exemptions for taxes, and expansion of the state's highway system.

Under Rivers's leadership, electrical services were expanded to rural areas of the state. Georgia moved from the lowest-ranked state to the top of the list in the number of rural electrification associations. While he was in office, the State Bureau of Unemployment Compensation was created, allowing Georgians to receive unemployment benefits.

After Rivers's re-election in 1938, he ran into problems financing many of his improvement programs. Although the budget was reduced by 25 percent, he was able to convince the legislature to create the Georgia Housing Authority and obtain federal funds to build public housing. It was during this time that Atlanta's Techwood Homes and University Homes were built. Several other Georgia cities also began public housing programs.

During Rivers's second term, there were political scandals and charges of corruption. Some staff members did not follow proper procedures in awarding highway contracts. Some of them sold prison pardons. Many of Rivers's appointees and staff members were charged with corrupt practices, and the charges reflected poorly on the governor.

Talmadge Re-Elected

In 1940, Eugene Talmadge ran for governor again and was elected. Talmadge had softened his anti-Roosevelt stand and began using modified versions of New Deal legislation. The state's economy grew. Then, a series of events angered the voters and put Georgia in a bad light.

A Talmadge supporter was an instructor at the University of Georgia. He told the governor that one of the deans at the university and the president of the Teachers College in Statesboro (now known as Georgia Southern University) had plans to integrate the school (open it to members of all races and ethnic groups). Talmadge convinced the board of regents to fire the two individuals. He also got rid of several members of the board of regents who publicly opposed his interference in the university system.

Above: During the 1936 governor's race, Eurith "Ed" Rivers campaigned across the state in support of New Deal policies.

Did You Know?

When Arnall became governor in 1943, he was the youngest governor in the nation.

There was a great deal of national publicity, strongly against the governor's stand. The situation so offended the Southern Association of Colleges and Schools that they voted to take away the accreditation of white Georgia colleges. Georgians were upset with both the association and the governor.

Ellis Arnall

Ellis Gibbs Arnall defeated Talmadge in the governor's race in 1942, taking office in 1943. A native of Newnan, Arnall had served as the state's attorney general. A constitutional amendment passed during Governor Talmadge's third term made Arnall the first Georgia governor to serve a four-year term.

Arnall quickly took steps to correct the problems with university accreditation. The General Assembly passed a constitutional amendment that made the board of regents a separate entity, no longer under the influence of the governor's office. The terms of regents were staggered so there were always

experienced members serving on the board. These actions led the Southern Association of Colleges and Schools to restore accreditation to Georgia's colleges and universities.

Arnall also removed the prison system from the governor's control. He established a board of corrections to oversee state prisons and a pardon and parole board to handle those requests. Arnall abolished the poll tax, and, under his leadership, a new state constitution was adopted in 1945.

Governor Arnall is probably best known for leading Georgia to become the first state in the nation to grant eighteen-year-olds the right to vote. When young men were drafted into the armed forces during World War II, Arnall argued that youths old enough to fight for their country were old enough to vote for their country's leadership.

It's Your Turn

1. What were the four aims of New Deal legislation?
2. What did the term *stretch out* mean in the textile mills?
3. Who made up Roosevelt's "Black Cabinet" during the New Deal?
4. Which New Deal governor do you think brought about the most changes in Georgia?
5. Which New Deal programs do you think were most important? List your top five choices and indicate why each made your list.

Top: This photograph shows Eugene Talmadge in his trademark white shirtsleeves and red suspenders. **Above:** Ellis Arnall was the first Georgia governor to serve a four-year term.

Section Preview

As you read, look for:
- the reasons for World War II,
- why the United States entered the war,
- how the war affected Georgia's economy,
- how Georgians contributed to the war effort, and
- vocabulary terms: isolationism, dictator, appeasement, World War II, Holocaust, ration, and G. I. Bill.

World War II

The United States was still struggling to get out of the Great Depression when war broke out in Europe in September 1939. In the late 1930s, the United States tried to maintain a policy of isolationism (not taking part in the affairs of other nations), but that came to an end as the war came to America's shores.

Increasing Tensions

The 1930s was a time for the rise of dictators, individuals who wanted to rule countries through military might. Four nations—Japan, Italy, Germany, and the Soviet Union—were trying to expand their power and territory. Germany was led by Adolf Hitler, Italy was led by Benito Mussolini, Japan was led by Emperor Hirohito, and the Soviet Union was led by Joseph Stalin.

Japan was an industrial nation, but it did not have basic raw materials such as coal, iron ore, and rubber. In 1937, Japan seized most of the coastal area of China. It then announced a "new order in Asia." It would take the resources it needed from China.

In 1935, Benito Mussolini sent Italian troops into the African nation of Ethiopia. In 1939, Italy conquered Albania.

Adolf Hitler came to power in Germany in 1933. He had promised to make Germany a great nation again and to regain the territory it lost after World

Below: In this photograph, Adolf Hitler is shown in a triumphal procession after the fall of France in June 1941.

War I. Hitler began a program of economic improvements. He also rebuilt the German military forces, which violated the treaty ending World War I. Because he believed that German Jews were responsible for Germany's defeat in World War I, he began to persecute them. At the same time, Hitler and his followers (called Nazis) silenced all opponents.

In 1936, Hitler and Mussolini signed a treaty and formed the "Berlin-Rome Axis." In 1940, Japan joined the Axis Powers.

By 1930, Joseph Stalin had seized control in the Soviet Union. He quickly built up the country's industries, but he also forced the peasants onto collective farms. In 1939, Hitler and Stalin signed a nonagression pact; that is, they agreed not to wage war against each other.

The War Begins

In Hitler's quest for power, he tried to unite all the Germanic peoples of Europe. By early 1938, he had seized the Rhineland (an area between France and Germany) and annexed Austria. In 1938, Great Britain and France agreed to let Hitler take over the Sudetenland, a part of Czechoslovakia. This action by Great Britain and France was appeasement, the policy of giving an aggressor what it wants in order to avoid war. When Hitler seized the rest of Czechoslovakia in 1939, Great Britain and France warned Hitler not to seize any more territory.

On September 1, 1939, German troops invaded Poland. Shortly thereafter, Great Britain and France declared war on Germany. But before Great Britain or France could send troops, German and Soviet forces had divided Poland between them. The Soviet Army also took over Estonia, Latvia, and Lithuania and invaded Finland. World War II had begun.

Hitler struck again in April 1940. Within a month, the German army conquered Denmark and Norway. In May, German troops overran Holland, Belgium, Luxembourg, and a large part of France. The British Army retreated from the continent across the English Channel. Hitler then made plans to invade Great Britain. His air force heavily bombed British cities from August through December 1940. The Royal Air Force, however, was able to hold off the German bombers, and Great Britain was not invaded.

Below: This man is standing on a London roof looking for enemy planes. Bottom: This World War II poster celebrates the bravery of British fighter pilots during the Battle of Britain.

"NEVER WAS SO MUCH OWED BY SO MANY TO SO FEW"
THE PRIME MINISTER

Did You Know?

People in England were urged to eat carrots during the war so that they would have better nighttime vision to watch for enemy planes.

A Neutral United States

President Roosevelt watched as Japan, Italy, the Soviet Union, and Germany carved up the world. Most Americans felt strongly that we should not get involved, but Great Britain was an ally and Roosevelt wanted to help. He thought that only the British could stop Hitler from crossing the Atlantic Ocean.

In the 1930s, Congress had passed neutrality acts to keep the United States out of another war. One of those acts would not allow the president to sell weapons to any warring nation. In 1939, Roosevelt asked for and got a new law that allowed the Allied Powers to buy arms if they paid cash and carried them in their own ships. In 1940, Roosevelt gave Great Britain old weapons and traded fifty destroyers for British bases in the Western Hemisphere.

In early 1941, when the British ran out of cash with which to buy American supplies, Congress authorized Roosevelt to lend or lease arms to them. After Germany turned on and invaded the Soviet Union in June 1941, Roosevelt gave lend-lease aid to the Soviets as well. To make sure the supplies got to them, Roosevelt built air bases in Greenland and Iceland. Planes from these bases tracked German submarines. Roosevelt also ordered the U.S. Navy to convoy (escort) British ships part of the way across the Atlantic. In late 1941, German submarines sank an American destroyer. The United States was engaged in an undeclared war that was about to become a declared one.

"A Day That Will Live in Infamy"

Meanwhile, American-Japanese relations got worse. To protest Japanese expansion, the United States stopped exporting airplanes, metals, aircraft parts, and aviation gasoline to Japan. After Japan invaded French Indochina in 1941, Roosevelt seized all Japanese property in the United States.

Badly needing the oil that Roosevelt had cut off, Japan decided to invade the Dutch East Indies (now Indonesia) in late 1941. The only force that could stop the Japanese was the U.S. Navy stationed at Pearl Harbor, Hawaii.

December 7, 1941, was a peaceful Sunday morning. Many of the sailors stationed on the island were eating breakfast or going about their early morning routines. Suddenly, around 8:00 a.m., the air was filled with the sounds of machine gun fire and low level bombing. The Japanese attack on Pearl Harbor was over by 10:00 a.m., but the damage to the Navy's Pacific fleet was incredible. All eight battleships in port were destroyed or severely damaged; more than 180 planes were destroyed. Over two thousand people were killed, and over one thousand were wounded. President Roosevelt called the attack a "day that will live in infamy."

On December 8, Congress declared war on Japan, and the United States entered World War II. A few days later, Germany and Italy declared war on the United States. Now it was a full-fledged war between the *Allied Powers*

Top: The Italian foreign minister (left) and the German foreign minister in Berlin for the signing of the alliance between Germany, Italy, and Japan. Above: Lend-Lease supplies—in this case, bacon—being unloaded in England.

led by the United States, Great Britain, and the Soviet Union and the *Axis Powers* of Germany, Japan, and Italy. Joining the Allies meant the United States had to fight on two fronts, facing Germany and Italy in Europe and Africa and Japan in the Pacific.

American Military Forces

Millions of Americans enlisted in the armed forces after the Pearl Harbor attack. The nation's military effort in World War II was not limited to any one group, race, or gender. Close to 400,000 Mexican Americans served in the armed forces during the war.

Over 330,000 women served in the war in jobs that ranged from nurses to clerks to aides and drivers. Women in World War II were not allowed to go into combat, but they took over jobs to free men to fight on the battlefronts. The WASPs (Women's Air Force Service Pilots) trained as pilots and delivered planes from factories to airfields. They also served as pilots testing the newest planes the Army Air Force was building, and they flew target planes, pulling targets behind them for male pilots to practice on.

Above: Within two hours, Japanese bombers destroyed, sank, or capsized 18 ships and over 180 airplanes. Most of the casualties were on the U.S.S. *Arizona*.

The Tuskegee Airmen

In World War I, Eugene Bullard had made history in France as the first African American to fly in combat. World War II did not represent much of an improvement in the area of discrimination in the military. However, one group of flyers made the Pentagon rethink its position on the role of African Americans in combat. The military referred to their flying as an "experiment," but the Germans, who faced the fighters, called them the "Black Bird Men."

Each flight crew was composed of six men. Working out of a training facility at Tuskegee Institute in Alabama, these men made history as the "Tuskegee Airmen." At first, funding for the training facility was a huge problem. Few gave the program any chance of succeeding. But the training continued under the direction of Chief Flight Instructor Charles Anderson who, twelve years earlier, had taught himself to fly in a plane he purchased.

One day in May 1941, Eleanor Roosevelt arrived at Tuskegee to visit while the president rested at Warm Springs. She arrived at the airstrip, visited briefly, and told the small assembled group that she wanted to fly with Mr. Anderson. After the successful and highly publicized flight, the training facility received money to continue its program.

After their training, the airmen were assigned as escorts for allied bombers. At first, the bomber flight crews wanted nothing to do with their escorts, but the airmen's reputation quickly spread, and flyers clamored to have the Tuskegee Airmen by their side. In over two hundred missions, the flight squadron never lost a single bomber they were escorting.

By the end of the war, close to 1,000 young African Americans had completed the training. Their skills were demonstrated by shooting down or damaging over 4,000 enemy planes and flying over 1,500 missions, while losing only 98 pilots. One hundred fifty pilots received decorations, including Flying Crosses, Purple Hearts, and Silver Stars.

Many of these pilots' names are familiar today. Daniel "Chappie" James became America's first black four-star general. General Benjamin O. Davis, Jr., became the Air Force's first black lieutenant general. Others included Coleman Young, who served as Detroit's mayor; cable television mongol Percy Sutton; and Roscoe Brown, president of Bronx Community College in New York.

The Tuskegee "experiment" was a success and led the way for the integration of the armed forces.

Restrictions and segregation reduced the participation of African Americans in the war effort at first. Those who did participate served in segregated units. But military records indicate that approximately 700,000 African Americans served in the Army, 165,000 in the Navy, 5,000 in the Coast Guard, and 17,000 in the Marines. The Red Ball Express, a trucking unit that supplied gasoline and supplies to the American soldiers moving through France and into Germany, was manned primarily by African Americans. The Tuskegee Airmen flew more than 15,000 sorties and completed 1,578 missions with the Army Air Force.

Native Indians had their role in America's war efforts too. Over 425 Navajo served in the Marine Corps as communication specialists using their native language as a code that was never broken. Navajo "Code Talkers" took part in every assault the U.S. Marines conducted in the Pacific from 1942 to 1945. When the war ended, the Navajo were told to keep their part in the war effort a secret in case the code was needed again. It was not until 1969 that the truth about the role of the Navajo in World War II became public knowledge.

Did You Know?

The **highest-ranking African American officer** in the armed forces was **Brigadier General Benjamin O. Davis, Jr., who** was the **first African American general** in the **U.S. Army.**

The War in Europe

In late 1942, British and American troops invaded North Africa and won control of the area by May 1943. From Africa, the Allied armies moved into Sicily and Italy. The Italian people overthrew Mussolini and joined the Allies. Germany and Japan were the remaining Axis Powers.

In 1943, American General Dwight D. Eisenhower was named Supreme Commander of Allied Forces. It was his responsibility to coordinate and plan the Allies' efforts to recapture Europe. On June 6,

Top and above: During World War II, women served in all branches of the service. At home, they worked in factories, as nurses, journalists, farmers, mail deliverers, garbage collectors, builders, and mechanics. Women made major contributions to the war effort.

Above: On June 6, 1944, Allied forces invaded the beaches of Normandy, France, in an action called Operation Overload. Future President Dwight D. Eisenhower led the assault that involved 4,000 ships, 11,000 planes, and 176,000 soldiers.

1944, D-Day, Allied forces landed at Normandy in northern France. By early 1945, Allied troops had pushed the German army out of France and across the Rhine River to Germany. At the same time, the Russian Army recaptured four smaller countries that were part of the German alliance: Bulgaria, Finland, Hungary, and Romania.

Europe was freed from Hitler's control in April 1945, when the Soviet and American troops came together at the river Elbe in central Germany. Adolf Hitler committed suicide on April 30, and the last German forces surrendered to the Allies in May.

Did You Know?

May 8, 1945, was declared VE Day—Victory in Europe Day.

Georgia Loses a Friend

President Roosevelt had been a frequent visitor to Georgia, spending time at the "Little White House" in Warm Springs. On March 30, the president returned to the Little White House. He planned to rest and work on a speech for the United Nations. On April 24, Roosevelt was sitting for a portrait. Suddenly, the president put his hand to his head and said, "I have a terrific headache." At 5:48 p.m., a stunned nation learned of the death of the man who had led the country through recovery from the depression, through the New Deal, and to the brink of victory in World War II. He had suffered a massive stroke.

As Roosevelt's body was carried by train from Warm Springs back to the nation's capital, the tracks were lined by thousands of crying Georgians who had come to think of Roosevelt as one of their own. Whole families stood alongside the railroad tracks to say goodbye to their beloved president. And, it was not just Georgia. All along the route to Washington, Americans stood with their hands over their hearts in a final salute.

Vice President Harry S Truman became president on the death of Roosevelt and was the nation's commander-in-chief during the final months of World War II.

The War in the Pacific

By early 1942, Japan had captured Burma, Hong Kong, Malaya, Thailand, and the Philippines. Japan threatened New Guinea and Australia before its advance in the Pacific was stopped.

Allied forces began to retake the Pacific islands, the Philippines, and Burma. In the summer of 1945, Allied forces began daily air raids on Japan. On July 26, Allied leaders demanded that Japan surrender. Japan refused. To bring an earlier end to the war and avoid the loss of perhaps half a million American lives, President Truman authorized the use of a new weapon. On August 6, the *Enola Gay*, a U.S. bomber, dropped an atomic bomb on Hiroshima. It virtually destroyed the city of 255,000 people.

Top: President Roosevelt was sitting for this portrait, now unfinished, when he was stricken. Above: A U.S. Navy corpsman helps a wounded Marine on Guam. Japan captured Guam in 1942; the Allies were not able to retake it until 1944.

Still, the Japanese refused to surrender. A second atomic bomb was dropped on the city of Nagasaki on August 9. Japan surrendered to the Allies on August 15, 1945. The bombings of Hiroshima and Nagasaki were the first and last times to date that atomic warfare has been used to settle differences between nations. At last, World War II was over.

The war had been costly. Over 50 million people—military and civilian—died in the war. The United States lost over 300,000 soldiers; Great Britain lost over 450,000. The Soviet Union lost some 20 million people during the war. In addition to casualties, the war cost a great deal of money. The United States alone spent over $360 billion.

Carl Vinson, Father of the Two-Ocean Navy

It is impossible to review World War II without examining the contributions of one of Georgia's most influential leaders, Carl Vinson. Vinson is often referred to as the "father of the two-ocean navy." He served twenty-five consecutive terms representing Georgia in the U.S. House of Representatives, from 1914 to 1965. When he retired, he had established a record for longevity in the House.

Vinson, a native of Baldwin County, served as chairman of the House Naval Affairs Committee for 16 years and its successor, the House Armed Services Committee for 14 years. Even before World War II, Georgia's economy had grown to depend heavily on the state's military installations, and Vinson represented Georgia's interest in the military through his committee work.

Vinson was a major influence in promoting a strong national defense. Alarmed by rising tensions in Europe, President Roosevelt and Vinson worked to increase the country's military readiness. Almost two years before Japan's attack on Pearl Harbor, Vinson maneuvered two important bills through Congress. One bill expanded the naval aviation system to 10,000 planes, trained 16,000 pilots, and established 20 air bases. The second piece of legislation eased labor restrictions in the shipbuilding industry and allowed faster construction of navy ships.

Even after World War II, Vinson continued his dominance in Congress, pushing for a strong defense throughout the Cold War with the Soviet Union. In 1964, President Lyndon B. Johnson awarded Carl Vinson the Presidential Medal of

Above: Congressman Carl Vinson was a powerful force in the growth of America's land, sea, and air forces.

Freedom. After serving for over 50 years in the nation's Congress, Vinson retired to his Milledgeville farm in 1965. In 1972, President Richard M. Nixon honored Vinson by naming the country's third nuclear carrier for him. He died in 1981.

The Holocaust

In the spring of 1945, as Allied troops pushed into Poland, Austria, and Germany, nothing could have prepared them for what they found. Auschwitz, Buckenwald, Dachau, Treblinka, Bergen-Belsen, and other concentration camps were set up by the Nazis as the "final solution to the Jewish problem." Those who were left alive in the camps were emaciated skeletons from years of starvation, disease, cruel treatment, and forced labor.

The Holocaust was the name given to the systematic extermination (killing) of 6 million Jews. An additional 5-6 million people, labeled as "undesirables," were also killed by the Nazis. In the camps, many died from starvation; others died from disease, mistreatment, and medical experiments. Prisoners, including children, were gassed in chambers they thought were showers. Their bodies were incinerated in huge ovens or thrown into mass graves. The deaths of these Jews, Poles, Czechs, Russians, Gypsies, homosexuals, and the mentally or physically disabled all fit Hitler's plan to rid Europe of what he called "inferior" people.

Those who survived the German concentration camps had a daily reminder of the horrors they experienced—a number branded into their arms.

The United States Holocaust Memorial Museum, established by an act of Congress, opened in Washington, D.C., in April 1993. The museum was created as a memorial to the 6 million Jews and millions of other victims who perished in the Holocaust.

Georgia During World War II

After the United States's declaration of war, over 320,000 Georgians between the ages of 21 and 35 put on military uniforms. Of that number, 7,388 died in battle. Eight Georgians received the Medal of Honor, the nation's highest military decoration.

A Boost to the Economy

World War II brought prosperity to Georgia. Millions of federal dollars poured into the state, strengthening the economy. Because of its climate and the influence of politicians like Senator Richard Russell, Jr., Senator Walter F. George, and Representative Carl Vinson, the state became the site of several military installations.

Major military bases included Fort Benning in Columbus, Camp Gordon in Augusta, Fort Stewart and Hunter Air Field in Savannah, and Warner Robins Air Field near Macon. Airmen from Glynco Naval Air Station, near Brunswick, flew blimps along the southern Atlantic coast in search of German submarines.

In fact in April 1942, the war came frighteningly close to Georgia's shores. A German submarine sank the S.S. *Oklahoma*, a merchant marine vessel, and the Esso *Baton Rouge* tanker off the coast of St. Simons Island. The community rallied quickly, and fishing boats and yachts raced to the waters to pick up survivors of both boats.

Fort McPherson, in the Atlanta area, was a major induction center for newly drafted soldiers from all over the country. A military hospital, which had been

Above: The German government set up concentration camps to imprison and later kill Jews, Gypsies, other victims of ethnic and racial hatred, and political opponents of Nazism. This is a survivor of the Gusen camp in Austria.

Holocaust is a word of Greek origin that means "sacrifice by fire."

Above: Aircraft mechanics work on the nose and cockpit of a B-26 bomber at Warner Robins Air Field near Macon in July 1943.

Did You Know?

During 1943 alone, school children across the country bought enough stamps and bonds to pay for 13,500 airplanes and 44,200 jeeps.

used in World War I, was reopened in Atlanta. In nearby Clayton County, Fort Gillem, an army storage facility and railroad yard, began operation.

In 1943, the Cobb County Airport became the Marietta Army Airfield. At Fort Oglethorpe, some of the 150,000 women who served in the WAAC (Women's Army Auxiliary Corp, later known as WACs) trained to become postal workers, clerks, typists, switchboard operators, code clerks, and drivers or aides.

In Marietta, 30,000 men and women built B-29 bombers at the Bell Bomber Plant. Thousands of Georgians were also employed in automobile and textile plants that were being used to produce military vehicles and uniforms. The Atlanta airport became an air base in 1941, and Delta Airlines named Atlanta the home of its fast growing fleet.

Georgians Support the War Effort

Georgia farmers planted peanuts for their oil, grew vegetables, and raised cotton and livestock to help feed the country and its allies. By 1944, the annual farm income was $454, over three times what it had been in 1940.

Gasoline, shoes, and food items such as meat, butter, and sugar were rationed; that is, their consumption was limited. Women used leg makeup because it was hard to get silk and nylon stockings. Georgia joined the rest of the nation in donating 13 million pints of blood for the war wounded.

Children and young people helped in the war effort too. Students collected everyday items soldiers might need like toothbrushes or a washcloth, soap, pencils, or small writing pads. In some schools, students made candles to send to Great Britain, where much of the household electricity had been destroyed by German air raids.

Spotlight on the Economy

Georgia's Wartime Industries

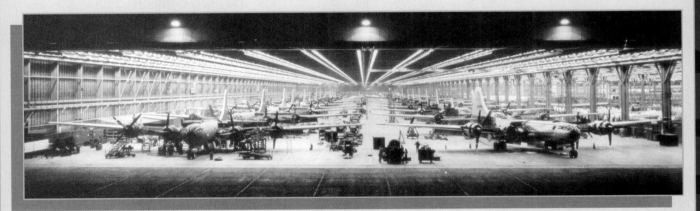

A large part of Georgia's contribution in World War II came from the military installations in our state, which trained men and women to function in a variety of military activities. Georgia's thirteen military installations add over $25 billion to Georgia's economy each year.

But, as World War II opened, industries in Georgia were also contributing to the war effort. One effort was the building of Liberty ships at Brunswick and Savannah shipyards. President Roosevelt named the cargo ships "Liberty ships" after Patrick Henry's famous quotation, and the ships were essential to the war effort. The first of Georgia's Liberty ships was launched in November 1942—the U.S.S. *James Oglethorpe*, which was sunk by a German submarine the next year. In all, eighty-eight Liberty ships were built in Savannah by 15,000 workers, many of whom were women.

In Brunswick, over 16,000 men and women worked around the clock in 1943 and 1944 on six ships at a time. In December 1944, they set a national record by building seven ships in just one month. The crews even worked on Christmas Day and donated their checks for that day to the war effort. In all, Brunswick's shipyards produced ninety-nine Liberty ships. Both of Georgia's port cities can be proud of their tremendous contributions to the war effort.

Another massive effort was undertaken at Warner Robins Air Force Base. During the war years, 23,670 employees repaired thousands of planes and trained 60,000 field

Above: In Marietta, a bomber plant was built to produce B-29 aircraft, called the "Superfortress" because of its size and bomb-carrying capacity.

mechanics who were deployed throughout the world wherever there was fighting. They also supplied needed equipment like spark plugs, parachutes, and radio sets, even small arms.

While coastal Georgians were building ships, Marietta was transformed from a bedroom community of Atlanta to a major industrial area. In spring 1943, Bell Aircraft Company began assembling B-29 bombers for the U.S. Army Air Force. The bomber plant was the largest facility in the Deep South, with over 4.2 million square feet. Between the end of 1943 and the close of the war, over 28,158 employees finished 668 planes.

In addition to those major efforts, many other mills and factories in the state switched to making war supplies, weapons, equipment, and even military vehicles. While Georgia did not enter this period as a major industrial state, at the close of World War II, the industrial base in Georgia was fully developed. A boom in industry and manufacturing after the close of the war led to some of the state's most prosperous times. As the decade drew to a close, more Georgians were engaged in manufacturing than in agriculture for the first time in the state's history.

The popular student magazine, *The Weekly Reader*, kept students informed about the war and had instructions for spotting enemy planes. Students were encouraged to save their money and buy war bonds and defense stamps to finance the war effort.

Students were also expected to help plant, maintain, harvest, and even can foods from the family's "Victory Garden." Young people took children's wagons and collected any scrap metals along the roadside or in vacant fields. Those scraps were melted down and reused in American factories. Children picked milkweed floss, which was used in making life jackets and clothing for the sailors and soldiers.

POW Camps in Georgia

Many Georgians do not realize that many of our military bases were also POW (Prisoner of War) camps for German, Austrian, and Italian soldiers captured during the war. Fort Oglethorpe, Fort Benning, Fort Gordon, Fort Stewart, and Camp Wheeler provided housing for hundreds of POWs. At one point during the war, there were over four thousand prisoners. POWs received housing, medical care, food, and canteen visits. In some places, the POWs had educational opportunities; in others, they took part in work programs, toiling in fields or nearby factories.

At the end of the war, the POWs were "re-educated" about what to expect when they returned to their war-torn countries. Some of the prisoners, when released, chose to make Georgia their permanent home.

Figure 40 Social Effects of World War II

● In 1944, Congress passed the Serviceman's Readjustment Act. The G. I. Bill, as it was called, made low-cost loans to veterans who wanted to buy homes or start businesses. The G.I. Bill also gave all returning soldiers the opportunity for a college education, which, in turn, changed job availability and heralded a new middle working class.

● In 1943, Congress imposed a withholding system on taxpayers. Federal income tax was withheld from workers' pay and sent directly to the U.S. Treasury. The number of taxpayers jumped from 4 million in 1939 to 42.7 million in 1945.

● Racial segregation was no longer acceptable to returning African American soldiers.

● Women who had experienced a new sense of freedom and independence were not ready to leave the workplace and return to the homemaker roles that had been their only option before the war. And, new inventions were releasing women from many of the time-consuming "homemaking" responsibilities.

● The horrors of the Holocaust forced Americans to re-examine their policy of isolationism.

The War's Effects on Society

Once the United States declared war on Japan and joined the Allies, the nation turned its full attention to the war effort. Almost overnight, women replaced men in the workplace, rationing became a way of life, and everyone (including children) was expected to share in ensuring an American, and an Allied, victory. In addition, war production pulled the United States out of the last stages of the Great Depression and pushed the throttle fully open on the economy.

When the war finally ended in 1945, many changes faced the nation and returning GIs (see Figure 40). The war changed the role of women and helped attack prejudice and discrimination.

1. Why did President Roosevelt feel so strongly about helping the British?
2. What event finally led the United States to enter the war?
3. What events led to the surrender of Japan?
4. Which military installation was located in Columbus?

A Final Note

Our Constitution ensures that we have the freedom to believe as we wish. The pledge that is said daily in our schools along with the words on the coins in our pockets—"In God We Trust"—are reminders for us to have respect for our creator. In a sermon given about the 1942 Bataan Death March, in which thousands of Filipinos and Americans died or were imprisoned, William T. Cummings said, "There are no atheists in foxholes." What do you think he meant by that comment?

In World War II, 2,278 Catholic priests, 243 rabbis, and 5,620 Protestant chaplains served our country. In what ways do you think the military Chaplain Corps helped soldiers maintain respect for their creator?

Above: In August 1945, the Japanese cities of Hiroshima and Nagasaki were destroyed by atomic bombs in an attempt by the United States to shorten the war.

Chapter Summary

- The 1920s, known as the Roaring Twenties, was a time of prohibition, illegal liquor, mobs and speakeasies, flappers, jazz, and the blues.
- The prosperity of the 1920s ended with the stock market crash.
- Failures of banks and businesses caused massive, widespread unemployment across the country.
- After Roosevelt's election, a series of New Deal programs put people back to work, provided insurance and pensions for retirees, and delivered electrical power to the nation's rural areas.
- During this period, most Georgia governors supported New Deal legislation.
- Governor Talmadge did not at first support Roosevelt's economic policies, but he later softened his opposition.
- World War II broke out in Europe in 1939, and the United States entered the war in 1941 after the Japanese attack on Pearl Harbor.
- Germany surrendered in May 1945, and Japan followed suit in August 1945.
- During the war, the economies of both the United States and Georgia prospered, pulling the country and the state out of the Great Depression.
- World War II made the United States a superpower and changed the nature of the American work force and the roles of women.

Chapter Review

Reviewing People, Places, and Terms

Use the following terms in a paragraph describing the United States during the Great Depression and World War II.

1. dictator

2. Great Depression

3. isolationism

4. laissez-faire

5. New Deal

6. ration

7. rural electrification

8. Social Security Act

9. stock market

Understanding the Facts

1. What was Georgia's first radio station?

2. What natural disaster struck Georgia's cotton growers during the 1920s?

3. What were some of the reasons that African Americans moved in large numbers from the South to the North during this era?

4. Name two ways in which President Hoover tried to help the economy recover.

5. Name three problems in the U.S. economy that led to the Great Depression.

6. After President Roosevelt took office, what was his first act to prevent the nation's banks from failing?

7. What New Deal laws were intended to help the nation's workers?

8. Which Georgia governor refused to go along with New Deal programs?

9. In what ways did the United States protest Japanese aggression in the Far East?

10. What was the country's "Little White House" during Roosevelt's presidency?

Developing Critical Thinking

1. Do you believe that another stock market crash is possible in this country today? Why or why not?

2. Do you think a guaranteed minimum wage is a good thing? Why or why not?

3. What might have been the impact on history if the United States had not entered World War II?

4. Why do you think gasoline, shoes, women's nylons, and certain food items were rationed during World War II?

5. How do you think minority soldiers felt when they returned to their own country after the war and found segregation and discrimination still in place?

Checking It Out

1. Check local historical records and find out what CCC projects took place in your county and whether those projects are still in place today. Which major CCC projects happened in the section of the state where you now live?

2. Research the Bataan Death March and answer the following question: Could the May 6, 1942,

surrender of Corregidor have been prevented? How? What role did Douglas MacArthur have?

3. Use your research skills to find information on the Manhattan Project. What would have been the likely outcome of the Japanese war had we not developed and used the atomic bomb? How might our world be different today?

4. Use your research skills to find out more about Winnie the Pooh. Did you know she was an actual bear and was a mascot for a Canadian regiment of soldiers? Pooh died in 1934 at age 20, but she was the very bear A. A. Milne wrote about.

Writing Across the Curriculum

1. Prepare a short report on one of the New Deal programs or laws. Include information on when the program was created or when the law was passed, its purpose, and its effectiveness.

2. Political cartoons and propaganda slogans were widely used in World War II.

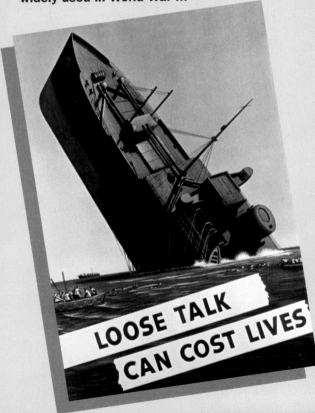

LOOSE TALK CAN COST LIVES

"Loose lips sink ships" was one favorite that reminded people not to talk about war secrets to anyone, especially civilian workers in defense plants. Examine some of the cartoons of the famous World War II cartoonist Bill Mauldin and some of the recruitment posters used in World War II, then try your own hand. Either be a cartoonist and represent an attitude about any event that happened in Georgia during this period or be an editorialist and develop wartime slogans for Georgia during this period. Try to prepare at least two cartoons or two slogans that will teach your classmates some facts about this chapter's time period.

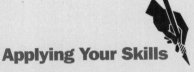

Applying Your Skills

1. The number of shares of stock traded on the New York Stock Exchange for certain years between 1920 and 1935 are shown below. Prepare a bar chart using this information. What does the chart suggest about the nation's attitude toward buying stock after the stock market crash?

1920	227,636,000 shares
1925	459,717,623 shares
1929	1,124,800,410 shares
1930	810,632,546 shares
1935	381,635,752 shares

2. Timelines are an important way of looking at history. Use your research skills and prepare a timeline that shows the twenty-five most famous Georgians who were born between 1920 and 1945. The individuals could be politicians, noted sports people, entertainers, or business people. Post the chart so that you can compare the list with the information in upcoming chapters.

Above: The idea of "two Georgias" can be seen in the photographs on these pages. This is Atlanta. Opposite page: The small town of Flowery Branch is near Lake Lanier.

Georgia in the Modern World

We are referring to the period after World War II as the Modern Era, the one in which you are now living. The past sixty years have been a time of incredible technological and scientific advancements. They have also been a period of social upheaval and change at home and political entanglements abroad including two wars and three "conflicts." Pivotal to the period was the introduction of terrorism on America's soil.

In addition, for the first time in our history, four generations are living together, as life expectancy has increased. This turn of events has also resulted in a huge "generation gap" as the cultural customs and folkways of each succeeding generation have changed.

It is up to your generation to take the events and lessons learned during the mid-1940s through today and determine the direction in which our nation will go. Remember the saying "Those who do not learn from history are doomed to repeat it." We have no doubt that you will be up to the task.

Baby Boomers, Rebellion, and Wars

Above:
This is the main street of Plains,
Georgia, the home town of President Jimmy Carter.

he thirty years after the end of World War II marked a period of great changes in Georgia and the United States. Millions of babies were born between the late 1940s and the early 1960s. Families grew, as did the economy. Television appeared, and highways were built. African Americans became more visible in their demand for equal treatment. It was also a time of tension, as the Cold War developed and young people protested.

Signs of the Times
1946-1979

Population: In 1950, 3,444,578; in 1970, 4,589,575

Life Expectancy: In 1950, women could expect to live 71.1 years and men 65.6 years. By 1970, that was 74.8 years for women and 67.1 years for men.

Costs of Living: In 1949, the average new home cost $7,450. By 1978, that price had jumped to $54,749. A new car cost $1,420 in 1949; by 1978, the car cost $5,405. Food prices also increased steadily. A dozen eggs cost $0.24 in 1950, and $0.42 in 1970. A loaf of bread jumped from $0.14 a loaf in 1949 to $0.42 a loaf in 1979. Movie tickets that were $0.60 in 1949 cost $2.00 by 1978.

Wages/Salaries: In 1950, the average salary was $2,992; in 1970, it was $7,562. The minimum wage jumped from $0.43 an hour in the 1950s to $2.90 in 1979.

Art/Architecture: In the years after World War II, leading artists included Jackson Pollock, Willem de Kooning, Mark Rothko, Andy Warhol, and Robert Smithson. Suburbs developed around major cities, the first being Levittown, New Jersey. The ranch-style home was popular.

Fads/Fashions: Fads of the period included hula hoops, silly putty, G.I. Joe dolls, trolls, mood rings, Rubik's cube, and pet rocks. 3-D movies, complete with goggles, were popular. Fashions began the era with blue jeans, poodle skirts, pony tails for girls, and flat tops or crew cuts for boys. The 1960s brought button-down shirts, go-go boots, miniskirts, hot pants, Nehru jackets, and turtlenecks. At the end of the period, men favored long hair, bell-bottom pants, and leisure suits. Women wore hip huggers, platform shoes, pants suits, and T-shirts.

Music: In the late 1940s, the big band sound gave way to soloists and then to be-bop and rhythm-and-blues. In the 1950s, rock-and-roll, a blending of southern blues and gospel music, hit the airwaves. The Beatles arrived from England, and the top American group was the Beach Boys. Woodstock drew over 400,000 young people to a three-day concert. The 1970s saw the rise of hard rock, soft rock, country rock, folk rock, punk rock, and disco.

Literature: Important books of the period included George Orwell's *1984*, Richard Wright's *Black Boy*, Ray Bradbury's *The Martian Chronicles*, Ernest Hemingway's *Old Man and the Sea*, Ralph Ellison's *Invisible Man*, Truman Capote's *In Cold Blood*, Rachel Carson's *The Silent Spring*, Harper Lee's *To Kill a Mockingbird*, Woodward and Bernstein's *All the President's Men*, and *The Pentagon Papers* by Daniel Ellsberg.

Religion: Mother Frances X. Cabrini became the first American saint in the Catholic Church. The Presbyterian Church approved ordination of women in 1955. U.S. Supreme Court ruled that prayer in schools was unconstitutional. The United Methodist Church formed in 1968 and the National Presbyterian Church in 1973. Episcopal bishops ordained women as priests in 1972.

Science/Inventions: Jonas Salk developed a vaccine for polio. National Hurricane Center established. New devices included the copy machine, transistor radio, color television, microchips, the laser, communications satellites. America entered the space age and put a man on the moon in 1969. In 1977, the trans-Alaska pipeline began operation and the Apple II computer was introduced.

Education: The 1950s and 1960s saw the integration of public schools and colleges. The era also saw a national emphasis on reading problems of school children and the spread of back-to-basics movements emphasizing basic skills. Antiwar protests and sit-ins spread across most college campuses in the 1970s.

Transportation: The Federal Highway Act of 1956 gave rise to the interstate highway system. Idlewild International Airport (Kennedy Airport) in New York was dedicated in 1948. Pan American Airways began transatlantic jet service in 1958. American automobile manufacturers began making smaller cars in the 1960s to combat foreign import sales. By 1966, there were 78 million cars and 16 million trucks registered in the U.S.

Leisure Time: Drive-in movie theaters were popular. Influential movies included *The Graduate*, the *James Bond* series, *E.T.*, *Jaws*, *The Godfather*, *American Graffiti*, *Saturday Night Fever*, and *Star Wars*. Popular television shows included *Gunsmoke*, *I Love Lucy*, *All in the Family*, *Saturday Night Live*, and *Sesame Street*. The miniseries *Roots* aired in 1977. *American Bandstand* featured the newest music and the latest dances. Disneyland opened and became an instant success.

Figure 41 Timeline: 1940–1980

1971 International flights began at Hartsfield International Airport

1974 Hank Aaron broke Babe Ruth's home run record

1976 Jimmy Carter elected president

WTBS became first cable "superstation"

1968 Dr. Martin L. King, Jr. assassinated in Memphis, Tennessee

1964 Martin L. King, Jr. awarded Nobel Peace Prize

1962 County unit system struck down

1961 University of Georgia integrated

1946 Winecoff Hotel fire

Three Governors episode

1955 Legislature stopped funds for integrated schools

1960 Sibley Commission

1977 Kelly Barnes Dam broke

1979 First MARTA rapid rail service

1940   1950   1960   1970   1980

1946 National School Lunch Act

1950 Korean War began

1953 Korean War ended

1954 *Brown v. Board of Education*

1955 Montgomery bus boycott

1963 President John F. Kennedy assassinated

1964 Civil Rights Act passed

1965 Voting Rights Act passed

1972 Watergate break-in

Title IX passed

1973 Vietnam cease fire

Oil embargo

1979 Iranian hostage crisis

The Postwar Period

The 1950s were a good time for most people. Returning veterans were able to attend college on the G.I. Bill and to buy homes. Enrollment in colleges and universities soared, and **suburbs** (residential areas around cities) sprang up. So many children were born that this period was known for its **baby boom**. The economy was strong, with an average family income of $4,421.

America's love affair with the automobile reached full bloom. Riding around and "hanging out" at drive-in restaurants was a favorite pastime of young people. The first McDonald's opened with 15-cent hamburgers. New words added to the dictionary told a lot about the period: *rock and roll, UFO, junk mail,* and *credit card*.

Inventions of the period changed the way people lived. Dr. Jonas Salk developed a vaccine to erase the single greatest fear of the decade—polio. Johnson & Johnson provided the nation with no-tears baby shampoo. We also got super glue, radial tires, contact paper, Saran wrap, appliances in color, and Velcro.

Rock and roll dominated the period, led by performers such as Bill Haley and Georgia's Chuck Berry. Many adults believed that such music was dangerous and damaging for American teens! Perhaps the most important influence on this and later periods was television.

Below: During the 1950s, cars became more than just a means of transportation. They became status symbols.

Television Changes America

Teenagers in the 1950s grew up with television. At first, television programs ran only six or seven hours *a day*. Families gathered around the small black-and-white sets to watch such popular performers as Jackie Gleason in "The Honeymooners," Lucille Ball in "I Love Lucy," comics Sid Caesar and Milton Berle, and major productions such as the "Ed Sullivan Show," "Gunsmoke," and "Bonanza." Television shows like "The Adventures of Rin Tin Tin," "Lassie," and "Captain Kangaroo" made an appearance for young children. The "Mickey Mouse Club" made its debut, and "Dragnet" was a television favorite. "Your Hit Parade" kept teenagers informed about the latest musical hits.

Television viewing began to replace family games and conversation as the evening entertainment of choice. Even food changed. Frozen TV dinners were developed to shorten the time spent preparing evening meals. They were designed to be eaten in front of the television set, not at a dining table.

Television also brought about a change in organized religion, which flourished in the 1950s. Evangelists such as Billy Graham and Oral Roberts developed national followings through their use of the television screen. Bishop Fulton J. Sheen, a nationally known Roman Catholic priest, joined his Protestant counterparts in using the new medium to promote family values and the fight against communism.

In 1956, the appearance of Elvis Presley on the "Ed Sullivan Show" drew a record 54 million viewers. Cameramen on the show were ordered to show Presley only from the waist up since many considered the singer's "hip swinging gyrations" to be unsuitable for family audiences. Less than ten years later, the Beatles appeared on the "Ed Sullivan Show" and drew a record 70 million viewers.

In 1950, only 9 percent of the nation's households had a television. By 1955, that percentage had spiraled to 65 percent, and by 1979, 99 percent of American households had televisions. The number of hours spent watching those television sets also grew. In 1950, the average viewer watched 5 hours of television a day; by the 1970s, the average viewer watched over 6½ hours of television a day.

In the 1970s, the major commercial broadcasting stations (ABC, CBS, NBC) were joined by commercial cable television stations. By the end of the decade, about 20 percent of

Top: In the 1950s, the television took a prominent place in American homes. Above: One of the most popular television shows of the 1950s was "I Love Lucy." These are the cast members.

Did You Know?

In 1951, Diner's Club introduced the first credit card to two hundred customers who could use it at twenty-seven restaurants in New York.

American households had access to both network and cable television. Time, Inc., established the first cable television network —HBO—in 1972. In 1976, Ted Turner turned Atlanta's WTBS into the first "superstation." Turner was also responsible for the nation's first 24-hour news network, CNN, which began broadcasting from its Atlanta headquarters in 1980 and which today reaches over a billion viewers daily worldwide.

In addition to changing the nation's entertainment habits, television contributed greatly to our nation's cultural and educational growth. Television allowed Americans to travel throughout the nation and the world from the safety of their living rooms. It presented live news so that viewers could see events as they actually happened and not as groups of editors or broadcasters interpreted them. Americans in the 1970s, for example, watched as John F. Kennedy and Bobby Kennedy were assassinated; they watched gun battles in Vietnam; and, they watched as Neil Armstrong walked on the moon.

The Cold War

While some people focused on the social and cultural changes, others turned their attention to world tensions. The relations between the United States and the Soviet Union grew strained after World War II. This hostility was called the Cold War because it was fought mainly with words and diplomacy.

The hostility arose for several reasons. At the end of the war, the United States and the Soviet Union were the two most powerful countries in the world. The United States expected the Soviet Union to permit free elections in the East European countries it occupied. Instead, the Soviets held them in an iron grip. Winston Churchill called it an "Iron Curtain."

The Soviets believed that communism would triumph over democracy and capitalism, and they supported communist revolutions in other nations. The United States thus feared for its security. The United States adopted a foreign policy called *containment*, which was intended to prevent the Soviet Union from expanding its control to other nations. As part of this policy, the United States formed military alliances with nations on both sides of the Soviet Union. Containment led the United States into wars in Korea and Vietnam, a confrontation over nuclear weapons in Cuba, and the "arms race."

Above: After World War II, Germany was partitioned. The United States, Great Britain, France, and the Soviet Union each controlled a section. Berlin, the German capital, was also partitioned. In 1948, the Soviet Union set up a blockade of Berlin, refusing to allow trucks to drive across the Soviet sector to resupply the western sectors. The United States responded by airlifting supplies to Berlin. The pilots often dropped candy to the waiting children.

Did You Know?

Sir Winston Churchill **first referred to the** "Iron Curtain" **in a speech at** Westminster College **in Missouri.**

The Cold War ended with the breakup of the Soviet Union in the 1980s and Russia's movement toward democratic government. The fear of nuclear war has lessened, but regional conflicts are emerging all over the world.

The Korean War

At the end of World War II, Korea had been divided along the 38th parallel of latitude. The United States supervised the government of South Korea, and the Soviet Union that of North Korea. On June 25, 1950, North Korea invaded South Korea, hoping to make one unified communist country. Instead, the Korean War broke out.

Seventeen United Nations countries immediately sent troops to South Korea to stop the North Korean invasion forces. The UN troops, led by divisions of American soldiers that included 75,000 Georgians, pushed the North Korean troops back almost to the border of China. However, the United Nations forces were not prepared when China's huge army came to North Korea's aid. There seemed to be no way to avoid another world war.

After many attacks and counterattacks, a battle line was drawn between the two countries in July 1951. Peace was finally declared in July 1953 with no clear victor.

The Korean War was a costly one, with 2,500,000 killed or wounded. Of those killed, 25,000 were Americans and over 500 were Georgians. Today, Korea remains divided along the 38th parallel. Some U.S. troops are still in South Korea to help with its protection, although efforts toward the reunification of Korea continue on both sides.

Georgia During the Cold War

The economy of Georgia—like that of many other states—benefitted from the arms race and by the need for military preparedness. Businesses like Martin-Marietta employed thousands of workers. Military installations such as Dobbins, Warner Robins, and Fort Benning created employment for many other Georgians. Even textile firms were kept busy supplying clothing, sheets, and other items for the armed forces.

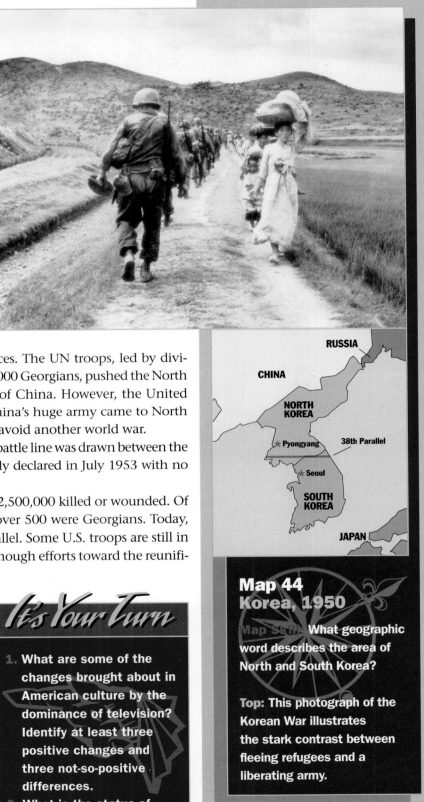

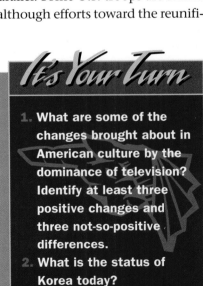

It's Your Turn

1. What are some of the changes brought about in American culture by the dominance of television? Identify at least three positive changes and three not-so-positive differences.
2. What is the status of Korea today?

Map 44
Korea, 1950

Map Skill: What geographic word describes the area of North and South Korea?

Top: This photograph of the Korean War illustrates the stark contrast between fleeing refugees and a liberating army.

Georgia After World War II

Section Preview

As you read, look for:
- the growth of business and industry after the war,
- the "Three Governors Episode,"
- Georgia's postwar governors, and
- **vocabulary terms:** National School Lunch Act, Georgia Minimum Foundation Program for Education Act, one-person, one-vote concept, and reapportion.

Below: As you can see in this photograph, the ladders of the fire company did not reach to the higher floors of the Winecoff Hotel.

When Georgia's soldiers and sailors returned home after World War II, they found the state in the midst of rapid change. Like the rest of the nation, Georgia had to shift from a wartime economy back to a peacetime economy. Agriculture was no longer as dominant in the state as it had been; manufacturing was now more important. That led to a significant growth of our cities.

In 1946, Georgia Senator Richard B. Russell sponsored a bill in Congress that affected the entire nation. It was called the National School Lunch Act. The act outlined a program to ensure that schoolchildren received nutritious lunches. It also encouraged school cafeterias to use government surplus food items such as cheese, flour, and peanut butter. Because of his work, Senator Russell is known as the "father of the school lunch program."

Did You Know?

In 2003, more than 191 million school lunches were served in Georgia alone.

An Atlanta Tragedy

On December 7, 1946, one of Georgia's greatest tragedies occurred in Atlanta. At fifteen stories, the Winecoff Hotel was the city's tallest hotel. A brick-and-stone structure, it was advertised as "fireproof." However, the hotel had one spiral staircase, an operator-controlled elevator, no sprinkler system, and no fire escapes.

That night, the hotel was filled with guests commemorating the fifth anniversary of Pearl Harbor and with teenagers from across the state who were attending the Youth Assembly at the Capitol. About 3 a.m., fire broke out on the third floor. By the time fire trucks arrived about forty-five minutes later, much of the building was ablaze. Some guests had already died either from the flames, from smoke inhalation, or from injuries suffered after jumping out of windows to the streets below. The firemen worked frantically to put out the blaze and to rescue guests, but their hoses would only reach to the eighth floor. Two and one-half hours later, the incident was over. Of the more than 280 guests, 119 died. Many more were severely injured.

The cause of the fire is still under debate. Some blamed it on arson, others on careless smoking. Whatever the cause, it remains one of the nation's worst hotel fires. Within days of the incident, states across the nation updated their fire codes for hotels and other public buildings to avoid a repeat of the tragedy. In 1948, Georgia's General Assembly adopted the building exits code to ensure that all buildings would have enough fire exits in the event of a fire.

Industries Move into Georgia

After the war, businesses continued to move into the state. Georgia's mild climate lured many northern companies that wanted to escape cold winters, high heating costs, and transportation slowdowns caused by snow and ice. Georgia still had one weather drawback—the intense summer heat.

Rich's Department Store had been the first air-conditioned building in Atlanta. After the war, air-conditioning was slowly introduced in other stores and office buildings. But it was not until the 1960s that the climate controls we take for granted today were installed in most businesses. Most homes and automobiles did not become air-conditioned until the 1970s and early 1980s.

In addition to favorable weather, the state also had low business and individual tax rates. In 1949, a typical Georgian paid only $38 in state taxes. Most importantly from a business owner's standpoint, Georgia was a non-union state. Workers could be hired at lower wages and with fewer labor demands than in states controlled by unions.

The growth of aviation created even more expansion during this period. By the close of the 1950s, Lockheed was the state's largest employer. In 1946, another company that was to become important to the world arrived in Atlanta—the Centers for Disease Control. The CDC is the world leader in protecting us from old and new diseases, including those created by humans.

Top: A number of different types of planes were built at Lockheed's Marietta plant. Above: Headquartered in Atlanta, the CDC is an agency of the Department of Health and Human Services.

Georgia Politics

Georgia politics during the early postwar years meant business as usual. But no political event in Georgia during this period got more publicity or caused greater confusion than the "three governors episode."

The Three Governors Episode

In 1946, Governor Ellis Arnall's term was drawing to a close. Because he could not succeed himself, Georgians had to elect a new governor. The field of candidates in the Democratic primary included Arnall's arch rival, segregationist Eugene Talmadge; former governor Eurith Rivers; and James Carmichael, who had headed the Marietta Bell bomber plant during the war. In the primary, Carmichael won the popular vote. In large part, Carmichael's victory was due to the fact that, for the first time since Reconstruction, black voters could take part in the primary election. However, Talmadge won the county unit vote, and he became the Democratic candidate.

The Republicans did not have a candidate, so Talmadge ran unopposed in the November general election. Talmadge was sixty-two years old and in poor health. Because his close advi-

sors were afraid he would not live long enough to begin his term, they made a secret plan. The plan was for a few hundred selected supporters to write the name of Eugene Talmadge's son Herman on the ballot as their second gubernatorial choice. When the general election was over, Eugene Talmadge had been elected governor; Melvin Thompson had been elected lieutenant governor. Shortly before Christmas, and before he was sworn in, Eugene Talmadge died, and the confusion began.

The legislature chose Herman Talmadge as governor, based on the size of the write-in votes for him—a good number of which were suddenly "found" after the election. Governor Arnall declared that Lieutenant Governor Thompson was the rightful successor. However, in the early morning hours of January 15, 1947, a group of Eugene Talmadge's men broke into the governor's office, changed the locks on the doors, and readied themselves to run the state.

Because he was locked out of his own office, Governor Arnall set up a temporary office at the Capitol information counter. Three days later, with news cameras flashing, Arnall officially resigned. In the meantime, Lieutenant Governor Thompson opened an office in downtown Atlanta and began legal proceedings to become governor. The government was in a state of total confusion.

Secretary of State Ben Fortson refused to give the official state seal (used for legalizing documents) to either Talmadge or Thompson. As a result, no

Opposite page, above: James V. Carmichael won the popular vote in the 1946 gubernatorial primary, but lost the county unit vote to Eugene Talmadge. **Opposite page, below:** Herman Talmadge (center, to right of smiling woman), just after the legislature put him in the governor's chair. **Above:** Ellis Arnall set up his office at the information counter in the Capitol rotunda after being locked out of his office.

Did You Know?

State law **limits** development on **Jekyll Island to 35** percent of the land.

one was in a position to run the state. The national news media had a field day reporting Georgia's political chaos.

Finally, in March, the Georgia Supreme Court ruled that Thompson was the rightful head of state until a special election could be held in 1948 to fill the unexpired term of Governor-elect Eugene Talmadge. In that election, and again in 1950, Herman Talmadge was legally elected as Georgia's governor.

Melvin Thompson

Among Melvin Thompson's accomplishments during his brief time in office was a plan for the state to convert Jekyll Island into a state resort. He bought Jekyll Island for $675,000, a bargain that has been compared to the original purchase of Manhattan. Jekyll Island has proven to be one of Georgia's major assets as a tourist attraction and year-round resort area. Thompson also built the University of Georgia's School of Veterinary Medicine and the textile engineering building at Georgia Tech.

Herman Talmadge

During Herman Talmadge's tenure as governor, he restructured the state highway department, created the Georgia Forestry Commission, and provided leadership for improvements in soil conservation programs, county health departments, and the state's prison system.

Above: Herman Talmadge (left) shakes hands with Melvin Thompson (right).

Most of Talmadge's legacy is in the field of education. He provided leadership for a new state constitution that expanded schools to include grades 1-12. In 1949, the General Assembly passed the **Minimum Foundation Program for Education Act**. This act lengthened the school year to nine months and raised standards for buildings, equipment, transportation, and school curricula. A 3 percent sales tax was passed in 1951 to pay for these changes.

After leaving office, Talmadge was elected to the U.S. Senate in 1956. He served there until 1981.

Marvin Griffin

Education advancements also marked the term of Governor Talmadge's successor, Marvin Griffin. During his term, educational television was begun, classrooms were constructed, and over three thousand new teachers were hired. As enrollment in Georgia's colleges and universities grew, Griffin worked to provide campuses and facilities to meet those needs.

Governor Griffin, a native of Bainbridge, oversaw the remodeling of the State Capitol and the purchase of Stone Mountain as a state park area. He

provided leadership for the development of new public health facilities and improved medical services, senior citizens care, vocational rehabilitation, and child services. He also obtained funding to build an atomic reactor at Georgia Tech and a new science center for the University of Georgia.

In 1968, Griffin was briefly the vice presidential running mate of American Independent party presidential candidate George Wallace.

"One Person, One Vote"

In the 1960s, two rulings by the federal district court brought dramatic change to Georgia's political structure. The first involved the county unit system. As you learned in Chapter 11, this system had been in place since 1917. It was designed to maintain the power of the rural areas of the state even though the greatest population growth was in urban areas.

Did You Know?

The federal court decision was appealed to the U.S. Supreme Court in *Gray v. Sanders*. It was in the decision in that case that "one person, one vote" was first used.

In April 1962, the Georgia federal court ruled that the county unit system violated the Fourteenth Amendment. The ruling was the basis for the one-person, one-vote concept; that is, every citizen's vote should be equal to every other citizen's vote no matter where the person lived. Once the county unit system was ruled unconstitutional, the majority of representatives in

Above: The State of Georgia bought Stone Mountain in September 1958 for use as a park. Governor Griffin was convinced that the purchase "will be of everlasting benefit to the present generation and all future citizens of this state, and the entire southland." Do you agree?

the Georgia house came from the urban areas. Political power shifted from rural to urban areas. This also gave predominantly black population areas an equal opportunity to elect legislative representatives. In a 1962 election, Atlanta attorney Leroy Johnson became the first African American state senator in Georgia since Reconstruction.

In 1964, the federal court again ruled that Georgia's constitution, which ensured each county in the state at least one seat in the legislature, violated the one-person, one-vote concept. The courts stated that legislative districts should depend solely on population rather than on county boundary lines. The General Assembly had to **reapportion** (redraw) voting districts to ensure districts of equal population sizes.

These two decisions did more than just shift political power from rural to urban areas; they also influenced the campaign styles and election of the state's governor.

Carl Sanders

In 1962, Carl Sanders defeated Governor Marvin Griffin in the gubernatorial race. Griffin was a rural Democrat who campaigned the "old-fashioned" way. He toured the state, speaking from county to county at political barbecues and rallies. Sanders was a native of Augusta. In addition to the rallies and fund-raisers, Sanders relied on television to appeal to the state's urban voters. He soundly defeated Griffin.

Sanders campaigned on a promise to modernize state government. Once in office, he appointed study commissions and used their recommendations to streamline and modernize key state agencies. He also worked to improve Georgia's infrastructure and bring more industry to the state.

Sanders dealt fairly with the periods of racial unrest and disturbances that took place in the state in the 1960s, especially in Savannah, Americus, and Atlanta. Because he insisted that all Georgians obey the law and settle disputes in the courtrooms rather than in the streets, Georgia avoided the racial violence that took place in states such as Alabama. This moderation was another reason for leaders of business and industry to move into the state.

However, Governor Sanders's most significant achievements may have been in education. He used almost sixty cents of every tax dollar in his budgets for education. He opened new junior colleges and vocational schools throughout the state, established a dental school, added 10,000 new public school teachers, reorganized the state's Department of Education, and raised university faculty salaries 32 percent. He was responsible for more university construction projects than all of the state's previous governors.

Above: When he was elected in 1962, Carl Sanders was, at age thirty-seven, the nation's youngest governor. After serving one term, he ran for governor again in 1970, losing to future president Jimmy Carter. Disappointed by his defeat, he left politics and founded the Atlanta law firm of Troutman Sanders, which today is one of the largest and most prestigious law firms in Georgia.

Governor Sanders was a new breed of southern governor—a state leader who developed a strong and vocal place in national Democratic party politics and maintained a positive working relationship with national administrations. When his term ended in 1967, he returned to his law practice and built one of the state's largest and most prestigious law firms.

Lester Maddox

In 1967, segregationist and restaurant owner Lester Maddox of Atlanta became governor. The 1966 gubernatorial election was "another one for the books." When no candidate received a majority in the Democratic primary, there was a runoff. Maddox was a surprise winner over former Governor Ellis Arnall. In the general election, Maddox faced Republican Howard "Bo" Callaway. While Callaway had more votes than Maddox, a write-in campaign for Arnall prevented Callaway from getting a majority of the vote. The election then went to the Democratic legislature, which chose Maddox.

Maddox surprised many Georgians by appointing more African Americans to state boards and commissions than all prior governors combined. He named the first black member of the Board of Pardons and Paroles, reformed state prisons, and integrated the Georgia State Patrol. The governor increased spending on teacher salaries and higher education. Governor Maddox also established "People's Days." Twice a month, any Georgian could visit the governor's mansion to talk about anything they wished.

Since he could not succeed himself, Maddox ran for lieutenant governor in 1970 and was elected overwhelmingly.

Above: Lester Maddox was an unlikely choice for governor, but he was an able governor. In 1970, Maddox became the first governor to be elected lieutenant governor.

It's Your Turn

1. What legislation did Senator Richard B. Russell introduce in 1946?
2. What made Georgia so attractive to new industries in the postwar period?
3. Why was the county unit system considered a violation of the Fourteenth Amendment?
4. Of the five governors discussed in this section of the chapter, each accomplished much on behalf of Georgia. Which of these leaders do you think was the most outstanding leader of this era and why?

Section Preview

As you read, look for:
- **important legislation and the desegregation of Georgia schools,**
- **key people in the civil rights movement,**
- **notable events in the civil rights movement, and**
- **vocabulary terms: Brown v. Board of Education, Southern Christian Leadership Conference, sit-in, Student Nonviolent Coordinating Committee, Civil Rights Act of 1964, and Voting Rights Act of 1965.**

The Civil Rights Movement

African Americans returning from the war found little change in attitudes toward blacks. In the South, and other parts of the country as well, Jim Crow was still in full throttle. There were still separate entrances to doctor and dentist offices, signs labeling drinking fountains for "Whites" and "Colored," and separate entrances to movie theaters where "balcony seating" was available for African Americans. Lunch counters and restaurants were segregated, as were public schools, libraries, city pools, transportation services, and other facilities.

In 1946, President Truman set up the President's Committee on Civil Rights to study the problem of discrimination. Two years later, in 1948, Truman signed an executive order that outlawed racial segregation in the armed forces. By the time of the Korean War, African Americans and whites were serving in the same units. The Federal Housing Act, passed in 1949, banned racial discrimination in federally financed housing.

But no matter how important these measures were to the cause of civil rights, it was in the field of education that the most far-reaching changes occurred.

The Supreme Court and Education

In earlier chapters, you learned that the U.S. Supreme Court struck down the Civil Rights Act of 1875. In addition, in its 1896 decision in *Plessy v. Ferguson*, the Court essentially legalized the separate-but-equal doctrine.

In 1935, the National Association for the Advancement of Colored People (NAACP) began the fight to end segregation in schools. Charles Houston and Thurgood Marshall, who later became a U.S. Supreme Court justice, presented NAACP-supported cases in many of the twenty states where schools were still segregated. One of those cases resulted in the desegregation of Georgia's schools.

In 1950, seven-year-old Linda Brown, a black student, tried to enroll in an all-white school in Topeka, Kansas. When entry was denied, the NAACP helped Brown's father sue the Topeka Board of Education. The case, referred

Above: These three attorneys successfully argued the *Brown v. Board of Education* case. Future Supreme Court justice Thurgood Marshall is in the middle.

By the Side of the Road

Jack Roosevelt Robinson was born in Cairo in 1919, but his family moved to California when he was a young child. A tremendous athlete, Jackie was the first student at UCLA to earn varsity letters in four different sports in one year—baseball, basketball, football, and track. He played professional football for the Los Angeles Bulldogs of the Pacific Coast League until World War II broke out.

Robinson broke onto the national scene in 1945 when he was hired as the first African American baseball player to play for the Montreal Royals, a Brooklyn Dodgers farm club. In 1947, Robinson was called up to the major leagues as a Dodger, the first African American baseball player in the major leagues. He spent his entire playing career with the Dodgers, winning many honors including MVP in 1949. When you next visit Grady county, look on Hadley Ferry Road for the historical marker showing where Robinson was born.

Birthplace of Jackie Robinson
First African American in Major League Baseball

Robinson was born here on January 31, 1919 before he and his family moved to California in 1920. After attending U.C.L.A., serving in the U.S. Army, and playing in the Negro American Baseball and International Leagues, Robinson joined the Brooklyn Dodgers in 1947, breaking major league baseball's color barrier. Adding to his many sports accomplishments, he served as special assistant to New York Governor Nelson Rockefeller, established the first African American Modern Bank/Freedom National Bank, and provided housing for the underprivileged through his construction firm. Robinson died in 1972. The house burned in 1996.

Erected by the Georgia Historical Society and
The Jackie Robinson Cairo Memorial Institute, Inc.

2001.22   65-1

to as *Brown v. Board of Education*, reached the Supreme Court. In its 1954 ruling, the Court said separate-but-equal schools were unconstitutional. It ordered racial integration of schools "with all deliberate speed." After nearly sixty years of court-approved segregation, the ruling in the *Plessy* case was finally overturned. Although the Court had spoken, many states were slow to carry out its orders.

The Sibley Commission

In Georgia, most of the state's school systems refused desegregation. Indeed, the opposition to desegregation was so strong that the General Assembly voted in 1955 to cut off state funds to any system that integrated its schools. Ernest Vandiver, who became governor in 1959, was elected, in part, on his promise to keep Georgia's schools segregated.

But in 1960, the Georgia General Assembly recognized change was at hand. It organized a fourteen-member commission, headed by Atlanta attorney and banker John Sibley, to study the problem of integration.

The Sibley Commission held hearings all over the state to learn how the public felt about integration. Reaction was swift and direct. By a three-to-two margin, Georgians said they would rather close the schools than integrate them. The commission recommended that local school systems be allowed to decide if they would abide by a probable court order to integrate public schools or if they would close them. In many communities, private schools were opened to avoid the issue.

Georgia Begins to Integrate Schools

Despite resistance from many states, including Georgia, the Supreme Court and federal district courts held their ground. On January 6, 1961, the University of Georgia, with the backing of Governor Vandiver, allowed its first two black students to be escorted into the school by state patrol officers. One of these students was Charlayne Hunter, who graduated from the Henry W. Grady School of Journalism and later, as Charlayne Hunter-Gault, became a

nationally known newspaper and public television reporter. The other was Hamilton Holmes, who was installed in Phi Beta Kappa, graduated with honors from the university, and later practiced medicine as an orthopedic surgeon in Atlanta until his death in 1995.

Many university alumni and Georgia politicians had pleaded with Governor Vandiver to close the university rather than allow the two students to enroll. Refusing to bend to pressure, the governor instructed the president of the university, Dr. O. C. Aderhold, to open the doors. This move by the governor shocked and angered many Georgians who had voted for the Lavonia resident based on his pledge not to integrate the state's schools.

During the heated discussions that followed, Vandiver admitted that he had been wrong in his pre-election speeches. After the two students were enrolled, he went even further. The governor asked the legislature to repeal other segregation laws in Georgia. Vandiver's actions were one of the main reasons that Georgia's subsequent efforts at desegregating schools were calmer and smoother than those in many other school systems in both the South and North.

The state's largest school system also began token integration in 1961. The Atlanta city school system allowed nine black students to enroll in a formerly all-white high school. The peaceful integration of four high schools by the end of the year prompted President John F. Kennedy to praise the system. During the next three years, the courts ordered all systems in the state to integrate schools. After the Civil Rights Act of 1964 passed, the federal government refused federal funds to any system that did not end segregation. Some chose to take the cut in funding, but integration continued to come about across the state.

In 1969, the U.S. Department of Justice sued the Georgia State Board of Education, demanding that the

Opposite page, above: A pro-segregation protest in front of the governor's mansion in 1959. Opposite page, below: Charlayne Hunter and Hamilton Holmes leave campus at the end of their first day. Below: Ernest Vandiver was governor during most of the turbulent years of integration. Bottom: Counselor Dorothy Morr shows Mary McMullen her new locker at Grady High School, 1961.

state withhold funds from systems that refused to follow court-ordered desegregation plans. Communities moved to comply with federal laws, and by 1971 all Georgia's public schools were integrated. This made Georgia the first state with a sizable African American population to have a statewide integrated school system.

The Montgomery Bus Boycott

The desegregation of transportation systems in the South began at 5:30 p.m. on Thursday, December 1, 1955. Along with it began a movement that forever changed race relations in America.

Rosa Parks, a middle-aged African American seamstress was tired from a long day of work. She boarded a public bus in Montgomery, Alabama, paid her fare, and sat down in the first empty seat just behind the "whites only" section. At a stop, six white passengers got on the bus. Because there were not enough empty seats in the white section, the driver ordered all African Americans to move to the back. Three rose to move, but Mrs. Parks stayed where she was. The driver called for a policeman. Mrs. Parks was arrested, booked, fingerprinted, and briefly jailed. She had violated a city ordinance that gave bus drivers the right to decide where passengers sat. Her trial was set for December 5.

Above: Mrs. Rosa Parks and her attorney are seen on the way to the Montgomery courthouse. Reporters often asked Mrs. Parks about her bravery when she refused to give up her seat on the bus. She replied that she was just tired.

Rosa Parks was a former officer in the Montgomery chapter of NAACP. News of her arrest quickly spread among the 50,000 members of the African American community, and a group of ministers gathered to talk about ways to support her. They asked Atlanta-born Dr. Martin Luther King, Jr., to be their spokesperson and agreed to boycott the city buses on the day of Mrs. Parks's trial.

On Sunday, December 4, African American ministers and civic leaders asked all African Americans to stay off the buses on the next day. Even though Rosa Parks was found guilty, the bus boycott was 90 percent successful. The community decided to continue the boycott until the following demands were met: (1) African American passengers would be treated with courtesy; (2) African American drivers would be assigned to primarily black routes; and (3) seating would be on a first-come, first-served basis.

Dr. Martin Luther King, Jr., began making speeches all over the city in support of the boycott. Car pools formed in African American neighborhoods, and African American-owned taxi cabs charged only a dime for a ride to or from work. In a matter of weeks, the city's bus revenue fell by 65 percent.

In March 1956, three months after the boycott started, Dr. King and eighty-nine other leaders were found guilty of violating an outdated 1921 antilabor law forbidding boycotts. They appealed their convictions. In November, the city went to court again, demanding an end to the car pools and asking to be paid the money it had lost on bus service.

Dr. King entered the courtroom on November 13 to face the same judge who had found Rosa Parks guilty. About noon, a reporter handed Dr. King a teletyped message from one of the national news services. The U.S. Supreme Court had just upheld a district court ruling that made segregation on public transportation unconstitutional. When the Supreme Court decision officially reached Montgomery on December 21, 1956, Dr. King and a white minister boarded a city bus and rode through the streets without incident. The Montgomery bus boycott was over, but the movement for civil rights was just beginning.

A Nonviolent Movement Is Born

The success of the Montgomery bus boycott thrust Martin Luther King, Jr., into the national spotlight. Dr. King was a third-generation minister, the second of three children. He lived in Atlanta and attended Booker T. Washington High School. The school was Atlanta's first African American secondary school and had been built largely because of the efforts of Dr. King's grandfather, A. D. Williams, and other community leaders.

Above: This portrait of Dr. Martin Luther King, Jr., hangs in the state Capitol as a memorial to his civil rights leadership.

In 1944, when he was fifteen, King entered Morehouse College. In 1947, he was ordained to the ministry at Ebenezer Baptist Church, after which he enrolled at Crozer Theological Seminary in Pennsylvania. In 1948, he earned a doctorate in theology from Boston University. While in Boston, he met and married Coretta Scott, who was studying at the New England Conservatory of Music.

During his years of study, Dr. King developed a nonviolent approach to social change. He based his ideas on the writings of Henry David Thoreau

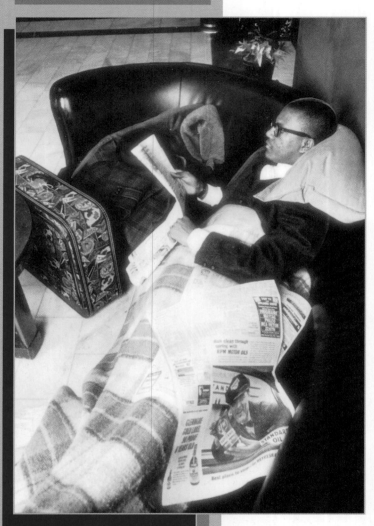

Above: Before the Civil Rights Act of 1964, African Americans often had difficulty finding a motel or hotel that would accept them. In 1963, one of the many nonviolent protests—a "lie-in"—took place at Atlanta's Grady Hotel.

(the author of *On Civil Disobedience*) and on the teachings of India's Hindu leader, Mahatma Gandhi. King first practiced nonviolence during the Montgomery bus boycott. He was aided by other ministers and civic leaders, including Edward Nixon and the Reverend Ralph Abernathy.

King called the boycott a conflict "between justice and injustice." He believed in a four-pronged approach for gaining civil rights for all Americans: (1) direct, nonviolent actions, (2) legal remedies, (3) ballots, and (4) economic boycotts.

Encouraged by the success of the boycott, King carried his message of a nonviolent approach to social change to other parts of the South. Dr. King often traveled two or three thousand miles a week spreading the message of nonviolence. He moved to Atlanta in January 1960 as head of the Southern Christian Leadership Conference (SCLC), a group he had helped form the year before.

During the early 1960s, King held lunch counter sit-ins to protest the segregated lunch counters of department and chain stores in the South. A sit-in is a type of demonstration where people enter a public building and refuse to leave until they are served or their demands are met. In 1960, Rich's Department Store had been the site of the first Georgia sit-in, where King was joined by Julian Bond, Lonnie King, and other students from Morehouse College. Fifty of the students were arrested. However, their efforts continued in spite of anti-trespass laws passed by the Georgia General Assembly making sit-ins illegal.

The Albany Movement

In 1961, Albany, Georgia, became a center of civil rights activity. Mainly a farming community, Albany had a population that was about 40 percent African American. Six years after *Brown v. Board of Education*, Albany schools were still segregated. Only a small number of African Americans were allowed to register to vote.

In 1955, the Interstate Commerce Commission, following the Supreme Court decision, prohibited segregation in interstate bus and train stations. On November 1, 1961, workers with the NAACP and Student Nonviolent Coordinating Committee (SNCC) decided to test the ruling by sitting in the "whites only" waiting room at the city's bus station. They were quickly arrested. This prompted the African American community to unite and form the Albany Movement, which was led by Dr. William Anderson.

In December, black and white "freedom riders" arrived in Albany to support the Albany Movement. They were arrested at the Central Railway Termi-

nal. The next day, SNCC organizer James Forman led a march of African American high school students to the same train station. The students were arrested and jailed while members of the national press watched. At one point during the months of protest in Albany, five hundred people were either in jail or out on bond. Civil rights leaders arrested included Dr. King and Reverend Ralph Abernathy, who had traveled to Albany to ask city officials for a meeting to resolve the dispute. Before the year's end, a biracial committee was formed to study concerns of the African American community in Albany.

Protests Move to Alabama

In April 1963, Dr. Martin Luther King, Jr., began a campaign in Birmingham, Alabama, to end discrimination in all areas of that city's public life. For several nights, television news showed police attempts to control demonstrators with attack dogs and high-pressure fire hoses. Over three thousand persons, including Dr. King, were arrested.

On September 15, 1963, during Sunday School at Birmingham's Sixteenth Street Baptist Church, a bomb killed four black children and injured fourteen others. Even though a riot followed the tragedy, many African Americans and whites joined together to stop further violence. One of those individuals was Atlanta's Reverend Austin Ford, who ran Emmaus House, an inner-city mission. He was one of a small group who supported and encouraged the integration of churches in the 1960s. Other supporters, some lawyers and even a few judges, joined with white students from the North and South. In their own way, all did what they could to help the effort.

Above: In August 1962, protestors tried to integrate the Carnegie Library. The library closed rather than open its doors to African Americans. In March 1963, African Americans were admitted to the library for the first time.

The Civil Rights Act

In June 1963, President John F. Kennedy went on national television and described segregation as a moral crisis for the country. He told of his plans to ask Congress to pass a new civil rights law. Later that month, Kennedy sent to Congress the strongest civil rights bill in history.

Unfortunately, President Kennedy did not live to see that civil rights bill become law. President Kennedy was assassinated on November 23, 1963, in Dallas. On the presidential jet that carried Kennedy's body back to the nation's capital, Vice President Lyndon B. Johnson was sworn in as the thirty-sixth president of the United States.

In a speech to Congress shortly after Kennedy's assassination, President Johnson vowed to continue fighting for the earliest possible passage of President Kennedy's civil rights bill. Under President Johnson's leadership, and with the political pressure of both black and white supporters, the Civil Rights Act of 1964 became law. This was the most far-reaching and important civil rights legislation since Reconstruction. Basically, the equal protection clause of the Fourteenth Amendment was given greater influence. The legislation made segregation of all public facilities illegal. This included restaurants, theaters, hotels, public recreational areas, schools, and libraries. It also prohibited discrimination in businesses and labor unions.

The Voting Rights Act

In spite of the Civil Rights Act, African Americans in many sections of the South still could not vote. Dr. Martin Luther King, Jr., who had been awarded the Nobel Peace Prize in 1964, began to turn his attention to voting rights.

In the summer of 1964, dubbed "Freedom Summer," people from all over the country came to the South to help African Americans register to vote. One group very involved in the effort was SNCC, a group that included Georgia's Julian Bond as one of its founders and Georgia's John Lewis as its national chairman.

In March 1965, Dr. King met with civil rights leaders in Selma, Alabama, to plan demonstrations and marches in support of voting rights. As he led marchers to the Dallas County (Alabama) courthouse, King and over five hundred students were arrested and jailed.

To call attention to the cause of voter's rights, King planned a march from Selma to the state capital in Montgomery. On March 7, over six hundred marchers approached the Edmund Pettus Bridge that spans the Alabama River. There, they were met by about two hundred state troopers armed with billy clubs and tear gas. The marchers fell back into Selma, followed by the county sheriff's mounted posse.

Dr. King went to Montgomery to request a march permit, which was granted by a federal district court judge. President Johnson activated the Alabama National Guard and sent army troops, federal marshals, and FBI agents to Selma to protect the marchers.

On March 21, more than four thousand Americans of different races, led by Dr. King and Rabbi Abraham Herchel, began the fifty-mile walk to Montgomery. About twenty-five thousand others joined the group in Montgomery to complete the march to the Alabama State Capitol.

The march influenced Congress to pass the Voting Rights Act of 1965. Within eighteen months, a million African Americans were added to the registers of voters in the South.

A Shift in Mood

After the Selma-to-Montgomery march, the mood of many seeking equal civil rights changed. These people abandoned the moderate, nonviolent approach of Dr. King to follow much more aggressive activists. SNCC replaced John Lewis with the more radical Stokely Carmichael and later H. Rap Brown. The group began to speak of "black power." Eldridge Cleaver helped found a militant group called the Black Panthers, which had many confrontations with police. As a member of the Nation of Islam, Malcolm X (born Malcolm Little) rejected the

Below: Dr. King leads the Selma-to-Montgomery march in 1965. Dr. King told the group that "we are on the move and no wave of racism will stop us."

Above: On April 4, 1969, Dr. Martin Luther King, Jr., was shot to death on the balcony of the Lorraine Motel in Memphis, Tennessee. The motel is now the National Civil Rights Museum.

civil rights movement and instead preached black separatism, black pride, and black self-dependence. In the summer of 1967, there were riots in black communities in places like Watts in Los Angeles, Detroit, and Newark.

Dr. King and his supporters urged an end to the violence. On April 3, 1968, King was in Memphis, Tennessee, to organize support for 1,300 striking sanitation workers. There had been threats on King's life, but he said,

It really doesn't matter what happens to me now because I've been to the mountain top . . . and I've looked over and seen the promised land. I may not get there with you. . . . But we, as a people, will get to the promised land . . . . Like anybody, I would like to live a long life. Longevity has its place. . . but I'm not concerned about that now.

The next day, the 39-year-old King was on the balcony of a Memphis motel talking with Jesse Jackson, standing below. A shot from a high-powered rifle left Martin Luther King, Jr., dead.

On March 11, 1969, James Earl Ray, a forty-year-old high school dropout, was tried and convicted for King's murder. He was sentenced to ninety-nine years in prison.

The movement toward civil rights for all Americans did not die with Martin Luther King, Jr. It continued through the work of many others, including Mrs. Coretta Scott King, Dr. Ralph Abernathy, Reverend Jesse Jackson, and Georgia political leaders Andrew Young, John Lewis, and Julian Bond. The movement for equality and fair treatment for all Americans continues today with new leaders and new participants, building on the contributions of those who came before.

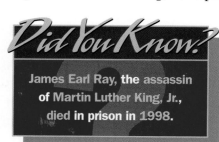

Did You Know?

James Earl Ray, **the** assassin **of** Martin Luther King, Jr., died **in prison in** 1998.

Atlanta: A Case Study in Change

During the midst of the civil rights movement, riots and demonstrations were taking place in cities like Boston, Newark, Los Angeles, and Birmingham. But in the city of Atlanta, with the exception of two fairly minor breakouts, the desegregation and integration of business, city government, and schools were peaceful. This was due in part to the influence of Atlanta's African American church leaders such as Ebenezer Baptist pastor Martin Luther King, Sr., and Wheat Street Baptist pastor William Holmes Borders. Other leaders included Walter White, Martin Luther King, Jr., and Andrew Young. The peaceful transition is also credited to Atlanta's business and civic leaders such as William Hartsfield and Ivan Allen. In Atlanta, changes started long before the Civil Rights Act of 1965.

William Hartsfield served as mayor of the city for an astonishing six terms (1937-1941 and 1942-1961). Although he is widely acknowledged for his leadership in making Atlanta an aviation hub of the Southeast, he also helped lead the city in the area of civil rights. In 1946, after the Georgia white primary was outlawed and elections were opened to African Americans, Hartsfield organized a biracial coalition that included Dr. King, Sr., and Reverend Borders. African American leaders worked on voter registration drives.

In 1948, Mayor Hartsfield hired eight African American police officers for restricted duties, a move unheard of throughout most of the South. Slowly

Below: The demonstrators outside the Atlanta City Hall in 1947 are protesting the lack of black policemen.

but surely, Atlanta became known as a city of racial moderation. In 1955, as the result of a U.S. Supreme Court ruling, the city's golf courses were integrated without incident. In 1957, Reverend Borders and a small group of ministers quietly and without fanfare boarded a segregated city transit bus and sat in front. Their arrest and the resulting court hearings led to the integration of the city's bus system.

In October 1958, the Hebrew Benevolent Congregation was bombed. The rabbi at the temple was well known for his commitment to working for equality for all Georgians, and his stance was not popular with Atlantans who wanted to maintain the "status quo." The following day, Mayor Hartsfield received a letter from Dr. Martin Luther King, Jr., on behalf of the Southern Christian Leadership Conference. In his letter, Dr. King said,

Since this tragic incident has occurred in Atlanta, a city long prided as a shining example of civility and tolerance in the South, we pray God that it will challenge the decent people of our city, state, and region to speak up for the "due process of law" and peaceful settling of differences and with equal clarity, to speak out against those who use their elective positions of trust to peddle hatred and to inflame the dynamiters and cross-burners to commit their dastardly deeds of destruction. Surely we who love the South must find the courage and intelligence to provide the constructive leadership so sorely needed now.

Above: Mayor Ivan Allen's conversations with Dr. Martin Luther King, Jr., helped keep Atlanta calm during the sometimes contentious civil rights movement.

In 1958, the mayor asked the state to allow Atlantans to decide whether or not to keep integrated schools open. At that time, the state was refusing to fund integrated schools. A state committee finally visited Atlanta in 1960 in response to Hartsfield's request. They found overwhelming support for keeping the public schools open. To the citizens, that issue was far more important than issues involving school integration.

Also in 1960, Dr. King helped organize sit-ins at eight different Atlanta cafeterias, including the one at City Hall. The peaceful sit-ins resulted in Dr. King's arrest, along with others involved in the protest movement.

On August 30, 1961, nine African American students integrated four previously all-white high schools without incident. Within months, the local chamber of commerce joined Mayor Hartsfield and local African American leaders in ending lunch counter segregation.

In 1962, businessman Ivan Allen was elected mayor. On the day he took office, Mayor Allen ordered the immediate removal of the "Colored" and "White" signs on all entrances and exits to City Hall. Shortly thereafter, he removed the restrictions on the African American policemen, and integrated the city's fire department and city government.

In July 1963, area theater owners opened the main doors to six African American patrons each night. When there were no incidents, a total open-door policy followed. By October, all of Georgia had followed the Atlanta lead and desegregated public facilities. The following year, Georgia State College opened its doors to all students, and other Atlanta area schools followed suit. Westminister became the first private school to desegregate in the city.

This timeline is not to suggest that there were no racial problems in Atlanta. Segregationist Lester Maddox used a gun and ax handles to chase African Americans away from his restaurant. Other business owners, less brazen than Maddox, admitted African Americans into their establishments but offered them less than the "usual Southern hospitality" in serving them. And, in 1963, when the newly elected African American legislators entered the Capitol cafeteria for the first time, there was, according to Leroy Johnson, a "mass evacuation."

In September 1966, a six-day race riot broke out in the Summerhill area of the city across from the stadium. A suspected car thief trying to escape

Below: In the 1960s, a number of Atlanta's civil rights leaders marched to support Julian Bond as he sought to take his seat in the Georgia house of representatives. These leaders included Reverend Ralph Abernathy (second from left), James Forman (fourth from left), Coretta Scott King (fifth from left), Reverend Martin Luther King, Jr. (sixth from left), and John Lewis (right).

Above: Former Mayor Andrew Young is covered in tickertape during a parade through downtown Atlanta to celebrate the city's being named the site of the 1996 Olympic Games.

was shot by a white police officer. According to eyewitnesses, he was then shot a second time after he was down. In response, onlookers threw bricks and bottles at the police; 138 were arrested, 35 of whom were injured.

In 1968, during the funeral of fallen civil rights leader Martin Luther King, Jr., the eyes of the world turned again toward Atlanta. Those who hoped to see a repeat of racial troubles were disappointed. What the rest of the world saw, however, was a city united in mutual grief and mutual respect.

In 1969, the city that *Time* magazine called an "oasis of tolerance" showed its progress. Sam Massell became the city's first Jewish mayor, and African American Maynard Jackson became vice mayor. Another African American leader, Dr. Benjamin Mayes, became a member of the city's Board of Education. The mayors who followed Massell were Maynard Jackson, Andrew Young, Bill Campbell, and Shirley Franklin—all of whom were African Americans walking the path that made Atlanta a "city too busy to hate."

It's Your Turn

1. Who were the first two black students to enroll in the University of Georgia?
2. What two leaders influenced Dr. King's nonviolent approach to social change? What might have happened had Dr. King's approach not dominated in the civil rights struggle of the period?
3. What were the Southern Christian Leadership Conference and the Student Nonviolent Coordinating Committee? In which areas of civil rights did each group actively work?
4. What bill did the march from Selma to Montgomery influence Congress to pass?
5. Why do you think the tactic of organized sit-ins was effective in ending segregation? What other tactics might the protestors have chosen?

Of Special Interest

Hammerin' Hank Aaron

On a steamy Monday night, April 8, 1974, in Atlanta Fulton County Stadium, Hank Aaron leaned his weight into a pitch thrown by Dodger Al Dowling and lifted the ball high into the air and into the left field bullpen, where it was caught by relief pitcher Tom House. It was home run #715, breaking the career home run record held previously by the great Babe Ruth of the New York Yankees. As Aaron rounded the bases, tears welled up in his eyes, for he had chased that record for years.

The Dodgers players congratulated "Hammerin' Hank" as he rounded the bases, and a mob of fans, including his mother, met him at home plate. Dodger relief pitcher Tom House walked back onto the playing field to return the historic ball to Aaron.

Aaron began his professional career with the Negro American League's Indianapolis Clowns. He was the last African American player to play in both the Negro League and the major leagues. He joined the Braves in 1952, and in 1954 he became the Braves' first African American player. In 1972, Aaron signed a record-breaking, three-year, $600,000 contract with the Braves.

As Aaron approached the record, he was the target of intense racial criticism that an African American player would dare break the mighty Babe Ruth's record. He even received death threats. Aaron saved the hate mail, the letters that were sent to him as he neared Ruth's record. He explained that there are still problems in our country, and we occasionally need to be reminded that things are not always as good as we think they are.

When Hank Aaron retired from baseball, he held a number of career accomplishments: 3 Golden Glove awards, an MVP award, and 24 All Star selections. He still holds the records for extra base hits (1,477), total bases (6,856), and RBIs (2,297). But it was that 715th home

Above: Hank Aaron holds the ball he hit for his 715th home run, which broke the record held by Babe Ruth.

run that will always be associated with Aaron's game. Both the ball and the bat Aaron hit it with are on display at Turner Field in Atlanta.

After his retirement from baseball, Hank Aaron remained with the Atlanta Braves and works in Braves' management. In 1982, Aaron was inducted into the Baseball Hall of Fame at Cooperstown, New York.

A Period of Protests and Changes

Section Preview

As you read, look for:
* improvements in communication and transportation,
* the first Georgian elected president,
* the women's rights movement, and
* vocabulary terms: Metropolitan Atlanta Rapid Transit Authority, women's rights movement, affirmative action program, National Organization for Women, National Women's Political Caucus, Equal Rights Amendment, Title IX, Vietnam War, and Watergate.

The late 1960s and early 1970s was a period of frequent demonstrations by young people against a variety of issues, ranging from the war in Vietnam to public morality. Many of these protests were fueled by singers such as Bob Dylan and Joan Baez, who mixed traditional ballads with antiwar and pro-civil rights activist lyrics.

Hippies (young people who supported peace, love, and drugs) basically opposed any issue that the "establishment" supported. At first, these young people were an amusement to some and a bewilderment to most of their parents. But as their actions continued unchecked, this period marked the beginning of a widespread drug culture that was to plague the nation for decades.

Music also began to change as new, loud rock bands such as the Byrds, the Rolling Stones, the Doors, and the Who became wildly popular. For three days in August 1969, close to a half million young people converged on a farm in New York called Woodstock, where for seventy-two hours they carried on a free-for-all party of nonstop music and celebration.

Georgia in the 1970s

The decade began with more advancements in communications. Ted Turner bought Atlanta station WJRJ and renamed it WTCG. One of the features of Turner's broadcasting services was sports. Both the Atlanta Braves and the Atlanta Hawks were broadcast over WTCG. In 1976, Turner linked his television station's signal to a satellite and broadcast programs to cable operators throughout the nation. The "superstation"—later renamed TBS—was born.

Transportation was also in the Georgia spotlight during the 1970s. Atlanta's William B. Hartsfield International Airport offered its first international flights in 1971. The Metropolitan Atlanta Rapid Transit Authority (MARTA) had been established in 1966. In 1975, groundbreaking ceremonies were held for the first rapid rail line, the East Line. The first rapid rail service began in 1979.

Throughout the decade, weather made news. Tornadoes, hail storms, rains and flooding, ice storms, and even snowstorms resulted in injuries and loss of life and property damages in the billions of dollars. In 1973, Savannah recorded its heaviest snowfall in over 100 years (3.6 inches), while the counties in north Georgia received

Above: In 1980, Ted Turner founded CNN, the first 24-hour news channel. In 1995, CNN merged with Time-Warner.

Did You Know?

Ted Turner purchased the Atlanta Braves in 1976 and the Atlanta Hawks in 1977.

almost 20 inches of snow. Tornadoes swept through more than twenty-five counties during the decade. In 1977, heavy rains caused an earthen dam above Toccoa Falls to collapse. The Kelly Barnes Dam in Stephens County gave way during the early morning hours of November 6. Downstream from the dam, the students of Toccoa Falls College were sleeping. Within minutes of the dam collapse, a wall of water crashed into the small Christian college destroying buildings, killing thirty-nine people, and causing $2.5 million in property damage.

James Earl Carter

In 1970, Georgians elected former state senator James Earl "Jimmy" Carter as governor. He was born in Plains in 1924 and grew up on his parents' southwest Georgia peanut farm. Carter attended Georgia Southwestern College and Georgia Tech before receiving an appointment to the U.S. Naval Academy. After graduation, he was assigned to the Pacific Fleet. Later, Carter went to Union College and studied physics.

Above: Jimmy Carter was the first Georgian to be elected president of the United States. He served from 1977 to 1980.

During his term, Governor Carter reorganized the state's executive branch, cutting the number of government agencies from three hundred to twenty-five. He also influenced Georgia's court system, bringing a unified approach to the courts and changing the selection of judges to a merit process. Governor Carter appointed the first woman as a state judge.

He created the Georgia Heritage Trust, which is designed to protect our state's natural and cultural resources. He also worked to equalize funding for public schools across the state and expanded special education, vocational education, and preschool education. Governor Carter also expanded state mental health services for Georgians. At the end of his term, many Georgians were surprised when he announced that he was a candidate for the 1976 Democratic presidential nomination.

Carter was the first Georgian to become president of the United States, defeating President Gerald Ford. As president, Carter will likely best be remembered for his efforts to negotiate peace between Israel and Egypt.

Two events during his term probably cost Carter a second term. First, energy costs, interest rates, and inflation were high. In trying to reduce

Jeff MacNelly was a Pulitzer Prize winning political cartoonist. His targets were the "establishment," particularly those in Washington, D.C. One of his favorite targets, as you can see here, was Jimmy Carter.

Did You Know?

In 2002, Jimmy Carter was awarded the Nobel Peace Prize for his efforts in furthering the cause of peace throughout the world.

inflation, he created a brief recession. Second, in November 1979, militants took over the U.S. Embassy in Iran and held fifty-two Americans hostage for 444 days. The hostages were not released until January 20, 1981, the day Carter left office.

After leaving office, the Carters returned to Georgia. President Carter is much admired for his efforts to negotiate peace, to defeat diseases, to ensure fair elections, and to build housing.

Problems of the Cities

During the late 1970s, census figures showed that the population in thirty-seven of America's fifty-eight largest cities had declined. The middle class was moving out of the cities and into the suburbs. The result was lost revenue for businesses and restaurants, a lower property tax base, declines in the level of city services, strains on aging city infrastructures, and increases in drug use, crime, and gangs. As buildings became empty, vandalism and vagrancy increased. In many cities, the downward spiral lasted until the mid-1990s.

Slowly, urban development grants, special tax monies, business incentives, and the return of suburbanites who were tired of driving 2-4 hours a day to get to and from work began to turn things around. Special attractions, such as Underground Atlanta, the Augusta Riverwalk, and the Chattahoochee Riverwalk in Columbus, have encouraged tourism, which led to the return of downtown hotels, restaurants, galleries, shops, theaters, and other businesses.

Could there be another migration out of the cities? Perhaps, but the larger cities in Georgia have taken steps to avoid another exodus.

The Women's Rights Movement

"You've come a long way, baby" was the slogan in a cigarette ad aimed at women in 1968. That message also fits another civil rights movement of the late 1960s and the 1970s. The women's rights movement reflected major changes in the way women viewed themselves and their contributions to society.

World War II was a major watershed in changing gender roles. Millions of men went off to war, and women stepped in to fill their civilian jobs. Demonstrating their ability to do "man's work," women gained confidence that they could do many things besides clerk, type, nurse, teach, and tend house and children. When the war ended, many women wanted to continue to work outside the home. Some did, but many others were expected to give up their wartime jobs and turn them back over to men.

By the 1960s, many women were unhappy with their lot. The Civil Rights Act of 1964 made it illegal to discriminate against women in hiring practices. Federal affirmative action programs, designed to provide work opportunities for women and minorities, opened up some jobs to women. Still most were not being treated fairly at work. They were discriminated against, and their pay was not equal to men's pay for the same work. Most women held traditional women's jobs. Leadership positions in business were generally closed to them.

Women were also discriminated against in other places. Banks often refused to grant a woman credit without her husband's signature. Single women, including widows, were often unable to obtain credit—no matter what their level of income. Many women, therefore, were unable to buy a home, rent an apartment, buy an automobile, or take out a credit card in their own names. When making major purchases or even taking the family

Top: The Augusta Riverwalk winds along the Savannah River. Above: This 1970s rally was in support of the Equal Rights Amendment.

Above: Condoleezza Rice is a good example for young women. In 2005, President George W. Bush named her his secretary of state. She has also been a writer, a college professor and provost, and a member of the board of directors of a number of corporations.

car in for repairs, women were often asked for the approval of the "man of the house."

Women began questioning their roles in society. By the 1970s, women wanted far more than access to nursing, teaching, and secretarial careers; they wanted equal access to education, to jobs, to salaries, and to benefits. They also wanted equal respect.

Several organizations were established to work for equal rights for women. In 1966, feminist Betty Friedan and others formed the National Organization for Women (NOW) to work for the economic and legal rights of women. In 1971, Gloria Steinem, Betty Friedan, Bella Abzug, and Shirley Chisholm formed the National Women's Political Caucus to promote women's issues. *Ms.* magazine came out a year later and was the first magazine to popularize the issues of women's liberation.

These organizations and others supported a drive to add an Equal Rights Amendment (ERA) to the U.S. Constitution. The proposed amendment read: "Equality of rights under the law shall not be denied or abridged by the United States or by any state on account of sex." In 1972, Congress voted to send the proposed amendment to the states for ratification. Three-fourths of the state legislatures (38 of 50) had to approve the amendment for it to become law. During the fight for ratification, both sides were loud and vocal. By June 30, 1983—the deadline for its ratification—the proposal still lacked the necessary approval. The ERA failed by three votes. Fifteen states, including Georgia, never ratified the ERA.

In 1972, President Nixon signed into law legislation known as Title IX, which prohibited discrimination in education whether in academics or athletics. For the first time, girls could take auto mechanics or shop and boys could take home economics or typing. Some thirty years later, 84 percent of the nation's young women graduate from high school. Women with college doctoral degrees rose from 16 percent to over 46 percent. Female participation in athletics rose from 7.4 percent in high school to 41.5 percent and from 15 percent to 42 percent in college. There has also been a significant increase in the number of women who have become school principals and college professors. Today, female students your age can become anything they wish if they are willing to work for it, whether it is driving a bulldozer or working on power lines or serving in the President's Cabinet.

Vietnam Divides America

In the 1950s, the United States began providing money and a small group of advisors to the government of South Vietnam in its struggle with the communist government of North Vietnam. Slowly, however, the United States stepped up its involvement. As fighting escalated, more and more American troops were sent there until, by the end of 1968, there were 536,000 American troops in South Vietnam.

The Vietnam War was one of the most socially and politically divisive wars in American history. This was the first "televised" war. Americans could see what was happening on the evening news and compare that with what the government was telling them. The two were not always the same. Television helped increase the opposition to the war and citizens' distrust of the government. The distrust increased as American casualties rose and there were reports of Americans killing Vietnamese civilians. The distrust fueled antiwar sentiment, and hundreds of thousands of Americans protested against the war. Some of those protests turned violent, and federal

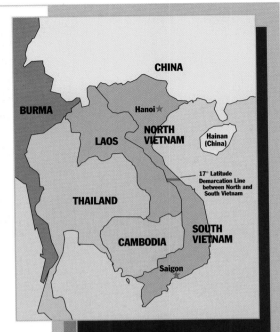

**Map 45
North and South Vietnam**

Map Skill In what part of the world is Vietnam located?

Left: As American soldiers slogged through the rice paddies of Vietnam, the nation was dividing over U.S. involvement in the war.

Dean Rusk

Above: Secretary of State Dean Rusk defended U.S. involvement in Vietnam.

One of the most outstanding national leaders during modern times has been Georgia native David Dean Rusk. A native of Cherokee County, Rusk graduated from Davidson College (in North Carolina) in 1931 and attended Oxford University as a Rhodes Scholar. When he returned to the United States, Rusk taught at Mills College in California. When World War II approached, he joined the U.S. Army, later serving with General George Marshall.

After the war, Rusk joined the Department of State and directed the Office of Special Political Affairs. In 1950, he was appointed Assistant Secretary of State for Far Eastern Affairs, where he worked to counter the continuing communist aggression in Korea.

Rusk left government service briefly in 1950 to serve as the president of the Rockefeller Foundation in New York. In 1961, President John F. Kennedy asked Rusk to serve as secretary of state. Rusk held that position until 1969.

As secretary of state, Rusk was responsible for a number of major diplomatic missions. In 1962, during the Cuban Missile Crisis, Secretary Rusk convinced President Kennedy to rely on a blockade instead of military force. Rusk also negotiated the Nuclear Test Ban Treaty between the Soviet Union and the United States, which ended the above-ground testing of nuclear bombs. It was, however, his position on the Vietnam War that most defined his years of public service. For his support of the war, Rusk was ridiculed on many college campuses across the nation where antiwar protests raged.

When Rusk retired, he returned to the University of Georgia to teach. In 1977, he was honored with the establishment of the Dean Rusk Center for International and Comparative Law. In 1985, Davidson College also established a Dean Rusk International Studies Program in his honor.

Secretary Rusk died in Athens in 1994 and was laid to rest in Oconee Hill Cemetery alongside the campus of the University he loved.

and state governments used heavy-handed methods to suppress the war's opponents. Belief that the war was necessary to contain communism decreased. Returning veterans were met with scorn and hostility rather than the victory parades that followed the return of the nation's soldiers in World Wars I and II.

After his election in 1968, President Richard Nixon promised to bring American troops home. He tried to force the communists to negotiate a peace by increasing bombings. As a result, thousands more were killed and injured, and the sentiment against the war grew even stronger.

Finally, in January 1973, a cease-fire was declared, and United States involvement in the war came to an end. More than 2,000,000 Vietnamese and 57,000 Americans died. At least 1,200 Americans were listed as missing. There was no clear victor, although Vietnam is now united under a communist government.

The war led to a reluctance to use military force. People feared being drawn into another long, divisive war. It was not until the Persian Gulf War of 1991 that the American people again supported large-scale military action.

Watergate

In June 1972, police arrested a group of men for breaking into and "bugging" the Democratic National Committee offices at the Watergate building in Washington, D.C. Investigating newspaper reporters discovered that some of the burglars had worked for a committee to re-elect President Richard Nixon. Nixon denied any connection between the burglary and the White House. However, the newspaper investigative teams probed further and uncovered additional information that pointed to a cover-up at the highest level of government. When the

burglars were tried in early 1973, one of them talked. What emerged was a story of the abuse of power by the White House.

During its investigations, the U.S. Senate committee discovered that Nixon tape-recorded all of his Oval Office conversations. President Nixon continued to deny any involvement in **Watergate** and refused to give up the tapes. Eventually the Supreme Court ruled that the president had to turn over the tapes. When the tapes were reviewed, they showed that President Nixon knew of the Watergate burglary and had tried to cover it up. A number of people connected to the administration were convicted of Watergate-related crimes. The House of Representatives prepared to impeach President Nixon, but he resigned on August 8, 1974. The new president, Gerald Ford, pardoned Nixon rather than see him tried in criminal court.

The Watergate affair showed first and foremost that no person was above the law, not even the president. The affair also led Americans to become more cynical about their government, a situation that continues to this day. And it popularized the practice of using investigative reporting teams to dig up and use all sorts of information to attract the eye of the reading and television viewing public. This practice has undoubtedly uncovered news items about which the public should be aware. However, it also has led to charges of the invasion of an individual's privacy and the trampling of his or her rights all in the cause of the public's "right to know."

Top: President Nixon is besieged by reporters seeking information about Watergate, the scandal that eventually drove him from office. **Above:** Sam Ervin chaired the U.S. Senate's Watergate hearings.

The Energy Crisis

In October 1973, war broke out in the Middle East between Egypt and Israel. U.S. support for Israel caused OPEC (the Organization of Petroleum Exporting Countries) to cut oil production and to place an embargo on oil to the United States. Fuel shortages hit America in 1973. Some schools closed temporarily. Employees faced workplaces where temperatures had been lowered. The lines to buy gasoline stretched for blocks at service stations. The price of airline tickets soared as airlines found themselves unable to afford jet fuel. Businesses dependent on oil or oil products had to lay off workers or even close down. People stopped buying large gas-guzzling cars, which led to layoffs in the automotive industry. They began buying European, high-mileage compact cars, forcing American automakers into the compact car market.

Although it was not quite that bad in Georgia, most thermostats were set at 68° or lower, and sweaters suddenly became quite popular. Georgians accustomed to leisurely four- and five-hour drives to the mountains or the beach canceled or postponed vacation or weekend plans. Teenagers who were used to "driving around" suddenly realized allowances would not cover gas costs. All over the state, people began car pooling to and from work. Mass transit systems took on a new life, and multilane highways started adding high occupancy lanes just for vehicles with two or more passengers.

One solution to America's dependence on foreign oil resources came with the oil discovered at Prudhoe Bay in the North Slope in northern Alaska. In 1977, a pipeline began carrying the oil over eight hundred miles through Alaskan wilderness to the port of Valdez. From there, it was

Spotlight on the Economy

Economic Cycles

As you have read about the history of our state in the twentieth century, you have covered all of the major steps in the state's economic cycle. Our state's economy does not stand still, it moves in cycles. Economic cycles have three critical points— inflation, recession, and depression.

Inflation occurs when there is enough money in circulation for people to spend, but not enough goods and services to spend the money on. For example, imagine that teenagers have enough spending money but that there is a shortage of the sneakers teenagers like. Prices for those sneakers would go up because teenagers would be willing to pay more for a product in short supply. As a result, inflation causes higher prices. Normally, inflation leads to an increase in demand for goods and services, an increase in the production of goods and services, an increase in employment, and an increase in wages and salaries because more people are working.

When prices get so high that people cannot afford to pay them, the economic cycle turns to a recession. Recessions occur because people will not or cannot afford goods and services. Recession leads to a decrease in the demand for products or services, a decrease in the sales of products because prices are too high, a decrease in production of goods since sales are declining, an increase in unemployment when businesses start laying off people, and a decrease in wages and salaries since fewer people are working.

Occasionally, when a recession lasts for too long and the economy does not recover, the cycle leads into a *depression*. A depression causes a decline in business, high unemployment, and low wages.

The economy never stands still. It continuously moves in a cycle from inflation to recession with an occasional tilt to a depression.

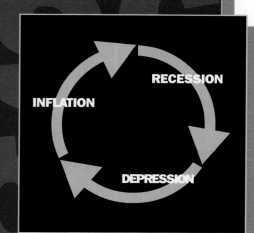

INFLATION • RECESSION • DEPRESSION

transported by tankers to refineries in the "lower 48" states. The success of the pipeline has led energy corporations to push for additional drilling in national park and wilderness areas despite protests by most of the nation's environmentalists.

The 1970s fuel shortage led Americans to question what the country could do to lessen our dependence on Middle East oil. Some argued we should drill for oil in wilderness areas and national preserves. Others argued for the development of renewable fuel sources. Thirty-five years later, the United States is still searching for solutions. Your expertise may be needed to solve this problem.

A Final Note

Few words in the English language have been more misunderstood than the term *tolerance*. What exactly does it mean? First of all, it does not mean that you have to approve of, like, or hang out with those whose values differ from yours.

Tolerance means respect. It means trying to understand and care for others who may be of a different race, color, sex, religious belief, or socioeconomic background. It means being kind to those with different abilities or talents. Tolerance means observing the human rights of all of those around you.

Much of this period in our history is about tolerance. Make a list of ten things you can do in school and at home or in the community to show your tolerance for others.

Chapter Summary

- Veterans of World War II returned to a state, and a nation, full of change.
- For most of the 1950s, prosperity marked our state and nation.
- The Cold War did have some hot spots, including Korea and Vietnam.
- Georgia moved from an economy dominated by agriculture to a more diversified economy as businesses and industries grew.
- The so-called Three Governors Episode was an embarrassment for the state.
- Governor Carl Sanders expanded the state's educational system, opening junior colleges and vocational programs.
- During the struggle for civil rights, Georgian Dr. Martin L. King, Jr., was a national leader of nonviolent protests and demonstrations to bring about change.
- The Civil Rights Act of 1964 and the Voting Rights Act of 1965 were hallmarks of the civil rights struggles of the 1960s.
- The 1960s and 1970s were marked by protests, first in the struggle for civil rights, then in the struggle for equal rights for women, and later in the protests against the Vietnam War.
- Watergate added to the lack of confidence Americans had in their government.
- Former Governor Jimmy Carter became the first Georgian to be elected president of the United States.

Chapter Review

Reviewing People, Places, and Terms

Use each of the following terms in a sentence describing Georgia or the United States during this period.

1. baby boom
2. *Brown v. Board of Education*
3. Civil Rights Act of 1964
4. Cold War
5. one-person, one-vote concept
6. reapportion
7. sit-in
8. Voting Rights Act of 1965
9. women's rights movement

Understanding the Facts

1. Explain Georgia's "Three Governors Episode." Who were the major characters involved and how was the issue resolved?

2. Why was Georgia's county unit system ended?

3. Which governor might be known as the father of the junior college system in Georgia?

4. What Supreme Court decision ended the separate-but-equal segregation of public schools?

5. Whose arrest led to the Montgomery bus boycott? Why was this person arrested?

6. What prize was awarded to Dr. Martin Luther King, Jr., in 1964?

7. What bill did the march from Selma to Montgomery influence Congress to pass?

8. What Georgian was elected president of the United States in 1976?

9. When were the Embassy hostages released by Iran? What was the significance of that date?

10. What are affirmative action programs?

Developing Critical Thinking

1. How do you think television influenced Americans' opinions and actions during the Vietnam War?

2. During this period there were significant changes to education in Georgia – the expansion of the school year to nine months, the addition of the twelfth grade in schools, the establishment of junior colleges, the use of a sales tax to fund education, and so on. Which do you think was the most significant?

3. Affirmative action programs have come under increasing criticism in recent years. Many white males claim they are victims of a form of "reverse discrimination." What is reverse discrimination? Do you agree or disagree with the criticism of affirmative action programs?

4. What do you think could be done to eliminate discrimination and prejudice that still exists?

5. In recent years, there have been court cases against large businesses for not employing persons with disabilities. How are these cases like those of the NAACP in the 1960s?

Checking It Out

1. During the 1960s, the slogan "Black is beautiful" became very popular with African Americans. Research the development of that slogan and explain what you think it means. Why did the slogan appeal to so many African Americans? Why did it serve as a challenge to so many whites? Is the slogan still in popular use today?

2. In the 1960s and 1970s, sightings of UFOs (unidentified flying objects) were common

throughout the nation including in Georgia. Use your research skills to find out about UFOs and sightings in our state. What is your explanation of such sightings?

3. During the 1970s, there was public debate over whether nuclear power plants were safe. The debate continues today, although "safe" has been expanded to include safe from terrorist attacks. Research the number, location, and uses of nuclear power plants in Georgia. Indicate their locations on a Georgia map.

4. A unique mystery of this time period was the "Bermuda Triangle." The strange, peculiar, and unexplained disappearances of ships and airplanes produced many theories. In 1945, five U.S. Navy bombers flew over the triangle and were never seen again. One of the pilots radioed, "Cannot see land. We seem to be off course." Silence followed. Try your hand at solving the mystery. Research the numbers of ships and planes lost and the variety of explanations. Choose one or two reasonable choices and defend your choices.

Writing Across the Curriculum

1. Suppose you could choose to interview one governor from this time period. Which governor would you select and why? Write out a list of interview questions that you would ask the governor.

2. Two aspects of the Cold War involved fear of an atomic or hydrogen bomb attack on the United States. Adults who were children in school during those years learned about three things: bomb shelters, civil defense shelters, and "duck and cover drills." Interview members of your own family, neighbors (with permission), or teachers about these three phenomena. Write a short report that explains what these shelters and drills were.

3. Imagine that you were present at a major event during this period such as the Montgomery bus

boycott. Write a letter to the editor of your school newspaper summarizing what happened, describing how you feel about what happened, and what influence the event is likely to have on your own future.

Exploring Technology

1. In the late 1960s, the Special Olympics was organized by Eunice Kennedy Shriver. Use your Internet research skills to learn more about this event. Share your findings with your classmates.

2. In the late 1970s, the Environmental Protection Agency (EPA) began alerting citizens that some of the water we were drinking was unsafe due to increased pollutants. Use your Internet skills to check out the situation today. Is the pollution of our water better or worse? Back up your opinion with specific details. Are there lakes, streams, or rivers in our state that are still considered polluted? Where are they and what steps are being taken to correct the problems?

Applying Your Skills

1. Georgia's voting districts are reapportioned each ten years based on federal census population statistics. Examine maps of Georgia's voting districts from the 1960 and 1970 census and compare them with the current voting map for our state. What changes in population have taken place that are reflected on those maps? Is your community in the same voting district as it was in 1960?

2. Make a timeline of Georgia's governors, U.S. senators, and legislators during the period from the end of World War II to the end of the Cold War. Select one national leader and one governor and prepare a chart of their major accomplishments in office.

Peace, Prosperity, and Peril

Opposite page: Stephen Kipkorir of Kenya leads the 1500 metre finals at the 1996 Olympics. Right: An ATF agent examines the sight of the Centennial Park bombing.

The final decades of the twentieth century and the arrival of the new millennium were periods of sharp contrasts in Georgia and the United States. The economies of the nation and the state struggled through the 1980s, often called the "Decade of Greed," only to give rise to an era of prosperity and surplus budgets in the 1990s. As a new millennium began, the free-spending, good times waned and both state and nation grappled once more with budget shortages and difficult financial decisions. Many problems that had been building through the end of the twentieth century came to the forefront as the twentieth-first century began.

As the Cold War with the Soviet Union drew to a close, Americans and Georgians focused their attention on international terrorism. We faced, and continue to face, rising threats to the security of our citizens both abroad and at home. Terrorism spread to include 2001's direct attack on the United States.

Signs of the Times 1980-2005

Population: 5,463,087 in 1980 and 8,186,453 in 2000

Life Expectancy: In the 1980s, males could expect to live 69.9 years, females 77.6 years. At the end of the century, that had risen to 73.1 years and 79.1 years, respectively.

Costs of Living: In the 1980s, a new home cost $76,400, a first-class stamp cost $0.15, a gallon of regular gas was $1.25, a dozen eggs cost $0.91, and a gallon of milk was $2.16. The minimum wage in 1980 was $3.10; in 2000, it was $5.15.

Art/Architecture: Outstanding artists of the period included Wayne Thiebaud, Christo, Keith Haring, Andy Warhol, Annie Liebowitz, William Eggleston, and Maya Lin. Famous architectural highlights included Trump Tower in New York, the High Museum in Atlanta, Union Station in Washington, and the Sunshine Skyway Bridge in St. Petersburg. There was an emphasis on making offices and homes energy efficient.

Fads/Fashions: Fast food restaurants such as McDonald's, Burger King, Hardee's, and Taco Bell grew in popularity. Favored candies included Skittles and Sweetarts. Cabbage Patch dolls became collectibles. Coca Cola introduced the New Coke, but sales plummeted. Leading clothing designers were Anne Klein, Perry Ellis, Donna Karan, Calvin Klein, Liz Claiborne, DKNY, Tommy Hilfiger. Dress down Fridays and casual Fridays became popular at work.

Music: MTV was born, and the CD revolutionized the music industry. Pop, rock, New Wave, punk, country, rap, and hip hop were all popular. Artists included L. L. Cool J., Talking Heads, David Bowie, Garth Brooks, George Strait, Willie Nelson, Mariah Carey, Billy Joel, Bruce Springsteen, U2, and Britney Spears. Musicals were big including *Cats, Les Miserables,* and *The Producers.*

Literature: Online bookstores such as Amazon.com debuted. Diet books, self-improvement books, and self-help titles became best-sellers. Popular writers included John Grisham, Stephen King, Scott Turow, Michael Crichton, Tom Clancy, Danielle Steele, Tom Wolfe, and Alice Walker. Nonfiction best-sellers included *All I Really Need to Know I Learned in Kindergarten, The Beverly Hills Diet,* and *Iacocca: An Autobiography.*

Religion: The National Council of Churches of Christ issued new Bibles using gender-free terms such as *humankind* and *humanity* rather than *mankind.*

Leisure Time: Video games became very popular. Team sports were popular in school especially football, basketball, baseball, and soccer. Favorite television programs included "Cheers," "Sixty Minutes," "Seinfeld," "Touched by an Angel," "Friends," "Frasier," "Survivor," "American Idol," "NYPD Blue," "CSI," "West Wing," and "Law and Order." Movies of the period were *Driving Miss Daisy, Cocoon, On Golden Pond, Tootsie, Dances with Wolves, Silence of the Lambs, Schindler's List, Forrest Gump* (filmed in Georgia), *Braveheart,* and *Titanic.*

Education: Statewide and national testing to measure student achievement spread throughout the educational systems of country, as did efforts to hold schools and teachers accountable. Federal and state "No Child Left Behind" legislation passed to provide educational accountability, eliminate social promotions, provide remedial resources for children unable to meet criteria for promotions.

Science/Inventions: Americans began using personal computers at offices and homes. The first reusable space shuttle, *Columbia,* was launched. VCR sales rose 72 percent in one year to become the fastest selling home appliance in history. Americans began trading on the stock market over the Internet.

Transportation: Discount airfares were popular. Minivans and RV's made travel and camping out popular.

Figure 42 Timeline: 1980–2005

1993
HOPE scholarship program begun

1995
Newt Gingrich became Speaker of the House

1992
Georgia Dome completed

1996
Georgia hosted Centennial Olympic Games

1982
New state constitution

1986
QBE Act passed

1990
Zell Miller elected governor

2003
Sonny Perdue became governor
New Georgia flag adopted

1980	1985	1990	1995	2000	2005

1983
Sally Ride became first American woman in space

1989
Berlin Wall torn down

1995
Oklahoma City bombing

2003
Operation Iraqi Freedom

1986
Space shuttle *Challenger* exploded

1990
World Wide Web developed

2001
Terrorists attack on U.S.
Operation Enduring Freedom

1991
Persian Gulf War

1993
First World Trade Center bombing

1998
President Clinton impeached but acquitted

Section Preview

As you read, look for:
• the end of the Cold War,
• Georgia's governors in the 1980s,
• the "two Georgias" debate, and
• vocabulary terms: telecommute, email, Reaganomics, Quality Basic Education, and per capita income.

The 1980s

The 1980s was the age of the personal computer. As small computers became more affordable, they became standard equipment in offices as well as homes. Adding personal computers in the home allowed people to telecommute, to work at home while keeping in touch with the office through the computer. Email (sending messages electronically on the computer) became standard as the World Wide Web was developed in 1990.

Did You Know?

"Snail mail" is the term used to describe the postal service.

Schools began to purchase computers for use in classrooms. The children of the decade became the first generation of Americans to grow up using computers as comfortably and naturally as their parents had used such common household appliances as dishwashers and toasters.

Personal computers were only a small part of the technology leaps of the period. Computers soon replaced cash registers and adding machines and led to the widespread use of automatic teller machines (ATMs). Computers were joined by other devices made possible by the use of transistors and microchips—fiber optics, fax machines, scanners, cellular telephones, and the Internet.

The children of the 1980s also grew up in front of television sets. During the decade, the rapid expansion in cable channels meant that two or three networks no longer had a hold on television programming. The growth in satellite dishes and cable services led to new television networks for specific, small audiences. There were channels that appealed only to men, only to women, only to children, only to animal lovers, only to shoppers, only to golfers. Channels appeared for doctors, for schools, for lawyers, for ministers. Homes received hundreds of channels, some from international sites. And the children of the 1980s watched plenty of television. It is estimated that the average American spent over thirty hours a week in front of the television set.

The End of the Cold War

The 1980s saw President Carter defeated in his bid for a second term as the nation turned to 69-year-old Ronald Reagan, a former actor and governor of California. Reagan was called the "Great Communicator" for his ease in using television to strike a positive cord with citizens throughout the nation.

Reagan, who served from 1981 to 1989, is remembered most for two aspects of his presidency. The first was an economic policy known as Reaganomics, which defined the 1980s. The major features of his policy included supply-side economics, tax cuts, heavy defense spending, limited government, reductions in government workers, and limited regulations on industry and growth.

Above: Rural residents often have few choices for their television viewing and usually cannot receive cable television programs at all. A satellite TV dish can pick up television signals from satellites. That gives dish users many more choices.

Spotlight on the Economy

Reaganomics

President Reagan believed in limiting the role of the federal government. As a part of that policy, he reduced federal spending on domestic programs and reduced the number of government employees. He also moved to deregulate industries such as the airlines and savings and loan associations by reducing government controls.

Reagan's supply-side economics was based on a theory that lowered taxes would lead to an expansion of the economy as business and industry, and even individuals, invested the money they saved on taxes in the economy. Reagan's massive tax cuts, which were a part of the Economic Recovery Tax Act of 1981, cut income taxes by 25 percent over a three-year period and cut capital gains taxes. Putting more money in the pockets of individuals and corporations was supposed to result in an expanding economy that would be stronger and healthier. But inflation still gripped the nation and the Federal Reserve Board had to raise interest rates, making it harder for banks, businesses, and industries to borrow money.

Reagan also believed that the nation's security depended upon a strong defense. He increased military spending in unprecedented amounts as he continued America's Cold War with the Soviet Union. While Reagan reduced domestic spending, he could not control Congress, which continued to fund social programs. Between Congress's spending on domestic issues and Reagan's spending on national defense, the nation spent far more than it took in. The federal deficit was almost $200 billion by the end of Reagan's first term.

In 1982, the nation entered a severe recession. Over 10 percent of the nation's work force was unemployed. In 1983, that recession slowed as the Federal Reserve Board cut interest rates to make borrowing easier. Armed with

Above: Ronald Reagan was one of the most popular presidents of the twentieth century. He had a remarkable ability to connect with millions of people across the country.

borrowing power and with the extra income from the tax cuts, citizens began to spend more and the economy improved. Businesses began to earn a profit again, and unemployed workers were hired back into their jobs. By the end of Reagan's tenure as president, unemployment had dropped to 5.5 percent, the lowest in over a decade. But, the national debt continued to rise as Reagan and Congress spent money they did not have.

Near the close of Reagan's presidency, in October 1987, the stock market lost over 500 points in one day. While the crash did not cause another "Great Depression," it did signal that the American economy was in trouble. The government, America's businesses and industry, and individual citizens were all spending more than they were making and were borrowing too much. Reaganomics had provided a good time for almost a full decade, but economic problems were looming in the nation's future.

The second aspect of his presidency was Reagan's transition from the tough, defense-minded Cold Warrior to an international peacemaker. In that role, he worked with the Soviet Union's Mikhail Gorbachev to end the Cold War, which had dominated American foreign policy since the close of World War II.

The end of the Cold War led to the tearing down of the wall that had split Germany in two since 1961. It was a symbol of the closed society of the communist-ruled Soviet Union. In 1989, crowds of German citizens literally tore down the wall that divided Berlin into East and West.

At the same time, the people in Poland, Czechoslovakia, Bulgaria, Romania, and East Germany overthrew their communist governments and demanded free elections. By 1991, the Soviet Union had collapsed as its satellite republics declared their independence.

Above: For almost thirty years, the Berlin Wall was a symbol of the Cold War. In November 1989, East and West German citizens tore the wall down.

Georgia During the 1980s

For most of the 1980s, two men led the state of Georgia—George Busbee and Joe Frank Harris. Both took office on plans for economic development and educational improvements, and both leaders delivered on their commitments to the voters.

George Busbee

Serving as Georgia's governor from 1975 through 1983, George Busbee had promised Georgians a businesslike approach to government and improvements in education. Busbee, a native of Vienna, focused on bringing new industries to the state. Each year from 1978 through 1983, Busbee brought over $1 billion in new and expanded industrial development to Georgia. Many of his economic expansions were the result of his efforts to have foreign companies invest in Georgia. Under his leadership, international facilities in the state jumped from 350 in 1978 to 1,255 in 1988. That expansion continued in the 1990s. Today, Georgia is known as a global business center. There are over 1,600 internationally owned facilities in Georgia, representing 39 different countries. Over 53 nations have consular, trade, or chamber of commerce offices in Georgia, and there are 10 international banks based in the state.

Busbee is also credited with expanding the Department of Industry and Trade and for opening state information offices in Canada, Europe, and the Far East. He provided

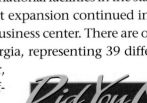

Did You Know?

As of September 2002, there were nearly 125,5000 employees working in international facilities in Georgia.

support to upgrade the state's ports and highway system, which helped the state's economy by allowing business expansions, increased imports and exports, and commerce.

Joe Frank Harris

Governor Joe Frank Harris served from 1983 to 1991 and had to deal with a slowing economy and the need for increased taxes. He too worked to ensure Georgia's economic growth, and he brought over 850,000 new jobs into the state.

In addition to the growth in jobs and investments, Harris provided leadership for the financing and construction of the Georgia Dome stadium in Atlanta and expansions of the World Congress Center. The domed stadium was located next to the Georgia World Congress Center, a convention hall and exhibition center, which had opened in 1976. The grand opening of the Georgia Dome was held in 1992; today, it serves as home to the Atlanta Falcons.

Above: Joe Frank Harris served nine terms in the Georgia House of Representatives before being elected governor in 1982.

The Georgia Dome, the Georgia World Congress Center, and Centennial Olympic Park are owned by the state of Georgia and are operated by the Georgia World Congress Center Authority. Together the three facilities make up one of the largest convention, sports, and entertainment complexes in the world and annually draw hundreds of thousands of tourists and convention-eers to the state. The complex has hosted the Centennial Olympic Games, two Super Bowls, an NCAA Final Four in basketball, and a long list of con-certs, conventions, and special events. All of these events bring millions of dollars into Georgia's economy each year.

Did You Know?

When it was completed in 1992, the Georgia Dome had the largest cable-supported fabric roof in the world.

Educational Improvements

Both Governor Busbee and Governor Harris worked to improve education in Georgia. Governor Busbee raised teacher salaries and established a statewide half-day kindergarten program. Governor Harris extended that kindergarten program to a full-day program. In addition, Harris organized business leaders, educators, legislators, and citizens to develop a legislative program called Quality Basic Education (QBE). That program standardized curriculum for all schools in the state, equalized funding for all 187 of the state's school sys-tems, implemented statewide testing of students, and required accountability performance testing for the certification of public school teachers.

In addition, Harris had a unique opportunity to exercise one of the most important informal powers of governor—the power to make appointments. During his two terms, Governor Harris appointed all fifteen members of the

Georgia Board of Regents (the group that controls the University System of Georgia and all public colleges and universities), all ten members of the Board of Education (the group that controls the public elementary, middle, and high schools of the state), and the State School Superintendent (the chief executive officer of the public schools). Such an opportunity will not likely happen again. Just through appointments alone, Governor Harris's influence on education was unparalleled.

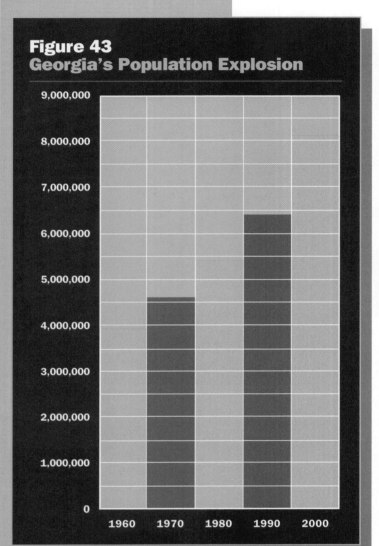

Figure 43
Georgia's Population Explosion

Georgia Gets a New Constitution

During the 1980s, Georgia also got a new state constitution. Governor Busbee recognized that the state had one of the longest and most complicated constitutions in the nation. It was over 600,000 words long. The U.S. Constitution contains only 1,800 words, quite a bit shorter and much easier to understand than Georgia's document.

The governor organized a commission of citizens, business leaders, educators, and government experts to draft a new constitution. The process took over five years, but the state's constitution was approved by the voters in 1982. It is the constitution under which Georgia operates today.

The Two-Georgia Debate Begins

During the 1980s, Georgia experienced a decade of economic growth. Georgia's population has expanded rapidly since the 1960s. Individuals and businesses moving into Georgia were attracted by the state's mild climate, low taxes, low fuel costs, abundant land, and a nonunionized labor force willing to work for lower salaries than workers in other parts of the country.

This pattern of population "in-migration" reversed a trend that saw Georgia losing population or remaining stagnant since the end of the Civil War. People had moved out of Georgia seeking more job opportunities, more educational opportunities for their children, and a higher standard of living. States like Georgia, with an economy based mainly on agriculture, energy, or heavy manufacturing, lost their most talented and educated young workers. In the 1960s, as the state's economy diversified and as air conditioning made life in the hot South more comfortable, more people moved into our state. The descendants of African American citizens who had fled Georgia after the Civil War also began to return to the state as decades of racial injustice and discrimination were replaced by moderation, by integrated schools, and by improved economic opportunities with a higher standard of living. Georgia is now one of the fastest growing states in the nation.

Population growth brings more jobs and opportunities. It also produces new tax sources that increase revenues needed for basic services. However, Georgia's population growth has not spread evenly across the state. One part of the state expanded and prospered, while the other did not. One part of the state increased in political power as the voter rolls grew, while the other part of the state lost political power as the numbers of its voters declined. One part of the state gained jobs and employment opportunities, while the other part lost jobs and employment opportunities dwindled. Soon, it appeared that there were really two Georgias. One was prosperous and expanding, making Georgia the fourth fastest-growing state in the country. The other Georgia was suffering from unemployment, a declining population, and diminishing influence and power.

At first, Georgia's rapid growth was in the city of Atlanta. But as the capital city expanded to become one of America's premier cities, the rural areas of the state began to receive less of the state's resources. Highway growth, business developments, educational opportunities, and industry focused on Atlanta. Georgia had the second fastest-growing **per capita income** (the total income of all people in an area divided by the total population of the area) in the Southeast over the past twenty years. But 139 of the 159 counties still had per capita income levels below the average for the Southeastern region, and over one million Georgians lived below the national poverty level. As fast as Atlanta grew, rural Georgia suffered. The two-Georgia conflict was Atlanta versus the rest of the state.

Atlanta's growth soon spread into the suburbs and then into the surrounding counties until the entire metropolitan area, which now includes forty-two counties, shared in the growth and prosperity. But large pockets of rural Georgia continued to decline. Their schools became less effective just as their citizens needed more technological training. Their job opportunities faltered as plants and mills closed, farms shut down, unemployment rates rose, and fewer dollars were available for essential services. Young people in these communities finished high school and fled to the cities. Suddenly the two-Georgia conflict was not just Atlanta versus

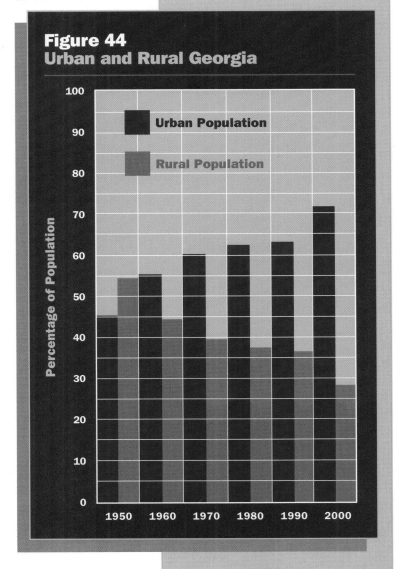

Figure 44
Urban and Rural Georgia

Urban Population

Rural Population

Percentage of Population

1950 1960 1970 1980 1990 2000

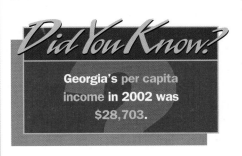

Did You Know?

Georgia's **per capita income in 2002 was** $28,703.

Above: One part of the two-Georgias debate has been the unequal educational opportunities available in urban and rural areas. The Blairsville campus of the North Georgia Technical College is part of the effort to bring more colleges to rural areas.

the rest of the state. It became the rural counties versus the metropolitan counties.

Today, the result of these population changes can be seen in the percentages of Georgia's residents who live in urban and rural areas. Just over 50 percent of Georgia's population lives in the Metropolitan Atlanta area, and just over 70 percent of the state's total population lives in an urban area. In contrast, just before the population migration began in the 1960s, only 45 percent of Georgia's citizens lived in urban areas, and the dominant industry was agriculture.

Are there two Georgias? Are the economies of the rural and the urban sections of the state so different that we have become two states? What has been done to pull all of Georgia together into one prosperous state?

Rural development programs, expanded highway and rail services into rural areas, expansion of the University System's community and technical colleges, improvements in the state's elementary and secondary schools, and the efforts of rural communities to improve their own economy have done much to eliminate the charge that there are two Georgias. Still, there is much more to do. Of the rural counties in Georgia, fifty continue to be classified by the Georgia Rural Development Council as lagging or declining in 2000. Only fifty Georgia counties were classified as developing or rapidly developing.

Georgia has begun a 25-year program to spend $1.6 billion to bring rural Georgia up to par with the more affluent urban and suburban areas. But even economic developments cannot quiet the argument about two Georgias. In 2004, for example, the issues of unfair differences between rural and urban Georgia focus on more than just population growth, jobs, and development. They also include inner city declines, educational equity, and water resources.

It's Your Turn

1. What was the strongest area of economic growth for Georgia during the 1980s? How will that impact Georgia's future?
2. What is the World Congress Center?
3. What was the massive reorganization of education and educational funding led by Governor Joe Frank Harris?
4. When was Georgia's current state constitution ratified? Which governor led the charge to streamline the state constitution?
5. What was the original basis for the "two Georgias" argument?

Section 2

The 1990s

In 1988, the voters selected George Herbert Walker Bush of Texas to be the nation's forty-first president. President Bush took over a nation in the midst of a recession.

One way companies tried to deal with the recession was through **downsizing**. Businesses downsized by firing or laying off workers to cut costs, maintain profits, and stay competitive with other businesses. Those cuts, however, put millions of Americans out of work, and unemployment skyrocketed again. As many as 10 million workers were unemployed in 1992, and businesses struggled to stay afloat and competitive.

The unemployment of the early 1990s hit everyone. Managers and middle-managers, corporate leaders, planners, and professionals alike faced sudden unemployment at a time when many families were in debt from the borrow-and-spend practices of the 1980s. People lost their homes and cars, and personal bankruptcies rose. (**Bankruptcy** occurs when people or businesses cannot pay their debts and seek the help of the courts to manage their affairs.) Generations of workers who did not remember the hard lessons of the Great Depression quickly found out why their parents and grandparents had been so frugal.

The Persian Gulf War

President Bush also had to deal with an international crisis. In August 1990, Iraq invaded Kuwait, hoping to seize Kuwait's oil and gain a port on the Persian Gulf. The United Nations demanded that Iraq withdraw.

The United States joined a coalition of twenty-six nations to free Kuwait. *Operation Desert Shield* was the name given to a five-month build-up of military forces in Saudi Arabia and the Persian Gulf region. President Bush and other world leaders hoped that Iraq would leave Kuwait; they set a deadline of January 15, 1991, for Saddam Hussein to withdraw his troops.

He refused, and *Operation Desert Storm* began on January 16, 1991. The allies

Section Preview

As you read, look for:
• the economic problems of the early 1990s,
• the Persian Gulf War,
• the 1996 Olympic Games, and
• vocabulary terms: downsizing, bankruptcy, HOPE scholarship program, and infrastructure.

Below: These humvees are carrying troops to the Persian Gulf War. **Bottom:** Georgia families greet troops returning from the Gulf War.

After the Persian Gulf War, the United Nations Special Commission (UNSCOM) was established to identify and destroy Saddam Hussein's weapons of mass destruction. The Iraqi leader was less than cooperative. What do you think cartoonist Walt Handelsman was trying to say here?

Above: John Lewis has been at the forefront of progressive social and political causes for more than forty years.

bombed Iraq for one month before ground troops landed under the leadership of General Norman Schwarzkopf. In one hundred hours, the US-led troops freed the Kuwaiti people and pushed Iraq back across its borders. On March 3, Iraq accepted the terms of a cease fire, and the fighting ended.

Left behind was an ecological disaster. Retreating Iraqi troops had blown up and set fire to oil wells across the country. Over 10 million barrels of oil had been released into the Persian Gulf, polluting the water for years. Marine wildlife was devastated, particularly birds.

Political Changes in a Conservative South

During the 1980s and 1990s, politics underwent a major shift in many southern states, including Georgia. While most citizens continued to elect Democrats to statewide offices, they were more conservative in national politics and tended to favor Republicans in national elections. This led to the election of more Republicans to the U.S. Congress from Georgia and, eventually, to the establishment of a real two-party system in the state for the first time since the Bourbon Redeemers over one hundred years ago.

In 1980, Mack Mattingly of St. Simons Island was the first Republican elected to the U.S. Senate from Georgia since Reconstruction. In the 1992 elections, Republicans won most of Georgia's congressional elections, although Atlanta Democrat Cynthia McKinney became the first African American woman from Georgia elected to Congress.

John Lewis

The senior member of Georgia's congressional delegation is John Lewis of Atlanta. Democrat Lewis was first elected to represent Georgia's Fifth Congressional District in the House of Representatives in November 1986.

Lewis was one of the civil rights leaders who worked with Dr. Martin Luther King, Jr., in the 1960s. He was a "freedom rider" who volunteered to help fight segregation at bus terminals across the South. He also was one of the founders of the Student Nonviolent Coordinating Committee and organized sit-ins and other activities during the civil rights movement. Lewis helped plan, and was a keynote speaker for, the famous 1963 March on Washington. He also took part in the march across the Edmund Pettus Bridge in Selma in March 1965.

From that background, Lewis won election to the Atlanta City Council in 1981. He resigned from the council to run for office in 1986.

Lewis has been a member of the House Budget Committee, the Ways and Means Committee, and the Subcommittee on Health. Lewis has also served as senior chief deputy to the Democratic whip (the party leader in Congress).

Newt Gingrich

In 1994, Republicans gained a majority in the U.S. House of Representatives for the first time in forty years, and Georgian Newt Gingrich was elected Speaker of the House. In the 1994 campaign, Gingrich designed a "Contract with America," a list of the actions Republicans would take once they became the majority party in the House. The document was given much of the credit for the party's success.

As the Republican House and the Democratic White House battled, Gingrich fought to reduce government spending while President Bill Clinton fought to save or increase government social programs. The government became deadlocked and could not agree on a budget in 1995; for a short while, the government was shut down completely. Voters and the party, rightly or wrongly, blamed Gingrich for the shutdown.

In 1996, the Republican party had expected to sweep the elections, but it did not happen. Instead, there was a disappointing turn-out of Republican voters, and the party held Gingrich somewhat responsible for the losses. In January 1997, Gingrich was again selected Speaker of the House. However, in November 1998 he resigned his speakership and resigned from his seat in Congress.

Sam Nunn

The most influential Georgia congressional leader of the era was Democratic Senator Sam Nunn, a native of Perry, who served in the U.S. Senate from 1972 to 1996. Nunn's career in the Senate included the chairmanship of the Senate Armed Services Committee from 1987 until 1996. Nunn was considered by many to be the nation's most influential civilian expert on military affairs.

Nunn also chaired the Senate Subcommittee on Investigations and served on the Governmental Affairs Committee and the Select Committee on Intelligence. He also served on

Top: New Gingrich was the chief architect of the Republican "Contract with America" and a key player in the Republican party's regaining control of Congress after forty years. **Above:** Sam Nunn represented Georgia for twenty-four years in the U.S. Senate, where he became an expert on military affairs.

Did You Know?

Gingrich was first elected to represent Georgia's Sixth Congressional District in the House of Representatives in 1978.

numerous subcommittees, including Government Information and Regulation, Small Business, Urban and Minority-Owned Business Development, and Rural Economy and Family Farming.

Since his retirement from the Senate in 1996, Nunn has been a partner in King and Spalding Law Firm in Atlanta, where he focuses on international and corporate issues. He is also a distinguished professor for the Sam Nunn School of International Affairs at Georgia Tech.

Zell Miller

Zell Miller, a native of Young Harris, served four consecutive terms as Georgia's lieutenant governor, beginning in 1974. He was first elected Georgia's governor in 1990. He served until 1999, almost the whole of the decade. During his two terms in office, Governor Miller addressed the rise in crime with tougher sentencing guidelines for criminals and "boot-camp" style prisons for non-violent offenders. He worked with the legislature to pass tougher ethics laws. He was the first governor to establish a policy to preserve Georgia's wild areas as public lands.

But Governor Miller will probably be most remembered for his impact on education in the state. He implemented a lottery designed to support a statewide pre-kindergarten program, the purchase of computers for schools and colleges, and the HOPE scholarship program.

The HOPE (Helping Outstanding Pupils Educationally) scholarship program provides money for tuition, fees, and books for Georgia high school students who graduate with a B average in core curriculum classes and who choose to attend one of Georgia's public colleges or universities. In addition, scholarships of up to $3,000 may be awarded to eligible students attending a private Georgia college or university. The PROMISE teacher scholarship program provides tuition assistance to undergraduate students who plan to become teachers in Georgia's public schools. The HOPE scholarship program, begun in 1993, has provided over $2 billion in assistance to over 700,000 college students. The program, which the *Los Angeles Times* called "the most far-reaching scholarship problem in the nation" has been copied by other states.

Governor Miller's HOPE program provided a pre-kindergarten program for four-year-olds, which began in 1993. That program has received more than $2 billion and has served over 560,000 children throughout the state.

The lottery monies are also used for technology grants to Georgia's schools and colleges. Since 1993, over $1.8 billion has been spent on technology advancements in education.

Above: Zell Miller has been a popular politician. He easily won four elections for lieutenant governor and two elections for governor.

Governor Miller also promoted the economic development of the north Georgia mountains. One major accomplishment was the completion of the Appalachian Developmental Highway, known as the Zell Miller Mountain Parkway. The highway runs from Atlanta's metropolitan area through the mountains of north Georgia and opened the area for tourism as well as business and industry.

Following his term as governor, Miller was appointed to complete the U.S. Senate term of Senator Paul Coverdell, who died in 2000. Miller chose not to run for re-election in 2004.

Georgia Hosts the Olympics

The games of the XXVI Olympiad were held in Atlanta in 1996. The Summer Olympics brought over 10,000 athletes representing 197 countries to Georgia, where more than 90,000 volunteers helped pr0duce an outstanding world event. Sites for the Olympic competitions were not just in Atlanta. Athens, Columbus, Jonesboro, and Savannah also hosted competitions for certain sports.

The Olympics brought four long-term benefits to the state. First, millions of dollars were spent to create world-class competition facilities such as the $189 million Olympic Stadium, the 1,400-acre Georgia Horse Park, the $17 million Wolf Creek Shooting Range complex, a Stone Mountain tennis facility, and the $10 million Lake Lanier Rowing Center. In addition, Georgia Tech and Georgia State University received new residence facilities, as well as renovated competition sites.

Below: More than 5,500 people, excluding athletes, took part in the Opening Ceremony of the 1996 Summer Olympic Games at Atlanta's Olympic Stadium. The flags of the various participating countries can be seen at the top of this photograph.

Second, the Olympics brought international recognition to Atlanta. Millions of visitors came to see the Games, and millions more watched on television. Atlanta and the state of Georgia received tremendous media coverage as one of the world's leading business centers.

Third, the Olympics brought volunteer programs, educational and training programs, and employment opportunities to thousands of Georgia's citizens. Fourth, the economic impact of the Olympic Games brought millions of dollars into Georgia's economy.

There were some moments at the Games when Georgia was not seen at its best. A bombing at Centennial Olympic Park on July 29, 1996, killed Alice Hawthorne of Albany and wounded 117, striking a note of fear into athletes and spectators alike. Severe traffic congestion in the Metropolitan Atlanta area made travel from one venue (event site) to another very difficult, and the world's press criticized the Olympic planners for their lack of **infrastructure** (basic facilities such as roads, bridges, and ports) to make transportation work smoothly. There were criticisms of the street vendors and salespersons who seemed to be on every corner. There was even criticism of the overly commercial advertising, particularly by Coca Cola, one of the major sponsors of the events. Nevertheless, the Olympic Games did show off Georgia like no other event ever has.

Southern hospitality, with volunteers working to make sure things ran correctly, was in full bloom. While transportation around the areas was difficult, once visitors arrived at a venue, the competition was unparalleled and excellent. While Atlanta's streets may have been congested, visitors got to see our state's diversity, our graciousness, and our own version of "southern hospitality."

Above: Lake Lanier was the venue (site) for the rowing competition. This is the Italian rowing team.

It's Your Turn

1. What does the term *downsizing* mean?
2. The war against Iraq was a result of its invasion of what nation?
3. Who was the first African American woman elected from Georgia to the U.S. Congress?
4. What does HOPE mean? Where does the HOPE money come from?
5. Who led the establishment of the HOPE program?

Section 3

Terrorism at Home and Abroad

Section Preview

As you read, look for:
• the events of September 11, 2001,
• the United States's reaction to 9/11, and
• vocabulary terms: terrorism and al-Qaeda.

In the 1990s, terrorism against the United States increased. Terrorism is acts of violence aimed at demoralizing or intimidating others.

In 1993, a bomb exploded in the parking garage under the World Trade Center in New York City. The explosion killed six people and injured more than a thousand people. In May 1994, four foreign terrorists were tried and convicted of the bombing. In 1995, the man thought to be the "mastermind" behind the bombing was tried and convicted.

In 1995, a bomb inside a van exploded outside the Murrah federal building in Oklahoma City. One hundred sixty-eight people were killed. Two Americans were later arrested, tried, and convicted in federal court for the terrorist act.

In 1998, U.S. embassies in Kenya and Tanzania were severely damaged by truck bombs that exploded outside the buildings. Over two hundred people were killed, and thousands were injured. The attacks were linked to al-Qaeda, an extremist group of Islamist terrorists led by Osama bin Laden. A number of men were convicted of the bombings.

In addition, there have been attacks on military facilities in Beirut (1983) and Saudi Arabia (1996) and on the guided missile destroyer U.S.S. *Cole* (2000).

In 2001, Republican George W. Bush became president in an election marked by charges of voting irregularities and challenges to election results. Bush was the son of former President George H. W. Bush. It was President George W. Bush who led the country during the worst terrorist attack ever on American soil.

Below: On April 19, 1995, a truck bomb explored at the Murrah Federal Building in Oklahoma City.

"The Day That Changed America"

It was 8:45 a.m. on September 11, 2001. Millions of Americans were finishing breakfast, driving their children to school, dressing for or heading to work, and either listening to the radio or watching morning news shows. One minute later, at 8:46 a.m., our world changed.

News reports said that an American Airlines plane filled with passengers had flown into the North Tower of New York City's World Trade Center. Fire and thick smoke poured out of the top floors of the building. People were shocked by what they thought was a terrible accident. Minutes later,

Below: After the terrorist attack on September 11, 2001, the World Trade Center in New York was reduced to twisted steel.

cameras caught a second passenger jet as it flew into the South Tower at 9:03. Instantly, any idea of an accident was forgotten. The United States had been attacked, and it was not over yet.

As stunned Americans watched the World Trade Center burning, American Airlines Flight 77 bound for Los Angeles was hijacked. It left Dulles International Airport in Washington, D.C., crossed the Potomac River, and crashed into the Pentagon, the symbol of the nation's military establishment. One hundred twenty-four people were killed on the ground, and seventy-six were injured. All of the passengers and crew members of Flight 77 were killed.

At 9:59 a.m., as millions were glued to their television sets, the South Tower of the World Trade Center collapsed, killing those occupants still in the building as well as those firefighters, police officers, Port Authority officers, and rescue personnel who had been trying to save those trapped inside. Twenty-nine minutes later, at 10:28 a.m., the North Tower fell. A total of 2,774 people were killed, and over 2,000 were injured. At about 5:30 p.m., a third tower in the World Trade Center Complex collapsed, and the next day, another building within the complex collapsed.

Most of the thirty-seven passengers on United Flight 93 were businessmen who left Newark International Airport at 8:41 a.m. By 9:35, with the Twin Towers and the Pentagon in flames, a thickly accented voice came over the Flight 93 intercom, "This is your captain. There is a bomb on board. We

are returning to the airport." In the passenger cabin, three men had taken control. When several passengers called spouses and friends to tell them they were being hijacked, the passengers learned of the other events of the morning. Realizing that their hijacked plane was about to be used as a weapon, a number of the passengers rushed the hijackers and the cockpit. There was silence for a few minutes, then the telephones went dead. The airplane crashed in a rural area in southwestern Pennsylvania, killing all aboard. No one knows the intended target of the hijackers; possibilities include the Capitol, the White House, or even Camp David, the presidential retreat. Whatever the terrorists had planned, the brave men and women aboard Flight 93 stopped yet another devastating attack on that day.

Operation Enduring Freedom

Right after September 11, President Bush declared a national emergency and called upon Congress to give him war powers. The United States determined that al-Qaeda was responsible for the September 11 attack. Al-Qaeda was based in Afghanistan, where the terrorist organization was protected by the political and religious Taliban. U.S. government leaders gave the Taliban an ultimatum to close terrorist training camps and hand over al-Qaeda leaders. The Taliban government refused.

President Bush led a coalition of seventy nations in an attack on Osama bin Laden's camps in Afghanistan. The operation was called "Enduring Freedom" and began on October 7, 2001. On December 22, 2001, America's military leaders met in Kabul for a ceremony marking the inauguration of the Afghan interim government, only seventy-eight days after the beginning of combat operations. By the end of March 2002, the Taliban had been removed from power and the al-Qaeda network in Afghanistan had been destroyed. Osama bin Laden, however, had escaped and continued to direct antiterrorist activities.

America's war on terrorism involved more than just military operations. One step in the war on terrorism was the creation of the Department of Homeland Security. Homeland Security is responsible for our nation's overall safety. Its specific role is still evolving and includes everything from

Map 46 Afghanistan

Map Skill: What country lies to the east of Afghanistan?

Top: Georgians in the National Guard and Reserves answered the call to serve in Afghanistan.

maintaining all of our borders to protecting all of our nation's critical installations. By 2004, this cabinet-level organization had a budget of $41 billion and 170,000 employees. U.S. officials have also worked with other nations to seize financial assets of groups like al-Qaeda and to disrupt their international fundraising activities.

Operation Iraqi Freedom

Following the attacks on September 11, 2001, the United States became more concerned about nations that might have weapons of mass destruction that could be used by terrorists throughout the world. One such nation was Iraq.

In September 2002, President Bush addressed the United Nations about the danger posed by Iraq and that country's violations of UN resolutions. In November 2002, the UN Security Council unanimously adopted Resolution 1441 warning Iraq that it faced "serious consequences" if it continued to violate the various UN resolutions.

On March 19, 2003, President Bush addressed the nation to explain that our nation was at war once again. In discussing what was called "Operation Iraqi Freedom," President Bush said,

My fellow citizens, at this hour, American and coalition forces are in the early stages of military operations to disarm Iraq, to free its people and to defend the world from grave danger. . . . Our nation enters this conflict reluctantly—yet, our purpose is sure. The people of the United States and our friends and allies will not live at the mercy of an outlaw regime that threatens the peace with weapons of mass murder. We will meet that threat now, with our Army, Air Force, Navy, Coast Guard and Marines, so that we do not have to meet it later with armies of fire fighters and police and doctors on the streets of our cities.

On May 1, 2003, President Bush declared the combat phase of the war with Iraq ended, although the Iraqis still needed our help to regain control of their country. Iraq's dictator, Saddam Hussein, was finally captured by U.S. troops in December 2003.

Among the Georgians who have lost their lives during the war with Iraq was 19-year-old, Colombia-born Army Pfc. Diego Fernando Rincon. Rincon

TURKEY

SYRIA

LEBANON

ISRAEL

JORDAN

EGYPT

SAUDI ARABIA

• Mosul

Kirkuk •

• Samarra   IRAN

Baghdad ★

Karbala •   • Al Kut

IRAQ

Basra •

KUWAIT

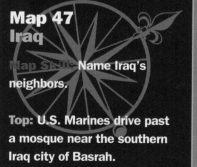

Map 47
Iraq

Map Skill: Name Iraq's neighbors.

Top: U.S. Marines drive past a mosque near the southern Iraq city of Basrah.

By the Side of the Road

Throughout our state are a number of Blue Star Memorial Highway markers. The blue star has been used as a symbol for heroism since 400 B.C. During World War I and World War II, American women formed the Blue Star Mothers to support their husbands and sons away at war. In 1945, the National Council of State Garden Clubs had the idea of a ribbon of highways across the United States, known as the Blue Star Memorial Highways, to honor all of those who served in the armed services. The first Blue Star Highway was a six-mile stretch in New Jersey. In 1981, it was decided that these stretches of highways should receive Blue Star markers. In 1994, the words "A tribute to the Armed Forces of America" were added to the markers.

There are quite a few Blue Star markers in Georgia. The one shown here is located in Bibb County on I-475 at the rest area just north of Exit 5.

and his family moved to the United States in 1989 to escape terrorism in Colombia. Rincon lived in Conyers, where he had been a 2001 graduate of Salem High School. He was killed in Iraq when a bomber dressed as a taxi driver detonated a suicide bomb at an army roadblock. Several days before his burial, President Bush granted citizenship to this young man posthumously so that he could be buried as an American citizen. He was already an American hero.

A Touch of Home

On April 7, 2003, news reporters were watching the men of the 3rd Battalion Infantry Division from Fort Benning, Georgia, raise a flag in front of one of Saddam Hussein's palaces in downtown Baghdad. The reporters kept trying to identify the flag, thinking at first that it must be an American flag, then realizing that it was not. Finally, one of the reporters shouted out, "It's a Georgia Bulldog. It's a Georgia Bulldog flag!"

Sure enough. The men had raised a 2003 SEC championship flag for the Georgia Bulldogs over the palace. Officers later explained that the soldiers were asked not to raise American flags over Iraq territory because the Iraqi people were not a conquered people; their dictator had just been deposed.

It's Your Turn

1. How has September 11, 2001 affected you?
2. What terrorist group and what leader were given credit for the September 11 attack?
3. What Iraqi leader was deposed by U.S. forces in 2003?
4. In your opinion, was America's involvement in Iraq justified? Why or why not?

Georgia in a New Century

At the start of a new millennium, Georgians faced some old problems and some new challenges.

Roy E. Barnes

In 1998, Georgians sent Democrat Roy E. Barnes to the Governor's Mansion. Barnes, a native of Mableton and a graduate of the University of Georgia, had served in the Georgia legislature for twenty-four years. His campaign for the governor's seat in 1998 was the costliest in the state's history, as Democrats fought to hang onto a governorship that they had held for 125 years. His term was marked by efforts to change the state flag, transportation projects such as the Northern Arc, and education reform.

Above: The state flag from 1956 to 2001, seen here flying in front of the state Capitol, included a representation of the Confederate battle flag.

The State Flag Issue

In 1956, Georgia's state flag was changed to incorporate the St. Andrew's cross, a Confederate battle emblem. The flag has long been a subject of controversy and division within the state. African Americans were offended by references to the slavery in the state's past. Many modern leaders were offended by the image of a state caught up in its past instead of its future. The use of the Confederate symbol was damaging Georgia's tourist industry, costing the state millions in lost convention and exhibition dollars, and portraying a negative "old-fashioned southern" impression of Georgia to the world's businesses. Other southern states that had used the battle symbol as a part of their flags found their tourism and resort industries damaged as conventions were cancelled and boycotts scheduled. The state that had hosted Super Bowls and the Olympics wanted to project a more modern image to the world.

Civic leaders, businessmen and developers, leaders of the hospitality industry, the powerful Atlanta Convention and Visitors Bureau, the legislative Black Caucus, and developers called on Governor Barnes to change the flag. Atlanta architect Cecil Alexander designed a new flag that featured the state seal in the center. Below the seal, a banner showed small images of Georgia's first three state flags and the first and the current images of the U.S. flag. The motto "In God We Trust" appeared below the banner.

The flag was introduced shortly after the 2001 legislative session got underway. With almost no time for discussion and dissent, the flag passed the house on January 24, 2001, and the Senate on January 30. On January 31,

Governor Barnes signed the bill authorizing the new flag into law. Most Georgians saw the new flag in the next day's newspapers and on TV news reports and were shocked at the speed of the change. The equally swift reaction could have been predicted.

Those citizens who saw the 1956 flag as a memorial to the Confederate war dead and the proud heritage of a people and a region were outraged that it had been changed. Others who saw the 1956 flag as a symbol of racism were glad for the change but upset that the 2001 flag still contained any Confederate emblem. The 2001 flag had few supporters. Critics even remarked that it would be too difficult for elementary school children to draw.

In the 2000 election, Barnes's Republican opponent, Sonny Perdue, made the changes in the flag a major campaign issue. Those who were offended that the flag had been changed voted against Barnes, and he was not re-elected. Newly elected Governor Sonny Perdue signed a new state flag into law on May 8, 2003. Georgia was to have its third state flag in under thirty months.

Georgia's 2003 flag was based on the first national flag of the Confederacy. It is a field of three horizontal bars, two red and one white. In the upper left corner is a square blue section containing Georgia's coat of arms and the words "In God We Trust." Surrounding the coat of arms is a circle of thirteen white stars representing the original thirteen states. In March 2004, the people of Georgia voted 3-1 in favor of keeping the 2003 flag as the state flag.

While changing Georgia's state flag may well have cost Barnes the re-election, he was honored by the John F. Kennedy Foundation with a Profiles in Courage Award in May 2003.

Above: The current flag was introduced in 2003 and approved by the state's voters in 2004. **Below:** The state flag from 2001 to 2003 included depictions of three of Georgia's previous flags. Many Georgians did not like this flag.

Global Warming

Many of the world's scientists believe that emissions of carbon dioxide and other gases function like the glass in a greenhouse to trap heat within the Earth's atmosphere. This trapped heat leads to a process called *global warming*. These scientists (and not all scientists agree with the global warming theory) argue that over a period of time, the global warming of Earth's atmosphere will cause glaciers to melt, sea levels to rise, land surface boundaries to change, and the world's ecosystems to change drastically. What can be done to reduce global warming?

Almost all energy experts and scientists can agree on one step that would improve the United States's production of greenhouse gases—improving the fuel economy of motor vehicles. Technology is available to improve the fuel economy of cars and trucks, and environmental leaders argue that such technology would not be too costly and would greatly reduce emissions of carbon monoxide. However, such changes would cause major shifts in America's automotive and oil industries and would certainly require that Americans give up their fuel-guzzling, fast and sleek cars.

Scientists argue that the nation should move away from a dependence on fossil fuels such as oil, coal, and natural gas and find other sources of energy. They urge us to begin to rely on renewable energy resources such as solar power. Alternative energy sources, however, have both advantages and disadvantages.

Global warming would, according to climate specialists, be a worldwide catastrophe. Are they correct? And, can we do more in our own country? Use your research skills to learn more about global warming and the controversy over what steps to take in Georgia, in the United States, and in the world.

Highway Issues

Governor Barnes had to deal with the staggering air pollution and traffic congestion caused by urban sprawl, particularly in the Metropolitan Atlanta area. He also had to confront environmental groups who believed that development was consuming about 50 acres of green space each day. Most immediately, he had to reverse the suspension of federal funds for highway projects in the thirteen-county metropolitan area because of Georgia's failure to meet federal Clean Air standards.

Working with the General Assembly, Barnes created the **Georgia Regional Transportation Authority** (GRTA) in 1999. GRTA was charged with combating air pollution, traffic congestion, and poorly planned development in the metropolitan region. It worked with the counties in the metropolitan area that were not meeting federal ozone standards—Cherokee, Clayton, Cobb, Coweta, DeKalb, Douglas, Fayette, Forsyth, Fulton, Gwinnett, Henry, Paulding, and Rockdale counties. As it succeeded in its task, GRTA was designed to give Georgia access to billions in federal highway funds that had been frozen.

The transportation plan developed by GRTA was approved, and highway funds were released for Georgia's metropolitan area road building projects. However, one part of the GRTA transportation plan faced a great deal of opposition. The so-called Northern Arc was a $2 billion, 59-mile freeway through four counties in the northern tier of Metropolitan Atlanta.

Finally, as his term drew to a close, Governor Barnes was forced to put the Northern Arc plans on hold because of the opposition. His successor, Sonny Perdue, had campaigned against the Northern Arc claiming that it would not be a part of his transportation plans at all.

Education Reform Issues

Despite the educational improvements and increased spending under Governors Busbee, Harris, and Miller, Georgia's schools were still ranked at or near the bottom on most national comparisons. Scholastic Aptitude Tests for college admissions showed that Georgia's high school graduates were not prepared to compete with the young people of other states. Business leaders in Georgia complained that graduates could not do the jobs created by our technologically advanced, information-age economy. Continuing problems with school drop-outs and social promotions had led to only minimal gains in student achievement even as education funding had risen.

Under Governor Barnes's leadership, school construction and renovation increased. By the opening day of school in 2002, the size of kindergarten and primary grade classes had been reduced, pre-kindergarten had spread throughout Georgia, and nurses had been added in every school system. The state had even funded counselors and technology specialists. Millions of federal and state dollars had been poured into innovative reading programs. Early intervention programs provided assistance for those who could not keep up. Additional funds had been provided for after-school programs and summer programs.

Despite those actions, student achievement was not sufficient. Governor Barnes focused on the poor quality of the state's schools. He worked with the General Assembly to create the Office of Educational Accountability in 2001. He called for more testing of Georgia's students. He wanted grade promotions based on student achievement and standardized testing. He proposed performance ratings for Georgia's schools and state takeover of failing schools.

However, Governor Barnes was not re-elected in 2002, and many of his suggestions were not implemented by his successor.

Figure 45
Building Blocks for Educational Reform

In testifying before a national Committee on Education and the Workforce in February 2001, Governor Barnes described four building blocks for educational reform:

1. Great teaching;

2. Leadership that is committed to serving the best interests of children;

3. Willingness to use innovation rather than defending the status quo;

4. Accountability . . . Absolute standards must be used in order to measure the success of educational reform.

Below: Governor Barnes visiting an elementary school class.

American Spotlight

Oprah Winfrey

Few Americans have had more of an impact than Oprah Gail Winfrey. Winfrey is an icon among television celebrities and one of the world's most recognized and respected women. Born January 29, 1954, in Kosciusko, Mississippi, she overcame many personal obstacles to become a millionaire businesswoman, an accomplished actress, a television and movie production company owner, a syndicated talk show hostess, and a major philanthropist.

After graduating from Tennessee State University with a degree in speech communications and theater, Winfrey knew that she wanted to enter broadcasting. She served as a reporter and co-anchor of a Baltimore television news broadcast in the late 1970s. From Baltimore, she went to Chicago, where she was the anchor of "A.M. Chicago," a morning talk show. There she found the television format that suited her personality perfectly. Within a year, the show was renamed the "Oprah Winfrey Show" and was expanded to a full hour. In 1985, her show was syndicated to over 120 American cities and rose to the top of the charts, where it has remained ever since. Her television audience now includes over 15 million viewers daily in our country and millions more in 132 other countries of the world.

By 1996, she was one of the world's highest paid entertainers according to *Forbes* magazine. She also began a lifestyle magazine for women called *O, The Oprah Winfrey Magazine.* Winfrey started her own motion picture and television production company, Harpo, Inc.

Winfrey has collected numerous Emmys for having television's best talk show, an Academy Award nomination for her acting in *The Color Purple,* Performer of the Year awards, Woman of the Year Achievement awards, People's

Above: In 1999, Winfrey received a National Book Foundation award.

Choice awards, and Horatio Alger awards. Since 1998, she has consistently been named one of the most powerful people in show business.

However, she may be best remembered for the social and philanthropic causes she has championed. One of her most successful projects is Oprah's Book Club. The books she features are often literary novels that do not attract large audiences but that do offer an uplifting spirit and message for the readers. Another successful project is Oprah's Angel Network, started in 1997, which raises money for college scholarships and funds to reward people for using their lives to help others. On her show, Oprah established the world's "largest piggy bank," and viewers all over the country sent in more than $1 million to send disadvantaged children to college. Winfrey matched the money raised dollar for dollar. She is involved with the Habitat for Humanity program, which builds houses for needy Americans, and with A Better Chance program, which funds scholarships for inner-city youths to attend college preparatory schools. She had attacked the AIDs epidemic in Africa through her Angel Network. Because of her international stature, Winfrey was chosen to co-host a memorial service held at Yankee Stadium in New York for the victims of the September 11 terrorist attacks.

Her personal philosophy has been to use her celebrity status as a force for good in the world. She said, in an interview in *Redbook* magazine, "My prayer to God every morning on my knees is that the power that is in the universe should use my life as a vessel, or a vehicle, for its work." You will have to agree, when you examine the causes Oprah Winfrey champions and the accomplishments she has attained, that her prayer is being answered.

Georgia Elects a Republican Governor

In November 2002, Perry native Sonny Perdue was elected Georgia's first Republican governor in 130 years. In that same election, the Democratic party maintained control of the General Assembly, but voters chose Republicans for the U.S. Senate seat and the majority of representatives for the U.S. House. Georgia had a two-party system for the first time since before the Civil War.

Challenges for the Future

There are three issues that continue to demand the attention of Georgia politicians and citizens—water resources, the differences between urban and rural Georgia, and Georgia's tremendous growth in population.

Water resources are limited in the state as development and population growth, especially in the Metropolitan Atlanta and north Georgia areas, have increased usage. Farmers in south Georgia complain that Metropolitan Atlanta uses too much water and pollutes the rivers feeding the southern agricultural area. Saltwater has seeped into the coastal water basins. Both Florida and Alabama have tried for years to reach an agreement with Georgia on reducing our state's water consumption; they continue to threaten court action if agreements cannot be reached. Federal officials have threatened the state with the loss of federal funds if more is not done to correct pollution in the state's streams, lakes, and rivers. Planning the future of this essential resource is an ongoing concern.

The continued growth in northern Georgia has served only to divide the rural, southern sections of the state from the rest of Georgia. Inequities between the two areas occur not only in population, services, businesses and industries, but also in education. Even though state leaders have tried to equalize education funding throughout the state, the areas of economic growth and prosperity have greater tax bases to support local school costs. Finding ways to lessen the burden on rural county property owners without sacrificing urban schools is an ongoing challenge.

Above: Georgia Governor Sonny Perdue (center) and Senator Saxby Chambliss (left) appeared with President Bush on one of his trips to our state.

Figure 46 Key Issues, 2004

Some of the key issues facing Governor Perdue and the General Assembly include:

- Saving the HOPE scholarship program when scholarship expenditures are about to exceed lottery revenues

- Developing legislation to protect children

- Reforming ethics legislation

- Resolving whether public displays of the ten commandments are legal

- Helping Atlanta fund infrastructure needs such as replacing an aging sewer system

- Dealing with the outcome of the 2004 vote on the state flag

- Dealing with state and local spending on education

Finally, the state's leaders must find a way to handle Georgia's tremendous population growth. Georgia is the tenth most populous state, with over 8 million residents. The 2000 census showed a population increase of 26 percent. But Georgia must also find ways to preserve some green space in the state's environment, to protect coastal marsh areas threatened by over-development, and to provide the infrastructure to serve the rising population. How Georgia's leaders and citizens handle these problems will determine much about our state's future.

A Final Note

The character word for the chapter is **pride**. To have pride is to have a sense of your own worth or to be satisfied with your achievements. For example, you can be proud of a good grade on a test for which you studied hard. You might be proud of something that makes you you— your heritage, your family, your school, your church, or the town in which you live.

Make a list of five things for which you are proud. Now, think of ten years from now. What other traits or accomplishments would you like to be proud of? For example, you might be proud of graduating from college or technical school or be proud of being a caring spouse.

You decide. Put your two lists in a "time capsule" and keep them safe. Every three years, open the capsule and see how you are doing.

Top: There are many users of Georgia's water resources. Government must find a way to balance the needs of industry, agriculture, cities and towns, individuals, and environmentalists. **Above:** One of the problems caused by the tremendous growth in the Atlanta area has been traffic congestion.

It's Your Turn

1. How do you feel about Georgia's state flag? What would you have done differently if you had been in charge?
2. Describe at least two key issues Governor Barnes faced during his term.
3. Explain at least four of the issues facing Governor Perdue.

Chapter Summary

- The Cold War ended in the early 1900s with the collapse of the Soviet Union.

- Georgia's population has grown steadily since the 1960s.

- Under Governor George Busbee, Georgia improved its educational system, expanded economic development, and revised its constitution.

- Voters approved the state's tenth constitution in 1982, and it took effect in 1983.

- Governor Joe Frank Harris expanded economic and educational improvements in the state, including the Quality Basic Education Act.

- The World Congress Center, the Georgia Dome, and Centennial Olympic Park make up one of the world's largest convention, sports, and entertainment centers.

- The two-Georgia argument dividing rural and urban areas began in the early 1980s and continues today despite state efforts to pour economic development funds into rural counties.

- The U.S. was involved in Operation Desert Storm (the Persian Gulf War) after Iraq's invasion of Kuwait.

- Georgia political leaders in the 1990s included Newt Gingrich, John Lewis, Sam Nunn, and Zell Miller.

- Under Zell Miller, Georgia established a state lottery and used the funds for scholarships, technology programs in schools, and a statewide pre-kindergarten program.

- Atlanta hosted the Summer Olympics in 1996.

- The World Trade Center in New York and the Pentagon were the targets of international terrorism on September 11, 2001.

- After September 11, 2001, the United States was involved in two wars—Operation Enduring Freedom against Afghanistan and Operation Iraqi Freedom with Iraq.

- Georgia leaders removed the Confederate battle emblem from the state's flag, and controversy ensued. The state has had three flags in a period of about thirty months.

- Education improvements featuring accountability were a focus of Governor Roy Barnes as the 1090s ended.

- In 2002, Republican Sonny Perdue was the first Republican elected governor of Georgia since Reconstruction.

- By 2002, Georgia had a viable two-party political system.

Above: Governor Sonny Perdue was the first Republican elected to that office in more than 125 years.

Chapter Review

Reviewing People, Places, and Terms

Use each of the following terms to write a factual statement about Georgia history.

1. Roy Barnes

2. Georgia Dome

3. Newt Gingrich

4. HOPE scholarship program

5. Zell Miller

6. per capita income

7. Quality Basic Education

8. terrorism

9. XXVI Olympiad

Understanding the Facts

1. What were the key features of Reaganomics?

2. Describe the "two-Georgia" controversy.

3. What was the "shift" that took place in Georgia politics in the 1980s and 1990s?

4. Give three examples of infrastructure.

5. How are the funds from Georgia's state lottery used?

6. Name at least three issues that have arisen because of Georgia's tremendous population growth between 1980 and today.

7. What pressures led Governor Barnes to change Georgia's state flag?

Developing Critical Thinking

1. How did the development of the personal computer affect our lives?

2. What are some of the changes in our lives that have resulted from September 11, 2001?

3. There were different opinions about Operation Iraqi Freedom. Some thought there should have been more time for diplomatic negotiations. Why do you think President Bush ordered troops to Iraq?

4. Georgia's flag controversy will not go away easily. Governor Barnes changed the flag, Governor Perdue changed it again, and in 2004 voters went to the polls to choose between those two flag choices. Should Georgia's flag be a subject of voter approval? What are the arguments for and against the use of Confederate heritage symbols as a part of current state symbols, such as the flag?

5. Of the issues facing Georgia since 2000, which concerns most directly impact you?

Checking It Out

1. In 1981, an assassination attempt was made on President Reagan's life. But during his term in office, two other world leaders and friends of the United States were victims of successful assassination attempts. Use your research skills to find out who these two leaders were and what happened to them. Share the information with the class.

2. The distribution of Georgia's population changed drastically in the last half of the twentieth century. Now, over 50 percent of the state lives in the metro-Atlanta area, and over 60 percent of the population lives in urban areas. In the mid-1800s, over 70 percent of the population lived in rural areas. Use your research skills to study the census data and prepare a graph of Georgia's population changes by area—rural, urban, suburban, and metropolitan.

3. Research the HOPE program that will be available for you to use when you are ready for college. What steps were taken in 2004 and 2005 to ensure that there would be enough funds to meet students' needs? Are these steps working, and what other steps must be taken in your opinion to save HOPE?

4. Use your research skills to investigate Georgia's water problems. Why do we need agreements with Alabama and Florida? Why are our rivers, streams, and lakes still so polluted? Why is water usage an issue between northern and southern Georgia? Prepare a report on the issues and the resources available. Who has to give up levels of water usage? Who should pay for pollution clean up? Why do we have to have an interstate agreement?

5. Research the use of the blue star as a symbol for heroism in history.

Writing Across the Curriculum

1. Politics is now a two-party affair in our state as both Republicans and Democrats field candidates for local and state offices and in national congressional races. Select one party or the other and prepare a campaign brochure outlining the improvements or changes called for in Georgia by that party.

2. Write a journal entry describing what you were doing or what you thought when you heard about the events of September 11, 2001.

Exploring Technology

1. Have Georgia's schools improved after two and a half decades of emphasis on educational reforms? Use your Internet research skills to track increases in student achievement and decreases in school drop-outs. How does the pattern look when you chart it on paper? Prepare that chart to share with your classmates. Do different regions of the state produce similar or dissimilar results in student achievement? Prepare that chart to show your classmates. What explanations can you find to match the results of your charts?

Applying Your Skills

1. "Wherever the highways are built, the businesses will follow" has long been a saying in Georgia politics. Examine a map and trace Georgia's major multilane and limited-access highways. Compare that with the patterns of growth in Georgia counties during the past ten years. Is that old saying true? Do the highways match the growth areas?

2. The federal census figures of Georgia's population are listed below. Prepare a chart that shows the percentage of increase for each decade.

1960	3,943,116
1970	4,589,575
1980	5,462,982
1990	6,478,216
2000	8,186,453

Unit 6

Making It All Work

The process of governing is not the duty or responsibility of one individual. It is shared by elected officials, various government employees, the voters, and you as a citizen. All are needed in order for our federal, state and local governments to work effectively and efficiently.

In this unit, you will learn about the workings of our federal government, whose offices are located in our national capital, Washington, D.C. This government is divided into three branches—executive (the president, vice president, and cabinet), legislative (Congress), and judicial (courts).

You will also read about our state government, whose offices are located in our state capital, Atlanta. Our state government has the same three branches as the federal government—the executive (governor and cabinet), legislative (General Assembly), and judicial (courts).

Finally, you will investigate the workings of your local government. Although the names are different, the jobs are similar to federal and state government. In your town, city, or county, there are a mayor or city manager (executive branch), a city council or board of commissioners (legislative branch), and a system of local law enforcement and courts (judicial branch).

Above: The White House. **Right:** Local government is represented by the Morgan County courthouse in Madison.

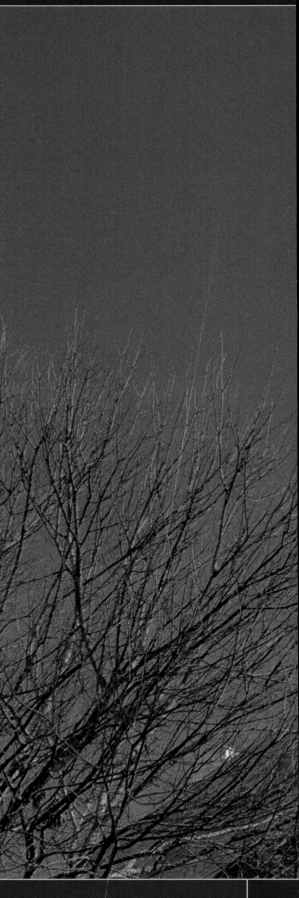

With Liberty and Justice, the Federal Government

The United States faced many challenges at the end of the American Revolution. One of the most important was the establishment of a stable national government. The first constitution, called the Articles of Confederation, was ratified by the states in 1781. But there were problems with the government created under the Articles of Confederation. A number of national leaders called for its revision. The Constitutional Convention met in Philadelphia in 1787 and drafted a totally new document—the United States Constitution.

Left: The U.S. Capitol building in Washington, D.C., is the seat of the legislative branch of the federal government.

Signs of the Times

U.S. Population: 281,421,906 according to 2000 census

Life Expectancy: 74 for males; 80 for females

Cost of Living: The salary of the president in 2003 was $400,000. The salary of the vice president was $186,300. The salary of a member of Congress was $158,100. The expenditures of the U.S. federal budget in 2003 were $1.8 trillion.

Literature: In 2003, the Librarian of Congress appointed Louise Glück as U.S. Poet Laureate.

Communication: In the United States, there are over 195 million telephone lines, over 75 million cellular phones, 575 million radios, over 10,000 radio stations, over 10,500 television stations, over 220 million televisions, and over 150 million Internet users.

Art/Architecture: The U.S. Capitol, built between 1783 and 1830, is a neoclassical style that resembles the Roman Pantheon with a circular domed rotunda.

Religion: The second amendment to the U.S. Constitution states, in part, "Congress shall make no law respecting an establishment of religion, or prohibiting the free exercise thereof. . . ."

Music: Our national anthem is "The Star-Spangled Banner," adopted in 1931. Before 1931, the patriotic song "My Country, 'Tis of Thee" was the national anthem.

Education: There are 94,112 public schools, 27,223 private schools, and 9,258 post-secondary institutions in the United States. There are nearly 3,000 charter schools.

Transportation: The United States has 99,260 miles of railroad lines, 3,948,335 miles of highways, 46,467 miles of interstates, 26,000 miles of navigable waterways, and 19,306 airports.

Science/Inventions: Inventors may register their inventions with the U.S. Patent and Trademark Office. A patent gives its holder the "the right to exclude others from making, using, offering for sale, or selling" the invention in the United States or "importing" the invention into the United States.

Figure 47 Timeline: 1750–2000

1856
J. C. Fremont ran unsuccessfully for U.S. president

1831
U.S. Supreme Court ruling in *Cherokee Nation v. Georgia*

1861
Georgia seceded from Union

1922
Rebecca Latimer Felton appointed first female U.S. senator

1788
Georgia officially became state

1870
Georgia readmitted to Union

1976
Jimmy Carter elected president

1750	1800	1850	1900	1950	2000

1781
Articles of Confederation & Perpetual Union ratified

1791
U.S. Bill of Rights ratified

1789
U.S. Constitution ratified

1913
Income tax established by Amendment 16

1971
18-year-olds given right to vote by Amendment 26

1787
Constitutional Convention drafted new constitution

1865
Slavery abolished by Amendment 13

1920
Women given right to vote by Amendment 19

1931
"Star Spangled Banner" became national anthem

Section Preview

As you read, look for:
* reasons for calling for a constitutional convention,
* important issues at the Constitutional Convention,
* method of amending the Constitution,
* basic principles of our government, and
* vocabulary terms: conservative, infrastructure, republic, proportional representation, Great Compromise, Three-Fifths Compromise, electoral college, Federalists, Antifederalists, sovereignty, electorate, constitutionalism, separation of powers, checks and balances, and federalism.

Toward a New Constitution

The colonists had just won the American Revolution. The founding fathers wanted to make sure that their new government would be very different from the government of Great Britain. The Articles of Confederation, ratified in 1781, intentionally established a weak national government. The new U.S. government consisted of a unicameral legislature—Congress—in which each state had one vote. There was no chief executive, and there was no national court system.

The weaknesses in the Articles of Confederation caused major problems for the new country. Under the Articles, the Confederation Congress that could not pay the colonial soldiers during the Revolutionary War found that it also could not pay them after the war. Some soldiers threatened to revolt. The Confederation Congress asked the states for help, but many states rejected or ignored the request.

The new government did not have the power to regulate trade between the states or between the United States and foreign countries. Each state had its own money system, which also created problems with trade. The British

reoccupied some of the forts in the Northwest Territory (the area north of the Ohio River), and the national government was powerless to do anything to stop them. As a result, foreign countries had little respect for the new country.

George Washington and others were alarmed at what they saw happening to the states under the Articles of Confederation. Some openly called for a change; others boldly called for a return to a monarchy. As a result, a movement began to examine and revise the Articles of Confederation.

However, the government leaders were afraid that the people might panic and chaos might result if they heard that the government was going to be changed. Therefore, the leaders decided that any change must take place quietly—without fanfare.

An opportunity to address some of the problems arose in 1786 when Virginia asked for a meeting in Annapolis, Maryland, to discuss the continuing trade problems among the states. Nine of the thirteen states agreed to send delegates to the meeting, but representatives from only five states attended. Because of the low attendance, nothing was accomplished. The delegates at Annapolis did ask that a second convention meet in Philadelphia the next year. They broadened the goals for the Philadelphia meeting and, instead of focusing only on trade problems, asked to discuss all the problems of the Articles of Confederation. It was hoped that some changes could be made that would make the national government stronger.

The Constitutional Convention

In February 1787, the Confederation Congress gave its support to the Philadelphia Convention. Three months later, delegates began to arrive at Independence Hall. Seventy delegates were named by their state legislatures, but only fifty-five actually attended. Rhode Island, however, did not send any delegates to the Constitutional Convention because it opposed a stronger national government.

George Washington attended and was elected to preside over the meeting, but many other well-know figures from the American Revolution were not present. Only eight people who had signed the Declaration of Independence served as delegates. Thomas Jefferson and Thomas Paine were in Europe at this time, and fiery radicals like Samuel and John Adams, John Hancock, and Patrick Henry did not attend. When the convention ended four months later, thirty-nine delegates were present to sign the document —the United States Constitution.

Convention Delegates

The fifty-five men who attended the Philadelphia Convention were for the most part well-educated, wealthy landowners. Forty-one of them had served in the Continental Congress, and a number of others had served in state government, including eight who were governors. The delegates were also relatively young. The average age was forty-two, but a number were under thirty.

Above: This painting of the members of the Constitutional Convention hangs in the east stairway in the House wing of the U.S. Capitol. **Opposite page:** A statue of George Washington stands in front of Independence Hall in Philadelphia. Washington presided over the meeting.

The delegates were more conservative (favoring traditional values and reluctant to make changes) than some others who supported widespread change. Charles Beard, a noted nineteenth-century historian, described the delegates as practical men who wanted to protect property and encourage business interests. Beard even suggested that the delegates might have been self-serving (more interested in furthering their own interests).

In reality, the delegates had experienced first-hand the problems of the weak national government under the Articles of Confederation. No one state was self-sufficient enough to fend for itself against a foreign foe. Nor could a single state build the infrastructure (basic facilities such as roads, bridges, and ports) to increase travel and commerce throughout the nation. However, a group of united states working together could accomplish these goals. Whatever their own agendas, the delegates put personal feelings aside and worked together to create an endurable form of government for all people—a form of government that has guided the United States for over two hundred years.

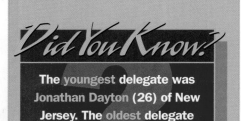

Figure 48 The Virginia Plan

The specific provisions were:

- A national government would be composed of three branches—legislative, executive, and judicial.

- A legislative branch would include a Congress of two houses. The House of Representatives was to be elected directly by the people of each state, and the Senate was to be elected by the members of the House of Representatives from persons nominated by each state legislature.

- Representation from each state in both the Senate and the House of Representatives would be based on population.

A Republican Form of Government

Before the delegates could decide how to change the government, they discussed what they knew about theories and ideas from the past. They had read the writings of philosophers and adopted many of their ideas about government. They had studied and were influenced by philosophers who had written about government, particularly the government of the ancient Romans. In the Roman system, the common people and the aristocracy shared political power and were able to govern themselves without a king. Instead of a king, they had a republic, which provided for the common welfare of its citizens.

As the delegates struggled to form their own definition of a republic, James Madison provided a clear image. In a republic, according to Madison, all the powers of government are given to the people. The people elect representatives to make the laws. The representatives have their jobs for a limited amount of time. Madison insisted that a large number of people, not a small number of special interest groups, should elect representatives. He wanted the lawmaking body of the United States to be elected directly by the people and not by the state legislatures. Madison defined a republic as a representative democracy, which gets its right to govern from the people it governs.

Organizing the Government

When the convention began, the delegates discussed their ideas on how the government should be organized. They wanted to make it strong enough to handle the nation's needs, but they also wanted to be certain it did not abuse its power. There were two major plans submitted to the delegates for their consideration.

The *Virginia Plan*, called for a strong national government. Under this plan, drafted by James Madison before the convention began, the national government would have the power to collect taxes, make laws, and enforce the laws in its own courts. The legislative branch would have the power to make laws, strike down state laws that violated national laws, mobilize the armed forces, and elect people to serve in the executive and judicial branches.

The Virginia Plan did not please all the delegates. Most delegates agreed that representation in the House of Representatives should be based on population, an idea known as **proportional representation**. The larger states wanted representation in the Senate to also be based on population because that would give those states more voice in the government. The smaller states objected. They wanted each state to have the same number of representatives in the Senate. The smaller states feared that, if the larger states had more votes, they would control the national government and thus be able to pass laws for their own special interests.

William Patterson, a delegate from New Jersey, proposed the *New Jersey Plan* to protect the interests of the small states. The New Jersey Plan, although it contained suggestions for solving some weaknesses, would have continued the government as it had been under the Articles of Confederation.

The Great Compromise

The small states continued to support equal representation (an equal number of delegates regardless of the population of the state), while the large states supported proportional representation. When it became evident that the two sides could not agree, the delegates established a special committee to work out a compromise. The result was the Great Compromise or, as it is sometimes called, the Connecticut Compromise.

The compromise called for a bicameral Congress. One house called the House of Representatives would be based on proportional representation; the second house called the Senate would have equal representation. It was also decided that all taxation and government spending bills would originate in the House, but they would have to be approved in the Senate.

After a bitter debate, the delegates passed the Great Compromise by a single vote.

> ### Figure 49 The New Jersey Plan
>
> The main provisions were:
>
> ● **Congress would have a one-house legislature that could levy taxes, control interstate and foreign trade, and make laws and treaties with foreign nations. State laws could not override the laws made by the national Congress.**
>
> ● **An executive branch would be composed of several persons selected by Congress.**
>
> ● **The executive branch would appoint a Supreme Court, which would have the power to handle conflicts.**

Above: Edmund Randolph, governor of Virginia and a delegate to the Constitutional Convention, introduced Madison's Virginia Plan to the rest of the delegates.

The Great Seal of the United States

The Great Seal of the United States was created between 1776 and 1782 as a graphic symbol of the nation. On the obverse, or main, side is an American bald eagle, our national bird and a symbol of power. An olive branch with thirteen olives and leaves is in the eagle's right talon. This is a symbol of the power of the nation to make peace. In its left talon are thirteen arrows, which indicate the power of the nation to make war. In its beak is a scroll inscribed with the national motto, *E pluribus unum*, which means "out of many, one." Above the head of the eagle is a golden circle of light surrounding a field of thirteen stars. Over the eagle's breast is a shield with thirteen vertical white and red stripes beneath a blue background. Do you see the pattern of thirteen in the Great Seal? Why thirteen?

The reverse of the seal features an unfinished pyramid, which signifies a nation yet unfinished. On the base of the pyramid are the Roman numerals for 1776. Above the pyramid is an eye in a triangle surrounded by a golden light. This is an ancient symbol for the total knowledge of humanity. Over the eye are the words *Annuit Coeptis*, which means "It [the eye of Providence] has favored our undertakings." This symbolizes the religious faith of the founding fathers. Underneath the pyramid is the motto *Novus Ordo Seciorum*, which means "A new order of the ages." This statement describes the revolutionary eighteenth-century concept of the rise of a new nation founded on the belief in freedom.

Compromises on Slavery

Slaves were a large percentage of the populations of the southern states. As a result, there was considerable debate over whether or not to include the slaves in the state's population to determine representation in the House of Representatives. Many northern states did not want to count slaves because that would give the southern states control of the House of Representatives.

After considerable discussion, the delegates reached a compromise. According to the **Three-Fifths Compromise**, the total number of free persons would be counted, but only three-fifths of all other persons (slaves) would be counted. Georgia had about 29,500 slaves in 1790, but it would only be allowed to count three-fifths of that number, or 17,700, in the state's official population.

The delegates also prohibited the importation of slaves after 1808 and agreed that fugitive slaves should be returned to their masters.

Compromise on the Presidency

The last major compromise of the Constitutional Convention involved the issue of who should elect the president—the citizens or the Congress. The solution was the creation of an **electoral college**. Each state's legislature was allowed to select as many "electors" as it had members in Congress (House and Senate). These electors would be allowed to vote for two people. The person who received the highest number of votes (provided it was a majority of the votes cast) would be named president. The person who received the second-highest number of votes would be named vice president. In this way, Congress would not be selecting the chief executive of the new nation. The people would be indirectly selecting the president and vice president because their state representatives would choose people to vote on their behalf.

The Art of Politics

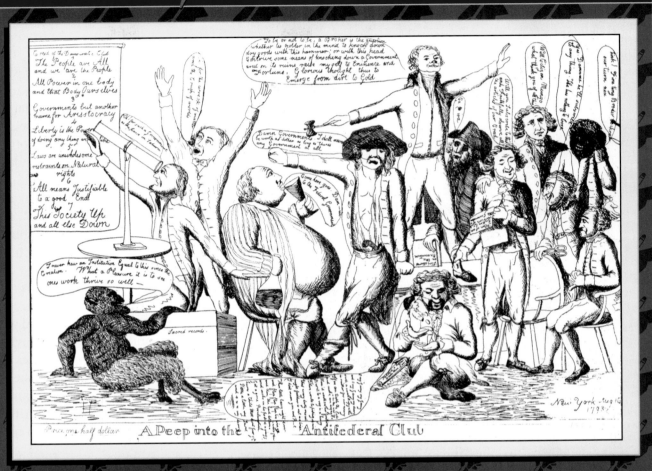

This 1793 political cartoon, entitled "A Peep into the Antifederal Club," ridicules the Jeffersonian Republicans, a political party formed by the Antifederalists. They are depicted as an unruly mob who consort with the devil (lower left). Thomas Jefferson is in the center, standing on a table with a gavel in his hand.

Ratification

The new United States Constitution was approved on September 17, 1787, by delegates from the twelve states present at the convention. On September 28, 1787, the new Constitution was sent to the states for ratification. Ratification was far from certain.

People who supported the strong national government established in the new constitution called themselves the Federalists; those who opposed a strong central government were called Antifederalists. Members of both groups had a strong sense of patriotism, a love and support of country and the Constitution.

The Antifederalists believed that the national government should not have too much power. They wanted the major powers left to state governments.

Figure 50   The Bill of Rights

First Amendment Freedom of religion, of speech, of the press, and the right to assemble and petition government

Second Amendment Right to keep and bear arms

Third Amendment Prohibits stationing of troops in homes without consent

Fourth Amendment Protects against unreasonable searches and seizures and requires probable cause for search warrants

Fifth Amendment Establishes grand jury; protects against double jeopardy and self-incrimination; guarantees due process and eminent domain

Sixth Amendment Ensures right to speedy trial, to be informed of charges against defendant, to counsel

Seventh Amendment Provides for trial by jury

Eighth Amendment Prohibits excessive bail or fines and prohibits cruel and unusual punishment

Ninth Amendment Does not deny people any rights that are not specifically mentioned in the Constitution

Tenth Amendment Gives the states or the people all powers not specifically granted to Congress or denied to states

Amending the U.S. Constitution is a very difficult task. In over two hundred years, only twenty-seven amendments have been added to the Constitution.

They also insisted that citizens' individual rights be specifically protected in the new Constitution. In order to gain their support, the first ten amendments to the Constitution were proposed in 1789 and approved in 1791. These amendments are called the Bill of Rights.

Nine states had to ratify the document before it could become the official Constitution of the young nation. Delaware was the first state to ratify the Constitution on December 7, 1787. Georgia was the fourth state to ratify the U.S. Constitution, as it voted its approval on a cold Wednesday morning, January 2, 1788. On June 21, 1788, New Hampshire became the ninth state to approve it.

Amending the Constitution

The U.S. Constitution is a very brief document. It is only about 1,800 words in length, and it has been changed or added to only twenty-seven times since it was first adopted. What makes the Constitution so effective? First, our forefathers wrote in a very terse (brief) and general style. Had they tried to be too specific, the document would have been much longer and could not have withstood the changes our nation has undergone since the late 1700s. Because it is so general, future generations of Americans have been able to interpret the document.

Second, our forefathers planned for a way to amend the Constitution. An amendment may be proposed by a two-thirds vote in both houses of Congress or by a national constitutional convention called for by two-thirds of the state legislatures. Once an amendment is proposed, it is sent to the states to be ratified. A proposed amendment must be approved by three-fourths (38) of the state legislatures.

All of the amendments to our Constitution except one have originated in Congress and have been approved by three-fourths of the states. That one amendment was the Twenty-First Amendment, which repealed the Eighteenth Amendment on prohibition.

Principles of the U.S. Government

The government of the United States is based on five principles. One principle is sovereignty, the idea of supreme power or source of authority. In our government, power rests with the citizens. The people of the United States are sovereign, and the power to govern comes from the people. This form of government is called a republic.

In a direct democracy, each individual in the country would be directly involved in making decisions about what the government should and should not do. That seemed impractical to our founding fathers, so they made our government a *representative democracy*. The citizens elect or appoint others to represent them in making decisions about what the government should do. The electorate (voters) choose the individuals who will be a part of the government and represent the people.

The second basic principle of American government is constitutionalism. The representatives selected by the voters cannot just make up laws or rules as they see fit. They are bound by the federal and the state constitutions. These written documents—the U.S. Constitution and the constitutions of the states—describe the rights of the people and the framework of the government.

When the U.S. Constitution was ratified by the states, it established a national government that was made up of three branches—the legislative branch, the executive branch, and the judicial branch. Responsibilities for government were divided among the three branches in what is known as a separation of powers. Separating government powers creates a "limited government." In addition, each branch of government was given some power to control or prevent some actions of the other two branches. This process is known as a system of checks and balances. The checks and balances ensure that no one branch becomes too powerful.

The U.S. government is also based on the principle of federalism. A federal system is one in which the national government and state governments share authority over the same territory and the same people. Georgians are state citizens, but they are also U.S. citizens. They are subject to both state and federal laws. If there is a conflict between the laws, the national law takes precedence.

Did You Know?

James Madison kept extensive notes of the proceedings of the convention. They are the most complete record of the debates that took place.

It's Your Turn

1. What were the major weaknesses in the Articles of Confederation? Why do you think the delegates chose to write an entirely new constitution rather than fix the Articles?
2. Identify the major debates that resulted in compromises at the Constitutional Convention.
3. Who were the Federalists and the Antifederalists?
4. How did the Bill of Rights come into being?
5. What are the five basic principles upon which our government is based?
6. What is the difference between a representative democracy and a direct democracy?

The Legislative Branch of Government

Section Preview

As you read, look for:
* the two houses of the national legislature,
* the powers of Congress,
* how a bill becomes law, and
* vocabulary terms: expressed powers, implied powers, elastic clause, bill, and veto.

The first article of the U.S. Constitution established the legislative branch of the federal government. It sets out the requirements for and responsibilities of those who serve in Congress.

The Members of Congress

The Constitution established a bicameral, or two-body, legislature composed of the Senate and the House of Representatives.

Figure 51
Georgia's Congressional Representatives (2003)

District	Representative
District 1	Jack Kingston (Republican)
District 2	Sanford Bishop (Democrat)
District 3	Jim Marshall (Democrat)
District 4	Denise Majette (Democrat)
District 5	John Lewis (Democrat)
District 6	Johnny Isakson (Republican)
District 7	John Linder (Republican)
District 8	Michael Collins (Republican)
District 9	Charles Norwood (Republican)
District 10	Nathan Deal (Republican)
District 11	Phil Gingrey (Republican)
District 12	Max Burns (Republican)
District 13	David Scott (Democrat)

The Senate

The Senate is made up of two representatives from each state, for a total of 100 members. A senator must be at least thirty years old, a citizen of the United States for at least nine years, and a resident of the state he or she represents. Originally, senators were chosen by their state legislatures to serve a six-year term. In 1913, the Seventeenth Amendment to the Constitution provided that the members of the Senate be elected by the people. Senate terms are now staggered so that only one-third of the entire Senate is elected in any one election year.

In 2003, Georgia's two U.S. senators were Zell Miller (a Democrat) and Saxby Chambliss (a Republican). Both senators represent the entire state of Georgia.

The vice president of the United States serves as the president of the Senate and presides over sessions. The vice president does not vote on any issues before the Senate unless there is a tie vote. The *president pro tempore* of the Senate (the senior member of the majority party) presides over the Senate in the absence of the vice president. There are also majority and minority leaders in the Senate. These individuals are the political leaders of the country's two dominant political parties—the Democratic and the Republican parties. These leaders work to promote and control legislation supported by their parties.

House of Representatives

A member of the U.S. House of Representatives must be at least twenty-five years of age, a citizen of the United States for at least seven years, and a resident of the state he or she represents. Representatives are elected to two-year terms and are chosen in November of even-numbered years.

Each state's population determines the number of representatives it has in the House of Representatives. The more populated states have more representatives. The Reapportionment Act of 1929 set a limit of 435 members in the U.S. House of Representatives. Every ten years, the 435 seats are reapportioned (divided) among the states according to federal census figures.

The political party that holds a majority of seats in the House (218 or more) is said to "control the House." The *Speaker of the House* is the leader of the House and is always a member of the majority party. The Speaker is responsible for the day-to-day functions of the House. At the beginning of each session of Congress, the two political parties select their leaders. The controlling party selects the *majority leader*, who controls the legislative agenda.

Based on its population in the 2000 census, Georgia has thirteen representatives. The state is divided into thirteen Congressional districts, and the voters of each district elect one member to the U.S. House of Representatives.

The Powers of Congress

The U.S. Constitution gives certain powers to Congress. These powers are both expressed and implied. Expressed powers are those powers specifically given to Congress in the U.S. Constitution. Implied powers are not specifically stated in the Constitution but are derived from Congress's right to make all laws necessary to carry out its expressed powers. This statement comes at the end of Article I, Section 8 of the Constitution, which is known as the elastic clause because it stretches the powers of Congress.

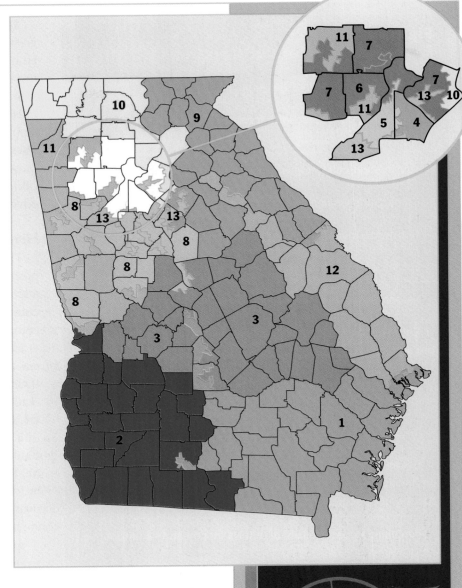

**Map 48
Georgia's
Congressional
Districts**

Map Skill: In which Congressional district do you live?

Figure 52
Expressed Powers of Congress

The expressed powers of Congress include:

● **Regulating commerce with foreign nations and among the states**

● **Levying and collecting revenues or taxes**

● **Coining and issuing money**

● **Borrowing money on the credit of the United States**

● **Establishing bankruptcy rules**

● **Establishing the naturalization procedure for citizenship**

● **Establishing post offices and post roads (routes used for the delivery of mail)**

● **Issuing copyrights and patents, which protect the rights of authors and inventors**

● **Regulating weights and measures**

● **Establishing federal courts, defining and punishing piracy on the high seas, and defining and punishing offenses against the law of nations (to punish for treason)**

● **Punishing counterfeiters of federal money and securities**

● **Providing legislation for territories of the United States, such as the District of Columbia, and providing for and maintaining national parks, federal buildings, and other federally owned lands**

● **Declaring war and making rules for warfare and the operation of the armed services**

Only a **very** small portion of bills, **about** 7½ percent, **actually** become laws. Most bills **never** make it out of committee.

The Constitution gives each house of Congress some powers not given to the other. The House of Representatives has the power to impeach; the power to try that impeached official, however, rests with the Senate. All bills to raise revenue must originate in the House of Representatives. The Senate has the sole power to ratify treaties and to confirm the president's selection of individuals to serve as cabinet members or in other high-ranking government positions.

How Congress Operates

The legislative work of Congress is accomplished primarily through committees. There are four basic types of committees: standing committees, select committees, conference committees, and joint committees.

Standing committees monitor the work of federal agencies and departments that fall under their areas. For example, the Department of Agriculture falls under the Agriculture Committee. Committees also control the progress of **bills** (proposed legislation). Committees can send legislation under their jurisdiction to the full House or Senate or they can kill the legislation. The House of Representatives has twenty-two standing committees, and the Senate has sixteen standing committees.

All members of Congress sit on several different committees. Their committee appointments are determined by their party's leadership and power, their personal interests, and the special needs and interests of their constituents (the voters they represent). For example, Georgia has a large number of federal military bases and receives significant federal military dollars. Georgia's congressional representatives seek seats on the powerful armed services committees. Since much of Georgia's economy is based on agriculture and agribusiness, Georgia's delegates also seek appointments to the agriculture committees.

At any time, Congress can form *select committees* to deal with specific issues, such as the Select Committee on Aging or the Select Committee on Narcotics Abuse and Control. Select committees usually have a limited life.

A bill must pass both houses of Congress in identical form before it is sent to the president. When the House and the Senate have approved different versions of a bill, they are sent to a *conference committee*. The committee contains representatives of both bodies. Committee members work to develop a compromise version of the bill that both the House and the Senate can support. If both bodies of Congress adopt the compromise version, it is sent to the president to be approved or vetoed. (To veto is to refuse to sign a bill.)

The fourth type of committee is the joint committee. *Joint committees* have members from both the House and the Senate and focus on issues of national concern. However, they do not propose legislation.

In addition to these four committees, much of the work of Congress is accomplished by *subcommittees*, which are smaller groups that examine issues and draft bills. All of the different committees make the work of Congress a complex, decentralized, and sometimes fragmented process.

Committees accomplish their work through two main activities—hearings and investigations. These activities are a part of Congress's "oversight power," meaning that hearings and investigations are used to oversee the activities of the executive branch of government and the federal bureaucracy.

How Laws Are Made

Bills can be introduced in either the House or the Senate; sometimes bills are introduced at the same time in both bodies. A bill must be introduced or sponsored by a member of the House or the Senate, and it may have more than one sponsor.

A bill is given a number and a prefix—*HR* in the House and *S* in the Senate. Bills are then sent to committees for consideration. The Speaker of the House or the presiding officer of the Senate decides which committees will receive which bills. Typically, bills are then referred to subcommittees, which investigate the issue, hold hearings, and hear evidence for and against a bill. The subcommittees report back to the full committees, either recommending action on a bill or offering a revised version of a bill. At that point, the committees either support the bill by allowing it "out of committee" or allow the bill to "die in committee."

Bills that reach the floor of the House or the Senate are debated and discussed. If a bill is passed by one house of Congress, it is then sent to the other house where it goes through the same procedures. If different versions of a bill are approved by the two house of Congress, a conference committee receives the two versions and works out a compromise. That compromise bill is sent back to both houses and must be voted on again. If a bill passes the House and the Senate in the same form, it is sent to the president who may sign or veto it.

If the president vetoes a bill, the bill is returned to Congress, along with the reasons for vetoing it. A two-thirds vote by both houses of Congress is required to override a presidential veto. If the president does not sign a bill into law within ten days and if Congress is still in session, the bill becomes law without the president's signature. However, if Congress adjourns during this ten-day period, the bill does not become a law and is dead. This type of inaction is often called a *pocket veto*.

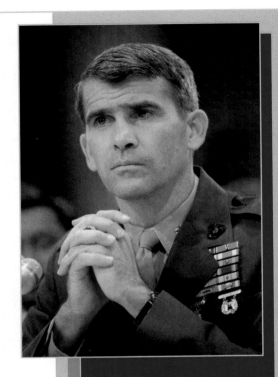

Above: Congressional committees often hold hearings and ask people to testify on an issue they are investigating. Here, Lieutenant Colonel Oliver North is testifying at the Iran-Contra hearings in 1987.

It's Your Turn

1. What are the basic requirements to be elected to Congress?
2. How often are the seats in the U.S. House of Representatives reapportioned?
3. How many Congressional districts does Georgia have?

The Executive Branch of Government

Section Preview

As you read, look for:
- the process of electing a president,
- the parts of the executive branch, and
- the powers of the president.

Our founding fathers wanted to give the executive branch of government enough power to carry out its duties, but not so much power that it might become abusive. They decided upon a single chief executive, a president. Next, the framers of our Constitution had to decide how the president should be elected. They believed that whoever chose the president would have a great deal of influence. They feared having the president elected by Congress or by the states, but they were not sure that the people had the knowledge to make the best choice. Finally, they decided that the president should be selected by a special committee known as the electoral college.

Figure 53
Important Dates in Electoral Process

Presidential election — Tuesday after the first Monday in November in years divisible by four

Electoral college meets to cast votes — Monday following the second Wednesday of December

President of U.S. Senate reads results of electoral vote — January 6

President inaugurated — January 20

The Electoral College

Members of the electoral college (electors) are selected from each state. The number of electors from any given state equals the number of its representatives in the Senate (always 2) and the House of Representatives. There are 538 electors in the electoral college because there are 100 U.S. senators, 435 representatives, and 3 electors from the District of Columbia. It takes 270 votes in the electoral college (a majority) to be elected.

Earlier you learned that, in the beginning, each elector voted for two people. The person who received the majority of the votes (at least one more than one-half of the votes cast) became president and the person who received the second-highest number of votes became vice president. If no one received a majority of electoral votes, the decision was given to the House of Representatives. In the House, each state had one vote and a candidate had to receive a majority of those votes to win.

Today, the electoral college operates somewhat differently. On the Tuesday following the first Monday of November in years divisible by four (2004, 2008, 2012, and so on), the people in each state cast their ballots for the candidates of their choice for president and vice president. In effect, a vote for a candidate is actually a vote for the candidate's electors. The candidate who wins the popular vote in a state usually wins all of that state's electoral votes. Although this is historically what happens, the electors are not legally bound to vote for the candidate who wins the popular vote in their state. There have been instances where an elector has

Above: On January 6, 2001, Senators Mitch McConnell (left) and Christopher Dodd monitor the counting of the electoral college votes for the 2000 presidential election.

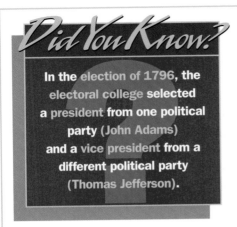

chosen to vote for a candidate other than the individual who won the popular vote in his or her state.

The electoral college meets on the Monday following the second Wednesday of December. Each state's electors meet in their respective state capitals and cast their electoral votes—one for president and one for vice president. The electoral votes are then transmitted to the president of the U.S. Senate who, on the following January 6, opens and reads them before both houses of Congress. The candidate with the majority of votes is declared the winner for the presidential and vice presidential races. These two individuals are sworn into office at noon on January 20 (Inauguration Day).

The Parts of the Executive Branch

The executive branch of government consists of far more than just the offices of the president and the vice president. First, let us look at those two individuals.

Qualifications for the president and vice president are the same. Both the president and the vice president must be at least thirty-five years of age, natural-born citizens, and residents of the United States for at least fourteen years. They are elected to serve four-year terms of office. The Twenty-second Amendment (ratified in 1951) limited the president to two consecutive terms.

The powers of the president are clearly spelled out in the Constitution and listed in Figure 54.

The vice president assumes the presidency if the president dies in office, resigns, or is removed by the impeachment process. If the vice president cannot assume those duties, the line of succession falls to the Speaker of the House of Representatives, followed by the president pro tempore of the Senate. The line of succession then follows through the cabinet officers, beginning with the secretary of state and continuing in the order each cabinet position was created.

The Twenty-fifth Amendment to the Constitution sets the procedure for the vice president to become "acting" president if the president is too ill to perform his or her duties. That

---

Figure 54
The Powers of the President

The president can:

● Appoint and dismiss thousands of federal employees including ambassadors, federal judges, judges of the Supreme Court, ministers and consuls, cabinet officers, and those who serve under them; major presidential appointments are made with the consent of the U.S. Senate

● Act as commander-in-chief of the nation's armed forces

● Call extra sessions of Congress

● Recommend legislation

● Veto bills or sign bills into law

● Receive diplomatic representatives

● Enter into treaties or compacts with foreign governments, with the approval of the Senate

● Issue proclamations, such as recognizing a sports team, honoring astronauts, or congratulating a 4-H group

● Pardon all offenses against the United States except in cases of impeachment, where a pardon can never be granted

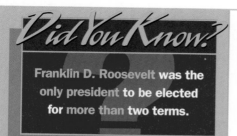
Figure 55
Presidential Line of Succession

1. Vice President
2. Speaker of the House of Representatives
3. President pro Tempore of the Senate
4. Secretary of State
5. Secretary of the Treasury
6. Secretary of Defense
7. Attorney General
8. Secretary of the Interior
9. Secretary of Agriculture
10. Secretary of Commerce
11. Secretary of Labor
12. Secretary of Health and Human Services
13. Secretary of Housing and Urban Development
14. Secretary of Transportation
15. Secretary of Energy
16. Secretary of Education
17. Secretary of Veterans Affairs
18. Secretary of Homeland Security

Amendment also sets the procedure for choosing a new vice president if the regular vice president becomes president.

Clearly, the job of administering the federal government in a nation as large and complex as ours requires more than just the two officials elected as president and vice president. The administrative groups that make up the executive branch of our government are generally known as the *executive bureaucracy*. It can be divided into five main groups: the Executive Office of the President, the Cabinet, independent agencies, regulatory commissions, and government corporations.

The Executive Office of the President

The Executive Office of the President includes major offices or agencies whose directors are appointed by the president with the consent of the Senate. These government leaders serve at the pleasure of the president and can be fired or asked to resign at any time by the president. Agencies in the Executive Office of the President include the Office of Management and Budget, the National Security Council, and the Council of Economic Advisors.

The Cabinet

Members of the Cabinet serve as official advisors to the president and as the heads of executive departments. The Cabinet members are appointed by the president, but they must be confirmed by the Senate. There are currently fifteen Cabinet positions.

Independent Agencies

Congress has created independent agencies to serve the public interest and keep the government and the economy working smoothly. The nature and purpose of independent agencies varies widely. The Environmental Protection Agency (EPA) is an example of an independent federal agency. It supervises national laws and programs involving clean air and water, waste disposal, radiation, and toxic substances. Another example of an independent agency is the General Services Administration. This agency oversees spending by all other government agencies. The heads of independent agencies in our federal government are appointed by the president with the consent of the Senate.

Dr. Antonia Coello Novello

Dr. Antonia Novello was the first female and the first Hispanic to be appointed surgeon general of the United States. The surgeon general is the nation's official spokesperson on all matters of public health. Dr. Novello served a three-year term from 1990 to 1993. As a practicing pediatrician, Dr. Novello's focus was on the health needs of the children and young people of America.

Novello was born in Puerto Rico in 1944. As a child, she suffered from a painful and serious illness of the colon, which was not corrected by surgery until she was eighteen. She had a second surgery two years later. She learned early what it felt like to be a helpless patient because she was hospitalized every summer for treatments of her colon disease. Her experiences led to an interest in medicine and a strong desire to help people. In an interview, Dr. Novello said, "I thought, when I grow up, no other person is going to wait 18 years for surgery."

Dr. Novello earned her medical degree from the University of Puerto Rico in 1970. She moved to Ann Arbor, Michigan, where she continued her medical training at the University of Michigan and, later, at Georgetown University in Washington, D.C. She joined the U.S. Public Health Service and, in 1982, earned a master's degree in public health from Johns Hopkins University.

As surgeon general, Dr. Novello was a strong advocate for preschool immunization programs, restraints on alcohol and tobacco advertising aimed at young people, and programs to increase AIDS awareness. She attacked the "Joe Camel" advertising campaign as a lure for teenage smokers. She initiated a "Spring Break '91" campaign against binge drinking among American college students.

Above: As Surgeon General, Dr. Novello focused her attention on the health of women, children, and minorities.

Dr. Novello felt that her time in office could be a signal of empowerment for women, children, and minorities. Her successes as surgeon general are evidence that she met that purpose. After leaving office, Dr. Novello accepted a position as New York Health Commissioner and also served as a representative for UNICEF (United Nations International Children's Emergency Fund). She lives in New York.

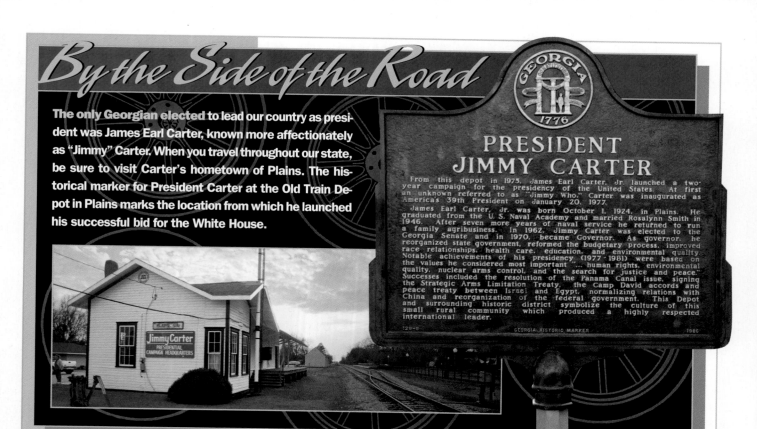

By the Side of the Road

The only Georgian elected to lead our country as president was James Earl Carter, known more affectionately as "Jimmy" Carter. When you travel throughout our state, be sure to visit Carter's hometown of Plains. The historical marker for President Carter at the Old Train Depot in Plains marks the location from which he launched his successful bid for the White House.

PRESIDENT JIMMY CARTER

From this depot in 1975, James Earl Carter, Jr. launched a two-year campaign for the presidency of the United States. At first an unknown referred to as "Jimmy Who," Carter was inaugurated as America's 39th President on January 20, 1977.

James Earl Carter, Jr. was born October 1, 1924, in Plains. He graduated from the U. S. Naval Academy and married Rosalynn Smith in 1946. After seven more years of naval service he returned to run a family agribusiness. In 1962, Jimmy Carter was elected to the Georgia Senate and in 1970, became Governor. As governor, he reorganized state government, reformed the budgetary process, improved race relationships, health care, education, and environmental quality. Notable achievements of his presidency (1977-1981) were based on the values he considered most important "... human rights, environmental quality, nuclear arms control, and the search for justice and peace." Successes included the resolution of the Panama Canal issue, signing the Strategic Arms Limitation Treaty, the Camp David accords and peace treaty between Israel and Egypt, normalizing relations with China and reorganization of the federal government. This Depot and surrounding historic district symbolize the culture of this small rural community which produced a highly respected international leader.

129-8   GEORGIA HISTORIC MARKER   1986

Federal Regulatory Commissions

Federal regulatory commissions have the power to make rules and to punish people or industries who break those rules. The heads of regulatory commissions are appointed by the president and must be approved by the Senate. Some regulatory commissions are a part of Cabinet departments, while others are separate from the major Cabinet divisions.

Examples of regulatory commissions are the Federal Communications Commission, the Securities and Exchange Commission, the Food and Drug Administration, and the National Labor Relations Board.

Government Corporations

The final branch of the federal bureaucracy is a group of government corporations that were established to provide a product or service for the American people. An example of a government corporation is the Federal Deposit Insurance Corporation (FDIC). The FDIC insures bank deposits to protect banking customers. Another well-known federal corporation is the United States Postal Service.

It's Your Turn

1. How many electors are in the electoral college?
2. How old does one have to be in order to be elected president of the United States? Why do you think that age requirement was set and do you think that age requirement is fair?
3. What is the Cabinet? How many Cabinet positions are there?

Federal Money

Where does the federal government get its money? How does the federal government prepare a budget (a plan for receiving and spending money)?

The federal government plans the year's budget in much the same way the typical family plans its budget. First, government financial planners estimate the amounts of money that they expect to take in. Most of the money that the federal government uses to pay the nation's bills comes from taxes.

Second, the federal government determines how much money it needs to spend for the year. Programs that the government must spend money on are called *mandatory programs*. Mandatory programs include social security, Medicare, and Medicaid, Other programs involve *discretionary spending*, where the amount of money allocated to a program changes from year to year. Discretionary spending programs include national defense, housing, transportation, education, foreign aid, and science and technology. Finally, the government must set aside some money to pay for interest payments on monies that the government has borrowed during previous years. In fiscal year 2001, the federal government spent $1.8 trillion.

In some years, the federal government has a surplus; that is, it takes in more money than it spends. In other years, the federal government has a deficit, which means that the government spends more money than it takes in.

What does the federal government do when a budget flares out of control? It operates at a deficit, borrows money, and raises the long-term interest rates for borrowed monies, until the next period of budget planning

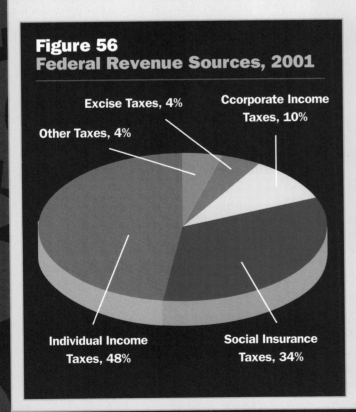

Figure 56
Federal Revenue Sources, 2001

Excise Taxes, 4%

Ccorporate Income Taxes, 10%

Other Taxes, 4%

Individual Income Taxes, 48%

Social Insurance Taxes, 34%

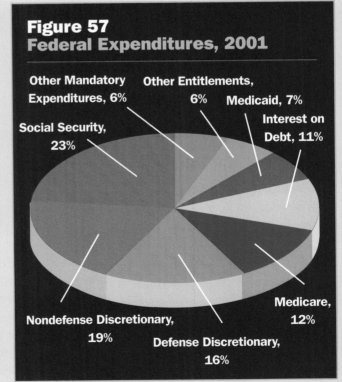

Figure 57
Federal Expenditures, 2001

Other Mandatory Expenditures, 6%

Other Entitlements, 6%

Medicaid, 7%

Social Security, 23%

Interest on Debt, 11%

Nondefense Discretionary, 19%

Defense Discretionary, 16%

Medicare, 12%

The Judicial Branch of Government

Section Preview

As you read, look for:
* the structure of the judicial branch,
* the system of checks and balances, and
* vocabulary term: judicial review.

The Supreme Court and all lower federal courts make up the judicial branch of the federal government. The duties of this branch include deciding on the meaning or interpretation of the Constitution and laws. The judicial branch protects individual citizens from mistreatment by other branches of government.

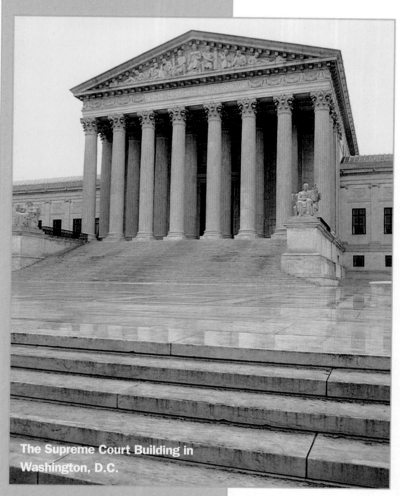

The Supreme Court Building in Washington, D.C.

The Supreme Court

The U.S. Constitution established the Supreme Court as the highest court in the land. Currently, the Court has a chief justice and eight associate justices. There are no set qualifications for Supreme Court justices; they usually serve for life or until they choose to retire. The president, with the consent of the Senate, makes appointments to the Supreme Court.

The Supreme Court has both original and appellate jurisdiction. The Court has original jurisdiction in cases involving a foreign country or in disputes between states and the federal government. It has *appellate jurisdiction* when reviewing decisions of lower-ranking federal courts and the decisions of the highest-ranking state courts. When the Supreme Court decides a case on constitutional grounds, that decision becomes the precedent (guideline) both for all lower courts to follow and for laws that deal with similar issues.

The greatest power of the Supreme Court is that of judicial review, the ability to set aside the actions of the legislative or executive branches of any government agency. By its decision in *Marbury v. Madison*, the Court established the principle that it could declare laws or presidential acts unconstitutional. The Court can also prevent executive action through injunctions (court orders) that forbid the action. In addition, the chief justice of the Supreme Court presides over impeachment proceedings against a president.

The Supreme Court decides which cases it will hear. This authority allows the Court to keep its case-load manageable and set its own constitutional priorities.

Did You Know?

George Washington appointed the greatest number of U.S. Supreme Court justices (11).

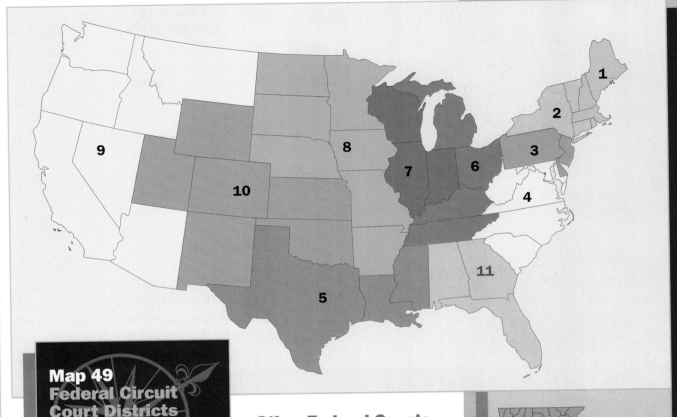

Map 49
Federal Circuit Court Districts

Map Skill In which circuit court district does California lie?

Other Federal Courts

The Constitution gave Congress the power to establish courts lower than the Supreme Court. In the Judiciary Act of 1789, Congress established circuit courts of appeal and district courts. Over time, other courts have been added.

Congress divided the nation into eleven judicial areas called *circuits* plus the District of Columbia. Each circuit has between one and twenty-four judges depending on the workload in a given area. Georgia is in the 11th Judicial Circuit, which includes all of Georgia, Florida, and Alabama.

The U.S. Court of Appeals for the 11th Circuit is based in Atlanta. The court has appellate jurisdiction for cases tried in lower courts or the judgments of administrative agencies. The Court of Appeals does not have juries or witnesses; only opposing lawyers appear to explain their positions.

Below the circuit courts of appeals are the ninety-four district courts, which have original jurisdiction. District courts are the federal trial courts and hear cases of civil and criminal violations of federal laws. District courts are the only federal courts that have juries and witnesses in trials. Georgia is divided into three district courts regions: the Northern District, the Middle District, and the Southern District.

In each district court region, there is also a U.S. Bankruptcy Court. *Bankruptcy* is a legal judgment that a person or an organization cannot pay its debts; the property of the bankrupt is administered to pay off creditors.

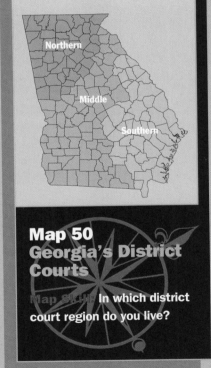

Map 50
Georgia's District Courts

Map Skill In which district court region do you live?

Special Courts

The final part of the federal judicial system is a series of courts created by Congress to deal with special kinds of cases. The U.S. Tax Court, for example, hears disputes between citizens and the Internal Revenue Service. The U.S. Court of Appeals for the Armed Forces reviews military court-martial convictions. The U.S. Court of International Trade decides civil suits against the United States involving trade with other nations. The U.S. Court of Federal Claims handles suits against the United States because of acts of Congress or contracts with the government.

Above: The U.S. Courthouse in Gainesville is one of Georgia's oldest federal buildings.

The System of Checks and Balances

The men who wrote our Constitution provided for a system of checks and balances to keep the branches of equal importance. For example, the power to pass a bill was given to the legislative branch, but the executive branch

Figure 58 Checks and Balances

Legislative Checks

As a check on the executive branch, Congress:

- Approves presidential appointments
- Controls the budget and money appropriations
- Can impeach and remove a president from office
- Can pass laws over the president's veto

As a check on the judicial branch, Congress:

- Votes to confirm the president's judicial appointments
- Can impeach and remove federal judges from office
- Can change laws overturned by the courts and can initiate a Constitutional amendment
- Can restrict the jurisdiction of courts to deal with certain types of cases
- Can create more court systems or do away with existing ones
- Can determine the times and places where federal courts hold sessions

Executive Checks

As a check on the legislative branch, the president has the power to:

- Veto Congressional legislation

As a check on the judicial branch, the president has the power to:

- Appoint or remove federal judges

Judicial Checks

As a check on the legislative branch, the Supreme Court can:

- Declare laws unconstitutional

As a check on the executive branch, the Supreme Court can:

- Declare presidential acts unconstitutional
- Prevent executive actions through injunctions
- The chief justice of the Supreme Court presides over impeachment proceedings against a president

must either sign the bill into law or veto it to keep it from becoming law. The judicial branch cannot write bills or sign them into law, but it can declare a law unconstitutional. In that way, each branch of government has a check on the power of the other two.

Checks and balances are meant to keep branches of government equal, but sometimes people find ways around them. For example, it is said that President Theodore Roosevelt wanted to send the U.S. Navy around the world so that the sailors would gain experience and other nations would see the strength of our naval forces. Congress did not like Roosevelt's plan and refused to provide the money. Roosevelt is said to have replied, "Very well, the existing appropriation will carry the navy halfway around the world and if Congress chooses to leave it on the other side, all right."

A Final Note

Every day, millions of people all over the world look at the United States and the actions of our government. What do they see?

They see a government based on a written constitution that has survived over 200 years by protecting the rights of its citizens. This is not true of most of the world's countries.

They see a government that is a representative democracy, where power rests with the citizens and the citizens elect representatives to manage the nation's affairs. This is not true of most of the world's countries.

They see a government that guarantees freedom of speech, freedom of religion, freedom to assemble peacefully, freedom to petition the government, freedom of the press, and the right to due process protections. These freedoms are not typical of most of the world's countries.

They see a government where almost anyone can be elected to public office at local, state, and national levels. A government where every citizen's vote counts, where each individual is important and is a part of the political process. This is not true of most of the world's countries.

To sum it up, they see liberty and individual freedom in a government that can disagree without violence and that can change without revolution. That is not true of most of the world's countries, and that makes us the envy of most of the world.

It's Your Turn

1. What is the age requirement for Supreme Court justices?
2. When would the U.S. Supreme Court have original jurisdiction over an issue?
3. Which federal judicial circuit includes Georgia?
4. Name one way the president checks Congress. Name one way the president checks the judicial branch.
5. Name one way the judicial branch checks Congress. Name one way the judicial branch checks the president.

Chapter Summary

- The U.S. Constitution established three branches of government: legislative, executive, and judicial.
- The United States is a republic.
- The United States has a bicameral legislature.
- Congress operates through a system of standing committees and select committees.
- A system of checks and balances ensures that no one branch of government becomes more powerful than the other branches.
- Georgia has two senators and thirteen representatives in Congress.
- Representation in the U.S. House of Representatives is based on population. Representation is recalculated every ten years after the federal census has been taken.
- Congress has both expressed and implied powers.
- The executive branch, headed by the president, also includes the vice president, major agencies, the Cabinet, independent agencies, federal regulatory commissions, and government corporations.
- The judicial branch includes the U.S. Supreme Court, circuit courts, district courts, bankruptcy courts, and special courts.

ChapterReview

Reviewing People and Terms

Use each of the following terms in a sentence that focuses on the U.S. Constitution or the federal government.

1. checks and balances

2. constitutionalism

3. elastic clause

4. electoral college

5. expressed powers

6. federalism

7. implied powers

8. judicial review

9. republic

10. separation of powers

11. sovereignty

Understanding the Facts

1. How did James Madison define a republic?

2. What was the difference between the Virginia Plan and the New Jersey Plan?

3. What are the three branches of the federal government?

4. Name four expressed powers given to Congress under the Constitution.

5. Who actually elects the president of the United States?

6. List four powers given to the president by the Constitution.

7. How many justices serve on the U.S. Supreme Court?

8. Discuss the basic principles on which our government is based.

Developing Critical Thinking

1. What were some of the problems with the Articles of Confederation and the unicameral legislature that led to the Constitutional Convention in 1787? How did those problems get resolved in the new Constitution?

2. Why do you think the men who drafted our Constitution set the particular age requirements for senators, representatives, presidents, and vice presidents that they did? Do you think these qualifications should be changed? Argue your position with specific examples.

3. Do you think the electoral college should be discontinued? Why or why not?

4. Do you think the U.S. Supreme Court should have the authority to select its own cases? Why or why not?

5. How effective do you think the system of checks and balances is in our federal government?

Checking It Out

1. Use your research skills to determine how many people are employed by our federal government. What is the annual payroll of federal government workers?

2. Symbols representing feelings and ideas are printed on the paper money of the United States. Look at a $1 bill and list the patriotic symbols that you find on it. Make a list of the patriotic pictures of leaders that are printed on all denominations of our paper money.

3. Use a dictionary or encyclopedia to find out the meaning of the term *Kitchen Cabinet*. Where did this term originate?

Writing Across the Curriculum

1. Who were Georgia's representatives at the Constitutional Convention? Prepare a short biography on each delegate to share with your classmates. Add pictures if you can locate them.

2. Write letters to your Congressional representative and your senators. Find out how they maintain contact with the voters in your community. Find out where their local offices are located and how those offices are staffed. Find out what to do if you have a problem and need assistance from them.

Exploring Technology

1. When our founding fathers came together to form a new government, the only model any of them had was the royal government in Great Britain. Where did the ideas the new government was based upon come from? Could the American Indians have contributed to our nation in this way? Using your favorite search engine, examine the "Iroquois Confederacy" and compare it to our government. Prepare a chart to show your comparison.

2. Using your favorite search engine, locate the websites of Georgia's Congressional delegation. Find out what committee assignments each delegate received. Why do you think Georgia's delegates serve on those particular standing committees? Are there standing committees that have no participation from any of Georgia's delegation? Why do you think Georgians were not appointed to these committees?

3. Go to Internet site www.usconstitution.net/elecvotes.html to learn how many electoral votes Georgia has. Click on "2004" to see how those votes were cast in the 2004 election. You may also want to look at Georgia's electoral votes in other elections.

Applying Your Skills

1. Thirty-nine of the fifty-five delegates who attended the Constitutional Convention had also served in the Continental Congress. What percentage of the delegates to the Constitutional Convention also participated in the Continental Congress?

2. Look up your Congressional district representative to the U.S. Congress. What is his or her voting record? Find out the person's background and some of his or her accomplishments since being elected to Congress. Share your findings with your classmates.

3. Find an example of an action by the federal government in a newspaper or news magazine. Identify which branch of government performed the action.

Government of the Empire State

Georgia's state government, like our federal government, has three branches: executive, legislative, and judicial. The tasks of these branches are, in many ways, like those branches of the federal government. That is, the executive branch enforces laws, the legislative branch enacts laws, and the judicial branch interprets laws. And, like the federal government, Georgia's local and state governments together are a massive enterprise providing employment for many of Georgia's citizens.

Left: The Georgia State Capitol building in Atlanta houses the General Assembly, the governor's office, the State Museum of Service and Industry, and the Hall of Flags. **Below:** The Georgia Governor's Mansion in Atlanta was built in 1967.

Signs of the Times

Georgia Population: 8,186,453 according to 2000 census

Life Expectancy: 74.9 years

Cost of Living: Georgia median household income is $42,433

Literature: Sixteen Georgia writers have been inducted into the Georgia Writers Hall of Fame: Conrad Aiken, Erskine Caldwell, Harry Crews, James Dickey, W.E.B. DuBois, Joel Chandler Harris, John Killens, Martin L. King, Jr, Sidney Lanier, Augusta Longstreet, Carson McCullers, Margaret Mitchell, Flannery O'Connor, Bryon Herbert Reece, Lillian Smith, and Alice Walker.

Fads/Fashions: Attire for Georgia's legislators and government officials is formal, conservative business dress. Traditionally, the evening before the opening day of a General Assembly session, delegates and lobbyists gather for the Wild Hog Supper, a "pork pickin' " barbecue to celebrate the arrival of another session.

Art/Architecture: The Louisville Capitol building had "Georgian style" architecture. The Milledgeville Capitol was a Gothic style. Georgia's current Capitol is a Classical Renaissance style based on styles popular in Italy in the 1400s and 1500s.

Education: Georgia has 34 public colleges and universities, 180 public school systems, and 367 public libraries.

Music: A number of songs have our state name in the song title including "Georgia On My Mind," "Rainy Night in Georgia," "Sweet Georgia Brown," "Midnight Train to Georgia," "The Night the Lights Went Out in Georgia," and "The Devil Went Down to Georgia."

Religion: The Georgia constitution protects freedom of religion in Article I, Section 1, Paragraph IV: "No inhabitant of this state shall be molested in person or property or be prohibited from holding any public office or trust on account of religious opinions. . . ."

Leisure Time: Georgia recreational opportunities include 63 state parks and historic sites and 360 golf clubs. Leading spectator sports include auto racing, golf, football, baseball, basketball, and wrestling.

Transportation: Georgia has 1,244 miles of interstate highways and 18,000 miles of federal and state highways. The total road mileage in Georgia is 115,533. Georgia has 5,000 miles of railroad track and over 260 airports, eight of which are regional airports.

Science/Inventions: The first fiber-optic cable was manufactured in Georgia, and there are now over 500,000 miles of fiber-optic cable buried beneath the state's highways. The Georgia Statewide Academic and Medical Systems video network (GSAMS) connects over four hundred distance-learning and teleconferencing sites including state universities and colleges, medical schools, technical and adult education centers, and K-12 schools.

Figure 59 Timeline: 1750–2000

1983
Current Georgia state constitution ratified

1953
Georgia allowed vote for persons 18 years of age

1796
Louisville became
Georgia capital

1804
Milledgeville became
Georgia capital

1945
Office of lieutenant governor established

1777
First Georgia state
constitution adopted

1868
Atlanta became
Georgia capital

1937
Georgia Bureau of
Investigation created

1985
QBE became
law

1750   **1800**   **1850**   **1900**   **1950**   **2000**

1788
Georgia ratified
U.S constitution

1870
Georgia readmitted to Union

1861
Georgia seceded from Union

The Executive Branch of State Government

Georgia was one of the original thirteen colonies and became a state after the American Revolution. Georgia adopted its first state constitution in 1777. In 1983, Georgians approved the state's tenth constitution. Even though there have been changes in the text of the various constitutions, the purpose of all of them has been the same. The state constitution declares:

> *To perpetuate the principles of free government, insure justice to all, preserve peace, promote the interest and happiness of the citizens and of the family, and transmit to posterity the enjoyment of liberty, we the people of Georgia, relying upon the protection and guidance of Almighty God, do ordain and establish this Constitution.*

Georgia's constitution states, "All government, of right, originates with the people, is founded upon their will only, and is instituted for the good of the whole. Public officers are the trustees and servants of the people and are at all times amenable to them." In other words, any power the government has is given to it by the citizens and is for the good of everyone. Persons elected to public office in state government work for the people and are accountable to the voters for their actions.

The constitution further states: "The people of this state have the inherent right of regulating their internal government. Government is instituted for the protection, security and benefit of the people; and at all times they have the right to alter or reform the same whenever the public good may require it." Therefore, Georgia's government is meant to serve the people, and the constitution allows the people to change the government when it fails to serve their needs.

The constitution gives voters the right to control state government by electing state officials. Citizens also may suggest laws that might improve the way the state is governed.

The largest branch of state government is the executive branch. The **governor** is the chief executive officer of the state. The governor is elected by a majority of the popular vote for a four-year term. The constitution allows governors to serve two consecutive terms, so it is

Above: Republican Sonny Perdue was elected governor of Georgia in 2002. He is seen here with the First Lady of Georgia, Mary Perdue.

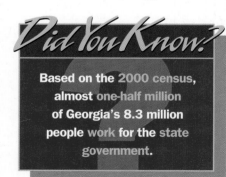

Did You Know?

Based on the 2000 census, almost one-half million of Georgia's 8.3 million people work for the state government.

Figure 60 Georgia State Government

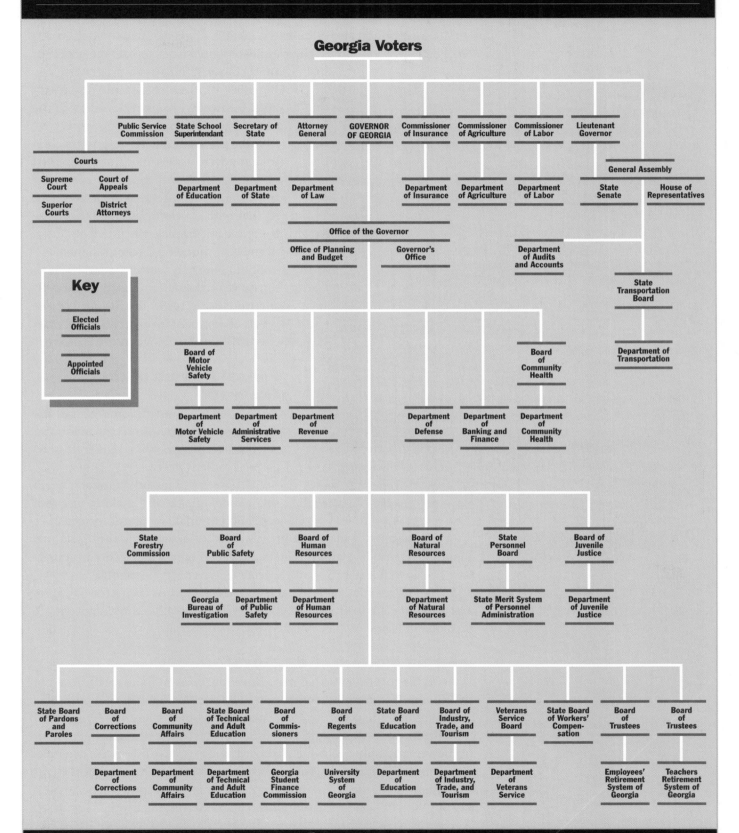

Georgia Voters

possible for one person to be the state's chief executive officer for eight years. After a second term, an individual has to wait four or more years before being able to run again.

The constitution also outlines the qualifications required to be elected as Georgia's chief executive. The candidate who wishes to become governor must be at least thirty years of age when taking office, a citizen of the United States for at least fifteen years, and a resident of the state for at least six years.

If the governor dies or resigns, the lieutenant governor becomes the state's chief executive officer until the next general election for members of the General Assembly. At that time, an election is held to choose someone to complete the unexpired term of the governor who died or resigned.

Should both the governor and the lieutenant governor die or resign from office in the midst of a term, the speaker of the house of representatives serves as the chief executive until a new governor is elected.

Formal Powers of the Governor

The Georgia constitution describes the governor's formal powers. They can be classified as executive powers, legislative powers, and judicial powers.

Executive powers include being able to appoint state officials and making sure that civil and criminal laws are enforced.

Legislative powers include sending requests and messages to the legislature, signing bills into law, and being able to veto a bill so it does not become a law. The governor may also call special sessions of the legislature.

Judicial powers include being able to pardon persons convicted of crimes and appoint state justices to fill unexpired terms. Other formal powers are included in Figure 61.

Informal Powers of the Governor

Georgia's governor also has many informal powers. Some are the result of tradition and custom; others are necessary to enforce the formal powers.

Sometimes, the governor's informal powers may seem more important than the formal powers. But a governor's greatest influence is through his or her power to appoint individuals to boards and executive offices. For example, Governor Joe Frank Harris, who served from 1983 to 1990, appointed all fifteen members of the Board of Regents (the board that controls the University System of Georgia and all public colleges and universities). He named

---

Figure 61
Formal Powers of the Governor

Formal powers of the governor include:

- managing the state's budget (the plan for receiving and spending money),

- directing the attorney general to act as a representative of the state in lower court cases involving state law,

- making an annual "State of the State" address to the legislature,

- preparing budget bills for consideration by the Georgia house of representatives,

- serving as commander-in-chief of the Georgia National Guard,

- heading the state's civil defense units, and

- sending Georgia Highway Patrol officers and the Georgia Bureau of Investigation into communities in times of danger.

Did You Know?

The Georgia Bureau of Investigation was created in 1937. It was first called the Division of Identification, Detection, Prevention and Investigation.

all ten members of the state Board of Education (the board that controls public elementary and secondary schools of the state). He also named a State Superintendent of Schools to complete an unexpired term.

In addition, he appointed a panel of business leaders, legislators, and citizens to write a legislative package called Quality Basic Education (QBE). When this package became law in 1985, it affected all public school students in Georgia. For example, an eighth-grade student in Ocilla has the same study objectives as an eighth-grade student in Columbus. Today, this standard state curriculum is called the Georgia Performance Standards. In several grades, all students take a state-prepared test during the spring. First-time teachers in the state of Georgia must pass tests during their first three years of teaching to show they are able to instruct students. This legislation also changed the way school systems are funded. In these ways, Governor Harris and his appointment powers had a great effect on education all over the state.

Office of Lieutenant Governor

The executive branch of state government also includes the office of **lieutenant governor**. The lieutenant governor is elected by popular vote at the same time the governor is elected. The lieutenant governor must meet the same qualifications for office as the govenor. However, unlike the governor, the lieutenant governor can serve an unlimited number of consecutive terms in office. For example, Zell Miller served four consecutive terms as lieutenant governor.

In the event of a governor's death, resignation, or impeachment, the lieutenant governor becomes the state's chief executive. The lieutenant governor also serves as the chief executive officer when the governor is out of the state.

The lieutenant governor is the presiding officer of the state senate. In that position, he or she makes senate committee appointments, assigns senate bills to committees, and recognizes members of the senate who wish to speak. Because of these powers, the lieutenant governor may affect the passage or failure of some senate bills.

Georgia's Other Elected Officials

The governor and lieutenant governor are not the only elected members of Georgia's executive branch. Voters statewide select the following officials: state

---

Figure 62
Informal Powers of the Governor

Informal powers of the governor include:

- communicating to the public a personal position on issues of interest to all Georgians,

- acting as honorary head of the political party that elected him or her to office,

- issuing proclamations to honor individuals, holidays, or special events and, with the legislature's approval, adding new state symbols,

- representing the state in meetings with other state officials, federal officers, or foreign dignitaries,

- meeting with business and industry leaders from other states or nations to encourage them to expand their businesses into Georgia,

- working with members of the legislature to get laws passed, and

- guiding state agencies.

Did You Know?

The office of lieutenant governor was created when the state constitution was rewritten in 1945.

Figure 63
Georgia's Elected Officials

● **State attorney general** is the chief legal officer for the state and the head of the Department of Law.

● **Commissioner of agriculture** is the head of the Agriculture Department. The commissioner directs agricultural or agribusiness programs, maintains state farmers' markets, supervises services such as inspections, and expands market opportunities for Georgia agriculture.

● **Commissioner of labor** is the head of the Labor Department. The labor commissioner regulates the health and safety of workers, enforces state labor laws, administers unemployment insurance programs, and maintains statistical data on labor.

● **Commissioner of insurance** regulates insurance carriers and issues insurance licenses.

● **Public service commissioners** regulate utilities in Georgia and control the rates and services of transportation companies, telephone companies, and electric companies.

● **Secretary of state** maintains the state's official records, publishes laws passed by the legislature, supervises elections, appoints examining boards, grants corporate charters, and regulates securities, stocks, and bonds.

● **State school superintendent** is the head of the Department of Education. The superintendent directs statewide educational programs, enforces state education regulations and laws, administers state and federal education funds, certifies and licenses teachers and other educators, and approves textbooks for use in Georgia schools.

attorney general, commissioner of agriculture, commissioner of labor, commissioner of insurance, public service commissioners, secretary of state, and the state school superintendent.

All of these officials serve four-year terms of office, except for the five members of the Public Service Commission, who serve six-year terms.

Appointed Officials, Boards, and Commissions

In addition to the officials named in the Georgia constitution, there are a large number of government officials known as *statutory officials*. Their positions are not provided for in the state's constitution, nor are they are elected officials. But their jobs are called for by statute (law). These officials are appointed either by the governor or by the head or directing boards of the department in which they serve. For example, the chief drug inspector is appointed by the commissioner of agriculture.

Another sector of Georgia's government are the boards and agencies that were created by the state constitution or by statute. Look again at Figure 60 on page 531. You can see that there are over thirty major agencies in our government. The State Board of Pardons and Paroles, the Board of Natural Resources, and the State Personnel Board are examples of governing boards created by Georgia's constitution. The Board of Human Resources and the Board of Public Safety were created by state statute. Members of most boards are appointed by the governor. Usually, board members have staggered terms of office so that the terms of all members do not expire at the same time.

Did You Know?

In 1997, Governor Zell Miller appointed Georgia's first black state attorney general, Thurbert E. Baker.

It's Your Turn

1. How many consecutive terms can a Georgia governor serve?
2. What are the three classifications of the governor's formal powers?
3. How does the lieutenant governor affect senate legislation?
4. Who is elected to head the Georgia Department of Education?

American Spotlight

Jimmy Carter

In the history of our nation, only one Georgian has served as president of our country—James Earl "Jimmy" Carter, Jr. Carter was born in Plains on October 1, 1924. He grew up on the family farm at nearby Archery and attended the public schools of Plains. In 1946, he married a neighbor, Rosalynn Smith. Carter graduated from the U.S. Naval Academy at Annapolis in 1946 and served in the Navy for seven years. In 1954, Carter resigned his Navy commission to return to Plains and take over the family's warehouse and cotton gin businesses and a peanut farm.

In 1962, Carter was elected to the Georgia senate and elected governor in 1970. As governor, his emphasis was on ecology, efficiency in government, and the removal of racial barriers. He completely re-organized the state government and reduced the number of state agencies.

In 1974, Carter announced his candidacy for president of the United States and began a two-year campaign across the country. Few gave the unknown governor from Georgia much of a chance, but he campaigned tirelessly on a platform of revival and reform in the Democratic party. Carter defeated President Gerald R. Ford in November 1976 and served one term in office.

During Carter's term as president, he established a national energy policy, completed major civil service reforms, expanded the national park system, deregulated the trucking and airline industries, and created the Department of Education. Carter also appointed record numbers of women, blacks, and Hispanics to government positions. However, domestic economic problems plagued his term. Inflation and interest rates were extremely high, and his efforts to reduce them created a short-term recession. Long gasoline lines and high prices make the public uneasy.

In foreign policy, Carter will probably be best remembered for the 1978 Camp David Peace Accords between Israel and Egypt, the first peace treaty between Israel and an Arab neighboring state. His perseverance in the face of obstacles to the peace efforts illustrate the Georgia character education term for this chapter. He obtained congressional

Above: Jimmy Carter waves from a train at Plains depot.

ratification of the Panama Canal treaties and established full diplomatic relations with the People's Republic of China. He also championed worldwide human rights.

However, in 1979, militants took control of the U.S. Embassy in Iran and seized 52 Americans, holding them captive for fourteen months. Iran did not release the hostages until 1981 on the day that Carter left office.

Following his term as president, Carter returned to his native Georgia where he established, in partnership with Emory University, the Carter Center. The Carter Center is committed to human rights and the easing of human suffering. It attempts to resolve conflicts, enhance freedom and democracy, and improve health worldwide. Carter has been an active leader internationally since 1981 working to monitor free elections throughout the world and to work toward peace in resolving national conflicts. He received the Nobel Peace Prize in 2002 for his many efforts.

The Legislative Branch of State Government

Section Preview

As you read, look for:
- the number of senators and representatives in the General Assembly,
- requirements for senators and representatives,
- committees in the legislature,
- how a bill is passed, and
- vocabulary term: public regulation.

The Tenth Amendment to the U.S. Constitution states that "The powers not delegated to the United States by the Constitution, nor prohibited by it to the States, are reserved to the States, respectively, or to the people."

The Georgia state constitution grants law-making power to the legislative branch. Georgia's legislature is officially known as the Georgia General Assembly. It was formed in 1777 as a one-house legislature. That makes it older than the Congress of the United States. In 1789, the Georgia General Assembly was reorganized as a bicameral, or two-house, legislature with a senate and a house of representatives.

The house of representatives and the senate operate in similar fashion except for two important differences. Only the house of representatives can write appropriations (spending) bills. Only the senate can confirm appointments the governor makes to executive offices. Either house can propose and pass bills, and all bills must be approved by both houses before being sent to the governor.

Members of the General Assembly

There are 180 members of the house of representatives and 56 members of the senate. Members of the legislature are elected by popular vote to two-year terms of office. There is no limit on the number of terms a representative or senator can serve. Each of these members is elected by voters in a house or senate district. Equally important, each house district contains about the same number of people as all of the other house districts. And each senate district contains about the same number of people as all the other senate districts.

At the time of their election, members of the senate are required by Georgia's constitution to be at least twenty-five years of age, citizens of the United States, and citizens of Georgia for at least two years. In addition, they must have been legal residents of the district from which they were elected for at least one year.

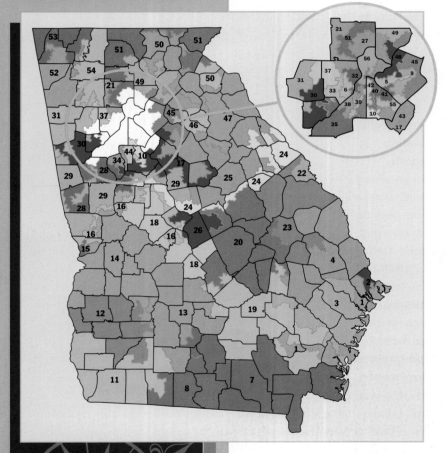

Map 51
Georgia State Senate Districts

Map Skill: In which senate district do you live?

Members of the house of representatives must be at least twenty-one years of age, citizens of the United States, citizens of Georgia for at least two years, and legal residents of the district from which they were elected for at least one year.

Legislative Sessions

The Georgia General Assembly meets each year for a forty-day session, beginning on the second Monday in January. Breaks and recesses do not count as part of the forty days, so the sessions usually last until the middle of March.

The lieutenant governor presides over the senate. Members of the house of representatives elect a speaker as their presiding officer. The speaker, like the lieutenant governor, appoints committees and their chairpersons and assigns bills to those committees.

The lieutenant governor does not have a vote in the senate, but the speaker of the house votes when it is necessary to break a tie.

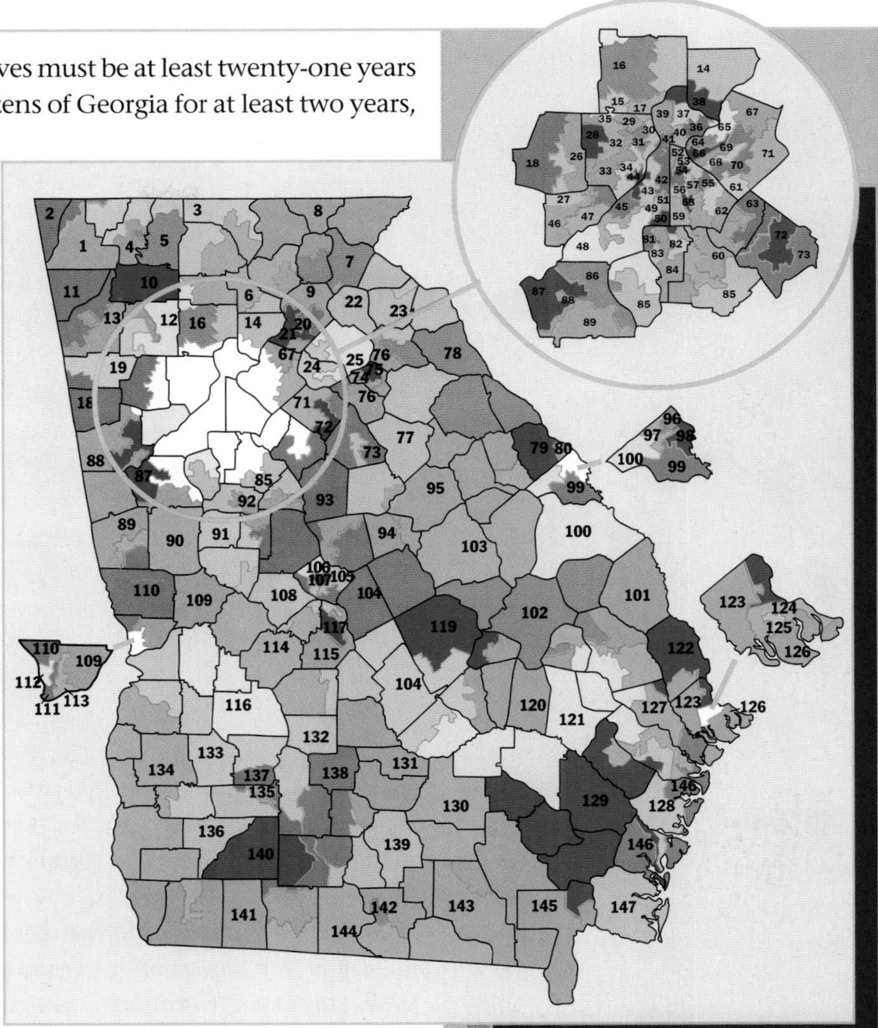

Committees

Like Congress, members of the Georgia house and senate are organized into committees. All bills must be reviewed by a house or senate committee before they can be brought to either the whole house or sent for a vote. The committee system makes it possible for members to study bills closely. There

Map 52
Georgia House of Representative Districts

Map Skill: In which house district do you live?

Figure 64 Powers of a Presiding Officer

A presiding officer has the power to

- determine the order of business,
- control debate,
- rule out proposed amendments to bills,
- enforce rules of procedure for the General Assembly,
- control meeting times and recesses of the General Assembly, and
- order a roll call vote on any issue.

would not be time for such study if each bill were discussed only by the entire house or senate.

Some committees are permanent, lasting from one session to the next. These are called *standing committees*. Some of the standing committees include the Ways and Means Committee, which handles bills involving taxes; the Appropriations Committee, which works on the budget; and the Judiciary Committee, which deals with bills concerning the state's laws and court system.

Other committees are organized for a special task and last only until their work is completed. One type of special committee is an *interim committee*, one that works on assigned issues and concerns between sessions of the legislature. Another special committee is the *conference committee*, which is appointed when the house and senate pass different versions of a bill. The conference committee is made up of three senators and three representatives. The committee takes the two versions and tries to write one bill that can be passed by both houses. A *joint committee*, another special committee, is made up of members from both houses and works on an assigned topic or issue.

A member of the Georgia General Assembly may serve on several committees. Committee chairpersons decide when their committees will meet. They choose the order in which assigned bills will be discussed and when the bills will be voted on.

Types of Legislation

The Georgia General Assembly can pass laws on any matter not denied it by the U.S. Constitution. It can amend state laws or do away with them. The General Assembly can pass legislation on such matters as taxes, education,

Spotlight on the Economy

Funding Georgia's Government

Like our federal government, Georgia must work each year from a budget that outlines sources of income for the state, called revenues, and plans for spending those funds, called expenditures. State budgets must often be adjusted during the year as economic conditions change.

Georgia basically works under three types of budgets—an original budget approved for a year, an amended budget, and a supplementary budget. The original budget is the first budget approved for a fiscal year (a budgetary spending year). An amended budget is one in which changes are made to add, delete, or transfer monies in order to keep Georgia's budget in line with state law. (Georgia's constitution requires that the state have a balanced budget, one that matches expenditures with revenues.) A *supplementary budget* is a change made in a budget to cover new spending when additional or unspent funds are available.

Georgia's revenues come from three basic sources—state funds, federal funds, and special fees collected by agencies. Most special fees are kept by the agencies that collect them. So Georgia's budget planners base their plans

on federal and state funding sources. Those sources include income taxes, sales taxes, other taxes and fees, lottery receipts, indigent care trust funds, and tobacco settlement funds. About 90 percent of Georgia's revenue comes from taxes. Georgians pay personal income taxes on salaries they receive as well as on interest, dividends, and any profits earned on rents. Corporations operating in Georgia also pay income tax on their profits. For 2004, as an example, individual and corporate income taxes were estimated at almost $8 billion. Another large source of taxes is the state sales tax, which consumers pay on the goods and services they purchase. Estimates of sales tax revenues for the 2004 budget were $4.7 billion. Special sales taxes are collected on motor fuel, cigar and cigarette products, and alcoholic beverages. These taxes are collected even before the products are sold to consumers. For the 2004 budget, special sales taxes were estimated to be $1.1 billion.

What are those funds normally spent on? Most state monies are spent to provide services directly to Georgia's citizens. Figure 66 illustrates where Georgia's money goes.

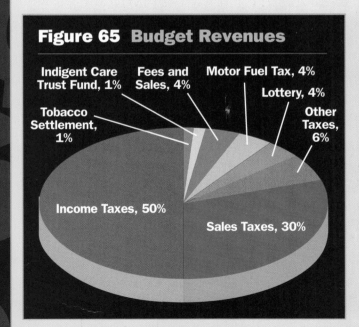

Figure 65 Budget Revenues

Indigent Care Trust Fund, 1%
Fees and Sales, 4%
Motor Fuel Tax, 4%
Lottery, 4%
Other Taxes, 6%
Tobacco Settlement, 1%
Income Taxes, 50%
Sales Taxes, 30%

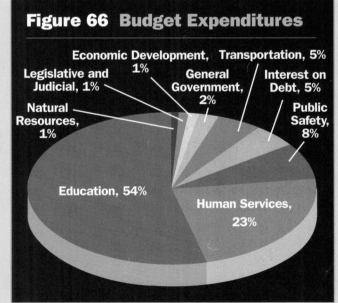

Figure 66 Budget Expenditures

Economic Development, 1%
Transportation, 5%
Legislative and Judicial, 1%
General Government, 2%
Interest on Debt, 5%
Natural Resources, 1%
Public Safety, 8%
Education, 54%
Human Services, 23%

Figure 67
Nine Steps from Proposal to Law

Bills in the Georgia General Assembly go through almost the same steps as those in the U.S. Congress before they become law. Let us look at a bill that starts in the state house of representatives.

1. A proposal is written in legal language and turned in to the clerk's office. There it is given a name and number. For example, the twelfth proposal turned in to the clerk of the house of representatives during a session will be "H.R. 12." After the proposal is given a number, it is called a bill.

2. Copies of the bill are made for members of the house. The bill is then assigned to a committee.

3. The committee to which the bill is assigned may hold public hearings so that interested persons may speak for or against the bill. The committee may also ask legislative staff members to gather information about the bill. The committee studies the bill and discusses its good and bad points.

4. The committee assigned to handle the bill can do several things: (a) It can hold the bill and not release it to the house; (b) It can vote the bill out of committee and recommend that it be passed; (c) It can vote the bill out of committee and recommend that it not be passed; (d) It can make changes in the bill and vote the new version out for consideration by the house; and (e) in the house only, it can vote the bill out of committee with no recommendation. If a bill is not voted out of committee, it is "killed" unless the full house votes to take the bill from the committee and assign it to another one.

5. A bill sent to the full house is discussed, debated, and perhaps amended. A majority vote is required to pass a bill.

6. When a bill is "certified" (passed) by the house, it is carried by messenger to the senate for consideration.

7. Again, the bill is assigned to a committee and studied. As before, the bill may be kept in committee, changed, or voted out without change to be handled by the entire senate.

8. If both the house and the senate pass a bill in the same form, it is signed by the presiding officers and clerks before being sent to the governor.

9. The governor can handle a bill in one of three ways. He or she can (a) sign it into law; (b) take no action, thus letting it become law automatically, or (c) veto it. If a bill is vetoed, the General Assembly can override the veto by a two-thirds vote of both houses. The bill then becomes law.

contracts, and real and personal property. Other subjects it deals with include inheritances, mortgages, corporations, and marriage and divorce. The legislature makes laws concerning fines, imprisonment, or death in criminal matters. It also considers public regulation, laws affecting such issues as morals, public health, business or professional regulations, or any general welfare rule that restricts personal property.

How a Bill Becomes Law

Any citizen may suggest an idea for a law, and any senator or representative can propose a bill for consideration. All bills that affect how the state raises or spends money must start in the house of representatives. Bills about anything else may begin in either house.

Remember that for a bill to become a law, the same version of the bill must be passed by both the house of representatives and the senate. Suppose that the senate passes a slightly different version of a bill than the one adopted by the house. When this happens, the amended bill must be sent back to the house to be reconsidered. If the two houses cannot agree to pass identical versions of a bill, the two versions are sent to a conference committee, which works out a compromise bill that both houses will accept. The compromise bill must be passed by both the senate and the house of representatives before it is sent to the governor.

Reapportionment

One task of the legislature every ten years is to redraw the maps dividing Georgia into voting districts. In Chapter 14, you learned that, af-

Figure 68 How a Bill Becomes Law

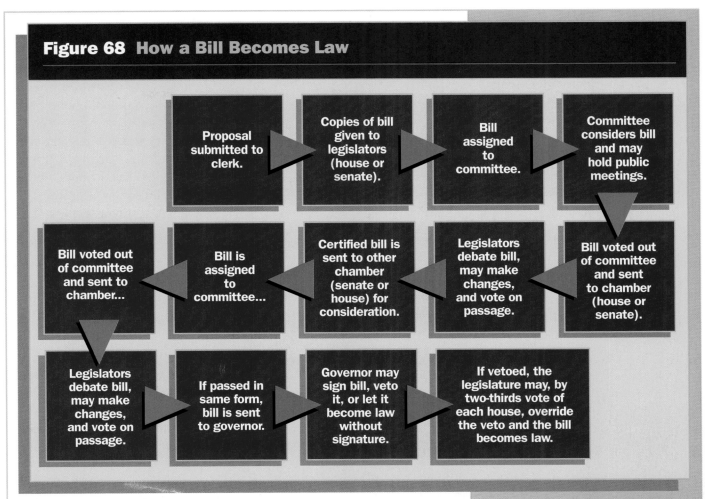

ter each census, seats in the U.S. House of Representatives are reapportioned based on the most recent population figures. In the 2000 census, Georgia's population increased. That meant that Georgia gained House seats, moving from 11 to 13 representatives.

In a special session of the 2001 legislature, the Georgia legislature redrew the voting districts. However, Republicans argued that the Democratic party, which controlled Georgia's legislature at that time, gerrymandered the districts lines to favor Democratic incumbents and dilute Republican voting strength. In effect, the new district voting lines spread Democratic voters over more districts and squeezed Republican voters into fewer districts.

In February 2004, a three-judge panel of the 11th Circuit Court of Appeals ruled that the state's redistricting plans did violate the one-person, one-vote concept. According to the court, district lines had to be redrawn before the 2004 party primaries and the November 2004 general election. If the legislature was unable to reach a decision on new voting district lines, the court would do it. When this textbook went to press, a special "master" appointed by the court had presented new district maps. They had not, however, been approved.

Two changes are likely to result from this redistricting effort. First, Republican party strength should increase in the state since the most populated

Did You Know?

During the 40-day session of the General Assembly, more than 1,000 bills will be proposed.

By the Side of the Road

The creation of counties and cities is, by Georgia law, a responsibility of the Georgia General Assembly. For example, Union County was created in by an act of the legislature 1832 from land that had been Cherokee County. John Thomas, a resident and politician, suggested "Name it Union, for none by union-like men reside in it." The historical marker that explains the creation of the county is in Blairsville at the old Union County Courthouse.

UNION COUNTY

Union County was created by Act of Dec. 3, 1832 from Cherokee. Originally, it contained part of Fannin and Towns Counties. In 1832 there was much discussion over Union and States' rights. John Thomas, chosen by the people as a representative for the new County, when asked to suggest a name, is reported to have said, "Name it Union, for none but union-like men reside in it." First officers of Union County, commissioned March 20, 1833 were: James Crow, Sheriff; Arthur Gilbert, Clerk Superior Court; Joseph Jackson, Clerk Inferior Court; James Gaddis, Sr., Coroner; Joseph Chaffin, Surveyor.

metro and northern counties have been Republican strongholds in recent years. Second and more significant, the shifting of power in Georgia politics from southern and rural areas to more populated metropolitan and urban areas will be complete. The situation will make the "One Georgia" ideal more difficult to achieve since funds and development for business, industry, and transportation will be controlled by metro and urban representatives.

It's Your Turn

1. Which house can propose a bill concerning how the state spends money?
2. When does the General Assembly convene each year and how long are the regular sessions?
3. What happens when the governor takes no action on a bill passed by both houses?
4. Who makes up the conference committee?

Georgia's Capitals

As you have read, Georgia has had several different capital cities. The capital rotated between Savannah and Augusta for much of the state's early history. Savannah was a coastal city. When most of Georgia's population moved inland, it became difficult for the state's citizens to travel to Savannah for state business. But Augusta was too far east for many of the state's citizens. In 1786, the legislature appointed a commission to find a site for a permanent, centrally located capital.

The commission was given funds to purchase 1,000 acres of land for a new city that was to be modeled after the U.S. capital of Philadelphia. The legislature also insisted that the new capital be called "Louisville" to honor King Louis XVI of France for his help in America's Revolutionary War. While finding the site was relatively easy, it was 1796 before a new Capitol building was constructed in Louisville. But Louisville served as the capital for only ten years before another move was necessary.

As more Indian lands opened to the settlers, Georgia's citizens continued to move west and wanted a capital that was more convenient for the western part of the state. In 1804, the legislature voted to build a new capital city in Baldwin County. It set aside funds to purchase 3,240 acres of land and agreed to name the newest capital "Milledgeville" in honor of Governor John Milledge. Milledgeville served as the state's capital for sixty years. Milledgeville had to be evacuated in 1864 during Sherman's March to the Sea. Macon served as a temporary capital while Milledgeville was occupied by Union troops. After the war, the government returned to Milledgeville.

Above: Milledgeville was the capital of Georgia for much of the state's early years, from 1803 until 1868. This building, which was twice destroyed by fire, was the Capitol. Today, it is part of the Georgia Military College.

A change in transportation led to the state's next capital city. The state's Western and Atlantic Railroad ended at a place called Terminus. Terminus was incorporated as a city in 1843 and renamed Marthasville to honor Governor Lumpkin's youngest daughter. In 1847, Marthasville officially became Atlanta and became the center of railroad activities in the state. After the Civil War, Atlanta also became the center of economic growth in the region. During Reconstruction, military authorities had their headquarters in Atlanta. Finally, in 1868, Georgia's new constitution called for the capital to be in the city of Atlanta. In July 1868, the legislature officially met in the newest capital city for the first time, and Atlanta has remained the capital ever since.

The Judicial Branch of State Government

The judicial branch of government consists of the state's courts. Their role is to interpret the state constitution, protect the legal rights of citizens, and enforce the laws of the state. Courts enforce constitutional laws, statutory laws (those passed by the General Assembly), administrative laws (regulations of executive branch agencies), and case laws (court interpretations of written laws).

The courts protect citizens from abuses by government by ensuring that each citizen has "due process of law." The U.S. Constitution says no state can deprive any citizen of life, liberty, or property without due process of law. This means that persons arrested for a crime have the right to have a lawyer present during questioning. Individuals must be given a speedy, public trial before a fair judge and jury. They may face and question witnesses, or they can remain silent so as not to incriminate (blame) themselves.

The courts also protect citizens from each other by handling civil cases (disputes between two or more persons or groups) and criminal cases (cases

Below: The Georgia supreme court has seven justices who are elected to six-year terms. Originally, there were three justices, but the number was expanded in 1896 to six and in 1945 to seven.

"FIAT JUSTITIA. RUAT CAELUM"

involving violations of the law). Crimes are divided into felonies and misdemeanors. A **felony** is a serious crime such as murder or burglary, punishable by a year or more in prison, a fine of at least $1,000, or both. A **misdemeanor** is a less serious crime punishable by less than a year in prison, a fine of less than $1,000, or both.

Georgia Courts

The highest-ranking court in the Georgia court system is the **supreme court**. The seven supreme court justices are elected by popular vote to six-year terms. If a supreme court justice resigns or dies before the end of a term, the governor may appoint a justice to complete his or her term of office. Supreme court justices elect the chief justice from among themselves.

The supreme court is an *appellate* court, which means it only reviews cases on appeal from lower-ranking courts. There are no witnesses and juries as there are in lower-ranking trial courts.

Another responsibility of the supreme court is to interpret the state constitution. It may review cases involving the constitutionality of laws, title to land, equity, wills, habeas corpus, divorce, and alimony. The supreme court automatically reviews all Georgia cases involving the death penalty. It also outlines a code of judicial conduct for the judges of the state, and regulates the admission of attorneys to practice law in Georgia. Decisions of the supreme court are binding. This means they have the final authority in matters of law at the state level.

The second highest-ranking state court is the **court of appeals**. Twelve judges serve on this court, and they elect one of their members to serve as the chief judge. The judges are elected to six-year terms. The court of appeals, like the supreme court, is an appellate court. It only hears cases appealed from lower-ranking courts.

Figure 69 Georgia Court System

Supreme Court
7 Justices

Court of Appeals
12 Judges
4 Divisions

Superior Court
188 Judges
49 Circuits

State Court	Juvenile Court	Probate Court	Magistrate Court
70 Courts	159 Courts	159 Courts	159 Courts
105 Judges	120 Judges and Associate Judges	159 Judges	159 Chief Magistrates
			346 Magistrates

Did You Know?

Women were not allowed to practice law in Georgia courts until 1915.

Figure 70 State Checks and Balances

● **The Executive Branch** can veto bills passed by the legislative branch and can call special sessions of the legislature. It also has some appointment powers when officers of the court resign or die.

● **The Legislative Branch** can impeach officials in the executive or judicial branches. It can override a governor's veto of bills to make them into laws. It must also confirm appointments made by the governor. It can also propose constitutional changes.

● **The Judicial Branch** determines whether or not laws are constitutional.

Above: The offices and courtroom of the Georgia Supreme Court are in the State Judicial Building in Atlanta. The Atlanta-based Court of Appeals also meets here.

Below the appellate courts are the trial courts of Georgia. The **trial courts** hear original cases, such as criminal cases and civil cases between private parties. The state's trial courts include 188 superior courts in 49 circuits (regions), 70 state courts, 159 probate courts, 159 juvenile courts, and 159 magistrate courts. Over 400 municipal (city) courts and special courts are also part of Georgia's judicial branch.

Each court has a special **jurisdiction** (the range of actions over which the court has control or influence). For example, the juvenile court handles cases involving persons under the age of seventeen. The probate court deals with the wills and estates of deceased persons. Magistrate courts can only hear civil cases involving sums under $15,000.

The Jury System

An important part of Georgia's court system is the concept of a jury trial, a trial before one's peers. There are two types of juries—a grand jury and a trial jury. The **grand jury** determines whether or not persons accused of crimes should be indicted (officially charged) and required to stand trial. A **trial jury** is a group of citizens who are charged with judging a person charged with a crime.

Separation of Powers

The Georgia constitution, like that of the United States, provides separate powers for each branch of government. It also provides for a system of checks and balances to ensure that no one branch becomes too powerful (see Figure 70).

In addition, each branch of government is responsive to the citizens of Georgia because most officials in each branch are directly elected by the voters.

It's Your Turn

1. What is the difference between appellate and original jurisdiction?
2. Which type of court normally handles cases involving persons under age seventeen?
3. Which type of jury decides whether to indict a person accused of a crime?

Section 4

Young People and the Law

Did you know that on any given day, over 2,500 children are locked up in Georgia? Most of these young people are jailed for nonviolent crimes such as shoplifting, breaking windows, truancy (failure to attend school), or running away from home. They fall under the jurisdiction of Georgia's juvenile justice system.

Juveniles are citizens under the age of seventeen. As citizens, juveniles must follow the same local, state, and federal laws that all other citizens follow. But juveniles have special status under the law, and they must also follow some laws that do not apply to adults. For example, they must attend school until at least age sixteen. They cannot run away from home. They cannot possess alcoholic beverages or tobacco until ages twenty-one and eighteen respectively. In addition, juveniles may not hang around public places or wander the streets breaking local curfews, which are usually 12 midnight to 5 a.m. Juveniles cannot enter bars where alcoholic beverages are sold unless accompanied by a parent or guardian. Finally, juveniles are required to obey all of the reasonable and lawful instructions or commands of their parents or guardian.

The Juvenile Court System

In 1906, the Georgia General Assembly passed a law establishing a special court for juveniles. In 1911, Fulton County became the first county in Georgia to set up a juvenile court. Today, every county in Georgia has one.

The juvenile courts have three main purposes: (1) to help and protect the well-being of children, (2) to make sure that any child coming under the jurisdiction of the court receives the care, guidance, and control needed, and (3) to provide care for children who have been removed from their homes.

Two terms are important to understand juvenile laws and courts. A *delinquent act* is an act that would be considered a crime if committed by an adult. A *status offense* refers to an act that would *not* be considered a crime if committed by an adult. When juveniles commit a delinquent act or a status offense and are captured by the police, they are said to be "taken into custody" rather than "under arrest."

Section Preview

As you read, look for:
- the steps in the juvenile justice system,
- the rights and responsibilities of juveniles, and
- vocabulary terms: truancy and juvenile.

Above: Juveniles—young people under the age of seventeen—have both rights and responsibilities. In Georgia, they have a special status and juvenile offenders are judged in a special court.

Did You Know?

The first juvenile court in the United States was established in Chicago in 1899.

Figure 71 Georgia's Juvenile Courts

Georgia's juvenile courts have jurisdiction over the following cases:

● Juveniles who commit traffic offenses;

● *Delinquent juveniles*, those under the age of seventeen who commit acts that would be crimes if committed by an adult (for example, burglary or car theft);

● *Unruly juveniles*, those under the age of eighteen who commit acts that would not be crimes if committed by adults (for example, running away from home, disobeying parents, being out between 12 midnight and 5 a.m., being repeatedly truant from school);

● Juveniles under the supervision or probation of the court;

● *Deprived juveniles*, children under the age of eighteen who are neglected or abused by parents or guardians or those who have no parents or legal guardians;

● Cases involving children who need mental health services; and

● Proceedings involving judicial consent for marriage, employment, or enlistment in the armed services when such consent is required by law.

Steps in the Juvenile Justice Process

When a juvenile is taken into custody, the first step is *intake*. At this time, the juvenile is turned over to a juvenile court intake officer, who investigates the case. The intake officer must decide if there is enough evidence (probable cause) to support the charges made against the juvenile. If there is not enough evidence, the intake officer must release the juvenile.

If there is enough evidence to think the juvenile may be guilty of the charges, the intake officer may (1) release the juvenile into the custody of his or her parents or legal guardian or (2) detain the juvenile.

In Georgia's juvenile system, most juveniles are not detained but are released into the custody of parents or guardians. Intake officers often detain juveniles who might be a risk to run away, who might have nowhere else to go if parents or guardians are unable or unwilling to take them, who might be a risk to harm themselves or others, or who have been in trouble with the law before. If a juvenile is detained, parents or a guardian must by law be notified.

Juveniles who are detained are housed in one of the state's Regional Youth Detention Centers, often known as RYDCs. In certain special circumstances, juveniles charged with serious crimes can be placed in adult jails and tried by adult courts rather than juvenile courts.

The second step is *detention*. If the juvenile is detained, a probable cause hearing before the juvenile judge must be held within seventy-two hours. At that point, the judge has three options: (1) dismiss the case, (2) have an *informal adjustment*, or (3) have a *formal hearing*.

Generally, an informal adjustment is held for first offenders. The juvenile and his or her parents or guardian must agree to the informal adjustment, and the young person must admit the wrongdoing. The juvenile is under the supervision of the court for at least ninety days. While under the court's supervision, the juvenile might be required to attend school regularly or participate in counseling programs. The juvenile may also be required to pay for any damages caused or to complete community service requirements.

If an informal adjustment is not held, the third step in the juvenile justice process is a *formal hearing*. First, the complaining witness files a petition outlining the wrongdoing. Once the petition is signed, a date is set for the formal hearing and a *summons* issued. The summons requires the juvenile, the parents or guardian, and those involved in the charges to attend the hearing.

The first part of a formal hearing is the *adjudicatory hearing*, which is somewhat like a trial. The juvenile judge hears the case against the juvenile and the juvenile's defense. There is no jury. After listening to all the evidence, the judge decides whether or not the child is guilty of committing a delinquent act. If found not guilty, the juvenile is released. If found guilty, the court schedules a second hearing.

The second part of the formal hearing is called the *dispositional hearing*. In this part, the judge determines the punishment for the offense. At this hearing, both the prosecutor and the defense can call witnesses and present evidence that might influence the judge's sentence.

The fourth step in the juvenile justice process is the *sentencing*. The judge may select from a number of options (see Figure 72).

As a final step in the process, a juvenile has the right to appeal his or her case. The court has the right to extend its custody or supervision of the juvenile for up to five years.

Did You Know?

Juvenile courts are charged with doing what is in the best interest of the child while keeping in mind the best interest of society.

Figure 72 Juvenile Sentencing

Once a juvenile has been judged guilty of committing a delinquent act, the judge has several ways to treat the child. The judge may

- Release the juvenile to the custody of parents or legal guardian with no court supervision.
- Place the juvenile on probation.
- Place the juvenile in a youth development center for up to ninety days.
- Commit the juvenile to the Department of Juvenile Justice.
- Send the juvenile to a special program such as boot camp.
- Assign other punishments (such as restitution and fines) and special conditions of probation (such as mandatory school attendance, community service, counseling, suspension or prohibition of driver's license).

Georgia's Seven Deadly Sins Act

In 1994, the Georgia legislature addressed the issue of increasingly violent youth crimes. It passed an amendment to the Georgia Juvenile Code that permits youths who are charged with certain violent crimes to be treated as though they were adults. These young offenders fall under the jurisdiction of the superior court and are treated as adult criminals.

The superior court has sole jurisdiction over juveniles charged with such serious crimes as murder, rape, and armed robbery with a firearm. These offenses were called the "Seven Deadly Sins" when the legislation was being debated in 1994. Mandatory ten-year sentence guidelines are a part of that change.

The Rights of Juveniles

Juveniles handled under the juvenile justice system have the same basic legal rights that other citizens have. They have the right to have their cases

Figure 73
Court Cases Involving Students' Rights

Case: *Tinker v. Des Moines*, 1969
Issue: Freedom of student expression
Explanation: School officials cannot limit a student's right to free expression unless there is evidence of a disruption in school operations or an invasion of rights of others.

Case: *Hazelwood v. Kuhlmier*, 1988
Issue: Student publications
Explanation: Although students have the right to publish and to distribute literature produced on and off campus, schools have the right to exercise editorial control over the style and content of school-sponsored student publications.

Case: *Bethel School District v. Fraser*, 1986
Issue: Disruptive speech
Explanation: School boards have the right to determine what speech is inappropriate, and they need not tolerate speech or conduct that is lewd or offensive.

Case: *Colorado Independent School District v. Barber*, 1995
Issue: Dress codes
Explanation: Schools can enact strict dress codes that prohibit students from wearing apparel or symbols of gang membership if it is shown that a gang problem exists.

Case: *New Jersey v. T.L.O.*, 1986
Issue: Unreasonable search and seizure
Explanation: School officials are not required to obtain a search warrant or to show probable cause to search a student, only a reasonable suspicion that the search will produce evidence of a violation of law or of school rules.

Case: *Gross v. Lopez*, 1975
Issue: Right to due process in suspensions and expulsions
Explanation: Students have a legal right to an education, and students cannot be expelled or suspended without due process protections.

decided quickly, just as adults have the right to a speedy trial. Juvenile cases, however, are decided by a judge, not a jury.

Juvenile court proceedings can result in the loss of liberty. As a result, juveniles have all of the rights to a fair trial: They must be notified of the charges against them; they are protected against self-incrimination; they have the right to an attorney; and they have the right to confront and to question witnesses against them. The accused juvenile has the right to present a defense, to introduce evidence, and to testify on his or her own behalf. Most importantly, the juvenile has the right to have a parent or a guardian present in all hearings. If a child's parents or guardian cannot afford a lawyer, the court must appoint an attorney to represent the child.

Students' Rights and Responsibilities Under School Law

Students do not leave their constitutional rights behind them when they enter the schoolhouse door. In particular, challenges have arisen over several areas of basic student freedoms when those freedoms seemed to conflict with a school's right to manage its environment. Students and schools have disagreed over the nature of school disciplinary procedures, protection of lockers and book bags against searches, freedom of expression in slogans on T-shirts, articles in student newspapers, public speech, and even school dress and hairstyle restrictions.

The courts have protected the First Amendment rights of students (freedom of religion, speech, the press, the right to assemble, and the right to petition) as well as their Fourth Amendment rights against unreasonable searches and seizures. Rulings have also protected the Fifth Amendment rights of students (equal protection under the law and right of due process of law).

Student Responsibilities Under School Law

According to Georgia law, students have a legal right to a free public education. But along with rights come responsibilities.

Students must attend school between the ages of six and sixteen. Students must follow reasonable rules and regulations, behavior codes, and even dress codes schools have established to provide an environment that is safe and conducive to learning.

Finally, students have a responsibility to work with school officials to prevent disruptions and violence in their schools. After the school shootings of the late 1990s, all students have a responsibility to work together to avoid weapons and fights on school campuses. And all students must work to prevent violence at school-sponsored activities, dances, ball games, and other events—not just in the school classrooms.

Schools will be as safe and successful as the students and teachers within them work to make them be.

A Final Note

The character education term for this chapter is perseverance. What does it mean and how does it apply? To persevere means to stick to the task, to "hang in there" and get a job done. People who show perseverance are those who do not quit just because they experience some failures or hardships or obstacles. For example, successful inventors exhibit perseverance. They experiment and fail many times before they succeed in developing a new product from a general idea or concept. Strong political and social leaders also exhibit perseverance. They too show a willingness to keep working on programs and reforms that will better their state.

Students have to have a touch of perseverance to make those high grades. Even when a project or assignment is a difficult task, the A student sticks to the job until it is completed satisfactorily. Perseverance is a trait we should all try to develop on our way to success. Good luck!

Chapter Summary

- Georgia's government is based on the state's constitution.
- Georgia's first constitution was adopted in 1777. The latest, the tenth, was adopted in 1983.
- Georgia has three branches of government—executive, legislative, and judicial.
- The executive branch, headed by the governor, is the largest branch of state government.
- Georgia has a bicameral legislature, a two-house body made up of the house of representatives and the senate.
- The supreme court is the highest-ranking court in Georgia, followed by the court of appeals and the state superior court.
- Georgia's government includes a system of checks and balances, just as the federal government does.
- The state is funded with both state and federal monies.
- The source of most state funds are individual and corporate income taxes and sales taxes.
- The majority of the state's budget is spent on education and social services.
- Young people under the age of seventeen or eighteen are subject to the juvenile justice system.

ChapterReview

Reviewing People, Places, and Terms

Use each of the following terms in a sentence about Georgia's government.

1. expenditures
2. governor
3. grand jury
4. jurisdiction
5. juvenile
6. revenues
7. supreme court

Understanding the Facts

1. What are the three branches of Georgia's state government?
2. How old does a person have to be to serve as Georgia's governor?
3. What length are the terms of the governor and the lieutenant governor?
4. Who prepares the annual budget, or appropriations package, for presentation to the Georgia General Assembly?
5. How many members make up the General Assembly?
6. Who presides over the Georgia senate? Who presides over the Georgia house of representatives?
7. How does the General Assembly manage to accomplish its work in a 40-day legislative session?
8. Which of Georgia's courts have appellate jurisdiction?

Developing Critical Thinking

1. Why is it important to have roughly the same number of people in each legislative district in the state?
2. Georgia is the fastest-growing state east of the Rockies. About 160,000 people move into the state each year. As more developments, businesses, and residences are built, land known as "green space" is lost. What is "green space"? How much do we have? Why is it a problem when a forested area is turned into condominiums, stores, or parking lots? How can we preserve some of the state's green space without turning away citizens?
3. In your opinion, what role does a student play in maintaining a safe school environment free of hate speech, violence, and weapons?

Checking It Out

1. You have read that the executive branch of Georgia's government is the largest branch, and that over one-half million people in Georgia are government employees. Research to find out how much it costs to pay Georgia's government workers. How much do your representative and senator make? How much do the governor and lieutenant governor make?
2. Two of Georgia's major recreational areas are Lake Lanier in north Georgia and West Point Lake in southern Georgia. Both lakes are served by the Chattahoochee River, which also goes through Metropolitan Atlanta and provides the city's water source. Interest groups and everyday citizens are concerned about overuse of the river's water and about pollution.

Research these two major lakes. How low is the water level in the lakes getting? What activities are underway to protect the water reservoirs and the river? Who are the opponents in the dispute over water use?

3. Use your local newspaper to locate the names and contact addresses of your state senators and representatives. How do you contact them if you need assistance? How do you contact them if you want information or want to share your ideas about issues?

Writing Across the Curriculum

1. There are a number of major issues that the General Assembly must confront in every session. Four of the problems are (1) the water supply and sharing available water resources both within the state and with neighboring states; (2) air pollution and traffic congestion, especially in Metropolitan Atlanta; (3) educational improvement; and (4) economic improvements. Select any one of these issues. Prepare a short report stating the problem, identifying proposed solutions, and giving your own recommendations for action.

2. Some of Georgia's most influential leaders have been writers, people like Gene Patterson and Ralph McGill of the *Atlanta Journal-Constitution* and Bill Shipp of *Georgia Trend* magazine. Through their editorials and stories, writers like these have greatly influenced the way ordinary Georgians think and act. Examine the writings of these three men, then try your hand at writing an editorial for your school or community newspaper. Select a current issue, explain that issue, and propose action in your editorial. Remember, you have to be fair, your facts have to be accurate, and your proposal has to be reasonable if your fellow students and community members are to accept your ideas.

Exploring Technology

1. Using your favorite search engine, find an Internet site about Georgia's military bases. Where are they located? What military installations are at each base? How many personnel are stationed at each base? How much does each base contribute to the state's economy? In what other ways are the bases important to Georgia?

2. Using your favorite search engine, find out about Georgia's most pressing environmental concerns such as air pollution, water pollution, recycling, toxic wastes, and waste dumps and landfills. What are the pollution issues in your own community? Who is working on those concerns, and what steps are being taken to find long range solutions? What can you and your classmates do?

Applying Your Skills

1. Research to find out how the state's current budget is being allocated. What percentage of the state's budget is being spent on education? on social services? Have these percentages changed over the past five years? How have they changed, and why do you think they have changed?

2. The HOPE scholarship program provides support for those high school graduates who want to go on to college. As the demands on HOPE scholarship monies grew, the Georgia lottery that funds HOPE began to run short of money. Recent changes in the HOPE grants are a result of this shortage. What are the requirements to receive HOPE funds today? How have the requirements changed since 2001? How much does HOPE provide for each student? How much is expended annually in HOPE scholarship funds?

Georgia's State Symbols

A symbol represents something else—a thing, an idea, or a concept. The bald eagle, for example, is a symbol of the United States. "Woody Owl" is a symbol for conservation. Closer to home, a birthday cake is a symbol of celebration for the day you were born. You have studied symbols in science (NaCl is the chemical symbol for table salt) and in mathematics (**+** is the addition symbol). Georgia too has many symbols—over forty. Some of them represent events that occurred in our history, some remind us of our heritage, and others are just fun celebrations enjoyed by Georgians. In this special section, you will read about many of Georgia's state symbols.

State Bird

The brown thrasher officially became Georgia's state bird in 1970, although Governor Eugene Talmadge had issued a proclamation in 1935 naming it a symbol of the state. Farmers, in particular, like to see the long-beaked bird nesting in low bushes on their land because the thrasher's diet includes grasshoppers, worms, and caterpillars, which can be destructive to crops.

State Butterfly

The tiger swallowtail butterfly was named the state butterfly in 1988. This gorgeous butterfly has large yellow and black striped markings on its wings. Like the honey bee, the tiger swallowtail butterfly helps pollinate plants.

State Creed

Georgia's official state creed was approved in March 1939. It reads:

Accepting, as I do, the principles upon which Georgia was founded, not for self but others;—its Democratic form of Government, based on 'Wisdom, Justice and Moderation';—its natural resources;—its Educational, Social and Religious advantages,

Top: Tiger swallowtail.
Middle: Brown thrasher.
Bottom: Peanuts.

making it a most desirable place to live—I will strive to be a pure upright Citizen, rejecting the evils—loving and emulating the good.

I further believe it is my duty to defend it against all enemies, to honor and obey its laws, to apply the Golden Rule in all my dealings with my fellow Georgians.

I feel a sense of pride in the history and heroic deeds accomplished by my forebears, and shall endeavor to so live that my State will be proud of me for doing my bit to make my State a better Commonwealth for future generations.

State Crop

The peanut was selected as Georgia's state crop because Georgia produces almost 50 percent of the total U.S. peanut crop and provides over 50 percent of the peanuts used in making peanut butter. The state leads the nation in peanut and peanut product exports. Originating in Brazil and Peru from the earliest days of Spanish explorers, the peanut was introduced to this country by Africans and quickly became a favorite food. In 2002, eighty Georgia counties produced over 2 billion pounds of peanuts.

State Fish

The state fish, the largemouth bass, is found mostly in warm water streams and lakes. Georgia boasts one of the world's records for the biggest largemouth bass ever caught.

Top: Largemouth bass.
Above: New state flag.

State Flag

The present state flag was adopted in 2003 after a long controversy. The flag features the "Stars and Bars" with the state's seal on a blue background in the upper left corner.

The 2003 flag replaced a flag that had been approved in January 2001. That flag had a Georgia state seal on a blue background. A banner entitled "Georgia's History" was placed under the seal and contained small versions of all five of the flags that had played a part of Georgia's history. The 2001 flag replaced the flag that had been adopted in 1956. The 1956 flag incorporated the Confederate battle flag, which many people believed was racist. Many believed that the 2001 flag was too much of a compromise.

The legislature ruled that Georgians would have an opportunity to vote on the issue in March 2004. In that vote, the people decided to keep the 2003 flag.

State Flower

The Cherokee Rose was adopted as a state symbol in 1916, making it one of the state's oldest symbols. The rose originally came from China and was introduced into the New World by Spanish settlers. According to the "Legend of the Cherokee Rose," the Cherokee women were so broken-hearted at leaving their lands in Georgia that the chiefs prayed for a sign to soothe their grief and give them strength. "The Great One" told them that each time the mothers' tears fell to the ground, a flower would spring up with white petals for the tears, a gold center to represent the gold stolen by the settlers who forced them off their lands, and seven leaves on each stem to represent the seven Cherokee clans. Today the rose grows along the path of the Trail of Tears from Georgia to Oklahoma.

State Fossil

The shark tooth, Georgia's state fossil, is a common fossil in the Coastal Plain region. In fossil form, the shark tooth can be traced back 375 million years, but the oldest shark tooth found in the state was 60 million years old. Fossilized shark teeth are found in a variety of colors ranging from black and gray to white, brown, blue, and reddish brown. If you are lucky enough to find a red shark tooth from the rivers around Camden County, you may really have something valuable because some are as much as 15 million years old.

State Fruit

The peach is our state fruit, and Georgia ranks third in the nation in peach production. One of the state's nicknames is "The Peach State." Our Georgia peaches are known for their superior flavor, texture, and appearance. They are good for our eyesight, fat-free, a source of fiber, and low in cholesterol and sodium!

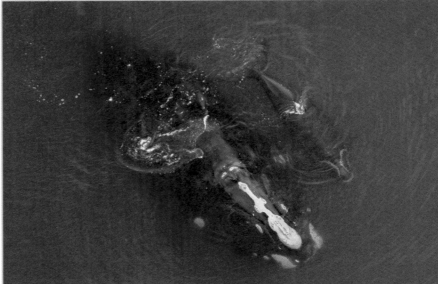

State Game Bird

The legislature selected the bobwhite quail as the official game bird of the state in 1970. The quail is best known for its distinctive "bob-bob-white" call. Georgia is known as the "Quail Capital of the World" and has several plants that process and ship the delicacy throughout the country.

State Gem

The state gem—quartz—is the second most abundant mineral on Earth. It can be found in the mountains of the state and comes in a wide variety of colors in Georgia. Quartz is most commonly recognized as the amethyst, often used in jewelry, and the clear quartz, which resembles a diamond when it is cut with many small flat surfaces.

State Insect

The state insect is the social honey bee, which has been around for 10 to 20 million years. The honey bee is important to agriculture because it pollinates more than fifty different crops. Honey produced by the bees is also a valuable commodity in Georgia's economy. In fact, the state is the seventh largest honey-producing state in the country.

State Marine Mammal

Georgia's state marine mammal is the right whale, considered to be one of the most endangered species in the world. Weighing up to seventy tons, the seventy-foot right whale is actually a baleen whale. Whalers thought they were the "right" whales to hunt since they were rich in blubber and they were easy to catch (they are relatively slow swimmers).

State Mineral

Old crystalline rocks are primarily found in northern Georgia. The reddish-brown or black staurolite, found in old crystalline rocks, was designated

Top left: Bobwhite quail. Top right: Right whale and calf. Above: Honey bee. Opposite page, top: Cherokee Rose. Opposite page, middle: A peach. Opposite page, below: Fossil shark's tooth (actual size!).

the official state mineral in 1976. The popular name for these good luck charms are "Fairy Crosses" or "Fairy Stones" because the crystals in the mineral form a cross. In fact, the name comes from the Greek word *stauros* meaning "cross."

State Poet Laureate

Georgia's poet laureate in 2003 was Dr. David Bottoms. Dr. Bottoms is a native of Canton. He is currently a professor of creative writing at Georgia State University and lives in Marietta. His books include both collections of poetry and works of fiction. A portion of one of his poems appears in Chapter 4.

State Possum

In 1992, Georgia's official possum became "Pogo Possum," the comic book character created by Walt Kelly. Pogo, who lives in Okefenokee swamp, has been featured in a nationally syndicated comic strip since 1949. His most famous expression is "We have met the enemy and he is us."

WE HAVE MET THE ENEMY AND HE IS US

Top: Live oak in Darien. Above: Bag of Vidalia onions by a roadside stand. Inset: Pogo sign at Okefenokee Swamp Park.

State Reptile

The gopher tortoise is the official state reptile. This type of tortoise is one of the oldest species native to our state and traces its ancestry back to land tortoises that originated in North America over 60 million years ago. The slow but appealing gophers burrow into the ground to create a maze of tunnels that can also serve as home to 360 other animal species from the armadillo to snakes and mice. The gopher tortoise can live up to 60 years.

State Seal

Georgia's state seal was adopted in 1799. It depicts an arch, which contains the word "Constitution," supported by three columns, representing the three branches of government. A man with a drawn sword stands between two of the columns. The man with the sword represented the military aid Georgia provided in defense of the Constitution.

A banner encircles the columns with the words *Wisdom*, *Justice*, and *Moderation* (the state motto). It was hoped that the legislature would use wisdom in making laws, that the judicial system's decisions would provide "justice," and that the executive branch of government would use "moderation" in administering the laws of the state.

The reverse side of the seal depicts a ship, two of Georgia's exports (cotton and tobacco), and a farmer plowing. These scenes are representative of the state's agriculture and commerce.

State Tree

The live oak was adopted as the state tree of Georgia in 1937. It is found primarily along the coastal plains and on the sea islands. The majestic tree sometimes has a trunk twenty-five feet in diameter. It can grow more than forty feet high and have a limb span of more than a hundred feet. A live oak tree often lives for several hundred years and is a host for clinging Spanish moss.

State Vegetable

Georgia's famous sweet Vidalia onion was named the state's vegetable in 1990. The onion is grown in a small area of southwest Georgia near Vidalia. Because of the makeup of the soil of this region, the granex seed, which produces hot onions in other soils, produces a sweet onion that is not hot to the taste.

State Wildflower

The azalea, also called bush honeysuckle, is a member of the Rhododendron family. Once you see azaleas in full bloom, you will understand why the azalea is our state wildflower. Our wild trumpet-shaped azaleas are a dazzling array of vibrant yellow, orange, scarlet, and crimson reds. They were growing wild in Georgia long before James Oglethorpe landed. You may see their wonderful colors from March until July or August.

Figure 74 Other State Symbols

Art Museum	Georgia Museum of Art
Atlas	*Atlas of Georgia*
Ballet	Atlanta Ballet
Beef Cook Off	"Shoot the Bull"
Folk Dance	Square Dancing
Folk Festival	The Georgia Folk Festival
Folk Life Play	"Swamp Gravy"
Historic Drama	"The Reach of Song"
Motto	"Wisdom, Justice & Moderation"
Musical Theater	"Jekyll Island Musical Theatre Festival"
Nicknames	Peach State, Empire State of the South
Peanut Monument	Turner County Peanut Monument
Pork Cook Off	"Slosheye Trail Big Pig Jig"
Poultry	Chicken
Prepared Food	Grits
Railroad Museum	Historic Railroad Shops
School	Plains High School
Song	"Georgia on My Mind"
Tartan	Georgia tartan
Theater	The Springer Opera House
Transportation History Museum	Southeastern Railway Museum
Waltz	"Our Georgia"

Local Government and Citizenship

Local governments are the most numerous of all governments in the United States. Georgia has 159 counties, and each of these counties has a government. In addition to the counties, there are almost six hundred cities in Georgia. Each of them has a government. Finally, there are special district governments with legal powers and jurisdictions.

Not only are local governments the most numerous, they are also the closest to the people and the most likely to affect people directly. Local governments get their powers and their right to exist from the Georgia state constitution. In this chapter, you will examine the different types of local government in Georgia.

Below: Thomas County was created in 1825 from portions of Decatur and Irwin counties. The county and its county seat, Thomasville, were named for a hero of the War of 1812, General Jett Thomas. The courthouse was built in 1858.

Signs of the Times

Population: Fulton County is the largest county, with a population of over 816,000 citizens in 2000. The least populous county in 2000 was Taliaferro, with a population of just over 2,000. The largest city is Atlanta, followed by Augusta, Columbus, Savannah, and Athens.

Life Expectancy: 74.9 years

Literature: Georgia writers include Eliot Wigginton of Raburn County, author of the *Foxfire* series. Joyce Blackburn of Glynn County has written biographies and children's books. Lewis Grizzard of Moreland wrote humorous books and newspaper columns. Atlantan Celestine Sibley has written newspaper columns and books, including *Christmas in Georgia*. Pat Conroy of Atlanta is known for such books as *The Prince of Tides*, *The Lords of Discipline*, and *The Great Santini*.

Cost of Living: Highest in Metropolitan Atlanta, where the average per capita income is $36,000; the lowest is in southwest Georgia, where the average per capita income is $22,393.

Education: Georgia has 180 local school systems, 159 are countywide systems and 21 are city school systems. There are 1,999 schools listed by the State Department of Education: 361 high schools, 406 middle schools, 1,224 elementary schools, and 8 K-12 schools.

Art/Architecture: Georgia's county governments are located in some famous and historic old courthouses. The Chattahoochee County Courthouse, built in 1854, is the only wood-frame courthouse left in Georgia. The Clay County Courthouse in Fort Gaines was built in 1873 and is a Greek Revival building made of red brick. The Randolph County Courthouse in Cuthbert was built in 1887 and is in Queen Anne style. Georgia has a Historic Courthouse Tour on famous courthouses located on Highway 27.

Music: Athens claims to be "Live Music Central." *Rolling Stone* magazine named the city as the #1 College Music Scene in America. The city is home to ten recording studios, a number of independent record labels, and major bands and musical groups including the B-52's, Pylon, REM, and Widespread Panic.

Fads/Fashions: **To save money, there is a move to consolidate county and city services. In some cases, county and city governments have merged. In other cases, counties and cities have agreed to merge selected services, such as fire protection.**

Leisure Time: **Today, the consumer-citizen allocates less time for leisure activities and spends much of that time with family-oriented events rather than individual pursuits.**

Transportation: **Georgia has over 113,000 miles of federal, state, and local roads. Nine Welcome Centers to greet visitors to our state are located along the five major interstate highways.**

Science/Inventions: **Electronic voting systems have replaced most older voting systems. Computerized state and regional records have made data available even to previously remote areas. The Internet facilitates access to information, services, goods, and products for Georgians in every community.**

Figure 75 Timeline, 1733–1945

1945
Legislature set a limit of 159 counties for state

1943
Warner Robins incorporated

1733
Savannah founded by
James Oglethorpe

1854
Conyers incorporated

1932
Milton, Campbell, and Fulton
merged into Fulton County

1837
Atlanta founded

1777
Georgia constitution
provided for 8 counties

1924
Georgia's youngest county,
Peach County, formed

1750   **1800**   **1850**   **1900**   **1950**

1841
Dallas, Texas, originally settled

1890
Oklahoma City incorporated

1858
Denver, Colorado, established

1881
Long Beach, California, laid out and settled

1870
Miami, Florida, founded

County Government

Counties are subdivisions of the state set up to carry out certain governmental functions. The state constitution sets out county powers. The state constitution also requires that all county governments be uniform (organized the same way). However, the General Assembly may, in any county, establish commissioners of roads and revenues, consolidate the offices of tax receiver and tax collector into the office of tax commissioner, and abolish the office of treasurer. Most county governments are headed by elected **boards of commissioners.** Because all county governments are similar, the governmental structure of one county, Camden County, can serve to show how a county operates.

A Look at One County

Camden County is located in southeast Georgia on the coast. It has about 45,000 residents. The major employer is Kings Bay Naval Submarine Base, which is the home of the Atlantic Trident nuclear submarine fleet and which employs about 6,700 people. The original industries that marked Camden's growth were pulp and naval stores industries, shipping, fishing, and paper mills. The last paper mill in Camden County closed in 2002, leaving tour-

ism, the naval base, and service industries that support the base as the major elements of the local economy.

The Spanish first settled the area in the 1500s. Camden was one of the first eight counties established by the Georgia state constitution on February 5, 1777. It was formed from St. Mary's and St. Thomas parishes. Camden County was named for the Earl of Camden, Charles Pratt, chief justice and lord chancellor of England, who had opposed the overly strict attitude of the British government toward the American colonies.

Did You Know?

Harris County was the first county to have a board of county commissioners. It was formed in 1868.

Figure 76 Camden County Services

The various services provided to the citizens of Camden County are typical of those provided by most of Georgia's county governments.

Animal Control Services: Collects stray animals, operates humane society, responds to dangerous animal threats, maintains animal disease-prevention and data collection programs, enforces animal protection and control ordinances.

Bryan Lang Library and Camden Public Library: Operates historical archives, county library, and public library for county residents.

Building and Planning Services: Regulates county building and zoning ordinances, issues building permits, and monitors flood plain regulations.

Children's and Family Services: Provides child support, child protection service, day care service, and administers Department of Family and Children's Services assistance programs.

Coroner: Provides death certificates, investigates suspicious deaths, and performs autopsies.

Court Services: Operates Department of Juvenile Justice, Juvenile Probation Office, District Attorney's Office, Magistrate Court, Probate Court, and Superior Court.

Emergency Services: Provides fire departments, emergency medical assistance technicians, ambulance services, and 911 emergency assistance program.

Environmental Health Services: Regulates wells and septic tanks, licenses and inspects food services establishments, monitors rabies and rabies-prevention programs, regulates travel and tourist accommodations, and monitors public swimming pools.

Health Department, Mental Health Department: Provides health services, child care programs, immunization and disease prevention programs, elderly assistance programs, and new mother assistance programs.

Parks and Recreation Services: Provides and maintains system of countywide parks and recreational areas and sponsors and monitors organized public sports and recreational programs.

Road Department: Responsible for roads, bridges, drainage maintenance, and right-of-way maintenance.

Sheriff's Department: Responsible for law enforcement, jail operations and maintenance, and legal services for court system.

Tax Assessor: Establishes appraisals for property values.

Tax Commissioner: Collects taxes and sells tags and licenses.

Waste Services: Operates yard waste facility and solid waste landfills.

Did You Know?

The 2000 census showed that 151 of Georgia's 159 counties increased in population.

Camden's county government consists of a five-member board of commissioners. The commissioners are elected by the voters for four-year, staggered terms. The board of commissioners has the authority to establish county policies, adopt county ordinances (laws), establish the county budget, establish tax rates, and provide services for the citizens of the county. A *county administrator*, appointed by the board of commissioners, serves as the chief administrative officer. The county administrator manages the day-to-day operations of the county and implements county policies.

Camden County includes three sizable cities—Woodbine, the **county seat** (the city or town where the county government is located), St. Marys, and Kingsland. The county and cities work together on some services for residents including parks and recreation programs and a business development and tourism authority.

The county's schools are managed by an elected five-member board of education and an elected school superintendent. The school district includes fifteen public schools that serve a student population of over 10,000 children.

Sharing Services

Some cities and counties cooperate in sharing services. Fulton County is the most populous county in Georgia and the center of Georgia's state government. It was originally created in 1853 by the Georgia General Assembly. Fulton County was enlarged in 1931 when Milton and Campbell counties merged with it. Fulton County covers 523 square miles; Atlanta occupies about 117 square miles, or 22 percent, of the county. Nine other incorporated cities are also located within Fulton County: Alpharetta, College Park, East Point, Fairburn, Hapeville, Mountain Park, Palmetto, Roswell, and Union City.

Fulton County's board of commissioners consists of seven members elected to four-year terms. Four commissioners are elected from geographic districts, and three are elected from the county at large. The Fulton County board of commissioners appoints a county manager as its chief executive officer. The county manager's chief function is to carry out policies set by the county commission. With the commission's approval, the county manager appoints all department heads except those who are elected or whose appointments are specifically provided for in the law.

Through contract agreements, the county provides financial support to shared ventures, such as the Fulton-DeKalb Hospital Authority, which operates Grady Memorial Hospital. Property zoning is a joint function of the county and Atlanta. Library services to residents of Fulton County are provided by Atlanta in a contract between the two governments.

The school system for the county, including all nine incorporated areas outside the Atlanta city limits, is operated by the Fulton County Board of Education, which is elected by the voters and which appoints a superintendent of schools. The elected Atlanta Board of Education appoints a superintendent of schools for the city.

Officials in County Government

Based on its population, each county has a different number of officials. Most counties have at least the following elected officials: commissioners, clerk of the superior court, judge of the probate court, tax commissioner, sheriff, and coroner.

Most county officials are appointed rather than elected. Examples of some appointed county officials include: county clerks, attorneys, tax assessors, emergency management services directors, fire chiefs, planning and building inspectors, registrars, roads supervisors, animal control officers, surveyors, and environmentalists.

Figure 77 Georgia's Ten Most Populous Counties, 2000

1. Fulton County
2. DeKalb County
3. Cobb County
4. Gwinnett County
5. Clayton County
6. Chatham County
7. Richmond County
8. Muscogee County
9. Bibb County
10. Cherokee County

It's Your Turn

1. What is the maximum number of counties allowed in Georgia by law?
2. How many counties were established in Georgia by the state's first constitution?
3. Name at least six services counties provide for Georgia's citizens.

Spotlight on the Economy

Levels of Taxes

The services that county governments and municipalities provide to citizens must be paid for, and the major source of revenue for local governments is taxes. In 2001, for example, Georgia's county governments collectively raised revenue totaling $5.7 billion. Georgia's municipal governments collectively raised revenues of just over $4.5 billion. The three consolidated county and city governments in that same year raised revenues of $625 million. Where did these local governments get this money?

The major source of revenue for local governments is taxes. In 2001, Georgia's counties collected about 36 percent of their revenues from property taxes, while the state's municipalities collected about 10 percent of their revenues from property taxes. There are basically three types of property taxes:

- Real property taxes on immovable property (real estate) such as land and buildings,
- Personal property taxes on movable items such as automobiles, boats, business machinery, and warehoused merchandise, and
- Intangible property taxes on such items as stocks and bonds.

According to Georgia law, property taxes may be charged on 40 percent of an item's *fair market value*, or what the item would be expected to bring if sold. This taxable amount is called an assessment.

Below: What do you suppose the fair market value of this home in Madison is?

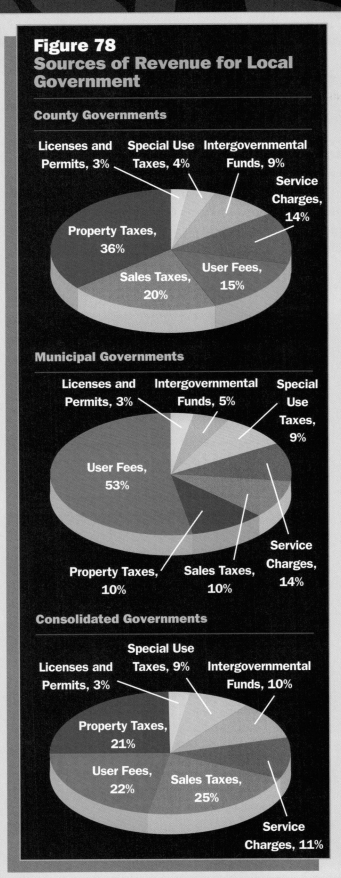

Figure 78
Sources of Revenue for Local Government

County Governments

- Licenses and Permits, 3%
- Special Use Taxes, 4%
- Intergovernmental Funds, 9%
- Service Charges, 14%
- Property Taxes, 36%
- User Fees, 15%
- Sales Taxes, 20%

Municipal Governments

- Licenses and Permits, 3%
- Intergovernmental Funds, 5%
- Special Use Taxes, 9%
- User Fees, 53%
- Service Charges, 14%
- Property Taxes, 10%
- Sales Taxes, 10%

Consolidated Governments

- Special Use Taxes, 9%
- Licenses and Permits, 3%
- Intergovernmental Funds, 10%
- Property Taxes, 21%
- User Fees, 22%
- Sales Taxes, 25%
- Service Charges, 11%

Above: These shoppers at Atlanta's Lenox Square will pay a sales tax on any of their purchases.

The sales tax is another source of funds for local governments. Sales taxes are placed on the sale, rental, and storage of goods and services. The state sets a base sales tax. Each county can add to that base rate by a general local option sales tax. Anytime you go to the store and purchase an item, you pay the state sales tax and the local sales taxes. In 2001, Georgia's counties took in about 20 percent of their total revenues, or $1.1 billion, from sales taxes. Georgia's municipalities received $458 million, or about 10 percent of their total revenues, from sales taxes.

Another source of tax revenue for local governments is the special use tax. One special use tax is on alcoholic beverages. Franchise taxes are imposed on utility companies (telephone, cable television, electricity, and gas companies) for the privilege of doing business in the state (having a franchise). Local governments collect insurance premium taxes on life, health, and accident insurance policies that Georgia citizens have. The taxes, collected by the state insurance commissioner, are sent back to the local counties where the citizens owning the policies reside. Hotel and motel taxes are paid by visitors traveling in an area and using local motels or hotels. Finally, local governments may collect occupational taxes on such businesses as builders and construction companies or plumbers.

Altogether, these special use taxes add up. In 2001, they accounted for 4 percent of the total revenues for counties and for 9 percent of the total revenues for municipalities.

Local governments also gain monies from user fees, licenses, and permits. In addition, local governments receive funds from federal and state governments through a variety of grants and funding programs.

City Government and Special-Purpose Districts

A city with its own government is called a **municipality**. Georgia's first city was Savannah, which was founded by James Oglethorpe in 1733. Augusta was the state's second city. Because of its Spanish ancestry, St. Marys claims to be the second oldest city in the United States after St. Augustine. There appears to be much pride and considerable dissent involved in the arguments over who was first.

Section Preview

As you read, look for:

- the three forms of city government,
- how local governments are funded, and
- vocabulary terms: **municipality, mayor-council form, figurehead, council-manager form, commission form, special-purpose district, ad valorem taxes, user fee, general local option sales tax, special purpose local option sales tax,** and **bond issue.**

Figure 79
Georgia's Ten Largest Cities, 2000

1.   Atlanta
2.   Augusta
3.   Columbus
4.   Savannah
5.   Athens
6.   Macon
7.   Roswell
8.   Albany
9.   Marietta
10. Warner Robins

Right: Savannah's City Hall is on Yamacraw Bluff overlooking the Savannah River.

American Spotlight

Maynard Jackson

To the sounds of the Atlanta Symphony Orchestra and Beethoven's "Ode to Joy" and the voice of famous soprano Mattiwilda Dobbs, Maynard Holbrook Jackson was sworn in as Atlanta's youngest and first African American mayor in January 1974. His swearing-in ceremony had to be held in the Atlanta Civic Center because the traditional site, City Hall, was not large enough for the thousands of Atlantans who were celebrating his election. On June 28, 2003, at that same civic center, Atlantans were joined by thousands from around the nation to say goodbye to Maynard Jackson. Who was Maynard Jackson, and what made his tenure as major of Georgia's largest city so special?

As a child, Jackson was very smart. He earned a B.A. degree in political science and history from Morehouse College at age 18. He graduated from North Carolina Central University Law School in 1964. He worked as an attorney in Atlanta until he entered politics and was elected mayor of Atlanta in 1973.

Called by many the "ultimate mayor," Jackson created "neighborhood planning units" to give local community citizens a voice in city politics. He tackled charges of police brutality and made changes in the organization and administration of the police and fire departments and city government. He led the development and expansion of MARTA. He expanded Hartsfield International Airport into one of the largest, busiest airports in the world, and he used airport construction to develop a minority participation plan that served as a model for governments throughout the nation. He put into action a belief that expanding economic opportunity for more people increased the prosperity of all people.

Jackson was a lifelong supporter of the arts. He established a Bureau of Cultural Affairs in 1975 and provided financial support to arts programs throughout the community. He used community development funds to hire artists

Above: Maynard Jackson, Atlanta's first black mayor.

and to found the Atlanta Contemporary Art Center, IMAGE, and Art Papers. He also had funds set aside in each construction project for works of art. In this way, MARTA stations, Hartsfield Airport, and City Hall became noted for their arts displays. He pushed for funds to restore the historic Cyclorama because it was such an important artistic representation of the city's history.

As one of his final legacies to Atlanta, Jackson led the efforts to secure Atlanta's selection as the host city for the 1996 Olympic Summer Games. His speech to the Olympic Committee, delivered in large part in fluent French, spoke eloquently of Atlanta's great record for racial diversity and humanitarianism. The committee recognized that record by awarding the games to Atlanta.

Maynard Holbrook Jackson died in 2003. In recognition of his many achievements, Atlanta's airport was renamed Hartsfield-Jackson Atlanta International Airport.

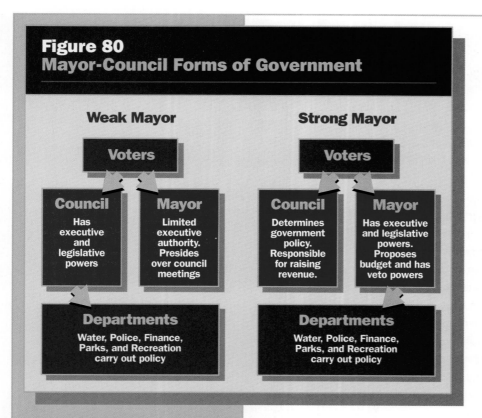

Figure 80
Mayor-Council Forms of Government

Weak Mayor

Voters

Council
Has executive and legislative powers

Mayor
Limited executive authority. Presides over council meetings

Departments
Water, Police, Finance, Parks, and Recreation carry out policy

Strong Mayor

Voters

Council
Determines government policy. Responsible for raising revenue.

Mayor
Has executive and legislative powers. Proposes budget and has veto powers

Departments
Water, Police, Finance, Parks, and Recreation carry out policy

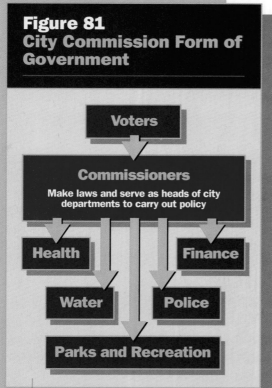

Figure 81
City Commission Form of Government

Voters

Commissioners
Make laws and serve as heads of city departments to carry out policy

Health

Finance

Water

Police

Parks and Recreation

A city exists as a political unit when it receives a charter from the state legislature. To be chartered as a city, an area must meet three requirements: (1) It must have at least 200 residents; (2) It must be located at least three miles from the boundaries of the nearest city; and (3) It must have 60 percent of its land divided into *tracts* (parcels of land) or being used for residential, business, industrial, institutional, or government purposes.

A city government can do only what it charter authorizes it to do. For example, most city charters allow cities to provide police protection, license businesses, maintain streets and sidewalks, control traffic, and provide water and sewerage services. Other services to the citizens may be provided if they are included specifically in a city's charter. For example, Atlanta and twenty other cities in the state operate their own school systems because that power was granted by the state in their charters.

Forms of City Government

The most common forms of city government are the mayor-council form, the council-manager form, and the commission form.

In the **mayor-council form** of government, the elected city council is responsible for making the laws. An elected mayor acts as the city's chief executive officer and is responsible for seeing that the laws are carried out and that city agencies do their jobs. The mayor may be either "weak" or "strong." In a *weak-mayor system*, the city council has both legislative and executive powers. The mayor has limited powers, appoints few city officials, and has little veto power. The mayor is primarily a **figurehead** (a person who is the head of an organization but who has no powers) who presides over council meetings and performs other ceremonial duties. Smyrna has a weak-mayor system. In the *strong-mayor system*, the mayor is a strong leader who proposes legislation, prepares the budget, appoints all department heads, and has veto power. Atlanta has a strong-mayor system.

In the **council-manager form** of government, the voters elect a city council that establishes laws and policies. There is a mayor who may be elected or named by the council. The council hires a city manager who is responsible for the day-to-day operation of the city. The city manager appoints the heads of city governments and sees that they carry out their jobs. Savannah has a council-manager form of government.

In cities with a **commission form** of government, the voters elect commissioners. Each commissioner is the head of a department within the city government, such as finance, streets, public safety, and so on. The mayor is elected by the commissioners from among themselves. Decatur has a commission form of government.

City-County Government

Some counties provide services outside of incorporated municipalities for things such as water, sewage, sanitation, and fire protection. As long as city and county governments provide different types of services in the same area, they do not get in each other's way. However, as a county becomes more urban, city and county governments may provide the same services to the same people.

One way to avoid this duplication is for city and county governments to form a single government. Several such mergers have taken place. For example, the city of Columbus and Muscogee County merged in 1971, and Athens and Clarke County formed a single government unit in 1991. Augusta and Richmond County merged in 1995, becoming the third consolidated government in Georgia.

Special-Purpose Districts

There are a number of special-purpose districts in Georgia. Generally, a **special-purpose district** is created for a single job or single group of tasks. Most such districts govern themselves. A school system is one example of a special district. State law requires children to attend school, but much of the control of that school is

Figure 82
Council-Manager Form of Government

Voters

Council
Determines policy and passes ordinances.
Hires city manager.
Mayor is a council member.

City Manager
Carries out policy set by the council.
Appoints all department heads and supervises all municipal affairs.

Health   **Finance**

Water   **Police**

Parks and Recreation

Left: The Athens-Clarke County City Hall houses the mayor's office and a variety of city-county government offices.

Above: Special-purpose districts, such as school systems, get most of their funding from local property taxes. Those taxes pay for such expenditures as teacher salaries and school buses.

left up to a local board of education and the school district office. Within the guidelines set by state law, local school systems can establish starting and stopping times for the school day, spell out standards of behavior and punishment, determine dress codes, and schedule students' time during the school day.

Within the metropolitan area of Atlanta, the Metropolitan Atlanta Rapid Transit Authority (MARTA) is another special-purpose district. MARTA runs a bus and rail system, determines the cost of fares, selects routes, and schedules public transportation times. The Public Housing Authority is a special-purpose district. It provides services such as determining the location of public housing, constructing and maintaining the buildings, renting the units, and drawing up tenants' rules and regulations.

Other special-purpose districts include community fire departments, parks and recreation authorities, and airport and port authorities. No matter what individual special-purpose districts are called, they all have one thing in common: they exist to provide for the public's welfare.

Funding Local Government

Local governments obtain money to provide services for their citizens from a variety of sources, including state and federal grants. However, the major source of funds comes from local property taxes, which are called ad valorem taxes. Property taxes are paid to local governments based on the value of the piece of *real property* (land, buildings or homes) or *personal property* (motor vehicles, boats, trailers, airplanes, mobile homes).

User fees paid by citizens are another source of funds for local governments. These fees might be for such services as garbage collection, recycling and waste disposal, water and sewerage, parking, and use of libraries and recreational facilities.

Two major types of sales taxes also provide funds for local government operations. A general local option sales tax is a countywide sales tax that is added onto and collected at the same time as the required state sales taxes. Counties can also approve special purpose local option sales taxes (SPLOST), which voters have agreed to support over a five-year period in order to finance specific local improvement projects such as public facilities, roads, and bridges. The SPLOST monies are divided between the county and the cities within that county.

Voters can also approve bond issues, in which some level of government asks permission to raise money for a public project. For example, some schools, libraries, and hospitals have been built with public money approved by the voters on a bond issue. The money raised from bond issues must be repaid, with interest.

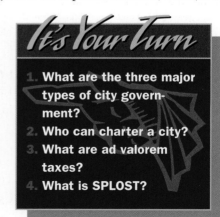

It's Your Turn

1. What are the three major types of city government?
2. Who can charter a city?
3. What are ad valorem taxes?
4. What is SPLOST?

Where Do Georgia's Citizens Live?

Section Preview

As you read, look for:
* how Georgia's population has changed,
* the growth of cities and suburban areas, and
* vocabulary terms: urban area, rural area, metropolitan area, and urban sprawl.

Georgia is one of the nation's fastest-growing states. Between 1990 and 2000, Georgia's population grew by over 26 percent, twice the rate for the United States as a whole. Georgia's population is estimated to be about 10 million people in 2010.

Georgia's Hispanic population quadrupled between 1990 and 2000, growing from 108,9000 to 435,200. You can see this in the growing number of multicultural restaurants and businesses and a rapid increase in Hispanic-language newspapers and magazine publications.

The number of Georgia citizens over sixty-five is growing twice as fast as the number of people under sixty-five. Georgians are living longer, and more people are retiring to the state from colder sections of the country.

Georgia's people live in urban areas and in rural areas. An **urban area** is a city with a population over 2,500 or a city and its surrounding area with over 50,000 residents. A **rural area** is a town or community of less than 2,500 people. Today, over two-thirds of all Georgians live in a **metropolitan area**, a central city of over 50,000 residents or a city and its surrounding counties with a total population of 100,000 or more.

Today, just over 50 percent of Georgians live in the Atlanta metropolitan area, and over 70 percent of the state's total population live in urban areas. This is in sharp contrast to fifty years ago when the majority of the state's citizens (almost 70 percent) lived in rural areas. At that time, Georgia was mainly an agricultural state. However, in the latter half of the twentieth century, agriculture began to decline and business and industry began to expand. Many Georgians moved from rural areas to the cities, where most businesses and industries were headquartered and where jobs were plentiful.

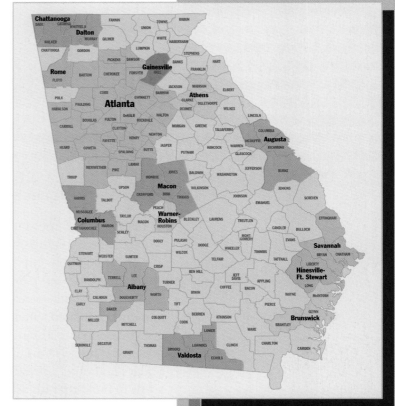

Map 54
Georgia's Metropolitan Areas

Map Skill: How many counties are considered part of the Atlanta metropolitan area?

Urban Sprawl

In the 1960s and 1970s, another population trend began in Georgia. People began moving out of the inner cities and into the suburbs. The growth of the suburbs was followed by an expansion of businesses to the suburban areas.

One of Atlanta's major tourist attractions is Grant Park, the city's largest park. The park is home to Lemuel Grant's antebellum home and the fortifications of Confederate Fort Walker. It is perhaps best know for the world's largest cyclorama, a big circular painting of the Battle of Atlanta. The painting revolves around the audience, with sound and light effects and a narrative about the highlights of the painting. Visiting Grant Park is a must for Georgia students interested in our state's history.

One of the major roles of city and county governments is providing parks, leisure opportunities, and recreational activities for local citizens. The citizens of Atlanta did just that with Grant Park in 1883 and it remains a thriving park, zoo, and historic site attracting visitors and residents alike.

GRANT PARK

Named for Col. Lemuel P. Grant (1817-1893), pioneer railroad builder and public-spirited citizen of Atlanta, who donated to the city 87.5 of this area for a park May 17, 1883. An additional 44 acres acquired by purchase from Col. Grant, increased it to 131.5 acres April 4, 1890.
Grant Park has the national distinction of being the location of one of the few extant cycloramas - the subject of which memorializes the major engagement fought by Confederate and Federal forces in the environs of the city - the Battle of Atlanta. July 22, 1864.

Above: *The Battle of Atlanta* depicts the intense battle that took place in the vicinity of the Troup-Hurt House.

In many parts of the state, inner cities have lost population and industry while the neighboring suburban areas have flourished.

This population shift has led to a problem generally known as **urban sprawl.** Because city planning laws and building codes and guidelines do not apply in suburban areas, the growth of the suburbs is generally unplanned and uncoordinated. Often the infrastructure does not exist to support rapid growth. Georgians leaving cities and moving into suburban areas need sewer systems, water systems, garbage collection services, streets and highways, bridges and other infrastructure. Local, state, and federal funds have to be spent to build that infrastructure. Often, adequate support systems do not come until after people have already moved into suburban areas.

Another problem resulting from urban sprawl is the economic hardship cities undergo. When people move out of the city to suburban areas, businesses leave to follow their customers. The residents and businesses and industries that move out take their property taxes with them, leaving a city with a declining tax base. However, many of the residents who move out of cities still travel to and from the city for work. They still need the infrastructure of the city, but they no longer pay city property taxes that maintain that infrastructure.

The millions of cars commuting to and from work daily create another major problem. Not only must new highways, perimeter roads, and bridges be built because of urban sprawl, but those same highways create massive traffic flow, traffic jams, and air pollution. State, regional, and federal officials have worked to reduce the numbers of commuter cars on highways by encouraging the use of public transportation services and car-pooling by commuters.

Urban Revitalization

As the tax base in cities decreases, the power of cities also declines. In many cases, political power (based on numbers of voters) belongs to the highly populated suburban areas. Cities are left with little money, little political power, and fewer jobs for those residents who would not or could not move out. Once-thriving parts of central cities are abandoned after the workday ends and left open for decay and crime.

Georgia's cities have been working to revitalize downtown and other areas. One successful venture has been to focus on tourism by building convention centers and attracting millions of tourists. Some cities have renovated historic areas and encouraged suburban dwellers to return to the city in restored neighborhoods such as Atlanta's Virginia Highlands, Little Five Points, and "Sweet Auburn" areas. Cities have renovated decaying business areas to attract new tenants. Savannah, for example, revived its historic waterfront by renovating the warehouses along Bay Street and Factor's Walk and by building new convention facilities along the waterfront.

Augusta has made "Riverwalk Augusta" the center of its restored downtown. The old river levee along the Savannah River has been converted to a brick esplanade with seating overlooking the river. The area is active day and night with playground and picnic areas, historical displays, major hotels, shops, and restaurants. The new Augusta Museum of History is a part of the Riverwalk area, along with the National Science Center's Fort Discovery and the Morris Museum of Art. As an attraction, the city commissioned replicas of a canal cargo boat to tour the Augusta Canal. The boats were built on Tybee Island.

Top: In northeast Atlanta lies the Virginia Highlands neighborhood. Many of the buildings and homes have been renovated, and the area now attracts many diners.
Above: The Riverwalk in Augusta is a popular destination for those looking to relax and enjoy the view of the Savannah River.

1. What are the fastest-growing segments of Georgia's population?
2. What do you think happens to a state when the population continues to diversify or change?
3. What is urban sprawl and how have cities combated the loss of residents and businesses?

Participation in a Representative Democracy

Section Preview

As you read, look for:
• the four factors that influence governments,
• the requirements to register to vote in Georgia, and
• vocabulary terms: political party, interest group, lobbyist, general election, citizenship, and naturalized citizen.

In Chapter 14, you learned that we live in a representative democracy. Who, or what, influences decision-making in the federal, state, and local governments of the United States? Obviously, you do! But major influences can be explained by considering four factors: (1) political parties, (2) interest groups, (3) voters, and (4) public opinion.

Political Parties

Political parties are organized groups of people who share common ideals and who seek to influence government policies and decisions by electing members of their party to government offices. The first political parties in the country were the Federalists and the Antifederalists who fought over the powers of a central government as the Constitution was being written and ratified. These two groups evolved into two political groups known as the Federalists and the Democratic-Republicans. While these early political parties have changed over the years, we have maintained a two-party system.

Today, America has two major political parties—the Republican party and the Democratic party. Members of these groups share common beliefs about government's role in American life and the policies that government should support. People who are not members of these two major parties are usually referred to as *independents*.

There are minor political parties that do not have enough members to win major elections, but who do have an important role in the democratic process. Minor parties bring attention to specific minority ideas. As minor parties gather political support from more people, their ideas influence the thinking and the principles of party leaders in the two major political groups.

Above: Democrat Al Gore (left) and Republican George W. Bush shake hands before the first televised debate of the 2000 presidential election.

Interest Groups

Interest groups are people who share common goals and objectives and who band together to influence government policies on issues related to their goals and objectives. Unlike political parties, interest groups do not typically exist to elect their representatives to government positions; instead, they

Cartoonist Thomas Nast developed the symbols for both the Republican and the Democratic parties. In 1874, Nast drew an elephant (above) to symbolize the size of the Republican party. Nast first drew the donkey in an 1870 cartoon. In the 1873 cartoon on the right, Democratic congressmen are shown as donkeys blowing inflation bubbles after the Panic of 1873.

try to influence office holders to act in a certain way when their particular issues arise.

There are many different types of interest groups. These interest groups may be concerned with economic issues, labor issues, agricultural issues, and particular professional issues.

Interest groups use basic persuasive tactics to influence government decision-making. They have lobbyists, people who are paid to represent them in Washington or Atlanta and to keep pressure on government officials to favor their interest group. Interest groups make contributions to political campaigns in hopes of gaining favor when legislation related to their interests is involved. They may endorse (support) particular candidates for office when those candidates favor the interests of their group.

On the Road Again

Lyndon House Arts Center

As you travel throughout the state, one "must stop" is the Lyndon House Arts Center at the end of Jackson Street in Athens. The house was originally known as the Ware-Lyndon House and has been listed on the National Register of Historic Places since 1976. The two-story home was built by local physician Dr. Edward R. Ware in 1850. It was purchased in 1880 by Dr. Edward S. Lyndon.

During World War II, the Lyndon House was used as a USO site. The city of Athens purchased by the house 1939 and used it as a park and recreation center for young people. Today the mission of Lyndon House is to support local artists and provide community education in the arts.

The Lyndon House Art Center offers classes as well as equipment, studio space and workshops, community art activities, and art education services. Each year, the Lyndon House holds a juried show (a professional art competition) featuring works in diverse media. It also has a gallery season featuring local artists. A stop by the Lyndon House is time well spent when you are visiting Athens.

Voters

The major influence on government decision-making is made at the polls on election day by people who vote. Voters in our democratic form of government elect representatives to political office and decide major questions and issues.

To register to vote in Georgia, a person must be at least eighteen years old and a citizen of the United States. An individual must also be a legal resident of Georgia and the county in which he or she registers.

Voting in national, state, and local elections takes place according to the Georgia Election Code. As the chief election official, the secretary of state makes sure candidates meet the qualifications to run for office. This official also schedules elections, prints ballots, and provides all election materials to Georgia's counties. After an election, the secretary of state checks the results in each county and publishes them.

A general election is held in November in at least every even-numbered year. This is when major federal and state officials are selected. Other elections are held as needed to select public officials at all levels of government: national, state, county, or city.

Voters select the most important state officials. These officials, in turn, appoint others who work for and with them. Therefore, a citizen can, by voting, influence all of government. Voters also have the right and responsibility to decide some issues. Because it requires a vote of the people to change the state constitution, proposed amendments sometimes appear on the ballot.

No matter what the purpose of an election, low voter turnout is a matter of serious concern. Many people fear that democratic government will not last if so few people are concerned enough about the issues and individuals to vote. Some fear that government will be taken over by wealthy, well-organized interests that have only their self-interest at heart. Effective, democratic government needs voters who are interested in the common good of all citizens of the nation, state, or community.

Public Opinion

A final major influence on government decision-making is public opinion. Since the men and women who run our governments receive their powers from the people, the opinions of the people make a difference. Today, television, radio, newspapers, and magazines keep the public informed about what is going on in Washington and Atlanta. Those news media also keep our elected officials aware of what the general public thinks about issues.

One of the best examples of the power of public opinion as expressed through the news media came in the 1960s and 1970s during the U.S. war in Vietnam. In the early 1970s, large numbers of the American people turned

Above: Cathy Cox was first elected secretary of state in 1998. She was re-elected in 2002. Cox is the first woman to serve as Georgia's secretary of state. **Below:** In the 1960s and '70s, students protested the Vietnam War and influenced the government.

against the war in Vietnam. They protested and demonstrated against the war. In both 1968 and 1972, U.S. involvement in Vietnam was a major political issue in the presidential and congressional elections. As public opinion ran more and more against the war, America's political leaders heard the people's message and U.S. involvement in Vietnam ended in 1974.

Above: These children are dressed in the traditional garb of their native countries at a July 4 naturalization ceremony. What countries do you suppose they represent?

Citizenship

When you studied the development of the U.S. Constitution at the Convention of 1787, you learned that one principle of the new government set up by our founding fathers was *sovereignty*, the concept that power and authority rest with the citizens. Another principle was *federalism*, a system where the national, state, and local governments share authority over the same land and the same people. The government gives to us, America's citizens, the status of citizenship. If your parents are U.S. citizens or if you were born in the United States, then you are a U.S. citizen. You are entitled to all of the protections and rights afforded by the federal and state constitutions.

Naturalized citizens are foreign nationals (those who were born in other countries) who choose to become American citizens and give up their citizenship in those other countries. People who are eighteen years of age, who have lived in this country for at least five years, and who entered the country legally can apply for citizenship. They must meet certain requirements – an ability to read, write, and speak English; a knowledge and understanding of U.S. history and government; good moral character; and a belief in the principles of the U.S. Constitution. Taking an oath of allegiance is the final step in the naturalization process.

Along with the rights that come with being a citizen of the United States, the state of Georgia, and a particular county and town are certain responsibilities. One is participation in government by running for office if you choose, but by voting for candidates for office even if you elect not to serve yourself. Another is upholding the laws of the nation. A third is defending the nation against its enemies. As a citizen, you may be called upon to serve in your community by participating in juries. You may also be called upon to serve in wartime by joining a branch of the military.

All young men are required to register with the Selective Service Board when they turn eighteen.

Most important, however, you can fulfill your responsibilities as a citizen by participating at local, state, and even national levels. You can serve on library boards, zoning commissions, and volunteer civic organizations. You can share your talents and your time with your community to make it a better place to live.

A Final Note

Voting, the most basic responsibility of citizens to participate in their government, is suffering in Georgia. In the last presidential election year, Georgia ranked 48th out of the 50 states in the percentage of eligible adults who voted. Never in the state's history have over 50 percent of the state's eligible voters actually gone to the polls. Who votes most frequently? Older residents between the ages of 60 and 64 are the most active voters, with 71 percent turning out. Unfortunately, the youngest voters, those between the ages of 18 and 24, have the lowest voter participation, with only 21 percent taking the time to vote.

Most of you are between the ages of 13 and 15. Now is the time to decide where Georgia will rank five years from now! It's up to you!

It's Your Turn

1. What are the two major political parties in the United States today?
2. How old does a person have to be to vote in Georgia?
3. When are general elections held in Georgia?
4. What are the two ways a child becomes a U.S. citizen?

Chapter Summary

- In the United States, government is carried out at three levels—federal, state, and local—but local government is the closest to the people.
- Local government includes county, city, and special-purpose governments.
- Georgia has 159 counties, the maximum number allowed by law, and over 600 cities or municipalities.
- Most county governments are led by elected boards of commissioners.
- The most common forms of municipal government are the mayor-council form, the council-manager form, and the commission form.
- Governments gain most of their operating funds from taxes, especially property, or ad valorem, taxes.
- Seventy percent of Georgia's citizens live in urban areas.
- Urban sprawl is one of Georgia's most pressing problems involving the state's continued population growth.
- Participation in a representative democracy stems from four areas: political parties, interest groups, voters, and public opinion.
- The minimum voting age in Georgia is eighteen.
- Effective government needs voters interested in the common good of all and who turn out to participate in elections at all levels.

ChapterReview

Reviewing People, Places, and Terms

Provide a brief definition of each of the following terms.

1. ad valorem taxes

2. citizenship

3. metropolitan area

4. SPLOST

5. urban sprawl

Understanding the Facts

1. What is the most common form of county government in Georgia?

2. Are counties or cities generally in charge of school systems?

3. What is Georgia's oldest city?

4. What are the requirements to become a city?

5. What major problems have been created by urban sprawl?

6. Where do counties and municipalities get most of their operating funds?

7. What are the major influences on government decision-making in America?

8. Name three responsibilities of citizenship.

9. What are the requirements for becoming a naturalized American citizen?

Developing Critical Thinking

1. Georgia, although a sizable land area, has a lot of counties. Critics argue that the state should redraw county lines and have a smaller, more manageable number of counties to reduce the costs of government. Do you think Georgia should reduce the number of counties? Why are some people opposed to such a reduction? List the arguments for and against reduction. List advantages and disadvantages to changing Georgia's county structure.

2. Duplication of services between cities and counties is expensive. A move to consolidate city and county governments has gained momentum in the state. Some areas are considering consolidating some services. Do you favor mergers of services, consolidations, or leaving city and county governments as they are? Explain and defend your answer.

3. Why do you think so few people now vote in general elections? Could the Untied States someday be governed only by special interest groups if citizens fail to exercise their right to vote?

Checking It Out

1. Investigate your own county and the cities within it. What shared or merged services do they provide? What duplicated services do the two governments provide?

2. Who do you turn to for help and for services? Once you have investigated your own local city and county government, check out where to

go for help in the following cases:

a. To obtain a driver's license

b. To obtain a marriage license

c. To establish that a will is valid

d. To complain about potholes in the road to your home

e. To get help for a wounded wild animal in your neighborhood

f. To report a rabies threat

g. To report a break-in at your home

h. To obtain a business license

Writing Across the Curriculum

1. Government documents are often difficult to understand because they are usually written in "bureaucratic language." Try your hand at being a journalist and translate a local ordinance into simple, everyday language for local residents. Remember, newspaper articles cover basic facts: *Who*, *What*, *Where*, *When*, *Why*, and *How*. They also cover information in a short or terse style and use graphics or illustrations and pictures to complement the story.

2. Write an open letter to the newspaper explaining why it is important that every citizen vote in the next election. In your letter, explain the concept of sovereignty, which is one of the basic principles of American government.

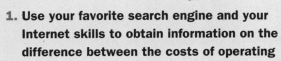

Exploring Technology

1. Use your favorite search engine and your Internet skills to obtain information on the difference between the costs of operating consolidated city-county governments such as Athens-Clarke, Augusta-Richmond, or Columbus-Muscogee and the cost of operating similar-sized governments in nonconsolidated cities and counties.

2. Local government is all about services. Explore the website of your local government if it has one. Compare the home page with comparable counties or cities across the state. Can you suggest changes to the web page that would improve an ordinary citizen's access to information? Work out a plan to improve citizens' access to information about government services in your own community.

Applying Your Skills

1. Every city and county government is a little bit different. Develop an organization chart that shows the operation of your county and your city governments. Identify the people who are elected and those who are appointed to positions of authority in those governments. Compare your county government with that of the two counties highlighted in the textbook— Fulton County and Camden County.

2. Examine historical maps of Georgia in the 1780s and county maps of today. The original parishes were converted to eight counties under Georgia's first constitution. Examine those counties' land areas and identify which modern-day counties were pulled from those original 8-county tracts.

3. Time is important. Which Georgia counties are the oldest and which are the youngest? You already know the eight original counties are the oldest, but find out which ten counties are Georgia's youngest counties. Using a county map, list the dates of creation of all Georgia counties.

Georgia Vital Statistics

Area
Land: 58,910 square miles (21st)
Water: 854 square miles
Coast: 100 miles (16th)
Shoreline: 2,344 miles (12th)

Distances
315 miles long
250 miles wide

Location
Between 30°31' and 35° north latitude
Between 81° and 85°53' west longitude

Bordering states
Alabama, Florida, North Carolina, South Carolina, Tennessee

Time zone
Eastern standard time

Average elevation
600 feet (16th)

Highest point
Brasstown Bald, 4,784 feet (25th)

Lowest point
Atlantic coastline, sea level (3rd)

Highest temperature
112°F, Louisville on July 24, 1953

Lowest temperature
-17°F, Floyd County on January 27, 1940

Admitted to Union
January 2, 1788 (4th)

Nicknames
Peach State, Empire State of the South

Capital
Atlanta

Population (2000)
8,186,453 (10th)

Largest cities (2000)
Atlanta, Augusta, Columbus, Savannah, Athens, Macon, Roswell, Albany, Marietta, Warner Robins

Oldest town
Savannah

Geographic center
Twiggs County, 18 miles southeast of Macon

Number of counties
159

Largest county
Ware County, 906 square miles

Smallest county
Clarke County, 121 square miles

Most populous county (2000)
Fulton County, 816,006

Least populous county (2000)
Taliaferro County, 2,077

Georgia Counties

County	2000 Population	Date Founded	County Seat	Named For
Appling	17,419	1818	Baxley	Colonel Daniel Appling
Atkinson	7,609	1917	Pearson	General William Y. Atkinson
Bacon	10,103	1914	Alma	Augustus O. Bacon
Baker	4,074	1825	Newton	Colonel John Baker
Baldwin	44,700	1803	Milledgeville	Abraham Baldwin
Banks	14,422	1858	Homer	Dr. Richard E. Banks
Barrow	46,144	1914	Winder	David C. Barrow
Bartow	76,019	1832	Cartersville	General Francis S. Bartow
Ben Hill	17,484	1906	Fitzgerald	Benjamin H. Hill
Berrien	16,235	1856	Nashville	John M. Berrien
Bibb	153,887	1822	Macon	Dr. William W. Bibb
Bleckley	11,666	1912	Cochran	Logan E. Bleckley
Brantley	14,629	1920	Nahunta	William G. Brantley
Brooks	16,450	1858	Quitman	Preston S. Brooks
Bryan	23,417	1793	Pembroke	Jonathan Bryan
Bulloch	55,983	1796	Statesboro	Governor Archibald Bulloch
Burke	22,243	1777	Waynesboro	Edmund Burke
Butts	19,522	1825	Jackson	Captain Samuel Butts
Calhoun	6,320	1854	Morgan	John C. Calhoun
Camden	43,664	1777	Woodbine	Sir Charles Pratt, Earl of Camden
Candler	9,577	1914	Metter	Governor Allen D. Candler
Carroll	87,268	1826	Carrollton	Charles Carroll
Catoosa	53,282	1853	Ringgold	Cherokee Indian word
Charlton	10,282	1854	Folkston	Robert M. Charlton
Chatham	232,048	1777	Savannah	William Pitt, Earl of Chatham
Chattahoochee	14,882	1854	Cusseta	Chattahoochee River
Chattooga	25,470	1838	Summerville	Chattooga River
Cherokee	141,903	1831	Canton	Cherokee tribe
Clarke	101,489	1805	Athens	General Elijah Clarke
Clay	3,357	1854	Fort Gaines	Henry Clay
Clayton	236,517	1858	Jonesboro	Augustin S. Clayton

County	2000 Population	Date Founded	County Seat	Named For
Clinch	6,878	1850	Homerville	General Duncan L. Clinch
Cobb	607,751	1832	Marietta	Thomas W. Cobb
Coffee	37,413	1854	Douglas	General John E. Coffee
Colquitt	42,053	1856	Moultrie	Walter T. Colquitt
Columbia	89,288	1790	Appling	Christopher Columbus
Cook	15,771	1918	Adel	General Phillip Cook
Coweta	89,215	1826	Newnan	Coweta tribe
Crawford	12,495	1822	Knoxville	William H. Crawford
Crisp	21,996	1905	Cordele	Charles F. Crisp
Dade	15,154	1837	Trenton	Major Francis L. Dade
Dawson	15,999	1857	Dawsonville	William C. Dawson
Decatur	28,240	1823	Bainbridge	Commodore Stephen Decatur
DeKalb	665,865	1822	Decatur	Johann DeKalb
Dodge	19,171	1870	Eastman	William E. Dodge
Dooly	11,525	1821	Vienna	Colonel John Dooly
Dougherty	96,065	1853	Albany	Charles Dougherty
Douglas	92,174	1870	Douglasville	Stephen A. Douglas
Early	12,354	1818	Blakely	Governor Peter Early
Echols	3,754	1858	Statenville	Robert M. Echols
Effingham	37,535	1777	Springfield	Francis Howard, Lord Effingham
Elbert	20,511	1790	Elberton	Governor Samuel Elbert
Emanuel	21,837	1812	Swainsboro	Governor David Emanuel
Evans	10,495	1914	Claxton	General Clement A. Evans
Fannin	19,798	1854	Blue Ridge	Colonel James W. Fannin
Fayette	91,263	1821	Fayetteville	Marquis de Lafayette
Floyd	90,565	1832	Rome	General John Floyd
Forsyth	98,407	1832	Cumming	Governor John Forsyth
Franklin	20,285	1784	Carnesville	Benjamin Franklin
Fulton	816,006	1853	Atlanta	Robert Fulton
Gilmer	23,456	1832	Ellijay	Governor George R. Gilmer
Glascock	2,556	1857	Gibson	General Thomas Glascock
Glynn	67,568	1777	Brunswick	John Glynn
Gordon	44,104	1850	Calhoun	William W. Gordon
Grady	23,659	1905	Cairo	Henry W. Grady
Greene	14,406	1786	Greensboro	General Nathaniel Greene
Gwinnett	588,448	1818	Lawrenceville	Governor Button Gwinnett
Habersham	35,902	1818	Clarkesville	Major Joseph Habersham
Hall	139,277	1818	Gainesville	Governor Lyman Hall
Hancock	10,076	1793	Sparta	John Hancock
Haralson	25,690	1856	Buchanan	General Hugh A. Haralson
Harris	23,695	1827	Hamilton	Charles Harris
Hart	22,997	1853	Hartwell	Nancy Morgan Hart

County	2000 Population	Date Founded	County Seat	Named For
Heard	11,012	1830	Franklin	Governor Stephen Heard
Henry	119,341	1821	McDonough	Patrick Henry
Houston	110,765	1821	Perry	Governor John Houstoun
Irwin	9,931	1818	Ocilla	Governor Jared Irwin
Jackson	41,589	1796	Jefferson	Governor James Jackson
Jasper	11,426	1807	Monticello	Sergeant William Jasper
Jeff Davis	12,684	1905	Hazlehurst	Jefferson Davis
Jefferson	17,266	1796	Louisville	President Thomas Jefferson
Jenkins	8,575	1905	Millen	Governor Charles J. Jenkins
Johnson	8,560	1858	Wrightsville	Governor Herschel V. Johnson
Jones	23,639	1807	Gray	James Jones
Lamar	15,912	1920	Barnesville	Lucius Q. C. Lamar
Lanier	7,241	1920	Lakeland	Sidney Clapton Lanier
Laurens	44,874	1807	Dublin	Colonel John Laurens
Lee	24,757	1826	Leesburg	General Henry Lee
Liberty	61,610	1777	Hinesville	Concept of freedom and liberty
Lincoln	8,348	1796	Lincolnton	General Benjamin Lincoln
Long	10,304	1920	Ludowici	Dr. Crawford W. Long
Lowndes	92,115	1825	Valdosta	William J. Lowndes
Lumpkin	21,016	1832	Dahlonega	Governor Wilson Lumpkin
McDuffie	21,231	1870	Thomson	George McDuffie
McIntosh	10,847	1793	Darien	William McIntosh, Creek chief
Macon	14,074	1837	Oglethorpe	General Nathaniel Macon
Madison	25,730	1811	Danielsville	President James Madison
Marion	7,144	1827	Buena Vista	General Francis Marion
Meriwether	22,534	1827	Greenville	General David Meriwether
Miller	6,383	1856	Colquitt	Andrew J. Miller
Mitchell	23,932	1857	Camilla	General Henry Mitchell
Monroe	21,757	1821	Forsyth	President James Monroe
Montgomery	8,270	1793	Mount Vernon	Major General Richard Montgomery
Morgan	15,457	1807	Madison	General Daniel Morgan
Murray	36,506	1832	Chatsworth	Thomas W. Murray
Muscogee	186,291	1825	Columbus	Muscogee tribe
Newton	62,001	1821	Covington	Sergeant John Newton
Oconee	26,225	1875	Watkinsville	Oconee River
Oglethorpe	12,635	1793	Lexington	James Edward Oglethorpe
Paulding	81,678	1832	Dallas	John Paulding
Peach	23,668	1924	Fort Valley	Georgia peach
Pickens	22,983	1853	Jasper	General Andrew Pickens
Pierce	15,636	1857	Blackshear	President Franklin Pierce
Pike	13,688	1822	Zebulon	General Zebulon M. Pike
Polk	38,127	1851	Cedartown	President James K. Polk

County	2000 Population	Date Founded	County Seat	Named For
Pulaski	9,588	1808	Hawkinsville	Count Casimir Pulaski
Putnam	18,812	1807	Eatonton	General Israel Putnam
Quitman	2,598	1858	Georgetown	General John A. Quitman
Rabun	15,050	1819	Clayton	Governor William Rabun
Randolph	7,791	1828	Cuthbert	John Randolph
Richmond	199,775	1777	Augusta	Charles Lenox, Duke of Richmond
Rockdale	70,111	1870	Conyers	Rockdale Church
Schley	3,766	1857	Ellaville	Governor William Schley
Screven	15,374	1793	Sylvania	General James Screven
Seminole	9,369	1920	Donalsonville	Seminole tribe
Spalding	58,417	1851	Gifffin	Thomas Spalding
Stephens	25,435	1905	Toccoa	Governor Alexander H. Stephens
Stewart	5,252	1830	Lumpkin	General Daniel Stewart
Sumter	33,200	1831	Americus	General Thomas Sumter
Talbot	6,498	1827	Talbotton	Governor Matthew Talbot
Taliaferro	2,077	1825	Crawfordville	Colonel Benjamin Taliaferro
Tattnall	22,305	1801	Reidsville	Governor Josiah Tattnall, Jr.
Taylor	8,815	1852	Butler	President Zachary Taylor
Telfair	11,794	1807	McRae	Governor Edward Telfair
Terrell	10,970	1856	Dawson	Dr. William Terrell
Thomas	42,737	1825	Thomasville	General Jett Thomas
Tift	38,407	1905	Tifton	Colonel Nelson Tift
Toombs	26,067	1905	Lyons	Robert Toombs
Towns	9,319	1856	Hiawassee	Governor George W. Towns
Treutlen	6,854	1917	Soperton	Governor John A. Treutlen
Troup	58,779	1825	LaGrange	Governor George M. Troup
Turner	9,504	1905	Ashburn	Captain Henry G. Turner
Twiggs	10,590	1809	Jeffersonville	General John Twiggs
Union	17,289	1832	Blairsville	Union loyalty
Upson	27,597	1824	Thomaston	Stephen Upson
Walker	61,053	1833	LaFayette	Major Freeman Walker
Walton	60,687	1818	Monroe	Governor George Walton
Ware	35,483	1824	Waycross	Nicholas Ware
Warren	6,336	1793	Warrenton	General Joseph Warren
Washington	21,176	1784	Sandersville	President George Washington
Wayne	26,565	1803	Jesup	General Anthony Wayne
Webster	2,390	1853	Preston	Daniel Webster
Wheeler	6,179	1912	Alamo	General Joseph E. Wheeler
White	19,944	1857	Cleveland	David Thomas White
Whitfield	83,525	1851	Dalton	Reverend George Whitfield
Wilcox	8,577	1857	Abbeville	Major General Mark Wilcox
Wilkes	10,687	1777	Washington	John Wilkes
Wilkinson	10,220	1803	Irwinton	General James Wilkinson
Worth	21,967	1853	Sylvester	General William J. Worth

Appendix III

Georgia Governors

TRUSTEES

Name	Birthplace	Term
James Edward Oglethorpe, Trustee	England	1733 - 1743
William Stephens, President	England	1743 - 1751
Henry Parker, President	England	1751 - 1752
Patrick Graham, President	England	1752 - 1754

ROYAL PERIOD

Name	Birthplace	Term
John Reynolds	England	1754 - 1757
Henry Ellis	Ireland	1757 - 1760
James Wright	England	1760 - 1776

PROVISIONAL GOVERNORS

Name	Birthplace	Term	Political Party
George Walton (President, Council of Safety)	Virginia	1775 - 1776	Whig/Federalist
Archibald Bulloch (President, Council of Safety)	South Carolina	1776 - 1777	Whig
Button Gwinnett (President, Council of Safety)	England	1777	Whig

STATE GOVERNORS

Name	Birthplace	Term	Political Party
John Adam Treutlen	Austria	1777 - 1778	Whig
John Houstoun	Georgia	1778 - 1779	Whig
John Wereat (President, Executive Council)	England	1779 - 1780	Whig
George Walton	Virginia	1779 - 1780	Whig
Richard Howley	Georgia	1780	Whig
Stephen Heard (President, Executive Council)	Virginia	1780 - 1781	Whig
Nathan Brownson	Connecticut	1781 - 1782	Whig
John Martin	Rhode Island	1782 - 1783	

Name	Birthplace	Term	Political Party
Lyman Hall	Connecticut	1783 - 1784	
John Houstoun	Georgia	1784 - 1785	
Samuel Elbert	South Carolina	1785 - 1786	
Edward Telfair	Scotland	1786 - 1787	
George Mathews	Virginia	1787 - 1788	
George Handley	England	1788 - 1789	
George Walton	Virginia	1789	Jeffersonian Republican
Edward Telfair	Scotland	1789 - 1793	Jeffersonian Republican
George Mathews	Virginia	1793 - 1796	Jeffersonian Republican
Jared Irwin	North Carolina	1796 - 1798	Democratic-Republican
James Jackson	England	1798 - 1801	Democratic-Republican
David Emanuel (President, State Senate)	Pennsylvania	1801	Democratic-Republican
Josiah Tattnall, Jr.	Georgia	1801 - 1802	Democratic-Republican
John Milledge	Georgia	1802 - 1806	Democratic-Republican
Jared Irwin (President, State Senate)	North Carolina	1806 - 1809	Democratic-Republican
David Brydie Mitchell	Scotland	1809 - 1813	Democratic-Republican
Peter Early	Virginia	1813 - 1815	Democratic-Republican
David Brydie Mitchell	Scotland	1815 - 1817	Democratic-Republican
William Rabun (President, State Senate)	North Carolina	1817 - 1819	Democratic-Republican
Matthew Talbot (President, State Senate)	Virginia	1819	Democratic-Republican
John Clark	North Carolina	1819 - 1823	Democratic-Republican
George Michael Troup	Georgia	1823 - 1827	Democratic-Republican
John Forsyth	Virginia	1827 - 1929	Democratic-Republican
George Rockingham Gilmer	Georgia	1829 - 1831	Democrat-Whig
Wilson Lumpkin	Virginia	1831 - 1835	Union Democrat
William Schley	Maryland	1835 - 1837	Union Democrat
George Rockingham Gilmer	Georgia	1837 - 1839	Democrat-Whig
Charles James McDonald	South Carolina	1839 - 1843	Democrat
George Walter Crawford	Georgia	1843 - 1847	Whig
George Washington Towns	Georgia	1847 - 1851	Democrat
Howell Cobb	Georgia	1851 - 1853	Union Democrat
Herschel Vespasian Johnson	Georgia	1853 - 1857	Union Democrat
Joseph Emerson Brown	South Carolina	1857 - 1865	Democrat
James Johnson (Provisional)	South Carolina	1865	Democrat
Charles Jones Jenkins	South Carolina	1865 - 1868	Democrat
Thomas Howard Ruger (Military)	New York	1868	
Rufus Brown Bullock	New York	1868 - 1871	Republican
Benjamin Conley (President, State Senate)	New Jersey	1871 - 1872	Republican
James Milton Smith	Georgia	1872 - 1877	Democrat
Alfred Holt Colquitt	Georgia	1877 - 1882	Democrat

Name	Birthplace	Term	Political Party
Alexander Hamilton Stephens (President, State Senate)	Georgia	1882 - 1883	Democrat-Whig
James Stoddard Boynton (President, State Senate)	Georgia	1883	Democrat
Henry Dickerson McDaniel	Georgia	1883 - 1886	Democrat
John Brown Gordon	Georgia	1886 - 1890	Democrat
William Jonathan Northen	Georgia	1890 - 1894	Democrat
William Yates Atkinson	Georgia	1894 - 1898	Democrat
Allen Daniel Candler	Georgia	1898 - 1902	Democrat
Joseph Meriwether Terrell	Georgia	1902 - 1907	Democrat
Hoke Smith	North Carolina	1907 - 1909	Democrat
Joseph Mackey Brown	Georgia	1909 - 1911	Democrat
Hoke Smith	North Carolina	1911	Democrat
John Marshall Slaton (President, State Senate)	Georgia	1911 - 1912	Democrat
Joseph Mackey Brown	Georgia	1912 - 1913	Democrat
John Marshall Slaton	Georgia	1913 - 1915	Democrat
Nathaniel Edwin Harris	Tennessee	1915 - 1917	Democrat
Hugh Manson Dorsey	Georgia	1917 - 1921	Democrat
Thomas William Hardwick	Georgia	1921 - 1923	Democrat
Clifford Walker	Georgia	1923 - 1927	Democrat
Lamartine Griffin Hardman	Georgia	1927 - 1931	Democrat
Richard Brevard Russell, Jr.	Georgia	1931 - 1933	Democrat
Eugene Talmadge	Georgia	1933 - 1937	Democrat
Eurith Dickinson Rivers	Arkansas	1937 - 1941	Democrat
Eugene Talmadge	Georgia	1941 - 1943	Democrat
Ellis Gibbs Arnall	Georgia	1943 - 1947	Democrat
Herman Eugene Talmadge	Georgia	1947	Democrat
Melvin E. Thompson	Georgia	1947 - 1948	Democrat
Herman Eugene Talmadge	Georgia	1948 - 1955	Democrat
S. Marvin Griffin	Georgia	1955 - 1959	Democrat
Samuel Ernest Vandiver, Jr.	Georgia	1959 - 1963	Democrat
Carl Edward Sanders	Georgia	1963 - 1967	Democrat
Lester Garfield Maddox	Georgia	1967 - 1971	Democrat
James Earl Carter	Georgia	1971 - 1975	Democrat
George D. Busbee	Georgia	1975 - 1983	Democrat
Joe Frank Harris	Georgia	1983 - 1991	Democrat
Zell Bryan Miller	Georgia	1991 - 1999	Democrat
Roy Barnes	Georgia	1999 - 2002	Democrat
Sonny Perdue	Georgia	2003 - Present	Republican

Georgia Colleges and Universities

University	City	Type
Abraham Baldwin Agricultural College	Tifton	Community College
Agnes Scott College	Decatur	Private (women)
Albany State University	Albany	Public
Andrew College	Cuthbert	Community College
Armstrong Atlantic State University	Savannah	Public
Athens Technical College	Athens	Community College
Atlanta Christian College	Atlanta	Private
Atlanta Metropolitan College	Atlanta	Community College
Augusta State University	Augusta	Public
Augusta Technical College	Augusta	Community College
Bainbridge College	Bainbridge	Community College
Bauder College	Atlanta	Community College
Berry College	Mount Berry	Private
Brenau University	Gainesville	Private (women)
Brewton Parker College	Mount Vernon	Private
Central Georgia Technical College	Macon	Community College
Chattahoochee Technical College	Marietta	Community College
Christian Life School of Theology	Columbus	Private
Clark Atlanta University	Atlanta	Private
Clayton College & State University	Morrow	Public
Coastal Georgia Community College	Brunswick	Community College
Columbia Theological Seminary	Decatur	Private
Columbus State University	Columbus	Public
Columbus Technical College	Columbus	Community College

University	City	Type
Coosa Valley Technical College	Rome	Community College
Covenant College	Lookout Mountain	Private
Dalton State College	Dalton	Public
Darton College	Albany	Community College
DeKalb Technical College	Covington	Community College
East Georgia College	Swainsboro	Community College
Emmanuel College	Franklin Springs	Private
Emory University	Atlanta	Private
Floyd College	Rome	Community College
Fort Valley State University	Fort Valley	Public
Gainesville College	Gainesville	Community College
Gammon Theological Seminary	Atlanta	Private
Georgia College & State University	Milledgeville	Public
George Institute of Technology	Atlanta	Public
Georgia Military College	Milledgeville	Community College
Georgia Perimeter College	Atlanta	Community College
Georgia Southern University	Statesboro	Public
Georgia Southwestern State University	Americus	Public
Georgia State University	Atlanta	Public
Gordon College	Barnesville	Community College
Griffin Technical College	Griffin	Community College
Gwinnett Technical College	Lawrenceville	Community College
Institute of Paper Science & Technology	Atlanta	Private
Interdenominational Theological Center	Atlanta	Private
John Marshall Law School	Atlanta	Public
Kennesaw State University	Kennesaw	Public
LaGrange College	LaGrange	Private
Life University	Marietta	Private
Macon State College	Macon	Public
Medical College of Georgia	Augusta	Public
Mercer University	Macon	Private
Middle Georgia College	Cochran	Community College
Morehouse College	Atlanta	Private

University	City	Type
Morehouse School of Medicine	Atlanta	Private
Morris Brown College	Atlanta	Private
North Georgia College & State University	Dahlonega	Public
North Georgia Technical College	Clarkesville	Community College
North Metro Technical College	Acworth	Community College
Northwestern Technical College	Rock Spring	Community College
Ogeechee Technical College	Statesboro	Community College
Oglethorpe University	Atlanta	Private
Paine College	Augusta	Private
Piedmont College	Demorest	Private
Reinhardt College	Waleska	Private
Savannah College of Art & Design	Savannah	Private
Savannah State University	Savannah	Public
Savannah Technical College	Savannah	Community College
Shorter College	Rome	Private
South Georgia College	Douglas	Community College
South University	Savannah	Private
Southern Polytechnic State University	Marietta	Public
Southwest Georgia Technical College	Thomasville	Community College
Spelman College	Atlanta	Private
State University of West Georgia	Carrollton	Public
Thomas University	Thomasville	Private
Toccoa Falls College	Toccoa	Private
Troy State University – Atlanta	Atlanta	Public
Troy State University – Fort Benning	Fort Benning	Public
Truett-McConnell College	Cleveland	Private
University of Georgia	Athens	Public
Valdosta State University	Valdosta	Public
Waycross College	Waycross	Community College
Wesleyan College	Macon	Private
West Central Technical College	Waco	Community College
West Georgia Technical College	LaGrange	Community College
Young Harris College	Young Harris	Private

An Atlas of GEORGIA

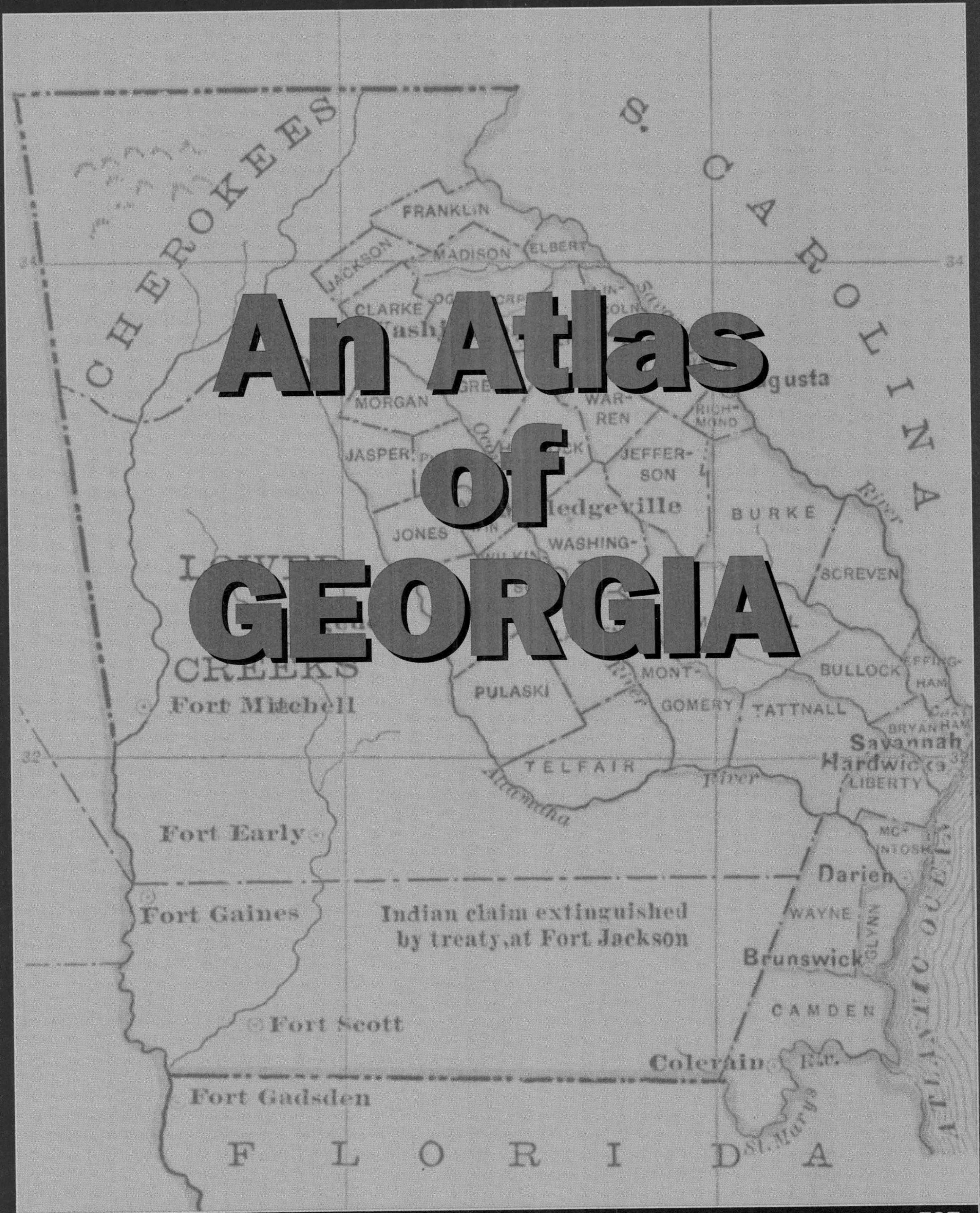

CHEROKEES

S. CAROLINA

FRANKLIN

JACKSON

MADISON

ELBERT

34

34

CLARKE

Washi

LINCOLN

Savan

MORGAN

GRE

gusta

WAR-
REN

RICH-
MOND

JASPER

JEFFER-
SON

ledgeville

BURKE

River

JONES

WASHING-

WILKINS

SCREVEN

LOWER

CREEKS

BULLOCK

EFFING-
HAM

Fort Mitchell

PULASKI

MONT-
GOMERY

TATTNALL

CHAT

BRYAN

HAM

Savannah

TELFAIR

River

Hardwic

LIBERTY

32

Altamaha

River

32

Fort Early

MC
INTOSH

Darien

Fort Gaines

Indian claim extinguished
by treaty, at Fort Jackson

WAYNE

GLYNN

ATLANTIC OCEAN

Brunswick

Fort Scott

CAMDEN

Colerain Riv.

Fort Gadsden

St. Marys

F L O R I D A

ARCTIC OCEAN

75°

GREENLAND

Arctic Circle

Arctic Circle

ICELAND

60°

CANADA

IRELAND

45°

UNITED STATES

PORTUGAL   SPA

PACIFIC OCEAN

ATLANTIC OCEAN

MOROCCO

30°

Canary Islands

WESTERN SAHARA

Tropic of Cancer

MEXICO

THE BAHAMAS

MAURITANIA

15° North Latitude

CUBA

DOM. REP.

JAMAICA   HAITI

BELIZE

SENEGAL

GUATEMALA   HONDURAS

GAMBIA

EL SALVADOR   NICARAGUA

GUINEA BISSAU   GUINEA

COSTA RICA

SIERRA LEONE

COTE

PANAMA

VENEZUELA

LIBERIA

0°   Equator

COLOMBIA

GUYANA   SURINAME   FRENCH GUIANA

Equator

ECUADOR

PERU

15° South Latitude

PACIFIC OCEAN

BRAZIL

ATLANTIC OCEAN

BOLIVIA

Tropic of Capricorn

PARAGUAY

Tropic of Ca

30°

CHILE

ARGENTINA   URUGUAY

180°   165°   150°   135°   120°   105°   90°   75°   60°   45°   30°   15°
       45°

West Longitude

60°

Seattle
★Olympia
WASHINGTON
Spokane

OREGON

Portland ·Vancouver
★Salem

Helena
★

MONTANA

NORTH DAKO

·Bismarck
★

·Boise
★
IDAHO

WYOMING

Pierre
·
★
SOUTH DAKO

Carson City
·
★Sacramento
·Oakland
San Francisco

NEVADA

Salt Lake City
★

Cheyenne
★

NEBRASKA

UTAH

Boulder·
·Denver

COLORADO

KAN

CALIFORNIA

Los Angeles
·

ARIZONA

Santa Fe
★

San Diego
·

Phoenix
★

NEW MEXICO

OK

Pacific
Ocean

TEXAS

ALASKA

Anchorage·

Juneau★

HAWAII

Honolulu★

San Antonio

CANADA

Lake Superior

MINNESOTA

St. Paul
Minneapolis

WISCONSIN

Milwaukee

Madison

Lake Michigan

MICHIGAN

Lansing

Detroit

Ann Arbor

Lake Huron

Lake Ontario

Rochester

Buffalo

Lake Erie

Cleveland

NEW YORK

MAINE

Augusta

VERMONT

Montpelier

Concord

NEW HAMPSHIRE

Boston

MASSACHUSETTS

Albany

Providence

Hartford

RHODE ISLAND

CONNECTICUT

New York

40°

IOWA

Des Moines

Omaha

Lincoln

Chicago

ILLINOIS

INDIANA

OHIO

Columbus

Indianapolis

Dayton

Cincinnati

Springfield

St. Louis

Louisville

Frankfort

Topeka

Kansas City

Jefferson City

MISSOURI

KENTUCKY

PENNSYLVANIA

Pittsburgh

Harrisburg

Baltimore

Washington D.C.

Annapolis

Trenton

NEW JERSEY

Philadelphia

Wilmington

Dover

DELAWARE

MARYLAND

70°

WEST VIRGINIA

Charleston

Richmond

Norfolk

VIRGINIA

Greensboro

Raleigh

NORTH CAROLINA

Charlotte

Atlantic Ocean

Nashville

TENNESSEE

Memphis

ARKANSAS

Little Rock

Columbia

SOUTH CAROLINA

Atlanta

Birmingham

MISSISSIPPI

ALABAMA

GEORGIA

Montgomery

Oklahoma City

AHOMA

Dallas

LOUISIANA

Jackson

Austin

Houston

Baton Rouge

New Orleans

30°

Jacksonville

Tallahassee

Orlando

Tampa

FLORIDA

Miami

Gulf of Mexico

90°

80°

DADE
Trenton •
Ringgold •
CATOOSA
WHITFIELD
Dalton •
LaFayette •
WALKER
CHATTOOGA
• Summerville
MURRAY
• Chatsworth
GILMER
• Ellijay
GORDON
• Calhoun
Jasper •
PICKENS
CHEROKEE
Canton •
Rome •
FLOYD
Cartersville •
BARTOW
FANNIN
Blairsville •
Blue
Ridge
UNION
WHITE
Cleveland •
Dahlonega •
LUMPKIN
DAWSON
Dawsonville •
FORSYTH
Cumming •
Hiawassee •
TOWNS
RABUN
• Clayton
HABERSHAM
Clarksville •
Toccoa •
STEPHENS
HALL
Gainesville •
BANKS
Homer •
Carnesville •
FRANKLIN
HART
Hartwell •

• Cedartown
POLK
PAULDING
Buchanan •
HARALSON
Dallas •
COBB
Marietta •
Atlanta •
Douglasville •
DOUGLAS
FULTON
• Decatur
DeKALB
Jefferson •
JACKSON
GWINNETT
Lawrenceville •
BARROW
Winder •
CLARKE
• Athens
Watkinsville •
OCONEE
Monroe •
WALTON
MADISON
Danielsville •
OGLETHORPE
Lexington •
Elberton •
ELBERT
WILKES
Washington •
Lincolnton •
LINCOLN
COLUMBIA
• Appling
Thomson •
McDUFFIE

CARROLL
Carrollton •
Newnan •
COWETA
HEARD
Franklin •
ROCKDALE
Conyers •
CLAYTON
Jonesboro •
FAYETTE
Fayetteville •
HENRY
McDonough •
Covington •
NEWTON
MORGAN
Madison •
GREENE
Greensboro •
TALIAFERRO
Crawfordville •
Warrenton •
WARREN
Augusta •
RICHMOND

MERIWETHER
Greenville •
PIKE
Zebulon •
Barnesville •
LAMAR
• Forsyth
MONROE
JASPER
Eatonton •
PUTNAM
Monticello •
HANCOCK
Sparta •
GLASCOCK
Gibson •

TROUP
LaGrange •
SPALDING
• Griffin
Thomaston •
UPSON
BUTTS
Jackson •
JONES
Gray •
BALDWIN
Milledgeville •
WASHINGTON
Sandersville •
JEFFERSON
Louisville •
Waynesboro •
BURKE

Hamilton •
HARRIS
MUSCOGEE
• Columbus
TALBOT
Talbotton •
Butler •
TAYLOR
CRAWFORD
Knoxville •
PEACH
Ft. Valley •
Perry •
BIBB
Macon •
TWIGGS
Irwinton •
Jeffersonville •
WILKINSON
LAURENS
Dublin •
JOHNSON
• Wrightsville
EMANUEL
Swainsboro •
JENKINS
Millen •
SCREVEN
Sylvania •

CHATTAHOOCHEE
Cussetta •
MARION
Buena
Vista •
SCHLEY
Ellaville •
Oglethorpe •
MACON
TAYLOR
HOUSTON
Hawkinsville •
BLECKLEY
Cochran •
Eastman •
DODGE
MONT-
GOMERY
Alamo •
WHEELER
• Mt.
Vernon
McRae •
TELFAIR
TOOMBS
Lyons •
Reidsville •
TATTNALL
Metter •
CANDLER
Statesboro •
BULLOCH
EVANS
Claxton •
Pembroke •
BRYAN
EFFINGHAM
Springfield •
Savannah •
CHATHAM

STEWART
Lumpkin •
WEBSTER
Preston •
SUMTER
Americus •
DOOLY
Vienna •
PULASKI
WILCOX
Abbeville •

QUITMAN
• Georgetown
RANDOLPH
• Cuthbert
Dawson •
TERRELL
LEE
Leesburg •
CRISP
Cordele •
BEN HILL
Ashburn •
TURNER
• Fitzgerald
JEFF
DAVIS
Hazlehurst •
APPLING
Baxley •
LIBERTY
LONG
• Hinesville
Ludowici •
Jesup •
WAYNE
McINTOSH
Darien •

CLAY
• Ft. Gaines
Morgan •
CALHOUN
Albany •
DOUGHERTY
Sylvester •
WORTH
IRWIN
Ocilla •
Tifton •
TIFT
COFFEE
• Douglas
BACON
• Alma
PIERCE
Blackshear •
Nahunta •
BRANTLEY
GLYNN
Brunswick •

EARLY
Blakely •
BAKER
Newton •
Camilla •
MILLER
Colquitt •
MITCHELL
COLQUITT
Moultrie •
COOK
Adel •
BERRIEN
Nashville •
LANIER
Lakeland •
ATKINSON
Pearson •
WARE
Waycross •
Homerville •
Woodbine •
CAMDEN

Donalsonville •
SEMINOLE
DECATUR
Bainbridge •
Cairo •
GRADY
Thomasville •
THOMAS
BROOKS
Quitman •
LOWNDES
Valdosta •
CLINCH
CHARLTON
Folkston •
ECHOLS
• Statenville

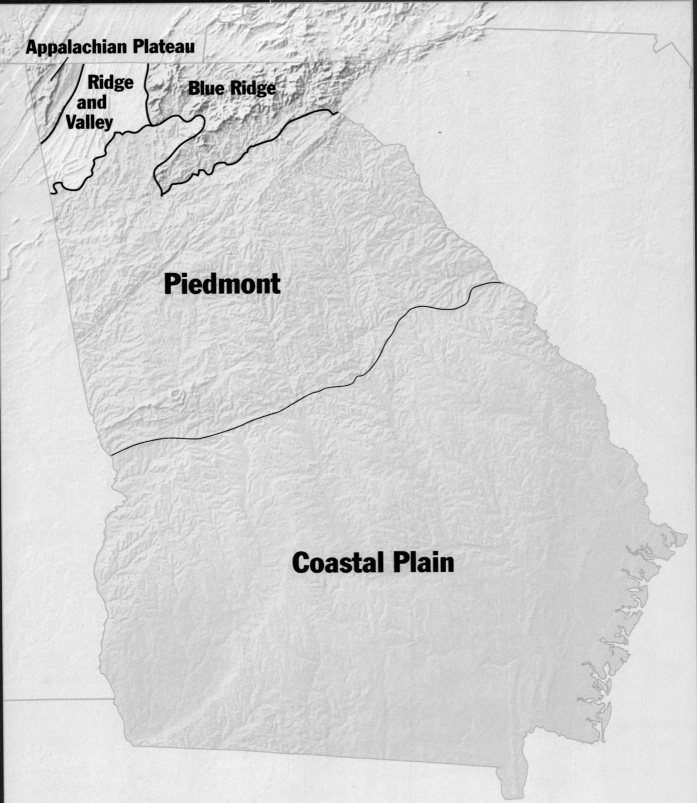

Appalachian Plateau

Ridge
and
Valley

Blue Ridge

Piedmont

Coastal Plain

Atlas of GEORGIA | Major Cities and Highways

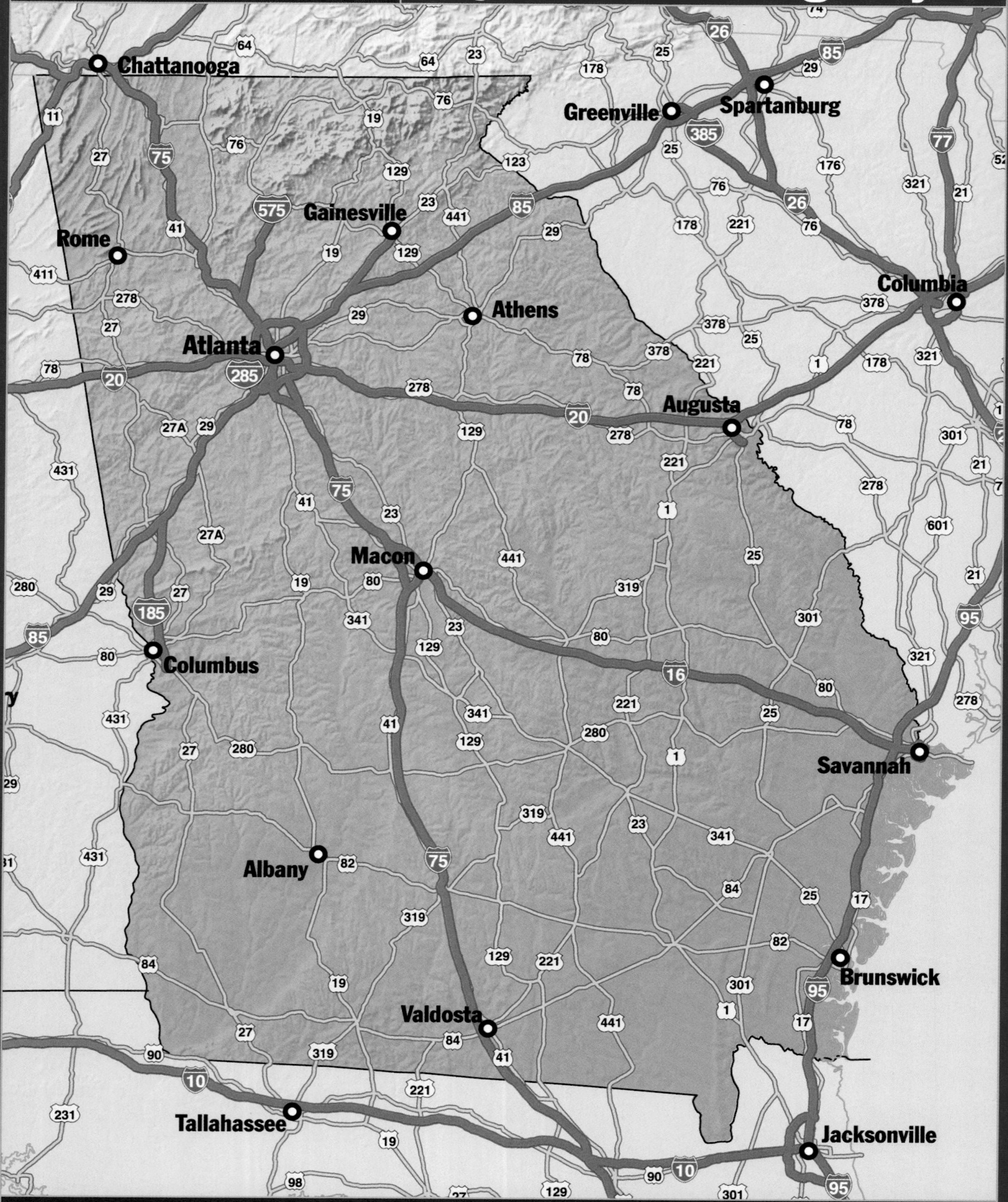

Chattanooga
Greenville
Spartanburg
Gainesville
Rome
Athens
Columbia
Atlanta
Augusta
Macon
Columbus
Savannah
Albany
Brunswick
Valdosta
Tallahassee
Jacksonville

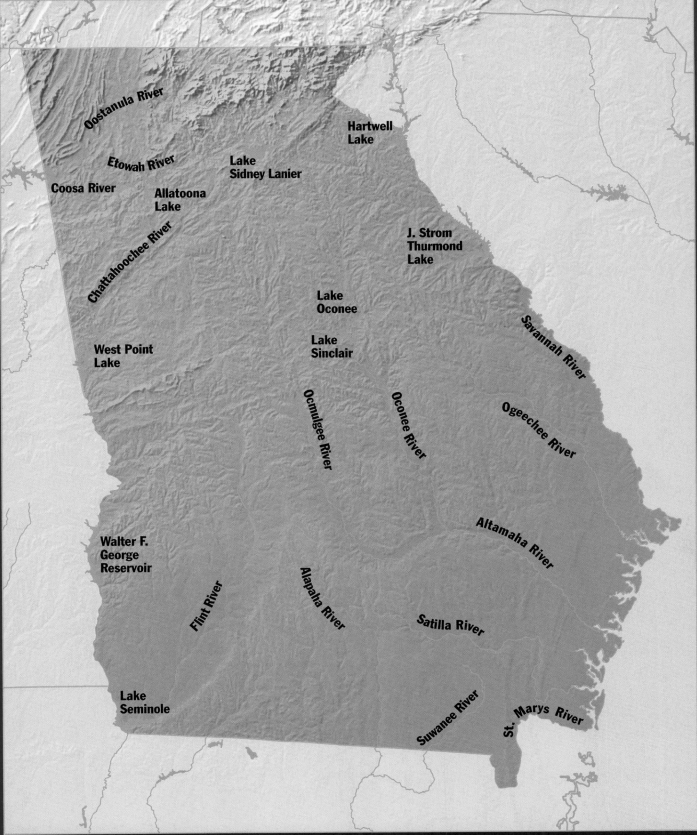

Oostanula River

Hartwell
Lake

Etowah River

Lake
Sidney Lanier

Coosa River

Allatoona
Lake

J. Strom
Thurmond
Lake

Chattahoochee River

Savannah River

Lake
Oconee

Lake
Sinclair

West Point
Lake

Ogeechee River

Ocmulgee River

Oconee River

Altamaha River

Walter F.
George
Reservoir

Flint River

Alapaha River

Satilla River

Lake
Seminole

Suwanee River

St. Marys River

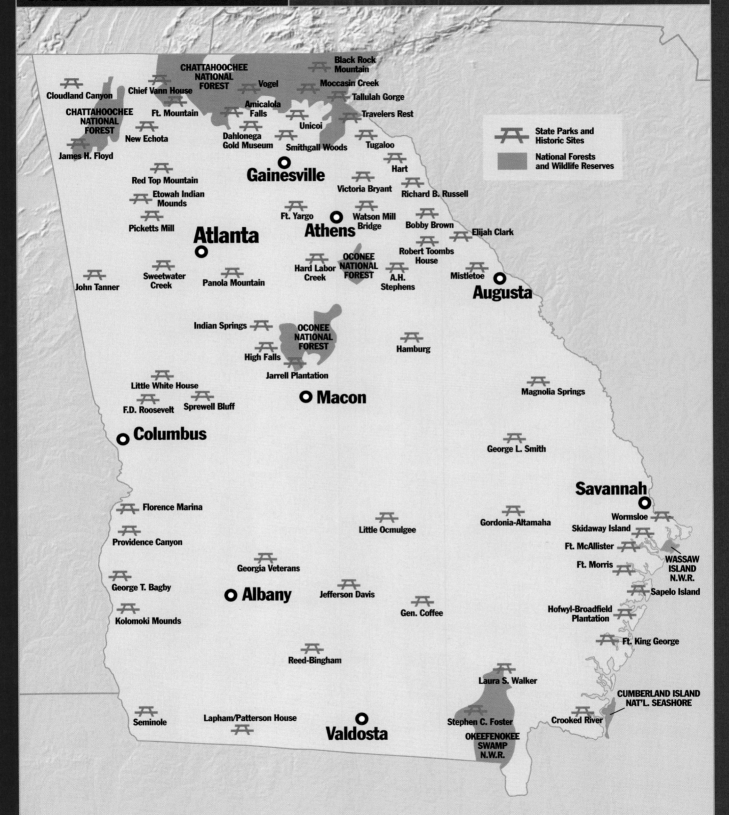

Cloudland Canyon

CHATTAHOOCHEE NATIONAL FOREST

Chief Vann House

Vogel

Black Rock Mountain

Moccasin Creek

Tallulah Gorge

Amicalola Falls

Travelers Rest

Ft. Mountain

CHATTAHOOCHEE NATIONAL FOREST

New Echota

Dahlonega Gold Museum

Unicoi

Smithgall Woods

Tugaloo

James H. Floyd

Red Top Mountain

Gainesville

Hart

Victoria Bryant

Etowah Indian Mounds

Ft. Yargo

Watson Mill Bridge

Richard B. Russell

Picketts Mill

Atlanta

Athens

Bobby Brown

Elijah Clark

John Tanner

Sweetwater Creek

Panola Mountain

Hard Labor Creek

OCONEE NATIONAL FOREST

Robert Toombs House

A.H. Stephens

Mistletoe

Augusta

Indian Springs

OCONEE NATIONAL FOREST

Hamburg

High Falls

Little White House

Jarrell Plantation

Magnolia Springs

F.D. Roosevelt

Sprewell Bluff

Macon

Columbus

George L. Smith

Savannah

Florence Marina

Little Ocmulgee

Gordonia-Altamaha

Wormsloe

Skidaway Island

Providence Canyon

Ft. McAllister

Georgia Veterans

Ft. Morris

WASSAW ISLAND N.W.R.

George T. Bagby

Albany

Jefferson Davis

Sapelo Island

Kolomoki Mounds

Gen. Coffee

Hofwyl-Broadfield Plantation

Ft. King George

Reed-Bingham

Laura S. Walker

CUMBERLAND ISLAND NAT'L. SEASHORE

Seminole

Lapham/Patterson House

Stephen C. Foster

Crooked River

Valdosta

OKEEFENOKEE SWAMP N.W.R.

State Parks and Historic Sites

National Forests and Wildlife Reserves

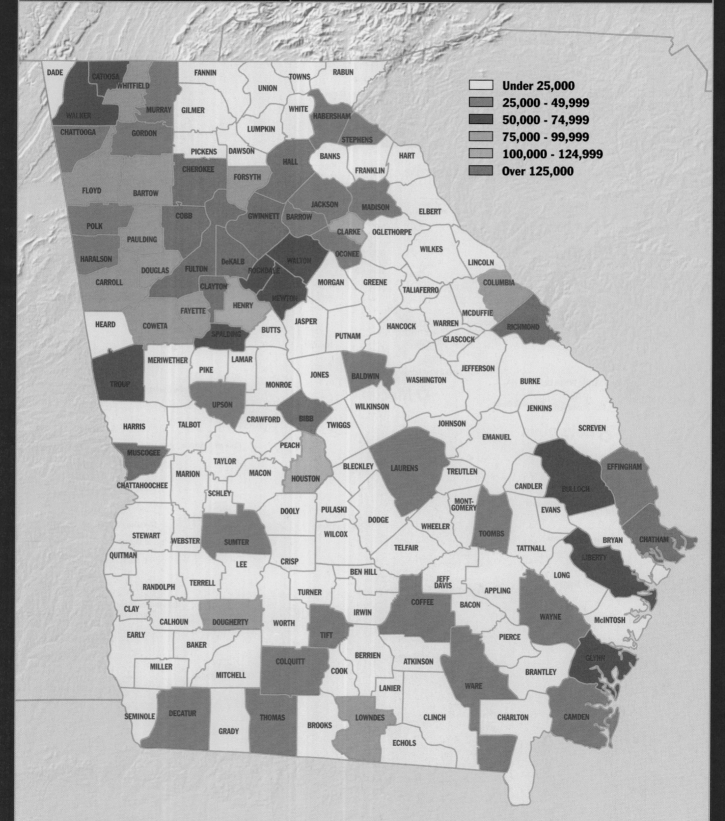

Under 25,000
25,000 - 49,999
50,000 - 74,999
75,000 - 99,999
100,000 - 124,999
Over 125,000

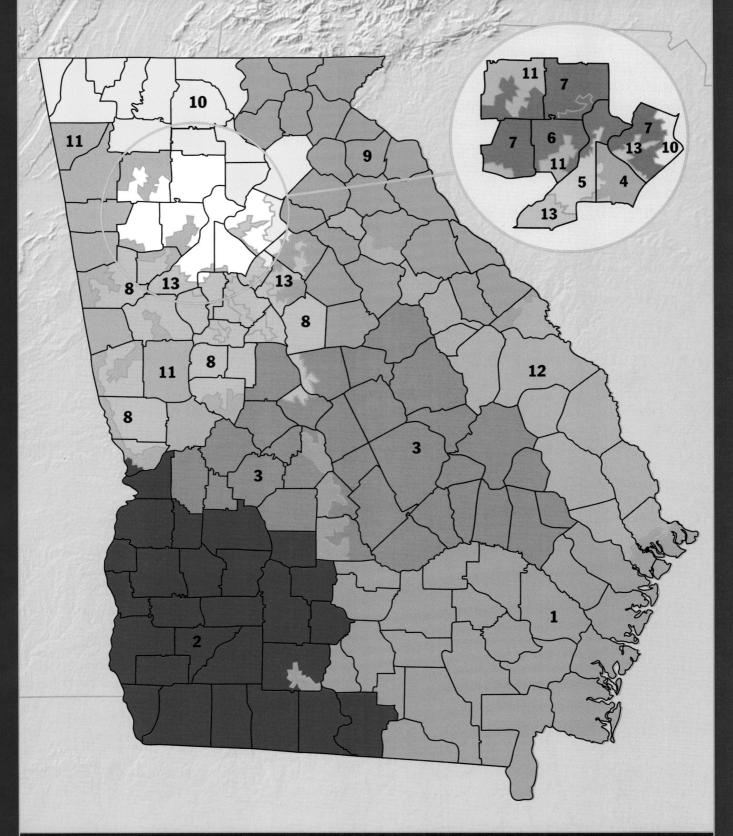

Glossary

This glossary contains those terms that are in bold color in the textbook. The chapter in which the term appears is shown in parentheses following the definition.

A

abolition the movement to do away with something, particularly slavery in the 1800s (7)

absolute location identifies a precise position on Earth's surface; often stated in longitude and latitude (1)

ad valorem tax a tax on real and personal property that is imposed on the property's fair market value (16)

affirmative action program a program designed to provide work and education opportunities for women and minorities (12)

Agricultural Extension Service a government agency that gave matching federal funds to states that spent money to teach young people better farming methods (10)

ally one who shares a common cause (9)

al-Qaeda an extremist group of Islamist terrorists led by Osama bin Laden; responsible for the September 11, 2001, terrorist attacks (13)

annex to add on, such as adding territory to an existing town, city, or state (7)

antebellum the period before the Civil War (7)

anthropologist a scientist who studies artifacts, cave drawings, well-traveled pathways, and oral history to learn about the culture of a group (3)

Antifederalists those who opposed a strong central government and did not favor ratification of the U.S. Constitution (14)

antiquities ancient relics (3)

Appalachian Plateau region a physiographic region of Georgia in the far northwestern corner of the state (1)

appeasement the policy of giving an aggressor what it wants in order to avoid war (11)

apprentice to learn a particular skill or craft from a master craftsman (5)

aquifer an underground natural water storage tank (2)

archaeologist a scientist who studies artifacts to learn about the lives of early peoples (3)

armistice an agreement to stop fighting (10)

arsenal an arms storehouse (7)

Articles of Confederation the first constitution of the United States; ratified in 1781, it created a weak federal government and was eventually replaced (5)

artifacts items such as pottery shards, weapons, tools, and jewelry that were made by humans; could also include fossils (3)

artisan a craftsperson (4)

assessment the fair market value set on a particular item (16)

Atlanta Compromise speech a speech given by Booker T. Washington in 1895 at the Cotton States and International Exposition that proposed that blacks and whites should agree to benefit from each other (10)

Atlantic Intracoastal Waterway a 1,000-mile-long inland waterway that runs from New York to Miami, Florida (2)

Australian ballot a reform supported by the Populist party in which a ballot is printed by the government, distributed at voting places, and collected in sealed boxes so that the votes would be kept secret (10)

axis an imaginary straight line around which an object rotates (1)

B

baby boom a period following World War II in which many children were born (12)

Back-to-Africa movement a movement popular in the 1890s that promised cheap transportation to Liberia for African Americans for the purpose of establishing colonies (10)

bankruptcy occurs when people or businesses cannot pay their debts and seek the help of the courts to manage their affairs (13)

barrier island an island that lies off the coast and protects the beaches by blocking much of the wind, sands, and water that could erode the mainland (1)

barter economy an economy based on the ability to trade or exchange goods or services without the use of money (3)

bauxite a mineral used in the manufacture of aluminum (9)

bill a proposed law (14)

Bill of Rights the first ten amendments to the U.S. Constitution (6)

Black Code a set of laws passed by Georgia, and most southern states, after the Civil War to restrict the rights of the freedmen (9)

blockade to obstruct or prevent access to (8)

blockade runner a ship that slipped around or through a blockade (8)

Blue Ridge region a physiographic region of Georgia located in the northeastern part of the state (1)

blues, the a form of music that was based on black folk music (11)

board of commissioners the elected governing body for most Georgia counties (16)

boll weevil a small, grayish, long-snouted beetle that attacked the cotton plant (11)

bond issue a way for local governments to raise money for a public project; the amount raised by the bonds must be repaid with interest (16)

Bourbon Triumvirate the name given to three Georgia leaders—Joseph E. Brown, Alfred H. Colquitt, and John B. Gordon (9)

boycott a protest in which people refuse to buy certain items until specific conditions are met (5)

Brown v. Board of Education a U.S. Supreme Court case in which the Court declared that the separate-but-equal schools were unconstitutional (12)

budget a plan for receiving and spending money (14)

C

carpetbagger a northerner who moved to the South after the Civil War (9)

cash crop crops like wheat or cotton that were grown to be sold (6)

chain gang a group of prisoners in a county work camp; replaced the convict lease system (10)

charter a legal document that grants special rights and privileges (4)

checks and balances the system that provides to each branch of government some power that controls or prevents some actions of the other two branches (14)

citizenship denotes the rights and responsibilities of a natural-born or naturalized citizen (16)

civil rights the rights that a person has simply because he or she is a citizen (10)

Civil Rights Act of 1964 federal legislation that refused federal funds to any school system that did not end segregation; the legislation also made racial discrimination in public places, such as theaters, restaurants, and hotels, illegal (12)

clan a group of people who believe themselves related by blood (3)

climate the type of weather a region experiences over a long period of time (1)

Coastal Plain region a physiographic region of Georgia that runs from the coast to the Piedmont Plateau (1)

Cold War a period of hostility between the United States and the Soviet Union following World War II (12)

collective bargaining discussions between a union and employer to determine such things as working conditions and employees' wages, hours, and benefits (11)

colony a group of people who settle in a new land but who keep their ties to their homeland (4)

commission form a form of municipal government in which voters elect commissioners, each of whom is the head of a department within city government (16)

Compromise of 1850 legislation passed by Congress by which California entered the Union as a free state, slave trading was ended in the District of Columbia, Texas gave up its claims to New Mexico in exchange for money, residents of the territories of New Mexico and Utah would be able to determine whether they wanted slavery, and a stronger Fugitive Slave Act was enacted (7)

Confederate States of America the name given to the government formed by the southern states that seceded from the Union in the early 1860s (7)

conscription the drafting of men to serve in the army (8)

conservative favoring traditional values and reluctant to make changes (14)

constitutionalism a principle that elected representatives are bound by a written constitution that describes the rights of the people and the framework of the government (14)

continental shelf that portion of the continent or the coastal plain that extends into the ocean (1)

convict lease system a system in Georgia after the Civil War in which prisoners were leased to companies for their labor; companies were supposed to provide housing and food (9)

co-op a cooperative buying store that allows members to buy goods and equipment directly from producers (9)

council-manager form a form of municipal government in which voters elect a city council, which hires a city manager responsible for the day-to-day operations of the city (16)

county a subdivision of the state set up to carry out certain governmental functions; Georgia has 159 counties (16)

county seat the city or town where the county government is located (16)

county unit system a procedure for political primaries that gave the more populous counties more unit votes; established by the Neill Primary Act (10)

court of appeals the second highest ranking court in the Georgia court system; an appellate court (15)

crackers a group of what plantation owners called "undesirable people" who moved from Virginia and the Carolinas to the middle and western parts of the colony (5)

credit the ability to buy something now and pay for it later or over a period of time (9)

culture the beliefs, traditions, music, art, and social institutions of a group of people who share common experiences (3)

D

Declaration of Independence document issued by the Second Continental Congress by which the delegates stated their intention to be free of British rule (5)

deficit spending owing and spending more than is available (5)

depression a sharp economic downturn; businesses and banks fail, farmers lose their land, people lose their jobs (6)

dictator an individual who rules a country through military might (11)

discrimination unfair treatment of a person or group because of prejudice (9)

disfranchise to take the right to vote away from someone or some group (9)

downsizing occurs when businesses fire or lay off workers to cut costs, maintain profits, and remain competitive with other businesses (13)

driver an older slave that a plantation owner thought was loyal and who supervised other slaves (7)

drought a lack of precipitation over a period of time that results in water shortages (1)

E

economics the study of how we made decisions to allocate limited resources (natural, human, capital) in order to meet our unlimited wants (3)

Eighteenth Amendment an amendment to the U.S. Constitution that prohibited the manufacture, sale, and transportation of alcoholic beverages (10)

El Niño warmer-than-normal Pacific Ocean surface temperatures (1)

elastic clause Article I, Section 8 of the U.S. Constitution, which gives Congress the right to make all laws necessary to carry out its expressed powers (14)

electoral college a group of representatives who formally elect the president and vice president; each state has electors equal to the number of its representatives in Congress (14)

electorate the voters (14)

email messages sent electronically on the computer (13)

Emancipation Proclamation a document issued by President Abraham Lincoln in 1862 that freed the slaves in the Confederacy (8)

embargo the stopping of all trade with a foreign country (6)

emigrate to move to another place (6)

Equal Rights Amendment (ERA) a proposed amendment to the U.S. Constitution to ensure equal rights for women; the amendment failed to get the required votes (12)

equator the imaginary line that goes around the globe exactly halfway between the North Pole and the South Pole (1)

estuary a body of water where freshwater rivers and salt water mix; examples include sounds, marsh creeks, and tidal rivers (2)

expenditure money spent or paid out (15)

expressed powers those powers specifically given to Congress in the U.S. Constitution (14)

F

Fall Line the point at which hilly or mountainous lands meet the coastal plain (1)

Farmers' Alliance a farmers organization founded in the late 1870s; it worked for lower railroad freight rates, lower interest rates, and a change in the government's tight money policy (9)

fauna animals, reptiles, birds, and sea life (2)

federalism a system in which the national and state governments share authority over the same territory and the same people (14)

Federalists those who supported a strong national government and ratification of the U.S. Constitution (14)

felony a serious crime such as murder or burglary punishable by a year or more in prison, a fine of at least $1,000, or both (15)

Fifteenth Amendment an amendment to the U.S. Constitution, ratified in 1870, that extended the right to vote to all males (9)

figurehead a person who is the head of an organization but who has no powers (16)

fiscal year a budgetary spending year; Georgia's fiscal year begins July 1 and ends June 30 (15)

flora plants, flowers, and trees (2)

Fourteenth Amendment an amendment to the U.S. Constitution, ratified in 1868, that granted citizenship to the former slaves and forbade the states from denying anyone the "equal protection of the law" (9)

freedmen the former slaves (9)

Freedmen's Bureau a federal government organization established in 1865 that helped the newly freed slaves after the Civil War (9)

free soiler those people in the Kansas and Nebraska territories who opposed slavery (7)

free state a state that did not allow slavery (7)

French and Indian War the war that took place in North America from 1754 to 1763 in which the French and their Indian allies fought the British for control of the Ohio River Valley (5)

freshwater slough small ponds, freshwater marshes, and swamps (2)

G

garrison a fort where troops are housed (4)

General Assembly the legislature of the state of Georgia; consists of a senate and a house of representatives (6)

general election an election held in November in at least every even-numbered year to choose major federal and state officials (16)

general local option sales tax a countywide sales tax added onto and collected at the same time as the state base sales tax (16)

geography the science of studying Earth as the home of humans (1)

Georgia Act legislation passed by Congress in 1869 that returned Georgia to military rule and required the state to ratify the Fifteenth Amendment (9)

Georgia Regional Transportation Authority a group established in 1999 to combat air pollution, traffic congestion, and poorly planned development in the Metropolitan Atlanta area (13)

gerrymander to draw up an election district in such a way that it benefits a certain group (10)

G. I. Bill legislation passed by Congress in 1944 that made low-cost loans to veterans and gave returning soldiers the opportunity for a college education; the Serviceman's Readjustment Act (11)

global warming the raising of the average temperature on Earth due to an excess of carbon dioxide in the atmosphere (1)

good any item that can be bought, sold, or traded (3)

governor the head of the executive branch of the state government (15)

grandfather clause a clause inserted in the Georgia constitution in 1908 that stated only those men whose fathers or grandfathers had been eligible to vote in 1867 were eligible to vote; the clause disfranchised most of Georgia's African Americans (10)

grand jury a group of citizens who determine whether or not a person accused of a crime should be indicted and required to stand trial (15)

Grange the Patrons of Husbandry, a farmers' organization, organized in 1867; it influenced the establishment of a state department of agriculture (9)

Great Compromise a compromise at the Constitutional Convention in which the states agreed that the House of Representatives would be based on proportional representation and the Senate would have equal representation (14)

Great Depression a severe economic downturn that began with the stock market crash of 1929 and lasted until World War II (11)

Great Migration the movement of southern blacks from the South to the North; it began after World War I and lasted until the 1960s (11)

H

headright system a system of distributing land by which each white male as the "head" of a family had the "right" to receive up to 1,000 acres (6)

hemisphere one-half of a sphere (1)

Holocaust the name given to the systematic extermination of 6 million Jews and other "undesirables" during World War II (11)

HOPE scholarship program a scholarship program established in 1993 that provides money for tuition, fees, and books for Georgia high school students who graduate with a B average and who choose to attend one of Georgia's public colleges or universities; students who choose to attend a private Georgia college or university may be eligible for scholarships of up to $3,000 (13)

horticulture the science of cultivating plants and trees (3)

hurricane a tropical storm spawned when waters of 80°F or more transform the heat energy of tropical waters into strong winds and heavy waves (1)

I

impeach to bring charges against a public official while that person is still in office (9)

implied powers powers not specifically stated in the Constitution but derived from Congress's right to make all laws necessary to carry out its expressed powers (14)

indentured servant a person who agreed to work for someone for a set period of time in exchange for passage to the New World (4)

independence political or economic freedom (5)

inflation a general increase in the prices of goods and services over time (8)

infrastructure basic facilities such as roads, bridges, and ports (13)

injunction a court order stating that something must or must not be done (10)

integrate to open something to members of all races and ethnic groups (11)

interest group people who share common goals and objectives and who band together to influence government policies on issues related to their goals and objectives (16)

ironclad an armored ship (8)

isolationism not taking part in the affairs of other nations (11)

J

jazz a form of music that relied on improvisation (11)

Jim Crow laws laws passed in the South to establish "separate-but-equal" facilities for whites and for blacks (10)

judicial review the ability to set aside the actions of the legislative or executive branches of any government agency (14)

jurisdiction the range of actions over which a court has control or influence (15)

juvenile a citizen under the age of seventeen (15)

K

Kansas-Nebraska Act legislation that created the territories of Kansas and Nebraska and that contained a clause on popular sovereignty that negated the Compromise of 1850 (7)

kaolin a white clay used in the manufacture of paper and other products (9)

King Cotton diplomacy the South's political strategy during the Civil War; it depended upon British and French dependency on southern cotton to the extent that those two countries would help the South in the war (8)

Know Nothing party a political party in the 1800s that did not want immigrants to become citizens or persons not born in the United States to hold political office (7)

Korean War a war that broke out in 1950 when communist North Korea invaded democratic South Korea (12)

Ku Klux Klan a secret racist organization, formed in 1865, that worked to keep the freedmen from voting after the Civil War (9)

L

labor union an organization of workers formed to improve their wages, benefits, and working conditions (10)

laissez-faire the doctrine that the government should not interfere in the private sector of the economy (11)

La Niña colder-than-normal Pacific Ocean surface temperatures (1)

latitude a measure of the distance north or south of the equator; expressed in degrees, minutes, and seconds (1)

Liberty Boys a group of Georgians who opposed the Stamp Act; part of the larger Sons of Liberty (5)

lieutenant governor an elected official who serves as a

deputy to the governor (15)

litigation legal court action (6)

lobbyist one who is paid to represent an interest group and to keep pressure on government officials to favor the interest group (16)

longitude a measure of the distance east or west of the prime meridian; expressed in degrees, minutes, and seconds (1)

Louisiana Purchase a transaction in which the United States, at the urging of President Jefferson, bought from France for $15 million a huge amount of land stretching from the Mississippi River to the Rocky Mountains (6)

loyalty a person's devotion or feeling of attachment to a person, group, or idea (7)

lynching an illegal hanging, usually by a mob (10)

M

manifest destiny the belief that it was the will of God that the United States expand its borders to the Pacific Coast (7)

market economy an economy in which production and costs of goods and services are determined by competition among individuals (6)

martial law the use of military forces to maintain order because civilian forces will not or cannot maintain order (10)

mayor-council form a form of municipal government where voters elect a mayor and a city council; mayors may be either "weak" or "strong" (16)

medium of exchange anything that is generally accepted as a standard of value in a society; usually refers to currency (3)

mercantilism a trade policy in which a country exports more than it imports; colonies are expected to supply raw materials to the mother country (4)

meridian a line that runs north and south from one pole to the other; a longitude measure (1)

metropolitan area a central city of over 50,000 residents or a city and its surrounding counties with a total population of 100,000 or more (16)

Metropolitan Atlanta Rapid Transit Authority (MARTA) a special-purpose district in metropolitan Atlanta that operates the bus and rail system (12)

middleman a trader who buys goods from producers and sells them to other traders and consumers (4)

militia a citizen army (4)

Minimum Foundation Program for Education Act legislation passed in 1949 that lengthened the school year to nine months and raised standards for buildings, equipment, transportation, and school curricula (12)

minimum wage the least amount an employer can pay an employee for a certain number of hours worked (11)

misdemeanor a less serious crime punishable by less than a year in prison, a fine of less than $1,000, or both (15)

Missouri Compromise legislation passed by Congress in 1820 by which Maine entered the Union as a free state, Missouri entered the Union as a slave state, and slavery was prohibited north of the southern border of Missouri (7)

monarch a king or queen (4)

muckraker name given to journalists and writers of the Progressive Era who wrote about dishonesty in business, corruption in government and politics, and the horrors of being poor (10)

municipality a city with its own government (16)

N

National Association for the Advancement of Colored People (NAACP) an organization formed in 1909 by white liberals and members of the Niagara Movement to work for the rights of African Americans (10)

National School Lunch Act legislation introduced by Georgia Senator Richard B. Russell in 1946 that outlined a program to ensure that schoolchildren received nutritious lunches (12)

National Organization for Women (NOW) an organization formed to work for the economic and legal rights of women (12)

National Urban League: an interracial organization formed in 1910 to help solve social problems facing African Americans who lived in the cities (10)

National Women's Political Caucus an organization to promote women's issues (12)

naturalized citizen a foreign national who chooses to become an American citizen, gives up his or her citizenship in another country, meets certain requirements, and takes an oath of allegiance to the United States (16)

naval stores turpentine, rosin, tar, and pitch (9)

neutral to not take sides in a disagreement (10)

New Deal the name given to the programs enacted by Congress in the 1930s to bring about economic recovery, relieve the suffering of the unemployed, reform defects in the economy, and improve society (11)

New South a term coined by Henry W. Grady and used to describe the southern states after Reconstruction (9)

Nineteenth Amendment an amendment to the U.S. Constitution that gave women the right to vote (10)

nor'easter a strong storm that blows from the northern Atlantic and is often accompanied by large amounts of rainfall (1)

normal school a teacher-training school (9)

nullify to declare invalid (9)

O

ocean currents rivers of ocean water (1)

Oconee War war along the Oconee River between the Creek led by Alexander McGillivray and the settlers (6)

one-person, one-vote concept the policy that every citizen's vote should be equal to every other citizen's vote no matter where the person lives (12)

ordinance a bill or local law (7)

overseer a person hired to manage slaves on a day-to-day basis (7)

P

palisades fences made of sharpened stakes (5)

parallel an imaginary line that runs east and west side-by-side with the equator; a latitude line (1)

parish in colonial Georgia, a church and British government district (5)

patriotism a love and support of country and the Constitution (14)

Patriots those colonists who wanted independence from Great Britain; also called Whigs, Liberty Boys, Colonials, Sons and Daughters of Liberty (5)

per capita income the total income of all people in an area divided by the total population in that area (13)

Piedmont Plateau region a physiographic region of Georgia that begins in the mountain foothills of northern Georgia and goes to the central part of the state (1)

platform a statement of the principles and policies a political party supports (7)

plurality the margin of victory for the winner over his or her nearest rival (10)

political party an organized group of people who share common ideals and who seek to influence government policies and decisions by electing members of their party to government office (16)

poll a voting place (10)

poll tax a tax paid to be able to vote (10)

popular sovereignty the ability of the residents of an area to decide upon an issue, such as whether they would allow slavery (7)

Populist party a political party formed in the late 1800s by labor organizations and the Farmers' Alliance (10)

precipitation rain, hail, sleet, or snow (1)

prevailing westerlies winds from around 30°E to 60°E north and south of the equator that generally blow from the west to the east (1)

prime meridian an imaginary line running from the North Pole through England and part of Africa to the South Pole; 0° (1)

Proclamation of 1763 a order issued by King George III that moved Georgia's southern boundary to the St. Marys River; it also forbade the colonists from moving west of the Appalachian Mountains (5)

progressive movement a series of movements in the late 1800s and early 1900s whose members believed that government was best able to correct the ills of society (10)

prohibition the banning of alcohol (10)

propaganda information that is spread for the purpose of promoting some cause (10)

proportional representation representation based on population (14)

proprietary colony a colony directed by those to whom a charter was given (5)

provisional temporary (9)

public regulation a law affecting such issues as morals, public health, business or professional regulations, or any general welfare rule (15)

Puritans a group of people who had broken away from the Church of England because of religious differences (5)

Q

Quality Basic Education a legislative program passed in 1986 that standardized curriculum for all schools in the state, equalized funding for all school systems, implemented statewide testing of students, and required accountability performance testing to certify public school teachers (13)

Quartering Act legislation passed by the British Parliament that required the colonists to house and feed British soldiers at their own expense; part of the Intolerable Acts (5)

R

ratify to approve or make valid (5)

ration to limit the consumption of something (11)

rations portions of food (8)

Reaganomics the economic policy followed by President Reagan that featured supply side economics, tax cuts, heavy defense spending, limited government, reductions in government workers, and limited regulations on industry and growth (13)

reapportion to redraw voting districts to ensure districts of equal population sizes (12)

recession an economic slowdown; characterized by decreased demand for products or services, decreased sales, increased unemployment, and decreased wages and salaries (12)

Reconstruction the period immediately after the Civil War when the South rebuilt and the southern states returned to the Union (9)

Redemption the period immediately following Reconstruction when Georgia worked to recover from Reconstruction (9)

Red Sticks those Native Americans in the early 1800s who wanted war with the white settlers (6)

region an area on Earth's surface that is defined by certain unifying characteristics (1)

regulations government orders (4)

relative location describes where a place is compared with other places (1)

relief money and food given to people in special need (11)

republic a form of government in which all of the powers of government are given to the people, who elect representatives to make the laws (14)

Republican party a political party formed in 1854 to oppose slavery (7)

reservoir a holding tank for surface water; many have been created when rivers have been dammed (2)

resource anything used to produce a good or service (3)

revenue a source of income (15)

Ridge and Valley region a physiographic region of Georgia that lies between the Blue Ridge Mountains and the Appalachian Mountains (1)

royal colony a colony directly governed by the king (5)

rural area defined as a town or community of less than 2,500 people (16)

rural electrification a New Deal program that provided funds to farmers' cooperatives to help them extend their power lines (11)

Rural Free Delivery bill legislation introduced by Georgia Representative Tom Watson that required the U.S. postmaster general to find a way to deliver mail to rural homes free of charge (10)

S

saltwater marsh a saltwater wetland occurring along the Atlantic coastline (2)

scalawag a southerner who supported the Republicans during Reconstruction (9)

scrip paper money that is not legal currency (10)

secession the act of pulling out of the Union (7)

Second Continental Congress a meeting of the colonists in 1775 to discuss the increasing tensions between the British Crown and the colonists; eventually the delegates issued the Declaration of Independence (5)

sectionalism the belief by the people in a given region or area that their ideas and interests are better and more important than those of another region or area (7)

segregate to separate by race (9)

semidiurnal tides two high tides and two low tides each day (2)

separation of powers a division of responsibilities for government among the three branches (legislative, executive, judicial) (14)

service any action that one person does for another in exchange for some form of payment (3)

shale a type of rock that is formed in successive layers (3)

sharecropping an agricultural system common after the Civil War where landless farmers worked the land of a landowner who also supplied a house, farming tools and animals, seed, and fertilizer in return for a share of the harvest (9)

siege a military action that occurs when forces try to capture a fortified fort or town by surrounding it and preventing any supplies from reaching it (5)

skirmish a minor, short-term battle

slave a person who had few rights and who spent his or her entire life in service to others (4)

slave code laws enacted in the South that took away nearly all the rights of slaves by regulating their actions (7)

slave state a state that allowed slavery (7)

Smith-Hughes Act legislation sponsored by Georgia Senator Hoke Smith that helped establish vocational programs in public schools across the nation and that helped states plan and carry out vocational training (10)

Smith-Lever Act legislation sponsored by Georgia Senator Hoke Smith that created the Agricultural Extension Service (10)

Southern Christian Leadership Conference (SCLC) an organization founded by Dr. Martin Luther King, Jr., to work for civil rights for African Americans (12)

sovereignty the idea of supreme power or source of authority (14)

special-purpose district a form of local government created for a single job or single group of tasks (16)

special purpose local option sales tax (SPLOST) a tax imposed over a five-year period in order to finance specific local improvement projects such as roads and bridges (16)

Stamp Act legislation passed by Parliament in 1765 that imposed a tax on newspapers, legal documents, and licenses (5)

states' rights the belief that a state's interests should take precedence over the interests of the national government (7)

stock market the place where shares of ownership in corporations (stock) are bought and sold (11)

strategy a plan of action to accomplish something (8)

stretch out a textile mill practice requiring workers to tend more machines (11)

strike a work stoppage in protest over some grievance (10)

Student Nonviolent Coordinating Committee (SNCC) an organization founded in 1960 to coordinate and publicize sit-ins (12)

subsidy a grant of money from the government (11)

suburban area residential areas around cities (16)

suburbs residential areas around cities (12)

suffrage the right to vote (9)

suffragette a woman who fought for women's right to vote in the early 1900s (10)

Sugar Act legislation passed by Parliament in 1764 that imposed a tax on sugar and molasses imported from the West Indies (5)

supply side economics the economic theory that lower taxes lead to an expansion of the economy as businesses and individuals invest the money saved on taxes in the economy (13)

supreme court the highest-ranking court in the Georgia court system (15)

sutler wagon a privately owned wagon that followed behind the troops and that had available for sale food, razors, writing papers and pens, sewing needles, and other items (8)

sweatshop factories with especially harsh working conditions (10)

syllabary a group of symbols that stand for whole syllables (6)

T

tariff a tax on imported goods (5)

telecommute to work at home while keeping in touch with the office through the computer (13)

temperance the antialcohol movement (9)

tenant farming an agricultural system common after the Civil War where a farmer worked the land of a landowner in exchange for cash or an agreed-upon share of the harvest; tenant farmers usually owned some agricultural equipment and animals (9)

terrorism acts of violence aimed at demoralizing or intimidating others (13)

textiles woven materials (9)

Thirteenth Amendment an amendment to the U.S. Constitution, ratified in 1865, that made slavery illegal (9)

Three-Fifths Compromise a compromise at the Constitutional Convention by which the delegates agreed that only three-fifths of the slave population would be counted toward the state's total population (14)

tide a rise or fall of the sea level caused by the gravitational pull of the sun and the moon (2)

Title IX federal legislation that prohibited discrimination in education whether in academics or athletics (12)

topography physical features such as mountains or plateaus (page 34)

Tories those colonists who were loyal to the British crown; also called Loyalists, British Royalists, "King's friends" (5)

tornado a storm of swirling cyclonic winds that moves from southwest to northeast and spins in a counterclockwise motion (1)

Townshend Acts a series of laws passed by Parliament in 1767 that placed import taxes on tea, paper, glass, and coloring for paints (5)

trade winds winds from the equator to around 30° north latitude that generally flow from the northeast (1)

Trail of Tears name given to the forced removal of the Cherokee to Indian Territory (present-day Oklahoma) (6)

Treaty of Indian Springs a treaty signed in 1825 by which the Lower Creek gave up the last Creek lands in Georgia to the federal government in return for $200,000 (6)

Treaty of New York the agreement that ended the Oconee War; the Creek gave up all of their land east of the Oconee River (6)

Treaty of Paris the treaty signed in 1783 by Great Britain, France, and the United States that ended the American Revolution (5)

trial court the court that has original jurisdiction in the Georgia court system; includes superior courts, state courts, probate courts, juvenile courts, and magistrate courts (15)

trial jury a group of citizens who are charged with judging a person charged with a crime (15)

tribe a group of people who share a common ancestry, name, and way of living (3)

truancy failure to attend school (15)

trustee a person who holds responsibility on behalf of others (4)

turnpike a road that travelers had to pay a fee, or "toll," to use (6)

U

underground railroad a series of roads, houses, river crossings, and people who helped southern slaves escape to the North or Canada (7)

U.S. Constitution the document that set up our current framework for government; written in 1787 and ratified in 1788 (6)

urban area defined as a city with a population over 2,500 or a city and its surrounding area with over 50,000 residents (16)

urban sprawl the generally unplanned and uncoordinated growth around an urban area (16)

user fee an amount paid by citizens for services such as garbage collection or water and sewage service (16)

V

vertical climate climate that is influenced by elevation; the higher the elevation, the cooler the temperature (1)

veto to refuse to sign a bill (14)

Vietnam War a war in which the United States helped the government of South Vietnam in its struggle with the communist government of North Vietnam (12)

Voting Rights Act of 1965 federal legislation that enforced equal voting rights among all races (12)

W

Watergate a political scandal in which the Nixon administration was accused of abuse of power (12)

watershed an area that catches rain and snow, which then drains into marshes, streams, rivers, lakes, and groundwater (2)

weather the day-to-day conditions and changes in the atmosphere (1)

wetland a low-lying land area where water lies close to the surface creating sloughs, swamps, bogs, ponds, and freshwater marshes; a lowland that is influenced by tidal water flows (1)

white supremacy the belief that the white race is superior to any other race (9)

White Sticks those Native Americans in the early 1800s who did not want war with white settlers (6)

wind current a continuous movement or flow of air (1)

women's rights movement an effort by women to change the way women viewed themselves and their contributions to society and to ensure equal rights for women (12)

World War I a war that began in Europe in 1914 between the Central Powers (Germany, Austria-Hungary) and the Allied Powers (France, Great Britain, Russia, and eventually the United States); the war ended in 1918 (10)

World War II a war that began in Europe in 1939 between the Allied Powers (France, Great Britain, and eventually the United States) and the Axis Powers (Germany, Italy, Japan, and the Soviet Union); the war ended in 1945 (11)

Y

Yazoo land fraud the sale of western land to four land companies after the governor and members of the General Assembly had been bribed (6)

yeoman farmer an independent farmer who often lived from season to season (7)

Index

The purpose of the index is to help you locate information quickly. The index contains references not only to text, but also to illustrations and maps. A page number with **m** before it indicates a map; a page number with a **p** before it indicates a photograph or painting; a page number with an **f** before it indicates a table or chart.

muckrakers, 336
mulberry trees, 117, 120-121, 124
municipal courts, 546
municipal government,
    courts, 546
    forms of, 572-573, f572, f573
    functions of, 572
    funding for, 568-569
municipality, 570
Murrah Federal Building bombing, 481, p481
Murray County, f83, 589
Muscogee County, f350, f567, 573, 589
Musgrove, John, 118
Musgrove, Mary, 118
music, 381, 424, 452

N

Nacoochee Indian Mound, 81
Nantahala Mountains, 99
Napier, Viola Ross, 380
Nation, Carrie, 339, p339
National Association for the Advancement of Colored People
    (NAACP), 357, 359, 436, 442
National Industrial Recovery Act, 392, 394
National Labor Relations Act, f393
National Organization for Women, 456
National School Lunch Act, 428
National Urban League, 359
National Women's Political Caucus, 456
National Youth Administration, (NYA), f393
Native Americans, 69, 74-97, 192-203
    and agriculture, 77, 79, 80, 85, 92
    Archaic culture, 76-78
    burial mounds, 80
    clans of, 86, f87
    clothing, 92
    commandments, 96
    and contact with Europeans, 97, 107-108, 111, 112, 113, 118
    cultures, 75-81
    foods, 76, 77, 78, 91-92
    and French and Indian War, 143, 144
    government systems of, 86
    Mississippian culture, 80-81, 82
    moundbuilders, 80-83, m83
    Paleo culture, 75-76
    pottery of, 78, 79
    religious beliefs of, 80, 82, 92-95
    and removal, 197-198, 237
    Trail of Tears, 201-202, m202
    treaties with, 195
    tribes, 78-79, 84-96
    villages, 79, 81, 84-85
    Woodland culture, 78-80
    in World War II, 407
    See also specific tribes.
naturalized citizen, 582
natural resources, 52-55, m53

naval stores, 18, 137, 323
Navigation Acts, 149
Neill Primary Act, 359, f349
neutral, 370, 371
New Deal, 293, 391-401
    agencies, 392. f393
    in Georgia, 392, 394-396, 399
New Ebenezer, 122
New Echota, p170-171, 194, 199, 200, 201
New England Colonies, 136, 138, 139, 140
New Hope Church, f270-271, 272
New Jersey Plan, 505, f505
New South era, 317-329
newspapers, 137, 148, 185, 243, 286, 358
Newton County, 589
Niagara Movement, 359
Nineteenth Amendment, to U.S. Constitution, 342, 343, 380
Nisbet, Eugenius, 248
nor'easter, 28
normal school, 320-321
North America, exploration and settlement of, see European
    exploration and settlement.
Northen, William Jonathan, 593
Northern Arc, 488-489
Novello, Dr. Antonia Coello, 517, p517
nullification crisis, 227
nullify, 301
Nunis, Samuel, 121
Nunn, Sam, 477-478, p477

O

ocean currents, 26-27, m27
Ocmulgee Indians, 84
Ocmulgee National Monument, p69, 82, f83
Ocmulgee River, 50, 63, 76, 84
Oconee County, 589
Oconee Indians, 84
Oconee Lake, 64
Oconee River, 59, 63, 177, 195, 366
Oconee War, 195
Ogeechee River, 51, 59, 145, 146
Oglethorpe, James Edward, 114-115, p117, 118, p118, 119, 120,
    121, 122, 123, 124, 125, 126, 127, p129, 589, 591
Oglethorpe County, 589
Oglethorpe University, 596
Okefenokee Swamp, 20, 34-35, p34, 44, 49, 558
Old Federal Road, 182
Old Governor's Mansion, p242
Old State Capitol Building, p242
Olympic Games, p464, p465, 479-480, p479, p480, 571
one-person, one-vote concept, 433-434, 541
Oostanaula River, 59, 265
Operation Enduring Freedom, 483-484
Operation Iraqi Freedom, 484–485
oral tradition, 74
ordinance of secession, 248
Oregon, 213

Orr, Dr. Gustavus James, 319, 321
Outer Coastal Plain, 18, 20
overseers, 218, 229

P

Paine, Thomas, 155
Paleo culture, 75-76
palisades, 147-148
Panic of 1837, 181
parallels, 7
Paris, Treaty of, 145
parish, 142, 156
Parker, Henry, 127, 591
Parks, Benjamin, 198
Parks, Rosa, 440, p440
patriotism, 507
Patriots, 149
Patrons of Husbandry, 326
Paulding County, 488, 589
Peach County, 589
peaches, 46
Peachtree Creek, f270-271
peanuts, 18, p554, 555
Pearl Harbor, 404
Pember, Phoebe, 287
Pemberton, John S., 364, p364
Pentagon, 482
People's party, 346, 348
per capita income, 473
Perdue, Sonny, 487, 491, p493, p530, 593
Persian Gulf War (1991), 475-476
physiographic regions, of the state, 9-21, m9
Pickens County, 52, 589
Pickett's Mill, f270-271
Piedmont Plateau, 9, 16-17, 21, 44, 64, 65
Pierce County, 589
Pigeon Mountain, 12
Pike County, 589
Pine Mountain, 36
Pitt, William, 144, 587
place, geography theme of, 5-8
Plains, 518
plank roads, 181
plantations, 136, 217, 228, 229, 230, 231, 237, 304
planters, 217
platform, 245
Plessy v. Ferguson, 352, 436
Plum Nelly, 12
Pocahontas, 112
Pogo, 558
Point Peter, 164
political cartoons, 150, 190, 246, 259, 316, 358, 381, 454, 476, 507, 579
political parties, 578
    Constitutional Union, 244
    Democratic, 242, 244, 245, 307, 312-314, 348, 349-350, 510, 578

    first, 578
    Know Nothing, 242, 244
    People's, 316, 328, 346, 348
    Republican, 245-246, 299, 301, 304, 305, 314, 491, 510, 578
    States' Rights, 244
    Whig, 242, 245
politics,
    in antebellum period, 242-242
    and county unit system, 349-350, 433-434
    interest groups, 578-579
    in postwar period, 430-435
    rise of two-party system, 476-479, 491
Polk, James, 211-212, 589
Polk County, 12, 589
Polo, Marco, 104
polls, 348
poll tax, 357, 401
pollution, 488, 491
poor whites, 218-219
Pope, John, 304
popular sovereignty, 225, 245
population, 472-474, f472, f473, 492, 575-576
populism, 346
Populist party, 316, 328, 346, 348
ports,
    deepwater, 60
    inland, 60, 471
powers, 511, f512
precipitation, 14, 23-25, m25, 64, 65
prehistory, 74-75
Presbyterian church, 139, 242
president, of United States, 506, 514, 515, 516, 518, 520
    line of succession, f516
    powers of, 515
prevailing westerlies, 26
primary elections, 447
prime meridian, m6, 8
principles, of government, 508-509
prisons,
    Civil War, 275-276
    reform, 293, 315-316, 336, 337, 401
probable cause, 548
probate courts, f545, 546
Proclamation of 1763, 145
progressive movement, 293, 336-343
    legislation passed, 336
prohibition, 339-340, 381, 382
propaganda, 371
property taxes, 568
proportional representation, 505
proprietary colony, 142
Prosser, Gabriel, 232
Providence Canyon, 34, 38, p38
Provincial Congress, 149, 152, 153-154
Public Housing Authority, 574
public opinion, 581-582
public regulation, 540

Rocky Face Ridge, f270-271
Roman Catholic Church, 186, 242
Rome, 46, 325, 344
Roosevelt, Franklin D., 36-37, 293
    death, 408-409
    election, 391
    and New Deal, 391-397
    in World War II, 404
Roosevelt State Park, 395
Ross, John, 200, p200, p202
Roswell, , f570
royal colony, 142-148
royal governors, 142, 146-148, 150-151, 153
Ruger, Thomas Howard, 592
rural areas of state, 472-474, f473, 575
rural electrification, 395
Rural Free Delivery bill, 347
Rusk, Dean, 458, p458
Russell, Richard B., 398
Russell, Richard B., Jr., 398-399, p398, 411, 428, 593

S

Saffir-Simpson Hurricane Scale, f28
St. Augustine, 108, 112, 124, 127, 157
St. Catherines Island, 108
St. Marys, 23, 570
St. Marys River, 56, 59, 145
St. Simons Island, 108, 125, 328, 395, 411
sales tax, 432, 539, 569, 574
Salomon, Haym, 160
saltwater marshes, 57-58, p57
Salzburg settlers, 121-122, 123, 124
Sanders, Carl, 434-435, p434, 593
Sand Mountain, 10
Sapelo, 108
Sapelo Island, 51
Satilla River, 59
Sautee Nacoochee, legend of, 91
Savannah, 7, 20, 23, 27, 46, 56, 126, 187, 282, 411, 452, 570, f570, 573
    in antebellum period, 181, 185
    as capital, 543
    and civil rights movement, 434
    during Civil War, 273, 274
    colonial period, 137, 146, 147-148, 150, 152, 153
    design of, 120, p121
    founding of, 119
    and Olympics, 479
    during Reconstruction, 309
    renovation efforts, 577
    in Revolutionary War, 157, 158, m158, 161
    seaport, 60
    siege of 157, 158, 161
    during World War II, 413
Savannah River, 56, 59, 61, 62, p62, 76, 114, 116, 145
scalawags, 304
Schley, William, 590, 592

Schley County, 590
schools, 187, 188, 287, p319, 448
    attendance, 338
    for blacks, 357, 383-384
    commissioner, 319
    funding for, 188, 239, 319, 321, 349, 437
    integration of, 437-440
    normal, 320-321
    public, 138
    school term, 319-320
    segregated, 321, 352-353, 436-437
    superintendent of, 534, f534, 567
    See also education.
Scott, Winfield, 201, 258
Screven County, 590
scrip, 362
seal, 142, 157
seal, U.S., 506
sea life, 50-51
seaports, 60
secession, 301, 302
    debate over, 247-248
Second Continental Congress, 153, 154
secretary of state, 534, f534, 580
sectionalism, f216, 223
Securities and Exchange Commission (SEC), f393
segregation, 321, 351, 384, 413, 436, 437, 440, 441, 442, 444
select committees, 512
semidiurnal tides, 57
Seminole County, 590
Seminole Lake, 64
senate, Georgia, 175, 533, 536
    committees of, 537-538
    districts, m536
    making laws, 540, f540, f541
    member requirements, 536
    See also General Assembly; house of representatives, Georgia.
Senate, U.S., 174, 510, 512, 513, 515, 516, 518, 520
separate-but-equal concept, 351, 352, 436
separation of powers, 156, 509, 546, f546
September 11th, 481-483
Sequoyah, 193, p193
services, 90
settlement,
    early attempts, 114
    of Georgia, 119, 120-124
    reasons for, 114-115
    settlers,
    early, 116, 120-125, 142, 147
    Highland Scots, 124, 147
    Jewish, 121, 139
    Moravians, 123, 139
    Salzburgers, 121-122, 123, 124, 147
"Seven Deadly Sins" Act, 549
seven natural wonders, 34-39
Seventeenth Amendment to U.S. Constitution, 510
Seven Years War see French and Indian War.

treaty,
    of Ghent, 190
    of Guadalupe Hidalgo, 213
    of Indian Springs, 196
    with Indian tribes, 124
    of New York, 195
    of Paris (1763), 145
    of Paris (1783), 161
    of Washington, 197
trees, 44, 46, 559
Treutlen, John Adam, 157, 590, 591
Treutlen County, , 590
trial courts, f545, 546
trial jury, 546
tribe, 78-79. *See also* specific tribes.
Troup, George, 196, 590, 592
Troup County, 590
truancy, 547
trustees, 116, 123, 124, 142
trusts, 363
Truth, Sojourner, 235, p235
Tubman, Harriett, 235
Turner, Henry McNeal, 305, p305, 352
Turner, Nat, 232
Turner, Ted, 426, 452, p452
Turner County, 590
turnpikes, 181-182
Tuskegee Airmen, 406, 407
Tuskegee Institute, 353, 406
TVA, f393
Twenty-fifth Amendment to U.S. Constitution, 515-516
Twenty-second Amendment to U.S. Constitution, 515
Twiggs County, 8, 590
two-Georgias debate, 473-474, 491
Tybee Island, 158, 269, 395

U

Uncle Tom's Cabin, 220, 222
underground railroad, 232, 234, m234, 236
unemployment, 475
Union blockade of coast, during Civil War, 260, 262, m262
Union County, 542, 590
Union League, 305
unions, labor, 338, 392, 429
U.S. Constitution, 174-175, 503
    amendments to, 175, 301, f301, 302, 303, f303, 304, 306, f306, 340, 342, 536
U.S. government,
    branches of, 174
    House of Representatives, 174
    Senate, 174
    See also government, federal.
University of Georgia, 45, 432, 433, 438-439, 485, 596
    establishment of, 187-188
Upson County, 590
urban area, 575
urban sprawl, 488, 575-576

user fees, 574
Utoy Creek, f270-271

V

Vandiver, Ernest, 437, 439, p493, 593
Vann, Chief James, 192
Velazquez, Loreta, 283
Venable, James, 238
Venable, Willis, 364-365
vertical climate, 23
Vesey, Denmark, 232
veto, 513
Vidalia onions, 559
Vidalia Upland, 18
Vietnam War, 452, 457-458, m457
Vinson, Carl, 410, p410, 411
Virginia Plan, f504, 505
vocational education, 349, 434
voting, 580-581, 582
    during colonial period, 142
    and disfranchisement, 301, 303, 336, 349
    districts, 358, 433-434
    electorate, 409
    grandfather clause, 357
    polls, 348
    requirements for, 357, 580
    and Voting Rights Bill, 444-445
    for women, 336, 340, 342
    See also suffrage.

W

Wade-Davis Bill, 300-301
Wagner Act, 394
Walker, Clifford, p398, 593
Walker County, 590
Walter F. George Reservoir, 62, 64
Walton, George, 155, p155, 157, 590, 592
Walton County, 590
war,
    of 1812, 189-191, 195
    Civil, 257-289
    Cold, 426-427, 468, 469, 470
    French and Indian, 143-146, m146, 149
    of Jenkins's Ear, 124-125, 127
    Korea, 427, m427
    Mexican-American, 211-213
    Operation Enduring Freedom, 483-484
    Operation Iraqi Freedom, 484–485
    Persian Gulf War, 458, 475-476
    Revolutionary, 153-165
    on terrorism, 481-485
    Vietnam, 452, 457-458, m457, 581-582
    World War I, 370-371
    World War II, 402-414
Ware County, 590
War Hawks, 189-190
Warm Springs, 34, 36-37, p36, 395, 408

Acknowledgments

Clairmont Press is grateful to the following educators who participated in a survey about state history and the development of this textbook. Much appreciation goes to each for their incisive comments and suggestions.

Karen Andrews, Jasper County Schools, Monticello
Benny Ashley, Chickamauga City Schools, Chickamauga
Janet Baxter, Cherokee County Schools, Woodstock
Lori Cash, Floyd County Schools, Rome
Ronnie Fender, Cook County Schools, Sparks
Bonnie Fletcher, Bibb County Schools, Macon
Paula Hitt, Bullock County Schools, Statesboro
Brenda Keith, Tift County Schools, Tifton
Carol Mathis, Buford City Schools, Buford
Julia Faye Smith, Decatur County Schools, Bainbridge
Kimerly Spears, Carroll County Schools, Carrollton
Geneva Sutton, Elbert County Schools, Elberton
Jack Todd, Treutlen County Schools, Soperton
Vanessa Wilburn, Jefferson County Schools, Wrens.

Picture Credits: The following abbreviations are used for sources from which several illustrations were obtained.

ADAH	Alabama Department of Archives and History
AMNH	Alabama Museum of Natural History
AHS	Atlanta Historical Society
AJ&C	*Atlanta Journal & Constitution*
AUSC	Atlanta University Special Collections
GDITT	Georgia Department of Industry, Trade and Tourism
GHS	Georgia Historical Society
GSA	Georgia State Archives
LC	Library of Congress
NA	National Archives
NCDAH	North Carolina Division of Archives and History
OHS	Oklahoma Historical Society
TSM	Tennessee State Museum
UASC	William S. Hoole Special Collections Library, University of Alabama

FRONT MATTER: Cover Robin McDonald (background); GDITT (capitol, peach). i Robin McDonald. ii-iii Robin McDonald. iv (left) courtesy Bonnie London; (right) Tommy Lankford; (below) AHS. v (left) Tommy Lankford; (right) courtesy Barbara Mathis. vii Robin McDonald. viii-xiii Robin McDonald. **UNIT ONE:** x-1 Robin McDonald. 1 GDITT **CHAPTER ONE:** 2-3 (both) Robin McDonald. 4 (background) Robin McDonald; (timeline, left to right) Robin McDonald, GDITT, Corbis. 10-11 (all) Robin McDonald. 12 (above and below) GDITT. 12-13 Robin McDonald.13 (above) GDITT; (below) Robin McDonald. 14 (above and below) GDITT. 14-15 Robin McDonald. 15 (both) Robin McDonald. 16 (above) GDITT; (below) Robin McDonald. 16-17 Robin McDonald. 17 (both) GDITT. 18-19 (all) Robin McDonald. 20 GDITT. 21 GDITT. 22 GDITT. 24 Robin McDonald. 25 GDITT. 29 Corbis. 31 Robin McDonald. 33 GDITT. **Special Section:** 34 (above) Robin McDonald; (below) GDITT. 35 Robin McDonald. 36-37 (all) GDITT. 38-39 (all) Robin McDonald. **CHAPTER TWO:** 40 (above) GDITT; (below) Robin McDonald. 40-41 Robin McDonald. 41 (both) GDITT. 42 (all) Robin McDonald. 43 (both) GDITT. 44 (top and center) GDITT; (above and right) GDITT. 45 GHS. 46 (above) Robin McDonald; (below) GDITT. 47 (both) Robin McDonald. 48 (below) Corbis; (bottom) Robin McDonald. 49 (top and left) Robin McDonald; (above) GDITT. 50 (above left) Robin McDonald; (above right) Old Jacksonville; (below) Georgia Department of Natural Resources. 51 (both) GDITT. 52 (all) Robin McDonald. 55 (both) GDITT. 56 GDITT. 57 (below) GDITT; (bottom) Robin McDonald. 58 Robin McDonald; 59 (below) GDITT. 60 GDITT. 61 Robin McDonald. 62 (both) Robin McDonald. 63 (top) Robin McDonald; (below) GDITT. 64 Robin McDonald. 67 Robin McDonald. **UNIT TWO:** 68-69 Robin McDonald. 69 GDITT. **CHAPTER THREE:** 70 (above) GDITT. 70-71 Robin McDonald. 72-73 (background) Robin McDonald; (timeline, all) Pinson Mounds State Archeological Area, TN. 74 Robin McDonald. 75 (above) AMNH; (below) Pinson Mounds State Archeological Area, TN. 76 (above) Cherry Bishop; (below) AMNH. 77 Pinson Mounds State Archeological Area, TN. 78 (both) Robin McDonald. 79 (above) Pinson Mounds State Archeological Area, TN; (below) AMNH. 80 (above) GDITT; (below) Pinson Mounds State Archeological Area, TN. 81 (all) Robin McDonald. 82 (both) Robin McDonald. 84 Robin McDonald. 85 (above) Smithsonian Institution; (below) Birmingham Public Library. 86 Cherokee Historical Association. 88 (both) Robin McDonald. 89 (below) Robin McDonald; (bottom) TSM. 90-91 (both) Robin McDonald. 92 (both) Robin McDonald. 93 Billy Barnes. 94 (above left) Robin McDonald; (above right) Public Domain; (below) Smithsonian Institution. 95 North Carolina Department of travel and Tourism. 96 (both) Robin McDonald. 97 Independence National Historic Park. 99 Robin McDonald. **CHAPTER FOUR:** 100-101 Robin McDonald. 102-103 (background) Robin McDonald. 103 (timeline, left to right) UASC, GSA, Robin McDonald, Corbis. Smithsonian Institution. 104 LC. 105 (top) Architect of the Capitol; (above) Corbis. 106 Corbis. 107 (top) Organisation of American States; (above) LC. 108 UASC. 109 Architect of the Capitol. 110 NCDAH. 111 (both) Jamestown-Yorktown Foundation. 112 U.S. Capitol. 113 (both) Robin McDonald. 114 GHS. 115 GSA 116 GSA.117 GSA. 118 (left) Smithsonian Institution; (right) GHS. 119 (both) Robin McDonald. 120 Robin McDonald. 121 Special Collections, University of Georgia 122-123 Winterthur Museum. GSA. 123 (all) Robin McDonald. 124 GHS. 125 (left) GSA; (right) Robin McDonald. 126 Robin McDonald. 127 (both) Robin McDonald. 128 GSA. 129 GHS. **CHAPTER FIVE:** 132-133 Architect of the Capitol. 134-135 (background) Architect of the Capitol. 135 (timeline, left to right) Wisconsin Historical Society, GSA, LC, GSA, Architect of the Capitol. 137 Painting by David Wright. 138 (top) NCDAH; (above) TSM. 139 Robin McDonald. 140 (both) Robin McDonald. 141 Kentucky Historical Society. 142 GSA. 144 Washington and Lee University. 145 Wisconsin Historical Society. 147 GSA. 148 Robin McDonald. 150 (top) LC; (above) GSA. 151 (top) Corbis; (above) LC. 152 GSA. 154 (top) Corbis (above) GSA. 155 (both) GSA. 156 NA. 157 GSA. 158 LC. 159 GSA. 160 NA. 161 Architect of the Capitol. 162 GSA. 163 LC. 164 (top) Robin McDonald; (above) Historic New Orleans Collection. 165 Historic New Orleans Collection. 167 Robin McDonald. UNIT THREE: 168-169 Robin McDonald. 169 GDITT. CHAPTER SIX: 170-171 Robin McDonald. 172-173 (background) Robin McDonald. 173 (timeline, left to right) GHS, GSA, OHS, Robin McDonald, Woolaroc Museum, Bartlesville, OK.174 (left) GSA; (right) Architect of the Capitol. 175 GSA. 176 Corbis. 177 GSA178 LC. 179 NA. 180 (top) GHS; (above) ADAH. 181 (top) U.S. Capitol; (above) NA. 182 GSA. 183 Robin McDonald. 183 LC. 184 NCDAH. 185 (both) Robin McDonald. 186 LC. 187 (both) LC.188 Robin McDonald. 189 LC. 190 LC. 191 Louisiana State Museum. 192 Robin McDonald. 193 (above) Robin McDonald; (below) OHS 194 (both) Robin McDonald. 195 (top) UASC; (above) Birmingham Public Library. 196 OHS. 197 TSM. 198 GSA. 199 (both) Robin McDonald. 200 (top and below right) OHS; (above) Tennessee Historical Society. 201 Woolaroc Museum, Bartlesville, OK. 202 OHS. 203 North Carolina Department of Travel and Tourism. 205 Robin McDonald. CHAPTER SEVEN: 206-207 Robin McDonald. 208-209 (background) Robin McDonald. 209 (timeline, left to right) AHS, LC, Robin McDonald, UASC. Smithsonian Institution. 210 LC. 211 (top) LC; (above) NCDAH. 212 (both) LC. 213 TSM. 214 LC. 217 Robin McDonald. 219 Robin McDonald. 220 LC. 221 LC. 222 LC. 223 LC. 224 LC. 225 LC. 226 Robin McDonald. 227 Greenville County Museum of Art. 228 Robin McDonald. 229 GSA. 230 University of South Carolina. 231 (below) NCDAH; (bottom) Corbis. 232 LC. 233 West Virginia State Archives. 234 Robin McDonald. 235 Corbis. 236 (top) LC (above) LC. 237 AHS. 238 AHS. 239 (both) Robin McDonald. 240 Robin McDonald. 241 (top left, top right, above right) GDITT; (above left and left) Robin McDonald. 242-243 (all) Robin McDonald. 244 GSA. 245 LC. 246 LC. 248 GSA. 249 (both) UASC. 251 Robin McDonald. CHAPTER EIGHT: 252 Bruce Roberts. 253 Robin McDonald. 254-255 (background) Robin McDonald. 255 (timeline, left to right) GDITT, Kurz and Allison, GDITT. 256-57 Greenville County Museum of Art. 257 LSM. 259 (both) LC. 260 LC. 262 Museum of the Confederacy. 263 LC. 264 (both) *Battles and Leaders of the Civil War*. 265 (above) GDITT; (below) *Battles and Leaders of the Civil War*. 266-267 *Battles and Leaders of the Civil War*. 268 (below) Bruce Roberts; (bottom) GDITT. 269 (top) GDITT; (above) Robin McDonald. 270-271 *Battles and Leaders of the Civil War*. 272 Kurz and Allison. 273 (top) Kurz and Allison; (above) GDITT. 274 LC. 275 (both) Robin McDonald. 276-277 (all) GDITT. 278-279 (all) *Battles and Leaders of the Civil War*. 280 GDITT. 281 *Battles and Leaders of the Civil War*. 282 Kurz and Allison. 283 Wadsworth Atheneum. 284 UASC. 285 University of Miami. 286 NCDAH. 287 LC. 288 LC. UNIT FOUR: 292-293 (both) Robin McDonald. CHAPTER NINE: 294-295 Robin McDonald. 296-297 (background) Robin McDonald. 255 (timeline, left to right) LC, LC, LC, AHS. 298 NCDAH. 299 (both) Robin McDonald. 300 LC. 301 NCDAH. 302 GSA. 303 Robin McDonald. 305 GSA. 306 LC. 307 Robin McDonald. 308 (both) Robin McDonald. 309 AHS. 310-311 (both) AHS. 311-312 (both) GSA. 314 GSA. 315 (above) AHS; (below) Robin McDonald. 316 LC. 317 Robin McDonald. 318 AHS. 319 (both) Robin McDonald. 320 AHS. 321 Robin McDonald. 322 LC. 323 (both) Robin McDonald. 324 AHS. 325 (top) AHS; (center and below) GSA. 326 LC. 327 (all) Robin McDonald. 327 GSA 328-329 (both) Robin McDonald. CHAPTER TEN: 332-333 Robin McDonald. 334-335 (background) Robin McDonald. 335 (timeline, left to right) LC, Robin McDonald, Girl Scouts of the U.S.A., LC. 336 (both) AHS. 337 NA. 338 Corbis. 339 (top) Corbis (above) LC. 340 AHS 341 (both) Girl Scouts of the U.S.A. 342 (both) Robin McDonald. 343 AHS. 344 (above) GSA. (below) Robin McDonald. 345 Robin McDonald. 346 GSA. 347 LC.

348 (both) GSA. 350 Robin McDonald. 351 AHS. 352 LC. 353 Corbis. 354 LC. 355 Corbis. 356 AUSC. 358 LC. 359 (top) AUSC; (above) *AJ&C*. 360 *AJ&C*. 361 GSA. 362 (both) *AJ&C*. 363 LC. 364-365 (all) Coca-Cola Company Archives. 366 (above) Tennessee Tourism Department; (below) LC. 367 AUSC. 368-369 (both) Robin McDonald. 370 U.S.A.F. Museum. 371 (top) AHS. (above) LC. 372 (all) GSA. 373 GSA. 375 Robin McDonald. CHAPTER ELEVEN: 376-377 AHS. 378-379 (background) AHS. 379 (timeline, left to right) AHS, Corbis, Corbis, GDITT. 380 LC. 381 (above) AHS; (below) LC. 382 (top and bottom) NCDAH; (center) Corbis. 383 Corbis. 384 LC. 385 (both) Robin McDonald. 386 LC. 387 Corbis. 388 LC. 389 (both) LC. 390 LC. 391. LC. 392 (above) LC; (below) Robin McDonald. 393 AHS. 394 Robin McDonald. 395 Corbis. 396 LC. 397 (above) LC; (left) AUSC. 398 AHS. 399 (both) GSA. 400 *AJ&C*. 401 (top) *AJ&C*; (above) GSA. 402-403 (all) LC. 404 (both) LC. 405 Corbis. 406 LC. 407 (top) University of South Alabama; (above and left) LC. 408 LC. 409 (top) GDITT; (above) LC. 410 GSA. 411 LC. 412 LC. 413 AHS 415 LC. 417 LC. UNIT FIVE: 418-419 GDITT. 419 Robin McDonald. CHAPTER TWELVE: 420-421 Robin McDonald. 422-423 (background) Robin McDonald. 423 (timeline, left to right) Corbis, AJ&C, GSA, Corbis, GSA. 424 AHS. 425 (top) LC, (above) Corbis. 426-427 (both) Corbis. 428 Corbis. 429 (top) GDITT; (above) Robin McDonald. 430 (both) *AJ&C*. 431 AHS. 432 *AJ&C*. 433 Robin McDonald. 434 *Fulton County Daily Report*. 435 GSA. 436 Corbis. 437 (left) Corbis; (right) Robin McDonald. 437 AUSC. 438 (both) *AJ&C*. 439 (below) GSA; (bottom) AHS. 440 Corbis. 441 GSA. 442 *AJ&C*. 443 Corbis. 444-445 (all) Corbis. 446 Robin McDonald. 447 *AJ&C*. 448 Corbis. 449 *AJ&C*. 450 *AJ&C*. 451 Corbis. 452 Corbis. 453 GSA. 454 Corbis. 455 (top) Robin Mcdonald; (above) Billy Barnes. 456 Corbis. 457 Corbis. 458 Corbis. 459 (both) LC. CHAPTER THIRTEEN: 464-465 (both) Corbis. 466-467 (background) Corbis. 467 (timeline, left to right) *AJ&C*, *AJ&C*, Corbis, Office of the Governor, Robin McDonald. 468 Corbis. 469 Corbis. 470 Corbis. 471 *AJ&C*. 474 Robin McDonald. 475 (below) Corbis; (above) *AJ&C*. 476 (top) courtesy Tribune Media Services; (above) courtesy John Lewis 477 (both) *AJ&C*. 478 *AJ&C*. 479 Corbis. 480 Corbis. 481 Corbis. 482 Corbis. 483 Corbis. 484 Corbis. 485 Robin McDonald. 486 GDITT. 487 (top) Robin McDonald; (below) Office of the Secretary of State. 488 Corbis. 489 courtesy Roy Barnes. 490 Corbis. 491 Corbis. 492 (both) Robin McDonald. 493 Office of the Governor. UNIT SIX: 496-497 Robin McDonald. CHAPTER FOURTEEN: 496 Corbis. 496-497 Robin McDonald. 498-499 Robin McDonald. 500-501 (background) Robin McDonald. 501 (timeline, left to right) Robin McDonald, Corbis, Robin McDonald. 504 *AJ&C*. 502 Robin McDonald. 503 Architect of the Capitol. 505 Library of Virginia. 506 U.S. Bureau of Engraving. 507 LC 509 LC. 510 (top) AHS. (right) *AJ&C*. 512-513 Corbis. 514 Corbis. 517 courtesy Dr. Antonia Coello Novello. 518 (both) Robin McDonald. 520 Robin McDonald 522 Robin McDonald. CHAPTER FIFTEEN: 526-527 Robin McDonald. 527 GDITT. 528-529 (background) Robin McDonald. 529 (timeline, left to right) GDITT, GDITT, Robin McDonald. 530 Office of the Governor. 535 GDITT. 538 GDITT. 542 (both) Robin McDonald. 543 GSA. 544 courtesy Georgia Supreme Court. 546 Robin McDonald. 547 GDITT. Special Section: 554 (top) GDITT; (center and below) Robin McDonald. 555 (top) Kentucky Department of Tourism Development; (above) Robin McDonald. 556 (top right) painting by Louis Aggasiz Fuentes; (top right) Georgia Department of Natural Resources; (above) Robin McDonald. 558 (top and inset) Robin McDonald; (above) GDITT. CHAPTER SIXTEEN: 560-561 Robin McDonald. 562-263 (background) Robin McDonald. 263 (timeline, left to right) Robin McDonald, AHS, LC. 564 Robin McDonald. 568 Robin McDonald. 569 GDITT. 570 Robin McDonald. 571 *AJ&C*. 573 Robin McDonald. 574 Robin McDonald. 576 (left) GDITT; (right) Robin McDonald. 577 (both) GDITT. 578 Corbis. 579 (both) LC. 580 Robin McDonald. 581 (above) Office of the Secretary of State; (below) LC. 582 Corbis. 597 GSA.